Cisco Catalyst SD-WAN: Design, Deploy, and Secure Your WAN

Companion Website and Pearson Test Prep Access Code

Access interactive study tools on this book's companion website, including practice test software, review exercises, Key Term flash card application, and more!

To access the companion website, simply follow these steps:

1. Go to **www.ciscopress.com/register**.

2. Enter the **print book ISBN**: 9780138313906.

3. Answer the security question to validate your purchase.

4. Go to your account page.

5. Click on the **Registered Products** tab.

6. Under the book listing, click on the **Access Bonus Content** link.

When you register your book, your Pearson Test Prep practice test access code will automatically be populated with the book listing under the Registered Products tab. You will need this code to access the practice test that comes with this book. You can redeem the code at **PearsonTestPrep.com**. Simply choose Pearson IT Certification as your product group and log into the site with the same credentials you used to register your book. Click the **Activate New Product** button and enter the access code. More detailed instructions on how to redeem your access code for both the online and desktop versions can be found on the companion website.

If you have any issues accessing the companion website or obtaining your Pearson Test Prep practice test access code, you can contact our support team by going to **pearsonitp.echelp.org**.

Cisco Catalyst SD-WAN

Design, Deploy, and Secure Your WAN

ANASTASIYA VOLKOVA, CCIE No. 54378

OSVALDO SALAZAR TOVAR

CONSTANTIN MOHOREA, CCDE No. 20170054, CCIE No. 16623

DUSTIN SCHUEMANN, CCIE No. 59235

Cisco Press

221 River St.

Hoboken, NJ 07030 USA

Cisco Catalyst SD-WAN: Design, Deploy, and Secure Your WAN

Anastasiya Volkova, Osvaldo Salazar Tovar, Constantin Mohorea, and Dustin Schuemann

Published by:
Cisco Press

$PrintCode

Library of Congress Control Number: 2024941644

ISBN-13: 978-0-13-831390-6

ISBN-10: 0-13-831390-3

Warning and Disclaimer

This book is designed to provide information about Cisco Software-Defined Wide-Area Networks. Every effort has been made to make this book as complete and as accurate as possible, but no warranty or fitness is implied.

The information is provided on an "as is" basis. The authors, Cisco Press, and Cisco Systems, Inc. shall have neither liability nor responsibility to any person or entity with respect to any loss or damages arising from the information contained in this book or from the use of the discs or programs that may accompany it.

The opinions expressed in this book belong to the authors and are not necessarily those of Cisco Systems, Inc.

Please contact us with concerns about any potential bias at https://www.pearson.com/report-bias.html.

Trademark Acknowledgments

All terms mentioned in this book that are known to be trademarks or service marks have been appropriately capitalized. Cisco Press or Cisco Systems, Inc., cannot attest to the accuracy of this information. Use of a term in this book should not be regarded as affecting the validity of any trademark or service mark.

Special Sales

For information about buying this title in bulk quantities, or for special sales opportunities (which may include electronic versions; custom cover designs; and content particular to your business, training goals, marketing focus, or branding interests), please contact our corporate sales department at corpsales@pearsoned.com or (800) 382-3419.

For government sales inquiries, please contact governmentsales@pearsoned.com.

For questions about sales outside the U.S., please contact intlcs@pearson.com.

Feedback Information

At Cisco Press, our goal is to create in-depth technical books of the highest quality and value. Each book is crafted with care and precision, undergoing rigorous development that involves the unique expertise of members from the professional technical community.

Readers' feedback is a natural continuation of this process. If you have any comments regarding how we could improve the quality of this book, or otherwise alter it to better suit your needs, you can contact us through email at feedback@ciscopress.com. Please make sure to include the book title and ISBN in your message.

We greatly appreciate your assistance.

GM K12, Early Career and Professional Learning: Soo Kang

Alliances Manager, Cisco Press: Caroline Antonio

Director, ITP Product Management: Brett Bartow

Senior Sponsoring Editor: Malobika Chakraborty

Managing Editor: Sandra Schroeder

Development Editor: Ellie C. Bru

Senior Project Editor: Mandie Frank

Technical Editors: Brad Edgeworth, Gina Cornett

Editorial Assistant: Cindy Teeters

Designer: Chuti Prasertsith

Composition: codeMantra

Indexer: Cheryl Ann Lenser

Proofreader: Donna E. Mulder

About the Authors

Anastasiya Volkova, CCIE No. 54378 (EN and Security), is a Solutions Architect on the Cisco Global Demo Engineering team, with a focus on Enterprise networking, Security and Cloud solutions, and multi-domain integrations. Anastasiya has more than 12 years of industry experience. Her background includes different areas of expertise, from hands-on experience in design, implementation, and support of network solutions to conducting trainings and technical presentations. She is very passionate about sharing her knowledge with others, hoping to help more people fall in love with the technology.

Osvaldo Salazar Tovar is a Technical Solutions Architect/Solutions Engineer in the Cisco Enterprise Routing and SD-WAN group. Throughout his career, he has supported the Global Service Provider and Enterprise Networking teams in LATAM through various technical sales engineering roles. He is currently working with different verticals in the United States, assisting customers and partners in designing and implementing next-generation WANs and emphasizing the importance of the WAN. He holds a bachelor of science degree in information and communication technologies from Instituto Tecnologico y de Estudios Superiores de Monterrey (ITESM).

Constantin Mohorea, CCIE No. 16223, CCDE No. 20170054, is a Customer Delivery Technical Leader at Cisco with more than 20 years of experience in the networking industry. He specializes in designing and delivering Cisco SD-WAN technologies to clients across various industries and has a strong history of helping clients achieve their business goals. He is passionate about the evolving trends in programmability and automation within the networking sector and has authored a Cisco Press DevNet certification book. Constantin resides in Toronto, Canada.

Dustin Schuemann, CCIE No. 59235 (R&S), is very passionate about giving back through mentoring and building communities in the IT industry. Dustin has 22 years of experience in the networking field, and before joining Cisco he worked in the manufacturing, retail, and finance industries. Dustin currently works in Cisco's Global Demo Engineering organization as a Solutions Architect, leading the demo strategic direction. Dustin speaks on SD-WAN at Cisco Live globally and has been inducted into the Cisco Live Hall of Fame by achieving Distinguished Speaker status at five different events.

About the Technical Reviewers

Brad Edgeworth, CCIE No. 31574 (R&S and SP), is an SD-WAN technical solutions architect at Cisco Systems. Brad is a distinguished speaker at Cisco Live, where he has presented on various topics. Before joining Cisco, Brad worked as a network architect and consultant for various Fortune 500 companies. Brad's expertise is based on enterprise and service provider environments, with an emphasis on architectural and operational simplicity. Brad holds a bachelor of arts degree in computer systems management from St. Edward's University in Austin, Texas. Brad can be found on Twitter as @BradEdgeworth.

Gina Cornett, CCIE Emeritus No. 3311 (R&S and Security), is a Technical Marketing Engineer in the Enterprise Business Unit, where she focuses on design and customer adoption of Cisco Catalyst SD-WAN technology. In addition to this customer-focused design work, Gina has also worked in Customer Support, Systems Test, and the Customer Proof of Concept Labs (CPOC) for a career at Cisco lasting more than 28 years. Her background is in campus switching, security, and SD-WAN.

Dedications

Anastasiya Volkova:

I dedicate this book to my husband, Vitaly, whose endless patience and wholehearted support made a huge contribution not only to this book but to many other ambitious projects as well. You believe in me more than I believe in myself!

I also dedicate it to my parents, who have always been a great example of unprecedented love and constant readiness to develop new skills and share knowledge. Now we have one more book author in our family!

Osvaldo Salazar Tovar:

I dedicate this book to my wife, Cinthia. Thanks for supporting and encouraging me to always do my best and thanks for your love and partnership. You (and the cats —Mia, Salem, and Dexter) are my engine to keep moving.

I also dedicate this project to my mom, Teresa, my dad, Fidencio, and my brother, Fidencio Jr., for putting so much of your dreams in my career. I will endlessly be in debt to you.

Tessa, as I write this, your mom and I can't wait to meet you. No matter what, always chase your dreams, don't be scared of new challenges, always try your best, and we will be here for you.

To the reader, if you are looking for an answer or simply trying to be a better engineer in this technology, keep up the good work; you will make it. Thanks for getting here.

Constantin Mohorea:

I dedicate this book to my family: my parents, my wife, and especially my children. Thank you for all your support!

I also dedicate this work to the Transplant Team at Toronto General Hospital. Your incredible work and daily miracles have profoundly impacted my life, and I am forever grateful.

In memory of Alexi Laiho, Tomas "Quorthon" Forsberg, and Darrell Lance Abbott, whose music provided the inspiring soundtrack to the creation of this book.

Finally, I dedicate this book to everyone committed to continuous study and self-improvement. Keep pushing forward; your dedication inspires me!

Dustin Schuemann:

I dedicate this book to my father. As I write this, it is Father's Day, and I can't help but remember all the good times I had with him. My father lost his battle with cancer two years ago, but without the life lessons my dad instilled in me, this book would have never come to fruition. My father taught me first and foremost that if you believe in something do it no matter what stands in the way and secondly to make sure you are always focused on the greater good. This book is a testament to both of those examples he set in his own life, and I hope to carry on.

I love you, Dad.

Acknowledgments

Anastasiya Volkova:

I want to thank my friend and colleague Dustin Schuemann. I wouldn't have been involved in so many interesting projects if it were not for you. Thank you for the inspiration, support, and for being a great example!

I also want to acknowledge our GDE leadership team, in particular Charlie Lewis and Jason Angelus. Thank you for all the opportunities you've given us, and for the incredible culture you've created in our organization. I am happy and proud to be a part of this team!

Finally, a very big appreciation goes to Prashant Tripathi. Your level of expertise and willingness to help significantly improved not only this book but my personal knowledge as well. Thank you for providing detailed explanations and answering a million questions about Catalyst SD-WAN in general and Cloud OnRamp in particular.

Osvaldo Salazar Tovar:

First, I would like to thank and recognize my coauthors, Anastasiya, Dustin, and Constantin. You are such hard workers and lead by example, and I'm glad we met and came to achieve this book as a result. Dustin, how can somebody invite you to be busier and still ask why are you working on a holiday or late night? I really appreciate your leadership on this amazing project. Thanks for considering me.

Second, to our technical reviewers, Brad Edgeworth and Gina Cornett. I have learned a lot from you.

Finally, to my friends and mentors Paquito, Dana, Prashant, Ali, Adam, Brendan, Lee, Luis, Adilson, Jason, and Jeffry: Thanks for your friendship, mentorship, encouragement, and trust in me. To the TME, PM, and Escalations teams that have always tolerated my questions and provided me light and knowledge: Thanks.

Greg, thanks a lot for all the support, brother. And thanks to all my other colleagues and management that has contributed to my growth. The best is yet to come!

Constantin Mohorea:

I would like to express my deepest gratitude to my coauthors, Anastasiya, Osvaldo, and Dustin. Working with you was a true pleasure, and your collaboration made this journey memorable.

Special thanks go to our technical reviewers, Gina Cornett and Brad Edgeworth. Your time, expertise, and patience have been greatly appreciated.

I am grateful to my immediate Cisco team for their direct and indirect support. Thank you, Doug, for your unwavering encouragement. Nikhail, your questions always sparked deeper thinking. Iftikhar, your exemplary thoroughness set a high standard for us all.

To the many wonderful people at Cisco who contributed to my growth by patiently addressing my questions and leading by example, I am sincerely grateful.

Finally, to you, my reader: Thank you for dedicating your time to this book. Your interest and engagement give meaning to my efforts.

Dustin Schuemann:

First off, I want to send a special thanks to my coauthors, Anastasiya, Osvaldo, and Constantin. Throughout this experience, you have shown just how dedicated you are to your craft and, more importantly, passing on your knowledge to help others grow. Your focus on the reader was apparent, and every choice you made was grounded in what is best for them. I know there were a lot of long hours, weekends, and time away from your families while writing this, and I'm grateful for everything you have done here. Each of you should be very happy with what you've accomplished. Thank you! When are we doing the third edition?

I would like to also thank our Cisco Press team for their support and for providing us with the opportunity. Ellie Bru, thank you for dealing with my endless questions, keeping us on track, and ensuring that this book was successfully delivered. From the entire team, I would like to thank Gina Cornett and Brad Edgeworth for technical editing. Your knowledge and expertise on all things SD-WAN were instrumental in the delivery of this book, even if we didn't completely agree on the IP addresses we used in the book.

Finally, I want to thank my leadership team at Cisco. Charlie Lewis and Jason Angelus, you've supported me in everything I have done personally and professionally. Over the past few years, it hasn't been easy for me, and your desire to make sure I had the time and freedom to deal with those things is greatly appreciated. The team you have created and the people you have surrounded me with are exceptional in everything they do, and this has made me a better person. Thank you!

Contents at a Glance

Reader Services

Register your copy of this book at www.ciscopress.com/title/9780138313906 for convenient access to downloads, updates, and corrections as they become available. To start the registration process, go to www.ciscopress.com/register and log in or create an account.* Enter the product ISBN 9780138313906 and click Submit. When the process is complete, you will find any available bonus content under Registered Products.

*Be sure to check the box indicating that you would like to hear from us to receive exclusive discounts on future editions of this product.

Contents

Command Syntax Conventions

The conventions used to present command syntax in this book are the same conventions used in the IOS Command Reference. The Command Reference describes these conventions as follows:

- **Boldface** indicates commands and keywords that are entered literally as shown. In actual configuration examples and output (not general command syntax), boldface indicates commands that are manually input by the user (such as a **show** command).

- *Italic* indicates arguments for which you supply actual values.

- Vertical bars (|) separate alternative, mutually exclusive elements.

- Square brackets ([ ]) indicate an optional element.

- Braces ({ }) indicate a required choice.

- Braces within brackets ([{ }]) indicate a required choice within an optional element.

Cover Credit

Cover Photo: Jacob Lund/Shutterstock

Introduction

The Implementing Cisco SD-WAN Solutions (ENSDWI 300-415) exam is a concentration exam for the CCNP Enterprise certification. If you pass the ENSDWI 300-415 exam, you also obtain the Cisco Certified Specialist—Enterprise SD-WAN Implementation certification. This exam covers core SD-WAN technologies, including SD-WAN architecture, controller deployment, edge router deployment, policies, security, quality of service, multicast, and management and operations.

TIP   You can review the exam blueprint at https://learningnetwork.cisco.com/s/ ensdwi-exam-topics.

This book gives you the foundation and covers the topics necessary to start the CCNP Enterprise certification, with a focus on the SD-WAN concentration exam or the Cisco Certified Specialist—Enterprise SD-WAN Implementation certification.

The CCNP Enterprise Certification

The CCNP Enterprise certification is one of the industry's most respected certifications. In order to earn the CCNP Enterprise certification, you must pass two exams—the ENCOR exam and one concentration exam of your choice—so you can customize your certification to your technical area of focus. This book focuses on the Implementing Cisco SD-WAN Solutions (ENSDWI 300-415) concentration exam.

TIP   The ENCOR core exam is also the qualifying exam for the CCIE Enterprise Infrastructure and CCIE Enterprise Wireless certifications. Passing this exam is the first step toward earning both of these certifications.

The following are the CCNP Enterprise concentration exams:

- Implementing Cisco Enterprise Advanced Routing and Services (300-410 ENARSI)

- Implementing Cisco SD-WAN Solutions (300-415 ENSDWI)

- Designing Cisco Enterprise Networks (300-420 ENSLD)

- Designing Cisco Enterprise Wireless Networks (300-425 ENWLSD)

- Implementing Cisco Enterprise Wireless Networks (300-430 ENWLSI)

- Implementing Automation for Cisco Enterprise Solutions (300-435 ENAUTO)

TIP   CCNP Enterprise now includes automation and programmability to help you scale your enterprise infrastructure. If you pass the Developing Applications Using Cisco Core Platforms and APIs v1.0 (DEVCOR 350-901) exam, the ENCOR exam, and the Implementing Automation for Cisco Enterprise Solutions (ENAUTO 300-435) exam, you will achieve the CCNP Enterprise and DevNet Professional certifications with only three exams. Every exam earns an individual Specialist certification, allowing you to get recognized for each of your accomplishments instead of waiting until you pass all the exams.

There are no formal prerequisites for CCNP Enterprise. In other words, you do not have to pass the CCNA or any other certifications in order to take CCNP-level exams. The same goes for the CCIE exams. On the other hand, CCNP candidates often have 3 to 5 years of experience in implementation enterprise networking solutions.

The Exam Objectives (Domains)

The Implementing Cisco SD-WAN Solutions (ENSDWI 300-415) exam is broken down into six major domains. This book covers each of the domains and the subtopics included in them, as illustrated here. The following table lists the breakdown of each of the domains represented in the exam.

Domain	Percentage of Representation in Exam
1: Architecture	20%
2: Controller Deployment	15%
3: Router Deployment	20%
4: Policies	20%
5: Security and Quality of Service	15%
6: Management and Operations	10%
	Total 100%

Here are the details of each domain:

Domain 1: Architecture: This domain is covered in Chapters 1, 2, and 3.

1.1 Describe Cisco SD-WAN Architecture and Components

1.1.a Orchestration plane (vBond, NAT)

1.1.b Management plane (vManage)

1.1.c Control plane (vSmart, OMP)

1.1.c.(i) TLOC

1.1.c.(ii) vRoute

1.1.d Data plane (WAN Edge)

1.1.d(i) IPsec and GRE

1.1.d(ii) BFD

1.1.e Multi-Region Fabric

1.2 Describe Cisco SD-WAN Edge platforms and capabilities

1.3 Describe Cisco SD-WAN Cloud OnRamp

1.3.a SaaS

1.3.b IaaS

1.3.c Colocation

1.3.d Multicloud (Cloud and Interconnect)

Domain 2: Controller Deployment: This domain is covered primarily in Chapters 2 and 5.

2.1 Describe controller cloud deployment

2.2 Describe controller on-premises deployment

2.2.a Hosting platforms (Public and Private)

2.2.b Installing controllers

2.2.c Scalability and redundancy

2.3 Configure certificates and device lists

2.4 Troubleshoot control plane connectivity

Domain 3: Router Deployment: This domain is covered primarily in Chapters 3 and 4.

3.1 Describe WAN Edge deployment

3.1.a On-boarding (ZTP and Bootstrap)

3.1.b Data center and regional hub deployments

3.2 Configure Cisco SD-WAN data plane

3.2.a Circuit termination and TLOC-extension

3.2.b Dynamic Tunnels

3.2.c Underlay–overlay connectivity

3.3 Configure OMP

3.4 Configure TLOCs

3.5 Configure CLI and vManage feature configuration templates

3.5.a VRRP

3.5.b OSPF

3.5.c BGP

3.5.d EIGRP

3.6 Describe multicast support in Cisco SD-WAN

3.7 Describe configuration groups, feature profiles, and workflows

Domain 4: Policies: This domain is covered primarily in Chapters 6, 7, 8, 9, and 10.

4.1 Configure control policies

4.2 Configure data policies

4.3 Configure end-to-end segmentation

4.3.a VPN segmentation

4.3.b Topologies

4.4 Configure Cisco SD-WAN application-aware routing

4.5 Configure direct Internet access

Domain 5: Security and Quality of Service: This domain is covered primarily in Chapters 10 and 11.

5.1 Configure service insertion

5.2 Describe Cisco SD-WAN security features

5.2.a Application-aware enterprise firewall

5.2.b IPS

5.2.c URL filtering

5.2.d AMP

5.2.e SSL and TLS proxy

5.2.f TrustSec

5.3 Describe Cloud security integration

5.3.a DNS security

5.3.b Secure Internet Gateway (SIG)

5.4 Configure QoS treatment on WAN Edge routers

5.4.a Scheduling

5.4.b Queuing

5.4.c Shaping

5.4.d Policing

5.4.e Marking

5.4.f Per-tunnel and adaptive QoS

5.5 Describe Application Quality of Experience (App-QoE)

5.5.a TCP optimization

5.5.b Data Redundancy elimination (DRE)

5.5.c Packet duplication

5.5.d Forward error correction (FEC)

5.5.e AppNav

Domain 6: Management and Operations: This domain is covered primarily in Chapters 4, 13, and 14.

6.1 Describe authentication, monitoring, and reporting from vManage

6.2 Configure authentication, monitoring, and reporting

6.3 Describe REST API monitoring

6.4 Describe software image management from vManage

Steps to Passing the Implementing Cisco SD-WAN Solutions (ENSDWI 300-415) Exam

There are no prerequisites for the ENSDWI exam; however, students must have an understanding of implementing networking solutions.

Signing Up for the Exam

The steps required to sign up for the ENSDWI exam as follows:

Step 1.   Create an account at https://home.pearsonvue.com/cisco.

Step 2.   Complete the Examination Agreement, attesting to the truth of your assertions regarding professional experience and legally committing to adhering to the testing policies.

Step 3.   Submit the examination fee.

Facts About the Exam

The ENSDWI 300-415 exam is a 90-minute exam. It is a computer-based test that consists of multiple-choice questions only. You must bring a government-issued identification card. No other forms of ID will be accepted.

TIP   Refer to the Cisco Certification site at https://cisco.com/go/certifications for more information regarding this and other Cisco certifications.

About This Book

This book maps directly to the topic areas of the ENSDWI exam and uses a number of features to help you understand the topics and prepare for the exam.

Objectives and Methods

This book uses several key methodologies to help you discover the exam topics on which you need more review, to help you fully understand and remember those details, and to help you prove to yourself that you have retained your knowledge of those topics. This book does not try to help you pass the exam only by memorization; it seeks to help you to truly learn and understand the topics. This book is designed to help you pass the Implementing Cisco SD-WAN Solutions (ENSDWI 300-415) exam by using the following methods:

- Helping you discover which exam topics you have not learned thoroughly enough

- Providing explanations and information to fill in your knowledge gaps

- Supplying review questions that enhance your ability to recall and deduce the answers to test questions

- Providing practice exercises on the topics and the testing process via test questions on the companion website

Book Features

To help you customize your study time using this book, each chapter has several features that help you make the best use of your time:

- **Review All Key Topics:** The Key Topic icon appears next to the most important items in the chapter. The "Review All Key Topics" activity near the end of the chapter lists the key topics from the chapter, along with their page numbers. Although the contents of the entire chapter could be on the exam, you should definitely know the information listed in each key topic, so you should review these.

- **Define Key Terms:** This section lists the most important terms from the chapter, asking you to write a short definition and compare your answer to the glossary at the end of the book.

- **Review Questions:** Confirm that you understand the content you just covered by answering these questions and reading the answer explanations.

In addition, the companion website includes the Pearson Cert Practice Test engine, which allows you to answer practice exam questions. Use it to prepare with a sample exam and to pinpoint topics where you need more study.

How This Book Is Organized

This book contains 14 chapters, each of which covers a subset of the topics on the Implementing Cisco SD-WAN Solutions (ENSDWI 300-415) exam. The chapters map to the ENSDWI topic areas and cover the concepts and technologies that you will encounter on the exam.

Here's a brief summary of each chapter:

- **Chapter 1, "Introduction to Cisco Catalyst SD-WAN,"** provides an introduction to software-defined networking, controllers, and automation. This chapter also covers the benefits and value of automating management and operations.

- **Chapter 2, "Cisco Catalyst SD-WAN Components,"** provides an introduction to the SD-WAN components, including the various controllers, as well as the various types of deployment models. The chapter also introduces the control plane, data plane, and cloud integration.

- **Chapter 3, "Control Plane and Data Plane Operations,"** covers Overlay Management Protocol (OMP) and how it works to facilitate the orchestration of the control plane and ultimately influences the data plane. This chapter also covers how a secure data plane is constructed with IPsec. As with all routing protocols, there needs to be a loop-prevention mechanism, and this chapter discusses the various types of loop prevention within OMP.

- **Chapter 4, "Onboarding and Provisioning,"** covers how to provision data plane devices, either manually or via plug and play/zero-touch provisioning. It also discusses using templates as a means of gaining flexibility and scalability with configuration management.

- **Chapter 5, "Cisco Catalyst SD-WAN Design and Migration,"** covers the methodology behind SD-WAN design across the enterprise. This chapter also discusses preparation for SD-WAN migration, data center design, and branch design, as well as overlay and underlay routing integration.

- **Chapter 6, "Introduction to Cisco Catalyst SD-WAN Policies,"** covers the basics of Cisco SD-WAN policies, including the different types of policies, how policies are constructed, and how policies are applied to the Cisco SD-WAN fabric.

- **Chapter 7, "Centralized Control Policies,"** covers centralized control policies, which are used to manipulate or filter OMP updates in order to manipulate the structure and forwarding patterns in the Cisco SD-WAN fabric. This chapter also covers packet loss recovery techniques, including Forward Error Correction and packet duplication. It also provides a series of use cases that solve for different business requirements.

- **Chapter 8, "Centralized Data Policies,"** covers centralized data policies that are used to manipulate or filter flows in the data plane and override the natural forwarding behavior that is propagated through OMP. This chapter provides a series of use cases that solve for different business requirements.

- **Chapter 9, "Application-Aware Routing Policies,"** covers app-route policies and how they can be used to ensure that traffic is forwarded across the SD-WAN fabric using links that meet a required service-level agreement (SLA).

- **Chapter 10, "Localized Policies,"** covers localized policies, including local route policies, access control lists (ACLs), and quality of service (QoS).

- **Chapter 11, "Cisco Catalyst SD-WAN Security,"** covers what SD-WAN security is and why it is relevant to your organization. This chapter also covers how to deploy Enterprise Firewall with Application Awareness, intrusion detection and prevention, URL filtering, advanced malware protection (AMP) and Threat Grid, DNS web layer security, cloud security, and SD-WAN Manager authentication and authorization.

- **Chapter 12, "Cisco Catalyst SD-WAN Cloud OnRamp,"** covers what Cisco SD-WAN Cloud OnRamp is and how it can optimize your organization's application experience. This chapter also covers how to deploy OnRamp for SaaS, OnRamp for Multicloud, and SD-WAN Cloud Interconnect.

- **Chapter 13, "Cisco Catalyst SD-WAN Programmability,"** covers features and functionality of Cisco Catalyst SD-WAN APIs and using Python with Catalyst SD-WAN APIs such as REST. Finally, this chapter covers using infrastructure as code (IaC) tools such as Terraform and Ansible.

- **Chapter 14, "Cisco Catalyst SD-WAN Monitoring and Operations,"** covers SD-WAN Manager tools for monitoring the entire SD-WAN overlay and its individual components as well as troubleshooting tools to verify and troubleshoot SD-WAN operations in the SD-WAN fabric. It also discusses monitoring your SD-WAN fabric with ThousandEyes and provides an overview of SD-WAN Analytics.

- Appendix A, "Answers to Chapter Review Questions," provides the answers to the review questions at the end of each chapter.

- The **Glossary of Key Terms** provides definitions for the key terms in each chapter.

The Companion Website for Online Content Review

All the electronic review elements, as well as other electronic components of the book, are available on this book's companion website.

How to Access the Companion Website

To access the companion website, which gives you access to the electronic content with this book, start by establishing a login at www.ciscopress.com and register your book.

To do so, simply go to www.ciscopress.com/register and enter the ISBN of the print book: 9780138313906. After you have registered your book, go to your account page and click the **Registered Products** tab. From there, click the **Access Bonus Content** link to get access to the book's companion website.

Note that if you buy the Premium Edition eBook and Practice Test version of this book from Cisco Press, your book will automatically be registered on your account page. Simply go to your account page, click the **Registered Products** tab, and select **Access Bonus Content** to access the book's companion website.

Please note that many of our companion content files can be very large, especially image and video files.

If you are unable to locate the files for this title, please visit ciscopress.com/support. Our customer service representatives will assist you.

How to Access the Pearson Test Prep (PTP) App

You have two options for installing and using the Pearson Test Prep application: a web app and a desktop app. To use the Pearson Test Prep application, start by finding the registration code that comes with the book. You can find the code in these ways:

- You can get your access code by registering the print ISBN (9780138313906) on ciscopress.com/register. Make sure to use the print book ISBN regardless of whether you purchased an eBook or the print book. Once you register the book, your access code will be populated on your account page under the Registered Products tab. Instructions for how to redeem the code are available on the book's companion website by clicking the Access Bonus Content link.

- If you purchase the Premium Edition eBook and Practice Test directly from the Cisco Press website, the code will be populated on your account page after purchase. Just log in at ciscopress.com click Account to see details of your account, and click the digital purchases tab.

NOTE   After you register your book, your code can always be found in your account under the Registered Products tab.

Once you have the access code, to find instructions about both the PTP web app and the desktop app, follow these steps:

Step 1:   Open this book's companion website as shown earlier in this Introduction under the heading, "How to Access the Companion Website."

Step 2:   Click the **Practice Exams** button.

Step 3:   Follow the instructions listed there for both installing the desktop app and for using the web app.

Note that if you want to use the web app only at this point, just navigate to pearsontestprep.com, log in using the same credentials used to register your book or purchase the Premium Edition, and register this book's practice tests using the registration code you just found. The process should take only a couple of minutes.

Customizing Your Exams

Once you are in the exam settings screen, you can choose to take exams in one of three modes:

■ **Study mode:** This mode allows you to fully customize your exams and review answers as you are taking an exam. This is typically the mode you use to assess your knowledge and identify information gaps.

■ **Practice Exam mode:** This mode locks certain customization options in order to present a realistic exam experience. Use this mode when you are preparing to test your exam readiness.

■ **Flash Card mode:** This mode strips out the answers and presents you with only the question stem. This mode is great for late-stage preparation, when you really want to challenge yourself to provide answers without the benefit of seeing multiple-choice options. This mode does not provide the detailed score reports that the other two modes do, so you should not use it if you are trying to identify knowledge gaps.

In addition to these three modes, you will be able to select the source of your questions. You can choose to take exams that cover all of the chapters, or you can narrow your selection to just a single chapter or the chapters that make up a specific part of the book. All chapters are selected by default. If you want to narrow your focus to individual chapters, simply deselect all the chapters and then select only those on which you wish to focus in the Objectives area.

You can also select the exam banks on which to focus. Each exam bank comes complete with a full exam of questions that cover topics in every chapter. The two online exams that accompany this book are available to you, as are two additional exams of unique questions. You can have the test engine serve up exams from all four banks or just from one individual bank by selecting the desired banks in the exam bank area.

There are several other customizations you can make to your exam from the exam settings screen, such as the time you are allotted to take the exam, the number of questions served up, whether to randomize questions and answers, whether to show the number of correct answers for multiple-answer questions, and whether to serve up only specific types of questions. You can also create custom test banks by selecting only questions that you have marked or questions for which you have added notes.

Updating Your Exams

If you are using the online version of the Pearson Test Prep software, you should always have access to the latest version of the software as well as the exam data. If you are using the Windows desktop version, every time you launch the software while connected to the Internet, it checks whether there are any updates to your exam data and automatically downloads any changes made since the last time you used the software.

Sometimes, for many possible reasons, the exam data may not fully download when you activate your exam. If you find that figures or exhibits are missing, you may need to manually update your exams. To update a particular exam that you have already activated and downloaded, simply click the Tools tab and click the Update Products button. Again, this is only an issue with the desktop Windows application.

If you wish to check for updates to the Windows desktop version of the Pearson Test Prep exam engine software and ensure that you are running the latest version of the software engine, simply click the Tools tab and click the Update Application button.

## CHAPTER 1

Introduction to Cisco Catalyst SD-WAN

This chapter covers the following topics:

- **Introduction to Cisco Catalyst Software-Defined WAN (SD-WAN):** This section examines the benefits and drivers of Cisco Catalyst SD-WAN.

- **Use Cases Demanding Changes in the WAN:** This section covers a variety of use cases that businesses are adopting that are putting pressure on the WAN environment.

- **Cloud Trends and Adoption:** This section explores what is driving businesses to move their business-critical applications to the public cloud and SaaS providers.

Transitioning from a network-centric model to a business intent–based WAN network represents a significant and powerful shift. This change allows for greater simplicity in application deployment and management within the WAN architecture. At the same time, it requires a shift in mindset from focusing on network topology to prioritizing application services. A key challenge for network operations teams is effectively supporting both new and existing applications on the WAN, especially considering their substantial bandwidth consumption and sensitivity to variations in bandwidth quality, such as jitter, loss, and delay.

Improving the WAN environment for these applications is crucial. Moreover, the increasing demand to migrate to cloud-based applications further exacerbates bandwidth requirements on the WAN. Limited flexibility in connectivity options to accommodate the growing number of cloud applications can lead to costly and challenging provisioning of new applications and services. Many businesses rely on service providers for MPLS L3VPN to manage their WAN routing and network service-level agreements (SLAs). However, this reliance can hinder their ability to adapt to evolving application delivery methods, such as cloud and software as a service (SaaS), in a timely manner. Service providers may take months to implement necessary changes to support these applications, and they may charge exorbitant fees or refuse to make changes altogether. In addition, because service providers control the WAN core, instantiating VPNs independent of the underlying transport becomes extremely challenging, making it difficult, if not impossible, to implement differentiated service levels for individual applications.

Hybrid WANs were originated to address these issues. With a hybrid WAN, businesses acquire additional non-MPLS links and add them to the WAN to provide alternate paths that the applications can take across the WAN environment. Businesses have complete control over these circuits—from routing control to application performance.

Typically, VPN tunnels are created over the top of these circuits to provide secure transport over any type of link. Examples of these types of links are commodity broadband Internet, L2VPN, wireless, and 5G/LTE. This provides what is called *transport independence*, which makes it possible to use any type of transport underneath the VPN and get deterministic routing and application performance. Some applications can be sent over these commodity links rather than over the traditional service provider–controlled L3VPN MPLS links, and the more latency-sensitive traffic can be sent via the MPLS circuits. A hybrid WAN provides unique granularity of traffic control, redundancy, and resiliency. Figure 1-1 illustrates three common hybrid WAN topologies.

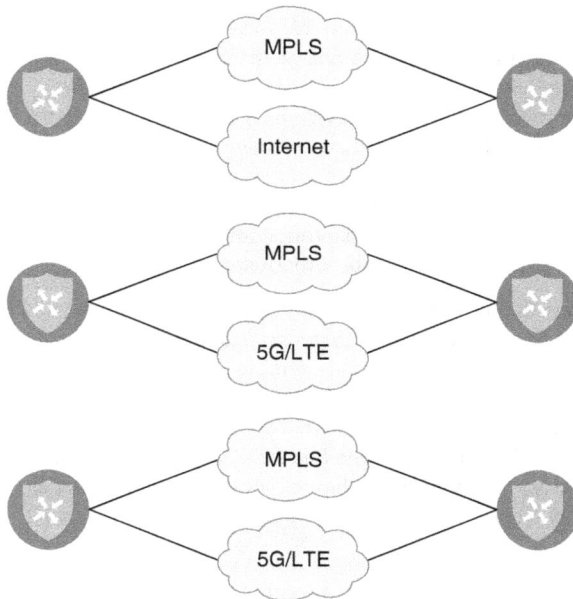

Figure 1-1 *Common Hybrid WAN Topologies*

Hybrid WANs need connectivity that is based on a service topology and can be centrally managed using policies. Currently, WAN connectivity is based on the network topology and managed using a peer-to-peer model. This means routing relationships are established by multiple control planes that operate independently of each other. Routing protocols such as Open Shortest Path First (OSPF) and Border Gateway Protocol (BGP) are used to establish routing domains across these connections, and IPsec is commonly used to secure the transport. These routing and security control planes run independently of each other and have their own scaling limitations, convergence requirements, and policy enforcement. This means each control plane is required to have its own independent policy and configuration. As a result, when a configuration change is required in the network, it has to be provisioned and propagated across all the control plane peers and for all transports, which creates operational pitfalls and also creates a potential risk of misconfiguration or missing configuration that might cause applications to suffer.

Transport Independence

Cisco Catalyst SD-WAN leverages a transport-independent fabric technology that is used to connect remote locations together. This is accomplished by using overlay technology.

The overlay works by tunneling traffic over any kind of transport between any destination within the WAN environment. This is the VPN concept that was mentioned earlier in this chapter—where, for example, it is possible to connect remote branches, regardless of whether they use MPLS or broadband Internet circuits. Using overlay technology gives true flexibility to routing applications across any portion of the network, regardless of what type of circuit or transport is in use. This is the definition of transport independence.

With a fabric overlay network, every remote site, regardless of physical or logical separation, is always a single hop away from another. This is of great benefit in terms of application latency and dynamic communication scenarios such as voice or interactive video. It not only provides increased simplicity in terms of network operations but also provides seamless mobility from a user experience perspective. Transport independence is also one of the primary aspects of Cisco Catalyst SD-WAN that allows for the use of flexible, lower-cost commodity circuits rather than high-cost, inflexible static bandwidth. Although service providers can upgrade the bandwidth of a circuit, cost is usually a barrier. In addition, there are many times that, based on the type of circuit the bandwidth is riding on, an entire physical circuit upgrade or swap may be more likely. An example of this is having a 100 Mbps MPLS handoff wherein the physical circuit it is delivered on is also only 100 Mbps. In cases like this, another higher-speed port on the provider side is required, such as a Gigabit or 10 Gigabit Ethernet port.

Many times, the circuit may ride over a different type of medium, and the entire circuit and delivery mechanism must be changed—for example, trying to go from a 45 Mbps DS3 to a Gigabit Ethernet link. All of this takes time—sometimes a considerable amount of time— and it is one of the things SD-WAN was created to address. A business can typically order a high-speed commodity Internet circuit and have it delivered within weeks. The new Internet circuit can be immediately added to the environment, and the business can take advantage of it by using SD-WAN. There are situations where multiple branch locations need to act as a single large branch across the WAN. This means having a virtual fabric over disparate transports such as MPLS and the Internet.

Given everything that has been covered thus far, it is important to now look at an example of a Cisco Catalyst SD-WAN diagram. Figure 1-2 provides a high-level overview of a Cisco Catalyst SD-WAN environment and how users, devices, and applications fit into the overall design.

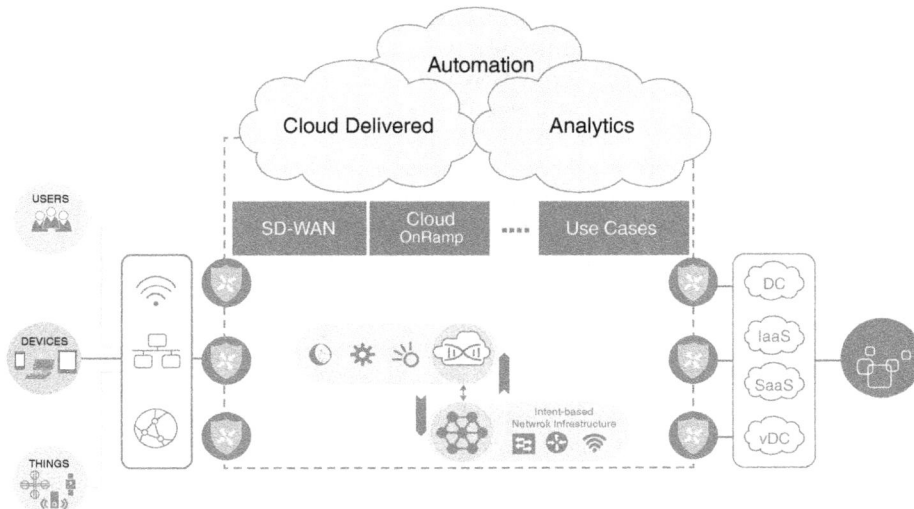

Figure 1-2 *High-Level SD-WAN Overview*

Moving from a network-centric WAN to an application- and services-focused WAN requires a different view of the WAN. Figure 1-3 illustrates a business intent–based network, its components, and how they fit within the new model.

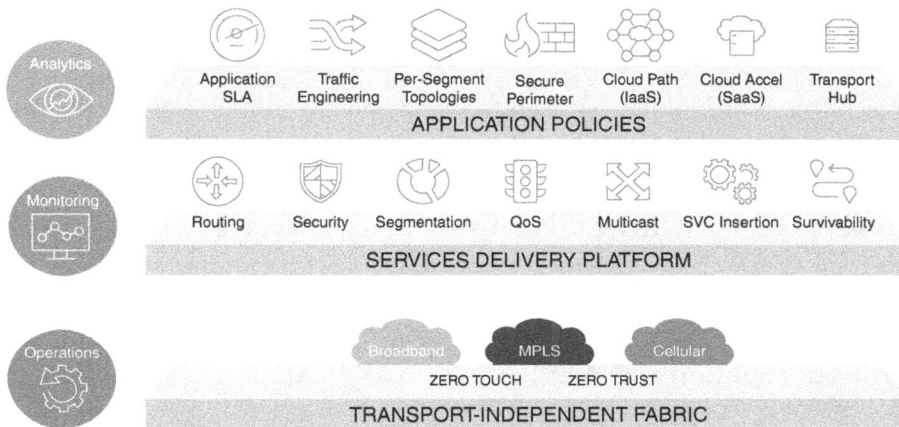

Figure 1-3   *Business Intent–Based Network Components*

Rethinking the WAN

If we were to redefine the current WAN technology and approach, we would want to make some fundamental changes to how WANs are constructed and managed today to address modern business and application requirements. These changes would involve the following key areas:

- Secure elastic connectivity

- Cloud-first approach

- Application quality of experience

- Agile operations

From a security perspective, end-to-end segmentation and policy are critical. The control, data, and management planes must be separated across the entire environment. The environment should be able to support native encryption that is robust and scalable, and it should offer lightweight key management and leverage a zero-trust model, meaning every aspect of the onboarding process must be authenticated and verified.

Rethinking the WAN from a connectivity perspective, these elements would be built on top of security functionality by integrating routing, security, and policy for optimal use of connectivity. The solution must allow for multiple types of transport connectivity options simultaneously and ultimately create a transport-independent operation model. Scalability, both horizontally and vertically, is necessary at any layer. In addition, advanced VPN capabilities and topologies to address any business intent or requirements are critical.

In terms of application support, the solution should support full application awareness across all elements in the system and offer built-in optimization techniques for the networks and applications. The network has evolved to be application aware, and it must be capable of choosing the most optimal path to connect to on-premises or cloud-based applications. The application experience must be optimal in terms of both access and security.

When it comes to the operation of this new application- and services-oriented WAN, network operations staff must be able to define networkwide policies that leverage templates rather than just use a device- or node-level policy. The controller must have the ability to coordinate the paths between the WAN edge routers, based on centralized policy orchestration. As organizations' network requirements change and evolve over time, the policy should be able to be changed in a single place. This not only reduces the amount of time spent on configuration but also lowers the risk associated with misconfiguration errors. Programmable, open application programming interfaces (APIs) should be available to provide northbound access for automation and orchestration capabilities. Support for southbound APIs for integration with other solutions should also be included.

Use Cases Demanding Changes in the WAN

Currently there are many reasons to look at enhancing the WAN environment—from load balancing traffic to ensuring that applications have the best performance possible. The following sections cover some of the use cases that are causing changes to the WAN.

Bandwidth Aggregation and Application Load Balancing

There are many different use cases that demand changes to traditional WAN architectures. Some are as simple as businesses wanting bandwidth aggregation, which is the ability to use both public and private transports together at the same time. For example, an organization might use A + B rather than A or B, meaning the secondary transport link (Link B) usually sits idle without any traffic using it until Link A fails. However, in a hybrid WAN approach, being able to leverage multiple links at the same time provides the ability to use bandwidth from both links. This is considered an A + A, or active/active, scenario.

Application load balancing is achieved using these types of designs as well. A hybrid environment featuring application load balancing allows for greater application performance at a fraction of the cost of two premium transport links. It also increases scalability and flexibility without any security compromise. Figure 1-4 illustrates the various options of application load balancing over multiple links in a hybrid environment. You can see that, by default, per-session active/active load sharing is achieved. Weighted per-session round-robin is also configurable on a device basis. Application pinning, or forcing an application to take a specific transport, is also something that can be enforced via policy. Similarly, application-aware routing or SLA-compliant routing is achieved by enforcing a policy that looks for specific traffic characteristics, such as jitter, loss, and delay, to determine the path the application should take over the available transports.

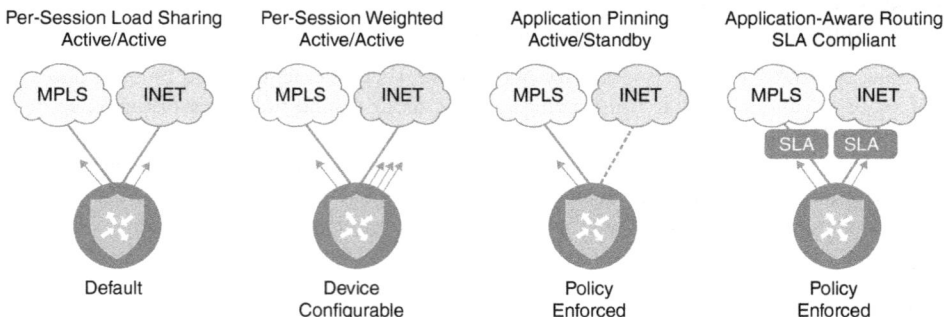

Figure 1-4 *Application Load-Balancing Options*

Protecting Critical Applications with SLAs

The requirement and capability to provide SLA for critical applications is another use case that drives changes in the WAN. This is accomplished by being able to route traffic based on the application requirements, as mentioned briefly earlier. This type of routing provides statistics on how the applications are performing. An SLA determines whether an application is adhering to the policy that has been created and whether it is performing properly. If the application is experiencing some sort of impairment, such as jitter, loss, or delay, the application can be routed to another transport, which will ensure that the application is within policy and able to perform to the SLA. Figure 1-5 illustrates this scenario.

A good example of providing SLA for critical applications in a hybrid WAN environment would be an MPLS link and an Internet link. If the MPLS link is experiencing >2% packet loss and the Internet link is not, it might be appropriate to route the application over the Internet link to ensure that the application is functioning properly and users are having the best possible experience interacting with the application. In the example in Figure 1-5, the policy says that if the application is experiencing any jitter greater than or equal to 10 ms, then it should prefer another transport. In this example, Path 2 and Path 3 are above the threshold, so Path 1 will be preferred.

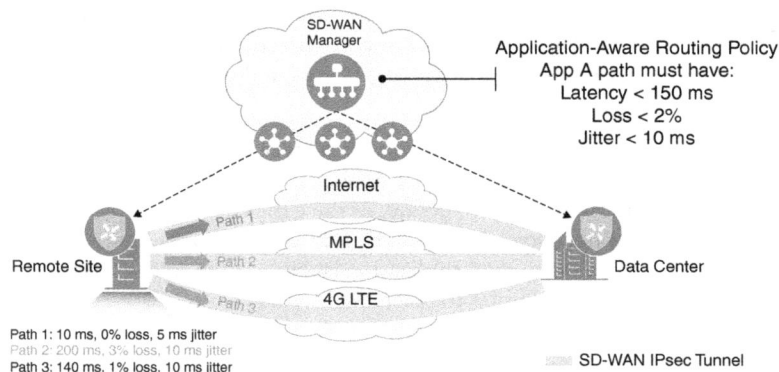

Path 1: 10 ms, 0% loss, 5 ms jitter
Path 2: 200 ms, 3% loss, 10 ms jitter
Path 3: 140 ms, 1% loss, 10 ms jitter

Figure 1-5 *Routing Based on Application Performance*

End-to-End Segmentation

Segmentation is another use case that drives changes in the WAN. Oftentimes, businesses face different corporate or regulatory requirements that require separation. For example, research and development may need to be segmented from the production environment. There may be extranets that connect to partners, or the business may be merging or acquiring another business; the networks may need to be able to communicate, but segmentation may still be required between the two. This type of situation might require multiple topologies that can be managed as one. Figure 1-6 illustrates an end-to-end segmentation topology, along with how different VPNs are carried over the tunnels. Each of these tunnels terminates at an edge router within the environment.

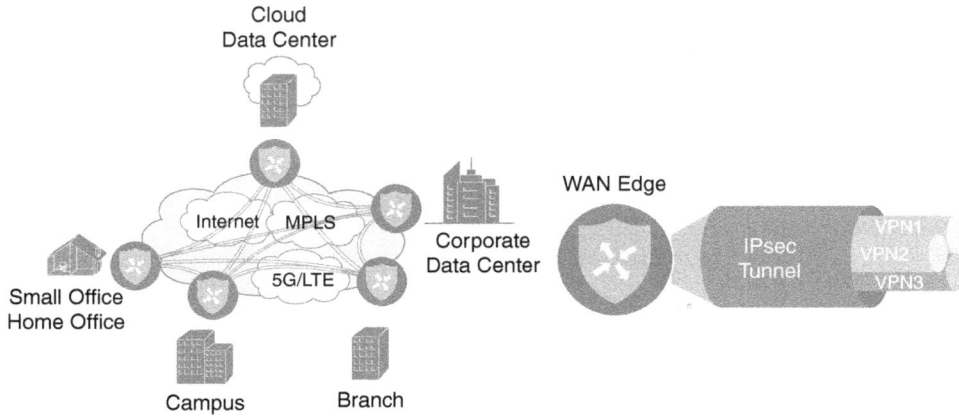

Figure 1-6   *End-to-End Segmentation*

Key Topic

Direct Internet Access

Direct Internet Access (DIA) gives branches the capability to send traffic directly out the local Internet transport instead of carrying it all the way back to a centralized data center to be inspected. This allows for cloud-based applications to go directly to the Internet and cloud service providers without having to use unnecessary WAN bandwidth. This method is increasingly being adopted.

Figure 1-7 illustrates the traditional way that cloud applications are accessed, which causes suboptimal performance for users trying to access these applications. As mentioned earlier, this method also puts a strain on the WAN infrastructure, as the expensive and limited WAN bandwidth is being consumed by applications that could be sent directly to the Internet from the remote site. It also introduces increased application latency, as the traffic has to cross the entire network to get to the data center to reach the Internet.

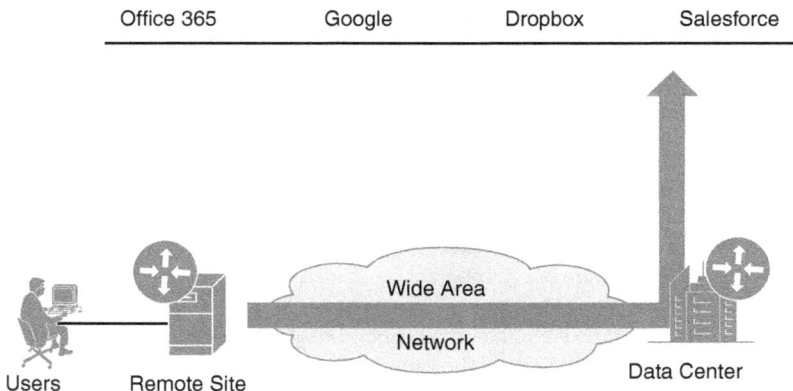

Figure 1-7   *Traditional Cloud Application Access via WAN*

Redesigning the WAN allows for different mechanisms that will allow for better performance and scalability. A great example of this is using the Direct Internet Access design to offload latency-sensitive cloud applications directly to the Internet. This method also provides the flexibility of allowing a local firewall or inspection device in the branch to ensure that the branch is protected from any malicious threats coming into the local branch Internet link. Figure 1-8 shows an example of what this would look like in a new WAN environment.

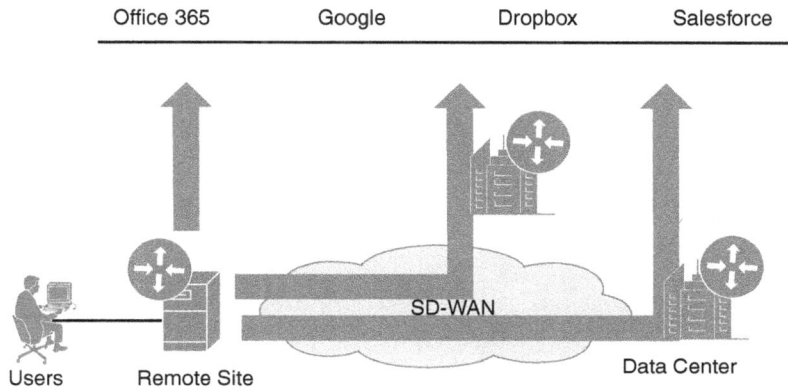

Figure 1-8 *Direct Internet Access and Cloud Access Topologies*

Fully Managed Network Solution

Finally, there is a use case that allows for the business to simply let someone else, such as Cisco or a Cisco partner, manage the network as a fully managed solution. This option provides the flexibility to have the network managed as a whole for the business and also allows the business to have control over the policy and reporting portion of the managed service. This is becoming a more attractive option for customers that want to move to an OpEx model. They can pay for their network on a subscription basis rather than use the traditional CapEx model and is analogous to paying an electric or cell phone bill. The consumption models available today are really opening up new options for customers.

NOTE   All of these use cases and technologies are covered in detail in this book.

Cloud Trends and Adoption

Cloud adoption has been taking the industry by storm. Over the years, the reliance on the cloud has grown significantly, starting with music, movies, and storage and moving into software as a service (SaaS) and infrastructure as a service (IaaS). Today, there are many aspects of businesses—such as application development, quality assurance, and production—that are running in the cloud. To make things even more complicated, companies are relying on multiple cloud vendors to operate their businesses.

Companies are also struggling with things such as shadow IT and backdoor applications in their environments. Lines of business are going to cloud providers on their own, without any knowledge or guidance from IT departments, and spinning up applications on demand in the cloud. As companies migrate workloads to the cloud, they are typically looking to keep the same set of policies they use on premises when carrying traffic into the cloud. Security and privacy are both concerns, and the potential loss of confidential information or intellectual property could damage an organization's brand and reputation. The risks are significant.

Furthermore, the applications in the cloud, whether legitimate production or development applications, still require certain levels of priority and treatment to ensure that they are being delivered properly to the users who consume them. Cisco Catalyst SD-WAN can help ensure that the applications are being treated appropriately and that the experience for the users is adequate.

Figure 1-9 illustrates the demand on the WAN and how the Internet is becoming critical to the operations of the business.

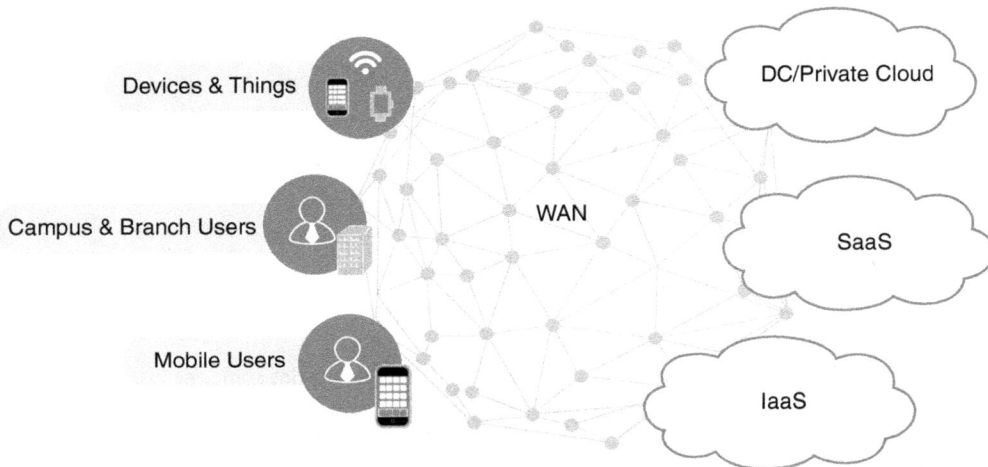

Figure 1-9   *Demand on the WAN for Internet-Based Applications*

Direct Internet Access can assist with this, as mentioned earlier. By being able to detect application performance through one or more Direct Internet Access circuits, the edge routers are able to choose the best-performing path based on the application-specific parameters. If one of the links to the cloud application fails or experiences performance degradation, the application can automatically fail over to another Direct Internet Access link. This process is fully automated and requires no interaction from the network operations staff. Figure 1-10 shows this scenario with multiple Direct Internet Access links.

This concept also works in an environment that has a remote branch site that has a local directly attached Internet link as well as an Internet link within a centralized data center. The same process takes place: The application performance is measured and the path that provides the best performance is chosen for the application. Similarly, Direct Internet Access can protect against blackout or link failures because of the redundancy built into the solution via the multiple available paths. Figure 1-11 illustrates a scenario with a local directly attached Internet link and an Internet link available in a centralized data center. Again, this leaves the router to make the decision based on the policy and application parameters configured. These decisions are fully automated and made on a per-application and per-VPN basis, which ultimately provides an amazing amount of flexibility and control over the application performance within the environment.

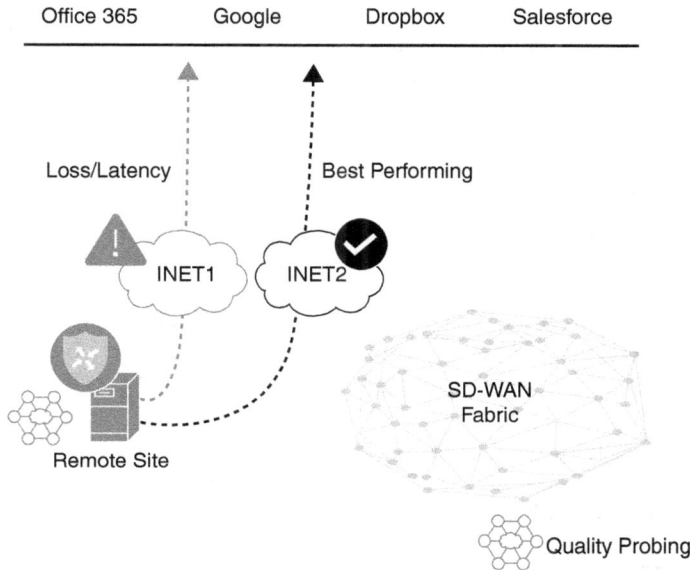

Figure 1-10   *Multiple Direct Internet Access Links to Cloud Applications*

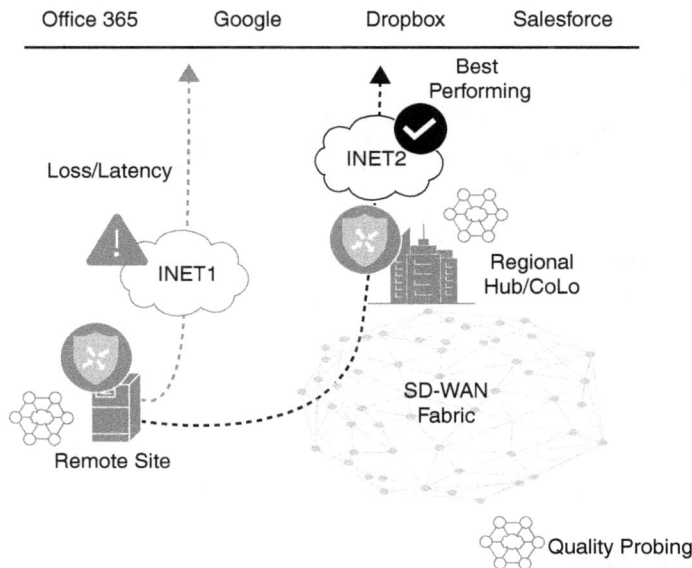

Figure 1-11   *Direct Internet Access and Centralized Internet Link to Cloud Applications*

There is one more force driving organizations to the cloud that we need to mention: As companies are moving their custom-developed applications to public cloud providers such as Amazon Web Services, Microsoft Azure, and Google Compute, the companies want to connect these cloud providers to their WANs. By connecting these cloud providers to your WAN, you can continue to maintain a common routing policy while also enforcing your business's security policy. In some cases, you can now leverage a cloud provider's network for transport for your WAN sites; this is referred to as middle-mile optimization. By taking advantage of middle-mile optimization, you can provide a simpler, more efficient, and scalable solution, using the cloud provider's global infrastructure.

Summary

This chapter provides a high-level overview of network challenges for businesses and their operations staff. It also covers common business and IT trends the industry is seeing and how they impact networks today. Organizations and their IT staff are rethinking the WAN environment in order to attain certain benefits. Cloud applications and the influx of large amounts traffic the network are causing strain on the WAN. Businesses are looking at ways to alleviate the pressure being put on the WAN—and on the organization as a whole. The use cases introduced in this chapter are all covered in depth in the upcoming chapters in this book.

As you have seen, cost is not the only factor driving organizations to look at SD-WAN. Application performance, security, segmentation, user experience, redundancy, and resiliency are also key drivers that point to SD-WAN.

Review All Key Topics

Review the most important topics in this chapter, noted with the Key Topic icon in the outer margin of the page. Table 1-1 lists these key topics and the page number on which each is found.

Key Topic

Table 1-1   Key Topics for Chapter 1

Key Topic Element	Description	Page Number
Section	Transport independence	3
Section	Protecting critical applications with SLAs	7
Paragraph	Cisco Direct Internet Access	8
Section	Cloud Trends and Adoption	9

Key Terms

Define the following key terms from this chapter and check your answers in the glossary:

application programming interface (API), Cisco Software-Defined WAN (Cisco SD-WAN), cloud, infrastructure as a service (IaaS), service-level agreement (SLA), software as a service (SaaS)

Chapter Review Questions

1.   What are some benefits businesses are looking for from their WAN? (Choose three.)

   a.   Lower operational complexity

   b.   Increased usable bandwidth

   c.   Reduced uptime in branch locations

   d.   Topology dependence

   e.   Improved overall user experience

2. What are some of the tools or technologies that may need to be implemented when redundant links are used in branch locations? (Choose three.)

   a. Administrative distance

   b. Traffic engineering

   c. Redistribution

   d. Loop prevention

   e. Preferred path selection

3. For what reasons are organizations looking to deploy SD-WAN? (Choose two.)

   a. To take all routing control from the service provider

   b. To create end-to-end SLAs for the organization's traffic

   c. To offload all routing control to the service provider

   d. To leverage the service provider's SLA for end-to-end traffic

4. What are some of the benefits of SD-WAN? (Choose four.)

   a. Lower cost

   b. Improved user experience

   c. Transport independence

   d. Increased cloud consumption

   e. IoT devices

   f. Increased bandwidth

5. What are some of the transport options for SD-WAN? (Choose three.)

   a. Dual MPLS

   b. Hybrid WAN

   c. Dual route processor

   d. Hybrid single link

   e. Dual Internet

6. True or false: Direct Internet Access is used to offload applications directly to the data center.

   a. True

   b. False

7. What are two of the driving forces for cloud adoption? (Choose two.)

   a. Middle-mile optimization

   b. Cloud application migration

   c. Increased costs

   d. Increased complexity

## CHAPTER 2

Cisco Catalyst SD-WAN Components

This chapter covers the following topics:

- **Data Plane:** This section discusses the physical and virtual routers that actually carry data traffic.

- **Management Plane:** This section introduces the component that handles most of the day-to-day tasks in managing the Cisco Catalyst SD-WAN fabric.

- **Control Plane:** This section covers the component that handles all policies and routing.

- **Orchestration Plane:** This section introduces the component that facilitates discovery, authentication, and facilitation of the fabric.

- **Multi-tenancy Options:** This section introduces the various multi-tenancy options available in Cisco Catalyst SD-WAN.

- **Deployment Options:** This section covers the various deployment options, including Cisco cloud, private cloud, and on-premises deployments.

This chapter introduces the various components that make up the Cisco Catalyst SD-WAN architecture as well as the various deployment options. At a high level, these components can be grouped based on the purpose they play in Cisco Catalyst SD-WAN:

- Data plane

- Management plane

- Control plane

- Orchestration plane

In traditional networks, the management plane, data plane, and control plane are all on the same router, and together they facilitate communication within the network. A traditional router has network interfaces and line cards (which handle forwarding of data packets); this is a data plane. A CPU module, which handles calculating a routing table and advertising networks to the rest of the network, is a control plane, and the command-line interface (CLI) that is used to configure the router is a management plane. At the CLI, you type commands, and those commands program the CPU and line cards to act on your intent. Each router in a network has these three components.

A traditional network has a number of routers, each of which needs to be programmed independently to achieve the desired operational state of the network. As networks get larger, the amount of human intervention required to configure the environment dramatically increases, potentially creating complexity. Each router must calculate its own routing table from its perspective of the network. For example, suppose you have a network with 6000 routes. Whenever there is a change in the network, each router may potentially have to process routing updates for each of these routes. This means the router must have the available CPU and memory required to process these updates, and this creates a lot of overhead. Tuning the routing table on a network with a large number of sites and routes—whether the network is full mesh, hub and spoke, partial mesh, and so on—can quickly become very complex. In addition, because each router is programmed individually, when you program the network on a router-by-router basis, you run the risk of undesired results due to improper design or human error on the CLI.

Cisco Catalyst SD-WAN is a distributed architecture that provides a clear separation between the management plane, control plane, and data plane. Figure 2-1 illustrates how the components fit into the architecture.

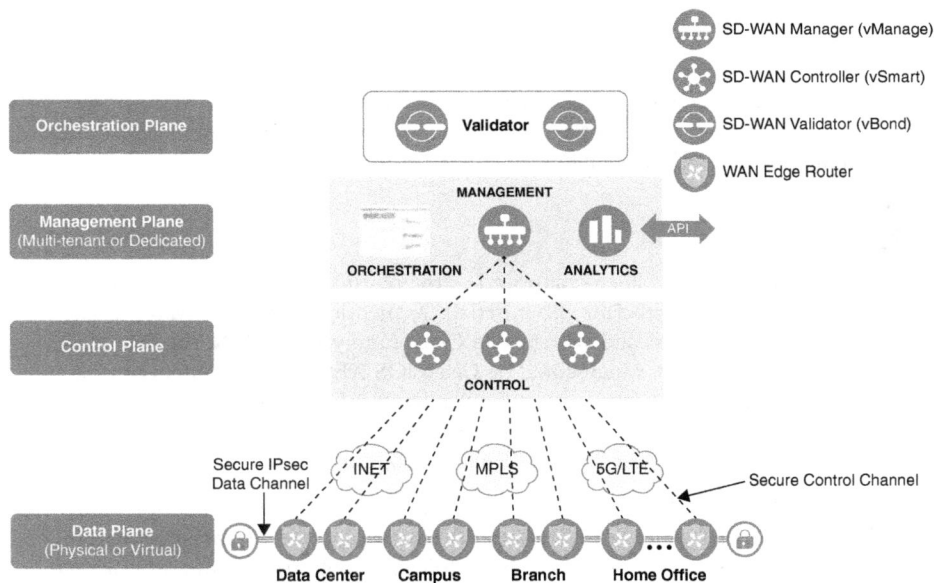

Figure 2-1 *Cisco Catalyst SD-WAN Distributed Architecture*

The Cisco Catalyst SD-WAN distributed architecture differs from traditional network architectures in that it allows you to support large-scale networks while reducing operational and computational overhead. Catalyst SD-WAN separates the data plane, the control plane, and the management plane from each other.

Because the control plane knows about all routes and nodes on the network, you have to calculate the routing table only once and can distribute the information to all the necessary nodes as a single routing update rather than have every router send routing updates to the others, with each determining its own Routing Information Base (RIB). This greatly reduces the overhead on the network and enables you to reduce required resources on the routers so that you can bring additional features and capabilities to your edge devices. Because you have a complete view of the network, you can create a common network policy across the entire SD-WAN fabric—and the management plane needs to program it only once. As new devices are added to the network, they receive the same policy as well, ensuring that the network is operating as expected. This book shows how you can create various topologies and policies with ease while increasing scale and capability.

NOTE   In 2023 Cisco SD-WAN was rebranded as Cisco Catalyst SD-WAN. In addition, starting with Cisco Catalyst SD-WAN Release 20.12, the following component changes apply:

- Cisco vManage is now Cisco Catalyst SD-WAN Manager.
- Cisco vAnalytics is now Cisco Catalyst SD-WAN Analytics.
- Cisco vBond is now Cisco Catalyst SD-WAN Validator.
- Cisco vSmart is now Cisco Catalyst SD-WAN Controller.
- Cisco SD-WAN Controllers (vManage, vSmart, and vBond together) are now Cisco Catalyst SD-WAN Control Components.

This change is reflected in the GUI and the official documentation. However, because the older names are more familiar to customers and are used in the ENSDWI certification exam, this book uses the new names but reminds you of the old names where appropriate.

Key Topic

Data Plane

Traditionally, the data plane has been composed of the physical interfaces that the physical layer plugs into (for example, Ethernet, fiber, serial). As mentioned previously, this is analogous to the line cards on routers and switches. In Cisco Catalyst SD-WAN, the data plane consists of WAN Edge devices, which could be Cisco IOS XE SD-WAN routers or legacy Cisco vEdge routers. Data plane devices may be deployed at branches, data centers, large campuses, colocation facilities, or in the cloud. At each site, you can have a single WAN Edge router or multiple WAN Edge routers, depending on your redundancy requirements.

The data plane is where the SD-WAN overlay resides and is the layer that forwards user, server, and other network traffic. Both IPv4 and IPv6 are supported for transport within the data plane. In addition, data policies (such as QoS and Application-Aware Routing) are enforced within the data plane.

Each WAN Edge router forms data plane connections to other WAN Edge routers within the SD-WAN overlay for the purposes of transporting user traffic. Data plane connections are only established between data plane devices. These tunnels are typically secured via Internet Protocol Security (IPsec). As described previously, the data plane has native segmentation. The segmentation information is encapsulated as defined in RFC 4023 and is carried across the SD-WAN overlay. Segmentation allows the network administrator to build separate instances of the data plane, depending on business requirements and regulations. The original data packets are typically encapsulated with IPsec, providing encryption and authentication.

Cisco Catalyst SD-WAN supports GRE as another method of data encapsulation. GRE provides less overhead but lacks all the security that IPsec provides, and it is used less often. Throughout this book, you can assume that IPsec encapsulation is being used unless noted otherwise.

Figure 2-2 illustrates the Cisco Catalyst SD-WAN packet structure.

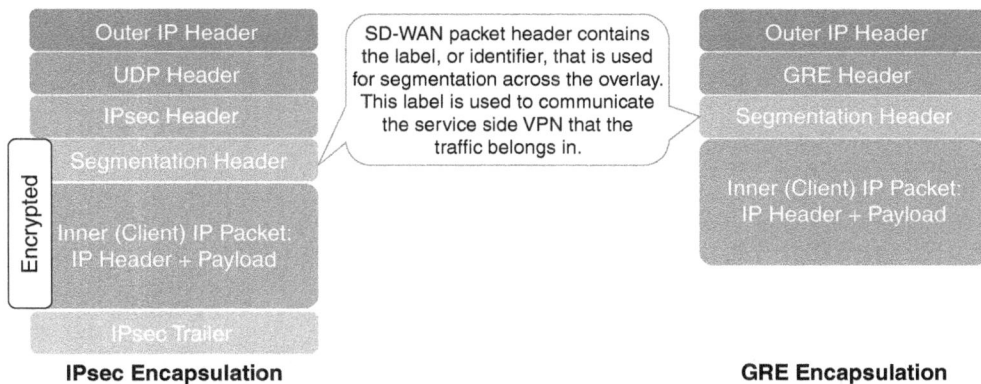

IPsec Encapsulation   **GRE Encapsulation**

Figure 2-2 *Cisco Catalyst SD-WAN Packet Format*

Cisco Catalyst SD-WAN can support diverse topologies that are unique to each VPN segment or data plane instantiation. These VPN segments are completely isolated from communicating with each other unless policy explicitly allows communication. These VPNs are carried in a single IPsec tunnel. For example, corporate users could have a full-mesh topology, while PCI or HIPAA requirements could dictate the use of a hub-and-spoke topology for other devices. Figure 2-3 provides a graphical representation of this concept.

On the LAN, or service, side, the data plane supports OSPF, EIGRP, RIPv2, and BGP for routing protocols. For smaller locations that don't utilize a routing protocol, VRRP is supported to provide first-hop gateway redundancy.

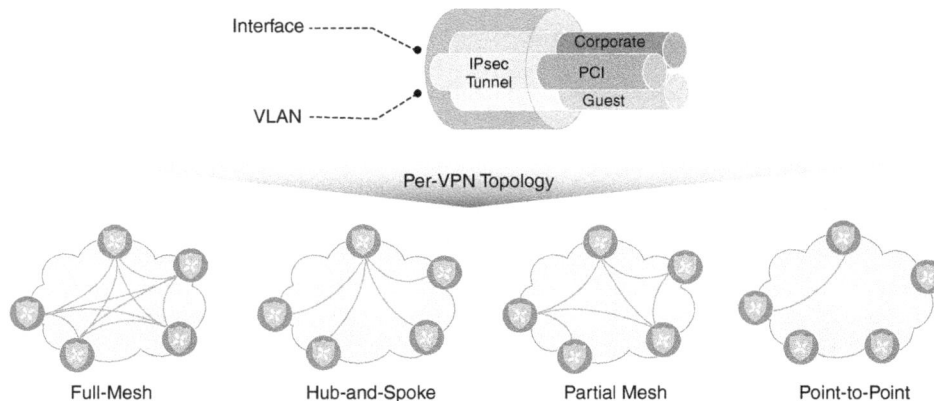

Figure 2-3 *Segmentation and Per-VPN Topologies*

NOTE   In Cisco Catalyst SD-WAN, Virtual Private Networks (VPN) are synonymous with Virtual Routing and Forwarding (VRF) instances from a generic routing perspective. VRF instances and VPNs provide a method to separate the control and data planes into different logical parts. Segmentation in the data plane is accomplished by building multiple isolated routing table instances and binding specific interfaces to those instances.

WAN Edge routers have built-in security to prevent unauthorized access from the network. The WAN-facing interfaces only allow connections from authenticated SD-WAN fabric components, such as SD-WAN Manager (formerly vManage) and SD-WAN Controllers (formerly vSmarts) and from other WAN Edge devices in the fabric (as learned from SD-WAN Controllers). For the rest of the traffic, the WAN-facing interface firewall on the WAN Edge router, by default, will block everything coming in from the outside that isn't allowed explicitly; this is also called an "implicit ACL." By default, a WAN Edge router only allows inbound DHCP, DNS, ICMP, and HTTP services. Other inbound services that can be enabled are SSH, NETCONF, NTP, OSPF, BGP, SNMP, and STUN.

NOTE   If a connection is initiated from a WAN Edge device and network address translation (NAT) is enabled on the WAN interface (for example, if Direct Internet Access is configured), return traffic is allowed by the NAT entry even if the implicit ACL has been configured as **no allow-service**. You can still block this traffic with an explicit ACL, as you will discover in later chapters.

Bidirectional Forwarding Detection (BFD) is used inside IPsec tunnels between all WAN Edge routers. BFD sends Hello packets to measure link liveness as well as packet loss, jitter, and delay. Each WAN Edge router makes its own determination about how to react to this BFD information. Depending on the policy defined by the management plane, routing across the data plane could be adjusted, such as having applications prefer one transport over the other, depending on the transport performance. BFD operates in echo mode, which means the neighbor doesn't actually participate in the processing of the BFD packet; instead, the BFD packet is simply echoed back to the original sender. This greatly reduces the impact on the CPU, as the neighbor doesn't need to process the packets. However, if the neighbor was involved in the processing of the BFD packets, and the remote neighbor's CPU were busy with some other processing, there could be potential delay in responding to the BFD packet. By eliminating this, you can reduce outage detection time and improve user experience. BFD cannot be turned off, but timers can be tuned in the SD-WAN fabric to identify and illicit a response to potential issues more quickly. Another advantage of using echo mode is that the original packet is echoed back to the original sender, and from this information, the WAN Edge router has a complete round-trip view of the transport.

When the WAN Edge router initially gets connected to the network and has no configuration present, it first tries to reach out to a Plug and Play (PNP) or Zero-Touch Provisioning (ZTP) server. Figure 2-4 provides a high-level overview of the PNP/ZTP process. This process will be discussed further in Chapter 4, "Onboarding and Provisioning," but for now, you just need to know that this is the process in which the router connects to the orchestration plane, learns about all of the various components in the network, and receives its configuration. Once the control plane is established, the last step is to build data plane connections to all other WAN Edge routers. By default, a full-mesh topology will be built, though policy can be built to limit data plane connections and influence the routing topology. It should be noted, as well, that if PNP or ZTP isn't available, there are other options available to manually bootstrap the configuration using the CLI or a USB thumb drive.

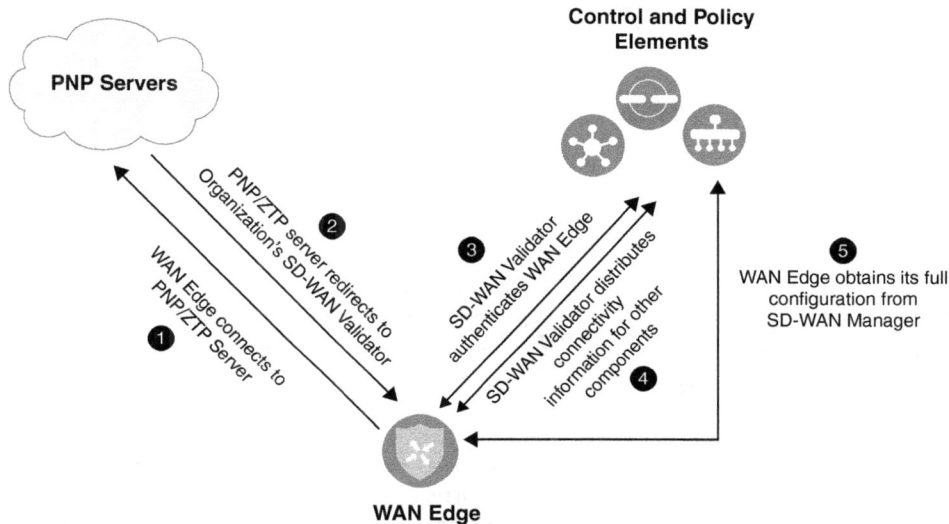

Figure 2-4 *High-Level Overview of the PNP/ZTP Process*

NOTE   There are two auto-provisioning methods for WAN Edge devices: PNP for Cisco IOS-XE Catalyst SD-WAN routers and ZTP, originally developed for Cisco vEdge routers. While the processes are quite similar, they rely on two different services. Both services are cloud based, but there's also an on-premises deployment option for ZTP that supports both device types. On-premises deployment can help in scenarios where Internet access is not available or local hosting of the PNP functionality is desirable.

SD-WAN Supported Platforms

Cisco offers the wide selection of platforms and appliances so that you can deploy SD-WAN anywhere, as illustrated in Figure 2-5. With Cisco Catalyst SD-WAN, you can create a comprehensive fabric and scale your entire network into hybrid and multicloud environments with ease.

In the ever-evolving landscape of networking, keeping up with product offerings can be challenging. At this writing, the leading Cisco Catalyst SD-WAN hardware platforms include Cisco Catalyst 8500, 8300, and 8200 Series Edge platforms, along with Cisco 1100 Series Integrated Services Routers (ISRs). Cisco Catalyst SD-WAN can also be deployed on SD-Branch solutions such as the Catalyst 8200 Series Edge uCPE and Cisco 5000 Enterprise Network Compute System (ENCS) using Network Functions Virtualization (NFV).

While Cisco Catalyst SD-WAN remains compatible with earlier hardware generations, like Cisco 4000 Series ISRs, Cisco Advanced Services Routers (ASRs), and original vEdge routers, it is important to note that these platforms are at different stages of their end-of-life lifecycle. Consequently, they are not recommended for new deployments.

SD-WAN platforms for any deployment

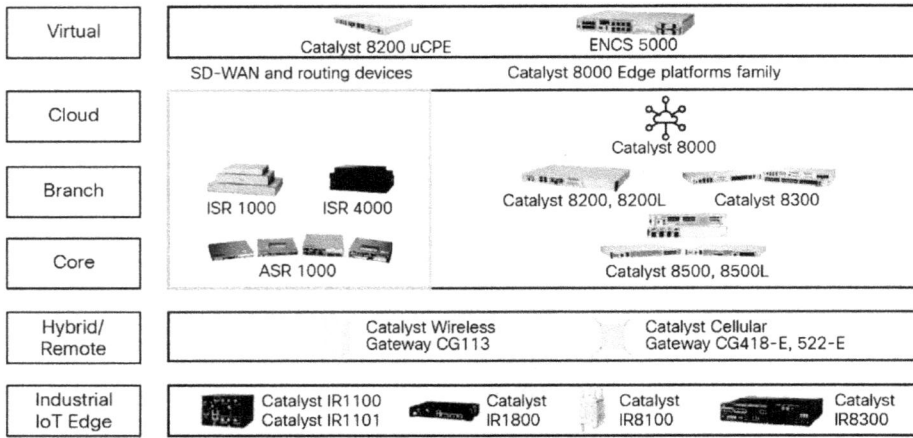

Figure 2-5   *Cisco Catalyst SD-WAN Supported Platforms*

A noteworthy feature of Cisco Catalyst SD-WAN is its seamless integration with public cloud environments, made possible through the Cisco Catalyst 8000V Edge Software and the legacy Cloud Services Router 1000V Series virtual platforms. Deployments in Amazon Web Services, Google Cloud, and Microsoft Azure are supported, offering flexibility and scalability. Virtual platforms can also be deployed in private clouds, running on either VMware ESXi or KVM hypervisors.

When deciding on WAN Edge platform, it's crucial to assess your specific requirements, including deployment type (physical or virtual), throughput needs, data plane tunnel scalability (such as the number of branches the router will communicate with), and the required interface types.

NOTE   Information about the Cisco Catalyst SD-WAN platform is accurate as of this writing. For the most current details, please consult the Cisco Catalyst SD-WAN home page or refer to the "SD-WAN Platforms" section in the Cisco Catalyst SD-WAN Solution Overview document on the Cisco documentation site.

NOTE   While Cisco Catalyst SD-WAN continues to support the original Cisco Viptela vEdge hardware models, including vEdge 100, vEdge 1000, vEdge 2000, and vEdge 5000, it is imperative to acknowledge the announced end of life for these devices. (For specific milestones and dates, please consult the product end-of-sale and end-of-life announcements.) Consequently, software development for this platform is concluding, with Version 20.6 marking the final release of Cisco Catalyst SD-WAN that includes support for Cisco vEdge 100 and vEdge 1000 devices. Version 20.9 is the last release for Cisco vEdge 2000 and vEdge 5000 routers.

Given these changes, this book focuses on the Cisco IOS XE SD-WAN platforms. All functionalities and features are described as they are implemented on Cisco IOS XE devices. Throughout the book, examples exclusively use Cisco IOS XE commands and configuration syntax, unless explicitly stated otherwise.

Some of the most important features supported on Cisco Catalyst SD-WAN routers are for advanced security use cases. While accessing the Internet directly via a local Internet circuit might pose security risks at the branch, overlaying security on top of Cisco Catalyst SD-WAN enables safe implementation of new use cases such as Direct Internet Access (DIA) and Direct Cloud Access (DCA).

Direct Internet Access allows certain Internet-bound traffic (for example, Facebook traffic, YouTube traffic) to be forwarded from the branch directly to the Internet instead of being backhauled to data center via SD-WAN fabric. Direct Cloud Access enables cloud traffic (for example, Office365 traffic, Salesforce traffic, Box traffic, Google traffic) to be sent from the branch directly to the Internet or, optionally, backhauled to data centers based on path performance. Figure 2-6 illustrates these concepts.

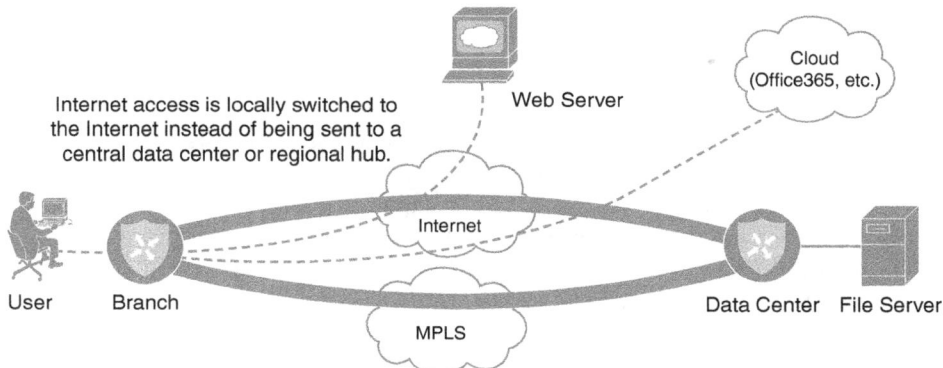

Figure 2-6   *Direct Internet Access/Direct Cloud Access Overview*

Security use cases are discussed in more detail in Chapter 11, "Cisco Catalyst SD-WAN Security," but here is a list of some of the currently supported security features:

- DNS security (Cisco Umbrella)

- Secure Internet Gateways (SIGs) and Cisco Secure Access integration

- Cisco Enterprise Firewall with Application Awareness

- Intrusion Prevention Systems (IPSs)

- URL Filtering

- Cisco Advanced Malware Protection

- SSL/TLS Proxy for Decryption of TLS Traffic

Traditionally, security requirements dictated centralization of the Internet access where all Internet traffic is backhauled to data centers, colocation, or regional sites. It was cost-effective to implement security at a central location rather than deal with the management and costs of disparate security components across many sites. With Cisco Catalyst SD-WAN security, businesses can now decentralize security functions, moving them to the branch level. This movement allows organizations to offload Internet access at remote sites. Here are some other areas where a business might see benefits from DIA:

■ Reduced bandwidth requirements and latency on costly WAN circuits

■ Guest access

■ Improved user experience to cloud SaaS and IaaS applications

Chapter 8, "Centralized Data Policies," discusses DIA in more detail.

When a WAN Edge router joins the fabric, it attempts to build control connections to SD-WAN Control Components across each transport deployed at that site. By default, if a transport doesn't have control connectivity to any of the SD-WAN Control Components, then it won't build a data plane connection across that transport either. This may be the case with cloud deployments where the controllers are in a public cloud and MPLS transport has no connectivity to the Internet.

NOTE   There are a few options to still activate the data plane for a transport with no control connectivity. One option is to disable control connections on that transport via the **max-control-connections 0** command. Be aware that when control connections aren't established on an interface, there will be no control plane monitoring over that transport. You still have monitoring from a data plane perspective, however.

Management Plane

As mentioned previously, network devices of the past were managed individually via the CLI. Cisco Catalyst SD-WAN, however, introduces SD-WAN Manager (formerly vManage), which is a network management system (NMS) that provides a single pane of glass to manage Catalyst SD-WAN. SD-WAN Manager can be used for device onboarding, provisioning, policy creation, software management, troubleshooting, and monitoring.

While SD-WAN Manager offers a rich feature set, if the preference is to interface with it programmatically, SD-WAN Manager also supports communication via REST APIs. In fact, the SD-WAN Manager GUI is fully API driven, meaning that actions performed in it are executed using REST API calls. With full access to SD-WAN APIs, users can automate tasks, build scripts, and interface with SD-WAN Manager programmatically.

As you can see in Figure 2-7, SD-WAN Manager provides an intuitive and easy-to-consume dashboard. When you first log in to SD-WAN Manager, you are presented with an overview of the current state of the network.

vManage deployment options range from standalone nodes to three- or six-node clustered setups, offering enhanced scale and redundancy. A single SD-WAN Manager can potentially handle up to 1000 to 1500 devices, and a six-node SD-WAN Manager cluster may support more than 10,000 devices. It's important to note that these numbers may vary based on a number of factors, such as SD-WAN Manager resources (instances/CPU/RAM/storage), the statistics load, and the version of SD-WAN software in use. (Numbers mentioned in this chapter are specific to Version 20.12.) For more accurate specifications, please consult the "Recommended Computing Resources for Cisco Catalyst SD-WAN Control Components" document for the SD-WAN software version you are using or are planning to use, available on the Cisco website.

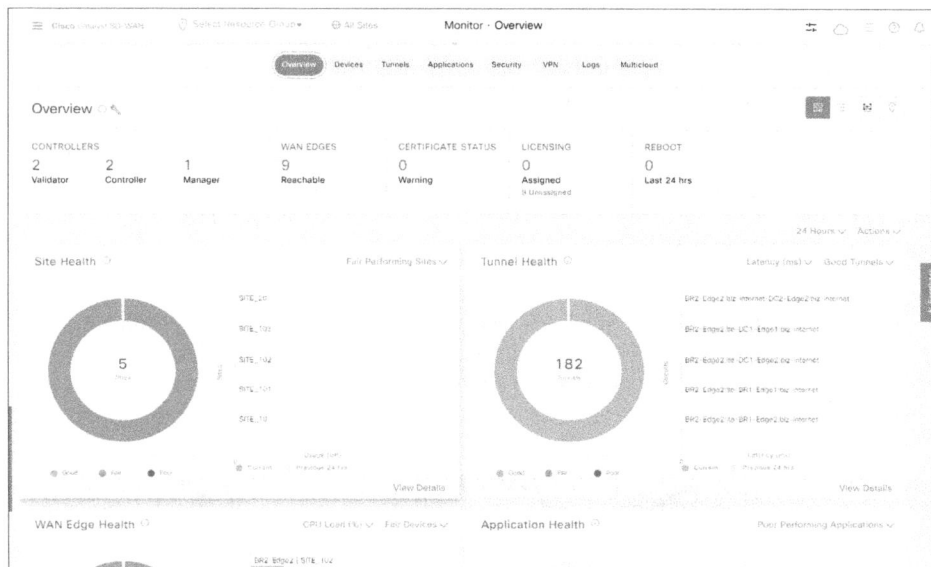

Figure 2-7 *Cisco SD-WAN Manager*

An SD-WAN Manager cluster is designed to tolerate the failure of a single server, but for high availability, a standby cluster should be implemented to handle a complete cluster failure. Typically, it is deployed in a geographically redundant location, such as a secondary data center in another region.

SD-WAN Manager can use multiple authentication sources, including RADIUS, TACACS, and SAML 2.0, for external user connectivity. By default, SD-WAN Manager is deployed in a single-tenant mode; however, if the requirements call for support of a service provider model, multi-tenancy may be used.

All configuration for the SD-WAN fabric should be performed via SD-WAN Manager in order to maintain consistency and scalability. As discussed further in Chapter 4, you can build device configurations in SD-WAN Manager via configuration groups, feature templates, or CLI templates. You can also configure policies to control things such as network topology, routing, QoS, and security in SD-WAN Manager. SD-WAN Manager is also where you perform troubleshooting and monitoring of the network. Network administrators can simulate traffic flows to show data paths, troubleshoot WAN impairment, analyze traffic flows in the network with Network-Wide Path Insights (NWPI), and access real-time operational information (such as routing tables) for all network devices. This greatly simplifies operations as there is no longer a need to log in to each WAN Edge router individually. Instead, troubleshooting can be accomplished via a single dashboard.

Each WAN Edge router forms a single management plane connection to SD-WAN Manager. If a device has multiple transports available, only one will be used for management plane connectivity to SD-WAN Manager. If a cluster is in place, the control connection will be load balanced across cluster nodes. If a transport hosting the management plane connection experiences an outage, the WAN Edge router will briefly lose connectivity to SD-WAN Manager, and any changes made will be pushed when the device reconnects.

The last component in the management plane is SD-WAN Analytics (formerly vAnalytics). As shown in Figure 2-8, SD-WAN Analytics gives the network administrator predictive analytics to provide actionable insight into the WAN. With SD-WAN Analytics, the business can perform trending and capacity planning of circuits, and it can review how application performance is trending globally. With capacity planning, you can see how new applications may interact on your WAN before actually deploying them, allowing your business to right-size connectivity. SD-WAN Analytics ingests data from the network and uses machine learning to predict capacity trends. SD-WAN Analytics is cloud based, it requires additional licensing, and it is not enabled by default.

NOTE It is important to note that SD-WAN Manager should be used for a real-time, raw data view of the network, while SD-WAN Analytics should be used as a tool to review the historical performance of the network and get forward-looking insight into network adjustments.

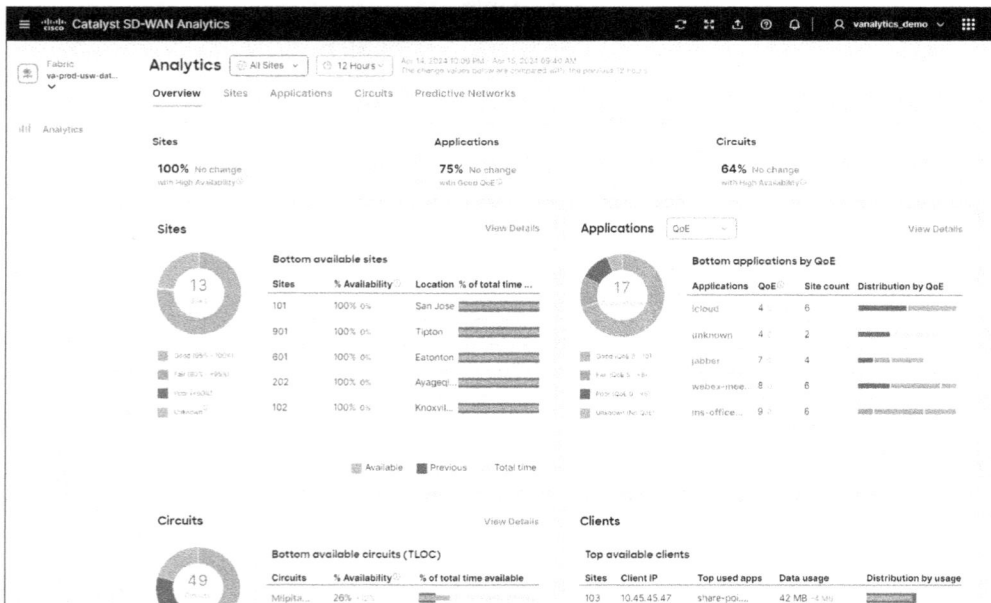

Figure 2-8 *Cisco SD-WAN Analytics*

Key Topic Control Plane

Previously, you learned how the control plane has traditionally been separated from the data plane. SD-WAN Controller (vSmart) is the component that provides control plane functionality and is the brain of the SD-WAN fabric. It is highly scalable and can handle up to 5000 control connections per instance, with up to 12 SD-WAN Controllers in a single production deployment (as of SD-WAN Version 20.12). With these numbers, a deployment can support very large SD-WAN networks.

SD-WAN Controller is responsible for the implementation of control plane policies, centralized data polices, service chaining, and VPN topologies. It also handles key management, which is an important part in the security and encryption of the fabric.

Separating the control plane from the data and management planes allows a solution to achieve greater scale while simplifying network operations. With Cisco Catalyst SD-WAN, all SD-WAN Controllers learn all the routing information. Then they calculate the routing table and distribute it to the WAN Edge routers, taking into consideration applicable centralized control policies.

A WAN Edge router can connect to multiple SD-WAN Controllers at a time but needs connectivity to only one to get its routing and policy information.

The protocol that SD-WAN Controllers use to communicate all this information is called *Overlay Management Protocol (OMP)*. Although OMP handles routing, it would be a disservice to consider it simply a routing protocol. OMP is used to manage and control the overlay beyond just routing (key management, configuration updates, and so on). As illustrated in Figure 2-9, OMP runs between SD-WAN Controller and WAN Edge routers inside a secured tunnel. When a policy is built via the management plane, it is distributed to SD-WAN Controller via NETCONF, and SD-WAN Controller then distributes this policy via an OMP update to WAN Edge routers.

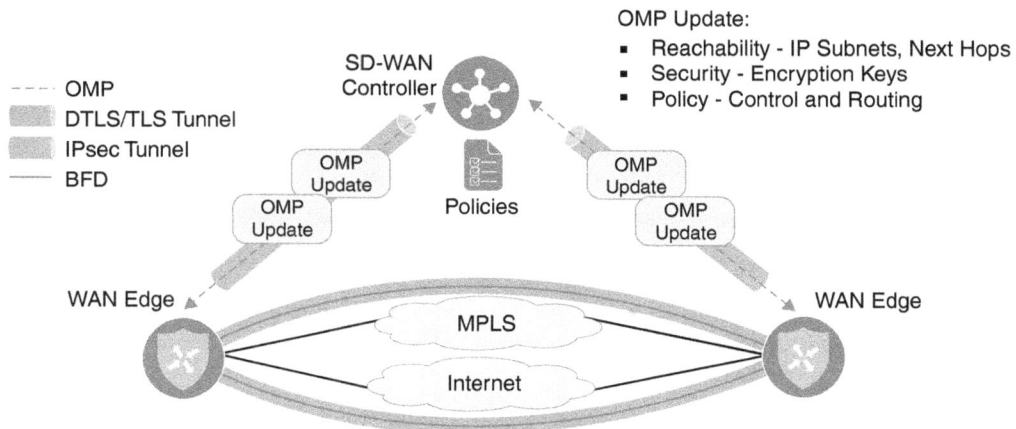

Figure 2-9 *Cisco Control Plane and Data Plane Overview*

SD-WAN Controller operates similarly to a BGP route reflector in iBGP. It receives routing information from each WAN Edge router and can apply policies before advertising this information back out to other WAN Edge routers. One example of these policies is the creation of distinct per-VPN topologies. To achieve it, the control policy is defined in SD-WAN Manager, which then distributes the policy through the management plane. Then, SD-WAN Controller applies the policy to the fabric. In this example, topology modification is achieved by manipulating what routes get distributed and how the data plane is built between WAN Edge routers.

NOTE   Note that SD-WAN Controllers are only involved in control plane communication. SD-WAN Controllers help WAN Edge routers build the data plane but are never a part of the data plane and never forward data packets.

The control plane also plays an important role in the encryption of the fabric. In legacy WAN technologies, securing the network required a considerable amount of processing power, as each device would compute its own encryption keys per peer and distribute those keys to peers by using a protocol such as ISAKMP/IKE. For more efficient scaling in Cisco SD-WAN networks, key exchange and distribution have been moved to the SD-WAN Controller, and no IKE is implemented since identity has already been established between the WAN Edge routers and SD-WAN Control Components. Each WAN Edge router computes its own set of keys per transport and sends them to SD-WAN Controllers. SD-WAN Controllers then distribute them to each WAN Edge router, according to the defined policy. This process repeats when IPsec security associations (SAs) expire and new keys are generated. By moving the key exchange to a centralized location, you achieve greater scale as each WAN Edge router doesn't need to handle key negotiation or distribution. (Refer to Figure 2-9 for an overview of how the control and data planes are built.) Chapter 3, "Control Plane and Data Plane Operations," covers this in more detail.

If control connectivity has been established but has been lost due to an outage, data plane connectivity continues to work. By default, WAN Edge routers continue forwarding data plane traffic in the absence of control plane connectivity for up to 12 hours, utilizing the last-known state of the routing table, although this is configurable, depending on your requirements. When control plane connectivity is reestablished, WAN Edge routers are updated with any policy changes that were made during the outage. When the control connection is restored, the routing table is refreshed, and any stale routes are flushed.

For redundancy, it is the best practice to deploy at least two geographically dispersed SD-WAN Controllers. They should have identical policy configuration to ensure network stability. If these configurations differ, there's a risk of suboptimal routing and potential blackholing of traffic. SD-WAN Controllers maintain a full mesh of OMP sessions among themselves and exchange control and routing information, although each operates autonomously (that is, there is no database synchronized between them).

Figure 2-10 shows how OMP is established between multiple SD-WAN Controllers and WAN Edge routers. SD-WAN Controllers form a full mesh among themselves, which ensures that they stay synchronized. WAN Edge routers establish one OMP session to each of two (by default) SD-WAN Controllers, but they do not create OMP sessions with each other. When there are more than two SD-WAN Controllers in the network, their selection is based on an algorithm to ensure that load balancing occurs. In the event of the total failure of an SD-WAN Controller, the sessions are redistributed between the remaining SD-WAN Controllers to maintain network continuity and stability.

By default, each WAN Edge router establishes multiple secure control connections, one over each available transport, to each selected SD-WAN Controller. However, only one OMP session is established between the WAN Edge device and each SD-WAN Controller, using one of those control connections as a transport.

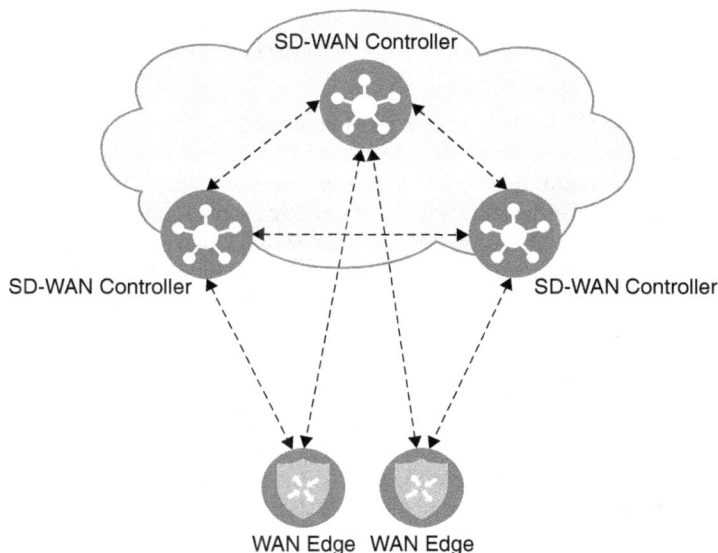

Figure 2-10   *OMP Session Establishment*

Orchestration Plane

The final, and probably the most important, component in Cisco Catalyst SD-WAN is SD-WAN Validator (formerly vBond). This component is very important because it provides initial authentication for participation in the fabric and acts as the glue that discovers and brings together all other components. Multiple SD-WAN Validator instances can be deployed to achieve high availability. Since a WAN Edge router can point to only a single SD-WAN Validator, it is recommended to configure WAN Edge routers to use a DNS name that has a single A record pointing to the IP addresses of all SD-WAN Validators. When the WAN Edge router tries to resolve the DNS record for the SD-WAN Validator, the DNS server provides multiple IP addresses for the hostname, and the WAN Edge router tries to connect to each of them sequentially until a successful control connection is made.

When a WAN Edge router first joins the overlay, the only thing it knows about the SD-WAN network is the IP address or DNS name of the SD-WAN Validator. It receives this information via one of these methods:

- PNP/ZTP

- Bootstrap configuration

- Manual configuration

The WAN Edge router attempts to build a temporary connection to the SD-WAN Validator over each transport. Once the control plane connectivity is up to SD-WAN Controller and SD-WAN Manager, the connection to the SD-WAN Validator is torn down. When the WAN Edge router connects to the SD-WAN Validator, they both go through an authentication process in which each component authenticates the other and, if successful, a Datagram Transport Layer Security (DTLS) tunnel is established. The SD-WAN Validator then distributes the connectivity information for the SD-WAN Controller and SD-WAN Manager to the WAN

Edge router. You can see why the SD-WAN Validator is referred to as the glue of the network: It tells all the components about each other. (This process is discussed in more detail in Chapters 3 and 4.)

One remaining functionality that the SD-WAN Validator provides is NAT traversal. By default, the SD-WAN Validator operates as a STUN server (RFC 5389). A WAN Edge router operates as a STUN client. What this means is that the SD-WAN Validator can detect when WAN Edge routers are behind a NAT device such as a firewall. When a WAN Edge router goes to establish its DTLS tunnel, the interface IP address it knows about is written into the outer IP header and noted within a payload of the message. When SD-WAN Validator receives this information, it compares the two values. If they are different, it can be inferred that NAT is in the transit path of the WAN Edge router (since the outer IP header was changed to a NAT IP address and no longer matches the IP address noted in the payload of the packet). The SD-WAN Validator communicates this back to the WAN Edge router, and the WAN Edge router can communicate this information to the rest of the overlay components—ultimately allowing data plane connectivity to be established through a NAT device. There are, however, some scenarios where this won't work, such as with symmetric NAT (as discussed in more detail in Chapters 3 and 4). Figure 2-11 explains how STUN is used to detect when a WAN Edge router or another SD-WAN Control Component is subject to NAT.

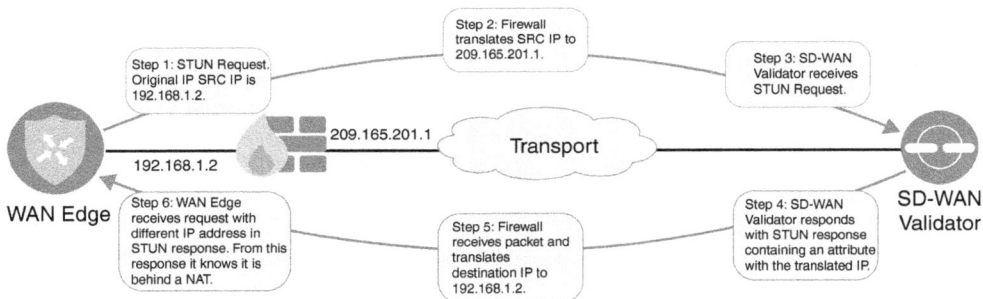

Figure 2-11   *STUN NAT Detection Method*

When deploying an SD-WAN Validator, one special consideration is that it must be reachable directly from all transports with enabled control connectivity. This implies that SD-WAN Validator needs a public IP address (or a private IP address with 1:1 static NAT) when Internet transports are used in SD-WAN fabric.

Other SD-WAN Control Components (including SD-WAN Managers and SD-WAN Controllers) can use private IP addresses as long as they have connectivity to SD-WAN Validator since they use the same NAT discovery method (STUN) as the WAN Edge routers.

Multi-tenancy Options

Cisco Catalyst SD-WAN supports multiple modes of segmentation in the control, data, management, and orchestration planes, as shown in Figure 2-12. One mode is dedicated tenancy. In this mode, each tenant has dedicated components, and the data plane is segmented as well. The second option is VPN tenancy. This mode segments only the data plane of the VPN topology and allows you to define read-only users who can view and monitor their VPN within SD-WAN Manager. VPN tenancy still shares the same SD-WAN components, however. The third option is multi-tenancy. With Cisco Catalyst SD-WAN multi-tenancy, a service provider can manage multiple customers, called tenants, from SD-WAN Manager.

The tenants share the same set of underlying SD-WAN Control Components: SD-WAN Manager, SD-WAN Validators, and SD-WAN Controllers. The tenant data is logically isolated on these shared SD-WAN Control Components. WAN Edge devices are typically tenant specific (that is, not shared), but service providers managing a multi-tenant SD-WAN deployment may deploy a multi-tenant WAN Edge device to serve as a shared gateway for traffic belonging to multiple tenants.

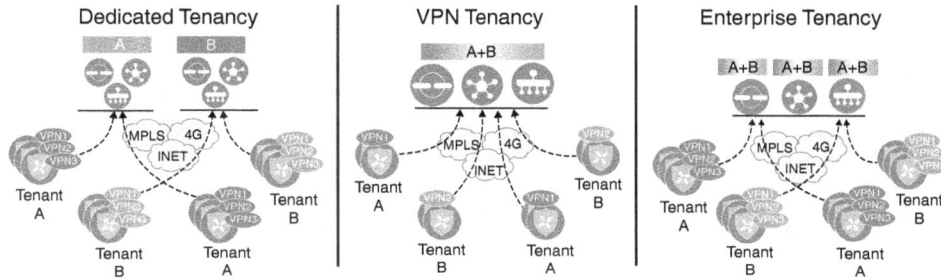

Figure 2-12   *Cisco Catalyst SD-WAN Multi-Tenancy Options*

Deployment Options

Cisco Catalyst SD-WAN supports multiple deployment options for SD-WAN Control Components:

- **Cisco cloud hosted:** This is the recommended and the most common deployment option, where Cisco builds, operates, and monitors all the SD-WAN Control Components introduced in this chapter. This greatly simplifies the deployment, allowing the network administrator to focus on the configuration and policy administration of the Cisco Catalyst SD-WAN fabric. Customers can manage their deployments through the Cisco Catalyst SD-WAN portal (https://ssp.sdwan.cisco.com), a cloud-infrastructure automation tool tailored for Cisco Catalyst SD-WAN. Using this portal, they can submit fabric provision requests, indicating the preferred cloud provider (AWS or Azure) and regions for hosting SD-WAN Control Components and data. The SD-WAN portal also offers additional functions, such as controller monitoring and fabric maintenance.

- **Managed service provider (MSP) or partner hosted:** SD-WAN Control Components are hosted in a private or public (AWS or Azure) cloud of an MSP or partner. The provider is responsible for provisioning of the SD-WAN Control Components and backups/disaster recovery.

- **On premises:** This option is suitable when business requirements dictate hosting SD-WAN Control Components in a traditional data center. With this approach, customers assume full responsibility for deploying, managing, and monitoring the SD-WAN Control Components. While it offers full control, customers must also manage the operations and maintenance of servers hosting these components. Another challenge is resource scaling, which is not as easy as with cloud-hosted solutions. On-premises deployment is particularly important for companies that are subject to strict regulations, such as those in the government, financial, healthcare, and utilities sectors.

- **Customer cloud hosted:** In this mix of previous options, SD-WAN Control Components are deployed in a public cloud (AWS or Azure), but customers are fully responsible for their deployment, management, and monitoring. Compared to on-premises hosting, customer cloud deployments have a low initial setup cost, as there is no need to purchase additional data center infrastructure. This option brings in traditional cloud benefits: ease of provisioning, stability, security, and scaling.

Summary

This chapter introduces the components that make up Cisco Catalyst SD-WAN. It discusses the data plane, wherein user traffic is routed and forwarded across the WAN. The data plane is similar to routers that would be deployed in a traditional WAN; in Cisco Catalyst SD-WAN, they are referred to as WAN Edge routers.

This chapter also introduces SD-WAN Manager, which is part of the management plane, where all Day 0, Day 1, and Day N functions are performed, including WAN Edge configuration, routing and control policies, troubleshooting, and monitoring.

You have seen that SD-WAN Controller, the brain of the Cisco Catalyst SD-WAN fabric, is responsible for calculating and deploying all control and data policies as well as handling the distribution of encryption keys for data plane connectivity.

You have also seen that SD-WAN Validator makes up the orchestration plane and is responsible for authenticating components on the fabric in addition to distributing control and management plane information to the WAN Edge routers. SD-WAN Validator is the component that aids in discovery of the fabric for all other components (such as when devices are behind NAT).

Finally, this chapter discusses deployment options. The most common deployment method is Cisco cloud hosted, but there are three other options to consider: on-premises, public cloud, and customer cloud hosted. By supporting all four deployment options, Cisco Catalyst SD-WAN can support all business requirements.

Review All Key Topics

Review the most important topics in the chapter, noted with the Key Topic icon in the outer margin of the page. Table 2-1 lists these key topics and the page number on which each is found.

Key Topic

Table 2-1   Key Topics

Key Topic Element	Description	Page
Figure 2-1	Cisco Catalyst SD-WAN distributed architecture	15
Section	Data plane	16
Section	Cisco Catalyst SD-WAN supported platforms	19
Section	Management plane	22
Section	Control plane	24
Section	Orchestration plane	27

Key Terms

Define the following key terms from this chapter and check your answers in the glossary:

control plane, data plane, management plane, orchestration plane, Overlay Management Protocol (OMP), SD-WAN Controller, SD-WAN Manager, SD-WAN Validator, WAN Edge

Chapter Review Questions

1. What are the three Cisco Catalyst SD-WAN Control Components? (Choose three.)

    a. SD-WAN Controller

    b. SD-WAN Validator

    c. WAN Edge

    d. SD-WAN Manager

    e. SD-WAN Orchestrator

2. How does the Cisco Catalyst SD-WAN architecture differ from traditional WAN technologies? (Choose three.)

    a. Single pane of glass

    b. Increased scale with centralized control plane

    c. Reduced uptime in branch locations

    d. Topology dependence

    e. Distributed architecture

3. What are the three functions of SD-WAN Manager in Cisco Catalyst SD-WAN?

    a. Troubleshooting

    b. Configuration

    c. Redistribution

    d. Loop prevention

    e. Monitoring

4. True or false: WAN Edge routers provide data plane encryption via IPsec.

    a. True

    b. False

5. What traditional networking concept does SD-WAN Controller closely relate to?

    a. OSPF designated router

    b. DHCP helper

    c. BGP route reflector

    d. PIM designated router

6. What functions does SD-WAN Validator provide in the SD-WAN environment? (Choose two.)

    a. Authentication and authorization of the SD-WAN components

    b. NAT detection and traversal

    c. Pushing configuration to WAN Edge routers

    d. Software upgrades

7. True or false: Cisco Catalyst SD-WAN supports multi-tenancy.

   a. True

   b. False

8. Which routing protocols are not supported on the service side of Cisco Catalyst SD-WAN? (Choose two.)

   a. EIGRP

   b. OSPF

   c. RIPv1

   d. OMP

   e. BGP

9. What attributes are measured with BFD? (Choose three.)

   a. Delay

   b. Loss

   c. Jitter

   d. Out-of-order packets

10. True or false: Cisco Catalyst SD-WAN is able to provide segmentation and different topologies per VPN.

    a. True

    b. False

11. Which is not a valid option for the deployment of SD-WAN Control Components?

    a. Cisco cloud hosted

    b. Customer on premises

    c. Partner cloud hosted

    d. Cisco on premises

References

RFC 4023, "Encapsulating MPLS in IP or Generic Routing Encapsulation (GRE)," https://tools.ietf.org/html/rfc4023, March 2005.

RFC 5389, "Session Traversal Utilities for NAT (STUN)," https://tools.ietf.org/html/rfc5389, October 2008.

"Cisco Catalyst SD-WAN," https://www.cisco.com/site/us/en/solutions/networking/sdwan/index.html.

"SD-WAN Platforms," https://www.cisco.com/c/en/us/solutions/collateral/enterprise-networks/sd-wan/nb-06-sd-wan-sol-overview-cte-en.html#SDWANplatforms.

CHAPTER 3

Control Plane and Data Plane Operations

This chapter covers the following topics:

- **Control Plane Operations:** This section covers Overlay Management Protocol (OMP) and how the three routing updates (TLOC, OMP route, and service routes) build the control plane. It also covers the multicast routing in SD-WAN overlay networks.

- **Data Plane Operations:** This section discusses how the data plane is established and secured, along with how Network Address Translation (NAT) interacts with overlay provisioning.

As discussed in Chapter 2, "Cisco Catalyst SD-WAN Components," and described in the list that follows, Cisco Catalyst SD-WAN consists of four operational functions (see Figure 3-1):

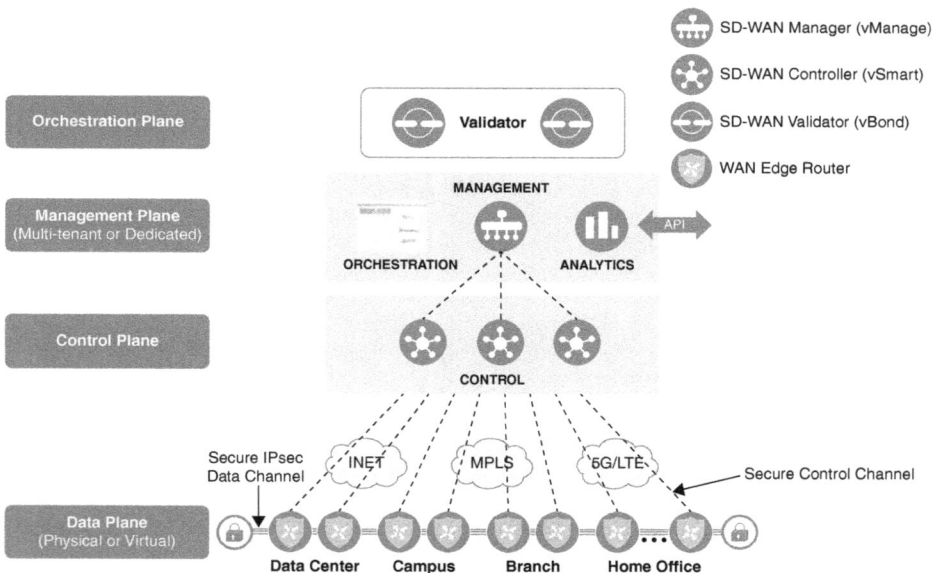

Figure 3-1 *Cisco Catalyst SD-WAN Distributed Architecture*

- **Data plane:** The data plane is where user traffic flows and utilizes information learned from the control plane to build connections between branches. The data plane can be full mesh, partial mesh, point-to-point, hub-and-spoke, or a combination thereof.

The data plane in Cisco Catalyst SD-WAN is extremely flexible and can be designed to meet the needs of most deployments.

- **Management plane:** The management plane is provided by SD-WAN Manager (formerly called vManage). SD-WAN Manager is a single pane of glass for onboarding, provisioning, monitoring, and troubleshooting. Once SD-WAN components are deployed, SD-WAN Manager is where most day-to-day operations are performed.

- **Orchestration plane:** Orchestration plane functionality is provided by SD-WAN Validator (formerly called vBond). SD-WAN Validator authenticates and authorizes all other SD-WAN components and provides connectivity information about SD-WAN Controller and SD-WAN Manager instances. In addition, SD-WAN Validator facilitates NAT-traversal capabilities.

- **Control plane:** The component responsible for control plane functionality is referred to as SD-WAN Controller (formerly called vSmart). SD-WAN Controller provides all routing and data plane policies to the routers in the environment.

This chapter is broken into two sections. The first section covers the SD-WAN control plane and how OMP facilitates building the control plane. This section introduces three route types: TLOC routes, OMP routes, and service routes. These routing updates are used to influence how WAN Edge routers build the data plane. It also covers multicast routing in SD-WAN overlay networks.

The second section of this chapter covers data plane operations. Multiple new concepts are introduced in this section, including colors, *restrict* option for TLOCs, VPNs, tunnel groups, and IPsec. NAT is integrated seamlessly in Catalyst SD-WAN and is covered in this section, too.

NOTE Please note that in both Cisco documentation and throughout this book, all three SD-WAN fabric components together are referred to as SD-WAN Control Components (that is, SD-WAN Manager, SD-WAN Controller, and SD-WAN Validator).

Control Plane Operations

In Cisco Catalyst SD-WAN, control plane mechanisms are facilitated by Overlay Management Protocol (OMP). OMP allows for a secure and scalable fabric across all transport types, whether private (MPLS, Layer 2 VPNs, and point-to-point networks) or public connectivity methods (Internet and LTE). As discussed in Chapter 2, the component responsible for the control plane is SD-WAN Controller. SD-WAN Controller facilitates a scalable control plane and is responsible for disseminating all policy information to the WAN Edge routers. SD-WAN Controller's functionality is often compared to that of a BGP route reflector. The SD-WAN Controller takes all routing and topology information received from the clients, calculates best-path information based on configured policy, and then advertises the results to the WAN Edge routers.

In traditional networks, the control plane is only focused on how the data flows through the network. This is accomplished by consuming routing updates, performing best-path selection operations, and feeding this information into forwarding tables. Configuring security with these protocols is usually an intensive and often manual process that generally requires downtime while the network administrator transitions to these security mechanisms. Security is often an afterthought and usually implemented after the routing domain is established. Security should be critical to any routing domain, as you need to validate and trust all routing updates so that no malicious routing information is processed.

Security is at the heart of Cisco Catalyst SD-WAN. Control plane tunnels are encrypted and authenticated via Datagram Transport Layer Security (DTLS) or Transport Layer Security (TLS). The WAN Edge routers form encrypted control connections to the SD-WAN Control Components (SD-WAN Validator, Controller, and Manager). SD-WAN Control Components also establish secure connections between themselves.

SD-WAN Manager and Controller support both UDP-based connections (DTLS) and TCP-based connections (TLS) for communication with WAN Edge devices and between themselves. However, all connections to SD-WAN Validator are always made using DTLS only.

When a WAN Edge has a sufficient number of control connections, it is considered to be in *equilibrium state*. By default, equilibrium state requires a WAN Edge to have an active DTLS/TLS connection to SD-WAN Manager, a DTLS/TLS connection for each transport to each of at least two SD-WAN Controllers, and one OMP session to each of two SD-WAN Controllers. When a WAN Edge is *in equilibrium state*, it does not keep a permanent connection with SD-WAN Validator. That's why normally you do not see control connections between a WAN Edge and Validator, and that is expected. However, if a WAN Edge goes *out of equilibrium* (that is, it cannot connect to the proper number of Control Components), it establishes a permanent connection to SD-WAN Validator and keeps it active until the correct number of control connections is reestablished.

Figure 3-2 provides an example of how DTLS/TLS connections are maintained between all personas in the SD-WAN overlay network. SD-WAN Controller and SD-WAN Manager are deployed as virtual machines that support multiple CPU cores (up to eight). In such case, they establish multiple simultaneous connections to SD-WAN Validator (one connection per CPU core).

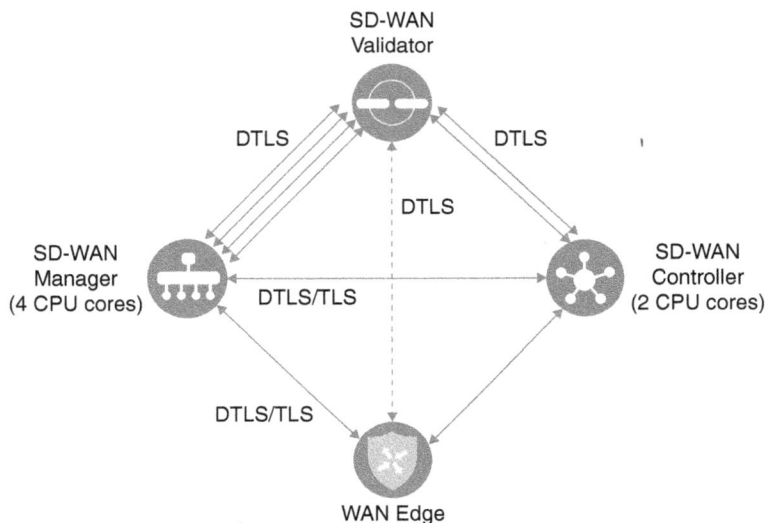

Figure 3-2 *Control Connections in SD-WAN Fabric*

DTLS/TLS secure tunnels are negotiated using SSL certificates, with each component authenticating the other peer. After two devices complete the bidirectional mutual authentication, the DTLS/TLS connection between them transitions from being a temporary connection to being a permanent one. This process of mutual authentication repeats for each pair of devices that tries to establish DTLS/TLS control connections (for example, between SD-WAN Controller and Validator, between two Controllers, between a WAN Edge and SD-WAN Manager).

For successful operation inside the SD-WAN fabric, each device must have a valid certificate that is signed by a trusted Root CA (certification authority) and has a valid certificate serial number with a matching Organization Name. See Figure 3-3 for an example of tunnel establishment between SD-WAN Controller and SD-WAN Validator. We use this pair of devices in our example because usually they are the first two devices on the SD-WAN Overlay network that validate and authenticate each other.

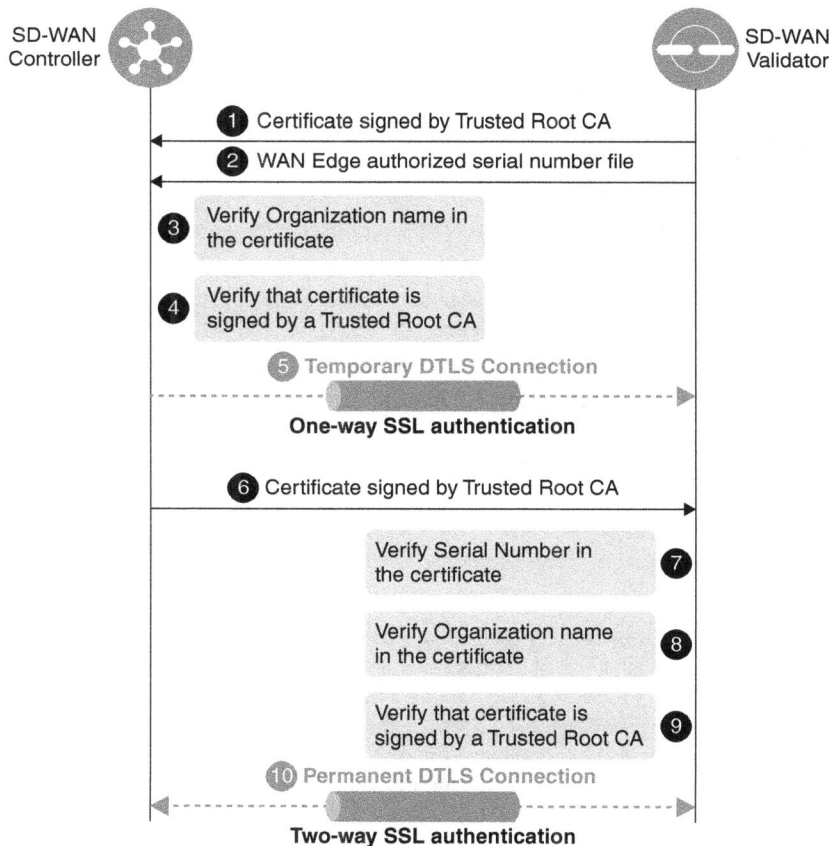

Figure 3-3   *DTLS Tunnel Authentication*

The process of mutual authentication shown in Figure 3-3 includes the following steps:

Step 1.   SD-WAN Validator sends its X.509 certificate, signed by the trusted root CA. This certificate represents SD-WAN Validator's identity.

Step 2.   SD-WAN Validator also sends the file with serial numbers of the authorized WAN Edge devices.

Step 3.   SD-WAN Controller compares the Organization Name from the received certificate with the Organization Name configured within SD-WAN Controller. If the names match, SD-WAN Controller knows that its peer belongs to the correct organization.

Step 4.   SD-WAN Controller verifies the root certification authority that signed the peer's certificate. If the signature is correct, SD-WAN Controller trusts the root CA and can also trust its peer.

Step 5.   If the checks in step 3 and step 4 succeed, SD-WAN Controller completes the authentication of SD-WAN Validator. At this point, a *temporary* DTLS connection is established.

Step 6.   SD-WAN Controller sends its own identity certificate to SD-WAN Validator so Validator can also authenticate its peer.

Step 7.   SD-WAN Validator extracts the serial number from the received certificate and verifies it against the file with serial numbers of the authorized SD-WAN Controllers. Only SD-WAN Controllers present in that list are allowed to join the SD-WAN fabric.

Step 8.   SD-WAN Validator compares the Organization Name from the received certificate with the Organization Name configured within SD-WAN Validator.

Step 9.   SD-WAN Validator verifies the root CA that signed the peer's certificate. If the signature is correct and SD-WAN Validator trusts the root CA, SD-WAN Validator can also trust its peer.

Step 10.   If all three checks from steps 7 through 9 succeed, SD-WAN Validator completes the authentication of SD-WAN Controller. Now both peers have mutually authenticated each other. The DTLS connection between them changes from being *temporary* to being *permanent*.

By default, DTLS is the protocol of choice. DTLS is a UDP-based protocol. As a first step, WAN Edge routers try to establish control connections with SD-WAN Control Components using UDP port 12346 as the source port. They can also use port hopping and try to establish control connections using different source ports in case the first connection fails. When using port hopping, WAN Edge routers increment the port by 20 and try ports 12366, 12386, 12406, and 12426 before returning to 12346. Port hopping is enabled on WAN Edge routers by default, but this configuration can be changed globally or on a per-tunnel-interface basis. It is important to consider all possible ports when planning an SD-WAN deployment and to make sure the devices can reach each other on all required ports. TLS is also supported if requirements call for it. (Note that TLS operates using TCP and is therefore stateful.) Both DTLS and TLS protocols are able to handle out-of-order or lost packets.

As we discussed previously, SD-WAN Manager and SD-WAN Controller can have multiple CPU cores. Each CPU core has a base port associated with it. Table 3-1 provides the core-to-port mappings for UDP and TCP. Inbound DTLS connections initially target UDP port 12346, while initial TLS connections target TCP port 23456. However, they can be transitioned to other base ports. This is how SD-WAN Manager and SD-WAN Controller are able to distribute the control connection load across the CPU cores. Recommended practice is to allow all base ports through transit devices so that SD-WAN Manager and SD-WAN Controller can properly balance inbound control plane connectivity.

Table 3-1 Core-to-Port Mappings

Core	UDP Port	TCP Port
Core 1	12346	23456
Core 2	12446	23556
Core 3	12546	23656
Core 4	12646	23756
Core 5	12746	23856
Core 6	12846	23956
Core 7	12946	24056
Core 8	13046	24156

In some scenarios, SD-WAN devices need to use different port numbers (for example, when several SD-WAN devices are connected behind the same NAT device and share the same public IP address). In such a case, having unique port numbers is mandatory so that other SD-WAN fabric members can uniquely identify their peers. To achieve that, you can configure every device with the unique *port-offset* value. The port-offset value represents the difference between the base port numbers and the actual ports used by the device. Actual ports are calculated using the formula **base port + *n***, where *n* is a port-offset value that can be configured between 0 and 19. For example, a device with a port-offset value of 1 will use UDP ports 12347, 12447, 12547, and so on. A device with a port-offset value of 2 will use UDP ports 12348, 12448, 12548, and so on. This logic can be applied to all fabric components except SD-WAN Validator.

NOTE The port-offset value is an advanced feature that is used in rare exceptional use cases only. We do not focus on it in this book. For a detailed feature description and implementation tips, please refer to the official Cisco documentation.

After control plane tunnels are up, other protocols can use these sessions as well. For example, SD-WAN Manager uses NETCONF to configure the WAN Edge devices, while SD-WAN Controller uses OMP to exchange the routing information with WAN Edge devices. By using established DTLS/TLS tunnels, you no longer need to be concerned about the disparate security that is native to these protocols or the flaws that may be present in them. Figure 3-4 shows an example of what resides inside the DTLS or TLS session between the components.

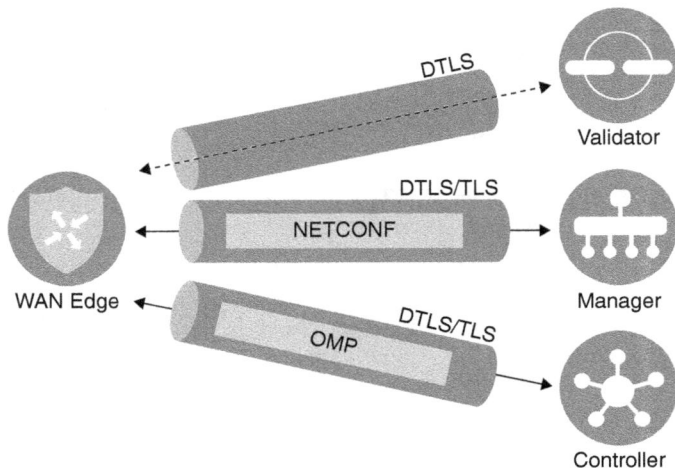

Figure 3-4   *Protocol Communications*

Control connection between WAN Edge and SD-WAN Validator is temporary. It is required for the initial authentication and device onboarding. Then a WAN Edge establishes permanent connections to SD-WAN Controller over every transport and a single permanent connection to SD-WAN Manager over one transport only. After that, the control connection between a WAN Edge and SD-WAN Validator is terminated.

Overlay Management Protocol

The routing protocol used with Cisco Catalyst SD-WAN is Overlay Management Protocol (OMP), but it would be a disservice to limit OMP to just routing. OMP is the director of all control plane information and provides the following services:

- Facilitation of network communication on the SD-WAN fabric, including data plane connectivity among sites, service chaining, and multi-VPN topology information

- Advertisement of services available to the fabric and their related locations

- Distribution of data plane security information, including encryption keys

- Best-path selection and routing policy advertisement

OMP is enabled by default and doesn't need to be explicitly enabled. As components in the fabric learn about their respective control elements, they automatically initiate control connections to them. With this information, reachability can be achieved, which ultimately allows for the orchestration of the topology.

As discussed in subsequent chapters, all of this information can be manipulated by user-defined policies via SD-WAN Manager. OMP interacts with all forms of legacy routing, including static routes and traditional interior gateway routing protocols, such as Open Shortest Path First (OSPF), Border Gateway Protocol (BGP), Enhanced Interior Gateway Routing Protocol (EIGRP), and Routing Information Protocol Version 2 (RIPv2). OMP differs from traditional IGPs in that the peering is not between all members in the routing domain. Peering occurs only between the WAN Edge routers and the SD-WAN Controller(s). This operates very similarly to a BGP route reflector in an Internal Border Gateway Protocol (iBGP) domain.

From a scaling perspective, this is beneficial as the domain starts to grow. By establishing peering with only SD-WAN Controllers, you reduce CPU cycles on the data plane devices since they don't need to handle and respond to excessive routing updates and best-path route recalculations.

OMP also supports graceful restart, which allows WAN Edge routers to cache forwarding information if connectivity to SD-WAN Controller becomes unavailable. In such a case, the WAN Edge will continue to use the routing information that was last received. Graceful restart is enabled by default on the SD-WAN Controllers and WAN Edge devices with a default timer of 12 hours. This timer can be modified with a minimum value of 1 second and a maximum value of 7 days. Keep in mind that there should be a valid IPsec encryption key throughout the duration of the graceful restart period; otherwise, you risk having the data plane tunnels being torn down before the graceful timer expires. By having a correct IPsec encryption key lifetime, you can ensure that there is no IPsec rekey while OMP is down. Best practice is to set your IPsec rekey timer to be twice the value of the graceful restart timer.

NOTE The graceful restart timer can be configured from SD-WAN Manager via an OMP feature template or an OMP parcel in the configuration group. Feature templates and configuration groups are discussed further in Chapter 4, "Onboarding and Provisioning."

When a peering session with the SD-WAN Controller becomes unavailable, a WAN Edge continuously tries to reestablish a connection. If the WAN Edge is reloaded, however, all the cached information is lost. The WAN Edge needs to reestablish an OMP session with SD-WAN Controller and receive new forwarding information before it can begin forwarding traffic on the SD-WAN fabric again. The same thing happens when the graceful restart timer expires.

As mentioned previously, OMP runs between the SD-WAN Controllers and WAN Edge routers and advertises the following types of routes:

- **TLOC routes (transport locations):** A TLOC is an attribute that uniquely identifies how a WAN Edge connects to the transport network. A TLOC route ties an OMP route to the transport attachment point of the remote WAN Edge. A TLOC route provides sufficient information how to reach the remote location and establish secure data tunnels with the remote WAN Edge router.

- **OMP routes:** Network prefixes provide overlay connectivity between the service-side VPN resources, such as data centers, branch offices, or any other endpoints in the SD-WAN fabric. OMP routes resolve their next hop to a TLOC.

- **Service routes:** A service route announces a network service to the SD-WAN overlay. It identifies the service's location, where the service could be a firewall, an IPS, an IDS, or any other device that can process network traffic. Service information is advertised from a WAN Edge to SD-WAN Controller in service routes.

Figure 3-5 shows examples of how these three types of routes interact in Cisco Catalyst SD-WAN.

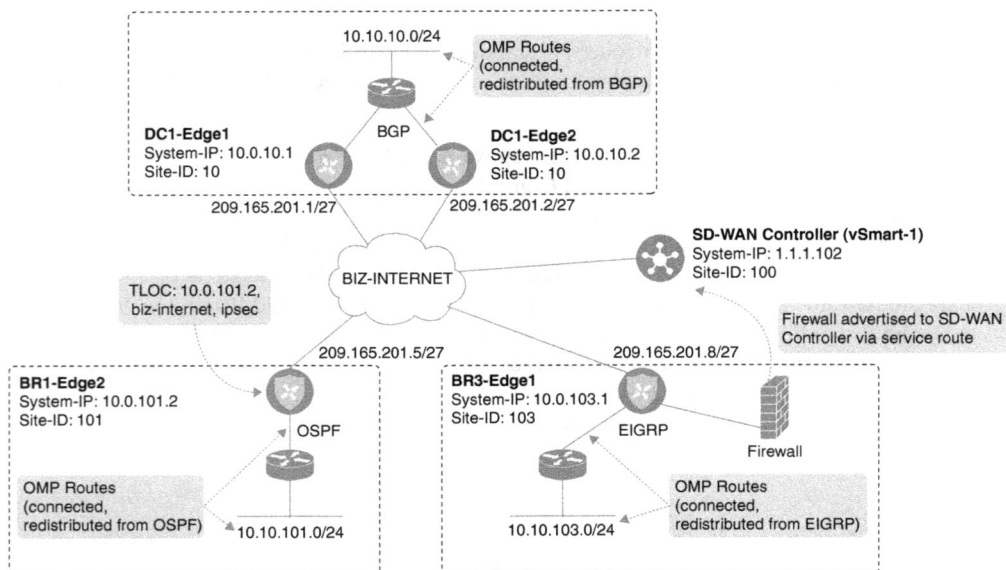

Figure 3-5   *Examples of the Three Types of SD-WAN Overlay Routes*

OMP Routes

Each WAN Edge at a site advertises service-side VPN routes to the SD-WAN Controllers. *Service-side VPNs* (sometimes also called *LAN service VPNs*) are used to connect the LAN-side resources, such as campus or data center networks. OMP updates are similar to traditional routing updates in that they include reachability information for prefixes the WAN Edge handles. OMP can advertise connected networks, static routes, and routing updates via redistribution from traditional protocols such as OSPF, EIGRP, RIPv2, and BGP. Along with reachability information, the following attributes are also advertised:

- TLOC
- Origin
- Originator
- Preference
- Service
- Site ID
- Tag
- VPN
- Tenant (for multi-tenant deployments)
- Region ID and Region Path (for multi-region fabrics)

A network administrator can modify some of these attributes to influence routing decisions:

- **TLOC:** The Transport Location identifier (TLOC) is the next hop of the OMP route. This attribute is very similar to the BGP_NEXT_HOP attribute. Within the TLOC, there are three values:

  - **System IP address:** This can be thought of as a router ID. This IP address doesn't need to be routable, but it needs to be unique across the entire SD-WAN fabric. The system IP address is a way to identify the WAN Edge that originally advertised the route.

  - **Color:** Color, as you'll see later in this chapter, is a way to label a specific WAN connection that can later be used for influencing routing policies and how the topology is built.

  - **Encapsulation type:** This value advertises what encapsulation type is being used for the data plane tunnel; possible options include IPsec and GRE.

- **Origin:** This is the source of the route. As the route is advertised into the routing domain, the original source of the route is inserted into the update. The source may contain an identifier (BGP, OSPF, EIGRP, RIPv2, Connected, or Static), along with the protocol's original metric. Origin is used in the best-path selection for OMP routes as well, and, as with most attributes, a custom policy can be configured to influence how this information is reacted to.

- **Originator:** The Originator attribute identifies where the route was originally learned. This value is the system IP address of the advertiser. The network administrator can construct a policy that takes this attribute into account.

- **Preference:** This is sometimes referred to as OMP Preference, though it should not be confused with TLOC Preference. The Preference value can be modified to influence the best-path selection criteria for a given route. A higher Preference value is preferred over a lower one. Preference operates similarly to LOCAL_PREF in BGP.

- **Service:** Catalyst SD-WAN also supports service insertion. If a service (a firewall, for example) is associated with a route, then it will be indicated in the Service attribute. Service routes are discussed in further detail later in this chapter.

- **Site ID:** The Site ID attribute is similar to a BGP Autonomous System Number (ASN). This value is used for policy orchestration and for influencing routing decisions. Every site should have a unique site ID. If there are multiple devices at a site, they should have the same site ID for loop prevention.

- **Tag:** This is an optional, transitive attribute that an OMP peer can apply to the route and that can be acted upon via policy. Redistributing to or from OMP does not carry the tag, however. This attribute functions like a route tag with traditional routing protocols.

- **VPN:** When discussing segmentation within Catalyst SD-WAN, this value communicates what VPN/VRF this route was advertised from. The VPN tag enables the use of overlapping subnets, provided that they are in different VPN/VRF instances (for example, 10.0.0.0/24 in VRF RED and 10.0.0.0/24 in VRF BLUE). Segmentation is discussed in more detail later in this chapter.

- **Tenant:** This attribute provides the tenant ID in a multi-tenant SD-WAN deployment. (Multi-tenancy is briefly discussed in Chapter 2.)

- **Region ID and Region Path:** These optional attributes are present in the routing updates only if a multi-region fabric was deployed. They describe to which region the destination prefix belongs and how to reach it. By default, the shortest path with fewest region hops is preferred. (Multi-region fabric is discussed in detail in Chapter 5, "Cisco SD-WAN Design and Migration.")

NOTE In Cisco Catalyst SD-WAN, the terms *VPN* and *VRF* are used interchangeably. VPN/VRF instances are used to logically segment a network into multiple data paths and to allow separate routing instances per VPN or VRF instance.

You can view OMP network prefixes on IOS XE WAN Edge devices by using the command **show sdwan omp [vpn** *vpnid*] [*network/prefix-length*] [**detail**]. Example 3-1 demonstrates the use of this command on the DC1-Edge1 router. (Refer to Figure 3-5 for the topology details.)

Example 3-1   *OMP Routing Update*

```
DC1-Edge1# show sdwan omp routes 10.10.101.0/24 detail
! Output omitted for brevity
omp route entries for tenant-id 0 vpn 10 route 10.10.101.0/24
          RECEIVED FROM:
peer            1.1.1.102
path-id         3
label           1003
status          C,I,R
loss-reason     not set
lost-to-peer    not set
lost-to-path-id not set
    Attributes:
    originator      10.0.101.2
    type            installed
    tloc            10.0.101.2, biz-internet, ipsec
    ultimate-tloc   not set
    domain-id       not set
    overlay-id      1
    site-id         101
    preference      not set
    affinity-group  None
    derived-affinity-group  None
    affinity-preference-order  None
    device-group    not set
```

```
region-id        None
br-preference    not set
mrf-route-originator     not set
region-path      not set
route-reoriginator       not set
tag              not set
origin-proto     OSPF-intra-area
origin-metric    2
as-path          not set
community        not set
site-type        not set
unknown-attr-len not set
management-gateway     not set
management-region      not
```

NOTE   In Example 3-1, the routing update was received from **peer 1.1.1.102**. On the SD-WAN overlay, all routing updates are received from the SD-WAN Controllers (in this example, the SD-WAN Controller has the system IP address of 1.1.1.102). The original route was advertised by the BR1-Edge2 router with the system IP address 10.0.101.2, which can be seen in the **originator** route attribute.

C,I,R stands for "chosen, installed, resolved." This designation means that the route was selected and installed into the routing information base (RIB). For a route to be selected, the next hop (TLOC) must be resolvable.

NOTE   OMP uses an administrative distance of 250 on legacy Viptela OS routers and 251 on IOS XE SD-WAN routers. IOS XE SD-WAN routers use 251 because Next Hop Resolution Protocol (NHRP) already uses an administrative distance of 250.

TLOC Routes

A TLOC identifies the transport location where a WAN Edge connects to a specific WAN transport. The TLOC must be reachable via its public or private IP address in the underlay, and it represents the endpoint of the data plane tunnels (similar to a GRE tunnel with **tunnel source** and **tunnel destination** commands). A TLOC is made up of three attributes: the system IP address of the WAN Edge, the transport color, and the encapsulation type. If a WAN Edge router has multiple transports, a TLOC route will be advertised for each interface. System IP addresses are used in the TLOC attribute due to the fact that IP addresses can change (for example, when DHCP is used). By using the system IP address, the TLOC remains easily identifiable. Figure 3-6 shows an example.

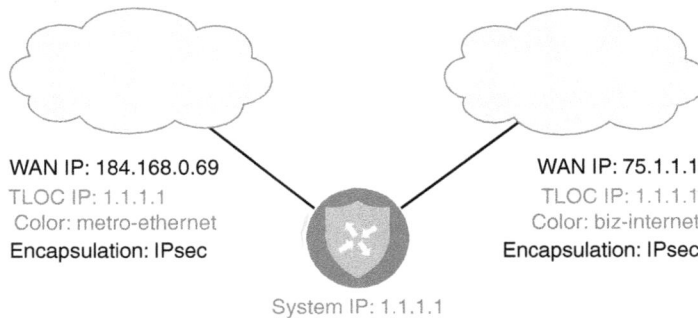

WAN IP: 184.168.0.69
TLOC IP: 1.1.1.1
  Color: metro-ethernet
Encapsulation: IPsec

WAN IP: 75.1.1.1
TLOC IP: 1.1.1.1
  Color: biz-internet
Encapsulation: IPsec

System IP: 1.1.1.1

Figure 3-6   *TLOC Route Example*

A critical attribute of the TLOC route is color, which is a mechanism to identify the transport. You cannot assign the same color to several transports on a WAN Edge, so each of your transports needs to have a different color on a router. Policy can then be constructed to use color to influence how the data plane is built. Currently, there are 22 predefined colors to choose from. Colors also indicate whether the underlying transport is private or public in nature and, hence, what IP address should be used when forming a data plane tunnel to the remote site. By default, WAN Edge routers attempt to build data plane tunnels to every other site using every color available. This may not be desirable, as it could lead to inefficient routing (for example, if MPLS sites attempt to build tunnels to public Internet sites). Although the connectivity may exist, the tunnels may have formed over an unintended path. This behavior can be controlled with the **restrict** command and/or tunnel groups, however. (The restrict option is covered in more detail later in this chapter.)

A TLOC route advertisement contains the following pieces of information:

- **TLOC Private Address:** This attribute contains the private IP address derived from the physical interface of the WAN Edge. When two WAN Edge devices are configured with *private colors*, they use private addresses to establish data plane tunnels between themselves.

- **TLOC Public Address:** As a WAN Edge builds its control plane connections, it is notified via STUN (RFC 5389) that it may be behind a device on a network that uses NAT. This attribute contains the publicly routable or outside IP address assigned to the WAN Edge. This is critical in supporting data plane connectivity across a NAT boundary. If both the public and private addresses match in a TLOC route, the device is considered to not be behind a NAT device. WAN Edge routers use public addresses to establish data plane tunnels with the remote site over a public color. Connections between a private color on one side and a public color on the remote side also use public addresses on both sides.

- **Color:** As discussed earlier, color is a unique identifier of the transport. Possible options are public **3g, biz-internet, blue, bronze, custom1, custom2, custom3, default, gold, green, lte, public-internet, red,** and **silver** colors and private **metro-ethernet, mpls, private1, private2, private3, private4, private5, private6** colors. The color **default** is used if no color is administratively defined.

■ **Encapsulation Type:** This attribute refers to the tunnel encapsulation type. Options available are IPsec and GRE. The two sides of the tunnel must match for data plane connectivity to occur.

■ **Preference:** Similar to OMP Preference, this attribute allows a network administrator to prefer one TLOC over another when comparing the same OMP route. A higher Preference value is preferred.

■ **Site ID:** This attribute identifies the originator of the TLOC route and is used to control how data plane tunnels are built.

■ **Tag:** This attribute is similar to route tags and OMP tags. A value can be defined that can control how prefixes are exchanged and, ultimately, how traffic will flow.

■ **Weight:** This attribute is used just like BGP Weight and is locally significant. A higher Weight value is preferred over a lower one.

Example 3-2 provides an example of a TLOC route to BR1-Edge2 router's interface connected to the **biz-internet** transport (refer to Figure 3-5). This TLOC route was received on DC1-Edge1 from the peer 1.1.1.102 (SD-WAN Controller). The command to retrieve this output is **show sdwan omp tlocs detail**.

Example 3-2 *Example of a TLOC Route*

```
DC1-Edge1# show sdwan omp tlocs detail
! Output omitted for brevity
---------------------------------------------------
tloc entries for 10.0.101.2
               biz-internet
               ipsec
---------------------------------------------------
            RECEIVED FROM:
tenant-id       0
peer            1.1.1.102
status          C,I,R
tenant-name     [Default]
loss-reason     not set
lost-to-peer    not set
lost-to-path-id not set
   Attributes:
    attribute-type     installed
    encap-key          not set
    encap-proto        0
    encap-spi          259
    encap-auth         sha1-hmac,ah-sha1-hmac
    encap-encrypt      aes256
    public-ip          209.165.201.5
    public-port        12346
    private-ip         209.165.201.5
```

```
        private-port       12346
        public-ip          ::
        public-port        0
        private-ip         ::
        private-port       0
        bfd-status         up
        domain-id          not set
        site-id            101
        overlay-id         not set
        preference         0
        device-group       not set
        region-id          None
        mrf-route-originator    not set
        affinity-group     None
        tag                not set
        stale              not set
        weight             1
        version            3
```

Service Routes

A service route advertises a specific service to the rest of the overlay. This advertisement can then be used for service chaining policies. Service chaining allows data traffic to be routed to a remote site through one or more services (such as firewalls, Intrusion Detection/Prevention systems, load balancers, IDP, or ThousandEyes) before being routed to the traffic's original destination. These services can be used on a per-VPN basis. For example, with compliance and regulations, a need exists for data to flow through firewalls that might be at a data center or regional hub, such as with Payment Card Industry Data Security Standard (PCI DSS).

To enable service chaining in the overlay, the following workflow should be used:

Step 1. The network administrator defines the service via a feature template or a configuration group.

Step 2. WAN Edge routers advertise the services available to the SD-WAN Controllers. Note that multiple WAN Edge routers can advertise the same service, if needed, for redundancy.

Step 3. WAN Edge routers also advertise their OMP and TLOC routes.

Step 4. The network administrator applies a policy defining traffic that must flow through the advertised service(s). Traffic is processed by the service before being forwarded to the final destination.

The example in Figure 3-7 describes how service chaining functions in Cisco Catalyst SD-WAN. The network has a central hub and two remote branches. Business requirements state that all traffic between Branch 1 and Branch 2 must flow through a firewall at the central hub. The following steps occur to enable this traffic flow:

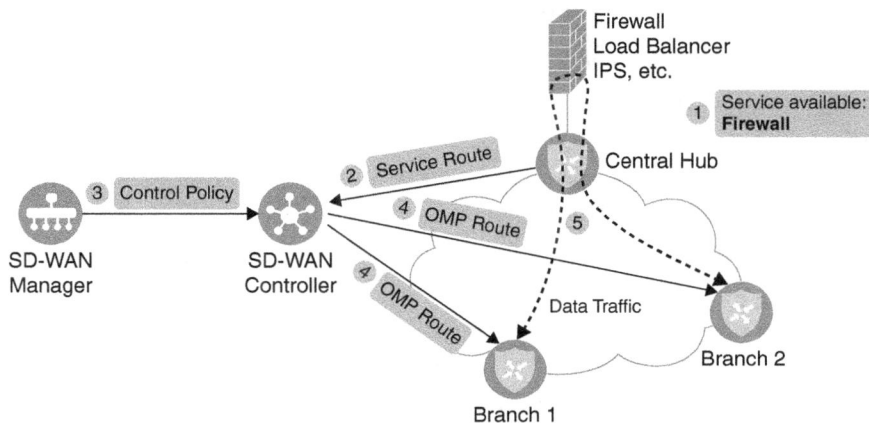

Figure 3-7 *Service Chaining Example*

Step 1.   The network administrator defines a new service of type *Firewall* in *Central Hub*. The configuration is pushed from SD-WAN Manager to the Central Hub WAN Edge router.

Step 2.   Central Hub WAN Edge advertises the *Firewall* service via the service route to SD-WAN Controller. The service route contains VPN ID, Service ID, Label, Originator ID, TLOC, and Path ID attributes. SD-WAN Controller keeps the service route locally, and does not advertise it to other WAN Edge devices.

Step 3.   The network administrator enables the service chaining policy and specifies that traffic between Branch 1 and Branch 2 must go through the firewall.

Step 4.   For the matching type of traffic, SD-WAN Controller changes the next hop for the OMP routes to the service landing point (the central hub) and sends OMP updates to Branch 1 and Branch 2 WAN Edge devices.

Step 5.   When Branch 1 and Branch 2 need to exchange the data traffic, it is sent via the central hub, as defined in the OMP routes.

The site offering the service (in this case, the central hub) advertises a service route via a Subsequent Address Family Identifier (SAFI) in the OMP Network Layer Reachability Information (NLRI). This information is advertised to SD-WAN Controller, where it is propagated to the WAN Edge devices. The service route update contains the following information:

■ **VPN ID:** This attribute defines what VPN this service applies to.

■ **Service ID:** This attribute defines the service type that is being advertised. Nine predefined services are available:

■ **FW:** Service type of Firewall (which maps to the value **svc-id 1**).

■ **IDS:** Service type of Intrusion Detection System (which maps to a value of **svc-id 2**).

- **IDP:** Service type of Identity provider (which maps to a value of **svc-id 3**).

- **netsvc1, netsvc2, netsvc3,** and **netsvc4:** These are reserved for custom services and map to the service values **svc-id 4, svc-id 5, svc-id 6,** and **svc-id 7,** respectively.

- **te:** Service type of ThousandEyes.

- **appqoe:** Service type of external Application Quality of Experience (AppQoE) service node.

- **Label:** OMP routes that have traffic that must flow through this service have the Label field in their advertisement replaced with this label.

- **Originator ID:** This attribute defines the system IP address of the node advertising the service.

- **TLOC:** This attribute defines the transport location address where the service is located.

- **Path ID:** This attribute defines an identifier for the OMP path.

Example 3-3 shows the output of **show omp services** from SD-WAN Controller. This output shows that WAN Edge 10.0.103.1 advertised an FW service. Similar to the OMP route, the Status field shows that the route is installed.

Example 3-3   *Example of a Service Route*

```
vSmart# show omp services
! Output omitted for brevity
ADDRESS                                         PATH    REGION
FAMILY   VPN    SERVICE  ORIGINATOR   FROM PEER  ID      ID      LABEL   STATUS
-----------------------------------------------------------------------------
ipv4     10     FW       10.0.103.1   10.0.103.1 66      None    1004    C,I,R
                                      10.0.103.1 68      None    1004    C,I,R
                                      10.0.103.1 70      None    1004    C,I,R
```

NOTE   This is just an introduction to service chaining. The process to construct and apply service chaining policies is covered in more depth in Chapter 6, "Introduction to Cisco Catalyst SD-WAN Policies," and Chapter 7, "Centralized Control Policies."

Path Selection

As with traditional routing protocols, OMP has best-path selection criteria to choose the best route available and avoid routing loops. The best-path selection process has some similarities to BGP. A WAN Edge installs an OMP route into its routing table only if the TLOC (next hop) is valid. A TLOC is valid if there is a Bidirectional Forwarding Detection (BFD) session that is associated to that TLOC.

As WAN Edge routers advertise OMP routes to SD-WAN Controller, SD-WAN Controller performs best-path selection and advertises the result to the WAN Edge routers. Best-path selection can be influenced by policy either inbound (before best-path selection) or outbound (after best-path selection).

NOTE This chapter covers the full process of best-path selection, including algorithms for a multi-region fabric. This topic is covered in Chapter 5.

The best-path selection occurs in the following order:

1. **Path validity:** For an OMP route to be considered valid, the TLOC needs to be valid. For a TLOC to be valid, there must be an active BFD adjacency for that TLOC. This is similar to BGP, where the next hop must be valid.

2. **Active vs. stale path:** An active path is a path from a peer with which an OMP session is up. A stale path is a path from a peer with which an OMP session is in graceful restart mode. An active path is preferred over a stale one.

3. **Lower administrative distance:** If multiple routes for the same prefix are received, the one with the lower administrative distance is preferred.

4. **Higher OMP Preference:** The route with a higher OMP Preference setting is preferred.

5. **(Multi-region fabric) Region path length:** The route with a lower region path length is preferred.

6. **(Multi-region fabric) Access region vs. Core region:** The access region path is preferred over a core region path.

7. **(Multi-region fabric) Direct vs. transport gateway path:** A direct path is preferred over a transport gateway path.

8. **(Multi-region fabric) Fabric subregion:** First, paths from the router's own subregion are preferred. When comparing routes that are not from the router's subregion, a path that is *not* part of any subregion is preferred.

9. **(Multi-region fabric) Border Router Preference:** A path with a higher Border Router Preference setting is preferred.

10. **(Multi-region fabric) Derived Affinity:** A lower Derived Affinity setting is preferred.

11. **(Multi-region fabric) Affinity preference:** When the affinity preference is configured, a path for which affinity is earlier in the preference list (higher priority) is preferred.

12. **Higher TLOC Preference:** A route with a higher TLOC Preference setting is preferred.

13. **Prefer origin:** The origin type setting is preferred in the following order (and the first match wins):
    - Connected
    - Static
    - LISP
    - EIGRP Summary
    - NAT routes
    - eBGP
    - EIGRP Internal
    - OSPF intra-area

- OSPF inter-area

- IS-IS Level 1

- EIGRP external

- OSPF external

- IS-IS Level 2

- RIPv2

- iBGP

- Unknown

14. Lowest origin metric: If origins match, the route with the lowest origin metric is preferred.

15. Path source: A path sourced from the WAN Edge over the same path coming from SD-WAN Controller is preferred.

16. Lowest private IP address: The OMP path with the lower private IP address is preferred.

If an SD-WAN Controller receives the same prefix from two different sites and if all attributes are equal, it chooses both of them. SD-WAN Controller can advertise up to 32 equal-cost routes to WAN Edge, if configured. By default, the advertisement is 4 equal-cost routes.

The following is an example of best-path selection when choosing routes that will be advertised to an OMP peer:

- An SD-WAN Controller receives four paths for the prefix 10.0.0.0/24.

- The first path doesn't have a valid TLOC.

- The second path has a TLOC Preference setting of 500 (and the default is 0).

- The third path has an OMP Preference setting of 300 (and the default is 0).

- The fourth path has an Administrative Distance setting of 249 (and the default OMP Administrative Distance is 250 or 251).

Walking through the process described previously, let's review these paths. The first path is ignored because the TLOC isn't valid. This leaves three valid paths. If we compare the remaining routes, the second has a TLOC Preference setting of 500, and the third has a higher OMP Preference setting. If we stop there, the third route wins, as it has a higher OMP Preference setting, which beats the TLOC Preference setting. However, in the example, the fourth path received wins because it has a modified Administrative Distance setting of 249.

OMP Route Redistribution and Loop Prevention

Just like other routing protocols, OMP supports redistribution. OMP supports mutual redistribution between OSPF, BGP, EIGRP, RIPv2, connected routes, and static routes. By default, OMP automatically redistributes connected, static, OSPF intra-area, and OSPF inter-area routes into OMP. To avoid routing loops and less-than-ideal routing, redistribution of BGP,

EIGRP, and OSPF external routes must be explicitly configured. A network administrator therefore needs to create OMP and OSPF templates, CLI template, or a configuration group.

Redistribution settings as defined in the OMP template are global—that is, they automatically apply to all the service VPNs. Also, by default, all routing information is redistributed into OMP without any filtering. If a more fine-tuned approach is required, you can enable redistribution per VPN and apply proper route maps using service VPN templates or configuration groups. (You may want to disable global redistribution for your routing protocol if you do so.)

Figure 3-8 shows the OMP Feature Template configuration, which defines the type of routes (connected, static) and the routing protocols that must be redistributed into OMP for all service-side VPNs.

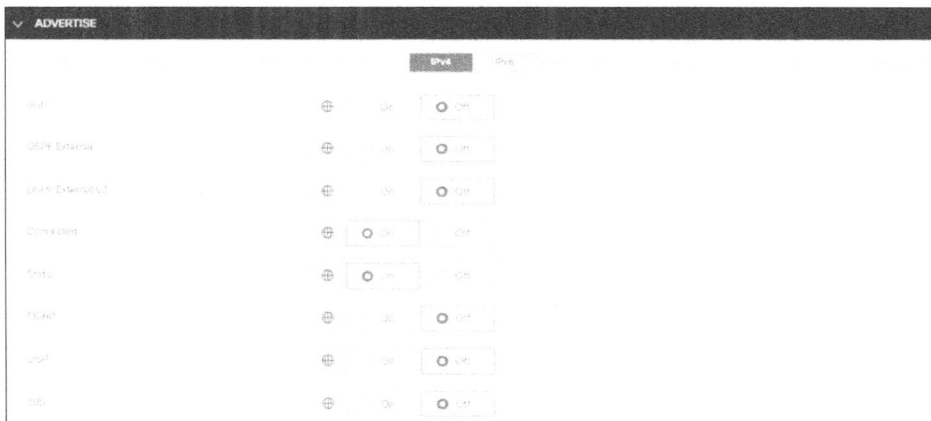

Figure 3-8   *OMP Template Configuration (for Redistribution into OMP)*

Figure 3-9 shows the OSPF Feature Template configuration, which enables redistribution from OMP into OSPF for a specific service-side VPN. Much as with OSPF, you can use Feature Templates to configure redistribution into other interior gateway protocols (IGPs).

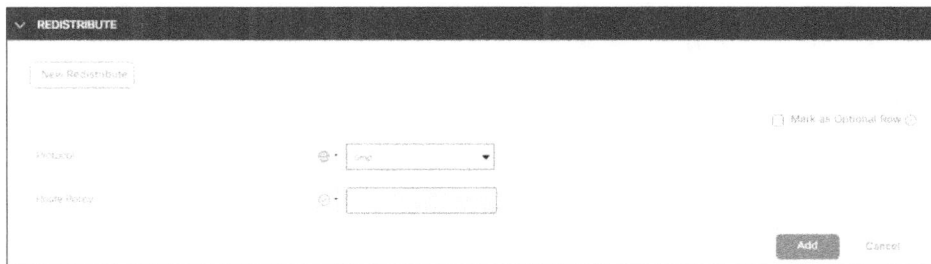

Figure 3-9   *OSPF Template Configuration (for Redistribution into IGP)*

Another way to configure WAN Edge devices is to use Configuration Groups. (Both Templates and Configuration Groups are covered in more detail in Chapter 4.) Redistribution from other routing protocols (such as OMP in this example) into OSPF is configured in the OSPF Feature Parcel, as illustrated in Figure 3-10.

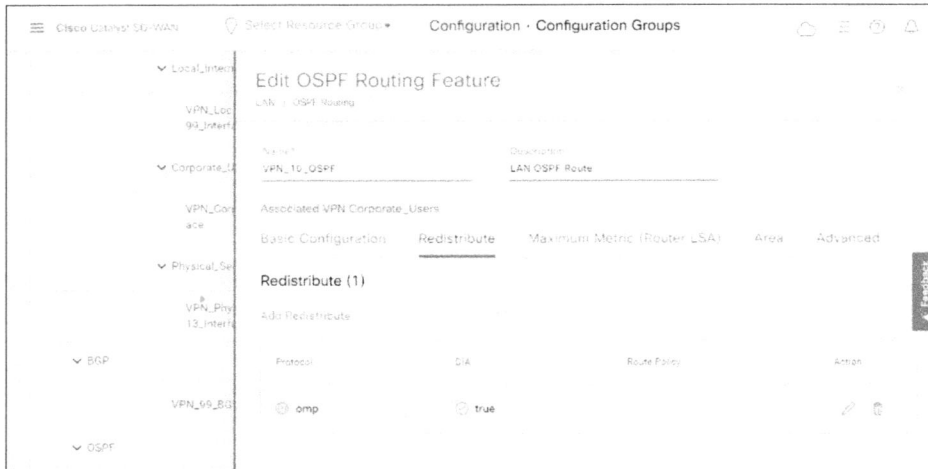

Figure 3-10   *Configuration Groups (for Redistribution from OMP into OSPF)*

Once the configuration is distributed from SD-WAN Manager to WAN Edge devices, you can verify it in the router's CLI by running the **show sdwan running-config** command. Example 3-4 shows the part of the configuration that is responsible for redistribution of connected, static, and OSPF external routes into OMP.

Example 3-4   *Redistribution into OMP*

```
BR1-Edge2# show sdwan running-config
! Output omitted for brevity
omp
 no shutdown
 send-path-limit  4
 ecmp-limit       4
 graceful-restart
 !
 address-family ipv4 vrf 10
  advertise ospf external
 !
 address-family ipv4
  advertise connected
  advertise static
 !
 address-family ipv6
  advertise connected
  advertise static
 !
```

Example 3-5 shows the part of configuration that is responsible for redistribution of routes from OMP into OSPF inside the service-side VPN 10.

Example 3-5   *Redistribution into IGP*

```
BR1-Edge2# show sdwan running-config
! Output omitted for brevity
router ospf 10 vrf 10
 auto-cost reference-bandwidth 100
 compatible rfc1583
 distance ospf intra-area 110 inter-area 110 external 110
 no local-rib-criteria
 max-lsa 50000
 redistribute maximum-prefix 10240
 redistribute omp
 router-id 10.0.101.2
 timers throttle spf 200 1000 10000
```

When redistributing into OMP, the origin and sub-origin are also set. This information is used in the best-path selection criteria mentioned earlier (specifically precedence 13, which involves the origin). Table 3-2 describes the various OMP origin types and their subtypes.

Table 3-2   OMP Origin Types

OMP Route Origin Type	OMP Route Origin Subtype
BGP	External
	Internal
Connected	N/A
OSPF, OSPFv3	Intra-area
	Inter-area
	External-1
	External-2
	NSSA-External-1
	NSSA-External-2
Static	N/A
EIGRP	Summary
	Internal
	External
LISP	N/A
IS-IS	Level 1
	Level 2
RIPv2	N/A

In addition, OMP carries the metric from the redistributed protocol. The metric 0 indicates a connected route. This is used to determine the lowest origin metric (precedence 14 in the best-path selection criteria described previously).

For reference, Table 3-3 lists the default administrative distances for WAN Edge routers.

Table 3-3   WAN Edge Default Administrative Distances

Route Source	Administrative Distance
Connected	0
Static	1
Learned via DHCP	1
eBGP	20
EIGRP Internal	90
OSPF	110
RIPv2	120
EIGRP External	170
iBGP	200
OMP	250 in ViptelaOS / 251 in Cisco IOS XE

Networks that have multiple exit points to the WAN are susceptible to routing loops. Loops commonly occur when two or more routers have mutual redistribution from the WAN routing protocol and the LAN routing protocol. Consider Figure 3-11, which features two WAN Edge routers and OMP and OSPF doing mutual redistribution.

OMP has native loop prevention mechanisms built into it when interfacing with EIGRP, OSPF, and BGP. In migration scenarios where the network is being migrated from a legacy site, the network administrator needs to take this into consideration and eliminate any potential loops by either filtering routes or using the traditional method of route tagging. At this time, OMP does not support filtering via a route tag, so this type of filtering needs to be handled outside the WAN Edge routers, such as at the core of the network.

Walking through the following process, you can see how the OSPF down bit can be used to prevent a routing loop:

Step 1.   DC1-Edge1 and DC1-Edge2 learn 10.10.101.0/24 via OMP.

Step 2.   DC1-Edge1 and DC1-Edge2 install 10.10.101.0/24 in their routing table with the administrative distance 251.

Step 3.   DC1-Edge1 and DC1-Edge2 advertise 10.10.101.0/24 into OSPF.

Step 4.   The core router(s) advertises the route received from DC1-Edge1 to DC1-Edge2 and the route received from DC1-Edge2 to DC1-Edge1 via OSPF.

Step 5.   (Here is where the loop can be formed.) Both WAN routers learn the same route via OSPF and OMP. Remember that OMP has an administrative distance of 251, and OSPF has an administrative distance of 110. In this case, the route via OSPF will be installed in the routing table due to its lower administrative distance. This will create a loop because the OSPF route will remove the route from OMP, which, in turn, will eventually remove the route via OSPF and blackhole traffic.

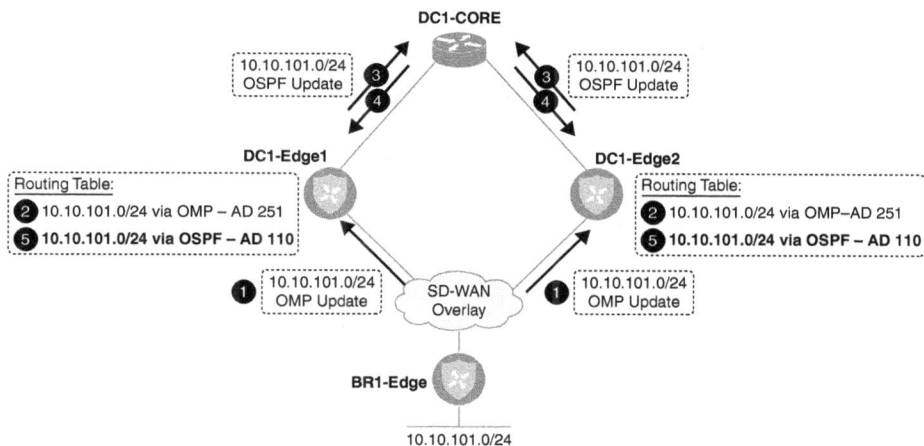

Figure 3-11   *Routing Loop*

RFC 4577 has been implemented to solve the loop prevention problem with OSPF. RFC 4577 implements a concept called a "down bit." When a route is being redistributed from OMP to OSPF, the WAN Edge sets this bit. As this link state advertisement (LSA) moves throughout the rest of the network and ultimately gets to the other WAN Edge, it is dropped due to the down bit being set. Example 3-6 shows the LSA in the database for 10.10.101.0/24 (with the **show ip ospf database external** command). Figure 3-12 shows this graphically.

Example 3-6   *OSPF Database Entry*

```
DC1-CORE# show ip ospf database external
! Output omitted for brevity
          OSPF Router with ID (10.10.10.1) (Process ID 1)


            Type-5 AS External Link States


  LS age: 203
  Options: (No TOS-capability, DC, Downward)
  LS Type: AS External Link
  Link State ID: 10.10.101.0 (External Network Number )
  Advertising Router: 10.0.10.2
  LS Seq Number: 80000001
  Checksum: 0x8A1B
  Length: 36
  Network Mask: /24
        Metric Type: 2 (Larger than any link state path)
        MTID: 0
        Metric: 16777214
        Forward Address: 0.0.0.0
        External Route Tag: 0
```

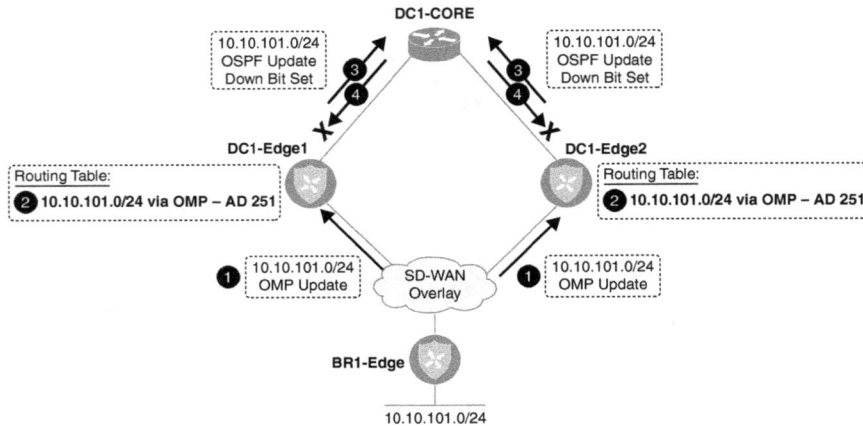

Figure 3-12 *OSPF Loop Prevention with the Down Bit*

In the following process, you can see how the OSPF down bit can be used to prevent a routing loop:

Step 1.   DC1-Edge1 and DC1-Edge2 learn 10.10.101.0/24 via OMP.

Step 2.   DC1-Edge1 and DC1-Edge2 install 10.10.101.0/24 in their routing table with the administrative distance 251.

Step 3.   DC1-Edge1 and DC1-Edge2 advertise 10.10.101.0/24 into OSPF and set the down bit.

Step 4.   The core router(s) advertises the route with the down bit set back to the WAN Edge routers via OSPF. The LSA is rejected.

Conversely, BGP loop prevention is handled with site of origin (SoO), which is a BGP extended community where the value is set to the OMP site ID. When the other WAN Edge receives the BGP update from the core network, it sees that the site of origin community matches its own site ID, and the BGP update is dropped. For this loop prevention mechanism to function properly, all BGP peers in the network must send BGP extended communities and must have the same site ID. Figure 3-13 shows this graphically.

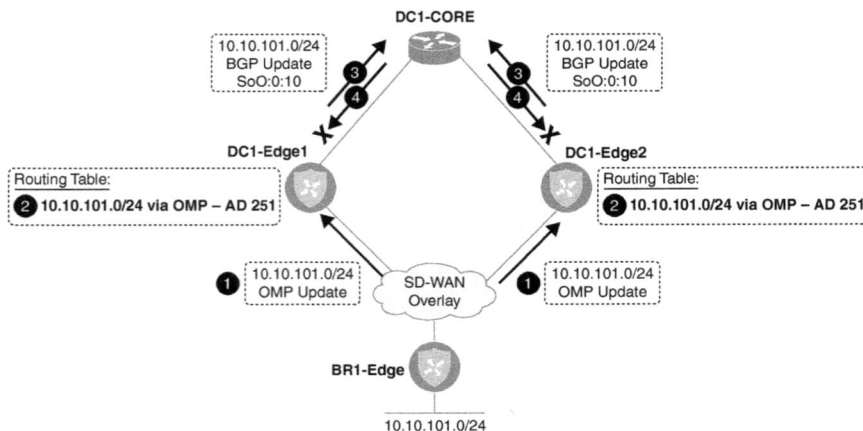

Figure 3-13 *BGP Loop Prevention with Site of Origin*

In this example, BGP site of origin is used to prevent a routing loop:

Step 1.   DC1-Edge1 and DC1-Edge2 learn 10.10.101.0/24 via OMP.

Step 2.   DC1-Edge1 and DC1-Edge2 install 10.10.101.0/24 in their routing table with the administrative distance 251.

Step 3.   DC1-Edge1 and DC1-Edge2 advertise 10.10.101.0/24 via BGP and set the site of origin extended community to 10. (That is DC1's Site ID.)

Step 4.   The core router(s) advertises the route with the extended community set. The WAN Edge devices drop the BGP update.

Example 3-7 shows a BGP routing update with an SoO extended community set (with the **show ip bgp 10.10.101.0** command). You can see that this matches the site ID of 10.

NOTE   For simplicity in this demonstration, we use the same setup to show redistribution between OMP and other routing protocols. BGP has multiple built-in loop prevention mechanisms, such as AS-Path attribute and iBGP route advertisement rules. Using the Extended Community attribute is one more way to prevent route loops in the event that other mechanisms are not applicable to the custom network design.

Example 3-7   *BGP Update with Site of Origin Set*

```
DC1-CORE# show ip bgp 10.10.101.0
! Output omitted for brevity
BGP routing table entry for 10.10.101.0/24, version 3
Paths: (2 available, best #2, table default)
  Advertised to update-groups:
     1
  Refresh Epoch 1
  65001
    172.16.10.1 from 172.16.10.1 (10.0.10.1)
      Origin incomplete, metric 1000, localpref 100, valid, external
      Extended Community: SoO:0:10 RT:65001:10
      rx pathid: 0, tx pathid: 0
```

Another built-in loop prevention mechanism with BGP is to use eBGP between WAN Edge devices and the core router. For example, when DC1-Edge1 and DC1-Edge2 use the same BGP ASN1 and the core router uses a different BGP ASN2, route advertisements from DC1-Edge1 will be accepted by the core router and sent to DC1-Edge2. However, when DC1-Edge2 receives this route update, it notices that its own ASN1 is already present in the BGP AS-Path attribute and drops that route, thus preventing the loop.

EIGRP also has embedded functionality to prevent such routing loops. When redistributing from OMP into EIGRP, the External Protocol field is set to the value OMP-Agent. When the other WAN Edge receives the update and installs the route into the EIGRP topology table, it sets the External Protocol field and sets its administrative distance to 252. This, in turn, makes OMP the preferred route because it has an administrative distance of 251. Figure 3-14 shows this graphically.

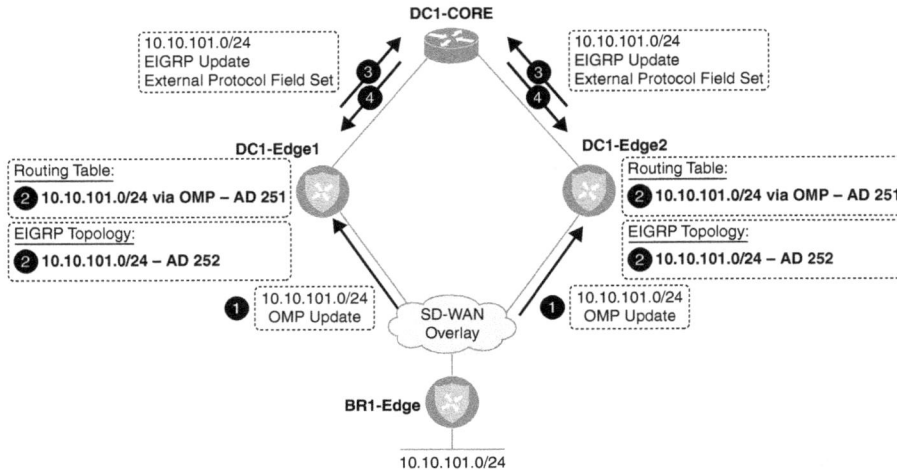

Figure 3-14 *EIGRP Loop Prevention with the External Protocol Field*

Here is how you can use EIGRP with the External Protocol field to prevent routing loops:

Step 1.   DC1-Edge1 and DC1-Edge2 learn 10.10.101.0/24 via OMP.

Step 2.   DC1-Edge1 and DC1-Edge2 install 10.10.101.0/24 in their routing table with the administrative distance 251.

Step 3.   DC1-Edge1 and DC1-Edge2 advertise 10.10.101.0/24 via EIGRP and set the External Protocol field to OMP-Agent.

Step 4.   The core router(s) advertises the route with the External Protocol field set.

Step 5.   When the WAN Edge routers receive this route, they place it into their EIGRP topology table with an administrative distance of 252. The routing table remains unchanged and continues to use the OMP route with the lower AD.

Example 3-8 provides an example of an EIGRP routing update with the External Protocol field set.

Example 3-8 *EIGRP Topology Table with the External Protocol Field Set*

```
DC1-CORE# show ip eigrp topology 10.10.101.0/24
EIGRP-IPv4 VR(eigrp-name) Topology Entry for AS(10)/ID(192.168.1.19) for
10.10.101.0/24
  State is Passive, Query origin flag is 1, 2 Successor(s), FD is 655361, RIB is 5120
  Descriptor Blocks:
  172.16.10.1 (GigabitEthernet1), from 172.16.10.1, Send flag is 0x0
      Composite metric is (655361/1), route is External
      Vector metric:
       Minimum bandwidth is 0 Kbit
        Total delay is 10000000 picoseconds
        Reliability is 0/255
        Load is 1/255
```

```
    Minimum MTU is 1500
    Hop count is 1
    Originating router is 172.16.10.1
 External data:
   AS number of route is 0
   External protocol is OMP-Agent, external metric is 4294967294
   Administrator tag is 0 (0x00000000)
```

Multicast Support

Multicast routing in an SD-WAN overlay network allows for efficient traffic distribution from one source to many recipients. The advantage of using multicast protocols over traditional unicast routing is that they provide enhanced efficiency and optimized network performance due to the significant reduction of redundant point-to-point traffic flowing through the same network links.

Cisco Catalyst SD-WAN supports the following protocols:

- **Protocol Independent Multicast v2 (PIM):** This protocol provides intra-domain multicast routing independent from the underlying unicast routing protocol. Cisco IOS XE SD-WAN routers support Source-Specific Multicast (SSM) and Any-Source Multicast (ASM).

- **Internet Group Management Protocol (IGMP v2 and v3):** This protocol allows multicast clients to announce their interest in receiving multicast traffic. IGMPv2 provides the possibility for the client to join the specific multicast group and to leave it when no longer needed. IGMPv3 extends the capabilities of IGMPv2 by adding support for SSM, which allows the clients to indicate their interest in receiving traffic only from the specific source.

- **Multicast Source Discovery Protocol (MSDP):** This protocol makes it possible to connect multiple PIM-SM domains. While every domain has its own rendezvous points (RPs) and does not rely on other domains, MSDP helps to exchange the source information between RPs in different domains. Starting from the software release 20.11, MSDP can also be used to interconnect Cisco Catalyst SD-WAN and non-SD-WAN domains.

Solution Overview

Figure 3-15 shows the multicast routing in a Cisco Catalyst SD-WAN Overlay network. On the service side, WAN Edge routers act as regular multicast-enabled routers in the service VPN. WAN Edge routers support IGMPv2/IGMPv3 and can receive group membership reports directly from the multicast clients. Also, a WAN Edge router can establish PIM neighborship with other routers in the local site network. Depending on the local network size and the design requirements, a WAN Edge can be an RP for the local site or can act as a first-hop router (FHR) with a directly connected multicast source.

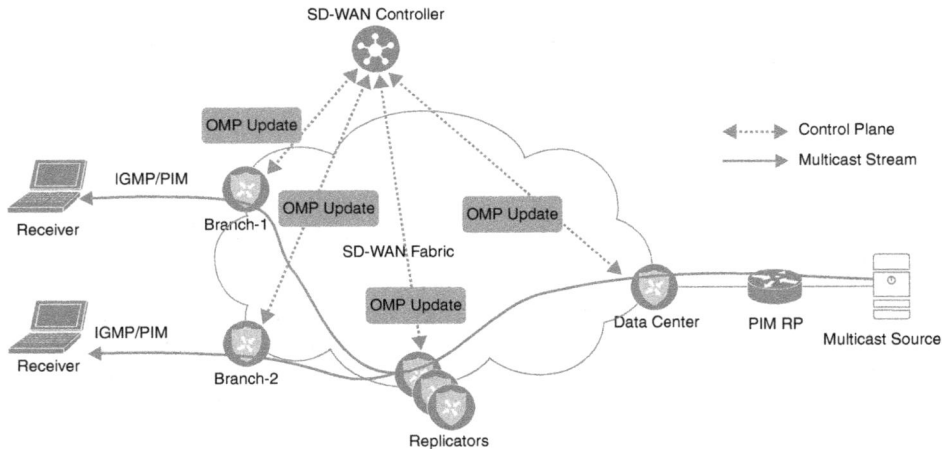

Figure 3-15 *Multicast Routing in an SD-WAN Overlay Network*

ASM relies on building a multicast shared tree, and requires an RP in the network. In Cisco Catalyst SD-WAN, an RP can be a WAN Edge or a non-SD-WAN router in the local site. These are the supported modes of RP discovery:

- Static RP

- Auto-RP

- Auto-RP Proxy

- Bootstrap Router (BSR)

On the transport side, OMP is responsible for exchanging multicast routing information. Similarly to unicast routing, WAN Edge devices share routing updates only with the SD-WAN Controller(s). Such information is included in *multicast service routes* (also known as *multicast autodiscover routes*). SD-WAN Controllers, in turn, send OMP updates to all other PIM-enabled WAN Edge devices.

OMP Replicators

In traditional IP networks, the ultimate goal for multicast traffic redistribution is to build the shortest-path source tree and make sure the traffic from the source to the receiver takes the most efficient path. This is achievable due to the fact that all routers in the same multicast domain are PIM enabled and have sufficient unicast routing information.

This concept changes, however, in WANs. You cannot expect all routers on the Internet to forward multicast traffic from your internal corporate domain. Also, in the SD-WAN network, there are encrypted data tunnels between WAN Edge routers located in different remote sites. All this makes it impossible to dynamically rebuild the multicast trees in WANs. As a result, the WAN Edge with the multicast source connected behind it would need to replicate the multicast stream a number of times that corresponds to the number of remote branches with active receivers in them (see Figure 3-16). This can become a problem in big networks with multiple branches if a multicast source is located in a small branch with a low-bandwidth Internet connection.

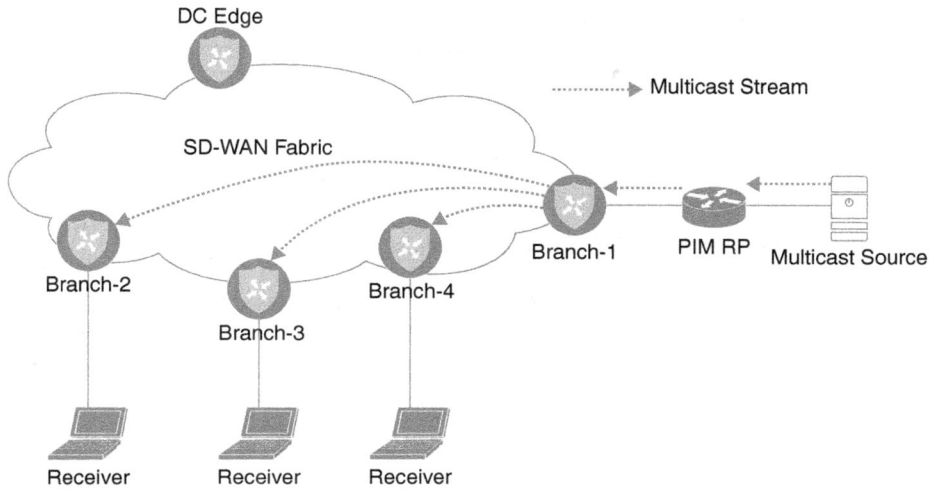

Figure 3-16 *Multicast Traffic Data Flow Without OMP Replicators*

To mitigate such issues and ensure the most efficient use of WAN bandwidth, a new device role called *OMP Replicator* was introduced. Typically a replicator is a PIM-enabled WAN Edge connected to the bigger site with a higher-speed Internet connection. The job of an OMP replicator is to receive multicast streams from the remote-branch sources, replicate them, and send to other sites with the multicast receivers in the same VPN (see Figure 3-17). Replicators advertise themselves to SD-WAN Controller using OMP multicast autodiscover route updates. Therefore, WAN Edge routers with the multicast sources do not need to replicate the multicast stream themselves; they only need to send it once to the OMP replicator(s).

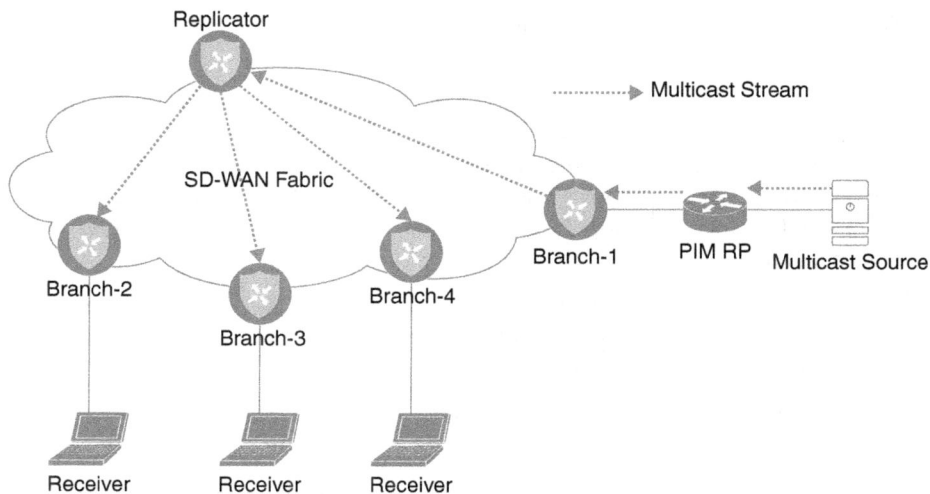

Figure 3-17 *Multicast Traffic Data Flow with OMP Replicators*

Control Plane Troubleshooting

This section shows several useful commands for troubleshooting the SD-WAN control plane. Most of the following commands can be run both on SD-WAN Control Components (SD-WAN Manager, SD-WAN Controller, SD-WAN Validator) and WAN Edge devices—but with one difference. Cisco IOS XE–based WAN Edge devices require the **sdwan** word before the command arguments (for example, **show sdwan running-config**), while legacy ViptelaOS devices and SD-WAN Control Components do not need it (for example, **show running-config**).

These are the most popular troubleshooting commands:

- **show (sdwan) control local-properties:** This command displays the SD-WAN properties of the current device. It can be used to verify local parameters like *system-ip*, *organization-name*, the configured IP address of SD-WAN Validator, X.509 certificate installation status and validity, and so on.

- **show (sdwan) control connections:** As shown in Example 3-9, this command shows the established control connections between WAN Edge routers and SD-WAN Control Components. Keep in mind that if a WAN Edge is in equilibrium state, it does not maintain a permanent control connection with SD-WAN Validator, and it is expected not to see it in the output.

- **show sdwan control connection-history** (or **show control connections-history** for legacy Viptela OS devices): This command shows all previous control connection attempts, including the failed ones. This command can be used to see the error details if the connection could not be established.

- **show orchestrator connections:** This command can be run on SD-WAN Validator only. It shows the control connections between SD-WAN Validator and other devices. It is expected to see permanent connections with SD-WAN Manager, SD-WAN Controller, and WAN Edge routers that are out of equilibrium state. Note that SD-WAN Manager and SD-WAN Controller establish multiple connections with SD-WAN Validator (one connection for every CPU core).

- **show (sdwan) omp peers:** This command shows the OMP peering sessions between WAN Edge and SD-WAN Controller, or between several SD-WAN Controllers. Such sessions are established using the device's System IP address, and there will always be only one session between a WAN Edge and an SD-WAN Controller, even if there are multiple DTLS/TLS connections between them. OMP Peering session is never established between WAN Edge routers.

- **show (sdwan) omp routes:** This command lists all received OMP routes together with the next-hop TLOC information and the route status (for example, chosen, installed, rejected, invalid).

- **show (sdwan) omp tlocs:** This command displays detailed information about received TLOC routes and their attributes.

- **show (sdwan) omp multicast-routes:** This command shows the overlay multicast routes, if present.

- **show (sdwan) omp services:** This command displays services available inside the SD-WAN fabric.

Example 3-9   *Control Connections Between a WAN Edge Router, SD-WAN Manager, and SD-WAN Controller*

```
WAN-Edge# show sdwan control connections
! Output omitted for brevity
                                    PEER              PEER
PEER     PEER        SITE  PEER     PRIV  PEER        PUB    LOCAL
TYPE     SYSTEM IP   ID    PRIVATE IP   PORT  PUBLIC IP    PORT   COLOR  STATE
-----------------------------------------------------------------------------
vsmart   1.1.1.102   100   209.165.201.10  12446  209.165.201.10  12446  lte    up
vsmart   1.1.1.103   100   209.165.201.11  12446  209.165.201.11  12446  lte    up
vsmart   1.1.1.102   100   209.165.201.10  12446  209.165.201.10  12446  mpls   up
vsmart   1.1.1.103   100   209.165.201.11  12446  209.165.201.11  12446  mpls   up
vmanage  1.1.1.101   100   209.165.201.9   12646  209.165.201.9   12646  lte    up
```

Data Plane Operations

The data plane in any traditional network is responsible for moving packets from one location to another. The data plane is therefore commonly referred to as the *forwarding plane*. From a WAN perspective, common transports used to transmit data packets consist of the public Internet and private WANs (such as DMVPN, MPLS, or point-to-point connections). All of these technologies build on some type of overlay for encapsulating and securing the data packets. As wide-area networks grow, the legacy transports start to have trouble scaling—particularly when securing the control and data planes becomes an issue. Processing key exchanges and routing updates consumes a lot of CPU cycles. Figure 3-18 shows a common deployment scenario for a WAN.

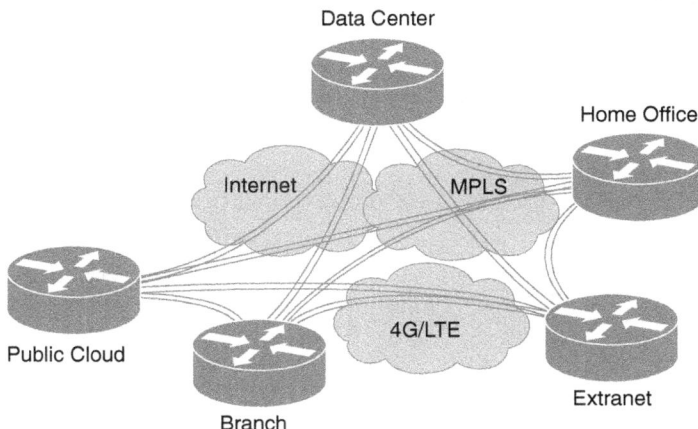

Figure 3-18   *Traditional Wide-Area Network*

Security in the data plane is usually achieved by encrypting the data with IPsec and its suite of tools. In networks that traditionally use IPsec to secure the data plane, scale becomes a concern, as the processing power to handle key exchanges is exponentially larger than the number of nodes in the WAN. For example, a full-mesh network that has 100 nodes would require 10,000 key exchanges (n^2). Each device would have to maintain 99 keys ($n - 1$).

With Cisco Catalyst SD-WAN, IPsec is used to secure the data plane. However, modifications have been made to support larger-scale deployments. To support larger numbers, a centralized SD-WAN Controller is used to distribute keys and routing information. Having SD-WAN Controller handle key distribution greatly increases the ability to scale out to larger networks by not requiring each WAN Edge to negotiate its keys with the other nodes in the network.

In addition, networks face scalability challenges when network requirements call for supporting segmentation or different topologies per network segment. Traditional methods of providing segmentation across a WAN using technologies such as MPLS L3VPN and 2547oDMVPN (MPLS over DMVPN) can be very complex, and their implementation, operation, and troubleshooting generally require more seasoned network engineers.

In Cisco Catalyst SD-WAN, segmentation is natively implemented, and advanced experience isn't required to implement and support it. Network segmentation also allows for different topologies per network segment. For example, corporate users could have a full-mesh topology, and PCI/HIPAA devices could be hub and spoke. (Later on in this chapter, we discuss segmentation and multi-topology.) Figure 3-19 shows an example of how network segmentation is achieved between Gidget and Mowgli.

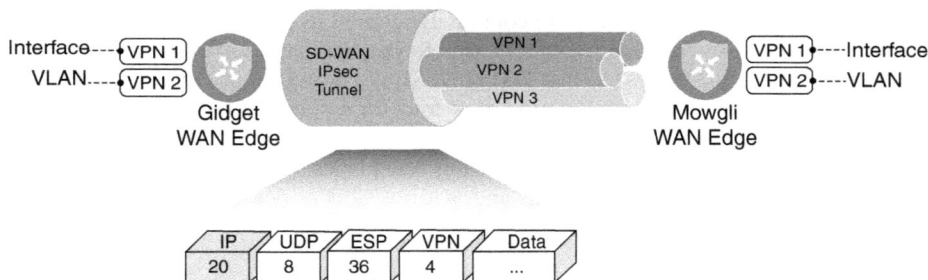

Figure 3-19   *Cisco Catalyst SD-WAN Segmentation*

The remainder of this chapter dives more deeply into these technologies and discusses how Cisco Catalyst SD-WAN implements data plane routing, encryption, authentication, and segmentation.

TLOC Colors

As discussed earlier, TLOC route is an OMP route type that provides WAN Edge reachability information on how to build the data plane to the rest of the WAN Edge routers in the network. The TLOC attribute identifies a WAN Edge attachment point to the physical underlay.

A key attribute of TLOCs is their color. Colors are used to label or categorize a specific transport. The network administrator assigns transports their respective colors when provisioning the routers. For example, all sites that have the same type of Internet circuit might use the same color. Policies can then be defined to control how data traffic flows across the overlay between these colors. Currently, there are 22 prebuilt colors, broken into two categories: public and private. The color selected signifies whether NAT is in play. Private colors are only used when there is no NAT between devices on the overlay. If there is a NAT device between WAN Edge routers, then a public color is used. Table 3-4 shows the breakdown of the colors.

Table 3-4   TLOC Colors by Category

Public Colors	Private Colors
default	metro-ethernet
3g	mpls
biz-internet	private1
public-internet	private2
lte	private3
blue	private4
bronze	private5
custom1	private6
custom2	
custom3	
gold	
green	
red	
silver	

NOTE   If there is no color defined, then **default** is the color that will be advertised with the TLOC route.

When establishing the IPsec data plane, WAN Edge devices by default attempt to establish full-mesh connectivity between all routers in the fabric. If two colors have IP reachability, they establish the data plane no matter what the color. For example, say that one router has only the color **biz-internet** and another router has only the color **public-internet**. Because they have IP connectivity, they will build an IPsec tunnel.

This may be desired, or it may not be desired. A common design where this decision comes into play is when a private WAN (MPLS) does not have IP connectivity to the Internet. In such a case, you don't want MPLS-connected routers attempting to build connections to Internet-connected routers. This decision also comes into play with global deployments. Depending on the country or region, you may want full mesh tunnels. However, across countries or regions (such as between the United States and Europe), you may want to use a point-to-point tunnel between hub sites.

Figure 3-20 illustrates the scenario when each of two routers has two transports: **biz-internet** and **public-internet**. When these devices establish their control plane connections, they advertise two TLOC routes each: one for the **public-internet** color and another for the **biz-internet** color. Both of these routers learn these TLOC routes and begin to establish data plane connectivity. Since these two colors have Internet connectivity as well as reachability between them, the routers will build data plane connections across all colors. This means that each router will have four IPsec tunnels to the other WAN Edge:

- WAN Edge 1: **biz-internet** ←→ WAN Edge 2: **biz-internet**
- WAN Edge 1: **public-internet** ←→ WAN Edge 2: **public-internet**

- WAN Edge 1: **biz-internet** ←—→ WAN Edge 2: **public-internet**

- WAN Edge 1: **public-internet** ←—→ WAN Edge 2: **biz-internet**

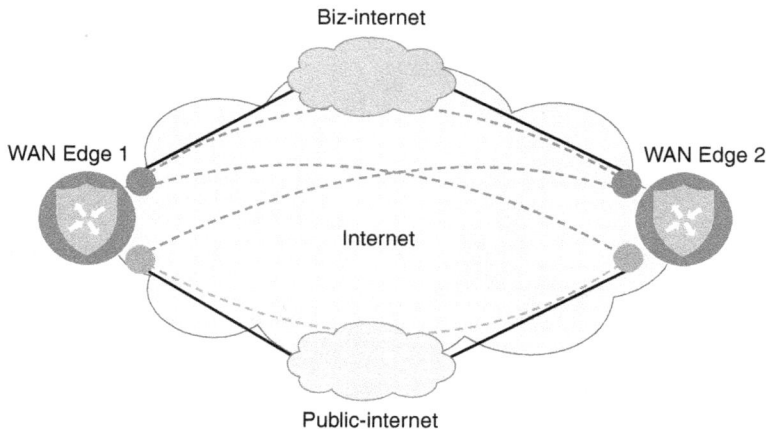

Figure 3-20   *TLOC Colors Without the restrict Keyword*

Let's say that either of the colors doesn't have IP connectivity between the TLOC or the design calls for them not to build data connectivity across colors. In this case, there are two options: You can advertise the **restrict** attribute with the TLOC, or you can configure tunnel groups. These attributes tell the other devices in the fabric not to attempt to build connectivity to the restricted color.

TLOC Colors with the restrict Keyword

Let's examine the concept of TLOC colors using the **restrict** keyword first. **restrict** is an OMP attribute inside a TLOC route. This value needs to be defined per site as either on or off. Example 3-10 provides an example of a TLOC route with **restrict**. Notice that this TLOC uses the color **biz-internet**. Toward the bottom of the advertisement, notice the **restrict** attribute that is set to 1. A **restrict** attribute of 1 means that this device will only form tunnels with other TLOCs advertising the **biz-internet** color. If this were 0, then the color would be unrestricted and could form tunnels with other colors. Look again at the example in Figure 3-20. In this case, if **restrict** is not set, you will end up with four data plane tunnels per device, with IPsec tunnels built across all colors.

Example 3-10   *A TLOC Route with restrict Set*

```
WAN-Edge1# show sdwan omp tlocs
! Output omitted for brevity
-----------------------------------------------------
tloc entries for 10.0.20.1
                biz-internet
                ipsec
-----------------------------------------------------
        RECEIVED FROM:
! Peer 1.1.1.102 is SD-WAN Controller (vSmart-2)
tenant-id        0
```

```
peer               1.1.1.102
status             C,I,R
tenant-name        [Default]
    Attributes:
    attribute-type    installed
    encap-key         not set
    encap-proto       0
    encap-spi         261
    encap-auth        sha1-hmac,ah-sha1-hmac
    encap-encrypt     aes256
    public-ip         209.165.201.3
    public-port       12346
    private-ip        209.165.201.3
    private-port      12346
<..>
    weight            1
    version           3
    gen-id            0x80000004
    carrier           default
    restrict          1
    on-demand         0
    groups            [ 0 ]
```

Figure 3-21 shows how the data plane would be established if **restrict** were set. Each WAN Edge would have two IPsec tunnels, one per color.

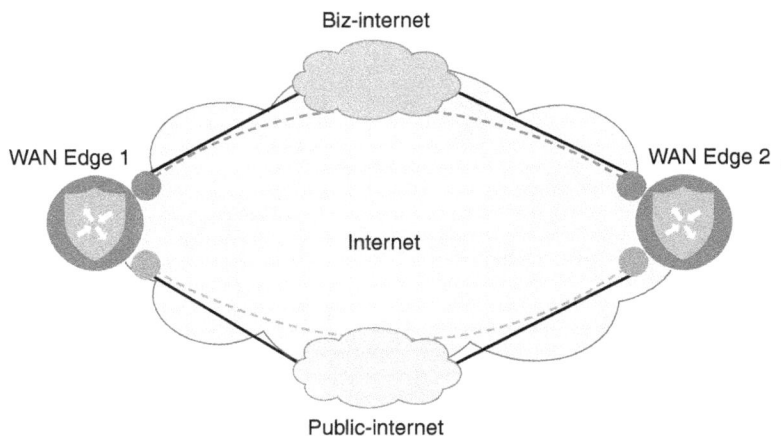

Figure 3-21 *TLOC Colors with the restrict Keyword*

Just as in the previous example, both routers have two transports: **biz-internet** and **public-internet**. In this case, **restrict** is configured on the two transports. When these devices establish their control plane connections, they advertise two TLOCs each: one for the **public-internet** color and another for the **biz-internet** color. Both of these routers learn these TLOCs and begin to establish data plane connectivity. Because **restrict** is configured, these routers will only build connections across their like colors. This means that each router will have two IPsec tunnels to the other WAN Edge:

- WAN Edge 1: **biz-internet** ←→ WAN Edge 2: **biz-internet**

- WAN Edge 1: **public-internet** ←→ WAN Edge 2: **public-internet**

Tunnel Groups

Another option for restricting data plane connectivity is using *tunnel groups*. Only tunnels with matching tunnel groups or no tunnel group defined can form data plane connectivity (independent of the color). It is recommended that, if using tunnel groups, all sites have tunnel groups defined. A common deployment for this is when a data center has two physical connections to the same MPLS provider, but each branch site has only one physical connection to that MPLS provider, though the design calls for building connectivity across both physical interfaces in the data center. The tunnel group is advertised as an attribute in the TLOC route, as demonstrated in Example 3-11. The possible values for tunnel groups are between 0 and 4294967295.

Example 3-11   *TLOC Route with Tunnel Groups*

```
DC-WAN-Edge# show sdwan omp tlocs
! Output omitted for brevity
---------------------------------------------------
tloc entries for 10.0.101.1
                 mpls
                 ipsec
---------------------------------------------------
          RECEIVED FROM:
! Peer 1.1.1.102 is SD-WAN Controller (vSmart-2)
tenant-id      0
peer           1.1.1.102
status         C,I,R
tenant-name    [Default]
    Attributes:
     attribute-type     installed
     encap-key          not set
     encap-proto        0
     encap-spi          314
     encap-auth         sha1-hmac,ah-sha1-hmac
     encap-encrypt      aes256
     public-ip          192.168.20.5
     public-port        12406
     private-ip         192.168.20.5
     private-port       12406
<..>
```

```
    weight          1
    version         3
    gen-id          0x80000004
    carrier         default
    restrict        1
    on-demand       0
    groups          [ 10 ]
```

In Figure 3-22, you can see three sites: a data center and two remote sites. The data center has three physical transports: two to the MPLS provider and one to the Internet provider. All of the MPLS transports have the tunnel group ID 10, and the Internet transports have the group ID 20.

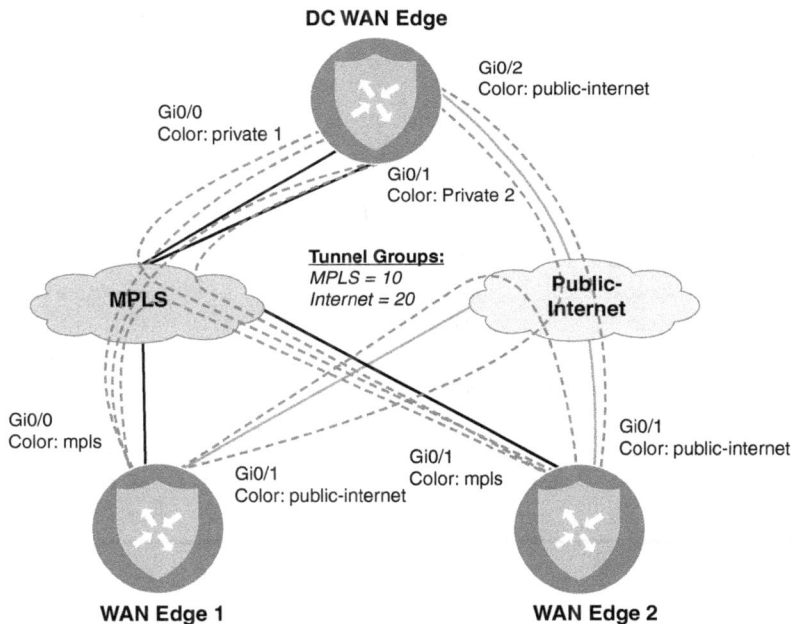

Figure 3-22 *TLOC Colors with Tunnel Groups*

Because the design calls for data connectivity to be built from the single MPLS connection at the remote sites to both MPLS physical interfaces at the data center, we are using two colors: **private 1** and **private 2**. The single color **mpls** is used at the remote branches on the MPLS transport. Each remote site builds five tunnels—three over the MPLS provider and two over the public Internet provider:

- WAN Edge 1 and 2: **public-internet** ⟷ DC WAN Edge: **public-internet**

- WAN Edge 1 and 2: **mpls** ⟷ DC WAN Edge: **private 1**

- WAN Edge 1 and 2: **mpls** ⟷ DC WAN Edge: **private 2**

- WAN Edge 1: **mpls** ⟷ WAN Edge 2: **mpls**

- WAN Edge 1: **public-internet** ⟷ WAN Edge 2: **public-internet**

Because the tunnel groups aren't the same between the **mpls** and **public-internet** transports, data connectivity between these colors will not be attempted. Example 3-11 shows the CLI output from these devices.

NOTE   An important note regarding color is that you can only have one interface per WAN Edge using that color. You can't have multiple interfaces on the same WAN Edge using the same color because using the same color would break the uniqueness of the TLOC route.

Example 3-12   *CLI Output from Each Device, Showing Data Plane BFD Sessions*

```
DC-WAN-Edge# show sdwan bfd sessions
                                SOURCE TLOC       REMOTE TLOC                       DST PUBLIC
SYSTEM IP  SITE ID  STATE       COLOR             COLOR             SOURCE IP       IP
-------------------------------------------------------------------------------------------
2.2.2.2    2        up          public-internet   public-internet   192.168.1.2     192.168.10.2
2.2.2.2    2        up          private1          mpls              100.64.0.2      100.64.10.2
2.2.2.2    2        up          private2          mpls              100.64.1.2      100.64.10.2
3.3.3.3    3        up          public-internet   public-internet   192.168.1.2     100.64.20.2
3.3.3.3    3        up          private1          mpls              100.64.0.2      100.64.30.2
3.3.3.3    3        up          private2          mpls              100.64.1.2      100.64.30.2

WAN-Edge-1# show sdwan bfd sessions
                                SOURCE TLOC       REMOTE TLOC                       DST PUBLIC
SYSTEM IP  SITE ID  STATE       COLOR             COLOR             SOURCE IP       IP
-------------------------------------------------------------------------------------------
1.1.1.1    1        up          public-internet   public-internet   192.168.10.2    192.168.1.2
1.1.1.1    1        up          mpls              private1          100.64.10.2     100.64.0.2
1.1.1.1    1        up          mpls              private2          100.64.10.2     100.64.1.2
3.3.3.3    3        up          public-internet   public-internet   192.168.10.2    100.64.20.2
3.3.3.3    3        up          mpls              mpls              100.64.10.2     100.64.30.2

WAN-Edge-2# show sdwan bfd sessions
                                SOURCE TLOC       REMOTE TLOC                       DST PUBLIC
SYSTEM IP  SITE ID  STATE       COLOR             COLOR             SOURCE IP       IP
-------------------------------------------------------------------------------------------
1.1.1.1    1        up          public-internet   public-internet   100.64.20.2     192.168.1.2
1.1.1.1    1        up          mpls              private1          100.64.30.2     100.64.0.2
1.1.1.1    1        up          mpls              private2          100.64.30.2     100.64.1.2
2.2.2.2    2        up          public-internet   public-internet   100.64.20.2     192.168.10.2
2.2.2.2    2        up          mpls              mpls              100.64.30.2     100.64.10.2
```

NOTE   Tunnel groups can be used with the **restrict** attribute as well. The rules of the two still follow, with **restrict** and **color** taking precedence. This means that if **restrict** is set on a color, and a tunnel group is set, the router will only build IPsec tunnels between routers with not only the same color but also the same tunnel group ID (or no tunnel group ID).

Dynamic Tunnels

Keeping data tunnels always in the active state requires additional network bandwidth and can increase the memory and CPU usage on the WAN Edge. In some deployments, it might not be necessary to have all data tunnels up and running all the time, and in some deployments, it might not be physically possible to have all data tunnels simultaneously up if the total number of data tunnels exceeds the capacity of the WAN Edge router.

In Figure 3-23, for example, the network has three sites (Datacenter, Branch 1, and Branch 2) connected to each other using a hub-and-spoke topology. There is Internet connectivity between the branches, but direct communication between them happens rarely, so it is very inefficient to keep the data tunnels between Branch 1 and Branch 2 always in the active state.

Cisco Catalyst SD-WAN has a feature that can reduce the performance demands and decrease the unnecessary network traffic in the spoke branches. *Dynamic on-demand tunnels* allow WAN Edge devices to establish data tunnels only when there is *bidirectional* traffic between the sites and to destroy those tunnels when they are no longer needed.

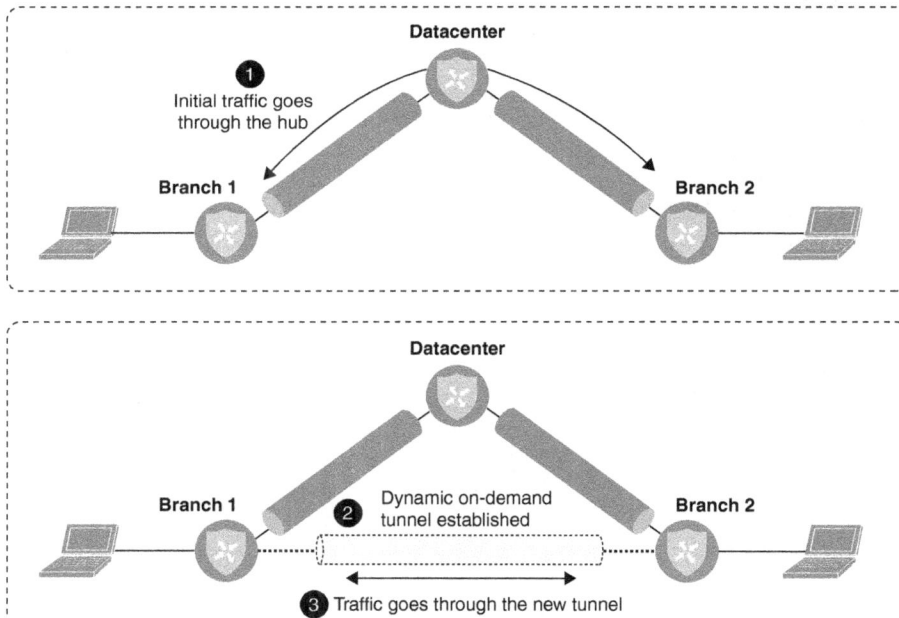

Figure 3-23 *Dynamic On-Demand Tunnels*

Let us look at how the traffic in Figure 3-23 goes. Initially there are no data tunnels between Branch 1 and Branch 2; that is, the tunnels are in inactive state. There must, however, be some connectivity between those sites. In this case, it will be achieved via the hub (Datacenter). When the hosts in Branch 1 and Branch 2 start to exchange packets, traffic initially takes the longer backup path through the hub. In the meantime, the branch WAN Edge routers provision the direct on-demand tunnel between their sites and start running Bidirectional Forwarding Detection (BFD) over this tunnel. When the tunnel state becomes active, the data traffic goes directly between Branch 1 and Branch 2. When the user traffic is finished, the WAN Edge devices will wait for the inactivity timer to expire and terminate the direct dynamic tunnel between the sites.

Network Address Translation

When discussing the data plane of any tunneling mechanism, it is important to examine Network Address Translation (NAT). As the IPv4 pool is exhausted further and further, WAN termination points are relying on NAT to conserve address space. As with most traditional tunneling technologies, there are some NAT designs that work in Cisco Catalyst SD-WAN, and some that don't work. The best possible solution is to assign your WAN Edge a public IP address to avoid having to worry about NAT, but that is not always possible. In this section, we'll discuss which designs work and which don't. Before we begin, let's review the various types of NAT deployments.

Static NAT

The first type of NAT deployment is *static NAT* (sometimes referred to as either *full cone NAT*, or *one-to-one NAT*). When static NAT is configured, the same *private* (internal) IP address and port are always translated to the same *public* IP address and port. The translation table on the NAT device is statically prepopulated with the configured translation, regardless of whether the traffic was already initiated. The assigned public IP address and port are always open, and any external hosts can initiate traffic to the internal Host A behind the static NAT device. You can have multiple static NAT translations configured to use the same public IP address, but the public ports must be different for each internal host. In addition, the internal and external ports don't need to match. You can configure NAT with static Port Address Translation (*static PAT*) when the same private ports will always be translated to the same public ports. Figure 3-24 provides an example of how static NAT works.

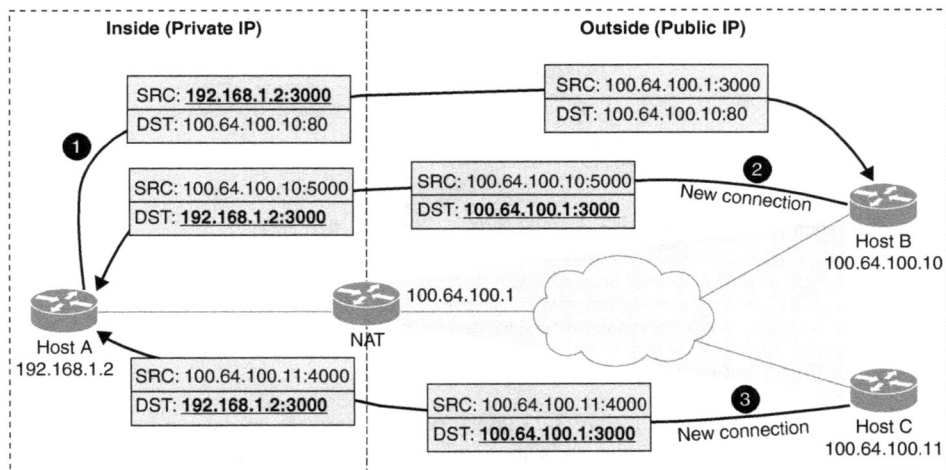

Figure 3-24 *Static NAT*

In this example, there are three hosts (Host A, Host B, and Host C) and a NAT device in the middle configured with static NAT. The internal Host A, 192.168.1.2, has a service running on port 3000. There is an external host, Host B, at 100.64.100.10.

Here is how the traffic flow occurs with static NAT:

Step 1.   Traffic initiated from inside Host A to outside Host B with source port 3000 will have its source IP address in the IP header translated to the outside zone with source IP address 100.64.100.1. So, SRC IP address 192.168.1.2 is translated to 100.64.100.1.

Step 2.   When the outside Host B initiates a connection to 100.64.100.1:3000, the NAT device translates the destination IP address in the IP header to the inside zone with destination IP address 192.168.1.2. So, DST IP address 100.64.100.1 is translated to 192.168.1.2.

Step 3.   Any other external host (for example, outside Host C) can initiate a connection to 100.64.100.1:3000 at any time. Similarly to step 2, the destination IP address is translated to the inside zone with destination IP address 192.168.1.2. So, DST IP address 100.64.100.1 is translated to 192.168.1.2.

Dynamic NAT

Whereas static NAT makes network connections more predictable and controllable by the administrator, multiple static translations for many internal hosts and ports can easily consume all public IP addresses and ports, even when they are not used. Also, sometimes company security policies dictate requirements that prohibit the possibility of establishing connections from the outside.

NOTE   Do not confuse dynamic NAT (also known as restricted cone NAT) with dynamic PAT (also known as symmetric NAT). Both of these options are explained later in this chapter.

In such cases, another type of address translation, *dynamic NAT*, can be used. Dynamic NAT is also referred to as *restricted cone NAT*. Depending on the implementation, there can be *address-restricted cone NAT* or *port-restricted cone NAT*. What they have in common is that the translation table on the NAT device is empty by default. The translation entry is created only when the inside host initiates the traffic toward the outside destination. The public IP address and/or port is assigned dynamically from the shared pool of resources. The mapping between private and public IP address and port exists temporarily. When the timeout expires and the translation is destroyed, the same public IP address and port can be reused by a different inside host or service.

Figure 3-25 illustrates the first variation of dynamic NAT: address-restricted cone NAT. This type of NAT allows an external Host B to communicate with internal Host A only if that Host A has communicated with Host B before on any port. After the first connection is established from the inside network and the translation entry is dynamically created on the NAT device, external Host B can initiate a connection with internal Host A, using any source ports. In this case, only the IP address of external Host B must match.

Let's review the conversations between the hosts shown in Figure 3-25:

Step 1.   Internal Host A behind the NAT device has initiated a connection to the destination IP address 100.64.100.10:80. As with all TCP/UDP conversations, there are a source port and a destination port in the header. On the NAT device, the source IP address is translated to 100.64.100.1, and the source port is translated from 3000 to 4000.

Step 2. Since internal Host A initially connected to Host B 100.64.100.10, Host B can now connect to 100.64.100.1 port 4000, and this traffic will be allowed. Host B uses a new source port 5000 for this new communication. The destination IP address and port are both translated to 192.168.1.2:3000.

Step 3. When external Host C, 100.64.100.11, tries to connect to 100.64.100.1 on port 4000, the traffic will be denied because internal Host A has never initiated a connection to 100.64.100.11 previously.

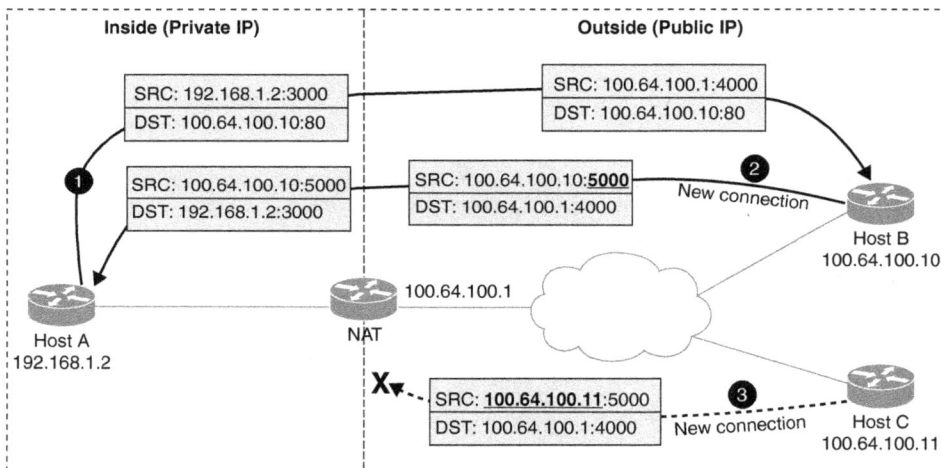

Figure 3-25 *Dynamic NAT (Address-Restricted Cone NAT)*

Another type of dynamic NAT, port-restricted cone NAT, works similarly to address-restricted cone NAT, but the restriction includes port numbers as well. External Host B can send packets to internal Host A only if Host A previously initiated a connection to that external host. Both the IP address and port of external Host B must match.

Figure 3-26 shows how port-restricted cone NAT works. This is the conversation that takes place:

Step 1. Internal Host A, 192.168.1.2:3000, initiates a connection to external Host B, 100.64.100.10, with destination port 80.

Step 2. Because Host A previously connected to 100.64.100.10 on port 80, external Host B is *only* allowed to initiate a connection to internal Host A if it uses source port 80.

Step 3. If the same external Host B tries to use source port 443, it will be denied because internal Host A has never connected to 100.64.100.10 on port 443.

Step 4. If external Host C, 100.64.100.11, tries to connect to 100.64.100.1 with source port 80, it is also denied because internal Host A has never established a connection to this IP address and port 100.64.100.11:80.

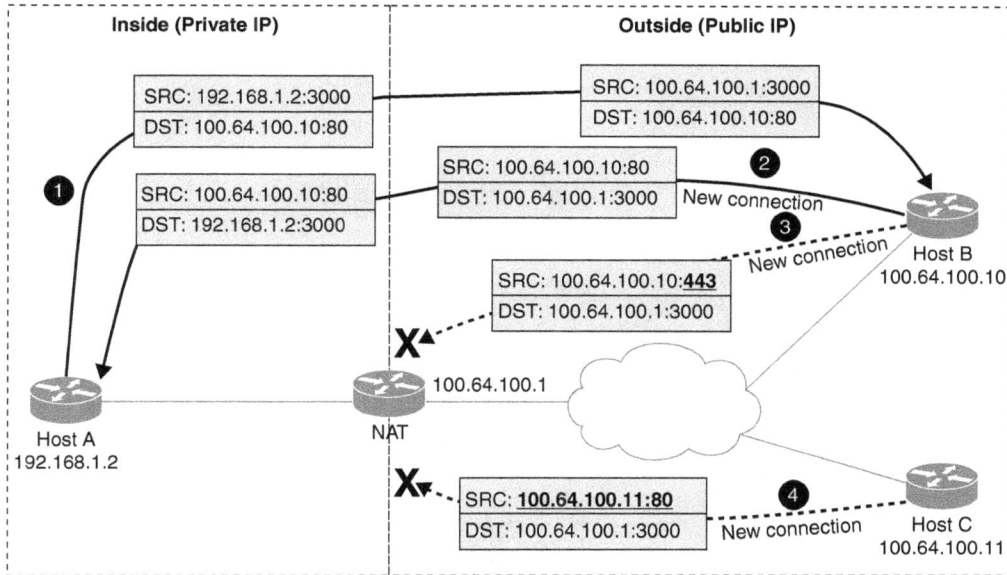

Figure 3-26 *Dynamic NAT (Port-Restricted Cone)*

Address-restricted cone NAT and port-restricted cone NAT are often grouped together and referred to as *dynamic NAT*. We will use this name throughout the chapter.

Dynamic PAT

Another type of NAT deployment, and probably the most common one, is *NAT with port address translation* (also referred to as *dynamic PAT* or *symmetric NAT*). Dynamic PAT has the advantage of allowing a large number of hosts behind a single IP address. It is common in deployments where a number of users need access to the Internet, but the administrator does not want to consume a unique IP address for each user. With dynamic PAT, the original source IP address is translated to the outside IP address, and the source port is translated to another port. This allows a theoretical limit of up to 63,335 hosts behind a single public IP address.

With dynamic PAT, each internally initiated conversation to the specific external IP address and port creates a mapping in the NAT translation table. If the same internal host sends the traffic from the same internal port but to a different external destination, a new NAT translation with the new public port is created. This is a key difference between dynamic PAT and static or dynamic NAT techniques that we discussed above. Because the mapping is created only when traffic is initiated from an internal host, external hosts cannot initiate connections to the internal host. This mapping is dynamic and eventually expires if there is no traffic matching that mapping entry.

Figure 3-27 illustrates how dynamic PAT works.

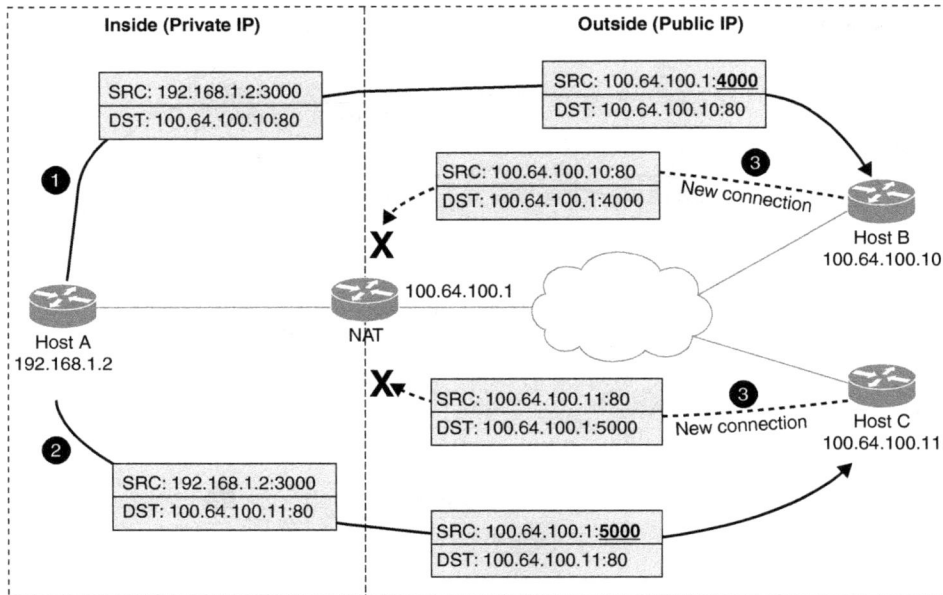

Figure 3-27   *Dynamic PAT*

In Figure 3-27, there are three hosts. Internal Host A, connected behind a dynamic PAT device, starts various connections to the external hosts 100.64.100.10 and 100.64.100.11. Let's review these conversations:

Step 1.   Internal Host A, 192.168.1.2, connects to external Host B, 100.64.100.10, port 80. In this case, the source IP address 192.168.1.2 and the source port 3000 are translated to 100.64.100.1:4000.

Step 2.   Similarly, internal Host A, 192.168.1.2, initiates another connection to external Host C, 100.64.100.11, port 80. The source IP address 192.168.1.2 is translated to the same public IP address 100.64.100.1, but the source port is different this time. For the second communication with Host C, the same source port 3000 is translated to 100.64.100.1:5000.

Step 3.   When external Hosts B and C try to send to internal Host A packets that are not part of the original conversations, this traffic is blocked. The initial NAT mappings created in steps 1 and 2 exist only for the original sessions started by Host A. These mappings cannot be reused in any other communications.

NOTE   Since the mapping entry is only created when traffic is initiated from the inside hosts, external hosts are unable to initiate connections unless there has been a prior conversation initiated from the internal host.

With Cisco Catalyst SD-WAN, there are certain types of NAT that work and some that have restrictions. Before discussing those restrictions, let's talk about how Cisco Catalyst SD-WAN handles NAT. As introduced in Chapter 2, the SD-WAN Validator operates on the orchestration plane and is the glue of the fabric in regard to how NAT is handled. WAN Edge routers always reach out to SD-WAN Validator first to learn about the rest of the components in the fabric. During this process, they also learn whether they are behind a NAT device. When a WAN Edge initially connects to SD-WAN Validator, it inserts its real IP address into the exchange. When this packet passes through the NAT device, the source IP address and possibly the source port are translated. Since the message still contains the WAN Edge's real IP address and port, SD-WAN Validator is able to send a message back to the WAN Edge, notifying it that it is behind a NAT device (since the real IP address differs from the NAT IP address received in the exchange). The WAN Edge then inserts this information into its OMP TLOC route and sends it to the SD-WAN Controller. If these values are different, then the WAN Edge is behind a NAT device. This information is then reflected to all WAN Edge devices in the overlay, and they use this information to build their data plane. The mechanism to achieve this NAT detection is STUN (RFC 5389). Review the output from Example 3-13 and see Figure 3-28 for a graphical depiction.

Example 3-13 *TLOC Route*

```
WAN-Edge# show sdwan omp tlocs
! Output omitted for brevity
-----------------------------------------------------
tloc entries for 10.1.0.1
                mpls
                ipsec
-----------------------------------------------------
            RECEIVED FROM:
peer              12.12.12.12
status            C,I,R
loss-reason       not set
lost-to-peer      not set
lost-to-path-id not set
    Attributes:
      attribute-type    installed
      encap-key         not set
      encap-proto       0
      encap-spi         256
      encap-auth        sha1-hmac,ah-sha1-hmac
      encap-encrypt     aes256
      public-ip         172.16.10.2
      public-port       12366
      private-ip        172.16.10.2
      private-port      12366
      public-ip         ::
      public-port       0
```

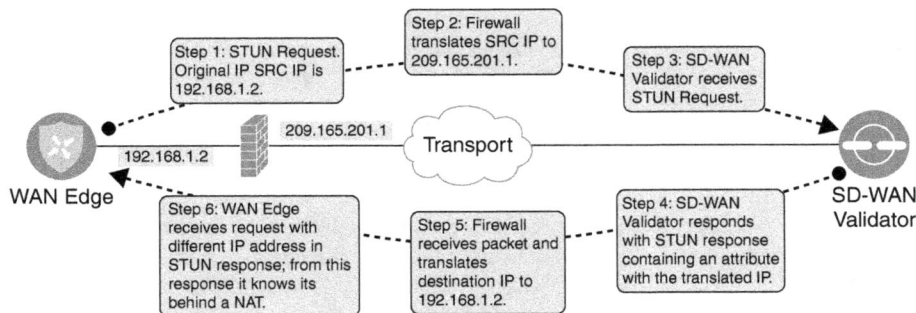

Figure 3-28 *NAT Traversal with STUN*

> **NOTE**   If the colors on both ends of the connection are private colors, then the private IP addresses and ports will be used to establish connectivity, even if the control connection with SD-WAN Validator is behind a NAT device. WAN Edge devices use the NAT address advertised only when connecting from private to public color or between public colors. It works the same way for data tunnels between WAN Edge devices, as well as for control connections between WAN Edge devices and SD-WAN Manager or Controller.

Dynamic PAT can cause issues for data plane connectivity. Dynamic PAT creates a new mapping for every outbound communication and only allows return traffic from the original destination IP address. For example, let's say you have one WAN Edge that is behind a NAT device using symmetric NAT. When the WAN Edge connects to SD-WAN Validator, the NAT device creates a NAT mapping with the source IP address of the WAN Edge, allowing only the SD-WAN Validator's return traffic. Now imagine that a second WAN Edge receives this TLOC with the public IP address and port that were used to communicate with SD-WAN Validator. When this WAN Edge tries to build an IPsec tunnel to the first WAN Edge using the public IP address and port from the advertised TLOC, it is unable to because the initial NAT mapping using that information is unique to the connection with SD-WAN Validator, as illustrated in Figure 3-29.

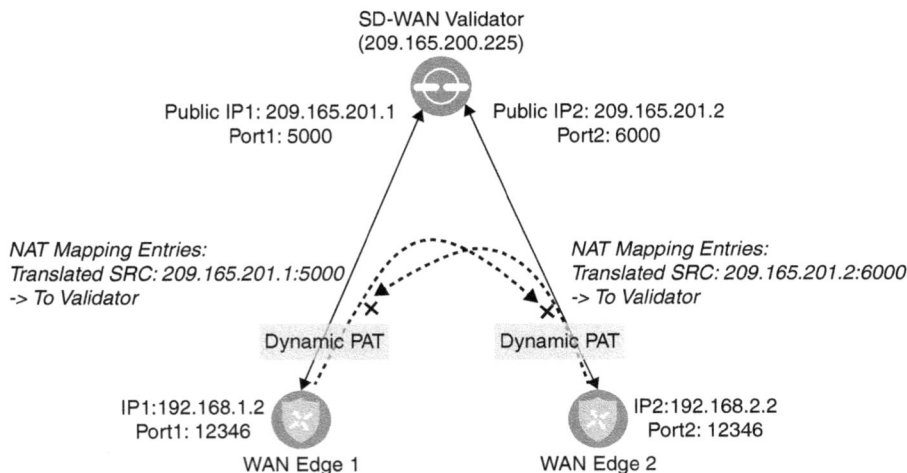

Figure 3-29 *Dynamic PAT Restrictions*

To resolve this, at least one of the WAN Edge routers must not use dynamic NAT/PAT. When WAN Edge 1 attempts to use the TLOC information of WAN Edge 2 (which is behind a dynamic PAT device) and establish data plane connectivity, it is dropped for the same reason as before. However, WAN Edge 2 also tries to establish a tunnel using WAN Edge 1's TLOC information. WAN Edge 1 is connected behind a static NAT device, and its public IP address and port will be always the same. This second connection creates a new NAT mapping, and the data plane connectivity is successful, as illustrated in Figure 3-30.

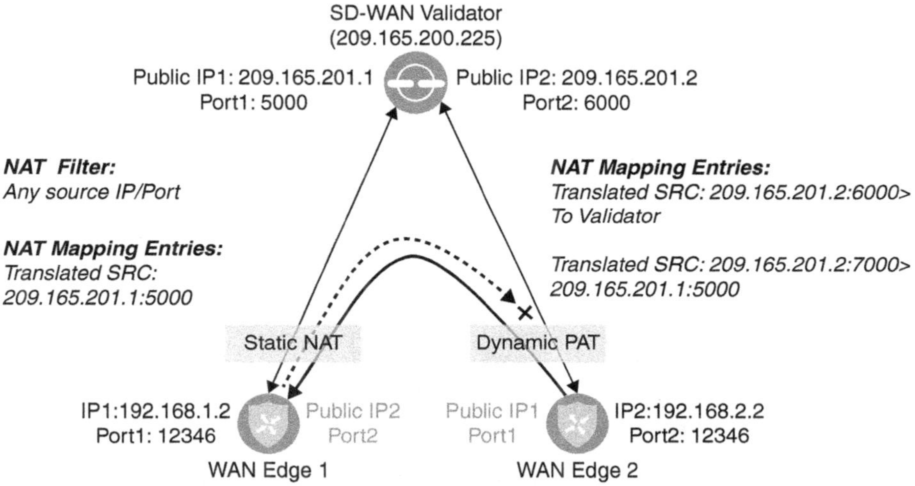

Figure 3-30   *Static and Dynamic NAT/PAT*

Table 3-5 provides a breakdown of how the various types of NAT interact with each other.

Table 3-5   NAT Types and Data Plane Status

Side A	Side B	Data Plane Status
Public IP address	Public IP address	Successful
Public IP address	Dynamic PAT (symmetric)	Successful
Static NAT (full cone)	Static NAT (full cone)	Successful
Static NAT (full cone)	Dynamic NAT (restricted cone)	Successful
Static NAT (full cone)	Dynamic PAT (symmetric)	Successful
Dynamic NAT (restricted cone)	Dynamic NAT (restricted cone)	Unsuccessful
Dynamic NAT (restricted cone)	Dynamic PAT (symmetric)	Unsuccessful
Dynamic PAT (symmetric)	Dynamic PAT (symmetric)	Unsuccessful

NOTE   Internet connections with dynamic PAT are used quite often, especially in small branches. If several branches behind a dynamic PAT device need to communicate with each other, you can achieve that connectivity by building a hub-and-spoke topology and sending the data traffic via an intermediary site (that is, a hub) that does not have NAT restrictions. The following chapters discuss the building of custom topologies.

Network Segmentation

Security is a growing concern for most network deployments, and more and more network administrators are looking at implementing network segmentation. Network segmentation is not new; network segmentation has been used for years, with solutions such as VLANs and VRF instances. Network segmentation enables a network to isolate different lines of business or users from each other unless specific policy allows communication between them. Here are a few common network segmentation use cases:

■ Segmenting corporate users from guest users

■ Allowing extranet partners to access selective parts of the network

■ Separating PCI and/or HIPAA networks due to regulatory requirements

By segmenting the control and data planes, you can build disparate topologies for each network segment. With Cisco Catalyst SD-WAN, network segmentation is accomplished via VPNs. Fundamentally, it is the same thing as a VRF instance, using legacy terminology. There are three different types of VPNs in Cisco Catalyst SD-WAN (see Figure 3-31):

■ **Service VPN:** A service VPN is where user traffic lives. Such a VPN is defined across the overlay and terminates the LAN side of a router (the service side). You can have multiple service VPNs in the fabric and have multiple topologies for different VPNs. These VPNs can have values from 1 to 511 and from 513 to 65527. (VPNs 65528 through 65530 are reserved.)

■ **Transport VPN:** A transport VPN is where the physical (WAN) underlay transport terminates. This VPN is usually referred to as VPN 0. VPN 0 is statically assigned as the WAN VPN and cannot be changed.

■ **Management VPN:** A management VPN is assigned to the out-of-band management interface. It uses VPN value 512, which cannot be changed.

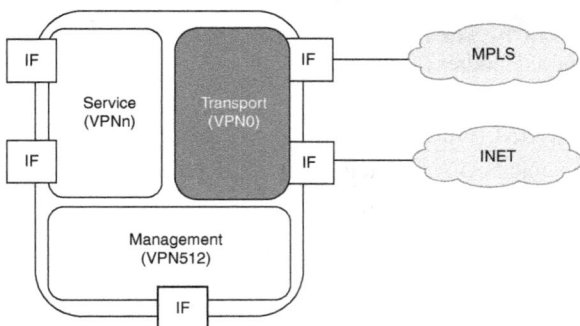

Figure 3-31 *VPN Types in Cisco Catalyst SD-WAN*

With Cisco Catalyst SD-WAN, segmentation is achieved by using VPN identifiers, as shown in Figure 3-32. Each data packet carries a VPN ID that identifies the VPN it belongs to on the overlay. Once the VPN is configured on WAN Edge devices, it has a label tied to it. As the WAN Edge builds its control plane, it sends the label along with the VPN ID to SD-WAN

Controller. SD-WAN Controller then distributes the VPN ID mapping information to other WAN Edge devices in the network. The remote WAN Edge devices in the network then use these labels to send traffic to the appropriate VPNs. This solution follows the standard defined in RFC 4023 and operates similarly to MPLS.

Because the control plane and data plane have been separated, the solution allows you to build different topologies for different VPNs. Common topology types are hub and spoke, point to point, full mesh, and partial mesh. With no topology defined, all VPNs are full mesh by default. Since the TLOC route influences how the data plane is built, you achieve the various topologies by filtering routes and TLOCs. (Topologies are defined in a centralized control policy, discussed later in this book.)

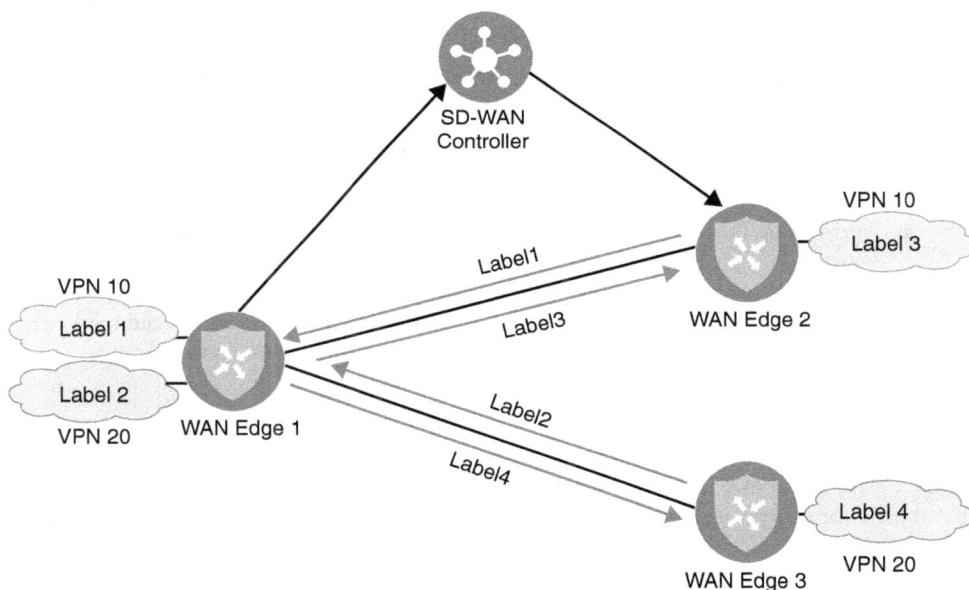

Figure 3-32 *Overlay Label Switching*

Data Plane Encryption

All of the concepts discussed up to this point in the chapter have been related to the control plane's role in building out the data plane. With most overlay technologies, including Cisco Catalyst SD-WAN, encryption and authentication are achieved with IPsec. As discussed previously, the biggest difference is how scale is achieved—particularly in how key exchange is handled.

Internet Key Exchange (IKE) protocol traditionally handles key exchange. In the first phase of the IKE process, two peers negotiate what type of encryption, authentication, hashing, and other techniques they want to use. This phase is used only to establish a secure channel to negotiate the second phase of the IPsec tunnel. The second phase of IKE establishes a tunnel in which user data is transmitted. For this tunnel to be established, a few things are negotiated. First, phase 2 of IKE negotiates the use of an encapsulation protocol (either Authentication Header or Encapsulation Security Protocol). Next, the encryption algorithm to use, the type of authentication, and the tunnel lifetime are agreed upon. These are the methods supported by Cisco Catalyst SD-WAN:

- **Authentication:** Authentication is the mechanism that ensures that the two endpoints communicating with each other are valid and authentic.

  - Cisco Catalyst SD-WAN uses 2048-bit keys with RSA encryption.

  - Starting from Release 20.6, Cisco Catalyst SD-WAN supports Encapsulation Security Payload (ESP) to authenticate the origin of the sender. Earlier releases supported Authentication Header (AH) protocol.

- **Encryption:** Cisco Catalyst SD-WAN uses AES with a 256-bit key length to encrypt data.

- **Integrity:** Data traffic is inspected to ensure that the traffic traversed the network without being tampered with.

  - The Galois Counter Mode (GCM) variant of AES-256 has a built-in hashing mechanism that is used to verify data integrity.

  - Anti-Replay Protection is also enabled to protect against duplication attacks.

It's easy to see how this process can become a scalability issue as a network grows larger and larger. Even after the negotiation takes place, the tunnel state must be tracked between devices, which, in turn, continues to burn CPU cycles. To remedy this, Cisco Catalyst SD-WAN implements these negotiations within the control plane.

The WAN Edge already has a tunnel established to the control plane (and these control tunnels have their own encryption, authentication, and integrity), and you can leverage this for data plane negotiations. Each WAN Edge generates an AES 256-bit key (per transport) that is used for encryption and integrity. This key is then advertised in an OMP update to SD-WAN Controller, along with the WAN Edge's corresponding TLOCs. These route advertisements are then reflected to the rest of the network. Remote WAN Edge routers then use this information to build IPsec tunnels between themselves. In essence, this model of key distribution removes the burden of individual negotiations brought forth with IKE. In addition, to provide enhanced encryption and authentication, WAN Edge routers regenerate their keys every 24 hours. This rekey timer can be tuned if requirements dictate. Renegotiation of keys does not drop existing traffic, as this negotiation happens in parallel with the existing tunnels.

Figure 3-33 illustrates the Cisco Catalyst SD-WAN key exchange process, which goes like this:

Step 1.   WAN Edge 1 generates an encryption key.

Step 2.   WAN Edge 1 advertises the key via an OMP route update. This key is received and reflected by SD-WAN Controller. (The same process happens on WAN Edge 2 and WAN Edge 3.)

Step 3.   Now that the WAN Edge routers have their respective peer keys, IPsec tunnels can be built.

By default, the key exchange between WAN Edge routers and SD-WAN Controller uses symmetric keys in an asymmetric fashion. This means that, not only is the same key used for encryption and decryption, but also the shared nature of that key allows WAN Edge routers to use a peer's key rather than their own when sending data. For example, say that WAN Edge 1 generates key 1. When WAN Edge 1 sends data to WAN Edge 2, it encrypts the data using WAN Edge 2's key. As WAN Edge 2 receives the data, it uses its key to decrypt that data. WAN Edge 2 does the same mechanism in reverse with WAN Edge 1's key.

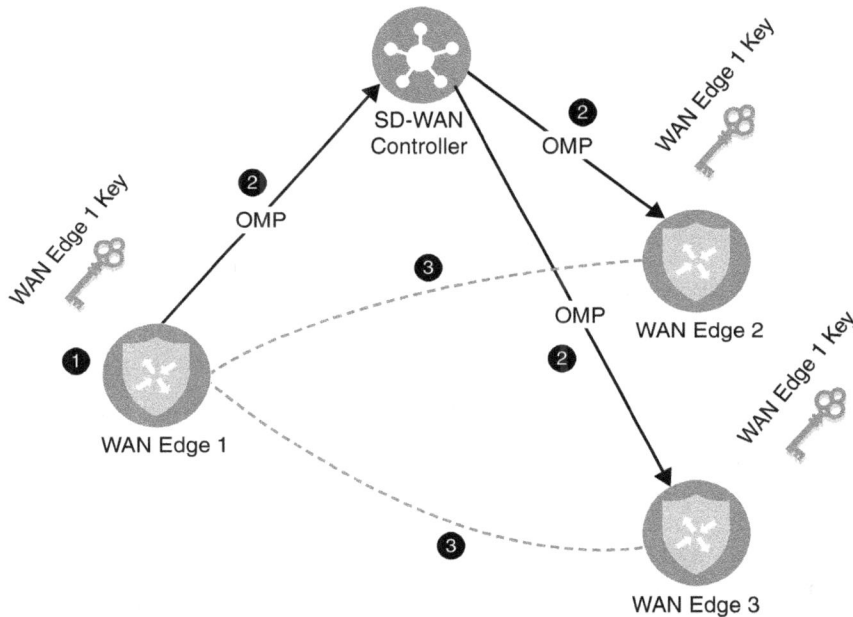

Figure 3-33 *SD-WAN Key Exchange*

Figure 3-34 illustrates how encryption and decryption occur with symmetric key exchange.

Now that both WAN Edge devices have the peers' respective keys, encryption and decryption occur using the following process:

Step 1.   WAN Edge 1 and WAN Edge 2 generate encryption keys (the WAN Edge 1 key and the WAN Edge 2 key).

Step 2.   Both routers advertise their keys via OMP.

Step 3.   If WAN Edge 1 sends traffic to WAN Edge 2, it uses WAN Edge 2's key. WAN Edge 2 uses the same key for decryption of that data. For traffic that WAN Edge 2 sends to WAN Edge 1, WAN Edge 1's key is used in the same fashion but in reverse.

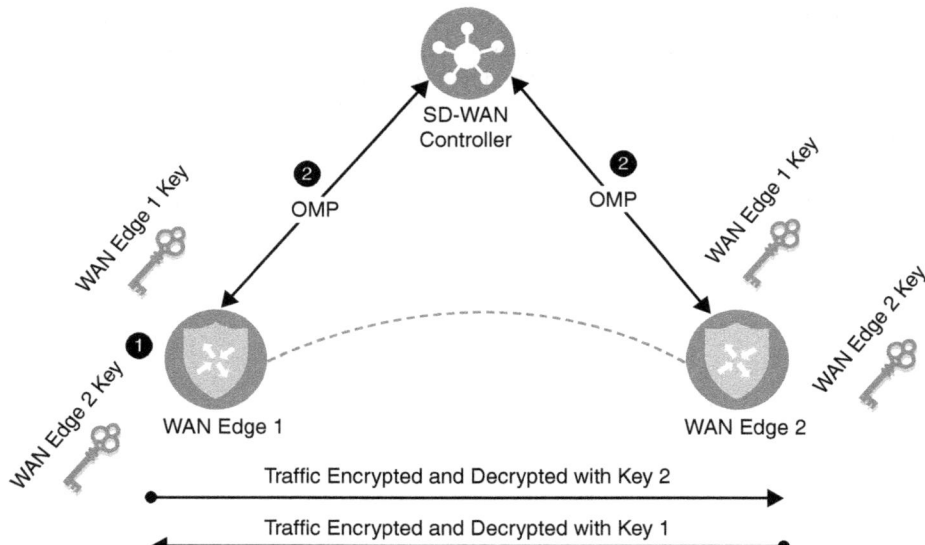

Figure 3-34   *Encryption and Decryption with Symmetric Key Exchange*

Data Plane Encryption with Pairwise Keys

An alternative to Cisco Catalyst SD-WAN's key exchange model described previously is the use of pairwise encryption keys. Pairwise keys provide some additional security measures in that the same key isn't used across all devices in the fabric for encryption and decryption. Specific key pairs are generated between two WAN Edge devices. For example, consider a fabric with three routers: WAN Edge 1, WAN Edge 2, and WAN Edge 3. Encryption and decryption between WAN Edge 1 and WAN Edge 2 uses a combination of public and private keys that is unique to that router pair. Traffic between WAN Edge 1 and WAN Edge 3 uses a different pair of keys.

WAN Edge devices use the Diffie-Hellman (DH) algorithm to generate the pairwise keys and authorize the peers. The public key is the only thing exchanged over OMP. The biggest benefit of this is that security-concerned customers don't have to worry about the private key being exchanged as well. Key exchange still occurs via SD-WAN Controller, and unique pairs are generated for each transport. Private keys are generated locally, stored on every WAN Edge device, and never shared with other peers. Figure 3-35 illustrates this process.

With pairwise keys, the process for encryption and decryption is as follows:

Step 1.   Each WAN Edge generates a key for each transport and each peer. This key will be advertised via OMP to SD-WAN Controller.

Step 2.   If WAN Edge A needs to send data to WAN Edge B, session key AB is used. In reverse, WAN Edge B uses session key BA.

Step 3.   If WAN Edge A sends data to WAN Edge C, session key AC is used. WAN Edge C uses session key CA when sending traffic in the reverse direction.

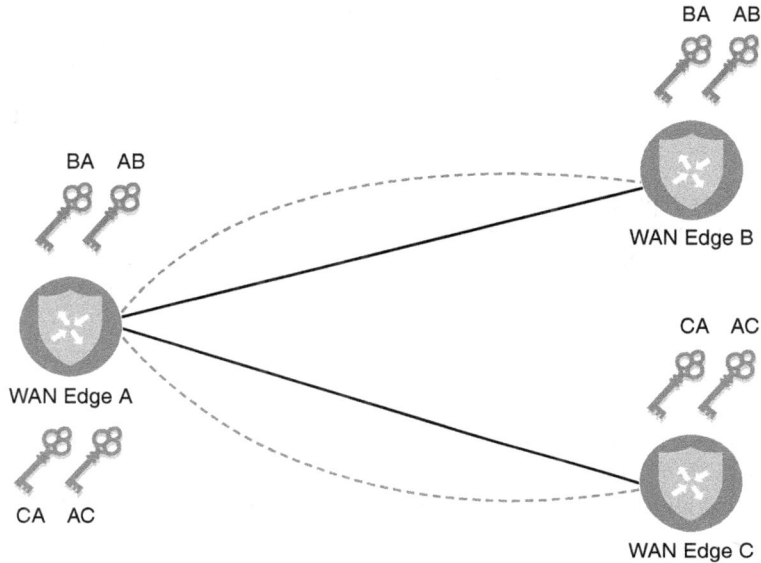

Figure 3-35 *Encryption and Decryption with Pairwise Keys*

It should be noted that pairwise keys are also backward compatible with devices that don't support pairwise keys. This functionality is disabled by default and can be configured via templates.

Finally, as with all IPsec tunnels, these technologies add overhead to data plane traffic, and this overhead reduces the amount of data that hosts can send into the fabric. To compound this issue, some transports (such as those utilizing PPPoE or LTE) have even further restrictions on payload size per packet (that is, Maximum Transmission Unit [MTU]). To address this, Cisco Catalyst SD-WAN uses a path MTU discovery mechanism via the BFD protocol. As discussed throughout this book, BFD is the protocol used in IPsec tunnels to measure loss, latency, and jitter for features such as Application-Aware Routing.

Path MTU (PMTU) discovery involves periodically probing the tunnel to determine the maximum packet size. Traditional PMTU discovery packets operate using ICMP. These packets are sent with the *Do Not Fragment* bit set. If a packet gets dropped, the sending router can assume that the transport does not support that packet's size. Another packet with a smaller packet size is sent. This process repeats until a packet is successful. With Cisco Catalyst SD-WAN, the PMTU discovery process is integrated within the BFD session. Specifically, the BFD header is padded to include PMTU information. Because BFD traffic (hellos, keepalives, and so on) is continuously sent, Cisco Catalyst SD-WAN is able to continually poll the MTU and adjust as needed. By default, the tunnel is checked every minute. In addition, because there are IPsec sessions per TLOC, MTU is calculated periodically per TLOC (or IPsec session). However, because this process sends varying packet sizes, issues may arise on low-bandwidth links. Large packets consume all available bandwidth while the learning process occurs. For this reason, it's recommended to turn PMTU discovery off on low-bandwidth links such as satellite, LTE, and metered links.

Summary

This chapter discusses the control plane process in Cisco Catalyst SD-WAN, how OMP is used as the overlay routing protocol, and how the data plane functions. It covers NAT and the specific constraints of dynamic NAT, and its associated requirements. It also covers IPsec and concepts related to controller-based key management, as well as BFD and how it is used for Application-Aware Routing and path MTU discovery.

You have learned that the control plane and data plane build-up process is as follows:

Step 1.   WAN Edge routers build DTLS or TLS tunnels to the Control Components. WAN Edge routers are authenticated and allowed on the fabric by SD-WAN Validator. SD-WAN Validator then facilities NAT traversal.

Step 2.   OMP routing information and encryption keys are distributed to SD-WAN Controller.

Step 3.   IPsec tunnels are built between WAN Edge routers by using symmetric keys or pairwise keys.

Step 4.   BFD sessions are established inside the IPsec tunnel. BFD is used to calculate MTU and monitor WAN metrics for Application-Aware Routing.

Review All Key Topics

Review the most important topics in this chapter, noted with the Key Topic icon in the outer margin of the page. Table 3-6 lists these key topics and the page number on which each is found.

Table 3-6   Key Topics

Key Topic Element	Description	Page
Section	OMP routes	42
Section	TLOC routes	45
Section	Service routes	48
Section	Network address translation	74
Paragraph	SD-WAN Validator as STUN server	79
Section	Data plane encryption	83
Figure 3-34	Encryption and decryption with symmetric key exchange	86
Section	Data plane encryption with pairwise keys	86

Key Terms

Define the following key terms from this chapter and check your answers in the glossary:

color, OMP route, SD-WAN Controller, service route, TLOC route

Chapter Review Questions

1. Which control component operates as a BGP route reflector and also is responsible for distributing encryption keys?

   a. SD-WAN Controller (formerly vSmart)

   b. SD-WAN Validator (formerly vBond)

   c. WAN Edge

   d. SD-WAN Manager (formerly vManage)

   e. SD-WAN Analytics (formerly vAnalytics)

2. What are the three different types of OMP route advertisements? (Choose three.)

   a. OMP route

   b. TLOC route

   c. LSA Type 5

   d. EIGRP update

   e. Service route

3. True or false: Data plane connectivity can be built between two routers that are behind dynamic NAT devices.

   a. True

   b. False

4. If you are using a NAT and a public color, which IP addresses and port attributes will be used for data plane connectivity?

   a. Public IP addresses (post-NAT)

   b. Private IP addresses (pre-NAT)

5. How does the Cisco Catalyst SD-WAN solution achieve scale with IPsec?

   a. Eliminating the need for IKE

   b. Decentralizing the control plane from the data plane

   c. Using NAT traversal

6. What port is used, by default, for WAN Edge devices to communicate with SD-WAN Validator (formerly vBond)?

   a. UDP 12346

   b. TCP 443

   c. TCP 1000

References

RFC 4577, "OSPF as the Provider/Customer Edge Protocol for BGP/MPLS IP Virtual Private Networks (VPNs)," https://tools.ietf.org/html/rfc4577, June 2006.

"Cisco Catalyst SD-WAN Command Reference," https://www.cisco.com/c/en/us/td/docs/routers/sdwan/configuration/cloudonramp/ios-xe-17/cloud-onramp-book-xe.html.

RFC 4587, "Network Address Translation (NAT) Behavioral Requirements for Unicast UDP," https://tools.ietf.org/html/rfc4587, January 2007.

RFC 5389, "Session Traversal Utilities for NAT (STUN)," https://tools.ietf.org/html/rfc5389, October 2008.

RFC 4023, "Encapsulating MPLS in IP or Generic Routing Encapsulation (GRE)," https://datatracker.ietf.org/doc/html/rfc4023, March 2005.

"Cisco Catalyst SD-WAN Routing Configuration Guide," https://www.cisco.com/c/en/us/td/docs/routers/sdwan/configuration/routing/ios-xe-17/routing-book-xe/m-multicast-routing.html#c_Multicast_Overlay_Routing_Overview_12198.xml.

"Cisco Catalyst SD-WAN Design Guide," https://www.cisco.com/c/en/us/td/docs/solutions/CVD/SDWAN/cisco-sdwan-design-guide.html.

CHAPTER 4

Onboarding and Provisioning

This chapter covers the following topics:

- **Configuration Templates:** This section discusses various template types, including CLI, device, and feature templates. This section also covers design and scaling techniques with templates.

- **Developing and Deploying Templates:** This section provides step-by-step instructions for building and deploying device and feature templates.

- **Configuration Groups and Feature Profiles:** This section explains the building blocks of configuration groups as a new way to easily configure devices in Cisco Catalyst SD-WAN.

- **Developing and Deploying Configuration Groups:** This section provides step-by-step instructions for building and deploying configuration groups and feature profiles.

- **Onboarding Devices:** This section covers onboarding of devices with manual setup and automatic provisioning with techniques such as using plug and play (PNP) and a bootstrap configuration file.

- **Key Settings in Device Templates and Configuration Groups:** This section describes some prevalent configuration settings that play important roles in common use cases, such as with Direct Internet Access breakout, tunnel count scoping, and transport preferences.

Current methods of managing configurations on network devices pose a lot of challenges, including version control, human error, and scaling considerations when deploying to a large number of devices. Traditionally, network engineers make individual changes to various network devices via the CLI. As networks grow, these configurations are often shared or piecemealed with other network devices (such as QoS or routing protocol configurations). Using QoS as an example, many questions must be answered before deployment and, depending on the device, there may be different options for modifying the configuration. Is it MLS queuing or MQC queuing? What hardware platform is it? How many queues has the service provider provided? What DSCP values are you using? This creates a lot of complexity when managing configuration options.

In a perfect world, all of our devices and configurations would be standardized across locations. But this isn't realistic for a multitude of reasons (such as different providers, hardware upgrade cycles, and business needs). As a network grows, the disparity among network devices and network functions makes operations and troubleshooting even more difficult. To compound this issue, network configurations tend to persist as devices are upgraded and replaced. The original intent of the network configuration is likely to get lost as the IT staff turns over or other factors change.

In most cases, network device configurations are rarely revisited for cleanup or optimization. Network administrators tend to make configuration changes on the fly, and the previous configuration gets lost. Version control is important, especially when there are outages. Having a working configuration to roll back to can save a lot of headache. Oftentimes, outages aren't noticed immediately after a change. With no version control or change management in place, rolling back to the last-known configuration becomes difficult because the previous configuration was not tracked.

With Cisco Catalyst SD-WAN, configuration management is maintained via a robust engine that supports automatic rollback. At this writing, two configuration approaches exist: using templates, which is a widely known configuration method, and using configuration groups, which involves presenting optimizations to the configuration engine.

You can build templates in a modular fashion and reuse them across differing device types. Templates allow network administrators to quickly roll out configurations or changes at a wide scale while also ensuring that the syntax is correct and is supported on any platform.

Thanks to automatic rollback in Cisco Catalyst SD-WAN, if a configuration option gets applied to a device and cuts off the device's ability to be managed by SD-WAN Manager (formerly vManage), the device automatically rolls back after 5 minutes (by default) and allows the network engineer to correct the issue.

With today's networks getting larger and larger, it's crucial to keep the work of provisioning and onboarding to a minimum. For example, onboarding a network device at a branch involves the following steps:

Step 1. The device ships from manufacturing to IT staff.

Step 2. The network administrator applies the required configuration to the device.

Step 3. The IT staff drives or ships the device to the appropriate location and physically installs it.

This process is expensive for an organization, especially when it needs to occur across thousands of devices. Issues such as a device's failure to connect to the network add further delay and operational expense as the IT team must perform troubleshooting.

In some cases, device installations are performed remotely. While remote installation reduces the cost of traveling, it can create a lot of frustration when issues arise. With a lack of local IT support at the site, network administrators often end up having to rely on non-IT staff to perform operations on the device. This requires a lot of faith in the remote staff and potentially takes them away from their day job.

Cisco Catalyst SD-WAN simplifies onboarding and provisioning of a device. WAN Edge devices support mechanisms such as PNP and ZTP to automatically bring a device online and into the fabric. These onboarding solutions work by allowing a network administrator to preconfigure a device within SD-WAN Manager. Once SD-WAN Manager sees the device, it automatically applies the specified configuration. WAN Edge devices can be shipped directly to the remote location and don't require initial configuration by IT staff. Once a device is physically installed at the remote site, it will automatically locate SD-WAN Control Components and begin the provisioning process. By reducing the time to bring up remote sites, IT staff can bring more devices online more quickly and with fewer errors. This time savings reduces operational cost and allows IT staff to focus on bringing additional capabilities to the business.

NOTE   The screen captures in this chapter show Catalyst SD-WAN Version 20.12. While newer versions of Catalyst SD-WAN might look slightly different, the basics of the configuration process flow will remain the same.

Configuration Templates

A network administrator can apply configurations in Cisco Catalyst SD-WAN in two different ways:

- They can apply a configuration by using the templates and Configuration Groups in the SD-WAN Manager GUI.

- They can programmatically leverage SD-WAN Manager APIs or configure devices manually via the CLI (that is, by using SSH to connect to a device or by connecting via the console port).

Using the SD-WAN Manager GUI is the preferred mechanism, as it is less error prone and provides support for automatic recovery. Configurations provisioned via SD-WAN Manager can be applied to both WAN Edge devices and SD-WAN Control Components. When SD-WAN Manager is responsible for applying the configuration, it is the single source of truth, and changes can only be applied via SD-WAN Manager.

NOTE   To apply centralized policy to the SD-WAN Controller, it needs to have a template assigned and be under the control of SD-WAN Manager. When a component is managed by SD-WAN Manager, an administrator cannot make changes to the device locally.

Key Topic

When applying a configuration to WAN Edge devices or controllers using the SD-WAN Manager GUI, a network administrator can apply a device template to a single device or to multiple devices of the same model. Device templates (see Figure 4-1) can either be CLI based or feature template based. When a CLI template is being built, the whole configuration must be in the template (not just specific configuration snippets). On the other hand, feature templates can be thought of as building blocks wherein each block is a specific technology feature.

A Feature Template defines the specific feature or technology to enable or configure, such as routing protocols, interface parameters, and Overlay Management Protocol (OMP). Feature templates can be reused between multiple device templates, and this flexibility brings greater scale to the solution (which is why using feature templates is the recommended way of configuring devices). Feature templates can be device type agnostic as well.

A network administrator needs only to be concerned with the functionality of the WAN Edge device. SD-WAN Manager is responsible for converting a template to a device's corresponding configuration syntax for the appropriate OS and platform.

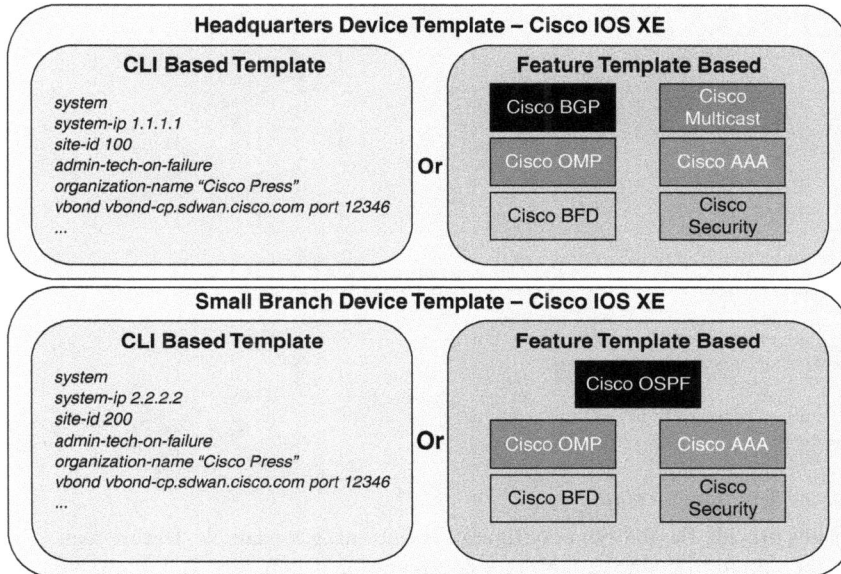

Figure 4-1   *Device Templates*

A Device Template is a collection of feature templates and can only be applied to specific device types. For this reason, you may have multiple device templates for the same model of hardware, depending on a particular device's location, connectivity options, or role in the network.

NOTE   A device template can't be shared across different device types, but a feature template can be used across multiple different device types. When a portion of the configuration from a device template needs to be reused, a template copy can be performed.

As illustrated in Figure 4-2, a device template has four main parts:

- **Basic Information:** This section includes items such as system, logging, AAA, BFD, and OMP feature templates.

- **Transport and Management VPN:** This section has templates for configuration of VPN 0 and VPN 512 (such as underlay routing protocol configuration and interface configuration).

- **Service VPN:** This section is where service VPNs are defined and LAN-facing template configurations will exist. It is where BGP, OSPF, and interface parameters are configured.

- **Additional Templates:** This section is for local policies, security policies, CLI add-on templates, ThousandEyes Agent, SNMP configuration templates, and so on.

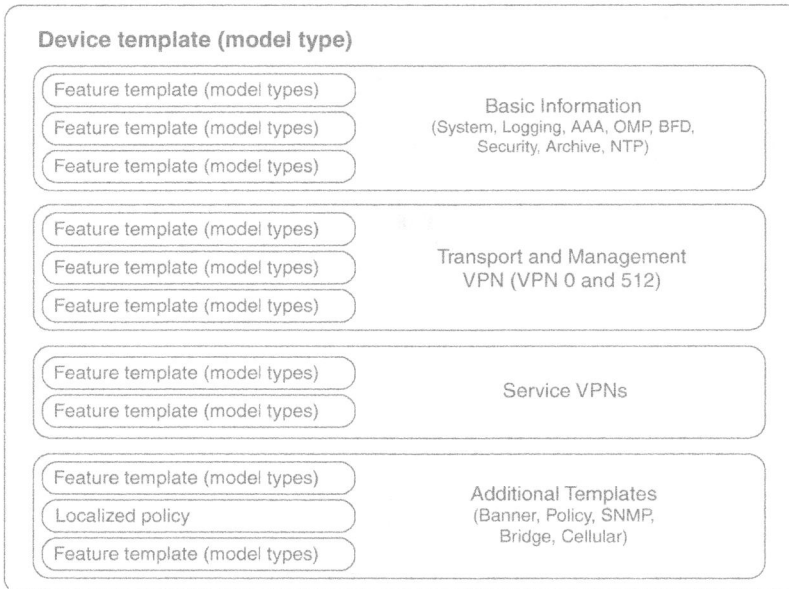

Figure 4-2   *Device Template Structure*

Key Topic

Feature Templates provide flexibility in configuration options. For example, feature templates provide the option to define variables for configuration parameters. This allows you to reduce the number of templates required in your deployment yet make the deployment much more modular. For example, suppose you have MPLS transports that use different physical interface numbers: GigabitEthernet0/0/0, GigabitEthernet0/0/1, GigabitEthernet0/0/2, and so on. Initially, you might want to build a feature template for each physical interface that has a different IP address. This would result in three different templates. By using variables for the physical interface and IP address options, you could condense this down to one feature template that can be used across all device templates.

Figure 4-3 shows how variables can be used to control template sprawl. This example involves nine different interface templates, and the one that is used depends on whether the IP address is assigned via DHCP and what interface is used. By using variables, a network administrator can reduce this down to three different feature templates.

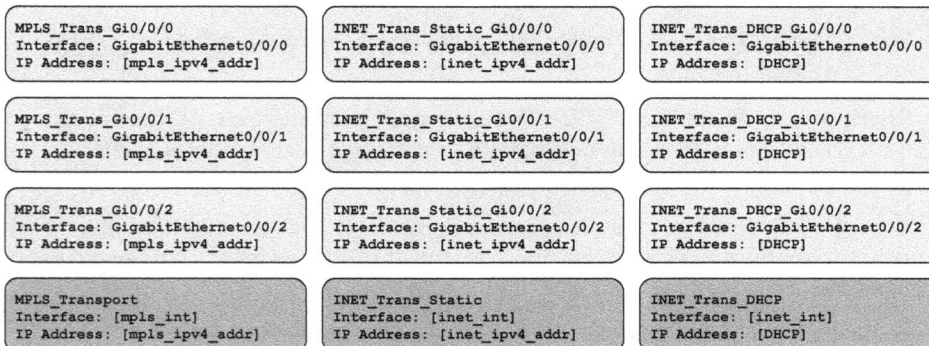

Figure 4-3   *Controlling Template Sprawl*

Three types of values can be defined in a template:

- **Default:** This is the factory default value, and it cannot be changed. An example might be using the default BFD timers.

- **Global:** Values set here are the same wherever this configuration option is used. An example could be SNMP community strings that you want to be globally applied to all devices using this template. The beauty of this is that, later on, if there needs to be a change to these values, you just update the feature template global option, and it updates every device template that is using this feature template.

- **Device specific:** The value is set via a user-defined variable (as in our earlier example with interface names). The values for these variables are set when the device template is attached to a specific device.

In Figure 4-4, you can see how these referenced values can be used. Some template options might not have all three of these options, depending on what is being configured. For example, a BGP AS number won't have a default value.

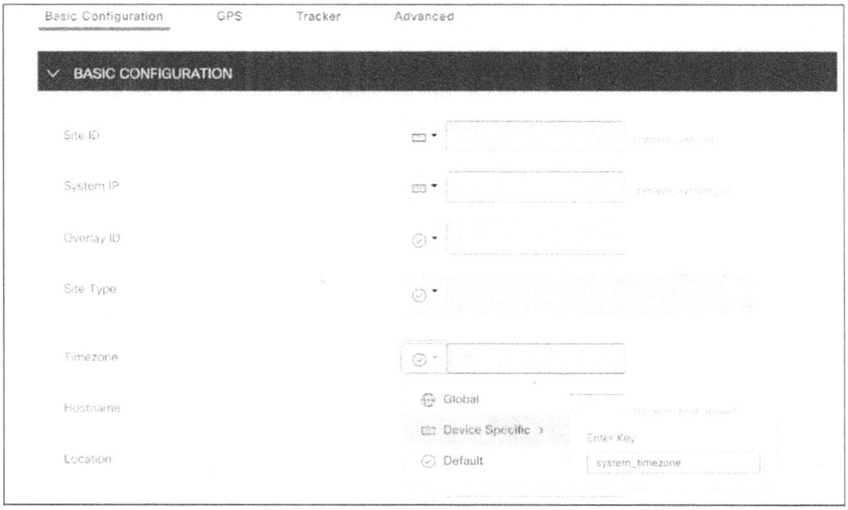

Figure 4-4 *Setting Variables*

A large number of feature template options can be configured. Here are some common feature templates:

- **System:** You can configure basic system information such as system IP address, site ID, and hostname.

- **BFD:** You can adjust BFD timers and app route multipliers for each transport or color. BFD timers are used for application-aware routing.

- **OMP:** You can change graceful restart timers or control redistribution from other routing protocols into OMP.

■ **Security:** You can change IPsec security settings such as anti-replay, authentication, and encryption settings.

■ **VPN:** You can define a service VPN, routing protocol redistribution, or static routing.

■ **BGP:** You can configure BGP in a VPN or VRF instance.

■ **OSPF:** You can configure OSPF in a VPN or VRF instance.

■ **VPN interface:** You can define an interface that is part of a service VPN or VRF instance. Common configuration options include IP address, QoS, ACLs, and NAT.

As feature templates are defined, they can be referenced via a device template. The device template can be applied to a specific device or to a group of devices. Remember that a device template can only be built for a specific device type. If there are any variables defined in the feature template, when the device template is attached, these values will need to be populated. Once these values are defined, a configuration syntax check is done in SD-WAN Manager. If it is successful, SD-WAN Manager notifies the WAN Edge device regarding the configuration that needs to be retrieved, and the device pulls it. Feature template variable values can be populated either within the SD-WAN Manager template attachment workflow or by using a CSV file. Populating feature template variables via CSV allows an administrator to quickly provision many devices at once.

If the need arises to change these values after the device template has been applied, it is possible to change these values on a device-by-device basis. If any changes are made to a feature template or device template (for example, changing the IP address of a device interface, changing the username and password of a device), SD-WAN Manager immediately pushes the updated configuration to all devices using that template.

NOTE   If at the time the configuration is pulled by the device, it loses control plane connectivity to SD-WAN Manager, by default the WAN Edge device starts a rollback timer of 5 minutes. If it doesn't reestablish connectivity within that 5 minutes, it rolls back its configuration and reconnects to SD-WAN Manager using the last-known-good configuration. At that time, the network administrator will see that the device is out of sync and can correct the issue.

Developing and Deploying Templates

Template configuration and creation is performed in the SD-WAN Manager GUI. After an SD-WAN Manager instance is deployed, some default templates are created. These templates can be used as a starting point to create customized templates. For example, to create a BFD template, you follow these steps:

Step 1.   Navigate to **Configuration > Templates** and go to the configuration section for templates, as illustrated in Figure 4-5.

Step 2.   In the template configuration window, you're presented with the option to configure device templates or feature templates, as shown in Figure 4-6.

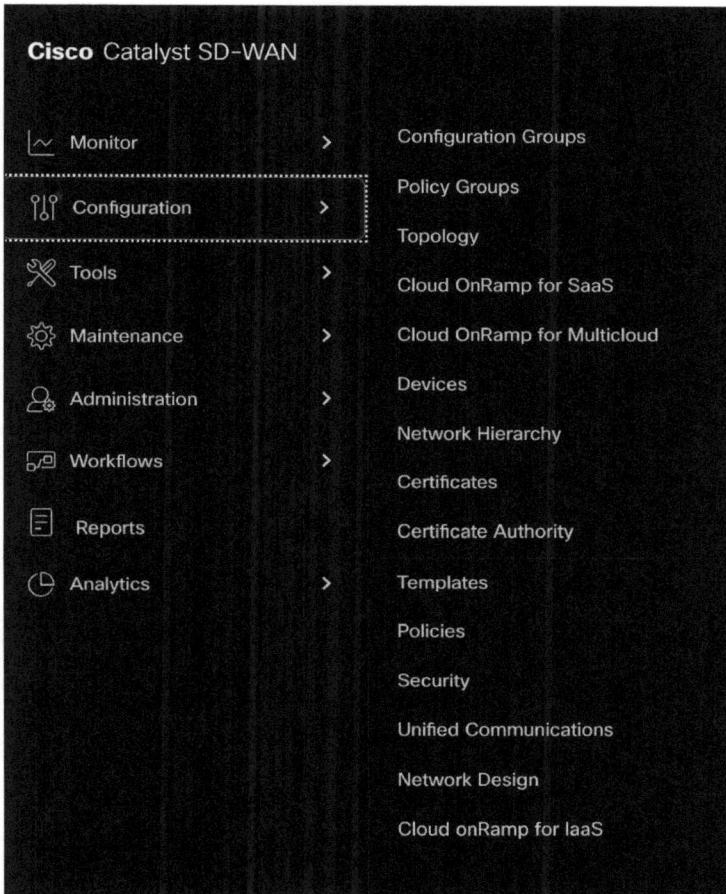

Figure 4-5 *Accessing the Template Configuration Interface*

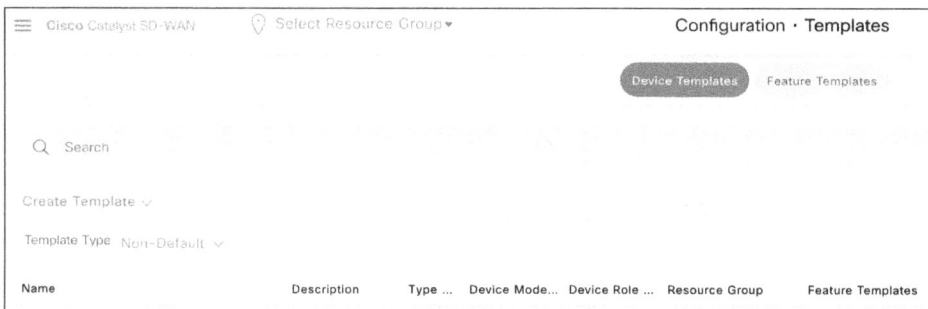

Figure 4-6 *Template Configuration Window*

Step 3. To begin creating a feature template, select **Feature Templates** and click **Add Template**. Select the devices that this template will apply to and select the type of template, as shown in Figure 4-7.

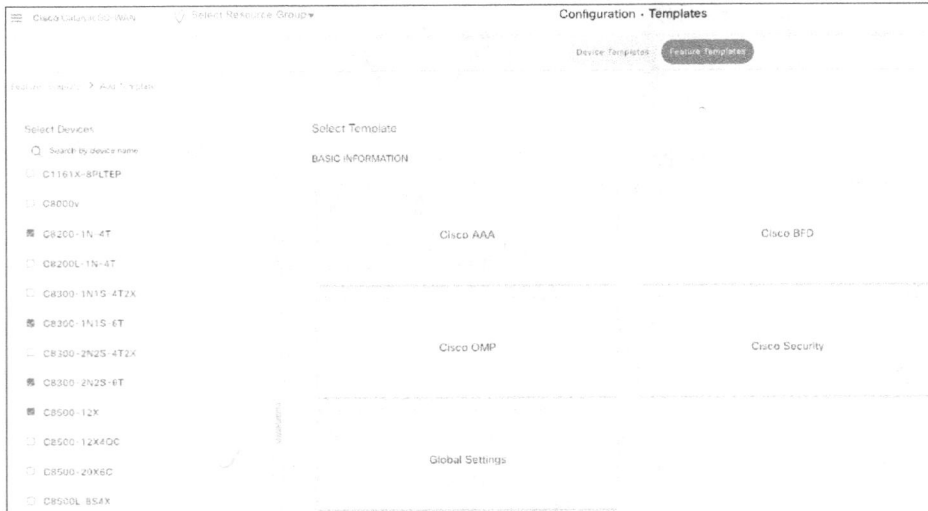

Figure 4-7   *Template Configuration: Device Selection Window*

Step 4.   Start setting values, as shown in Figure 4-8. These values can be either variables, global parameters, or the default parameter. When you're done setting configuration options, name the template **Sample-BFD-Template** and click **Save.**

Step 5.   To attach a feature template to a new device template, click **Device Templates** and then **Create Template.** (Note that you can also attach a feature template to existing device templates.) When you see the option to create a CLI-based template or a feature-based template, select **From Feature Template**, as shown in Figure 4-9.

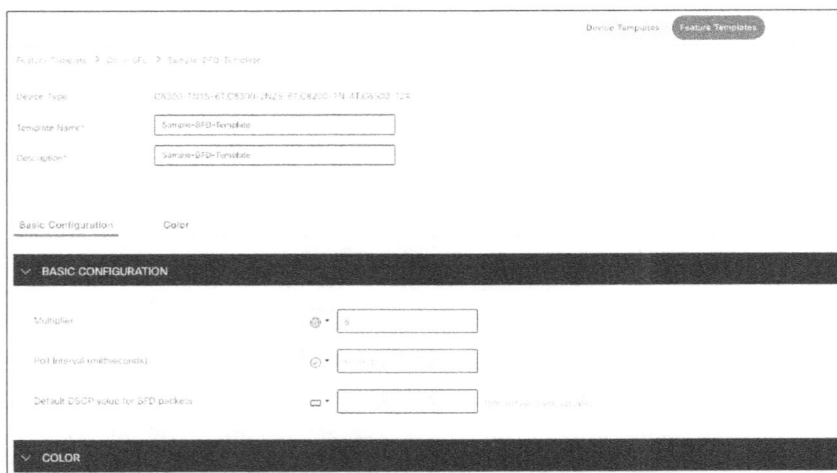

Figure 4-8   *Template Configuration: Setting Configuration Values*

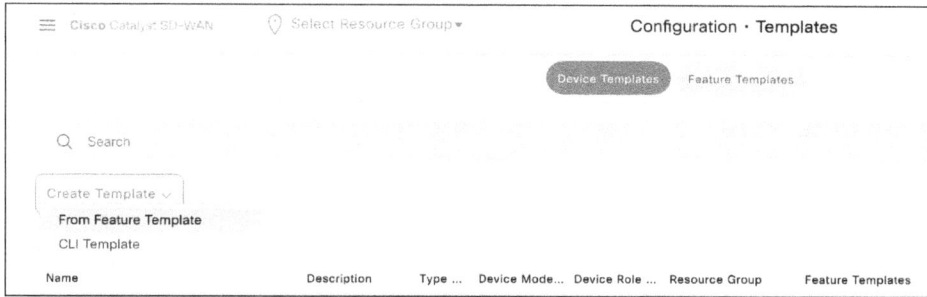

Figure 4-9 *Template Configuration: Selecting a Device Template*

Step 6. Select the device model this template will apply to, select the device role, name the template **HQ-Device_Template**, and provide a description for the template, as shown in Figure 4-10.

Step 7. To select the feature template to use, select the **Sample-BFD-Template** template you created earlier and click **Save**.

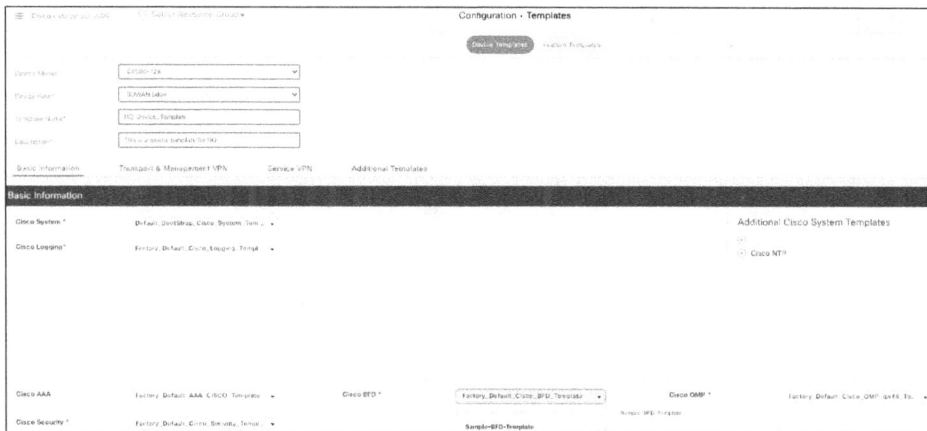

Figure 4-10 *Template Configuration: Selecting a Device Feature Template*

Step 8. To attach the device template to devices, on the Device Templates page, click the three dots next to the template you wish to attach. Select the option to **Attach Devices**, as shown in Figure 4-11.

Figure 4-11 *Attaching a Template to a Device*

Step 9. Select the devices to apply the configurations to, as shown in Figure 4-12. Once you select a device, you have the option to populate any variables.

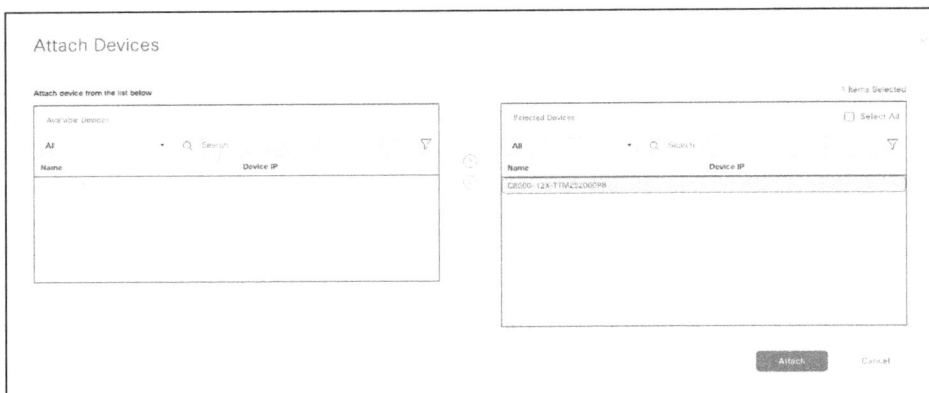

Figure 4-12 *Device Selection Window*

Once you have provided the values of the variables, you can deploy the configurations to the selected WAN Edge devices.

Configuration Groups and Feature Profiles

Starting with Catalyst SD-WAN Version 20.8, which provides backward compatibility with Version 17.6 for WAN Edge devices, Cisco introduced a new way to configure WAN Edge devices, adding benefits such as simplicity through intuitive and sequential configuration workflows, device-agnostic components that permit reusability, and structure that allows you to group devices that share common settings. You don't have to create a separate template for every device type, as you do with device templates. As illustrated in Figure 4-13, Configuration Groups method is composed of three main components:

- **Configuration Groups:** A Configuration Group is a logical grouping of devices or set of configurations that share a common purpose within the WAN fabric. These groups are customizable based on business needs, such as region (for example, East, West) or type of site (for example, retail store, distribution center).

- **Feature Profiles:** A Feature Profile is a flexible configuration bucket based on required similar features, such as WAN or LAN features.

- **Feature Parcels:** Feature Parcels are the building blocks of feature profiles. They are individual capabilities that can be used across Feature Profiles.

In Figure 4-13, the West Coast and East Coast Configuration Groups cater to different business needs, based on different regions. The figure also shows examples of Feature Profiles (Transport Profiles 1 and 2, System Profile, and Service Profile) that group individual functions, called Feature Parcels, like logging and WAN transport interfaces (such as MPLS or LTE).

NOTE You can associate a device to either a configuration group or a device template but not both.

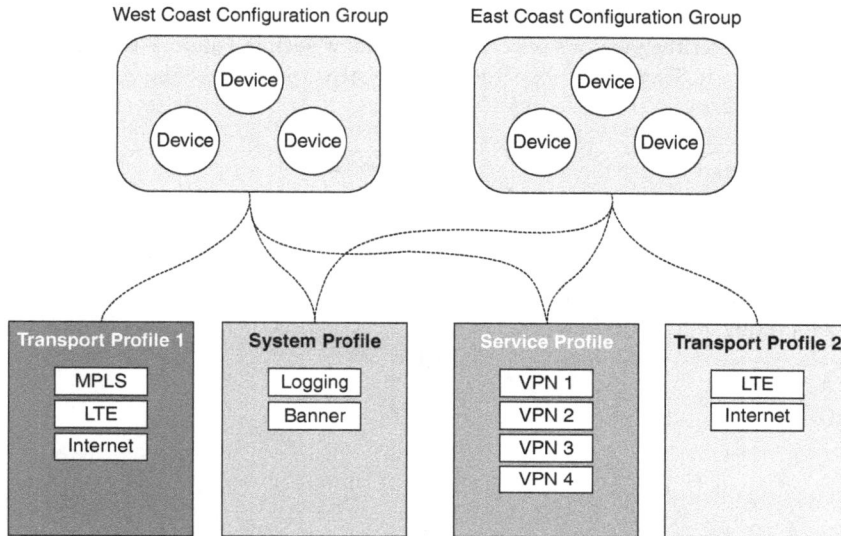

Figure 4-13 *Configuration Groups, Feature Profiles, and Feature Parcels Example*

Developing and Deploying Configuration Groups

Figure 4-14 shows two ways exist to create Configuration Groups:

- Select Configuration > Configuration Groups > Add Configuration Group

- Select Workflows > Workflows Library

NOTE Remember that the screen captures in this chapter show Catalyst SD-WAN Version 20.12.

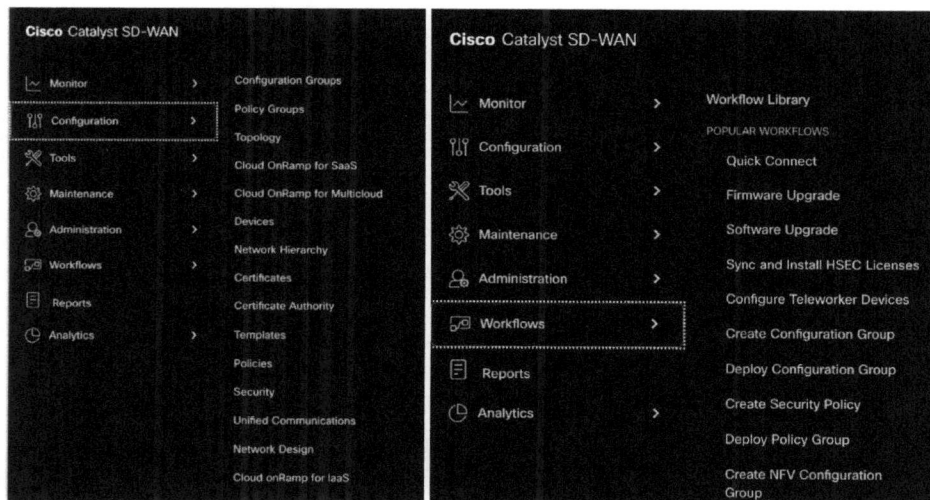

Figure 4-14 *Accessing the Configuration Groups Workflow Interface*

Regardless of the path previously taken, you need to select Create Configuration Group, as shown in Figure 4-15. After the previous selection, the window seen in Figure 4-16 pops up, where you click Let's Do It. Then, you follow these simple steps to complete the configuration group creation process:

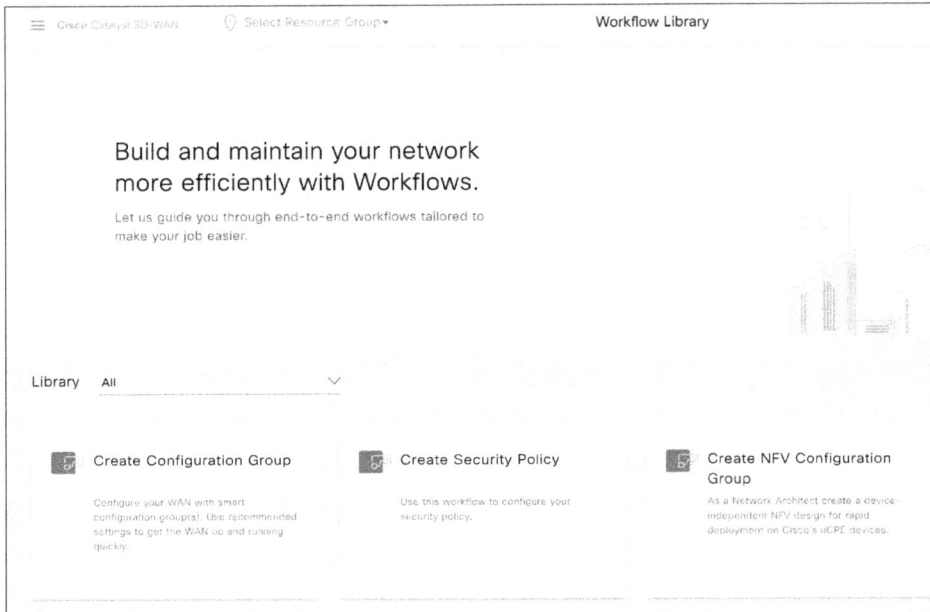

Figure 4-15 *Accessing the Configuration Groups Workflow Interface*

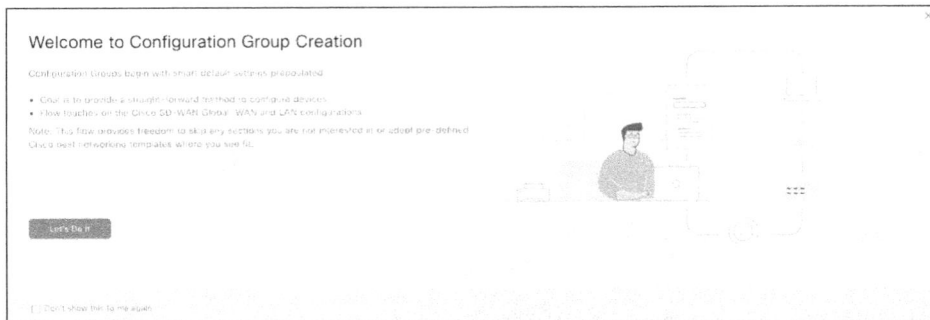

Figure 4-16 *Configuration Group Default Welcome Screen*

Step 1. Name the Configuration Group and provide a description for it, as shown in Figure 4-17. Then click **Next**.

Step 2. On the Site Configurations screen that appears, select **Single Router** or **Dual Router** under Site Type, depending on your configuration needs. Under Site Settings, choose the appropriate option, depending on whether you are working with global parameters, variables, or default parameters. Figure 4-18 shows these two first settings you can configure.

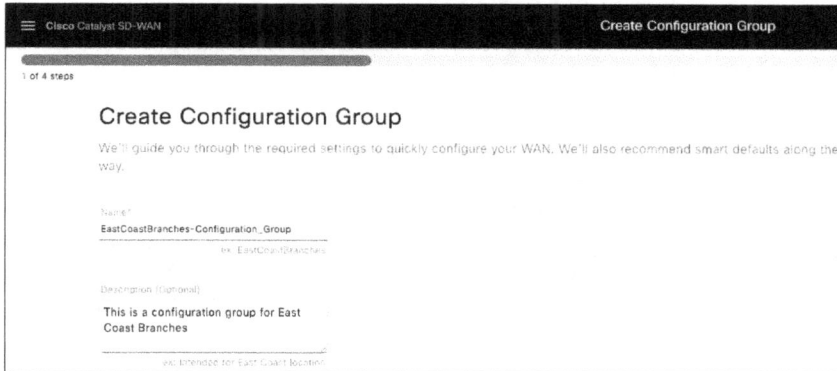

Figure 4-17 *Naming the Configuration Group*

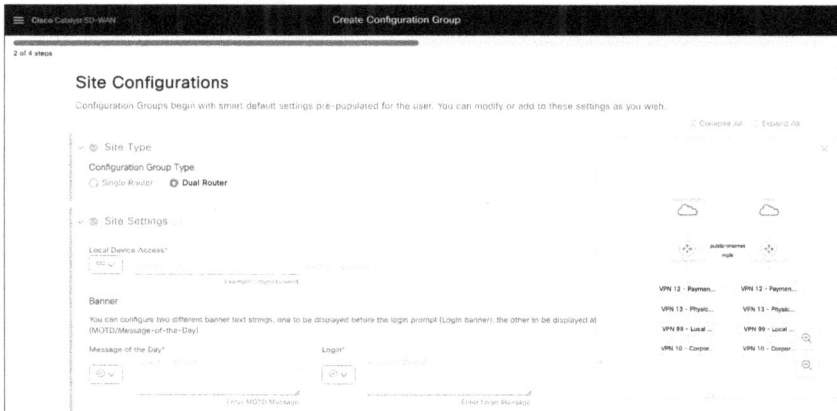

Figure 4-18 *Site Configurations*

Under WAN Interfaces, select the required WAN transports—either **DHCP** or **Static**. Full Mesh or Transport Extension appears as an option only if the Site Type selection is Dual Router. WAN routing and advanced capabilities are also options, as shown in Figure 4-19. This page presents a similar selection for a LAN and Service VPN profile. Click **Next**.

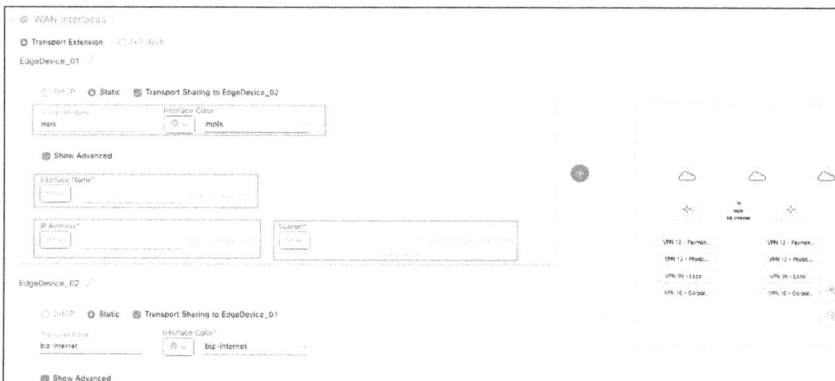

Figure 4-19 *WAN Interface Settings*

NOTE   Variables provide intelligent and intuitive names related to the interface's color, as you can see in the Show Advanced section in Figure 4-19. You can opt to leave default values to edit later in the process, as required.

Step 3.   On the screen that appears next, set additional features such as Remote access functionality if desired (see Figure 4-20).

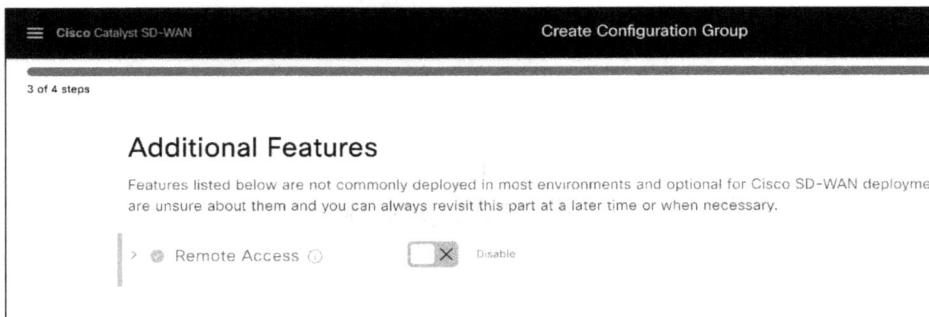

Figure 4-20   *Additional Features Step*

NOTE   Figure 4-20 shows that the only additional feature available is Remote Access. Recall that the figures in this chapter show SD-WAN Version 20.12, and newer releases may provide different options.

Step 4.   Review the summary that is provided and click **Create Configuration Group** (see Figure 4-21).

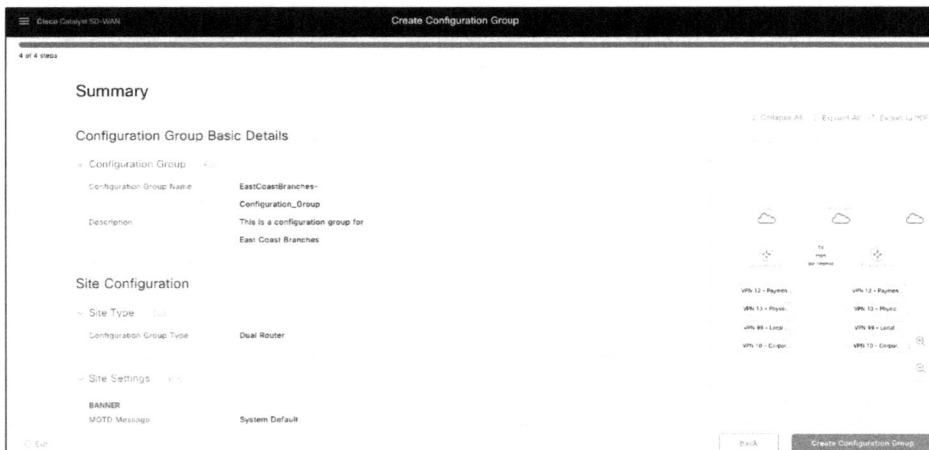

Figure 4-21   *Configuration Group Summary Screen*

Immediately after creating a Configuration Group, you need to associate this group to one or more devices, as shown in Figure 4-22.

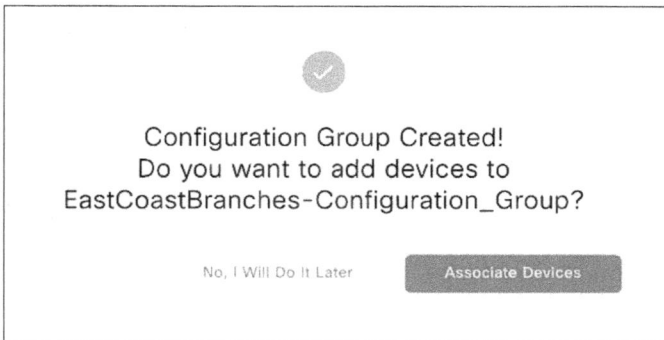

Configuration Group Created!
Do you want to add devices to
EastCoastBranches-Configuration_Group?

No, I Will Do It Later   Associate Devices

Figure 4-22   *Associate Devices Initial Workflow*

To associate a device to the recently created logical grouping, click **Associate Devices** in the popup window and follow these steps:

Step 1.   On the first screen, click **Next** (see Figure 4-23).

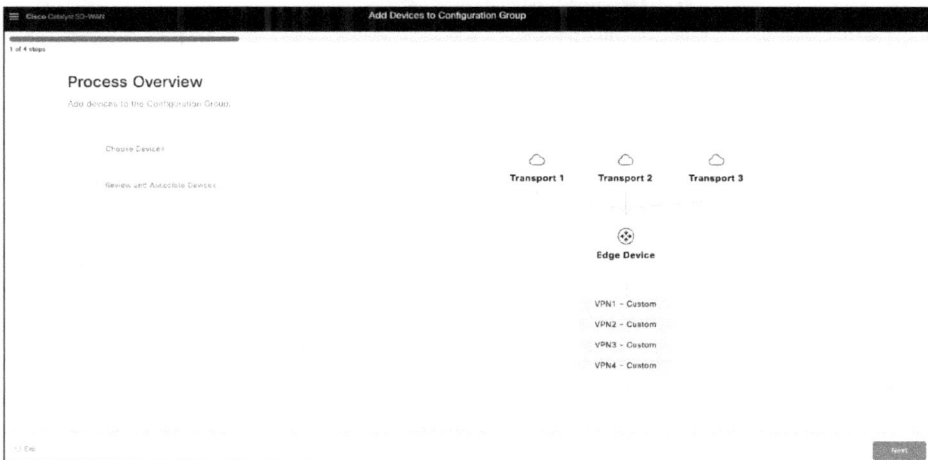

Figure 4-23   *Adding Devices to the Configuration Group Initial Flow*

Step 2.   On the screen that appears, select devices from the list of available devices and click **Next** (see Figure 4-24).

Step 3.   On the screen that appears, select the tags to use for grouping and describing the devices (see Figure 4-25). This makes it easier for operations teams in the future to differentiate the devices when a Dual Router Site Type selection is done. SD-WAN Manager creates smart default values—in this case, tag names—that can be modified based on needs. When you're finished with your selections, click **Next**.

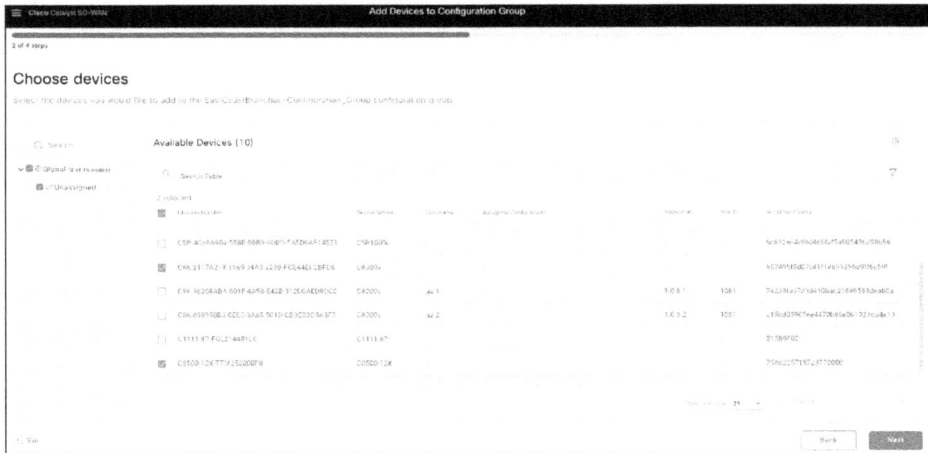

Figure 4-24 *Selecting Available Devices*

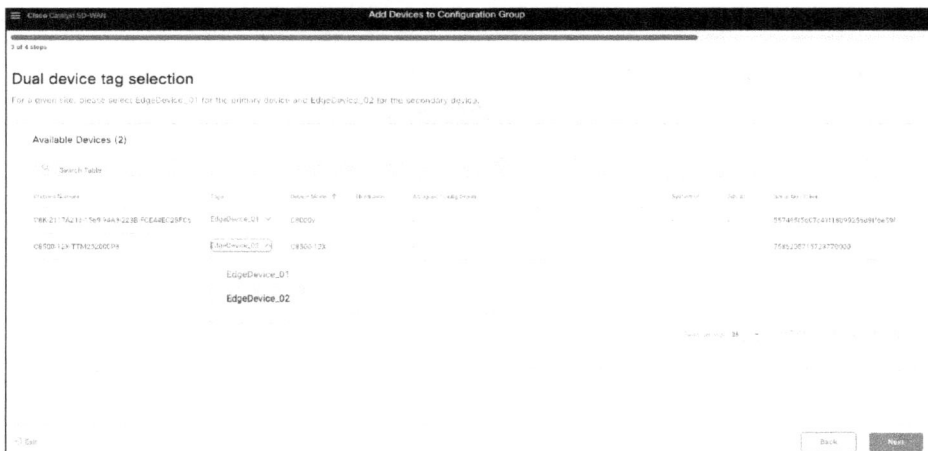

Figure 4-25 *Selecting Device Tags*

Step 4.   On the summary screen, which shows the devices to associate with the Configuration Group and allows you to edit the list to add devices, if everything looks good, click **Save** (see Figure 4-26).

Next, you have the option of provisioning devices with the Configuration Group you just created or selecting to provision it later, as shown in Figure 4-27. Select **Provision Devices** and then follow these steps:

Step 1.   Take a look at the workflow shown in Figure 4-28 and click **Next**.

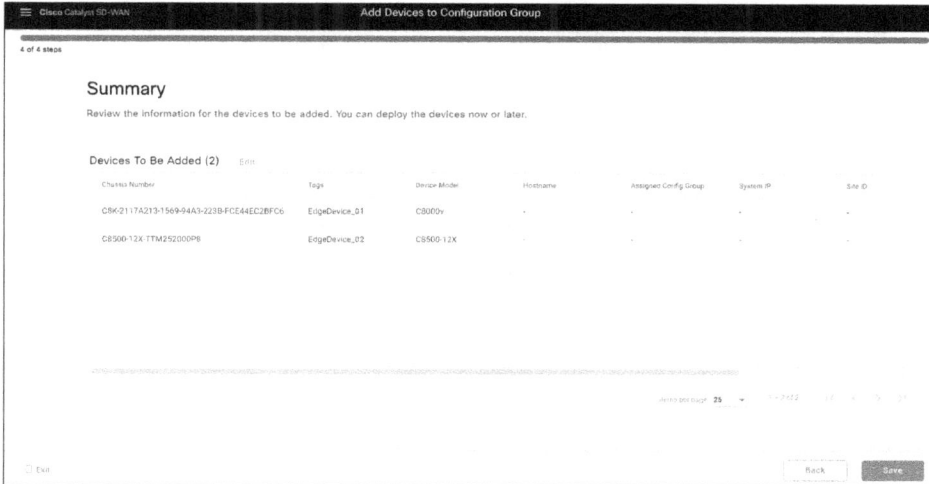

Figure 4-26   *Summary of Devices to Be Added to the Configuration Group*

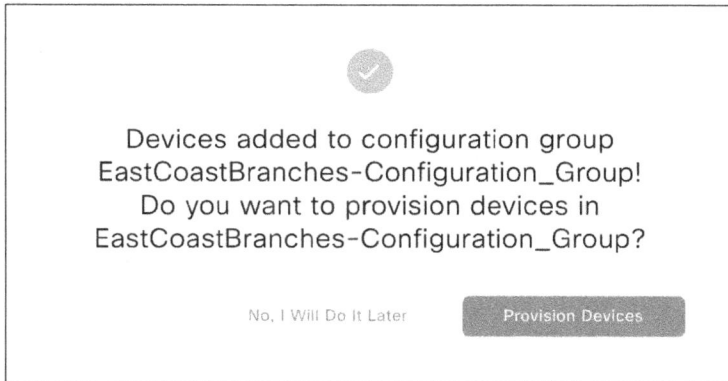

Figure 4-27   *Provisioning Step Prompt*

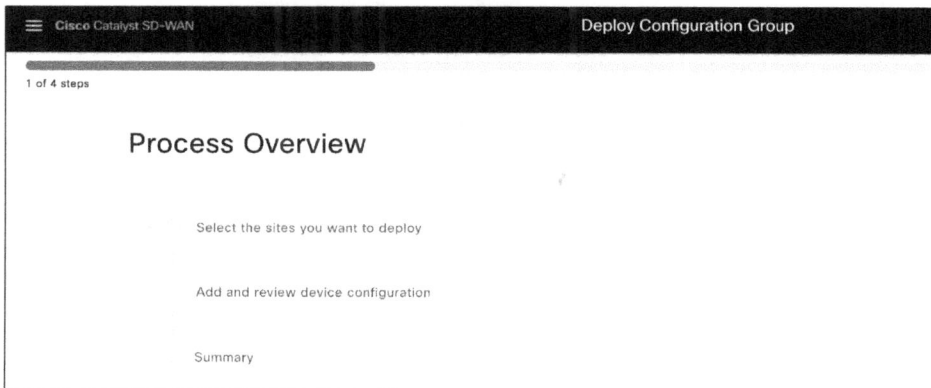

Figure 4-28   *Configuration Group Deployment Initial Screen*

Step 2.   To select the sites to deploy, check the boxes for both **EdgeDevice_01** and **EdgeDevice_02**, as shown in Figure 4-29, and click **Next**.

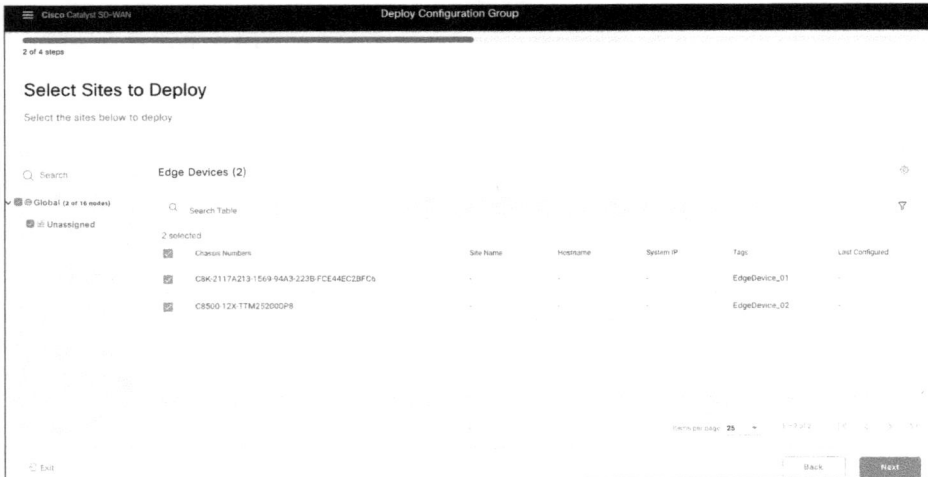

Figure 4-29   *Selecting Sites to Deploy*

Step 3.   Provide values for variables from nested feature parcels, either manually or via a comma-separated values file, as shown in Figure 4-30, and click **Next**. Notice that if mandatory values are missing, you won't be able to proceed to the next screen.

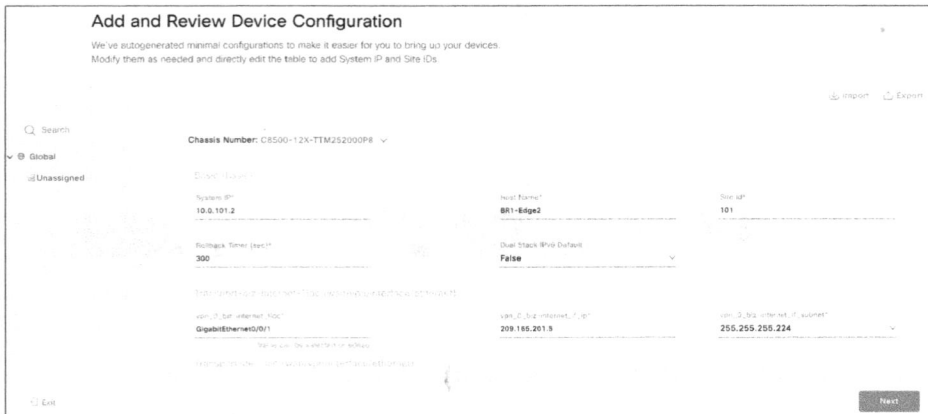

Figure 4-30   *Adding Devices and Reviewing the Device Configuration*

Step 4.   Examine the summary view that appears, which allows you to review the values provided during the workflow and preview the CLI configuration that you will send to devices (see Figure 4-31). If everything looks correct, click **Deploy**.

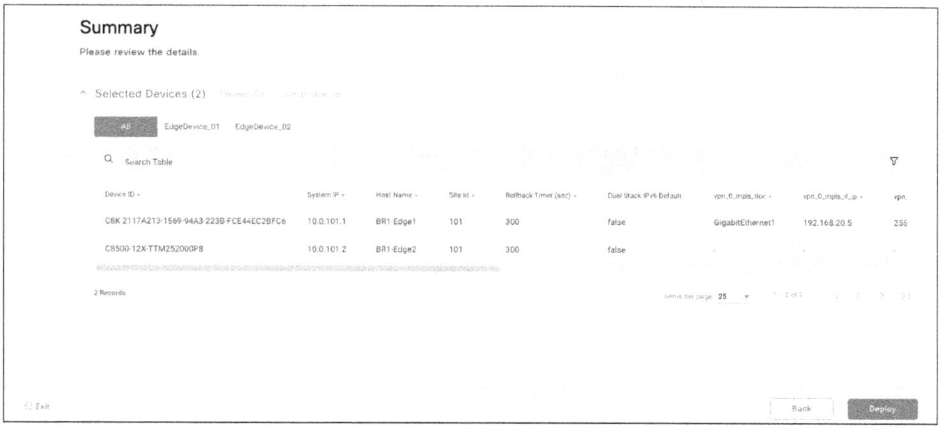

Figure 4-31 *Summary View*

> **NOTE** For both Device Templates and Configuration Groups, when a configuration change occurs, a preview CLI provides two widely used options: Inline Diff and Side by Side Diff. While both of these options highlight the differences, displaying deletions in red and additions in green, Side by Side Diff tends to be preferred because it clearly presents the old versus the new configuration the device will pull and makes it possible to revert and make required changes if needed.
>
> When using Device Templates, every single change must be implemented separately unless Draft Mode is enabled. Draft Mode allows for the aggregation of multiple changes and the generation of a config-diff, which can then be pulled by the WAN Edge Device. On the other hand, Configuration Groups two steps process inherently offers this change aggregation as they must be associated first to WAN Edge devices and then execute a Deploy to apply the configuration.

Configuration Groups offer a simplified, device-agnostic, efficient way to manage device configuration. All the relevant elements are grouped together instead of being split into many nonsequential pieces, as is the case with feature template creation and assignment to device templates. Configuration Groups also automatically create site topology to help you better visualize a site configuration's composition. You'll learn more about this in Chapter 14, "Cisco Catalyst SD-WAN Monitoring and Operations."

Be aware that feature parity between Configuration Groups and templates is progressing, and new phases are becoming available with the latest software versions. It is therefore important to test all the required functionality with Configuration Groups before you deploy them in a production environment.

As mentioned earlier, the recommended method for configuring WAN Edge routers is to leverage either Device Templates, Configuration Groups, or use the SD-WAN Manager programmatic API approach. The API option streamlines the configuration process and version control compared to manually configuring individual devices.

Onboarding Devices

For a WAN Edge Device to join the SD-WAN fabric, the device first needs to establish connectivity to SD-WAN Validator (formerly vBond). SD-WAN Validator facilitates discovery of SD-WAN Manager and SD-WAN Controller (formerly vSmart). As the WAN Edge device establishes connectivity to each of these control components, mutual authentication occurs. After the WAN Edge device has authenticated to the control components in the overlay, the device receives its full configuration from SD-WAN Manager.

There are two ways to bootstrap a device with an initial configuration so that it can reach SD-WAN Validator:

■ The less preferred, and more obvious, method is to manually apply minimal configuration to the device.

■ The second method is to automatically discover the network by using zero-touch provisioning (ZTP) or plug and play (PNP).

If a device is running Viptela OS, it will use ZTP. If the device is an IOS XE–based device and cloud-hosted controllers are in use, the device will use PNP, and if an on-premises ZTP server is in use, the device will use ZTP. The following sections elaborate on these processes.

A third option, generating a bootstrap file, allows an administrator to generate a basic configuration file for a WAN Edge device to initially connect to the fabric or in the event of configuration loss. This option is primarily used when a network is air-gapped, for devices without Secure Unique Device Identifier (SUDI), and when employing Catalyst 8000V Edge devices.

Manually Configuring a WAN Edge Device

To manually set up a WAN Edge device, a network administrator begins by applying a minimal configuration to the device, including IP addressing, SD-WAN Validator addressing (either DNS hostname or IP address), and system identification information. This information is used to establish initial connectivity and authentication. Example 4-1 illustrates the basic configuration required to set up a WAN Edge. The process to manually configure a device is as follows:

Step 1. Configure an interface, tunnel interface, IP address, and default gateway. If DHCP is available, you can use it to assign the IP address and gateway automatically.

Step 2. Configure the SD-WAN Validator IP address or hostname. If you are using a hostname, provide a DNS server address and ensure that the device has reachability from VPN 0.

Step 3. Configure device identification information, including the system IP address, site ID, and organization name.

Example 4-1   *Minimal Configuration for an IOS XE–Based Device*

```
!Configuration for BR3-Edge1
Router# config-transaction
Router(config)#system
Router(config-system)# system-ip 10.0.103.1
Router(config-system)# site-id 103
Router (config-system)# vbond validator.ciscopress.com port 12346
Router(config-system)# sp-organization-name Cisco-Press
```

```
Router(config-system)# organization-name Cisco-Press
Router(config-system)# exit
Router(config)# hostname BR3-Edge1
Router(config)# ip route 0.0.0.0 0.0.0.0 209.165.201.30
Router(config)# ip name-server 198.18.133.1
Router(config)# interface Tunnel 2
Router(config-if)# ip unnumbered  GigabitEthernet2
Router(config-if)# tunnel source  GigabitEthernet2
Router(config-if)# tunnel mode sdwan
Router(config)# interface  GigabitEthernet2
Router(config)# ip address 209.165.201.8 255.255.255.224
Router(config)# no shutdown
Router(config)# exit
Router(config)# sdwan
Router(config-sdwan)# interface GigabitEthernet2
Router(config-interface-interface-name)# tunnel-interface
Router(config-tunnel-interface)# color biz-internet
Router(config-tunnel-interface)# encapsulation ipsec
Router(config)# commit
BR3-Edge1# exit
```

The tunnel interface number may seem like a random number, but it is in fact tied to the physical interface type and number through a special formula, and those two must match for the configuration to be successful. This is the formula:

Tunnel # = (Interface number without slashes) + (1000*Subinterface number, if present) + (5000000 if interface is a serial interface) + (Channel group, if present * 1000) + (10000000, if interface is TenGigabit)

For example, GigabitEthernet0/0/0 maps to Tunnel0, GigabitEthernet0/0/1.5 maps to Tunnel5001, TenGigabitEthernet0/1/0.4 maps to Tunnel10004010, and so on.

One special case is when a loopback interface sources the tunnel. In this case, the formula is as follows:

Tunnel name = 14095000 + Loopback number

Automatic Provisioning with PNP or ZTP

Key Topic

When provisioning devices, another option is for a network administrator to automatically bring the devices online with minimal effort and involvement. Once a device is powered on, the default configuration on the device tries to receive an IP address via DHCP. Once the device has an IP address, it reaches out to the automatic provisioning server (hosted by Cisco) and learns about the organization's SD-WAN Validator. At this point, the process is exactly the same as the manual configuration process: The device connects and authenticates to SD-WAN Validator, learns about SD-WAN Manager and SD-WAN Controller, and then receives its configuration.

NOTE The automatic provisioning servers are managed via the PNP portal at https://software.cisco.com. As devices are purchased from Cisco, their serial numbers are populated at this portal. You can also configure SD-WAN Manager to synchronize with this portal to automatically populate your organization's devices into SD-WAN Manager.

Before the automatic provisioning process can be initiated, a network administrator needs to attach a device template or configuration group in SD-WAN Manager for the respective device. The device template must have the system IP address and site ID for the device populated as well. If none of this is completed, the process will not allow the administrator to proceed further in the workflow. When SD-WAN Manager sees the device for the first time, it pushes the template that is assigned to the matching serial number of the device performing ZTP or PNP.

The process is slightly different, depending on the type of device. Cisco IOS XE devices use PNP with cloud control components or ZTP with an on-premises ZTP server, and Viptela OS–based devices use ZTP.

When a device boots up, it starts the process of receiving an IP address and DNS server via DHCP. When this succeeds, a Viptela OS device tries to resolve ztp.cisco.com, and a Cisco IOS XE device tries to resolve devicehelper.cisco.com. If it succeeds, the device connects to the provisioning server, the server verifies what organization the device belongs to, and the server redirects the device to the correct SD-WAN Validator for the organization. The provisioning server is able to verify which organization the device belongs to by checking the serial number of the device against its serial number entries database. Once the device is connected to the SD-WAN Validator, the normal process continues.

For this type of automatic provisioning method to function, two things must happen: DHCP must be available on the WAN (VPN 0)-facing interface, and the device must be able to resolve ztp.cisco.com or devicehelper.cisco.com. The process is as follows (see Figure 4-32):

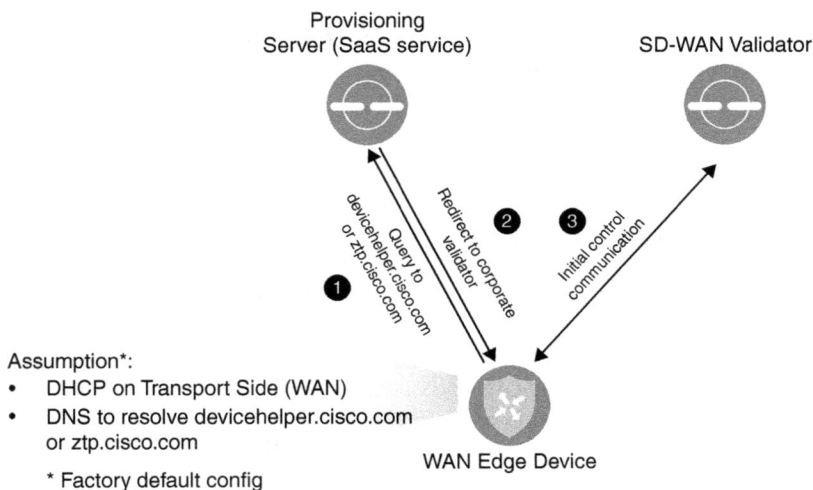

Figure 4-32 *Automatic Provisioning Workflow*

Step 1.   The WAN Edge router queries devicehelper.cisco.com or ztp.cisco.com. The provisioning server verifies that the device's serial number and organization exist in the serial numbers database.

Step 2.   If the WAN Edge router performing the automatic provisioning process exists in the database, the provisioning server responds, telling the WAN Edge router the connectivity information for the organization's SD-WAN Validator.

Step 3.   The WAN Edge device connects to the corporate SD-WAN Validator and goes through the authentication process. If the process is successful, SD-WAN Validator tells the router about SD-WAN Controller and SD-WAN Manager in the overlay. At this point, the WAN Edge device pulls the necessary configuration.

The process operates almost identically for PNP and ZTP, except instead of building a DTLS tunnel to the PNP server, the device communicates to the server via HTTPS. After the PNP server validates the device, it redirects the IOS XE–based WAN Edge device to the relevant SD-WAN Validator for the organization. An IOS XE–based device faces the same requirement as a ZTP device: It must get an IP address and DNS server via DHCP and must be able to resolve devicehelper.cisco.com.

An on-premises ZTP server can be used in air-gapped networks. The PNP agent in IOS XE–based devices attempts to connect to the local server before trying to connect to a cloud-based PNP server. (This feature was introduced to IOS XE, starting with SD-WAN Version 17.3.)

NOTE   Starting with Version 17.7 for IOS XE devices, Cisco provides an alternative when there is no DHCP server present. After not receiving a DHCP offer, the router proceeds to detect the IP address by examining ARP packets in the network and inferring the IP address of the interface to further progress in the PNP process. The official Cisco documentation Install and Upgrade Guides refers to this approach as "automatic IP address detection."

Using a Bootstrap Configuration File

In some scenarios, generating a bootstrap file and loading it to a WAN Edge device's memory can be useful. These scenarios include the lack of SUDI certificate, the use of software appliances like Catalyst 8000V, and instances where manual configuration, automatic IP address, PNP are all infeasible. There are various ways to generate a basic bootstrap file. One of the most prevalent examples is outlined in these steps.

Step 1.   Create a basic device template or configuration group and attach it to the target device. Then select **Configuration > Devices**, click the three dots under **Actions** for the intended device (see Figure 4-33), and choose **Generate Bootstrap Configuration**.

Step 2.   Click **OK** and save the generated bootstrap configuration file from the popup window, as shown in Figure 4-34.

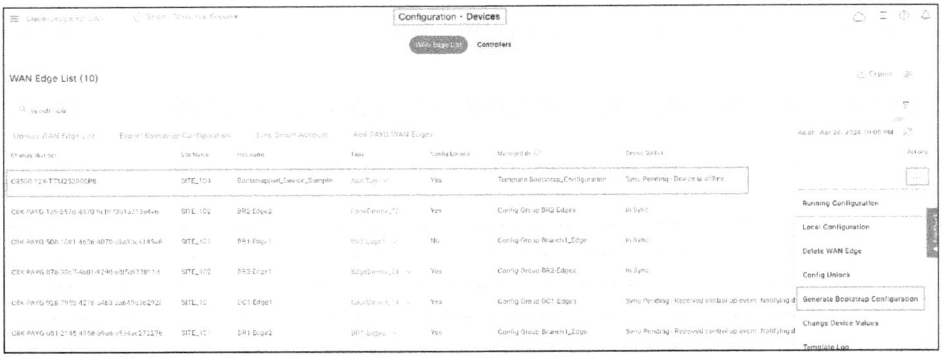

Figure 4-33   *Generating a Bootstrap Configuration*

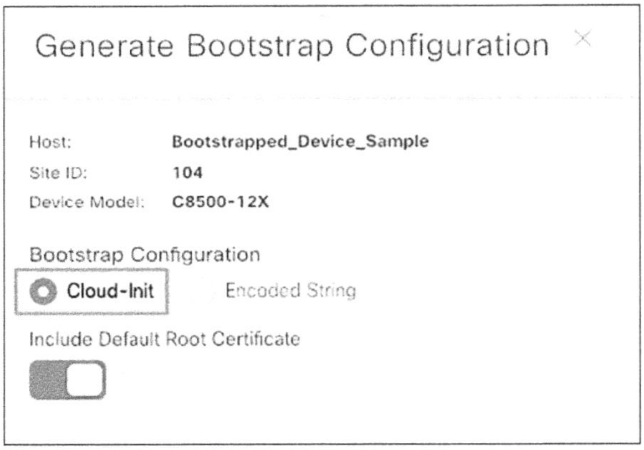

Figure 4-34   *Saving the Bootstrap Configuration*

Step 3.   Save the bootstrap configuration file to device memory or a USB stick or append it to the boot process of the virtual device.

NOTE   A bootstrap file needs to follow the naming *ciscosdwan*.**cfg** for all hardware devices except OTP-authenticated devices, such as ASR1002-X. For Cisco Catalyst 8000V Edge devices and ASR1002-X, use the bootstrap filename *ciscosdwan_cloud*_**init.cfg**. For detailed information about this process, refer to the official Cisco documentation Install and Upgrade Guides.

Depending on the network conditions, the number of steps required, or administrator preference, Cisco Catalyst SD-WAN provides flexibility by offering methods such as manual setup, automatic provisioning, or bootstrapping from a file in memory. These onboarding methods allow businesses to be adaptable.

Key Settings in Device Templates and Configuration Groups

Numerous settings can be used together depending on the business goal, particularly with Direct Internet Access, Cloud OnRamp for SaaS, and symmetric routing. Let's look at some of the frequently used settings and their use with Configuration Groups:

- **Transport interface settings:**

    - **NAT:** Public transports like the Internet are commonly used not only to source IPsec tunnels but also for Direct Internet Access (DIA). To support this, public TLOC interfaces require the NAT setting to be enabled, as shown in Figure 4-35. At this writing, Version 20.12 provides three options to enable NAT: interface (the option selected in the figure), pool, and loopback.

Figure 4-35   *Enabling NAT in a Public Transport Interface*

A NAT-enabled interface typically comes with a NAT DIA tracker, which is set in the Transport & Management as a Tracker Feature Parcel and then associated to the desired interface. This setting allows for probing the transport interface and detecting unavailability of the Internet or external networks. Enabling NAT on public interfaces is essential if you want to configure a NAT DIA route or selective DIA with policies. (Chapter 8, "Centralized Data Policies," discusses selective DIA.)

- **Tunnel interface attributes:** Throughout this book, you will see private transport mappings to MPLS TLOC colors. When the **restrict** attribute is set to this TLOC, the WAN Edge device exclusively tries to establish a tunnel to any remote TLOC matching exactly that TLOC color. This means only an MPLS-to-MPLS tunnel is permitted. This attribute is commonly used within private transports to prevent the establishment of sessions to other type of transports. This setting is illustrated in Figure 4-36.

Figure 4-36 *Restrict and Groups settings under Tunnel Interface*

A similar feature is Tunnel Group ID. Although it is not configured in the use cases later described, this feature is useful when more granular tunnel creation control is needed. When the tunnel group ID matches, a tunnel is created. If there is not a tunnel group ID associated, a tunnel can be created to any tunnel group ID. When this feature is used in conjunction with the **restrict** setting, both the remote color and tunnel group ID must match.

■ **TLOC preference and weight:** Under normal conditions, load is equally shared across different available transports (ECMP), and 0 is the default TLOC preference value. When symmetry needs to be influenced or active/standby usage of paths needs to be implemented, TLOC preference allows you to determine the preference for traffic in the outbound and inbound directions. This is discussed in Chapter 7, "Centralized Control Policies."

The Weight attribute operates when ECMP exists. It helps to weigh the session distribution across transports. It is commonly used for sharing loads in links proportionally to the allocated bandwidth. This means an administrator can set a distribution ratio of 1 session in a 10 Mbps link for each 10 sessions used in the 100 Mbps link. These two attributes are provided in the Tunnel Interface section, as shown in Figure 4-37.

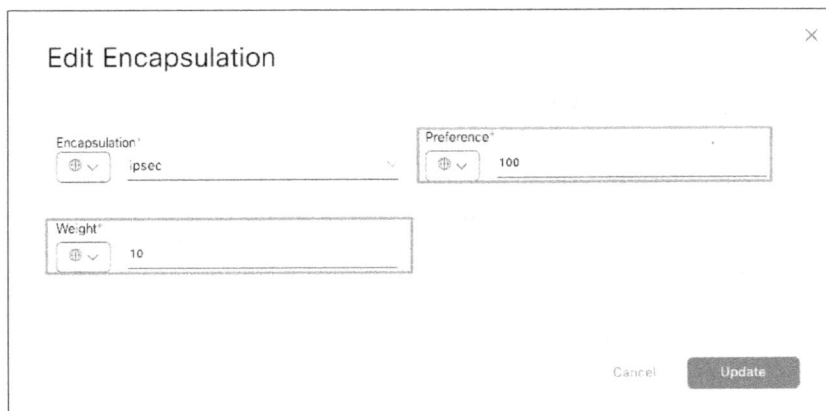

Figure 4-37 *Enabling TLOC Preference and Weight*

- **Service-side VPN settings:**

  - **NAT DIA route:** In scenarios where there is a guest VPN or any data segment that needs to be connected via Direct Internet Access, employing a NAT DIA route is an option. This type of route directs all default traffic out to the Internet. It can be set with the service-side VPN settings, as shown in Figure 4-38.

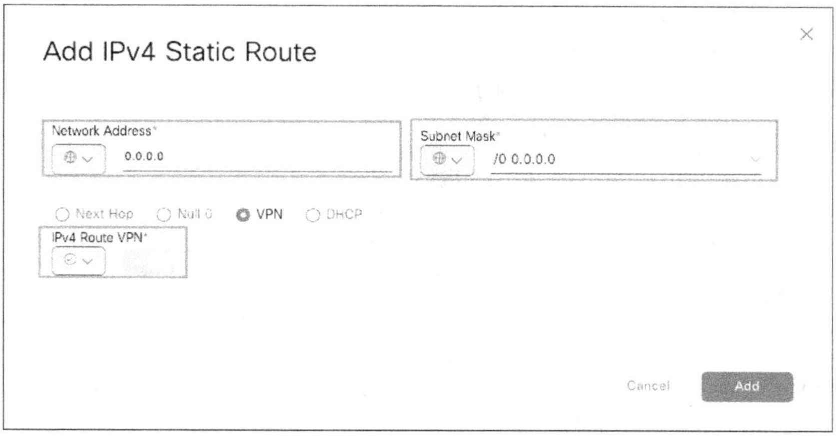

Figure 4-38   *IPv4 Route for NAT DIA*

  - **Service route:** You can use a service route for traffic that is to be redirected to a Secure Internet Gateway tunnel (see Figure 4-39).

When you need selective traffic redirection to the Internet or a Secure Internet Gateway provider, you want to use data policies, as discussed in Chapter 8.

As discussed earlier, numerous settings offer administrators options to fulfill various use cases, including ACLs, QoS, or route leaking of services between a global VPN and a service VPN. For more comprehensive information about available options, refer to the Cisco Catalyst SD-WAN Systems and Interfaces Configuration Guide for the software version you are using.

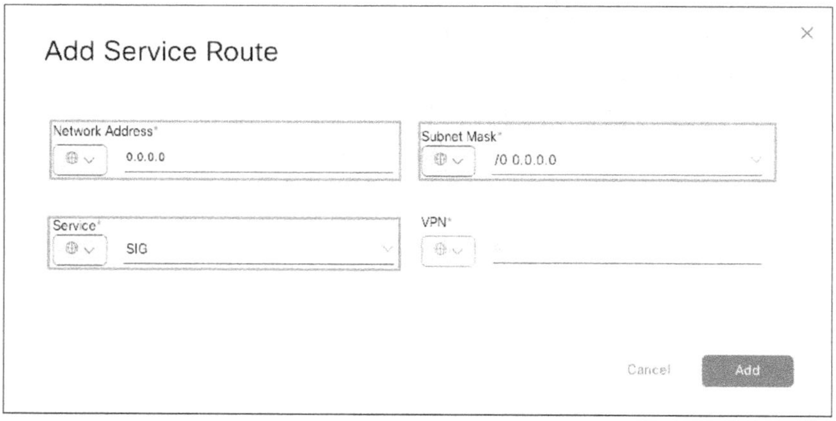

Figure 4-39   *Secure Internet Gateway Service Route*

Summary

With Cisco Catalyst SD-WAN, network settings are handled with ease via a powerful configuration engine and templates or configuration groups. Feature templates can be used to achieve modular configurations that can be reused across various platforms. Feature templates are used to form a device template. Configuration groups present a hierarchical approach that offers more structure and addresses scalability, reusability, and ease of configuration. By using variables within these two constructs, a network administrator can support a large range of configuration requirements.

Provisioning of devices can occur with one of the following methods: either manually, with an automatic process such as PNP or ZTP, or through the use of a bootstrap file. With the manual method, the amount of configuration is very small. The device must have a system IP address, site ID, organization name, and IP address information, and it must have a tunnel interface defined. When a device authenticates to the organization's SD-WAN Validator, it discovers the rest of the controller elements, and SD-WAN Manager can provide configuration to the device. The other option involves using an automatic onboarding process, via either ZTP or PNP, depending on whether it's a Viptela OS–based product or a Cisco IOS XE–based product. Once the device has gone through the automatic method and determined the SD-WAN Validator to use, the process works just the same as the manual method. Automatic onboarding allows a network administrator to deploy a large number of devices quickly, even if they have different configuration options.

Review All Key Topics

Review the most important topics in the chapter, noted with the Key Topic icon in the outer margin of the page. Table 4-1 lists these key topics and the page number on which each is found.

Key Topic

Table 4-1   Key Topics

Key Topic Element	Description	Page
Paragraph	Device templates	94
Paragraph	Feature templates	96
Section	Developing and Deploying Configuration Groups	103
Section	Onboarding Devices	111
Section	Automatic Provisioning with PNP or ZTP	113
Section	Using a Bootstrap Configuration File	115
Section	Key Settings in Device Templates and Configuration Groups	117

Key Terms

Define the following key terms from this chapter and check your answers in the glossary:

Device Template, Feature Template, Configuration Group, Feature Profile, Feature Parcel, SUDI

Chapter Review Questions

1. What methods can be used to construct device templates? (Choose three.)
   a. Using the CLI
   b. Using feature templates
   c. Directly using the device
   d. Using a programmatic approach (APIs)

2. What device value types can be used with feature templates? (Choose three.)
   a. Global
   b. Default
   c. Automatic
   d. Imported
   e. Device specific (variables)

3. True or false: A single device template supports multiple different device types.
   a. True
   b. False

4. True or false: CLI templates can be used modularly and achieve the same flexibility as feature templates.
   a. True
   b. False

5. Which automatic provisioning method uses HTTPS for communication?
   a. Plug and play
   b. Zero touch provisioning
   c. NAT traversal

6. What must a device have for automatic provisioning to be successful? (Choose three.)
   a. IP address and DNS server via DHCP
   b. Ability to resolve a ZTP/PNP domain name
   c. Connectivity to a ZTP or PNP server
   d. IPsec tunnel
   e. Connectivity to the data center

7. True or false: A single configuration group supports multiple different device types.
   a. True
   b. False

8. True or false: Devices can be associated with both configuration groups and templates at the same time.
   a. True
   b. False

9. True or false: In order to use Direct Internet Access over public interfaces, NAT needs to be enabled on them.
   a. True
   b. False

References

"Cisco Catalyst SD-WAN Command Line Reference," https://www.cisco.com/c/en/us/td/docs/routers/sdwan/command/sdwan-cr-book.html.

"Cisco Catalyst SD-WAN Control Components Certificates and Authorized Serial Number File Prescriptive Deployment Guide," https://www.cisco.com/c/en/us/td/docs/solutions/CVD/SDWAN/cisco-sdwan-controller-cert-deploy-guide.html, December 2023.

"Configuration Groups," https://www.cisco.com/c/en/us/td/docs/routers/sdwan/configuration/config-groups/configuration-group-guide/introduction.html.

CHAPTER 5

Cisco Catalyst SD-WAN Design and Migration

This chapter covers the following topics:

- **Cisco Catalyst SD-WAN Design:** This section outlines the methodology behind SD-WAN design across an enterprise.

- **Cisco Catalyst SD-WAN Control Components Design:** This section details the design options for Cisco Catalyst SD-WAN Control Components.

- **Cisco Catalyst SD-WAN Implementation Preparation:** This section covers the recommended steps to prepare for implementing Cisco Catalyst SD-WAN in an enterprise.

- **Cisco SD-WAN Transport Connectivity:** This section reviews various options for how WAN Edge routers can use available underlay transport connections.

- **Cisco Catalyst SD-WAN Data Center Design:** This section provides details on data center design options and migration techniques.

- **Cisco Catalyst SD-WAN Branch Design:** This section explores the details of branch design options and migration techniques.

- **Integrating Cisco SD-WAN with Existing Networks:** This section discusses optimal connectivity methods between migrated and non-migrated sites.

For many organizations, the chance to deploy Cisco Catalyst SD-WAN (Cisco SD-WAN) in a greenfield environment is rare. Instead, most opportunities to implement it occur in brownfield environments, offering a unique chance to re-architect the entire wide-area network.

The WAN is such a critical and sensitive component of a typical organization's business that approvals for lengthy outages necessitated by pervasive design changes are a rarity. Most organizations therefore see many years of incremental changes done by a multitude of individuals (with different skillsets and design methodologies) along with temporary fixes or adjustments that have never been reevaluated. Coupled with inconsistent configurations and connectivity models, this all results in complexities that, oftentimes, not a single person on staff may fully comprehend.

Designing your SD-WAN network is a golden opportunity to really dig deep into your WAN. You can learn how it operates, understand all the complexities and caveats that lie within, and propose a scalable, high-performing, easy-to-manage next-generation solution. It is crucial that the individuals leading the Cisco SD-WAN design and deployment dissect the existing WAN architecture in order to gain a solid understanding of routing, topology, high availability, failover, and traffic flow patterns as well areas where the current WAN architecture may not meet business requirements. The goal is to discover all the potential problems that may arise during implementation. With this information in hand, you can utilize the incredibly comprehensive tool sets provided by Cisco SD-WAN to effectively solve these problems intelligently and efficiently. During this process, the ultimate goal should be to remove unnecessary complexity, either through the evaluation of why that complexity existed initially and whether it is still required or through replacing it with the intelligent application-aware and flexible fabric that Cisco SD-WAN offers.

This section presents design recommendations garnered through years of Cisco SD-WAN implementation experience that will allow an organization to gracefully migrate to this new architecture while ensuring that the existing WAN is not disrupted. Ideally, the legacy WAN and the Cisco SD-WAN should be able to operate in parallel. An example of such a recommendation might be to selectively place Cisco SD-WAN hubs across your enterprise in order to act as transit points between migrated and non-migrated sites. Another recommendation might be to provide high availability at branch sites through the use of Virtual Router Redundancy Protocol (VRRP) between an existing router and the new SD-WAN router.

There are many ways to implement Cisco SD-WAN, and some may be better than others. In the end, however, everything always comes back to the fundamental routing and traffic engineering concepts we know and love today. Rest assured that Cisco SD-WAN provides comprehensive routing and traffic engineering tool sets, including best path manipulation options, advanced routing protocol features, filtering and tagging, and an overlay management protocol that delivers unprecedented traffic engineering flexibility.

Cisco SD-WAN Design Methodology

Key Topic

Crafting a well-thought-out design for the SD-WAN fabric is a crucial step in the journey to Cisco SD-WAN enablement. It is a key to ensuring success across all stages of implementation, including setting up SD-WAN Control Components, deploying data centers and branches, and configuring policies.

Cisco recommends taking a top-down approach to SD-WAN designs to ensure that the chosen platforms, use cases, and features align with the organization's implementation goals and business objectives. Implementations that follow SD-WAN design methodology typically include these considerations:

- **SD-WAN objectives and requirements:** Determine the reason for implementing an SD-WAN network, along with objectives and requirements for the network.

- **Network audit:** Identify current applications in the network, their latency and loss tolerances, and traffic patterns. Review current hardware, software, and transports, along with their utilization. Evaluate network performance to identify any problem areas.

- **WAN and site standards:** Develop standards for physical and logical topology (site types), dictating how the WAN Edge routers connect to the LAN and WAN infrastructure. Consider different site types to accommodate remote sites with varying business requirements, numbers of users, or available transports. Ensure that site standards account for future SD-WAN use cases and features that may impact traffic load, flow patterns, and other factors influencing decisions on bandwidth, redundancy, and WAN Edge platform selection.

■ **High-level design:** Make decisions regarding key elements of the SD-WAN deployment, such as budget allocation, implementation scope, and orders for circuits and hardware. High-level design includes the information needed to determine the platform choices, such as required features, circuits, bandwidth, and number of data tunnels per device for each site in the design.

■ **Low-level design:** Develop and validate specifics about configurations, policies, and other aspects of the implementation. This work can be done in parallel with the high-level design.

Subsequent sections of this chapter explore specific aspects of the SD-WAN design methodology in greater depth.

Cisco SD-WAN Objectives

Designing an SD-WAN network from scratch is a complex assignment. It is recommended to approach it in a structured manner, such as by taking a top-down design approach, analyzing business, functional, and technical (non-functional) requirements first before deciding on technologies and features.

Table 5-1 provides a few examples of common business objectives that can be addressed by a Cisco SD-WAN deployment.

Table 5-1   Business Objectives Addressed by Cisco SD-WAN

Objective	How Cisco SD-WAN Addresses Objective
Availability and performance	Cisco SD-WAN allows businesses to use all available network transports at full capacity, using automated path control to prioritize business-critical applications and improve performance.
Optimized cloud architecture	Cisco SD-WAN optimizes networks to connect to cloud-based applications easily and efficiently. It provides direct secure, high-performance connections to the cloud, avoiding backhauling traffic to data centers. With Cisco SD-WAN, the user experience with IaaS/Colo/SaaS-based applications is greatly improved.
Savings	Cisco SD-WAN makes it possible to replace expensive technologies (such as MPLS) with more cost-effective connectivity options (such as broadband and LTE). It reduces networking costs while easing demands on IT, thus increasing productivity and profitability.
Efficiency	Cisco SD-WAN provides a simplified and centralized configuration, policy management, network monitoring, and troubleshooting platform, making it easy to deploy and monitor individual sites and applications.
Security	Cisco SD-WAN delivers an integrated security platform with built-in user identity–based control, data encryption, and firewall support, using network intelligence to detect and respond to cyberattacks in real time.
Agility	Cisco SD-WAN enables zero-touch provisioning, reducing deployment time across the network.

Cisco SD-WAN Use Cases

As you analyze your specific requirements, you will likely find that the Cisco SD-WAN functionality that suits your needs aligns with one or more standard categories. There are four main use cases that Cisco SD-WAN is designed to efficiently address:

- Secure automated WAN

- Application performance optimization

- Secure direct Internet access

- Multicloud connectivity

These categories are not mutually exclusive, and a Cisco SD-WAN deployment may incorporate any combination of these use cases, depending on the specific needs and objectives of the network. Let's briefly review each of these use cases.

Use Case 1: Secure Automated WAN

The goal of the secure automated WAN use case is to establish secure connectivity between all network locations, including branches, data centers, colocations, and both public and private clouds, over a transport-independent network. This is the most typical use case for Cisco SD-WAN and forms the foundation for other use cases.

A secure automated WAN includes the following functionalities:

- **Transport flexibility and bandwidth augmentation:** Cisco SD-WAN supports various transport types, such as MPLS, Internet, 4G/5G LTE, satellite links, and more. Organizations can select the most suitable transport options based on cost, performance, and availability. Cisco SD-WAN can efficiently use available transports, whether by distributing traffic across all available WAN circuits in an active/active manner to increase overall WAN bandwidth or by intelligently offloading traffic from expensive circuits like MPLS to more cost-efficient broadband connections, all while maintaining equivalent availability and performance.

- **VPN segmentation:** Cisco SD-WAN creates routing table isolation, ensuring that a user in one VPN cannot transmit data to another VPN unless this capability is explicitly configured.

- **Zero-touch provisioning:** Cisco SD-WAN enables you to remotely provision a router anywhere in the WAN by simply connecting it to the transport network and powering it on.

- **Centralized management:** SD-WAN Manager offers a single pane of glass for centralized management of SD-WAN operations. It provides operational simplicity and streamlines deployment by using global policies and templates, resulting in reduced change control and deployment times.

Use Case 2: Application Performance Optimization

Achieving the best application experience is critical for user productivity, especially when a network experiences issues like packet loss, congested WAN links, and suboptimal WAN routing. Cisco SD-WAN excels at optimizing application performance and mitigating the impact of WAN latency and forwarding delays through the following capabilities:

- **Application-Aware Routing (AAR):** Transport performance is measured in real time and checked against customized SLA metrics. The application traffic is directed to WAN links that are in compliance with the SLAs for that application but can be directed to other paths during periods of performance degradation.

- **Quality of Service (QoS):** QoS uses classification, scheduling, queueing, shaping, and policing of traffic on the WAN router interfaces to minimize delay, jitter, and packet loss with critical application flows.

- **Forward Error Correction (FEC) and packet duplication:** These features are used to mitigate packet loss. With FEC, the transmitting WAN Edge router inserts a parity packet for every four data packets, and the receiving WAN Edge can reconstruct a lost packet based on the parity value. With packet duplication, the transmitting WAN Edge router replicates all packets for selected critical applications over two tunnels, and the receiving router reconstructs critical application flows, discarding duplicates.

- **TCP optimization and session persistence:** These features can address high latency and poor throughput for long-haul or high-latency links such as satellite.

- **Data Redundancy Elimination (DRE):** This feature is a type of TCP optimization that uses compression technology to remove redundant information, thus reducing the size of the transmitted data across the WAN.

Chapter 8, "Centralized Data Policies," and Chapter 9, "Application-Aware Routing Policies," cover application performance optimization use cases in more detail.

Use Case 3: Secure Direct Internet Access

In a traditional WAN, Internet traffic from a branch site is backhauled to centralized locations such as data centers, where it can be scrubbed by a security stack. Today, as more companies embrace cloud services for their applications, and the prevalence of Internet-based applications continues to grow, this approach leads to increased Internet traffic. This surge places additional strain on the security and network devices at central sites, increased bandwidth utilization, and suboptimal latency, negatively impacting application performance.

Direct Internet Access (DIA) and Direct Cloud Access (DCA) present a solution for these challenges by allowing Internet-bound user traffic—either all traffic or a subset of it—to exit locally from the remote site, as shown in Figure 5-1.

NOTE   Keep in mind that merely using Internet transport as an underlay to reach a data center through an SD-WAN tunnel for centralized Internet access does not constitute direct Internet access. The key distinction is a localized diversion of the Internet-bound traffic to a local Internet link.

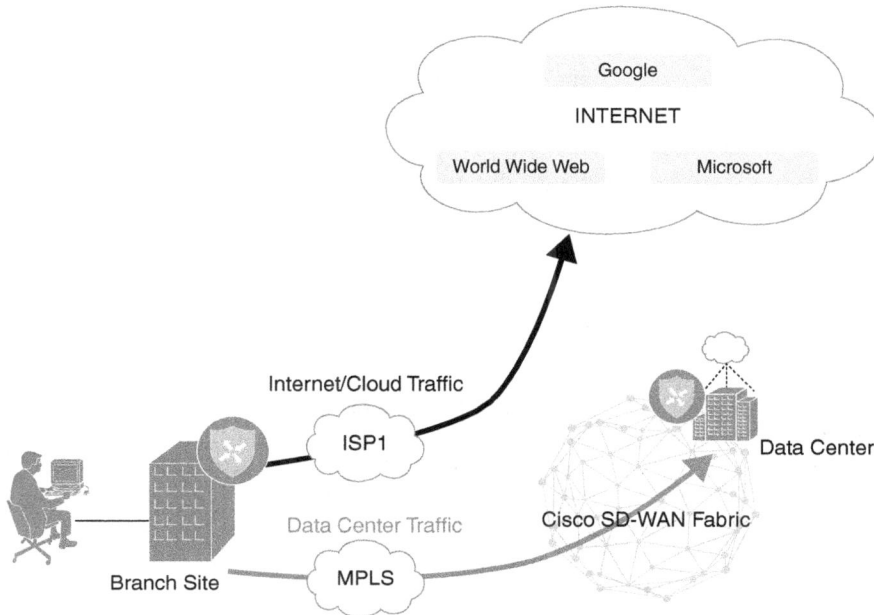

Figure 5-1   *Direct Internet Access/Direct Cloud Access*

While offering efficient Internet access, DIA introduces security challenges, such as safe-guarding remote site traffic against Internet threats. Cisco SD-WAN addresses this with the embedded security features on WAN Edge devices or by leveraging a secure access service edge (SASE) model with cloud-based security providers—or a combination of both. Cloud providers include Cisco Umbrella for DNS resolution, Cisco Secure Access Secure Service Edge (SSE), and other third-party secure Internet gateway (SIG) provides, like Zscaler and Netskope. The SASE model enhances security by consolidating various networking and security functions into a single integrated cloud service, ensuring secure application access for users regardless of their location.

The embedded security features in WAN Edge routers include an enterprise firewall with application awareness, an intrusion detection system (IDS)/intrusion prevention system (IPS), DNS security, URL Filtering, SSL proxy, and advanced malware protection.

The Cisco Umbrella cloud-based service provides a suite of security features, including a secure web gateway, DNS-layer security, cloud-delivered firewall, cloud access security broker functionality, and threat intelligence. In addition, the Cisco SASE model includes Cisco Duo, which offers two-factor authentication and endpoint security, and Cisco Thou-sandEyes, which offers Internet and cloud visibility to ensure exceptional user application experiences.

With Cisco Secure Access, Cisco Umbrella, and Zscaler, Cisco SD-WAN can leverage the SIG APIs to automate tunnel provisioning. This capability streamlines deployment for users, enabling quick and efficient setup with minimal configuration.

Chapter 8, "Centralized Data Policies," and Chapter 11, "Cisco Catalyst SD-WAN Security," cover secure direct Internet access use cases in more detail.

Use Case 4: Multicloud Connectivity

Organizations increasingly rely on a variety of cloud services, each with unique features and advantages. Multicloud connectivity use cases focus on ensuring that users consistently experience low latency and high performance when accessing cloud applications, regardless of the specific cloud services involved.

The following use cases are associated with this category:

■ **Infrastructure as a service (IaaS):** IaaS is a public cloud offering (such as AWS, Azure, or Google Cloud) that provides on-demand access to network, compute, and storage resources over the Internet. Traditionally, branches lacked direct access to cloud IaaS resources and required connectivity through a data center or colocation site, as highlighted in the previous section.

Cisco Cloud OnRamp for Multicloud simplifies connectivity to workloads in the public cloud. It automatically deploys WAN Edge router instances in the cloud and integrates them into the SD-WAN fabric, establishing data plane connectivity to the routers in data centers or branches. This extension of full SD-WAN capabilities into the cloud ensures a common policy framework across the entire SD-WAN fabric and cloud. Consequently, Cisco Cloud OnRamp for Multicloud enhances application performance by eliminating the need for SD-WAN traffic to traverse the data center when accessing applications hosted in the public cloud.

Figure 5-2 illustrates this use case:

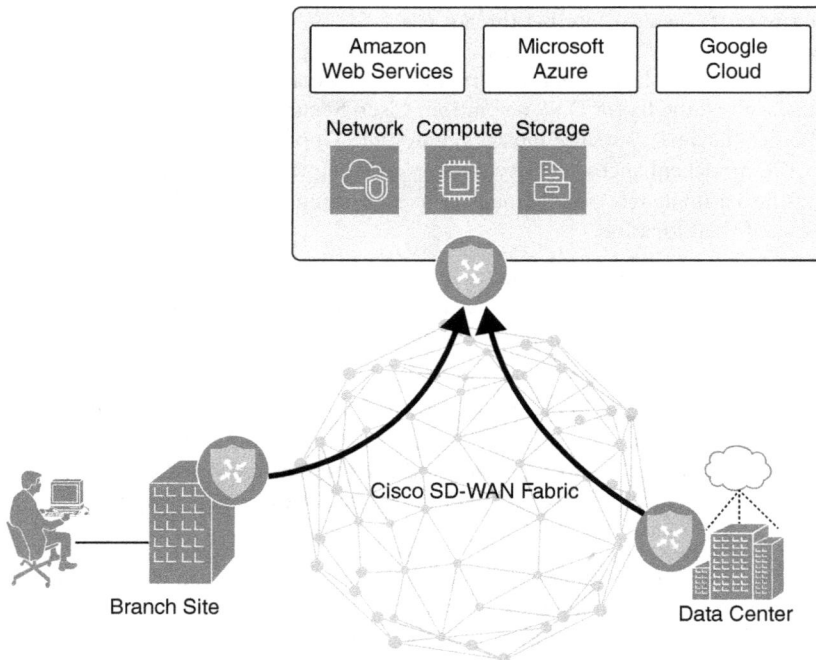

Figure 5-2 *Cisco Cloud OnRamp for Multicloud Use Case*

■ **Software as a service (SaaS):** Traditionally, branches accessed cloud SaaS applications (Office 365, Salesforce, Box, and so on) through centralized data centers, leading to increased latency and an unpredictable user experience. SD-WAN introduced additional network paths for accessing SaaS applications, such as direct Internet access and connections through regional gateways. However, optimal path selection for accessing SaaS applications becomes challenging when the network lacks visibility into the performance of these applications from remote sites.

Cloud OnRamp for SaaS facilitates easily configurable access to SaaS applications, offering the flexibility of direct access via the local Internet or through designated gateway locations. As shown in Figure 5-3, the router continuously probes, measures, and monitors the performance of each path to every SaaS application and dynamically selects the best-performing path based on loss and delay. In the event of any impairment, SaaS traffic is intelligently shifted to the updated optimal path, ensuring a seamless and optimal user experience.

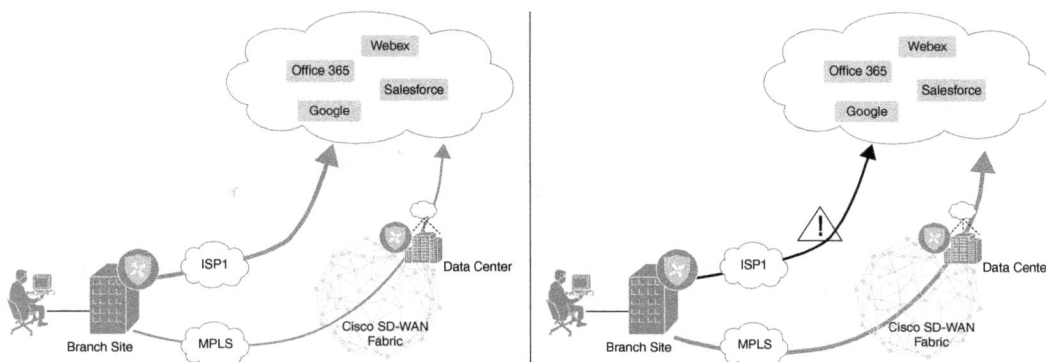

Figure 5-3 *Cisco Cloud OnRamp for SaaS Use Case*

Expanding on the basic benefits of Cloud OnRamp for SaaS, additional features have been introduced to enhance integration with Office 365. These features provide users with more insightful metrics, increased control over traffic flow for individual Office 365 applications, and automatic remediation of suboptimal performance, leveraging Microsoft telemetry metrics for a more refined and efficient user experience.

■ **Software-defined cloud interconnect (SDCI):** Traditionally, sites connecting to cloud applications often relied on using transports like the Internet and MPLS, which could be unreliable, insecure, or both. SDCI addresses these concerns by facilitating site-to-site and site-to-cloud connections through geographically dispersed points-of-presence (POPs) located in colocation facilities. These POPs interconnect with multiple ISPs and cloud providers at speeds of 100 Gbps and higher.

The SDCI approach offers quick and flexible software-defined onboarding that requires no additional hardware investment from the customer. This is accomplished by automatically deploying a virtual Catalyst 8000V WAN Edge router into the SDCI provider and integrating it into the SD-WAN fabric.

The customer can then use its preferred transports to reach the nearest SDCI provider's POP and rely on Cisco SD-WAN for optimized traffic flows. From there, user traffic moves onto the backbone of the SDCI provider, and it is then forwarded to the appropriate cloud providers. This technique provides reliable and dedicated bandwidth that is secure and cost-effective.

At this writing, Cisco SD-WAN supports Equinix and Megaport SDCI providers.

Chapter 12, "Cisco Catalyst SD-WAN Cloud OnRamp," covers multicloud connectivity use cases in more detail.

Cisco SD-WAN High-Level Design Considerations

During the high-level design phase, critical decisions are made regarding key elements of the SD-WAN deployment. The high-level design guides budget allocation and orders for hardware, software, licenses, control components, WAN transport circuits, and so on. Completing the high-level design early is crucial as some of these items may require extended lead times, especially when site construction is required to install new transports or hardware delivery is delayed due to manufacturing backlogs.

The high-level design should address the following topics:

- **Planned use cases and features:** Review the Cisco SD-WAN use cases and features, such as application visibility, VPN segmentation, AAR, QoS, FEC, cloud access, on-premises security, and multicast, and decide which of them will be implemented.

- **Cisco SD-WAN software version:** The code version used in the deployment can influence the design based on the features supported as well as the control plane scale. When choosing software for SD-WAN Control Components and WAN Edge routers, it is generally recommended to use versions that are marked with a gold star (based on software quality, stability, and longevity) at the Cisco Software Download site. However, you may require newer software that has new functionality or supports newer hardware, in which case it is recommended to use extended maintenance releases (for example, 20.9, 20.12, 20.15) wherever possible. You can find more details about current software recommendations from Cisco in the "Cisco Recommended SD-WAN Software Versions for Controllers and WAN Edge Routers" document at the Cisco website.

- **Transport strategy:** Evaluate the number of carriers and transport types for your SD-WAN design. Determine whether these transports will be interconnected or independent and determine their availability at data centers and in branches, bandwidth capacities, and whether there is a preferred transport. Keep in mind that while Cisco SD-WAN features such as AAR and FEC can mitigate WAN impairments, they are not a substitute for reliable transports provisioned with sufficient bandwidth.

- **Transport color scheme:** Determine what colors are assigned to transports in the SD-WAN overlay. Once the scheme is developed, you can use tools like color restriction, tunnel groups, and centralized control policies to manage the number of data tunnels between routers. Recall that WAN Edge routers by default attempt to build data tunnels from every local TLOC to every remote TLOC in the network, which increases the number of data tunnels in the SD-WAN network and limits the network's scalability.

■ **VPN segmentation:** Identify segmentation requirements and establish the number of service VPNs in the SD-WAN network. Assess whether certain VPNs need to enable communication with other VPNs within a single site or across multiple sites, such as connecting to a shared VPN in a data center.

■ **Overlay topology choices:** Based on the network audit and identified traffic flow patterns, decide whether remote sites should only form data tunnels to data centers in a hub-and-spoke topology, or if there's a need for full-mesh connectivity between sites for specific applications, such as voice.

■ **Deployment scale:** Evaluate the number of data center and branch sites, as well as the total count of routers. These factors significantly impact the network's scalability. Future-proof your design by planning for potential growth, ensuring that the network can adapt and scale as needed. Determine whether your network's scale requires a Multi-Region Fabric architecture (as discussed shortly).

■ **Deployment of SD-WAN Control Components:** Determine whether SD-WAN Control Components will be hosted in the cloud or on premises. Calculate the total number of control connections from WAN Edge routers based on the deployment scale and the color scheme. Use this information to establish the quantity of SD-WAN Control Components needed to effectively support the current and future scale of the network, considering potential growth.

For an on-premises deployment, identify the number of physical servers required to host SD-WAN Control Components, along with their characteristics (CPU, memory, interfaces, disk space, and so on). Plan for the worst case and future growth, as adding on-premises equipment is more complex compared to cloud deployment.

■ **Internet and cloud connectivity design:** Evaluate Internet access requirements for uses such as web browsing, cloud application access, or control connections to SD-WAN Control Components in the cloud. Determine how WAN Edge devices will connect to the Internet and the security policies needed to safeguard this traffic. Decide if localized security measures or cloud-based SASE security is required.

■ **Security planning:** In addition to securing the Internet access, consider other security aspects, such as encryption, data segmentation for protecting sensitive data, and consistent security policies across the SD-WAN fabric.

■ **High availability and disaster recovery:** Design for redundancy at multiple levels (such as link, device, and SD-WAN Control Components) to ensure high availability and reduce downtime. Consider various disaster recovery scenarios to ensure that the network supports business continuity.

■ **Compliance and regulatory adherence:** Ensure that the design aligns with industry-specific compliance and regulatory requirements, especially if dealing with sensitive data.

- **SD-WAN overlay tunnels:** Calculate the total number of data tunnels per router based on the deployment scale, color scheme, and overlay topology choices.

- **Cisco SD-WAN platforms:** Select WAN Edge routers that meet your current and future network requirements. Consider factors such as router type (physical or virtual), required throughput, number and type of interfaces, and number of supported data tunnels. Verify that your chosen WAN Edge routers support all the features that you plan to implement; keep in mind that Cisco ThousandEyes and advanced security features have additional memory requirements. In addition, ensure that WAN Edge devices are properly licensed.

By including these considerations in your design process, you can build a Cisco SD-WAN network that is functional, robust, and scalable. But remember: Every network is unique, and these considerations should be tailored to fit the specific needs and goals of your organization.

Cisco SD-WAN Multi-Region Fabric

Key Topic

Large SD-WAN fabrics may span multiple geographic regions, each with unique routing infrastructure, service providers, and traffic policies. While Cisco SD-WAN is fully capable of supporting such networks, configuring them can pose significant challenges.

To address complexities and streamline deployment, Cisco introduced a new architectural approach known as Multi-Region Fabric (formerly referred to as Hierarchical SD-WAN) that enables organizations to build unified, scalable, and resilient networks spanning multiple locations while ensuring consistent connectivity, security, and management.

Multi-Region Fabric introduces the capability to divide the overlay network into the following components:

- **Core region:** Designated as region 0, this network consists of border routers (BRs in Figure 5-4) that connect to regional overlays and to each other.

- **Access regions:** These networks consist of WAN Edge routers that connect to other WAN Edge routers within the same region. In addition, they can connect to core region border routers assigned to the region.

The division into regions creates a distinction between intra-region traffic and inter-region traffic:

- **Intra-region traffic:** Within a region, WAN Edge routers by default establish direct tunnels to other routers, allowing traffic to flow directly between source and destination devices without intermediate routing.

- **Inter-region traffic:** Conversely, for inter-region communications, WAN Edge routers in one region do not form direct tunnels to routers in different regions. Instead, they rely on core border routers to forward the traffic to the core border routers assigned to the target region. Subsequently, the traffic is directed to WAN Edge routers within the target region. In summary, inter-region traffic traverses at least three tunnels between the source device and the destination device to reach it.

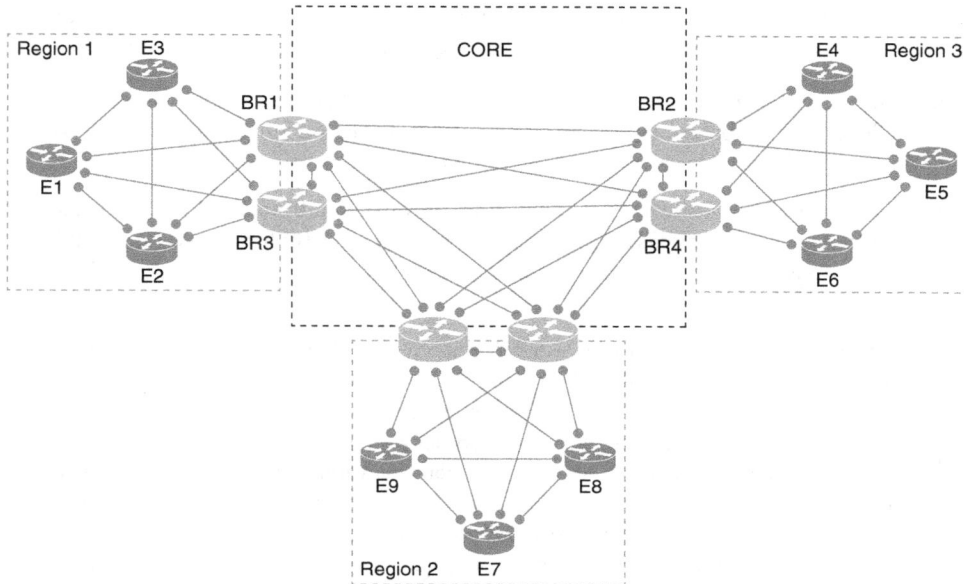

Figure 5-4 *Cisco SD-WAN Multi-Region Fabric*

Given the independence of routing within each region in a Multi-Region Fabric, it is possible to customize some aspects of the SD-WAN architecture in each region, including:

■ **Topology:** In the core region, it is recommended to use a full-mesh tunnel topology within the overlay network. This setup ensures optimal traffic forwarding between regions by allowing each border router in the core region to establish direct tunnels to every other border router.

Access regions, however, may adopt any suitable topology based on their specific requirements.

■ **Transport selection:** The core region's role is to ensure high performance and reliability for long-distance connectivity between distant geographic regions. Hence, premium transport services like premium WAN circuits, cloud backbones, or SDCI backbones are typically used in the core region.

In access regions, organizations may use the best available transport options based on their specific needs and constraints.

■ **Encapsulation:** In scenarios where the core region infrastructure is secure and does not require encryption, GRE encapsulation may be used for tunnels within the core region to provide better throughput. Conversely, if end-to-end encryption of inter-region traffic is necessary, IPsec encapsulation can be used to ensure secure transmission across the network.

However, the most significant advantage of Multi-Region Fabric is simplified policy design, incorporating functionalities that would typically require complex centralized control policies:

■ Traffic between regions is automatically routed via designated border routers. When multiple border routers are present in a region, you can use *router affinity groups* to indicate the order of preference for the routers.

■ *Secondary regions* allow direct connection between non-border WAN Edge routers in different regions, bypassing the core region. This is useful for high-volume traffic or applications that cannot tolerate additional latency introduced by routing via the core region.

■ Establishing paths between sites using disjointed providers is straightforward: Sites only require reachability to border routers, and then the core region's network facilitates connectivity between them. However, in some scenarios, it may be advantageous to offload this transit functionality from border routers due to factors such as traffic load, deployment location, or other design considerations. *Transport gateways* provide an alternative option to facilitate connectivity between disjointed providers. WAN Edge routers can be strategically deployed as transport gateways in access regions at points where different transport types converge. There they can handle translation and encapsulation of traffic between disparate transports, ensuring seamless communication across the network.

> **NOTE**   Router affinity, as a component of symmetric routing, and transport gateway features are available for standard, non-Multi-Region Fabric deployments beginning with Cisco Catalyst SD-WAN Version 20.12/IOS XE Version 17.12.

It is important to note that WAN Edge routers that are not configured for Multi-Region Fabric cannot establish connections with routers that are configured for it. This means that if you decided to use Multi-Region Fabric, all devices in the network must be configured to use it. Due to this restriction, enabling Multi-Region Fabric for an existing SD-WAN network could potentially disrupt connectivity between devices within the network, and so it needs to be planned carefully.

Key Topic   Cisco SD-WAN Control Components Design

As previously discussed, the Cisco Catalyst SD-WAN Control Components are SD-WAN Manager (formerly vManage) for network management, SD-WAN Controller (formerly vSmart) for the control plane, and SD-WAN Validator (formerly vBond) for the orchestration plane.

Early in any Cisco SD-WAN deployment, you need to deploy and configure SD-WAN Control Components and then set up data center and remote sites. The sequence is crucial because without a functional control plane in place, WAN Edge devices are unable to join the SD-WAN fabric and establish data plane connectivity.

The SD-WAN Control Components, which are software-based, offer deployment flexibility and can be implemented in several ways:

■ **Cisco cloud-hosted:** This is the recommended model, and it has been widely adopted due to its ease of deployment, scalability, reduced operational overhead, and cost efficiency. Cisco provisions SD-WAN Control Components in AWS or Azure Cloud, ensuring scale and redundancy, and enabling management of backups and disaster recovery. Customers are granted access to SD-WAN Control Components for network configuration and monitoring. Customers can submit fabric provision requests and manage their deployments through the Cisco Catalyst SD-WAN portal (https://ssp. sdwan.cisco.com), a cloud infrastructure automation tool for Cisco Catalyst SD-WAN. The SD-WAN portal also offers additional functions, such as controller monitoring, fabric maintenance, and more.

- **Managed service provider (MSP) or partner-hosted:** This model is similar to the Cisco cloud-hosted model, but in this case, the MSP or partner is typically responsible for provisioning of the SD-WAN Control Components, backups, and disaster recovery.

- **On-premises deployment in a private cloud or data center owned by an organization:** In this model, customers assume the responsibility of provisioning SD-WAN Control Components, managing backups, and disaster recovery. Some customers, especially those in the finance or government sectors, may opt for on-premises deployments for compliance and security reasons.

- **Deployment in a public cloud owned by your organization:** This model is similar to the on-premises option, but customers leverage their own public cloud infrastructure, eliminating the need for investing in their data center infrastructure.

Figure 5-5 highlights customer responsibilities for each of these SD-WAN Control Component deployment options.

	Cisco Hosted	MSP Hosted	On-Premises in a Private Cloud or Data Center	Customer-Owned Public Cloud
Physical Servers and Virtualization Platform	Cisco	MSP	Customer	Cloud Provider
Self-Service portal for easy SD-WAN Control Components provisioning and setup	Cisco	Not Available	Not Available	Not Available
SD-WAN Control Components deployment and initial setup	Cisco	MSP	Customer	Customer
SD-WAN Fabric Configuration (templates, configuration groups, policies, etc.)	Customer	Customer	Customer	Customer
SD-WAN Control Components Monitoring	Cisco	Customer or MSP	Customer	Customer
SD-WAN Control Components Backups and Disaster Recovery	Cisco	Customer or MSP	Customer	Customer

Figure 5-5 *Customer Responsibilities for Control Component Deployment Options*

All the deployment options involve the following common design considerations:

- **Connectivity channels:** Ensure that all SD-WAN Control Components and WAN Edge routers are reachable to each other via their VPN 0 interface.

- **IP address assignment:** Choose what kind of IP addresses (private or publicly routable) to assign to SD-WAN Control Components. When using private IP addresses with NAT, SD-WAN Validator learns about both private and public addresses of the SD-WAN Controller and SD-WAN Manager Control Components and sends this information to WAN Edge routers.

■ **Transport colors:** Choose transport colors assigned to SD-WAN Control Components. The type of color makes a difference since with public colors, WAN Edge routers will always connect to the public (post-NAT) IP addresses of Control Components, while with private colors on both sides, WAN Edge routers will try to connect to private (pre-NAT) IP addresses.

■ **Placement:** Decide where to strategically place SD-WAN Control Components in the network topology. Ensure that any firewall in the path allows communication between SD-WAN Control Components, as well as between WAN Edge routers and SD-WAN Control Components.

Note that with the Cisco cloud-hosted model, these considerations are addressed during provisioning. Connectivity channels are ensured during provisioning; SD-WAN Control Components are assigned private IP addresses and are mapped one-to-one via NAT to public IP addresses; and a public **default** color is assigned to transports (although it can be changed after provisioning). In addition, with SD-WAN Control Components hosted in the cloud, their persistent public IP addresses are assigned during provisioning and made known via the Cisco Catalyst SD-WAN portal so firewall rules can be properly configured.

Cloud-Hosted SD-WAN Control Components Deployments

Cloud-hosted deployments offer the advantages of ease of deployment and scalability, requiring only Internet accessibility. However, this convenience can turn into a disadvantage when SD-WAN fabric lacks Internet transports. Even if one Internet transport is available at a remote site, it introduces a vulnerability in terms of control connectivity redundancy.

Let's explore typical design scenarios for control connectivity, using a simple SD-WAN network with Internet and MPLS transports as an example.

With Option A, illustrated in Figure 5-6, MPLS transport provides native Internet reachability through some extranet connection. This configuration enables WAN Edge routers to establish direct connections to SD-WAN Control Components and form data tunnels using both transports. For WAN Edge routers to be able to reach the SD-WAN Control Components, they require either a default route or specific routes toward the publicly routable IP addresses of the SD-WAN Control Components. These routes can be configured statically or received dynamically via a routing protocol from the MPLS customer edge (CE) router. The choice between these approaches depends on the specific network requirements and the desired level of control.

In Option B, illustrated in Figure 5-7, the MPLS transport lacks direct Internet connectivity. Instead, control traffic is routed via a data center (or a regional hub) that is connected to both transports. In this configuration, data center routers may need to advertise either a default route or publicly routable IP addresses of SD-WAN Control Components into the MPLS network, depending on the specific network requirements.

A

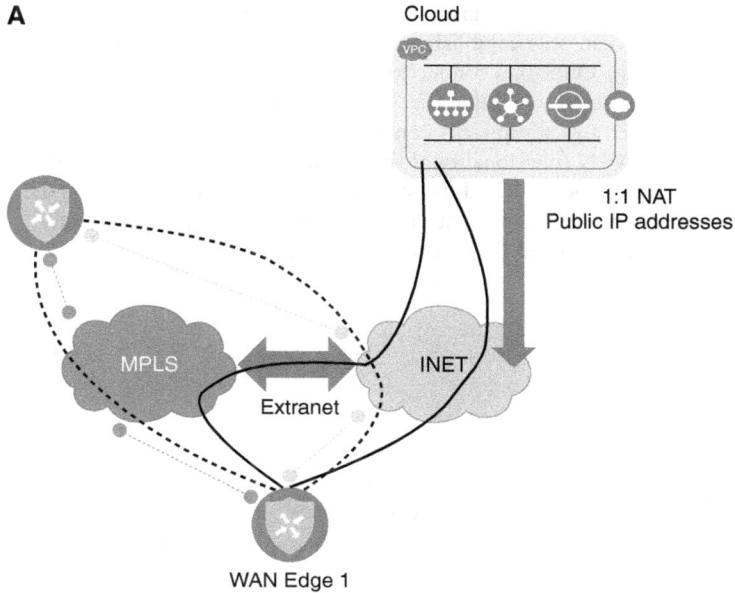

Figure 5-6 *Cloud-Hosted SD-WAN Control Components, Option A*

B

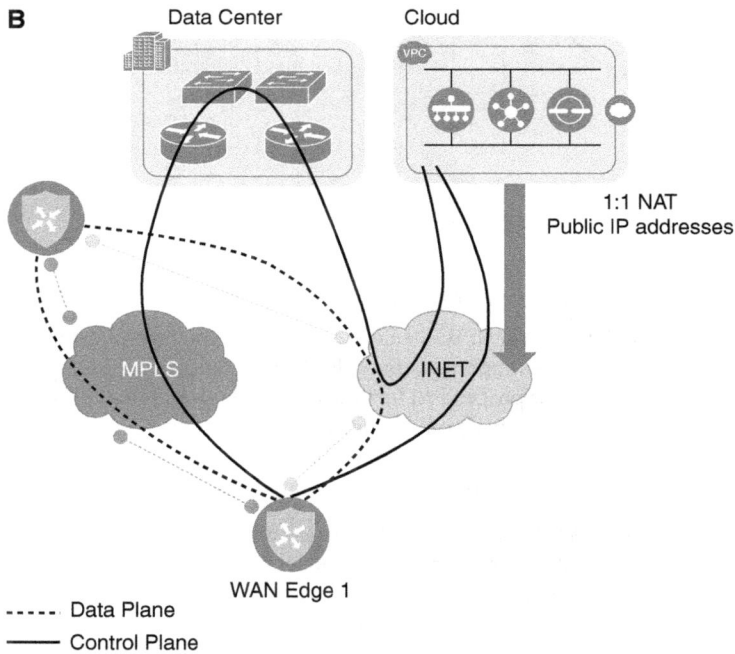

Figure 5-7 *Cloud-Hosted SD-WAN Control Components, Option B*

In Option C, shown in Figure 5-8, the MPLS transport does not provide Internet access. Consequently, WAN Edge routers can only establish connections to SD-WAN Control Components over the Internet transport. Once this connection is built, complete control information, including MPLS TLOCs, is received, enabling the WAN Edge to construct data tunnels over the MPLS transport. However, this setup lacks control plane redundancy. In the event of Internet transport failure, SD-WAN functionality at the site will degrade (for example, the WAN Edge will not receive routing updates), and the site will eventually go down when the IPsec rekey timer expires, the Overlay Management Protocol (OMP) graceful restart timer lapses, or the WAN Edge router is rebooted. This option is therefore the least preferred.

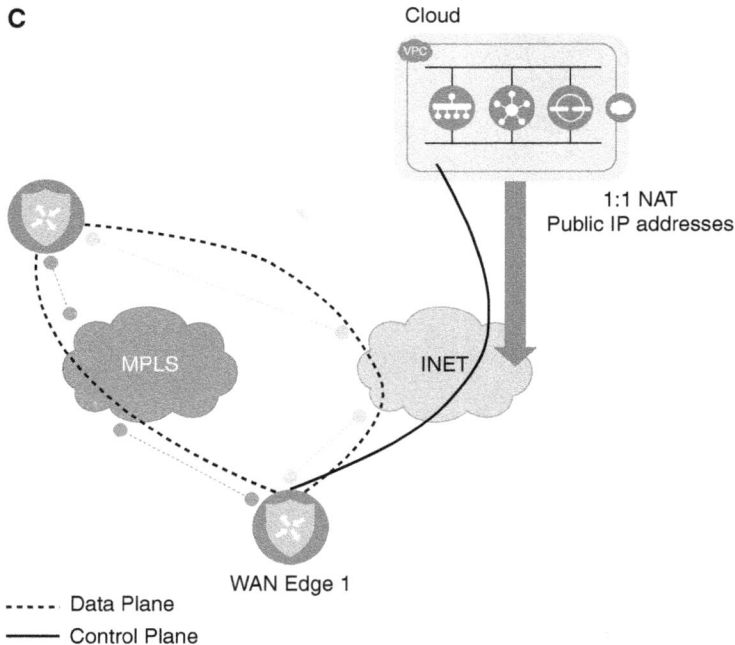

Figure 5-8   *Cloud-Hosted Control Components, Option C*

It is important to note that with default settings, WAN Edge routers will attempt to establish control connections to SD-WAN Control Components over the MPLS transport. If such an attempt is unsuccessful, the router will not proceed to form data tunnels over it, and SD-WAN will not use the transport. To address this, you should set the Maximum Control Connections option for the MPLS tunnel interface to 0. This tells the WAN Edge router that this TLOC is not expected to form control connections but still can build data tunnels.

In a cloud-hosted environment, SD-WAN Control Components are usually placed into a subnet behind a virtual gateway. Each SD-WAN Control Component is assigned a private IP address, and the cloud virtual gateway uses one-to-one NAT to translate that address into a unique public IP address that is accessible from the Internet.

A public color is assigned to the tunnel interfaces of SD-WAN Manager and SD-WAN Controller. This ensures that WAN Edge devices use public IP addresses of SD-WAN Control Components when communicating with them. The actual value of the color is not important and is often left unassigned, resulting in the use of the **default** color, which is public.

SD-WAN Validator is not configured with a tunnel interface, so the concept of color does not apply to it.

When SD-WAN Manager and SD-WAN Controller communicate with SD-WAN Validator, it is important for this interaction to use public IP addresses, even if all Control Components are in the same subnet. This is necessary because SD-WAN Validator needs to learn public IP addresses of other Control Components and relay this information to WAN Edge routers joining the SD-WAN overlay.

To meet this requirement, SD-WAN Manager and SD-WAN Controller are configured with the public IP address of SD-WAN Validator. This way, when they attempt to connect to SD-WAN Validator, the traffic is directed to a virtual gateway. The gateway then translates the private source IP addresses to the public IP addresses of SD-WAN Control Components, ensuring that SD-WAN Validator perceives the traffic as originating from the NAT public IP addresses of SD-WAN Manager and SD-WAN Controller. When SD-WAN Validator responds, it sends the returning traffic via the same virtual gateway where the reverse IP address translation process happens, achieving traffic symmetry.

SD-WAN Manager and SD-WAN Controller can communicate with each other both using private and public IP addresses. This is dictated by their site ID assignment: If the site IDs are the same, SD-WAN Manager and SD-WAN Controller communicate using private IP addresses. On the other hand, if the site IDs are different, Control Components communicate with each other via their NAT public IP addresses. This approach is used in Cisco cloud-hosted deployments.

On-Premises SD-WAN Control Components Deployments

Setting up SD-WAN Control Components on premises involves several considerations related to NAT, color usage, and the choice between public and private IP addresses. This section explores design options using a sample deployment featuring both public (Internet) and private (MPLS) circuits. In this scenario, the Internet TLOC is assigned the public color **biz-internet**, while the MPLS TLOC is assigned the private color **mpls**. In this configuration, control connections are established over both transports, as illustrated in Figure 5-9.

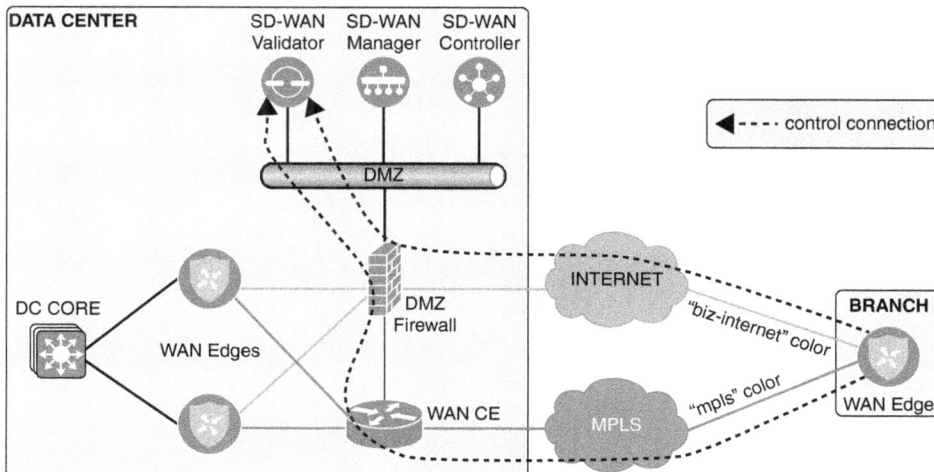

Figure 5-9 *On-Premises SD-WAN Control Components Deployment Example*

In this setup, all SD-WAN Control Components reside within a dedicated DMZ inside the data center. However, alternative deployment scenarios are possible, as long as they ensure connectivity between SD-WAN Control Components in VPN0 and allow SD-WAN Validator to discover the public (post-NAT) IP addresses of SD-WAN Manager and SD-WAN Controller.

To provide consistent connectivity to SD-WAN Control Components over both public and private transports, several IP addressing options are available:

- Public IP addresses:

    - SD-WAN Control Components are assigned public routable IP addresses.

    - Since public IP addresses are unknown within the MPLS cloud, the IP addresses of Control Components (or a default route) must be advertised into the MPLS network from the data center. This ensures that the Control Components are reachable by WAN Edge routers.

- Private IP addresses, mapped via one-to-one NAT to public IP addresses:

    - As in the previous case, post-NAT public IP addresses of SD-WAN Control Components need to be advertised into MPLS.

    - SD-WAN Controller and SD-WAN Manager are configured with a public color, so WAN Edge routers communicate using their public IP addresses over both transports.

    - Much as in cloud-hosted deployments, to facilitate discovery of their public IP addresses, SD-WAN Manager and SD-WAN Controller communicate with SD-WAN Validator using its public IP address. Meanwhile, connectivity between SD-WAN Manager and SD-WAN Controller uses private IP addressing because both are configured with the same site ID, as shown in Figure 5-10.

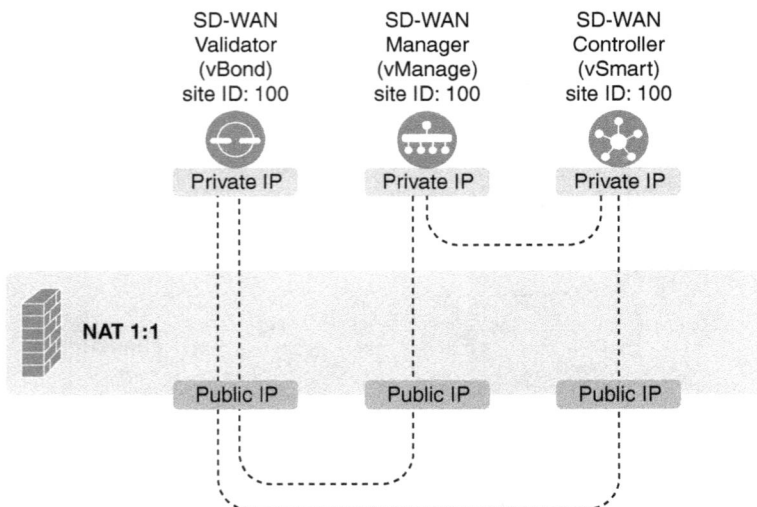

Figure 5-10   *On-Premises SD-WAN Control Components with Private IP Addresses and NAT*

> **NOTE** The firewall should properly implement hairpin NAT so that traffic from SD-WAN Control Components is correctly translated when traversing the firewall, even if the destination is in the same subnet. If this functionality is not supported, SD-WAN Validator may need to be implemented in its own dedicated DMZ.

- Mixed public and private IP addresses:

  - SD-WAN Control Components are assigned private IP addresses that are mapped via NAT to public IP addresses on public transport only.

  - The SD-WAN Validator DNS name is set to resolve to both its public and private IP addresses.

  - SD-WAN Controller and SD-WAN Manager are configured with a private color.

  - Over the Internet transport, WAN Edge devices communicate with the public IP addresses of SD-WAN Control Components because routers are configured with the public **biz-internet** color. (Remember that when one side of a control connection uses a private color and another uses a public color, the control connection is formed using the public IP addresses of devices.)

  - Over the MPLS transport, WAN Edge routers use the private IP addresses of SD-WAN Control Components since both routers and Control Components use private colors.

As you can see, these deployment options offer enough flexibility to tailor the implementation based on the requirements and constraints of specific networks.

SD-WAN Control Components Redundancy and High Availability

In any network setup, a standard best practice is to install redundant components at all levels, including duplicate routers, power supplies, and other components, as well as backup network connections. Similarly, it is important to provide high availability for SD-WAN Control Components. Networks designed for resilience should include redundant SD-WAN Manager, SD-WAN Controller, and SD-WAN Validator instances. By deploying duplicate instances of these SD-WAN Control Components, an organization can ensure uninterrupted operations even in the face of hardware failures, outages, or other unforeseen issues.

SD-WAN Manager Design

To enhance the availability of SD-WAN Manager, you can deploy it in one of the following ways:

- **SD-WAN Manager cluster:** A cluster consists of three or six SD-WAN Manager servers, all operating in active mode. This setup provides protection against a single node failure.

- **Standalone SD-WAN Manager in active/standby mode:** You can use one SD-WAN Manager instance in active mode as the primary with another instance in standby mode as a backup.

■ **SD-WAN Manager cluster in active/standby mode:** You can set up a primary SD-WAN Manager cluster in active mode, with another SD-WAN Manager cluster in standby mode to act as a backup.

When deployed in a cluster, SD-WAN Manager servers assume specific roles based on the services they run. This distribution of roles enables the cluster to balance the workload efficiently and share information among SD-WAN Manager servers. The role of a server in a cluster is determined by its persona. An SD-WAN Manager server can assume any of the following personas:

■ **Compute+Data:** This persona runs all services necessary for SD-WAN Manager, including application server, statistics database, configuration database, messaging server, and coordination server.

■ **Compute:** This persona runs all services except statistics database.

■ **Data:** This persona runs application server and statistics database services.

The persona for SD-WAN Manager is selected the first time that the server boots up after the SD-WAN Manager installation and cannot be changed. When deciding on the persona to configure for a server, note that the following deployments of nodes are the only officially supported combinations for an SD-WAN Manager cluster:

■ Three Compute+Data nodes

■ Three Compute+Data nodes and three Data nodes

If your network requires a different combination of nodes, it is advisable to contact your Cisco representative to validate the deployment.

When planning an SD-WAN Manager cluster, keep the following design considerations in mind:

■ A third interface is required in VPN 0 for communication and synchronization among SD-WAN Manager servers in the cluster. It is recommended to use a 10 Gbps interface for this purpose.

■ Database replication between cluster members requires 4 ms or less delay between cluster members. To achieve this, it's advisable to have all cluster members located at the same site.

■ All control sessions between the WAN Edge routers and SD-WAN Manager application servers are load balanced to optimize performance. A single SD-WAN Manager instance can potentially manage up to 1000 to 1500 routers, depending on the load. If your network exceeds this device count, or if the load is high for a single server, you need to deploy an SD-WAN Manager cluster.

■ A WAN Edge router establishes a single connection to SD-WAN Manager over one of the transports at any given time. You can specify the preferred transport by using the *vManage Connection Preference* setting under the tunnel interface on a WAN Edge, where a higher value indicates a higher preference. For instance, you might use a preference of 5 (default) for a high-bandwidth Internet link, a value of 3 for a lower-bandwidth MPLS link, and a value of 1 on a metered cellular interface to minimize the costs. A 0 value indicates that the tunnel interface will never be used to connect to the SD-WAN Manager. At least one tunnel interface must have a nonzero value.

It's important to recognize that the main purpose of an SD-WAN Manager cluster is scalability. While a cluster offers a level of redundancy against a single SD-WAN Manager failure, it does not protect against cluster-level failures. To achieve full redundancy, you need to deploy either a backup SD-WAN Manager or an SD-WAN Manager cluster in standby mode.

In common disaster recovery scenarios, an active SD-WAN Manager or SD-WAN Manager cluster is located in one data center site along with at least one SD-WAN Validator and SD-WAN Controller, and in a second data center, a standby (inactive) SD-WAN Manager or SD-WAN Manager cluster is deployed, also with at least one active SD-WAN Validator and SD-WAN Controller. The following disaster recovery methods are available:

- **Manual:** The backup SD-WAN Manager server or cluster is kept shut down in a cold standby state. Regular backups of the active database are taken manually, and if the primary SD-WAN Manager or SD-WAN Manager cluster goes down, the standby is brought up manually, and the backup database restored on it. This approach is applicable to both standalone SD-WAN Manager and SD-WAN Manager cluster deployments.

- **Administrator-triggered failover:** This is the recommended approach. In this method, the standby server or cluster is in a warm standby mode, and data is replicated automatically between the primary and secondary SD-WAN Manager instances at regular intervals. When needed, a switchover to the secondary SD-WAN Manager instance is performed manually from the GUI with a simple button click.

SD-WAN Controller Design

In a Cisco SD-WAN network designed for high availability, SD-WAN Controller redundancy is achieved by adding extra SD-WAN Controllers that operate in an active/active fashion. A network can have multiple SD-WAN Controllers (up to 12 have been tested), and each WAN Edge router, by default, connects to 2 of them at a time.

While the configurations on all SD-WAN Controllers must be functionally similar, the control policies must be completely identical. This ensures that, at any time, all WAN Edge devices receive consistent views of the network. The simplest and recommended approach to achieve this is by using SD-WAN Manager to manage SD-WAN Controllers and configure control policies rather than by configuring SD-WAN Controllers through the CLI.

SD-WAN Controllers assume the central control role within the network and maintain it by establishing the following connections:

- A full mesh of permanent DTLS/TLS control connections and OMP sessions among all SD-WAN Controllers to advertise routes, TLOCs, services, policies, and encryption keys. This exchange of information allows the SD-WAN Controllers to remain fully synchronized.

- A permanent DTLS connection to each SD-WAN Validator from each SD-WAN Controller's CPU core. These connections enable SD-WAN Validators to track the presence and operational status of SD-WAN Controllers.

- Permanent DTLS/TLS control connections and OMP sessions with the WAN Edge routers.

These connections keep SD-WAN Controllers constantly aware of any changes in the network topology. In the event of an SD-WAN Controller failure, the remaining SD-WAN Controllers seamlessly take over control of the network. They handle WAN Edge devices joining the network and continue sending route updates to the routers.

Let's review in more detail how WAN Edge routers interoperate with SD-WAN Controllers. When a WAN Edge device comes into the network, it receives a list of all available SD-WAN Controllers from SD-WAN Validator during the registration process; it selects which ones to use and designates them "assigned."

In cases where there are more SD-WAN Controllers in the network than a WAN Edge device is allowed to connect to (two by default), the router selects a subset of SD-WAN Controllers as "assigned." The selection is based on a hash that includes the system IP address of the SD-WAN router. This makes this process deterministic, meaning that WAN Edge routers consistently choose the same set of "assigned" SD-WAN Controllers while introducing enough randomness to ensure that different WAN Edge devices select different "assigned" SD-WAN controllers. This ensures that control connections and OMP sessions are load-balanced across all SD-WAN Controllers.

NOTE   To maximize the efficiency of the load-balancing among SD-WAN Controllers, it is recommended to use sequential numbers when assigning system IP addresses to the WAN Edge routers.

Control connections from WAN Edge routers to an SD-WAN Controller are also load-balanced across different cores on the same SD-WAN Controller. When the SD-WAN Validator sends the list of available SD-WAN Controllers to a WAN Edge router as part of the registration response, it includes only one of the available SD-WAN Controller cores. The SD-WAN Validator determines which core to send within a given registration response to balance control connections across all the cores of a given SD-WAN Controller.

Subsequently, WAN Edge routers establish permanent DTLS/TLS control connections and OMP sessions with the "assigned" SD-WAN Controllers. At this point, WAN Edge devices consider themselves to be in equilibrium if all the expected control connections and OMP sessions are successfully established.

Figure 5-11 illustrates this process. In this example, the WAN Edge router selected SD-WAN Controllers 1 and 3 as "assigned." However, it could have chosen another pair, such as SD-WAN Controllers 1 and 2 or SD-WAN Controllers 3 and 4, if it had a different system IP address.

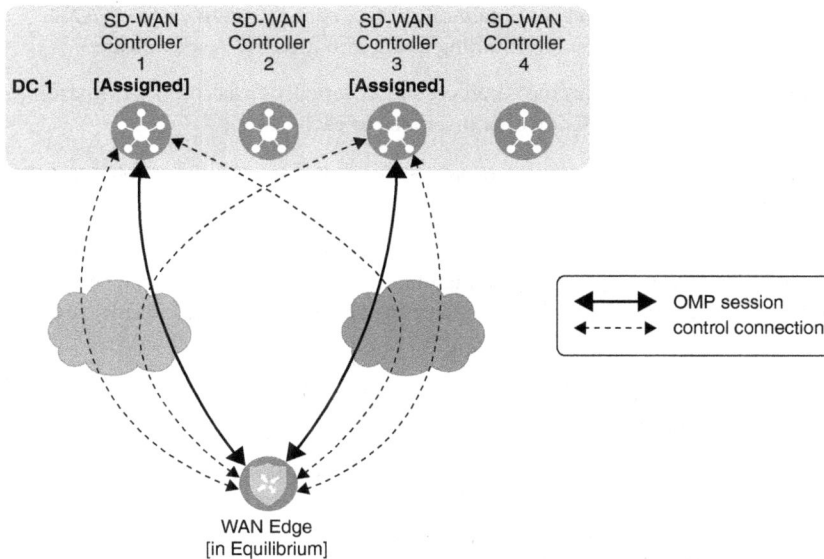

Figure 5-11   *WAN Edge Control Connections to SD-WAN Controllers*

By default, each WAN Edge router establishes DTLS/TLS control connections to two SD-WAN Controllers over each TLOC. This is controlled at the WAN transport tunnel interface level by the Maximum Control Connections setting. Similarly, each router establishes OMP sessions to two SD-WAN Controllers by default. This is controlled by the Maximum OMP Sessions setting in the System Configuration section. It is generally recommended to leave these settings unchanged as defaults, to minimize the number of connections made to the SD-WAN Controllers while still maintaining a good level of redundancy.

If an "assigned" SD-WAN Controller becomes unreachable, the WAN Edge device attempts to establish a connection to one of the remaining SD-WAN Controllers. At this time, it will be in the "out of equilibrium" state, continuously trying to reconnect to the unavailable "assigned" SD-WAN Controller to regain equilibrium. This way, when the "assigned" SD-WAN Controller comes back online, it restores all its previous sessions with WAN Edge routers, effectively rebalancing connections among SD-WAN Controllers.

As your network expands and more SD-WAN Controllers are added, you might need better control over which SD-WAN Controllers your WAN Edge routers connect to. Consider the following scenarios:

■ In geographically distributed networks, you may prefer to use local SD-WAN Controllers for better performance, with a backup available in more distant regions for redundancy.

■ When deploying multiple SD-WAN Controllers in separate data centers, you may want all your WAN Edge devices to connect to one SD-WAN Controller in one data center and one SD-WAN Controller in another during normal operations. In the event of a data center outage, all routers maintain one active connection to an SD-WAN Controller in a surviving data center, avoiding going into graceful restart mode.

■ You might want to group devices based on certain criteria (such as site type or size) and allocate specific SD-WAN Controller instances to each group.

SD-WAN Controller affinity allows you to manage scale and exercise control over which SD-WAN Controllers your WAN Edge routers connect to.

To participate in affinity, each SD-WAN Controller must be assigned a controller group identifier with the **controller-group-id** *number* command in the System Configuration section. SD-WAN Controllers in the same data center can have the same controller group identifier or different identifiers:

■ If SD-WAN Controllers share the same identifier, WAN Edge routers establish a control connection with any one of them.

■ If SD-WAN Controllers have different controller group identifiers, WAN Edge routers can designate one SD-WAN Controller as the preferred and the other(s) as a backup. This design, while offering redundancy among SD-WAN Controllers in a data center, also provides more granular control and additional fault isolation.

Configuring SD-WAN Controller affinity on a WAN Edge device is a two-part process:

■ At the system level, configure a list of affinity groups that the WAN Edge router belongs to in the Controller Groups setting. The router attempts to form connections to controller groups in the list sequentially, starting with the first group, so IDs should be entered in order of preference. It is recommended that this list contain all the controller groups in the overlay network. The total number of established sessions will be limited by the numbers set for the Maximum Control Connections and Maximum OMP Sessions settings.

■ Optionally, for each tunnel interface, exclude non-preferred controller groups with the Exclude Controller Group List setting. A WAN Edge router will make a connection to the excluded controller group(s) only as a last resort, when no other preferred controller groups are available. This helps avoid complete loss of connectivity to the SD-WAN network.

Figure 5-12 provides an example of how SD-WAN Controller affinity can be implemented in an SD-WAN deployment featuring two active data centers, with the third one designated for disaster recovery purposes.

In this example, a WAN Edge router first attempts to establish connections with SD-WAN Controllers in groups 1 and 2 over each transport. If group 1 becomes unavailable, the router will then attempt connections with the next group in the Controller Group list, which is group 4, bypassing group 3 due to its exclusion with the Exclude Controller Group List setting, and so forth. However, if no other controller groups are available, as a last resort, the router will try to connect to the excluded SD-WAN Controller in group 3 to avoid disconnection from the SD-WAN overlay.

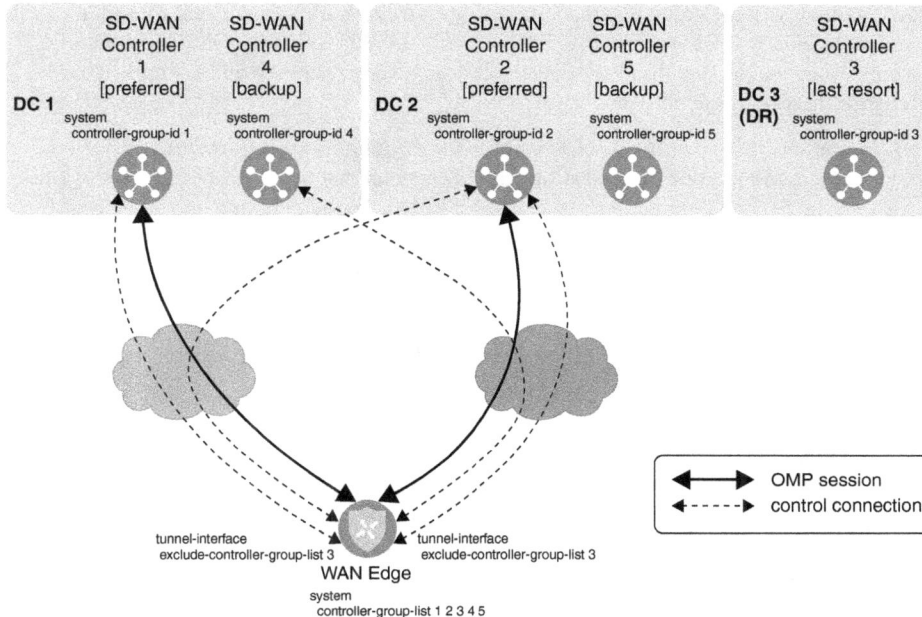

Figure 5-12 *SD-WAN Controller Affinity in a Dual Data Center Deployment with DR*

To monitor SD-WAN Controller association and affinity status on a WAN Edge router, you can use the **show sdwan control affinity config** and **show sdwan control affinity status** commands.

NOTE For an in-depth examination of SD-WAN Controller affinity design, we recommend referring to the "Cisco Catalyst SD-WAN Large Global WAN Design Case Study" and the "Cisco Catalyst SD-WAN High Availability Configuration Guide" documents, published on the Cisco documentation site. These resources provide comprehensive information beyond what we can cover in this book.

SD-WAN Validator Design

SD-WAN Validator plays a pivotal role in the Cisco SD-WAN overlay network, performing the following essential functions:

- Authenticating and validating all SD-WAN Controllers and WAN Edge routers attempting to join the SD-WAN network

- Facilitating the establishment of control connections between WAN Edge routers and the SD-WAN Manager for centralized management and configuration

- Orchestrating control plane connections between the SD-WAN Controllers and WAN Edge devices

- Serving as a STUN server to assist WAN Edge routers in determining their public IP addresses and establishing tunnels between them, even when they are located behind NAT devices

SD-WAN Validator runs as a virtual machine using a vEdge Cloud image, and due to its important role, it is advisable to deploy at least two SD-WAN Validators in your network. This ensures that one of them is always available whenever a router or an SD-WAN Controller is attempting to join the network.

vEdge Cloud learns its role as an SD-WAN Validator through its configuration when the **system vbond** command includes the **local** option. In this command, you also specify the local IP address of the SD-WAN Validator's interface in VPN0. The same command is used on SD-WAN Managers, SD-WAN Controllers, and WAN Edge routers to specify SD-WAN Validator orchestrator(s) for the SD-WAN network. Note that on WAN Edge routers managed by SD-WAN Manager, this command is not directly configurable. Instead, it is added to the configuration automatically by SD-WAN Manager with the value from the Validator (formerly vBond) setting in the Administration section of SD-WAN Manager.

In a network that has a single SD-WAN Validator, you can specify it either as an IP address or as a DNS name (such as validator.ciscopress.com). However, in networks with two or more SD-WAN Validators, the only option to use them is through a DNS name. The name is resolved to multiple IP addresses, and a router (or SD-WAN Controller) sequentially tries each IP address until a successful connection is established. Note that an external DNS server is not a requirement for an SD-WAN Validator DNS name resolution, as hostnames can be defined locally, as demonstrated in Example 5-1.

Example 5-1 *SD-WAN Validator Configuration Example (Configuration Snippets)*

```
vBond-1:
system
 vbond 209.165.201.12 local
```

```
vBond-2:
system
 vbond 209.165.201.13 local
```

```
vSmart-1:
system
 vbond validator.ciscopress.com
vpn 0
 host validator.ciscopress.com ip 209.165.201.12 209.165.201.13
```

```
BR1-Edge1:
system
 vbond validator.ciscopress.com
 !
ip host validator.ciscopress.com 209.165.201.12 209.165.201.13
```

NOTE Even when your SD-WAN network has only a single SD-WAN Validator, using a DNS name instead of an IP address is recommended as a best practice. This approach makes configuration more scalable. For example:

■ No configuration changes are needed on the network devices if additional SD-WAN Validators are introduced to the network.

■ In large geographically distributed networks, regional DNS names can be used to point to local SD-WAN Validator orchestrators.

In a network that has multiple SD-WAN Validators, each operates independently and is not even aware of the presence of other SD-WAN Validators. If one SD-WAN Validator fails, the remaining orchestrators simply continue to operate, handling all requests from Cisco devices attempting to join the network. As long as at least one SD-WAN Validator is operational in the domain, the SD-WAN network can continue operating without interruption because WAN Edge routers and SD-WAN Controllers can still locate each other and join the network.

From the control plane perspective, each SD-WAN Validator maintains permanent connections to each SD-WAN Manager and SD-WAN Controller. This ensures an up-to-date view of the network, preventing SD-WAN Validator from providing the IP address of an unavailable control component to devices joining the network. There are no control connections between SD-WAN Validators themselves, and no state is kept between them.

NOTE It is commonly thought that WAN Edge routers only establish transient control connections to SD-WAN Validator orchestrators when they join the network. However, there is a scenario when these connections become persistent.

When WAN Edge routers are unable to connect to at least one of their "assigned" SD-WAN Controllers due to issues like downtime, they enter the "out of equilibrium" state. In response, routers establish a persistent DTLS control connection from each of their TLOC to an SD-WAN Validator instance. This helps the WAN Edge devices determine whether the "assigned" SD-WAN Controller instances have been administratively removed from the network or are merely temporarily unavailable, meaning that routers should continue trying to connect to them. This strategy ensures that if the SD-WAN Controllers are down only temporarily, WAN Edge routers will reconnect to the same SD-WAN Controller instances once they are eventually back online. This approach prevents the permanent shift of load to a smaller number of SD-WAN Controller instances over time, which could happen in large-scale deployments due to failures, maintenance, or upgrades of SD-WAN Controllers.

WAN Edge routers maintain these connections with SD-WAN Validators until either the failed SD-WAN Controller comes back online or is removed from the SD-WAN network by a network administrator. It is important to understand this behavior when you're doing SD-WAN Validator capacity planning. For example, in a balanced dual data center design (similar to the one shown on Figure 5-12), a data center outage would lead to every WAN Edge device losing a control connection to one of its "assigned" SD-WAN Controllers. This

5

would result in all routers in the network establishing permanent, long-lived connections to SD-WAN Validators in the operational data center from each of their TLOCs. To handle such scenarios, it is crucial to provision enough SD-WAN Validators in each data center not only to handle all these long-lived connections but also to continue providing standard SD-WAN Validator services to devices attempting to join the network.

Note that SD-WAN Validators never participate in the data plane of the overlay network. Therefore, the failure of any SD-WAN Validator has no impact on data traffic.

SD-WAN Control Components Scalability

When designing a large Cisco SD-WAN network, it is important to be mindful of the capacity and scalability limitations of SD-WAN Control Components:

- **SD-WAN Manager:** Deployment options for SD-WAN Manager range from standalone nodes to 3- or 6-node clustered setups. A single instance can potentially handle up to 1000 to 1500 devices, while a 6-node SD-WAN Manager cluster may support up to 12,500 devices. However, the actual number of supported devices may vary significantly depending on factors such as SD-WAN Manager resources (instances/CPU/RAM/storage), the volume of generated statistics, and the version of the SD-WAN software. If the number of devices in the network exceeds the supported scale, another SD-WAN overlay may need to be considered.

- **SD-WAN Controller:** A single SD-WAN Controller can handle up to 5000 control connections and 2500 OMP sessions. The maximum number of tested SD-WAN Controller instances in a single Cisco SD-WAN overlay is 12.

  While two SD-WAN Controllers usually offer sufficient redundancy in many deployments, larger networks might need more SD-WAN Controllers, along with the use of affinity features.

  In a Multi-Region Fabric setup, SD-WAN Controllers can be configured to serve all regions. Alternatively, designated SD-WAN Controllers may be added and assigned to specific regions (both core and access), as needed.

- **SD-WAN Validator:** Each SD-WAN Validator supports up to 4000 connections, and up to eight SD-WAN Validators have been tested in a single Cisco SD-WAN domain. SD-WAN Validators can be oversubscribed under normal conditions as routers joining the network only make transient connections to SD-WAN Validator. However, additional SD-WAN Validators may be required to handle permanent long-lived connections from WAN Edge routers when they are out of equilibrium.

NOTE   All the scaling and sizing numbers discussed in this chapter are specific to Version 20.12 of the SD-WAN software. However, these numbers may vary depending on factors such as allocated resources, load, and the version of SD-WAN software in use. For more accurate specifications, please refer to the "Recommended Computing Resources for Cisco Catalyst SD-WAN Control Components" document for the SD-WAN software version you are using or are planning to use, available on the Cisco website.

Figure 5-13 summarizes these numbers.

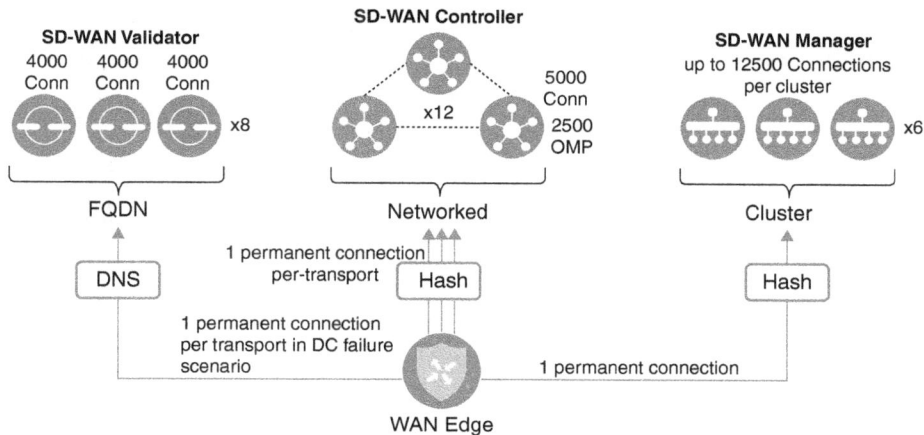

Figure 5-13 *Cisco SD-WAN Control Component Scalability*

Note that in a large-scale deployment, you may need to provide more resources to virtual machines running your SD-WAN Control Component instances. When designing an SD-WAN network, refer to the "Release Notes for Cisco Catalyst SD-WAN Control Components" and "Cisco Catalyst SD-WAN Control Components Compatibility Matrix and Recommended Computing Resources" documents, published on the Cisco website. These documents provide guidance on server resource requirements for SD-WAN Control Components, as well as the maximum number of devices supported in a specific software release, along with other considerations.

SD-WAN Control Components Sizing Exercise

Let's estimate an SD-WAN Control Components deployment for an imaginary network that has two data centers and 4000 sites in the following setup:

■ 1000 small sites, served by one router with two transports (two TLOC routes per router)

■ 1000 medium sites, with two routers with one MPLS and one Internet transport in each (two TLOCs per router)

■ 1000 large sites, with two routers with one MPLS and one Internet transport in each (Transports are extended between routers for increased availability; therefore, each router is configured with four TLOCs.)

■ SD-WAN Application Intelligence Engine (SAIE) enabled

■ Cisco SD-WAN Release 20.12

Without data center routers, this network has 5000 WAN Edge routers and 13,000 TLOCs, as summarized in Table 5-2. Routers are using the defaults of two OMP sessions and two control connections per TLOC.

Table 5-2   SD-WAN Control Components Sizing Example

Site Type	Number of Sites	Number of Routers per Site	Total Number of Routers	Number of TLOCs per Router	Number of TLOCs per Site	Total Number of TLOCs
Small	1000	1	1000	1	1	1000
Medium	1000	2	2000	2	4	4000
Large	1000	2	2000	4	8	8000
Total			5000			13,000

This network needs to be designed as fully redundant and should remain fully operational in the event of a data center outage. To meet these requirements, the following considerations apply to the SD-WAN Control Components:

■ SD-WAN Manager should support 5000 devices. Therefore, based on the "Recommended Computing Resources for Cisco Catalyst SD-WAN Control Components Release 20.12.x" document, this design will require a 6-node SD-WAN Manager cluster for each data center.

■ SD-WAN Controllers should support 10,000 OMP sessions (two per router) and 26,000 control connections (two per TLOC). That translates to 10,000/2500 = 4 SD-WAN Controllers to handle all OMP sessions and 26,000/5000 = 5.2 SD-WAN Controllers to handle all control connections. Rounding up, that is 6 SD-WAN Controllers in each data center.

■ SD-WAN Validator orchestrators should support 13,000 long-lived control connections in a data center failure scenario (one per TLOC). That translates into 4 SD-WAN Validators per data center (rounding up from 13,000/4000 = 3.25).

Based on these calculations, SD-WAN Control Components for this network should be deployed as follows:

■ **Data Center 1:** Active 6-node SD-WAN Manager cluster, six SD-WAN Controllers, and four SD-WAN Validator orchestrators

■ **Data Center 2:** Standby 6-node SD-WAN Manager cluster, six SD-WAN Controllers, and four SD-WAN Validator orchestrators

This exercise is just a high-level example. In real life, other considerations apply, such as sizing of the SD-WAN Control Components or statistics and route scale requirements. Therefore, for SD-WAN Control Components design in large networks, it is recommended to reach out to Cisco and validate the design before deployment.

Cisco SD-WAN Implementation Preparation

Once the design is finalized, the next crucial step for successful Cisco SD-WAN enablement is implementation planning. Thorough planning ensures success throughout all stages of SD-WAN implementation, including data center deployment, branch deployment, and policy configuration, as well as post-implementation day-to-day operations. The following are some of the most important preparations to make before starting the implementation:

■ **Create a system IP address structure:** A system IP address, a mandatory configuration element in Cisco SD-WAN, is a system-level IPv4 address that uniquely identifies the device. It acts much like a router ID, and it is not advertised or known by the underlay. However, best practice recommends assigning this system IP address to a loopback interface and advertising it within one of the service VPNs. It can then be used as a source IP address for SNMP and logging, making it easier to correlate network events with SD-WAN Manager information.

It is recommended to develop a logical scheme for system IP addresses to make sites more easily recognizable.

■ **Develop site ID scheme:** A site ID, another mandatory configuration element in Cisco SD-WAN, serves as a unique identifier of a site within the SD-WAN overlay network, with a numeric range from 1 to 4294967295. The site ID must be the same for all the Cisco SD-WAN devices that reside at the same site, where a "site" is a physical or virtual location within an organization's network infrastructure, like a branch office, data center, or cloud instance.

A site ID scheme should be chosen carefully to streamline the policy application. Centralized policies are applied to blocks of sites, defined as a list or range of site IDs (for example, 100,200–299), without wildcard support. To make an SD-WAN network more scalable, it is recommended to use ranges to group together sites with similar policies. This way, adding a new site with a site ID that falls into the matching range of policy will automatically cause the policy to be applied to it.

Table 5-3 provides an example of a six-digit site ID scheme suitable for a global organization with two data centers and two types of sites. In this example, policies specific to data centers in US/Canada West are applied to the site ID range 110000–110999. Policies specific to Type A sites in US/Canada East are applied to the site ID range 121000–121999. Policies specific to all Type B sites in all locations are applied to the site ID list that includes all the regional Type B sites ranges: [112000–112999, 122000–122999, 202000–202999, 302000–302999].

Table 5-3   Cisco SD-WAN Site ID Scheme Example

Digit	Representation	Values
First	Continent	1=North America, 2=Europe, 3=Africa
Second	Region	0=unused, 1=US/Canada West, 2=US/Canada East
Third	Site type	0=Data Center/Hub, 1=Site Type A, 2=Site Type B
Fourth through sixth	Site/store number	001, 002, 003, etc.

The example sites are grouped together based on their geography, which is helpful in cases where you might want to prefer a regional data center over another. These are some of the other potential grouping criteria:

■ Sites that access the Internet via a centrally located firewall versus those using Direct Internet Access

■ Sites with low-end routers and sites with more powerful devices (Low-end routers support only a handful of SD-WAN tunnels and require a hub-and-spoke topology, while sites with higher-end routers may use a full-mesh topology.)

■ Different SLA and transport requirements, such as certain sites using MPLS for all the traffic, with the Internet circuit serving only as backup, and some sites using MPLS for voice only while routing everything else through the Internet circuit

You can have overlapping types, but the general idea is to put them in categories that makes it easier to apply policy from a configuration perspective. It is strongly recommended to review the requirements and required policies before assigning site IDs.

■ **Design Cisco SD-WAN policy:** Cisco SD-WAN policy dictates the groups of interest (prefix lists, site lists, and so on), network topology, traffic engineering, overlay routing, application-aware routing, security posture, quality of service classification, application visibility, and more. Prior to implementation, the Cisco SD-WAN policy should be fully thought out so that sites rolling onto the fabric inherit the policy and adhere to it immediately. A well-constructed and well-executed policy will ensure that the implementation is smooth and that post-implementation performance is high.

■ **Collect physical and logical diagrams for data center and branch sites:** To have a good understanding of the existing architecture at data centers and branch sites, it is important to collect up-to-date physical and logical diagrams. This way, you can ensure that there is sufficient power, cooling, rack space, and port density, and you can visualize how the WAN Edge routers will be connected to the existing network.

■ **Collect existing device configurations:** Collecting and reviewing the existing device configurations ensures that all considerations have been made around Cisco SD-WAN feature support and enablement. You don't want to realize, in the middle of a site turnup, that a specific feature you were using prior to the Cisco SD-WAN migration is not yet supported or that you have not made provisions to ensure that the feature would still function as designed after the migration.

■ **Analyze existing topology, routing, and traffic engineering:** Having a good understanding of existing routing and traffic engineering in the network will allow you insert Cisco SD-WAN into the network with ease. It will allow you to determine if anything needs to be changed during the migration or if a specific consideration needs to be made to ensure that the same network behaviors exist post-migration. This might include topology design, data center affinity configuration, equal-cost multipath routing, high availability configuration, and failover behavior.

- **Allocate new physical and logical network resources:** If there are new WAN Edge routers added to the network (for example, in data centers), physical connectivity will need to be provided for the LAN and WAN. New subnets and IP addresses will need to be allocated for transit and management networking. Planning this ahead of time will allow you to scale consistently and contiguously.

- **Prepare integration with the existing infrastructure:** It is important to plan the integration process to ensure interoperability and a smooth transition from current setups to the SD-WAN environment.

- **Plan application performance management:** You need to classify applications in the network (for example, real-time, business-critical, standard, or best-effort) and understand their SLAs regarding packet loss, latency, and jitter tolerance. Consider whether applications have a preferred transport (for example, MPLS for voice) and plan for the scenarios where the preferred transport is unavailable or SLAs are not met.

- **Review QoS requirements:** If necessary, establish QoS policies across the SD-WAN to ensure that critical applications receive the bandwidth and priority they require.

Cisco SD-WAN Transport Connectivity

As detailed in previous chapters, a WAN Edge router has a transport-side VPN and a service-side VPN that need to be integrated into the existing network. For the transport side, Cisco highly recommends that all WAN Edge routers have connectivity into all available transports at a site in order for high availability and for application-aware routing to work optimally.

Transport Connectivity: Single-Router Sites

The most common way to integrate transport-side connections on a WAN Edge router into the network is by dedicating a single interface in VPN 0 for each carrier/transport. Routing can be as simple as a default route to the next-hop carrier edge equipment or gateway. The only requirement is that the IP address of the WAN Edge router transport interface must be reachable on that particular underlay.

One way to leverage an existing MPLS transport as a part of the Cisco SD-WAN overlay could be by connecting a VPN 0 interface directly to the MPLS CE router over a /30 transit network. A static default route toward that MPLS CE router is configured, and the MPLS CE router must advertise that transit network into the underlay.

Leveraging an Internet transport is nearly an identical process, except that the VPN 0 interface can connect to an existing DMZ or Internet edge firewall. It can be provided either a public or private IP address on a larger subnet, and it might or might not be behind NAT. Figure 5-14 details this type of connectivity.

NOTE   If NAT is required in order to provide connectivity to the Internet for the WAN Edge router, it is recommended to configure static one-to-one NAT whenever possible to avoid tunnel bring-up issues that might occur in some scenarios.

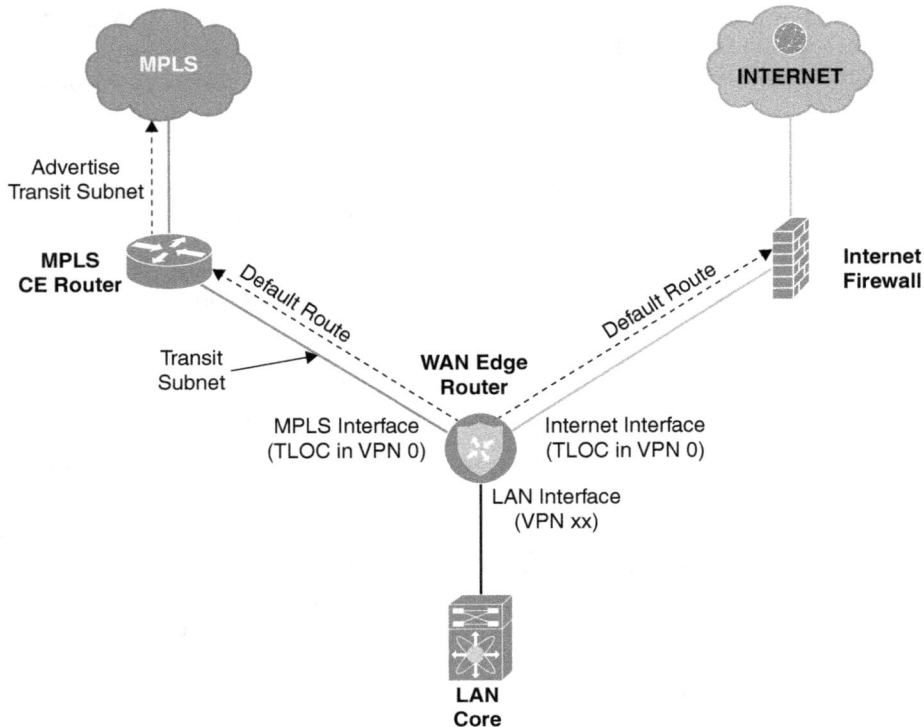

Figure 5-14   *Direct Transport Connectivity*

Indirect switched connectivity to transports is also an option and can be accomplished through the use of VLANs and dedicated interfaces or subinterfaces. In the example shown in Figure 5-15, the MPLS CE router and Internet firewall are physically connected to L2 ports on the LAN core, where three VLANs are provisioned: VLAN 10 for the LAN service-side connection, VLAN 20 for the MPLS transport connection, and VLAN 30 for the Internet transport connection. On the WAN Edge router, the subinterfaces for the MPLS and Internet transport connections share the same physical interface with the service-side link to the LAN core instead of using separate dedicated interfaces, minimizing the number of interfaces used. Routing to the MPLS CE router and Internet edge firewall remains the same as in the directly connected design.

In certain scenarios, a transport may not be exclusively dedicated to SD-WAN. For example, this could occur when Internet access at the data center is centralized and shared by all applications, including SD-WAN, or during a migration to Cisco SD-WAN when existing MPLS transport is used by both SD-WAN and legacy networks, and the MPLS CE router cannot be reconfigured to accommodate SD-WAN. In such cases, indirect routed connectivity may be used, where a WAN Edge device routes via another device(s), typically in the LAN core, to reach the appropriate transport, as illustrated in Figure 5-16.

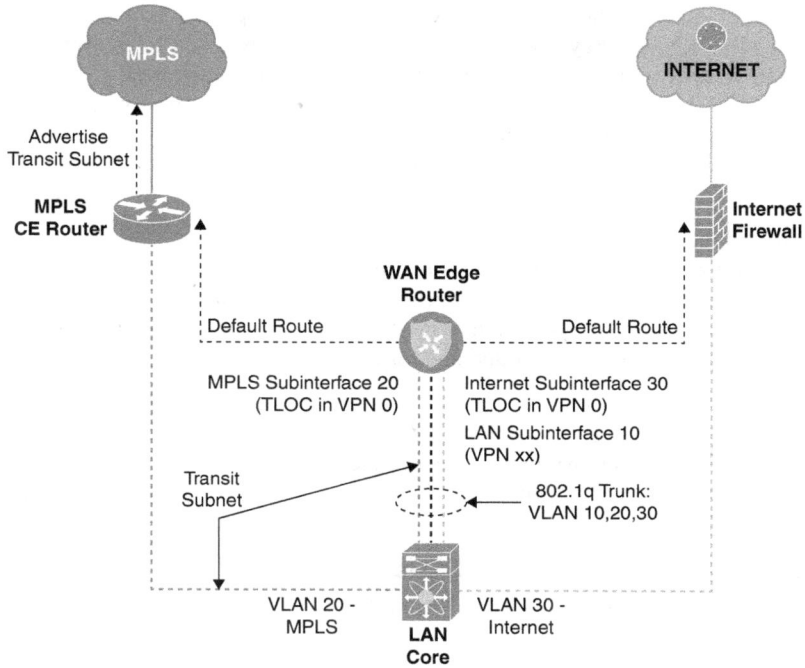

Figure 5-15   *Indirect Switched Transport-Side Connectivity*

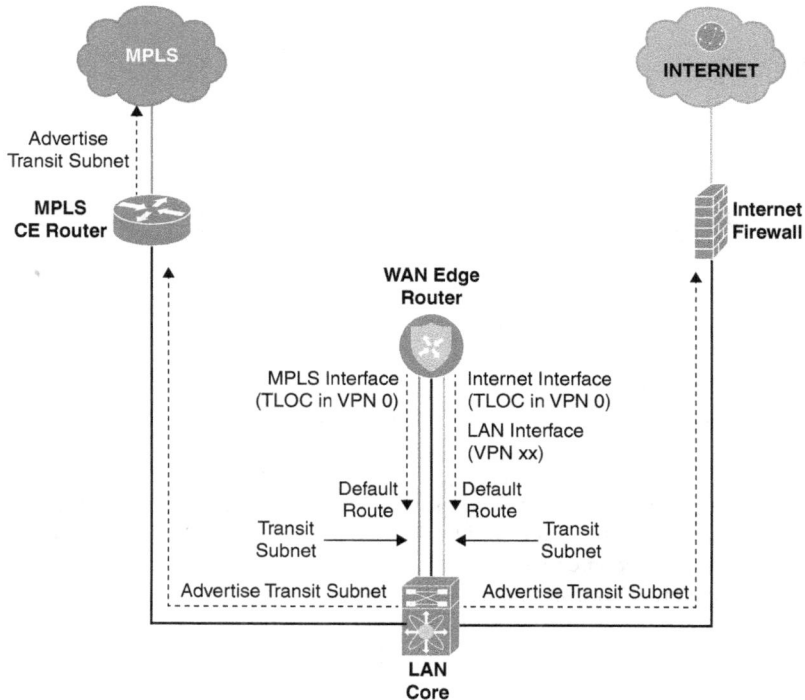

Figure 5-16   *Indirect Routed Transport-Side Connectivity*

However, this approach requires meticulous planning to prevent routing loops and route leaking between the SD-WAN underlay and overlay. Furthermore, there might be multiple redundant paths in the LAN core to reach the MPLS CE router or Internet firewall. Consequently, when Cisco SD-WAN measures path characteristics and evaluates performance, the results may be unpredictable, potentially impacting the efficiency of SD-WAN traffic handling. Therefore, this approach is the least preferred, and, if implemented, should be planned very carefully.

When implementing indirect routed transport connectivity, or in some other cases where underlay path manipulation or traffic engineering is required, enabling dynamic routing on a VPN 0 transport interface may be necessary. In such scenarios, a routing protocol such as BGP or OSPF can be configured in order for the router to learn more specific prefixes, and traditional route policies can be applied inbound and outbound.

> **NOTE**   When using a routing protocol on VPN 0 to gain access to the underlay, it is important to ensure that the correct and optimal path to peer tunnel endpoints for that particular transport is followed through the local network.

Transport Connectivity: Dual-Routers Sites

When deploying two WAN Edge routers at a site, one approach is to reuse single-router designs.

Figure 5-17 illustrates how direct transport connectivity may be implemented in a dual WAN Edge deployment, providing two options.

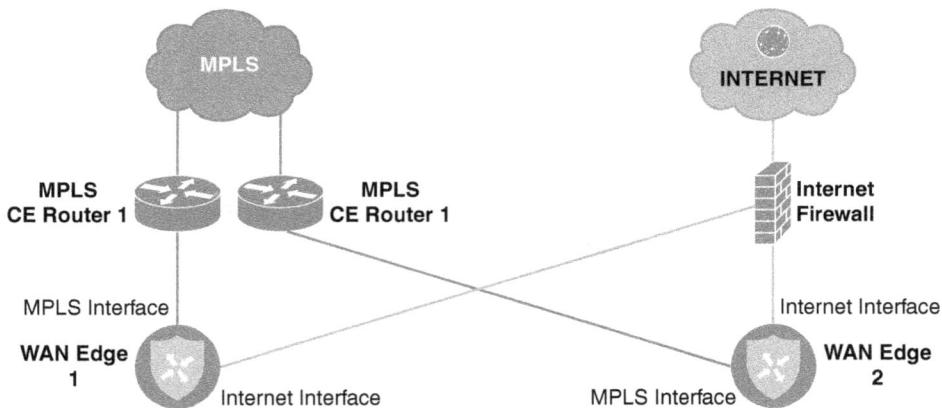

Figure 5-17   *Direct Transport-Side Connectivity with Dual Routers*

The first option, shown for MPLS transport, is to provision an additional MPLS CE router, with both WAN Edge routers directly connected to their own independent MPLS transports. This approach is suitable for environments where high availability is paramount, such as in the medical or financial sectors. However, it is generally not preferable due to increased costs.

For Internet transport, an additional port is provisioned on the Internet firewall. While simpler to implement, this method still requires an extra port on the firewall and additional cabling work. If this presents a challenge, an alternative is to use indirect switched connectivity, as illustrated in Figure 5-18.

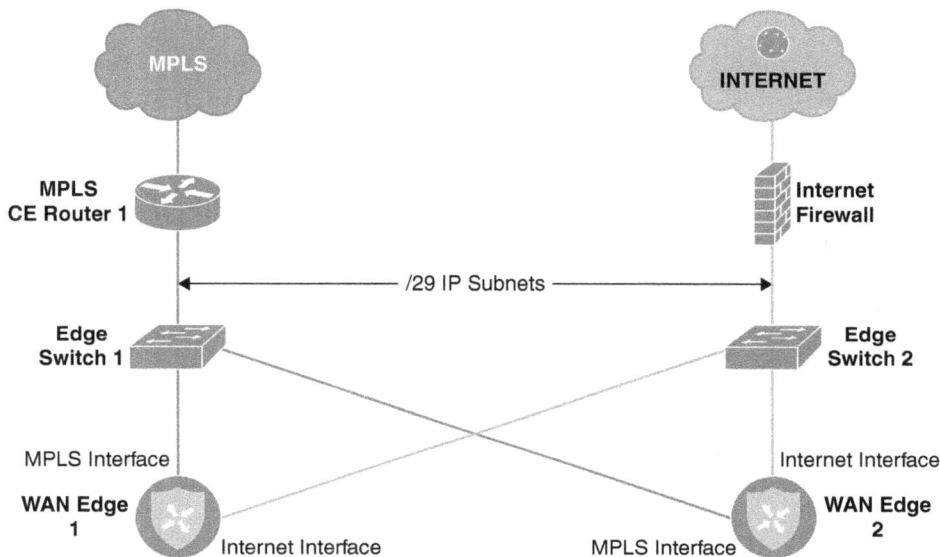

Figure 5-18 *Indirect Switched Transport-Side Connectivity with Dual Routers*

In this setup, interfaces of the transport gateway (the MPLS CE router or Internet firewall) and both WAN Edge routers are in the same VLAN and IP subnet. This configuration may be acceptable if switching infrastructure is already available but may require additional investment if not.

The bigger challenge is the need to increase the size of the transit network to /29 instead of /30 to accommodate all three devices in the same IP subnet; this needs to be negotiated with the MPLS provider.

TLOC Extensions

It is a very common scenario to have only a single physical handoff and a single IP address on a given transport and yet still need to have that transport terminated into two WAN Edge routers. In this scenario, public color and private color TLOC extensions can be used to meet the requirement.

A *TLOC extension* is a direct or indirect connection between two WAN Edge routers that extends a locally terminated TLOC to a peer router. This allows a WAN Edge router to leverage a non-locally connected transport as a part of the Cisco SD-WAN overlay. Figure 5-19 shows TLOC extensions configured between two WAN Edge routers.

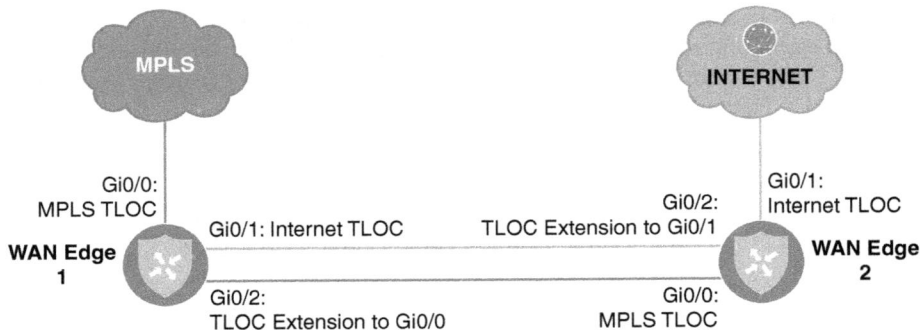

Figure 5-19 *TLOC Extension Dedicated Interfaces*

Multiple TLOCs can be extended from one WAN Edge router to another, but each TLOC extension requires its own dedicated interface on each router. In scenarios where there are not enough physical interfaces available, it is acceptable, if bandwidth allows, to use sub-interfaces on a physical interface to configure TLOC extensions. This can be done either directly between two routers or through a LAN core.

In addition, WAN Edge routers support Layer 3 TLOC extension via GRE. This removes the requirement for the routers to have direct Layer 2 adjacency to one another. Hence, they can be geographically separated (as might be the case in a campus environment with multiple data centers).

When extending a private color via TLOC extension, you need to allocate a new enterprise routable transit network for the connection between WAN Edge routers and ensure that it is reachable from the service provider's network. One way to achieve this is to ask the service provider to configure all the necessary routes statically. Alternatively, you can configure a dynamic routing protocol in VPN 0 on the router extending the locally connected private transport, peering with the service provider to advertise reachability of the new transit net-work. A route policy can be configured to filter inbound and outbound routes so that only the transit network is advertised out, and no other networks are learned. Remember that in most cases, a default route toward the service provider is all that is needed for tunnel build-ing and control plane connectivity.

The WAN Edge router receiving the extension is not aware of anything different and config-ures its end of the extension as a standard private TLOC with a default route pointing toward the adjacent next-hop IP address on the newly created transit network. Figure 5-20 high-lights the private TLOC extension.

> **NOTE** It is important to ensure that the WAN Edge router receiving the extension is able to build control connections through the peer by allowing the transit network to be learned by the data center (if the SD-WAN Control Components reside there) or is allowed through the Internet edge firewall, where it can egress to reach the cloud SD-WAN Control Components.

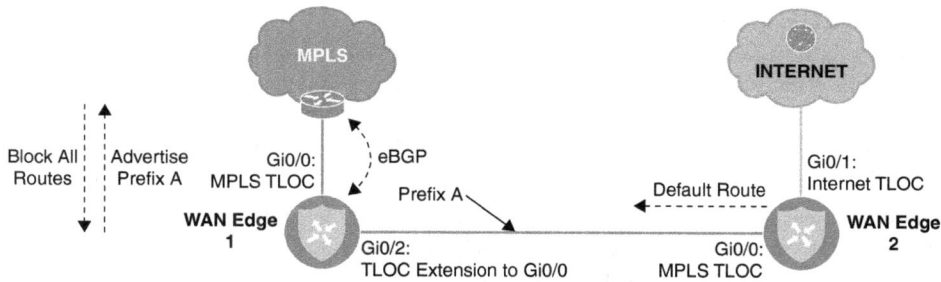

Figure 5-20   *Private TLOC Extension*

Extending a public color via TLOC extension is configured a bit differently than extending private TLOC extensions. For a public TLOC extension, it is necessary to enable NAT on the egress interface toward the transport on the router extending the public transport, if it's not already enabled. NAT facilitates private-to-public mapping, allowing WAN Edge routers to communicate with other remote sites and SD-WAN Control Components without needing to advertise the private transit network. This enables the allocation of any locally significant private transit network between WAN Edge routers to build connectivity.

As with a private TLOC extension, the WAN Edge router receiving the extension is not aware of anything different and configures its end of the extension as a standard public TLOC with a default route pointing toward the adjacent peer's next-hop IP address on the newly created transit network. Figure 5-21 shows an example of a public TLOC extension.

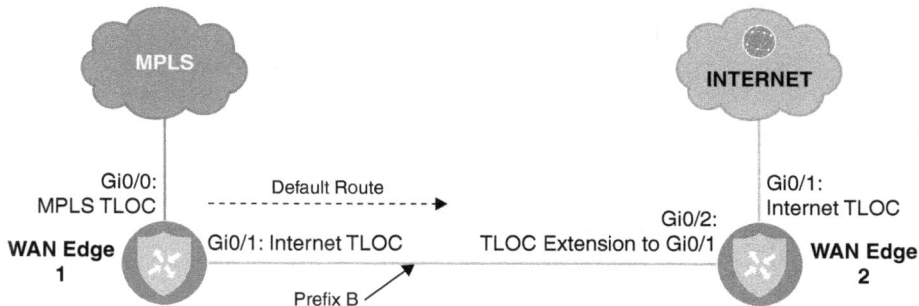

Figure 5-21   *Public TLOC Extension*

NOTE   Depending on your branch design, it is not always necessary to mutually extend TLOCs between WAN Edge routers. In an active/backup branch setup, extending a transport from the primary to the secondary WAN Edge router is redundant because the secondary backup router only becomes active when the primary goes offline. Therefore, when the secondary WAN Edge router is active, a path via the primary router is unavailable and cannot be used anyway. To implement this design, it is simpler to terminate the MPLS circuit on the primary WAN Edge router and the Internet circuit on the secondary WAN Edge router and extend it to the primary, as shown in Figure 5-21. This approach eliminates the need to manage routing for the transit network between routers.

Loopback TLOC Design

In some advanced topologies, an organization may want to leverage multiple CE routers and circuits to the same service provider for overlay connectivity and may also want to retain granular path selection and control via Cisco SD-WAN policy. Because a single transport color cannot be used twice by the same WAN Edge router, alternative TLOC designs involving Loopback interfaces exist to meet these requirements.

A loopback interface can be configured as a conventional TLOC and be advertised toward both CE routers via two connections (one to each CE). This way, both CE routers can reach the Cisco SD-WAN tunnel endpoint configured on the loopback, and the WAN Edge router can reach the underlay via both CE routers. The drawback to this solution is that it requires additional routing complexity. In addition, because there is only a single color configured, path selection granularity via Cisco SD-WAN policy is also limited.

Two modes exist for the loopback design: bind mode and the unbind mode. In bind mode, the loopback interface is bound to a physical interface, and traffic destined to the loopback interface will be carried to and from the mapped physical interface. This design can be used when you have connected subnets on the transport side and want to use a loopback to form control connections and data tunnels. Figure 5-22 shows the bind mode option.

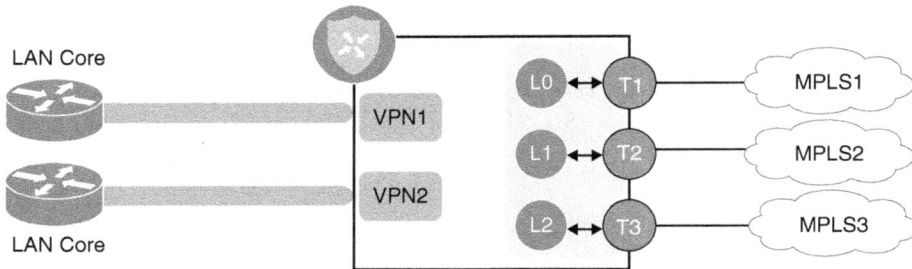

Figure 5-22 *Loopback TLOC Bind Mode*

In the unbind mode, the loopback interface is not bound to any physical interface. Traffic destined to the loopback interface can go through any physical interface based on a hash lookup. Figure 5-23 illustrates this.

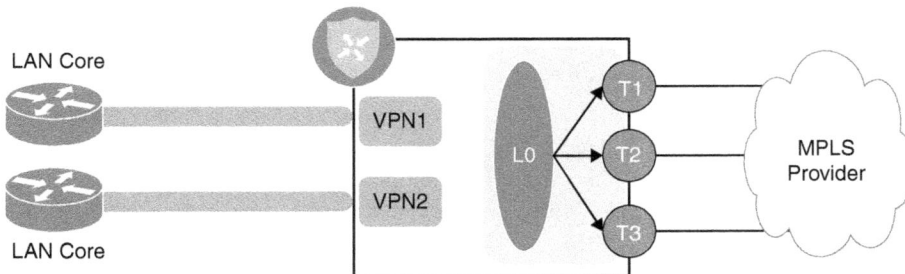

Figure 5-23 *Loopback TLOC Unbind Mode*

> **NOTE** It is important to note that in the unbind mode, information collected via Bidirectional Forwarding Detection (BFD) can be on any of the interfaces. Because of this, the liveliness info can be seen as different for each remote site, even though the remote sites are on the same local color at this location.

Another scenario where loopback interfaces prove beneficial is illustrated in Figure 5-24. This situation typically arises with the Internet, when you have multiple transport options in the same underlay at remote branches and a single transport at the hub or data center. With the current Cisco SD-WAN functionality, applying data or application-aware routing policies to prefer a specific transport from branch toward hub grants full control over traffic flow at the branch side. However, at the hub, where only one local transport is available during policy configuration, controlling which path to take to the remote site and which remote transport receives traffic from the hub becomes challenging.

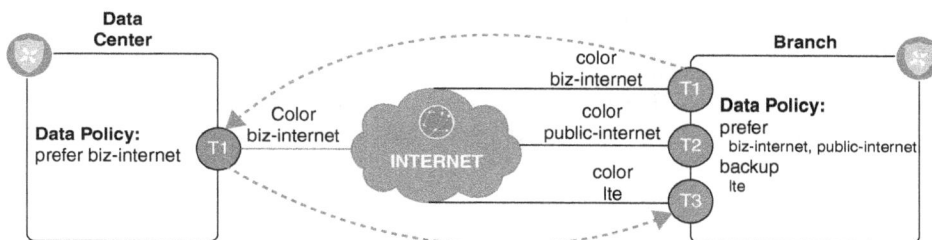

Figure 5-24 *Multiple Remote Colors*

In this example, there are three data tunnels present at the hub site WAN Edge router:

- Local **biz-internet** color to remote **biz-internet** color

- Local **biz-internet** color to remote **public-internet** color

- Local **biz-internet** color to remote **lte** color

When the policy prefers the local biz-internet color, all three tunnels match it, and traffic is load-balanced among them, potentially landing on any remote transport, including LTE, which, in this case, is costly and supposed to be used only as a backup.

The workaround is to create loopback interfaces in bind mode at the hub for remote branch colors that are not physically present there. This eliminates ambiguity during policy configuration, allowing for a desired level of policy granularity at hub sites, as shown in Figure 5-25.

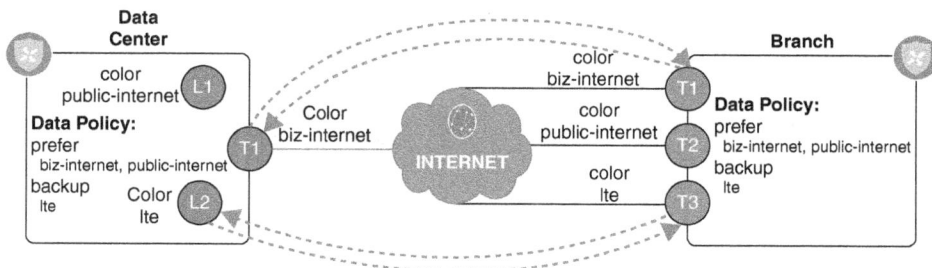

Figure 5-25 *Multiple Remote Colors with Loopback TLOCs*

In this case, there are three data tunnels present at the hub site WAN Edge router:

- Local **biz-internet** color to remote **biz-internet** color

- Local **public-internet** color to remote **public-internet** color

- Local **lte** color to remote **lte** color

Now, when policy prefers the local biz-internet color, traffic is only sent via the first tunnel, deterministically landing only on the biz-internet remote transport. Consequently, LTE is used solely as a backup, minimizing unnecessary usage charges. Moreover, this approach enables the configuration of transport parameters on the data center side, such as enabling the low-bandwidth-link feature for LTE, which further optimizes LTE bandwidth utilization.

Cisco SD-WAN Data Center Design

In nearly all cases, the data center is the first site to be implemented in Cisco SD-WAN deployments. While there are many ways to integrate SD-WAN into the data center, the most common and strongly recommended approach is to implement the solution in parallel with the existing WAN infrastructure. This is accomplished by standing up WAN Edge routers alongside the current WAN setup (behind the MPLS CE/PE routers and Internet edge firewalls) and providing the routers with indirect connectivity to WAN transports. This approach is particularly favored when an organization doesn't have the luxury of providing dedicated circuits for WAN Edge routers or when handoffs for all the transports are already in service.

It is common to see new WAN Edge devices leveraging private connectivity through an existing MPLS CE/PE router and public connectivity through an existing secure Internet edge firewall. Figure 5-26 illustrates this architecture.

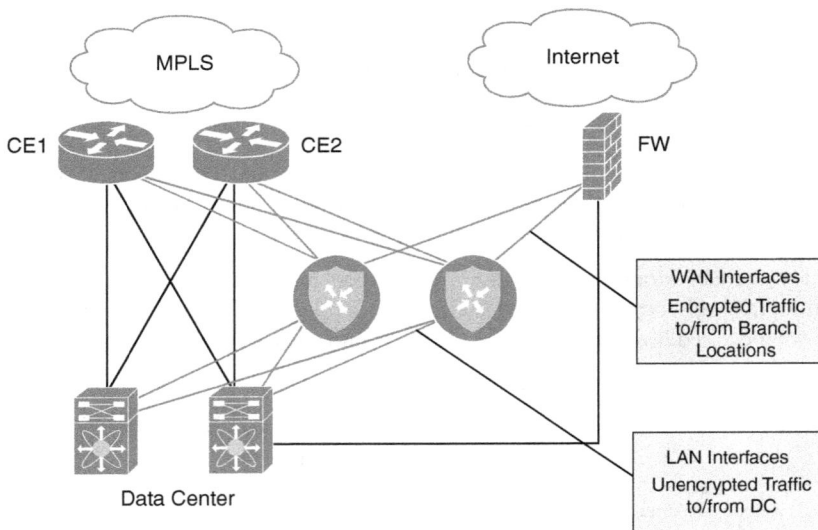

Figure 5-26 *Data Center Dedicated Pod*

NOTE   WAN Edge routers come with built-in security features and do not need to sit behind firewalls. In branches, WAN Edge routers often connect directly to the Internet transports. However, data centers typically have established Internet access segments protected by firewalls, which WAN Edge routers commonly leverage, as illustrated throughout this section.

Nevertheless, some organizations opt for dedicated Internet access within data centers solely for SD-WAN. In such cases, they procure new Internet circuits specifically for SD-WAN and often connect them directly to routers without firewalls in front of them. This approach is perfectly valid, as long as it aligns with the security policies of the organization.

This design allows the data center to act as a transit site for traffic between Cisco SD-WAN and non-SD-WAN sites and allows for a gradual migration of remote sites to Cisco SD-WAN without affecting the legacy network. This type of design also decouples and removes fate sharing between non-migrated and migrated sites, as they are landing on separate routers in the data center with distinct domains for routing and control. This same design can be used when migrating from legacy overlay technologies, such as Dynamic Multipoint VPN (DMVPN) and Group Encrypted Transport VPN (GETVPN), to Cisco SD-WAN.

In some environments, transiting the hub and the potential for added latency may be a concern. Designating multiple regional hubs as transit points for dedicated geographies and configuring the overlay routing to leverage these hubs intelligently is a common solution to this problem. For example, you may want to designate a U.S. West hub, a U.S. East hub, an APAC hub, and an EMEA hub, with each of these hubs handling the transit traffic between its respective regions.

An alternative, albeit much more complex and operationally expensive, method of solving the same latency problem is to mix overlay and underlay networking to provide a direct path between non-migrated and migrated sites. The section "Integrating Cisco SD-WAN with Existing Networks" addresses this approach later in the chapter.

Transport-Side Connectivity

Data centers form the heart of a network, offering extensive infrastructure and connectivity options. Typically, WAN Edge routers are deployed in data centers in pairs in a dual-router setup, with direct or indirect switched connectivity to transports, as previously discussed. TLOC extensions may also be used when transports are physically connected to WAN Edge routers and need to be accessible to other routers.

Service-Side Connectivity

Service-side connectivity is commonly achieved by provisioning one or two interfaces in a service VPN and connecting them into the data center core. The data center core is typically a point in the network where aggregation of legacy routes and Cisco SD-WAN routes occurs; it allows for natural transitive connectivity. Usually, a routing protocol (such as BGP) is run between the WAN Edge router and the data center core so that the WAN Edge router can learn both data center and legacy WAN routes as well as advertise migrated site routes back toward the data center.

External BGP (eBGP) is typically the protocol of choice, as it provides built-in loop prevention mechanisms (via AS_Path and Site of Origin attributes) and has a very flexible and comprehensive path selection algorithm. This algorithm can be manipulated in both directions via route policy. For instance, a route policy could match a set of routes from the overlay and set a local preference in order to influence the data center core routing. BGP Multi-Exit Discriminator (MED) attribute can also be leveraged for path selection in the overlay as it is carried within OMP. Finally, BGP provides granular tagging and filtering mechanisms through the use of route maps, prefix lists, and communities. Figure 5-27 shows this type of connectivity.

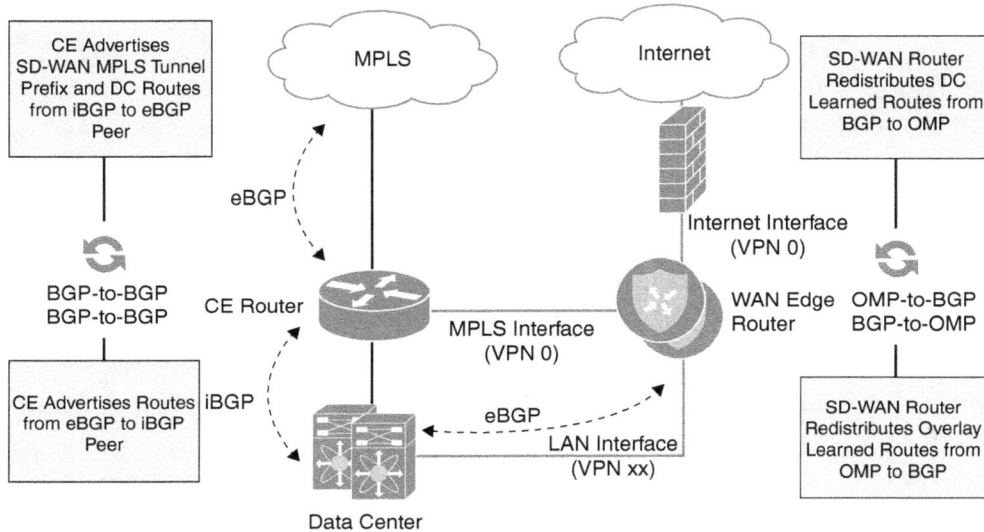

Figure 5-27   *Service-Side BGP*

While eBGP is usually the recommended service-side routing protocol, depending on the platform, Cisco SD-WAN supports iBGP, OSPF, EIGRP, RIPv2, static routing, and configuration of the first-hop redundancy protocol VRRP as well. Selecting an appropriate service-side routing protocol for an organization depends completely on the existing network configuration, required features and functionality, and operator comfort level.

In some instances, using a service-side routing protocol that is different from the existing routing protocol deployed in the data center core can add complexity—especially when it comes to route redistribution between the two protocols. To avoid this complexity, it may be worth considering the same routing protocol on the WAN Edge router that is found on the data center core.

An alternative approach is to connect and peer the service side of the WAN Edge router directly with an existing MPLS CE router that is already running BGP. This way, no additional redistribution needs to occur on the data center core since the MPLS CE router is already providing this functionality. Routes from the Cisco SD-WAN overlay would be learned by the MPLS CE router, and as long as the routing policy permits, these routes will be redistributed into the protocol running on the data center core. Conversely, the routes learned on the MPLS CE router from the data center core would be redistributed into BGP and learned by both the WAN Edge router and the service provider. Figure 5-28 details this type of connectivity.

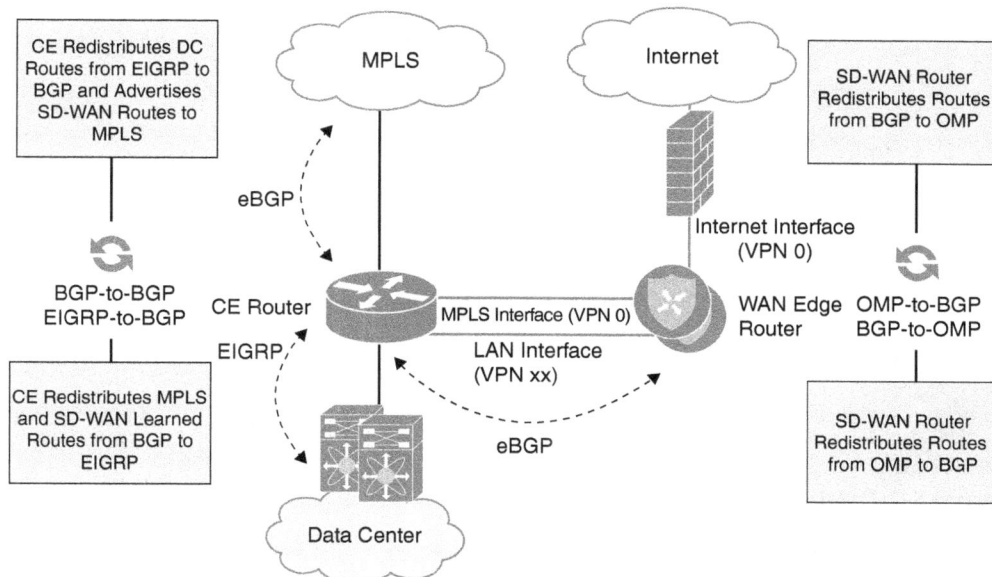

Figure 5-28   *Service-Side CE Integration*

NOTE   As with any other routing integration exercise, it is important to ensure that path selection occurs as desired, loops are avoided, failover performs as expected, and routing is optimal. To achieve these objectives, leverage the route manipulation, filtering, and tagging tools provided by Cisco SD-WAN.

Keep in mind that while the aforementioned Cisco SD-WAN data center designs are the most recommended and widely deployed, many other methods of providing transport and service-side connectivity do exist and can be investigated for their value, specific to the organization's needs. For instance, subinterfaces can be leveraged for both LAN and WAN connectivity if port density is a concern or if the requirement to transit through a switch or a transparent firewall is applicable. In the end, we are dealing with traditional routing and switching, and many basic design concepts still hold true.

Finally, once all remote sites have been migrated to Cisco SD-WAN, it is possible (but not mandatory) to decommission the legacy MPLS CE routers terminating the transport circuits. The transport circuits need to be re-terminated on the WAN Edge routers directly, which could potentially change the connectivity design and configuration.

In short, connectivity needs to be provided to VPN 0 in some manner. While decommissioning the legacy MPLS CE routers might seem like the right thing to do, many organizations opt to keep them in service to retain compartmentalization and minimize complexity. Figure 5-29 illustrates this potential post-migration design where the MPLS CE router is removed.

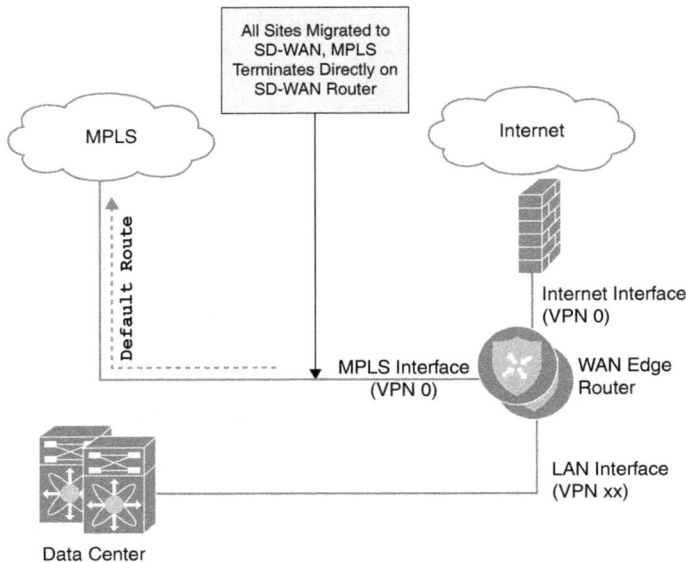

Figure 5-29 *Direct Transport Termination*

> **NOTE**   Refer to Cisco's published migration guides and Cisco Validated Design guides for detailed step-by-step instructions on migration and sample configurations.

Cisco SD-WAN Branch Design

Once the data centers have been migrated to Cisco SD-WAN, the branches can follow suit. Cisco SD-WAN branch design can be a bit tricky compared to data center design. Most organizations have branches that come in all shapes and sizes, with different topologies, WAN connectivity models, high availability, and additional services (such as voice and security) that need to be considered. The migration to Cisco SD-WAN could be your opportunity to enforce standardized branch designs and make use of the power of templates or configuration groups. Because it would not be feasible to detail how to migrate every single branch design, this section focuses on the designs that are most common.

Complete CE Replacement: Single WAN Edge Router

The replacement (or upgrade) of a single legacy router to an SD-WAN router requires downtime, as there is no other router to forward traffic during the migration. This design is very straightforward and simply requires you to terminate the circuits physically or logically on the transport side of the WAN Edge router as well as connect the service side to a LAN core. No routing protocol is required on the transport side, as a default route(s) is used to direct traffic to the respective carrier's next-hop IP address. Both Layer 2 and Layer 3 service-side connectivity is supported. A WAN Edge router can connect to the LAN via 802.1Q subinterfaces and act as the Layer 3 gateway for all of the service-side VLANs. Alternatively, depending on the platform, a WAN Edge router can peer with a Layer 3 LAN core router via BGP, OSPF, EIGRP, or RIPv2. In the Layer 2 design, the connected subnets are automatically redistributed into OMP, and end-to-end reachability is achieved. Figure 5-30 illustrates this type of Layer 2 design.

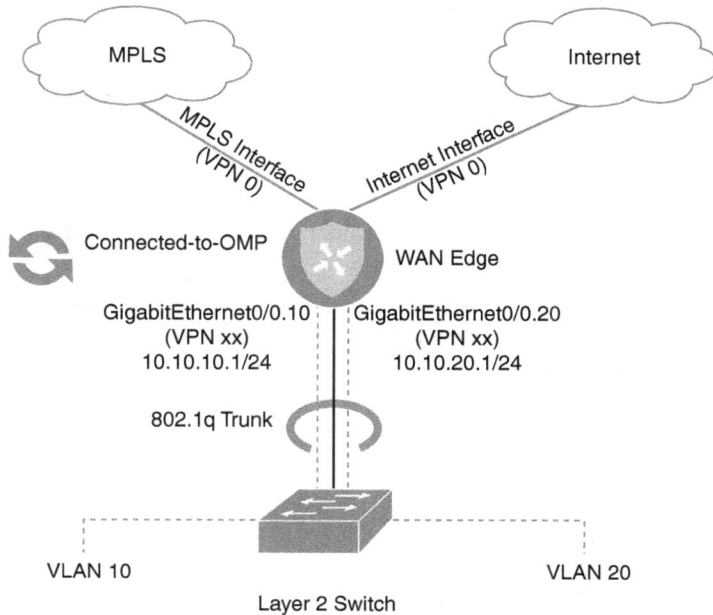

Figure 5-30 *Complete CE Replacement: Single-Router Layer 2 Branch*

In the Layer 3 design, the routing protocol used on the service side must be redistributed into OMP, and OMP must be redistributed into the service-side routing protocol. Figure 5-31 shows this design.

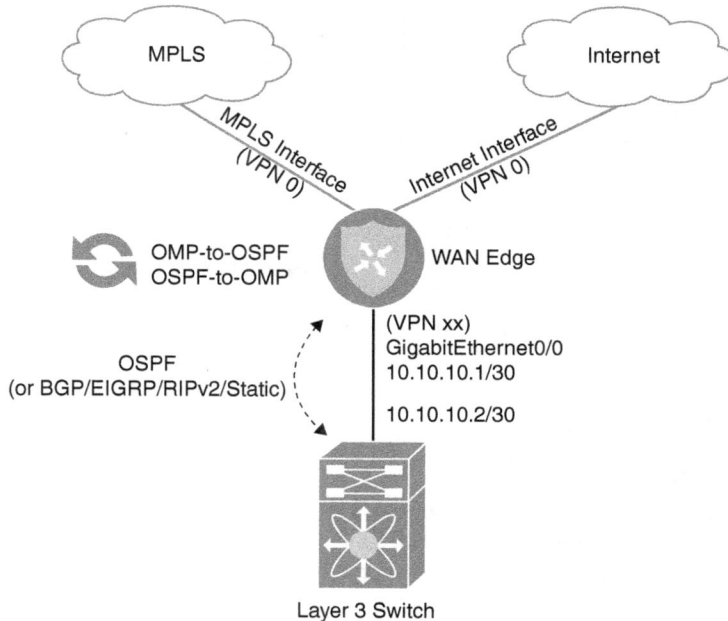

Figure 5-31 *Complete CE Replacement: Dual-Router Layer 3 Branch*

Complete CE Replacement: Dual WAN Edge Routers

A branch that requires high availability might have two WAN routers that need to be replaced. In this scenario, it is possible to provide a near hitless cutover since one router can be replaced or upgraded at a time while the other router continues forwarding traffic. Using routing protocol path manipulation and/or VRRP priority adjustment, it would be necessary to first ensure that all the inbound and outbound traffic is shifted to flow over the router that is not initially being upgraded. Once one of the routers is replaced or converted to Cisco SD-WAN, traffic can be shifted over to the newly brought up Cisco SD-WAN overlay network while the other router is then replaced or upgraded.

In this design, illustrated in Figure 5-32, both WAN Edge routers have access to all transports directly—either through multiple handoffs, by utilizing multiple IP addresses and switching infrastructure, or by using *TLOC extensions.*

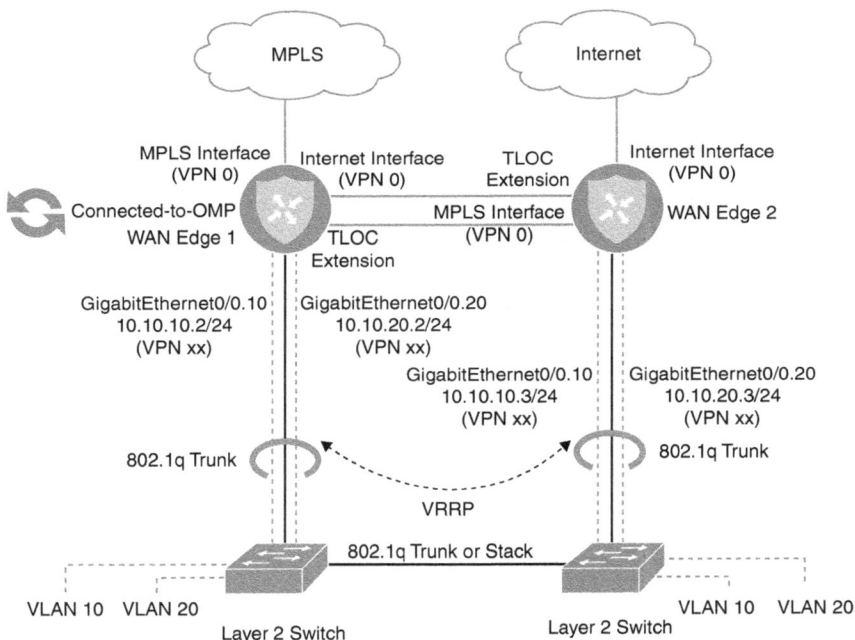

Figure 5-32   *Complete CE Replacement: Dual-Router Layer 2 Branch*

In addition, users have the choice of leveraging a routing protocol instead of VRRP for service-side integration, as illustrated in Figure 5-33.

Integration with an Existing CE Router

Sometimes a branch design calls for the integration of the WAN Edge router with an existing CE router. For example, some MPLS carriers provide and manage the CE router and, as a part of the contract, the router cannot be removed from the branch site. In other cases, the existing CE router may be providing other services for the branch that must stay intact post-migration (such as voice gateway functionality). In order for the WAN Edge router to have connectivity into the MPLS underlay, the design must be made such that the WAN Edge router can tunnel through the existing MPLS CE router. This can easily be accomplished by connecting a physical or logical transport-side interface, configured as a private TLOC in a /30 transit network, to an available interface or subinterface on the existing CE router. The WAN Edge router would then be configured with a default route pointing to the next-hop IP address of the MPLS CE router. In addition, to provide connectivity to the tunnel endpoint IP address, the MPLS CE router needs to advertise this transit network into the underlay network via a routing protocol such as BGP. Figure 5-34 illustrates this scenario.

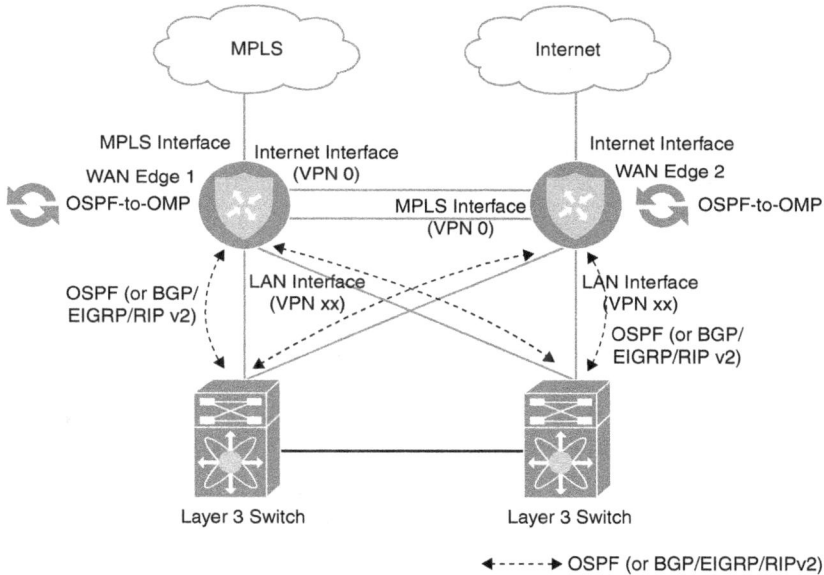

Figure 5-33   *Complete CE Replacement: Dual-Router Layer 3 Branch*

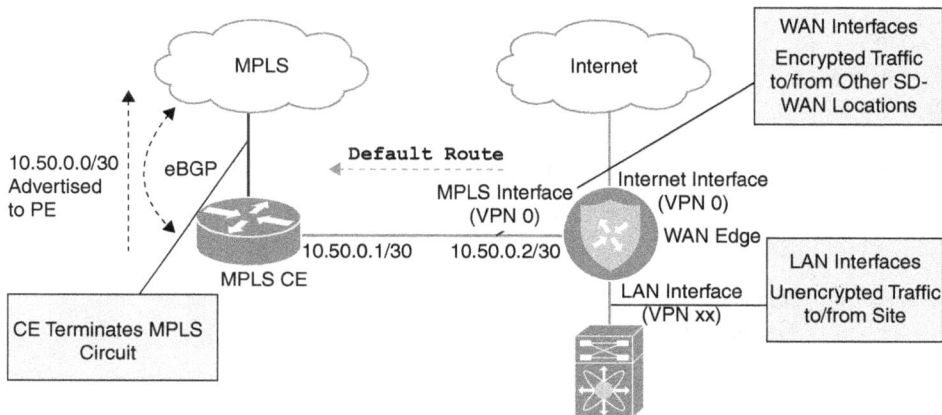

Figure 5-34   *Branch CE Integration*

Integration with a Branch Firewall

It isn't uncommon for a branch site to have a firewall terminating Internet connectivity and providing services such as direct Internet access, secure access control, zone-based segmentation, URL filtering, NAT, IDS/IPS, and so on. Because of the routing DNA embedded in Cisco SD-WAN, there are all sorts of methods for integrating with a branch firewall, depending on the desired traffic flow and traffic visibility requirements.

Firewalls can be inserted in front of the WAN Edge router, in parallel with the WAN Edge router, or even behind the WAN Edge router in either Layer 3 routed or Layer 2 transparent mode. The appropriate integration model depends on several factors, such as physical connectivity, logical traffic flow, traffic visibility requirements, segmentation architecture, and NAT requirements. The only requirement for the WAN Edge router is that it is provided transport-side Internet connectivity for control and data plane tunnels as well as service-side LAN connectivity to receive and forward user traffic into and out of the overlay.

If all Internet-bound traffic is backhauled to a data center or hub egress point, firewall integration is very straightforward. In this design, the firewall terminates the Internet connection directly and provides access to the WAN Edge router through either an allocated public IP address in a DMZ or through NAT (one-to-one NAT or PAT).

NOTE While Cisco SD-WAN supports tunneling through several types of NAT, some dynamic NAT and dynamic PAT combinations may cause tunnel establishment failures (especially if that type of NAT is on both sides of the tunnel). Refer to the "Network Address Translation" section in Chapter 3, "Control Plane and Data Plane Operations," for more details on supported NAT configurations.

Secure direct Internet access is one of the key benefits of migrating to Cisco SD-WAN, and the design options discussed in this section provide this functionality.

In some networks, it is beneficial for a firewall to provide direct Internet access functionality to clients since it may be running advanced security services such as URL filtering. With this design, Internet-bound traffic ingresses the service side of the WAN Edge router and, instead of performing NAT and local egress itself, the WAN Edge router forwards the traffic over another service-side link to the adjacent firewall. The firewall can then perform inspection, access control, and NAT prior to forwarding the traffic to the Internet. Traffic to private network destinations follows the Cisco SD-WAN overlay. This is most optimal when the Internet handoff has more than one physical port. Figure 5-35 details this design.

If a dedicated handoff to the Internet is not available, an alternative design would be to connect the transport side of the WAN Edge router to the firewall. In this way, the WAN Edge router has access to the Internet for control and data plane tunnels while also keeping a separate service-side connection to forward Internet-bound traffic to the firewall for processing and local egress. Figure 5-36 illustrates this design.

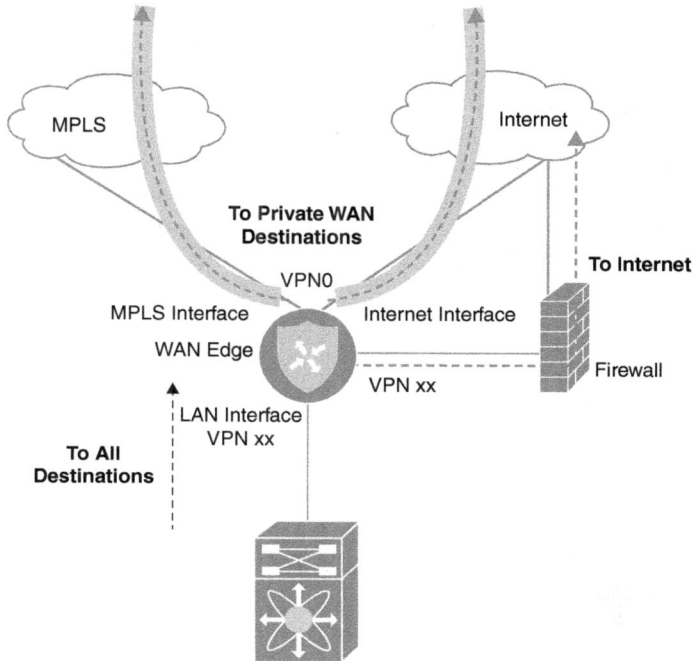

Figure 5-35   *Direct Internet Access Through a Firewall*

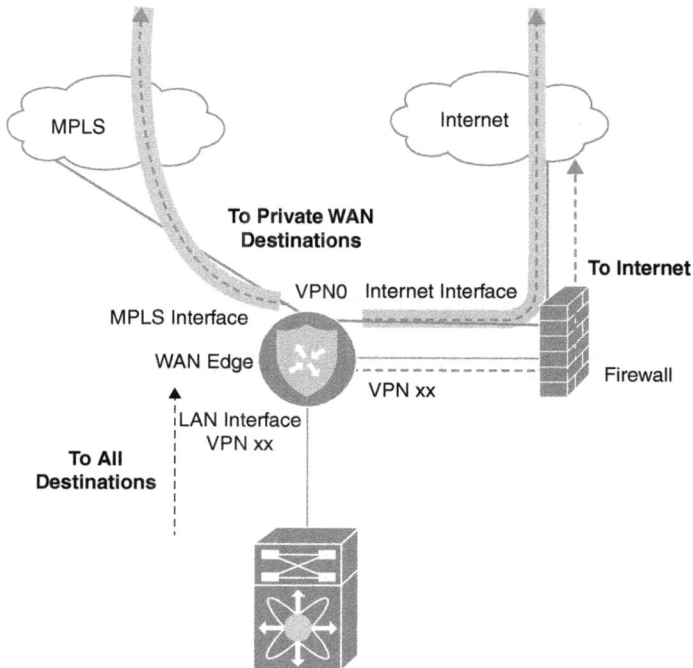

Figure 5-36   *Transport and Direct Internet Access Through a Firewall*

Finally, if you want all traffic to flow through the WAN Edge router and only a single connection exists between the router and the firewall, consider using a single transport-side connection for both tunneling and direct Internet access. NAT is configured on the transport-side interface connected to the firewall, and Cisco SD-WAN policy can selectively break out Internet-bound traffic to the underlay. The firewall receives this Internet-bound traffic and may perform NAT a second time, as it sends the traffic to the Internet. It is important to note that because the WAN Edge router is performing NAT (which is a requirement for WAN Edge routers to break out traffic locally), the firewall loses visibility into the original client source IP addresses. Figure 5-37 shows this design.

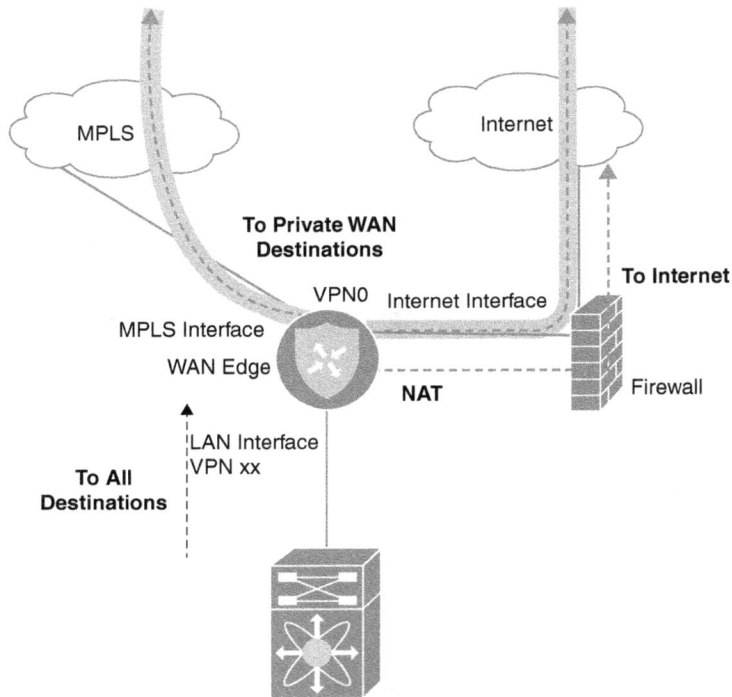

Figure 5-37 *Transport and Direct Internet Access Through a Firewall's Single Link*

Integrating Cisco SD-WAN with Existing Networks

This section details how integration between the existing network and SD-WAN overlay networks can be achieved through several design options.

Overlay Only

To minimize complexity and the potential for routing loops, it is recommended to adhere to the designs presented earlier in this chapter for data center and branch migration. These designs have been proven time and time again to provide a graceful migration solution for organizations of all sizes, complexities, and application types. Overlay-only migrations provide a clear and deterministic traffic flow and are easy to control, scale, and troubleshoot. Figure 5-38 shows traffic flow between a Cisco SD-WAN site and a legacy non-SD-WAN site with this design in place.

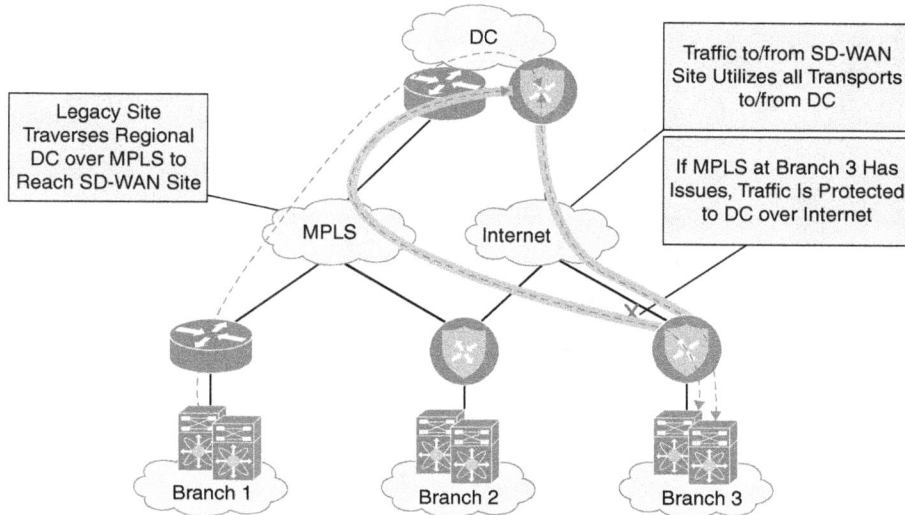

Figure 5-38 *SD-WAN to Non-SD-WAN Site Overlay-Only Traffic Flow*

Understanding the traffic flow from an SD-WAN site to another SD-WAN site is also critical. Figure 5-39 highlights the traffic flow patterns experienced when using an overlay-only design.

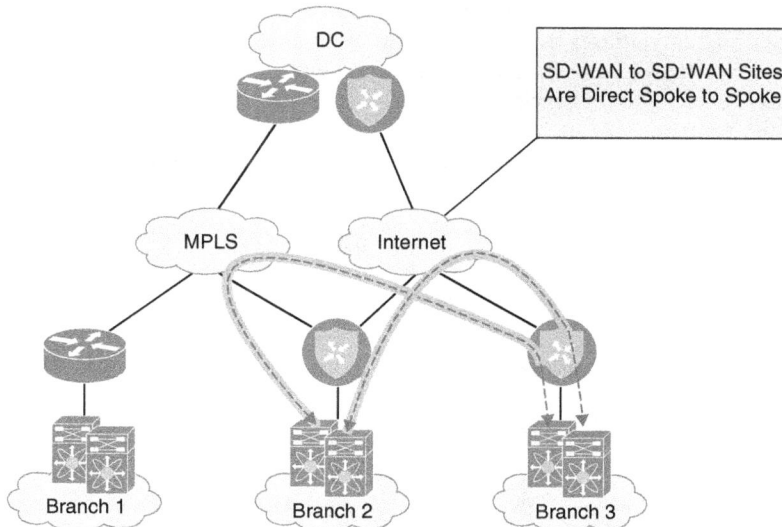

Figure 5-39 *SD-WAN to SD-WAN Site Overlay-Only Traffic Flow*

Overlay with Underlay Backup

If a branch site leveraging MPLS and Internet for the Cisco SD-WAN overlay has only a single WAN Edge router used alongside the MPLS CE router, another design opportunity exists that can allow for a backup path to become active if the WAN Edge router fails.

For this design to work properly, routing needs to be manipulated in such a way that the site prefixes advertised by the MPLS CE router into the underlay are less preferred in the network than those being advertised by the WAN Edge router into the overlay. Conversely, from the perspective of the LAN, the WAN Edge router should be the preferred path to reach remote networks. Figure 5-40 illustrates this.

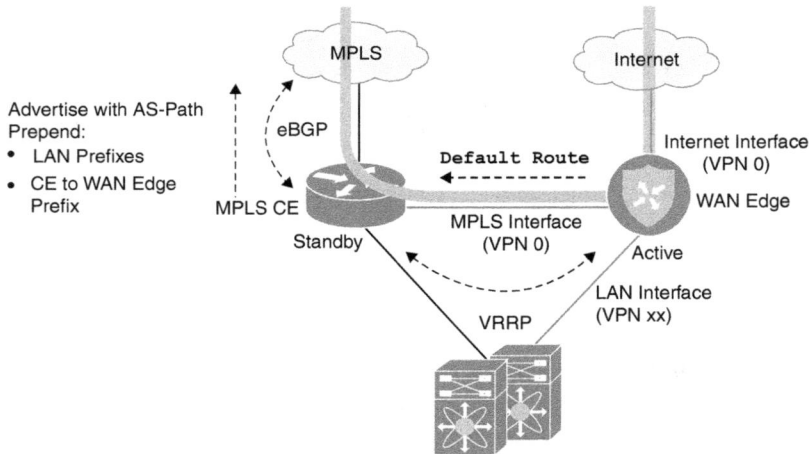

Figure 5-40   *Overlay with Underlay Backup: Layer 2 Design*

This manipulation of path preference ensures that the traffic flow stays symmetric over the Cisco SD-WAN fabric and only utilizes the underlay if the WAN Edge router were to fail. One way to manipulate path preference for the underlay is to only advertise local site prefixes from the MPLS CE router to the service provider and use BGP AS path prepending. Figure 5-41 shows this type of scenario. Naturally, the data center will advertise the remote site prefixes learned from the data center WAN Edge router into the underlay with a shorter AS path, ensuring a more preferred, symmetric flow.

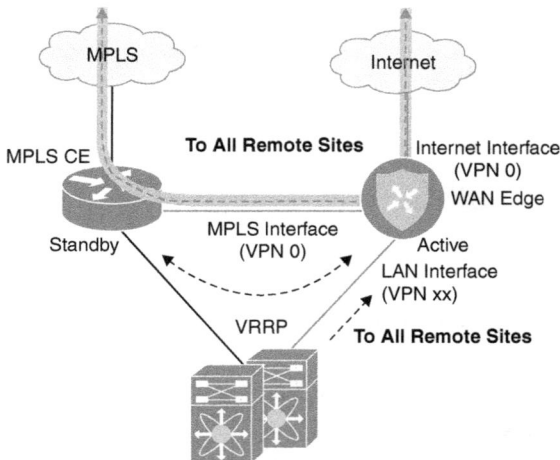

Figure 5-41   *Overlay with Underlay Backup: Layer 2 Design Traffic Flow*

It should be noted that LAN-side routing also needs to be manipulated in order to prefer the WAN Edge router (for normal operation) and fail over to the MPLS CE router during an impaired state. This can be accomplished in a Layer 2 branch by running VRRP between the WAN Edge router and the MPLS CE router (with the WAN Edge router having the higher priority). Figure 5-42 shows this design option.

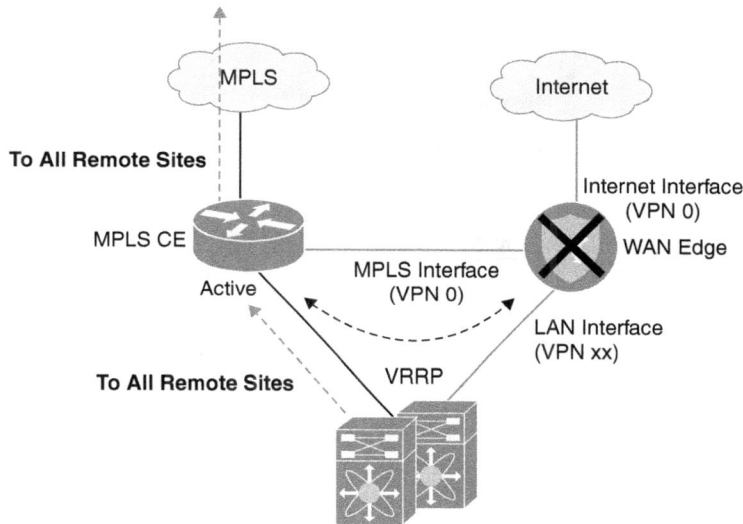

Figure 5-42 *Overlay with Underlay Backup: Layer 2 Design Traffic Flow During Failover*

In a Layer 3 branch design, advertising remote prefixes to the LAN with a more attractive metric from the WAN Edge router is also an option, as illustrated in Figure 5-43.

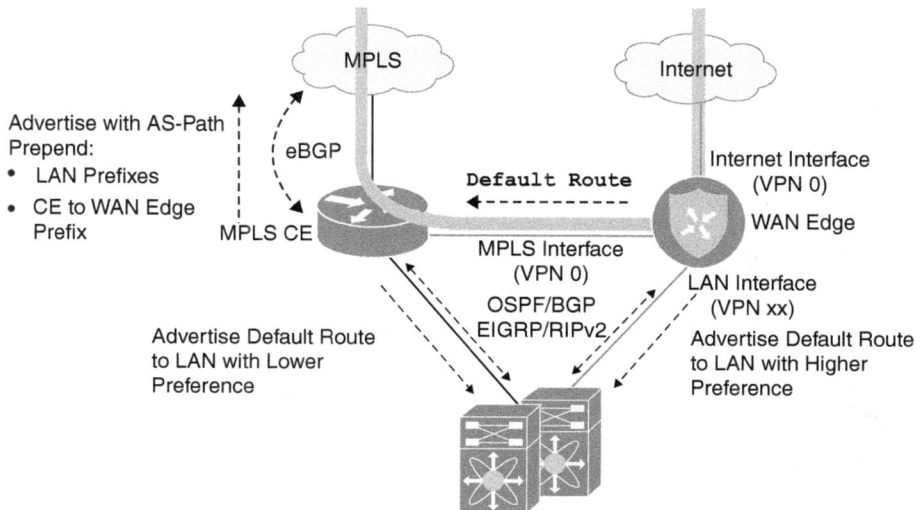

Figure 5-43 *Overlay with Underlay Backup: Layer 3 Design*

Finally, for the underlay backup architecture to work correctly, it is important to do some filtering at the data center. To ensure that remote branch routes are learned and preferred through the overlay (and asymmetry or route looping is avoided), create an outbound filter toward the WAN Edge router to limit the learned routes to those originating from the data center. Make sure to also advertise a default route or summary routes into the overlay. Figure 5-44 shows this design option.

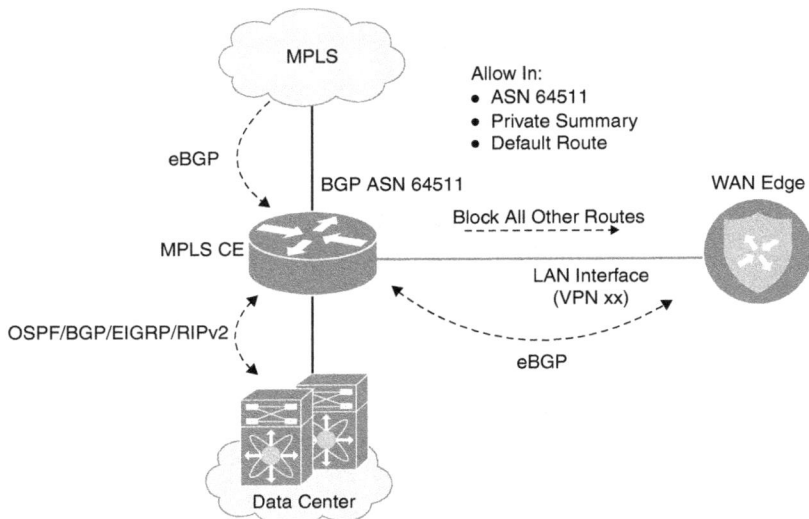

Figure 5-44   *Overlay with Underlay Backup: Data Center Considerations*

Figure 5-45 reviews the traffic flow patterns experienced when using an overlay with an underlay backup design.

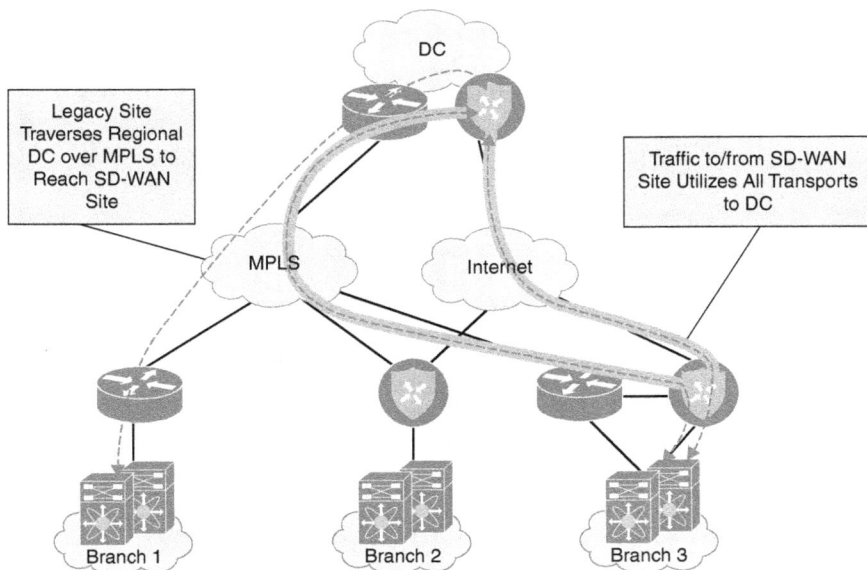

Figure 5-45   *Overlay with Underlay Backup Traffic Flow*

It is also important to see the traffic flow during a failover condition. This helps visualize the path the traffic will take during a failure scenario. Figure 5-46 highlights the backup traffic flow during a failover event.

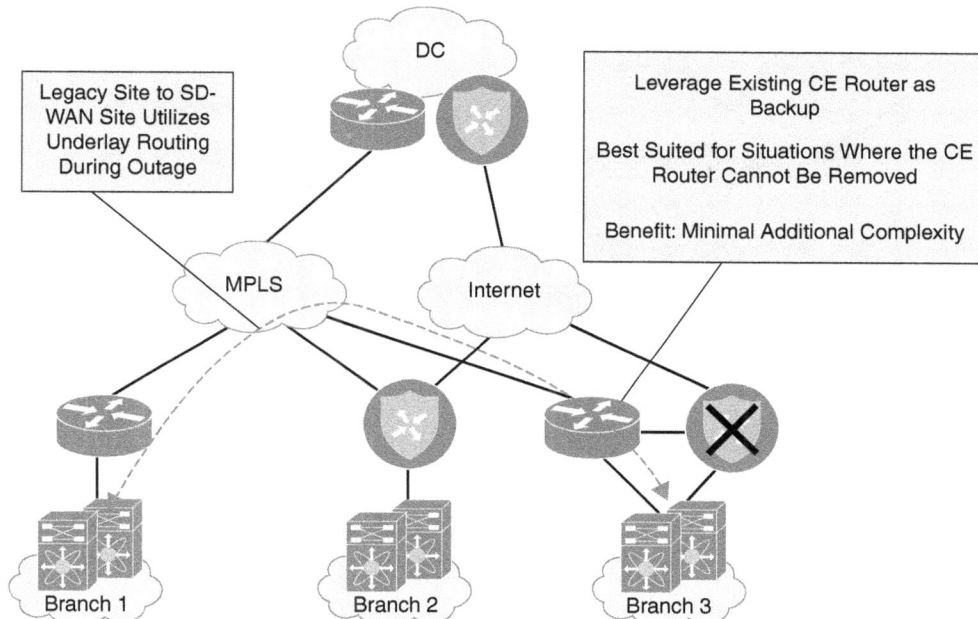

Figure 5-46 *Overlay with Underlay Backup Traffic Flow During Failover*

Full Overlay and Underlay Integration

For some organizations, due to strict application latency requirements, certain branches migrated to Cisco SD-WAN may need to communicate directly with non-migrated branches through a lower-latency underlay path. For example, CIFS traffic, which is relatively sensitive to latency, may suffer from going through additional hops at the data center for transit to another site. To address this latency requirement, SD-WAN network can be architected to use the overlay path for communication with migrated sites and the underlay path for communication with non-migrated sites, enabling full overlay and underlay integration. Figure 5-47 shows routing from a non-SD-WAN site to a Cisco SD-WAN site in this scenario. Figure 5-48 illustrates the traffic flow between two Cisco SD-WAN sites while leveraging a full overlay and underlay integration design.

NOTE In most cases, configuring full overlay and underlay integration at every site will add a significant amount of routing complexity to the network and, in some environments, can be a challenge to scale and control. Typically, voice applications can handle 300 ms of round-trip latency, and therefore this design might not even be required.

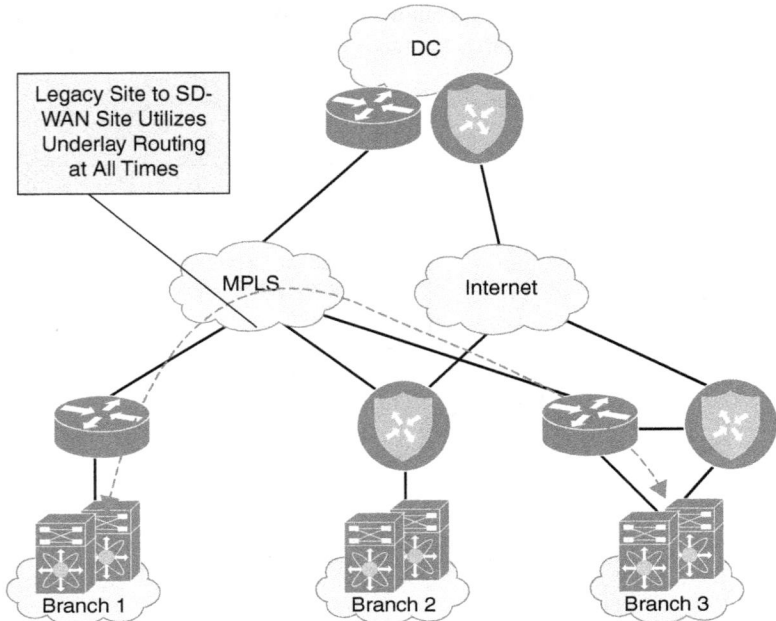

Figure 5-47   *Full Overlay with Underlay Routing: Legacy Site to SD-WAN Site Traffic Flow*

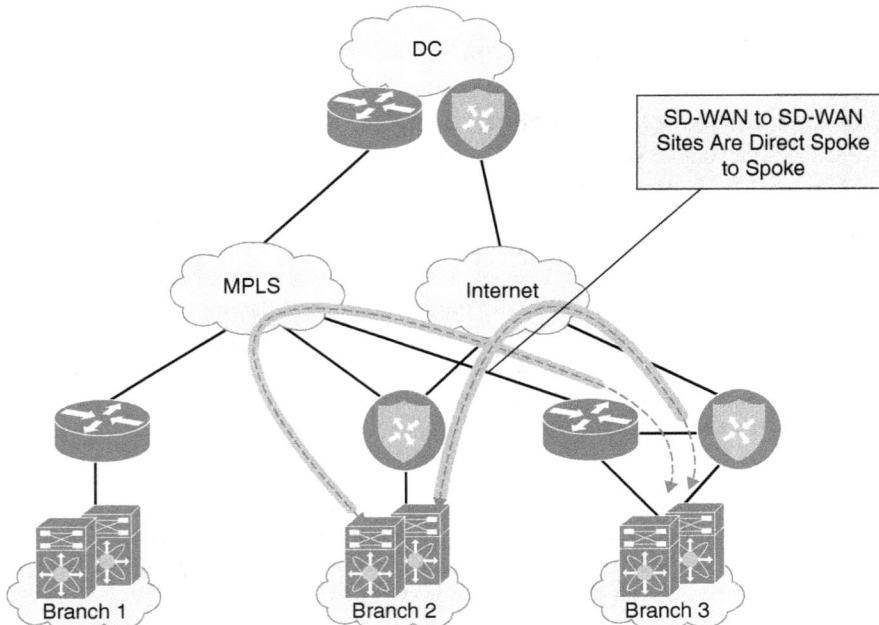

Figure 5-48   *Full Overlay with Underlay Routing: SD-WAN Site to SD-WAN Site Traffic Flow*

One way to implement full overlay and underlay integration at a branch is through the use of an existing MPLS CE router. This design is similar to the MPLS CE router integration solution discussed previously, with the difference being that the CE router continues to advertise the site prefixes into the MPLS underlay while the WAN Edge router simultaneously advertises the site prefixes into the overlay. Both the MPLS CE router and WAN Edge router advertise prefixes from the WAN into the LAN. However, the WAN Edge router should advertise SD-WAN migrated site prefixes (including data center prefixes) with a more attractive metric to retain traffic symmetry and to force Cisco SD-WAN sites to talk to each other via the overlay. While any routing protocol can be used to achieve this design, BGP is recommended for its native anti-transit logic. If any other routing protocol is used, tagging and filtering mechanisms should be used to avoid making the branch into a transit site. Figure 5-49 shows this design option.

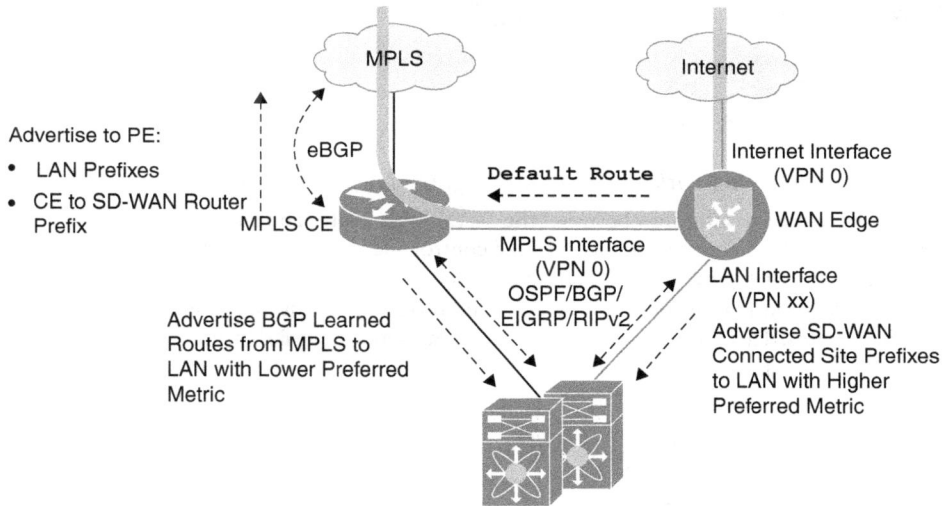

Figure 5-49 *Full Overlay with Underlay Routing: CE Integration*

Figure 5-50 shows the traffic flow for a branch with two transports. Traffic can flow directly through an Internet interface as well as through an interface that is connected to an existing MPLS CE router.

Full overlay and underlay integration can also be achieved without a dedicated MPLS CE router when only a WAN Edge router exists at the branch. The same principles apply as if there were a separate MPLS CE router; however, TLOC termination on the WAN Edge router is a bit different. Instead of configuring the TLOC on the physical interface connected to the MPLS carrier, a loopback interface is created in VPN 0, bound to the physical WAN interface, and configured as the TLOC. This configuration is required to remove TLOC configuration, along with the associated implicit ACL, from the physical interface. Without it, non-SD-WAN transit traffic received on MPLS from legacy sites will be dropped.

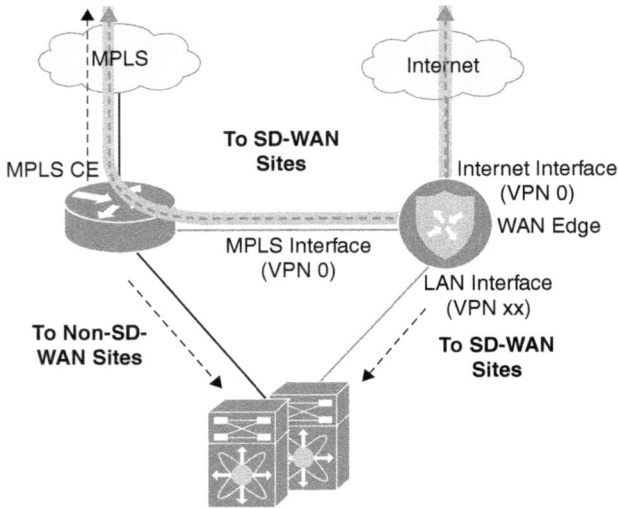

Figure 5-50 *Full Overlay with Underlay Routing: CE Integration Traffic Flow*

A routing protocol is configured between the WAN Edge router and the carrier in order to advertise the loopback interface IP address for control and data plane tunnel termination. A VPN 0 interface is then configured and connected to a downstream (LAN-side) Layer 3 switch. Finally, a routing protocol can be configured on this transit link to learn and advertise overlay routes. This configuration, in effect, creates a route leak between VPNs. Figure 5-51 shows this design option.

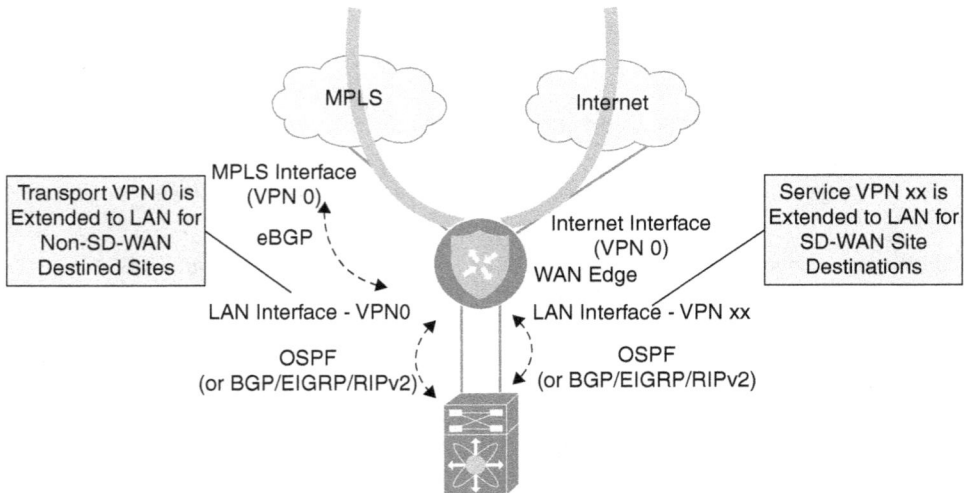

Figure 5-51 *Full Overlay with Underlay Routing: Without CE Integration*

Figure 5-52 illustrates the traffic flow for a site location with no integration with a CE device.

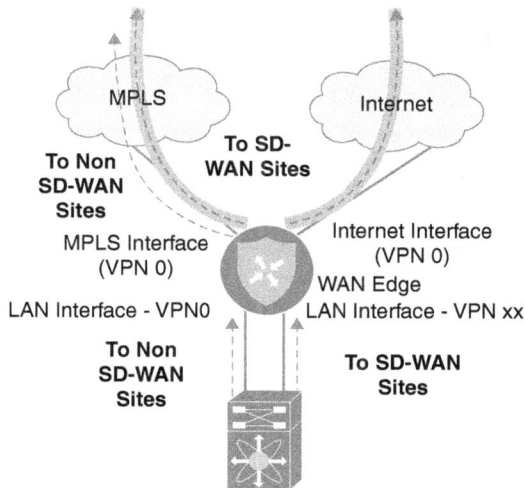

Figure 5-52   *Full Overlay with Underlay Routing: Without CE Integration Traffic Flow*

5

NOTE   Additional tagging, filtering, and best path manipulation may be required at both the data center and the remote sites participating in full overlay/underlay connectivity, depending on how routing between the overlay and underlay is accomplished. From a routing perspective, there are many valid ways to achieve full overlay and underlay integration. Each of these options deserves special attention to avoid routing loops and suboptimal routing. Every environment has unique complexities and caveats, so it's important to think through all the different possible scenarios specific to your organization's network that could affect the flow of traffic during and after migration.

Summary

This chapter covers the design methodology recommended for the implementation of Cisco SD-WAN. It discusses the importance of migration preparation, validated data center and branch designs, and overlay and underlay integration techniques. Cisco SD-WAN implementation requires a solid discovery and design period in which ample time is spent understanding the existing network thoroughly while also thinking about its future state. Preparation prior to deploying the Cisco SD-WAN network is key in ensuring that data center and branch cutovers are executed flawlessly. Understanding the benefits and caveats of all the supported data center and branch designs allows a network architect to select a design that meets the requirements of the business and provides additional Cisco SD-WAN functionalities while maintaining resiliency and performance. Every network has some degree of complexity, and the goal is to implement Cisco SD-WAN gracefully without increasing the complexity.

Review All Key Topics

Review the most important topics in the chapter, noted with the Key Topic icon in the outer margin of the page. Table 5-4 lists these key topics and the page number on which each is found.

Table 5-4   Key Topics

Key Topic Element	Description	Page
Section	Cisco SD-WAN Design Methodology	125
Section	Cisco SD-WAN Multi-Region Fabric	134
Section	Cisco SD-WAN Control Components Design	136
Section	TLOC Extensions	161
Section	Loopback TLOC Design	164
Section	Integrating Cisco SD-WAN with Existing Networks	176

Chapter Review Questions

1. What are some main use cases for Cisco Catalyst SD-WAN? (Choose three.)

    a. Application performance optimization

    b. Secure direct Internet access

    c. Multicloud connectivity

    d. Data center traffic segmentation

2. Cisco SD-WAN simplifies connectivity to what kind of resources in a cloud? (Choose two.)

    a. NaaS

    b. IaaS

    c. PaaS

    d. SaaS

3. Which of the following is not a consideration for Cisco SD-WAN design?

    a. Deployment scale

    b. Wireless authentication

    c. High availability and disaster recovery

    d. VPN segmentation

4. For what region in a Multi-Region Fabric do you need to add a topology control policy to ensure that traffic flow from one access region to another follows a certain preferred path?

    a. None

    b. Core region

    c. Source access region

    d. Destination access region

5. In which deployment model of Cisco SD-WAN Control Components does a customer assume the most responsibility?

    a. Cisco-hosted cloud

    b. MSP-hosted cloud

    c. On-premises private cloud

    d. Customer's public cloud

6. Which Cisco SD-WAN component does not support high availability configuration?

    a. Cisco Catalyst SD-WAN Analytics

    b. Cisco Catalyst SD-WAN Manager

    c. Cisco Catalyst SD-WAN Controller

    d. Cisco Catalyst SD-WAN Validator

7. What is the recommended disaster recovery mechanism for SD-WAN Manager?

    a. Manual

    b. Scheduled

    c. Administrator-triggered failover

    d. Arbitrator-triggered failover

8. How many SD-WAN Controllers are recommended for a deployment with 500 WAN Edge routers?

    a. 0 as this is an optional component

    b. 1 because 1 SD-WAN Controller has more than enough capacity for such a network

    c. 2 for the redundancy

    d. 3 because a clustered implementation requires an uneven number of devices

9. Which statement is true about SD-WAN Validator?

    a. Only two SD-WAN Validators can be provisioned in an SD-WAN network.

    b. It tracks the state of all the other SD-WAN Validators in the network.

    c. It can be entered in the WAN Edge configuration either as an IP address or as a DNS name.

    d. It runs the same virtual machine image as SD-WAN Controller, and the role is activated via the **system vbond** command with the **local** option.

10. True or false: Most SD-WAN deployments are done in a greenfield environment.

    a. True

    b. False

11. True or false: Migration to SD-WAN is a hard cut, with all data centers and remote sites migrated simultaneously.

    a. True

    b. False

12. What are some of the most important preparations that should be made prior to migration? (Choose two.)

    a. Reloading all routers

    b. Ensuring that every router has a maintenance contract

    c. Analyzing the existing topology, routing, and traffic engineering

    d. Cisco SD-WAN policy design and configuration

13. What type of SD-WAN-specific configuration values should be defined prior to migration? (Choose three.)

    a. Site IDs

    b. VPN IDs

5

    c. OSPF hello and dead timers

    d. BGP MED values

    e. TLOC colors

14. True or false: Standing up WAN Edge routers alongside the current WAN infrastructure is the preferred method for Cisco SD-WAN data center integration.

    a. True

    b. False

15. From a design perspective, how can you improve latency when migrating to Cisco SD-WAN while transiting hubs?

    a. Enable TCP optimization.

    b. Move the sites closer to each other.

    c. Designate multiple regional hubs as transit points.

    d. Use dedicated Layer 2 circuits.

16. True or false: The most common way to integrate transport-side connections on a WAN Edge router into the network is by sharing a single interface in VPN 0 for all carriers/transports.

    a. True

    b. False

17. What is the difference between bind mode and unbind mode when configuring a loopback TLOC?

    a. Bind mode forms control connections, and unbind mode does not.

    b. Unbind mode takes less router CPU than bind mode.

    c. Unbind mode allows for public and private color connectivity, whereas bind mode does not.

    d. Bind mode ensures that traffic destined to the loopback will be carried to and from the mapped physical interface. Unbind mode does not have this behavior.

18. What are three different Cisco SD-WAN branch migration options? (Choose three.)

    a. Complete CE replacement with a single WAN Edge router

    b. WAN Edge router running inline bridge mode

    c. Integration with an existing CE router

    d. Complete CE replacement with dual WAN Edge routers

19. True or false: A TLOC extension can only be configured for private colors.

    a. True

    b. False

20. Which routing protocols are supported for service-side integration with the LAN? (Choose three.)

    a. OMP

    b. OSPF

    c. ISIS

    d. EIGRP

    e. ODR

    f. eBGP

21. What important consideration needs to be made at the data center when implementing integration with existing networks?

   a. Only OSPF should be used.

   b. ECMP should be configured.

   c. WAN Edge routers should be running the latest code.

   d. Filtering toward the WAN Edge router should be configured.

References

"Cisco SD-WAN Design Guide," https://www.cisco.com/c/en/us/td/docs/solutions/CVD/SDWAN/cisco-sdwan-design-guide.html.

"Cisco SD-WAN Large Global WAN Design Case Study," https://www.cisco.com/c/en/us/td/docs/solutions/CVD/SDWAN/Cisco_SDWAN_Case_Study_Large_Global_WAN.html.

"Cisco Catalyst SD-WAN High Availability Configuration Guide, Cisco IOS XE Catalyst SD-WAN Release 17.x," https://www.cisco.com/c/en/us/td/docs/routers/sdwan/configuration/ha-scaling/ios-xe-17/high-availability-book-xe/m-high-availability-and-scaling.html.

"Cisco Recommended SD-WAN Software Versions for Controllers and WAN Edge Routers," https://www.cisco.com/c/en/us/support/docs/routers/sd-wan/215676-cisco-tac-and-bu-recommended-sd-wan-soft.htm

5

CHAPTER 6

Introduction to Cisco Catalyst SD-WAN Policies

This chapter covers the following topics:

- **Purpose of Cisco Catalyst SD-WAN Policies:** This section covers the reasons customers might choose to use Cisco Catalyst SD-WAN policies.

- **Types of Cisco Catalyst SD-WAN Policies:** This section introduces different types of Cisco Catalyst SD-WAN policies, including control, data, and security policies. It also explains the difference between centralized and localized policies.

- **Cisco Catalyst SD-WAN Policy Construction:** This section covers the building blocks of Cisco Catalyst SD-WAN policies and how their different components fit together.

- **Cisco Catalyst SD-WAN Policy Administration, Activation, and Enforcement:** This section discusses how Cisco Catalyst SD-WAN policies are activated and enforced throughout the Cisco Catalyst SD-WAN fabric.

- **Packet Forwarding Order of Operations:** This section examines how different Cisco Catalyst SD-WAN policies interact with each other when multiple policy types are applied at the same time.

Network administrators use policies in order to configure the Cisco Catalyst SD-WAN fabric to achieve specific business outcomes. This chapter introduces the different types of Cisco Catalyst SD-WAN policies. In addition, this chapter focuses on the necessary components and the process of building policies as well as how the policies are applied and where they are enforced within the network. Chapters 7 through 11 continue this conversation, with more detailed discussion of specific types of policies and how to use them to achieve the required business outcomes.

Purpose of Cisco Catalyst SD-WAN Policies

The ongoing transformation to digital business means that organizations are relying on their IT infrastructure more than ever before. There is more data flowing across the network, and that data is increasingly critical to ongoing business operations. Cisco Catalyst SD-WAN policies are the mechanism through which administrators can encode their intent into the network fabric, and organizations can start to realize new kinds of value.

IT administrators today are being tasked with meeting new demands from business leaders that have direct implications on the structure and operation of the network. One objective is to reduce the costs of the WAN transport infrastructure. Realizing this objective often involves moving from an active/standby design to a forwarding architecture where all links can be used in parallel. In addition, administrators are moving away from expensive, leased-line transports and relying more and more on commodity Internet circuits to meet their transport needs. At the same time, business stakeholders require the same application experience that they have traditionally had with MPLS transports. Policies allow network administrators to configure the Cisco Catalyst SD-WAN fabric in a flexible way in order to meet their business intentions.

In this chapter and the next several chapters, we discuss different types of policies and how they can be used with different use cases to solve business problems.

Types of Cisco Catalyst SD-WAN Policies

Network administrators use several different types of policies to meet their business objectives. Policies can be classified in several ways.

Based on the scope of impact, policies can be classified as either centralized policies or localized policies. Broadly speaking, a centralized policy is applied to the whole network and affects how routing information and data traffic are forwarded across the Cisco Catalyst SD-WAN fabric. Localized policies are provisioned locally to specific WAN Edge devices. Such policies control routing and traffic forwarding at the perimeter of the Cisco Catalyst SD-WAN fabric, where WAN Edge routers interface with traditional routers. Figure 6-1 illustrates the relationship between these types of policies.

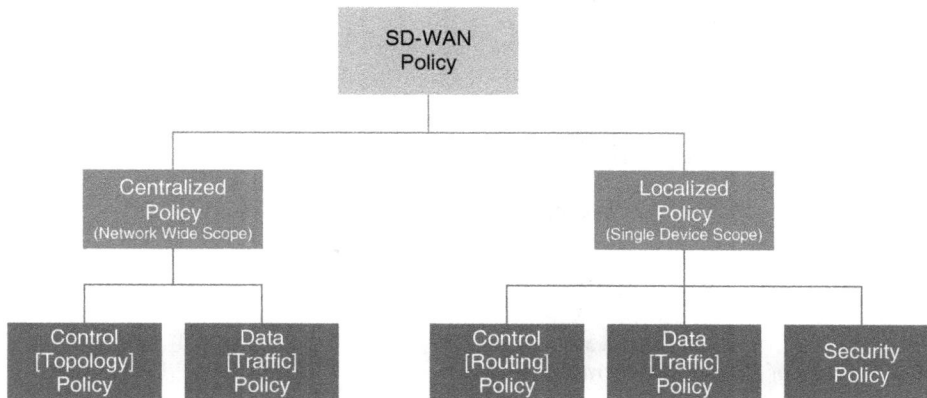

Figure 6-1 *Types of Cisco Catalyst SD-WAN Policies*

Based on the affected flow types, policies can be classified as either control policies or data policies. Control policies can be compared to the routing protocol policies in traditional networks. They affect the routing tables of WAN Edge devices and control how the routing information is exchanged between different devices. At a very high level, data policies can be compared to access control lists (ACLs) or policy maps. Data policies define how the data traffic flows through the SD-WAN overlay network.

Another type of policies in Cisco Catalyst SD-WAN fabric is security policies. Security policies control the security operations in the overlay network, such as zone-based firewall, Intrusion Prevention System (IPS), URL filtering, Advanced Malware Protection (AMP), DNS Security, and TLS/SSL decryption. (Security policies are covered in Chapter 11, "Cisco Catalyst SD-WAN Security.")

Centralized Policies

Figure 6-2 shows a deeper classification of centralized policies. Control policies (also called *Topology policies* in the SD-WAN Manager GUI) are used to manipulate the structure of the Cisco Catalyst SD-WAN fabric by altering the control plane information exchanged by Overlay Management Protocol (OMP). Data policies (called *Traffic rules* in the SD-WAN Manager GUI) are used to manipulate the data plane directly by altering the forwarding of traffic through the Cisco Catalyst SD-WAN fabric.

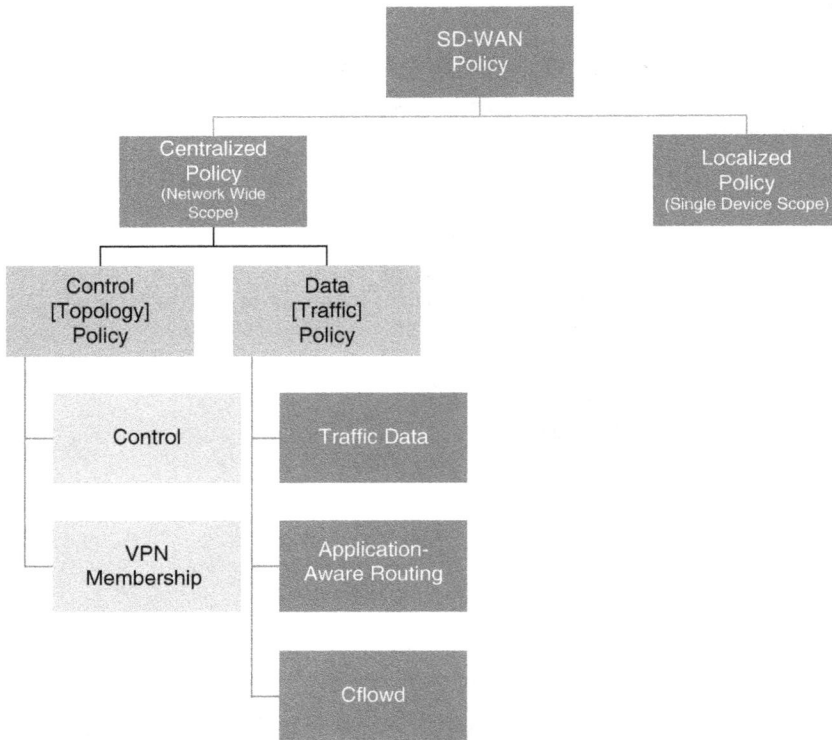

Figure 6-2   *Types of SD-WAN Centralized Policies*

Centralized Policies That Affect the Control Plane

Control policies and VPN membership policies are used to manipulate the propagation of routing information in the control plane, including manipulating or filtering OMP routes and Transport Locator (TLOC) routes. Chapter 7, "Centralized Control Policies," discusses control policies and VPN membership policies in more detail.

A *control policy* is used to control the exchange of routing information between different sites (for example, route advertisement, filtering rules), route manipulations (such as preferring one site over another for a specific destination or using default routing), building custom topologies on a per-VPN basis (for example, full mesh, partial mesh, hub and spoke), and limiting which sites can build tunnels directly across the fabric.

VPN membership policies are used to limit the distribution of routing information about particular VPNs to specific sites. One common use case for VPN membership policies is for guest segments where Internet access is permitted but site-to-site communication is denied.

Centralized Policies That Affect the Data Plane

Whereas control policies and VPN membership policies are used to manipulate the control plane, centralized data policies and application-aware routing policies directly affect the forwarding of traffic in the data plane.

A *centralized data policy* is a flexible and powerful form of policy-based routing and is commonly used to accomplish Internet access for specific applications, network service insertion, and data plane manipulations such as packet duplication and Forward Error Correction (FEC). Chapter 8, "Centralized Data Policies," covers centralized data policies in more detail.

An *Application-Aware Routing policy* is used to ensure that a particular class of traffic is always transported across a WAN link that meets a minimum service-level agreement (SLA). Chapter 9, "Application-Aware Routing Policies," covers these policies in more detail.

A *Cflowd policy* is a special type of centralized data policy that specifies the destination where flow records should be exported so that flow information is available on external systems for analysis.

Localized Policies

Much like centralized policies, localized policies can be used to manipulate both the control plane and the data plane. Figure 6-3 illustrates the three main types of localized policy: control plane, data plane, and security policies.

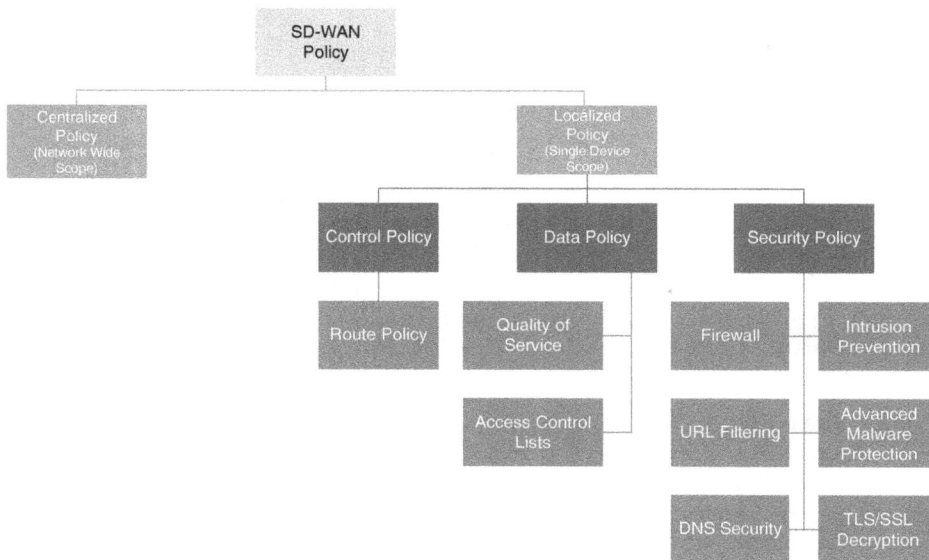

Figure 6-3 *Types of Cisco Catalyst SD-WAN Localized Policies*

Localized policies that affect the control plane, called *route policies*, control the WAN Edge routing behavior on the service-side network (that is, the LAN side). Route policies can be used to filter or manipulate routes exchanged or learned outside the SD-WAN fabric via protocols such as BGP, OSPF, and EIGRP. Route policies can also be used to filter routes as they are redistributed from one protocol to another—including into and out of OMP. Using a route policy is the only way to impact the control plane with localized policy.

Two main types of localized policies affect the data plane:

- **Quality of service:** Quality of Service (QoS) can be configured on WAN Edge routers to perform queueing, shaping, policing, congestion avoidance, and congestion management.

- **Access control lists:** Access control lists (ACLs) can be created with a localized policy to filter traffic at the interface level. ACLs can also be used to mark or remark traffic for QoS purposes.

Security policies allow network administrators to leverage the built-in advanced security features of Cisco Catalyst SD-WAN, such as next-generation firewall, IPS, URL filtering, Advanced Malware Protection, DNS Security, and TLS/SSL decryption (as of Version 20.12 of Catalyst SD-WAN).

NOTE   Sometimes a security policy is referred to as a different type of localized data policy because it is applied individually on the selected WAN Edge devices, and it affects the data traffic flow in the SD-WAN overlay network. At the same time, a security policy can be considered an independent type of policy because it adds a comprehensive set of features to provide full-stack multilayer security in the network.

Policy Domains

Figures 6-2 and 6-3 illustrate that both the control plane and the data plane can be manipulated with both centralized policies and localized policies. By comparison, Figure 6-4 illustrates the relationship between centralized control policies and localized control policies. Centralized policies are activated in SD-WAN Controller (formerly vSmart) and affect the control plane of the whole Cisco Catalyst SD-WAN fabric. Centralized control policies are present only on SD-WAN Controllers and are never sent to the WAN Edge devices. Localized control policies (which, you'll recall, are also referred to as *route policies*) are applied directly to the individual WAN Edge routers and affect the routing domain in the local site that is attached to the Cisco Catalyst SD-WAN fabric.

A similar distinction can be made about centralized data policies and localized data policies. Centralized data policies can affect the forwarding of data across the entire Cisco Catalyst SD-WAN fabric or the whole fabric site(s). Such policies are also activated on an SD-WAN Controller, but later they are distributed to WAN Edge routers via OMP. Localized data policies can be applied narrowly, such as to a single interface on a single router. Figure 6-5 illustrates these relationships.

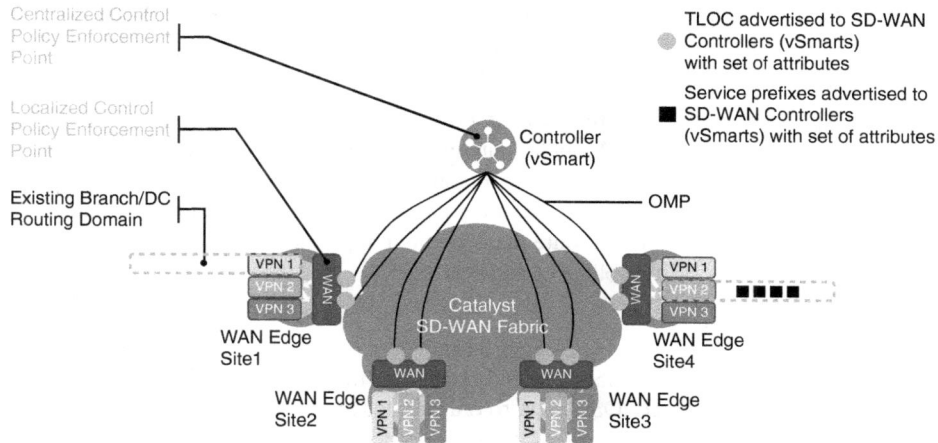

Figure 6-4 *Manipulating the Control Plane with Centralized and Localized Control Policies*

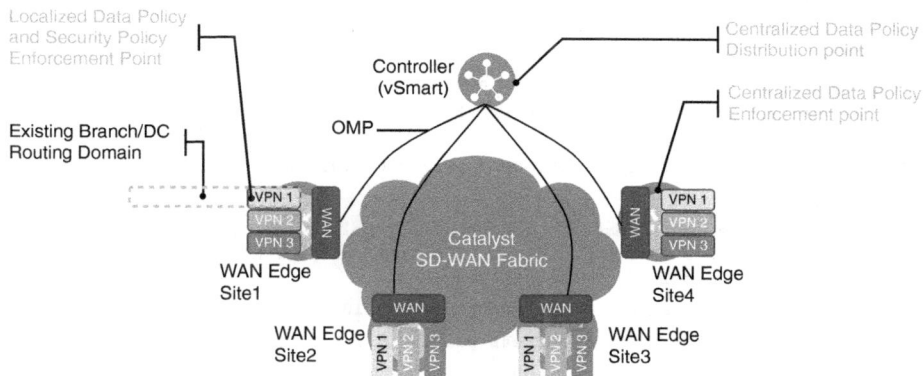

Figure 6-5 *Manipulating the Data Plane with Centralized and Localized Data Policies*

The remaining discussion in this chapter focuses primarily on centralized policies. While most of the concepts are applicable to both centralized and localized policies, there are some key differences in the way that localized and security policies are constructed and applied. These differences are discussed in further detail in Chapter 10, "Localized Policies," and Chapter 11, "Cisco Catalyst SD-WAN Security."

Cisco Catalyst SD-WAN Policy Construction

Cisco Catalyst SD-WAN policies may seem confusing at first look, but they are remarkably similar in construction and operation to routing policies created on traditional IOS routers. Creating a routing policy on a traditional IOS router is a three-step process:

Step 1.   Define lists to identify the groups of interest. Lists such as an access control list containing subnets of interest, an IP prefix list, and an autonomous system (AS) path list are commonly used for this purpose.

Step 2.   **Define a route map.** A route map is a structured sequence of match and set statements, where routes or traffic of interest from the list defined in the first step is matched and then the specific set of actions to be taken is listed.

Step 3.   **Apply the route map.** In order for a policy to have any effect at all, the route map must be applied. A single route map can be applied in a number of different ways, such as on an interface to configure policy routing in the data plane or on a routing neighbor to manipulate routing updates in the control plane. Configuring the list and route maps without applying them has no effect on the control plane or data plane of an IOS router.

Example 6-1 illustrates this process by showing a router at a remote site that has a BGP peering with a data center router (BGP neighbor 209.165.201.1). The network administrator creates and applies the policy in classic Cisco IOS syntax to only accept the default route advertisement from the data center router and to set a specific MED value for that default route.

Example 6-1   *Configuring a Routing Policy in Traditional Cisco IOS with a BGP Route Map*

```
REMOTE_R1#
REMOTE_R1#conf t
Enter configuration commands, one per line. End with CNTL/Z.
! Step 1: Define the list to identify the traffic of interest
! In this example, an IP prefix-list is defined to match only a default route
REMOTE_R1(config)#ip prefix-list DEFAULT_ONLY permit 0.0.0.0/0
REMOTE_R1(config)#
! Step 2: Define a route-map to execute the necessary policy actions
! In this example, sequence 10 permits the routes from our prefix-list,
! and sets the MED value to 1000; sequence 20 denies all other routes.
REMOTE_R1(config)#route-map PERMIT_ONLY_DEFAULT permit 10
REMOTE_R1(config-route-map)#match ip address prefix-list DEFAULT_ONLY
REMOTE_R1(config-route-map)#set metric 1000
REMOTE_R1(config-route-map)#route-map PERMIT_ONLY_DEFAULT deny 20
REMOTE_R1(config-route-map)#exit
REMOTE_R1(config)#
! Step 3: Apply the Route-Map
! In this example, the route-map is applied to one of the configured BGP neighbors
REMOTE_R1(config)#router bgp 101
REMOTE_R1(config-router)#neighbor 209.165.201.1 remote-as 10
REMOTE_R1(config-router)#neighbor 209.165.201.1 route-map PERMIT_ONLY_DEFAULT in
REMOTE_R1(config-router)#end
REMOTE_R1#
```

While Cisco Catalyst SD-WAN policies can appear intimidating to new engineers because they are much more flexible than traditional IOS-based policies, the same three-step process is used for configuring policies with Cisco Catalyst SD-WAN:

Step 1.   **Define lists to identify the groups of interest.** There are many more and different types of lists that can be used with Cisco Catalyst SD-WAN than with traditional IOS. This, in part, accounts for the greater flexibility with Catalyst SD-WAN than with traditional routing policy. In addition to using lists to identify traffic of interest, certain lists can also be used when defining actions and when applying policies. Lists are discussed in greater detail in the next section of this chapter.

Step 2.   **Define a policy.** Cisco Catalyst SD-WAN policies are defined in a structured sequence of **match** and **action** statements, where traffic of interest from the list defined in the first step is matched and then the specific set of actions to be taken is listed. There are many different types of policies that can be used with Catalyst SD-WAN to accomplish different objectives, but the structure of those policies is similar. The specific criteria that can be matched on and the different actions that can be taken differ between the types of policies.

Step 3.   **Activate the policy.** As with traditional Cisco IOS route maps, in order for a Cisco Catalyst SD-WAN policy to have any effect at all, the policy must be activated (that is, applied); a policy that has been configured but not applied does not affect the operation of the router. With Cisco Catalyst SD-WAN, centralized policies are always applied to a site list that matches one or more site IDs. If there are multiple WAN Edge routers at a single site, each of the routers configured with the same site ID will be subjected to the same centralized policy. Depending on the type of policy, the policy can also be applied to a specific VPN and to a specific direction of traffic flow.

Figure 6-6 illustrates this three-step process.

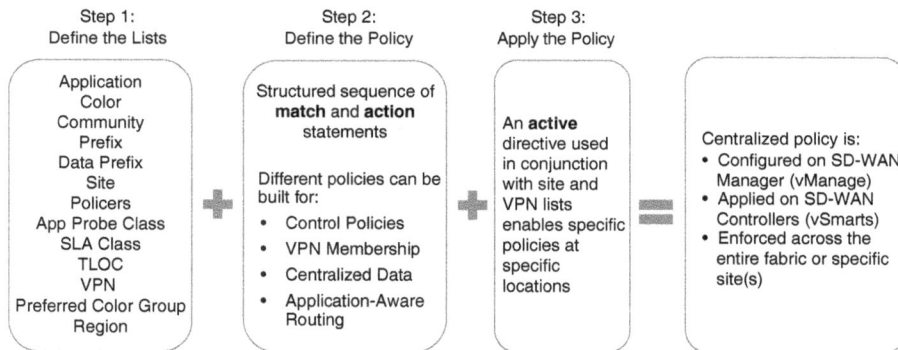

Figure 6-6   *SD-WAN Policy Building Blocks*

Figure 6-7 illustrates the configuration of the centralized control policy in Cisco SD-WAN Manager (formerly vManage). At this step, you define the sequence of **match** and **action** statements. Example 6-2 shows the configuration of such a centralized policy in the SD-WAN Controller CLI. As you can see, the three-step process for creating SD-WAN policies is similar to the process used with traditional routing policies, shown in Example 6-1.

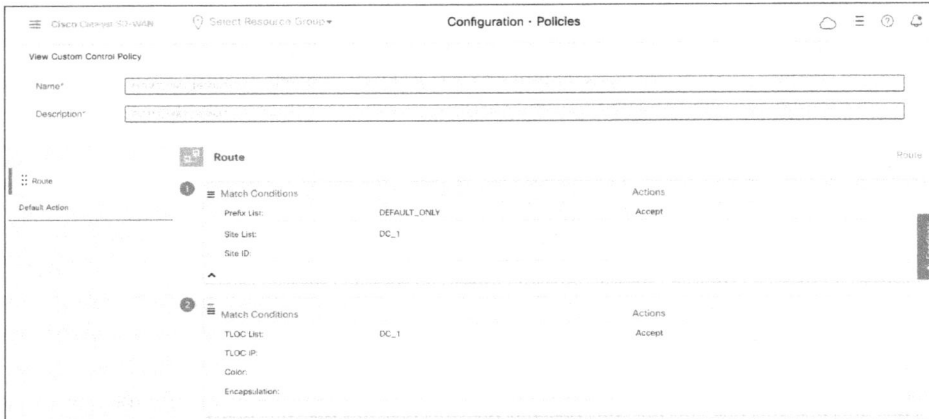

Figure 6-7　*Centralized Control Policy in Cisco SD-WAN Manager*

NOTE　In the SD-WAN Controller CLI configuration, centralized policies are always rendered in such a way that the policy definitions (step 2) are displayed first, the lists (step 1) are displayed second, and the policy applications (step 3) are displayed third, at the bottom. For this reason, some experienced engineers find it helpful to read policies from the bottom to the top, particularly when troubleshooting.

Example 6-2　*Configuring a Centralized Policy with Cisco Catalyst SD-WAN*

```
vSmart-1# show running-config
! Step 2: Define a control-policy to execute the necessary policy actions
! In this example, sequence 1 permits the routes from our prefix-list,
! and sequence 11 permits the TLOC Routes.
! The default action denies all other routes and TLOCs.
policy
 control-policy PERMIT_ONLY_DEFAULT
    sequence 1
     match route
      prefix-list DEFAULT_ONLY
      site-list DC_1
     !
     action accept
     !
    !
    sequence 11
     match tloc
      site-list DC_1
     !
     action accept
     !
    !
```

```
   default-action reject
 !
! Step 1: Define the list to identify the groups of interest
! In this example, a similar prefix-list is defined to match only a default
! route, as was done in Example 6-1.
 lists
  prefix-list DEFAULT_ONLY
   ip-prefix 0.0.0.0/0
  !
! Step 1 (continued): Two site-lists were defined to specify where
! the route is sourced from, and where the policy is applied.
  site-list REMOTE_1
   site-id 101
  !
  site-list DC_1
   site-id 10
  !
 !
 !
! Step 3: Apply the Policy
! In this example, the policy is applied to the remote site specified in the
! site-list REMOTE_1.
apply-policy
 site-list REMOTE_1
  control-policy PERMIT_ONLY_DEFAULT out
 !
 !
```

NOTE   Later chapters of this book review the construction of policies in much greater detail, so do not be concerned if the meaning of specific commands is not yet clear. The purpose of Examples 6-1 and 6-2 is to review the commonality of the structure of Cisco Catalyst SD-WAN policies with traditional control and data plane policies in Cisco IOS.

Types of Lists

Lists are the foundational building block of Cisco Catalyst SD-WAN policies. Lists allow for flexibility and extendibility in both how items are matched and how actions are taken in a Cisco Catalyst SD-WAN policy. Cisco Catalyst SD-WAN has many different types of lists that can be used to match different groups of interest in the control plane and the data plane. With centralized policies, the following types of lists can be used:

- **Application list:** An application list can match on a specific application or on an application family. These lists are used to assist administrators in creating business-relevant rules using Layer 7 application definitions rather than needing to specify Layers 3 and 4 (IP address and port) values. Common examples would include a VOICE_AND_VIDEO application list that matches applications such as RTP (VoIP) and WebEx, and a SCAVENGER application list that matches non-business-critical applications such as YouTube, Facebook, and Netflix. Application lists are only used as matching criteria.

- **Color list:** As discussed in Chapter 3, "Control Plane and Data Plane Operations," a *color* is an attribute of a TLOC. A color list can specify a single color or a group of colors. These lists can be used in both control plane and data plane policies, and they can be used as matching criteria as well as when specifying an action.

- **Community list:** A list of BGP communities can be used as both matching criteria and actions in the control policies. A community list defines which routes are accepted, preferred, distributed, or advertised. You can also use a community list under the actions to set, append, or modify the communities of a route.

- **Prefix list:** A prefix list is used to specify a range of routes in Classless Interdomain Routing (CIDR) notation. This list is used for matching routing information in the control plane exclusively and can only be used in control policies. Unlike in traditional IOS, where a single access list or prefix list can be used to match either control plane routes or data plane traffic (depending on how it is used in the policy), Cisco Catalyst SD-WAN defines two separate lists for these functions: a prefix list and a data prefix list.

- **Data prefix list:** A data prefix list is very similar to a prefix list; however, a data prefix list in Cisco Catalyst SD-WAN can only be used to match traffic in the data plane and is only used in data policies.

- **Site list:** Every site in the Cisco Catalyst SD-WAN fabric is assigned a site identifier called a *Site ID*. A site list can be a single Site ID, multiple Site IDs, or a range of Site IDs. Site lists are often used as matching criteria in policy statements and to specify which site or sites a particular policy gets applied to. This is discussed further in the following section.

- **Policers:** Much as with traditional Cisco IOS, with Cisco Catalyst SD-WAN, a policer is used for limiting the rate of ingress or egress traffic. A policer list can only be used as part of an action statement in a policy and not as part of a match statement.

- **SLA (Service-Level Agreement) class list:** An SLA class list is used with an Application-Aware Routing policy to define an SLA in terms of the maximum loss, latency, jitter, or a combination of the three, that a particular class of traffic should experience.

- **App probe class:** To measure the SLA metrics described previously, you can use passive traffic monitoring or active probing. Cisco Catalyst SD-WAN uses BFD probing for active measurements. An *App Probe Class* defines the forwarding class, color, and Differentiated Services Field Code Point (DSCP) value to be used when sending the probes. An *App Probe Class* can be used only inside the SLA class list and not directly in the policy. It is optional and needed only when active probing is used.

- **TLOC lists:** As discussed in Chapter 3, a TLOC (Transport Locator) serves as the next-hop address in routing lookups that happen across the SD-WAN fabric. A TLOC list is a set of next-hop addresses and can be used with both control and data policies to manipulate the next-hop address where the traffic should be forwarded over the SD-WAN fabric.

- **VPN list:** A VPN list is a list of service-side VPNs (or VRF instances) and is used to specify matching criteria in a control policy, such as which VPN segment a particular policy should be applied to.

- **Region list:** When Multi-Region Fabric is enabled globally, a list of regions can be used as matching criteria to specify the regions where the control policy should be applied.

- **Preferred color group list:** This list can be used in the Application-Aware Routing policy actions to define up to three levels of preferred transport priorities (primary, secondary, or tertiary) based on the color and the path type (direct or multi-hop) where the chosen application traffic should be preferably sent.

Policy Definition

While there are many different types of Cisco Catalyst SD-WAN policies, all of the policies are defined with a similar structure. Each policy is a numbered sequence of **match** and **action** clauses that are evaluated ordinally. Inside a particular sequence number, you may configure multiple matching conditions and multiple actions. If multiple conditions are specified, then a logical AND between the conditions is evaluated, and *all* of the criteria must be met in order to be matched by that sequence. In Example 6-3, the matching criteria of sequence 1 specifies that routes must match *both* (logical AND) the prefix list DEFAULT_ONLY and the site list DC_1_OR_2. Any default routes that are not from either Site 10 or Site 20 would not satisfy both of the criteria and therefore would not be matched by sequence 1 and would continue to be evaluated by additional sequences in the policy. Likewise, any routes from Site 10 or Site 20 that are not default routes would also not satisfy both of the criteria and would not be matched by sequence 1.

Example 6-3   *Centralized Policy with Multiple Matching Criteria*

```
vSmart-1# show running-config
! Output omitted for brevity
control-policy PERMIT_ONLY_DEFAULT
! Sequence 1 accepts routes that are matched by the prefix list DEFAULT_ONLY
! and the Site list DC_1_OR_2.
    sequence 1
     match route
      prefix-list DEFAULT_ONLY
      site-list DC_1_OR_2
     !
     action accept
     !
    !
    sequence 11
     match tloc
      site-list DC_1_OR_2
     !
     action accept
     !
    !
  default-action reject
 !
!
```

Sequence 1 in Example 6-3 shows that multiple lists can be specified as the matching criteria for a single sequence, and in that case, *all* of the matching criteria (both the prefix list and the site list in this example) must be met in order to be matched by sequence 1. At the same time, each of those lists can contain one or more values, as illustrated by the site list DC_1_ OR_2 in Example 6-4.

Example 6-4   *Lists That Match Multiple Values*

```
vSmart-1# show running-config
! Output omitted for brevity
lists
  prefix-list DEFAULT_ONLY
   ip-prefix 0.0.0.0/0
  !
  site-list REMOTE_1
   site-id 101
  !
  ! This list, when used as matching criteria, will match multiple values.
  ! Site 10 OR Site 20 will be matched by this list.
  site-list DC_1_OR_2
   site-id 10,20
  !
 !
!
```

In the event that the list being used as matching criteria contains multiple values, matching any one value will be sufficient for that criterion. In Example 6-3, sequence 1 will match routes sourced from the Site-ID list DC_1_OR_2, which is defined in Example 6-4 to be either Site-ID 10 or Site-ID 20. In this way, you can see that the multiple values within a single list, when used as a match condition, are treated as a logical OR. As each router is configured with a single Site ID, there is no way that a single route could fulfill the matching criteria to be from Site-ID 10 *and* Site-ID 20 at the same time.

NOTE   This chapter explains the fundamental principles of policy operations in the typical deployments where remote sites communicate with each other only via the SD-WAN fabric. The traffic flows might be different in more specialized and targeted use cases, such as when two sites are directly connected with a Data Center Interconnect (DCI) link. In such scenarios, the policy configuration may need to be adjusted to reflect the actual network requirements.

Key Topic

Much as in traditional Cisco route maps and ACLs, the matching logic applied in Cisco Catalyst SD-WAN policies is on a first-match basis. As soon as any given sequence in the policy is matched, those specific actions are taken, and no further match statements are evaluated. Therefore, it is a common practice to put the most specific matching criteria at the beginning of a policy and the broader, more general matches at the end of a policy.

Once a particular sequence number is matched, the first action that an administrator configures is to either "Accept or Reject" in a centralized control policy or "Accept or Deny" in a centralized data policy; this choice is mandatory. In addition, optional actions can be configured. If an entry in a control policy is rejected, no further actions can be taken. With a data policy, if the traffic is denied, you have the option to log or count the traffic. If the matching entry is accepted, there are many more possible options that can be taken in both cases. Example 6-5 provides an example of these **action** statements. (Subsequent chapters provide additional examples in much greater detail.)

Example 6-5 *Policy Actions and Default Action*

```
vSmart-1# show running-config
! Output omitted for brevity
control-policy PERMIT_ONLY_DEFAULT
    sequence 1
     match route
      prefix-list DEFAULT_ONLY
      site-list DC_1_OR_2
     !
! Every policy sequence either accepts or denies (for control policies),
! or accepts / rejects (for data policies) entries
     action accept
     !
    !
    sequence 11
     match tloc
      site-list DC_1_OR_2
     !
     action accept
     !
    !

! Every policy has a default action that applies when no other sequences
! have been matched
  default-action reject
 !
!
```

Each policy also has a default action as the very last sequence. This default action is similar to the implicit denial in traditional Cisco ACLs and route maps, but unlike with traditional Cisco route maps, the default action in a policy is always configured explicitly. When configuring centralized policies, it is important to keep in mind that the default action exists and by default is set to reject (for a control policy) or deny (for a data policy). Example 6-5 highlights the default action configuration.

Cisco Catalyst SD-WAN Policy Administration, Activation, and Enforcement

As discussed earlier in this chapter, each of the several different kinds of centralized policies (including control, VPN membership, centralized data policies, and Application-Aware Routing policies) are configured as individual component policies. Each of these component policies has its own specific sequence of **match** and **action** statements and is processed completely independently from the others. These individual policies are then combined into a single centralized policy.

Building a Centralized Policy

Example 6-6 demonstrates the process of combining multiple component policies together. This example continues to build on the policy that was created in Examples 6-4 and 6-5 and adds a centralized data policy to filter the traffic from a specific application on the network. This centralized data policy has a single sequence, sequence 1, that matches on an application list called BLOCKED_APPS. In addition to the new centralized data policy, Example 6-6 also includes several new lists, including the application list BLOCKED_APPS, the VPN list CORP_VPN, and the site list ALL_BRANCHES.

Finally, the apply-policy stanza at the end of the policy has been updated. This stanza now indicates that the new data policy has been applied to the sites indicated by the ALL_ BRANCHES site list.

Example 6-6   *Centralized Policy with Multiple Component Subpolicies*

```
vSmart-1# show running-config
! Output omitted for brevity
policy
 control-policy PERMIT_ONLY_DEFAULT
    sequence 1
     match route
      prefix-list DEFAULT_ONLY
      site-list DC_1_OR_2
     !
     action accept
     !
    !
    sequence 11
     match tloc
      site-list DC_1_OR_2
     !
     action accept
     !
    !
  default-action reject
 !
! The new data policy "_CORP_VPN_BLOCK_BAD_APPS" has been added
 data-policy _CORP_VPN_BLOCK_BAD_APPS
! This policy only applies to traffic in the specified VPN list
  vpn-list CORP_VPN
    sequence 1
     match
      app-list BLOCKED_APPS
     !
```

```
      action drop
      !
      !
  default-action accept

 lists
  app-list BLOCKED_APPS
   app youtube
   !
 prefix-list DEFAULT_ONLY
   ip-prefix 0.0.0.0/0
   !
 site-list ALL_BRANCHES
   site-id 101-103
   !
site-list REMOTE_1
   site-id 101
   !
  site-list DC_1_OR_2
   site-id 10,20
   !
 vpn-list CORP_VPN
   vpn 10
  !
 !
! The new data policy has been applied to all of the sites referenced
! by the site-list "ALL_BRANCHES".
 !
apply-policy
 site-list ALL_BRANCHES
  data-policy _CORP_VPN_BLOCK_BAD_APPS all
  !
 site-list REMOTE_1
  control-policy PERMIT_ONLY_DEFAULT out
  !
 !
```

As Example 6-6 shows, a single centralized policy can consist of many different component policies that can be applied to different subsets of sites in the apply-policy stanza to implement the intent of the administrator. The control policy PERMIT_ONLY_DEFAULT is only applied to Site ID 101, and at the same time, the data policy _CORP_VPN_BLOCK_BAD_ APPS is applied to Site IDs 101–103. In this way, a single site with the Site ID 101 would have both the control and data policies applied, while sites with Site IDs 102–103 would only have the data policy applied.

A Centralized data policy is always applied with a site list, a VPN list, and a direction. The direction is either configured as from-tunnel (which means from WAN to LAN), from-service (which means from LAN to WAN), or all. These policies can manipulate traffic that is both being received from the fabric and transmitted across the fabric. In Example 6-6, the data policy is configured with the *all* option, which indicates that this policy is applied to traffic flowing in both directions. Chapter 8 discusses these options in further detail.

An Application-Aware Routing policy is always configured with a VPN list and a site list, but not with explicitly configured directionality. As the purpose of an Application-Aware Routing policy is to select the specific tunnel in which the SD-WAN traffic should be forwarded (based on the real-time performance of the site-to-site tunnels), Application-Aware Routing policies can only be used when the traffic is destined across the fabric. The directionality of this policy is always fixed; it is not logical to configure an Application-Aware Routing policy for traffic that is already received across the Cisco Catalyst SD-WAN fabric and being forwarded out to a local service-side VPN interface. Chapter 9 discusses this in further detail.

Key Topic

Each Cisco Catalyst SD-WAN fabric can have only a single centralized policy that is active at any point in time. That single policy can have as many different component policies as necessary, and those component policies can apply to different sets of sites or VPNs in order to accomplish the desired business outcomes. In the case of Example 6-6, this complete centralized policy is the combined entirety of the named control and data policies, the lists that are referenced in those policies, and the apply-policy stanza that specifies where the policies will be enforced. All of these elements *together* make up a single centralized policy and are indented under the policy statement in the very first line.

Activating a Centralized Policy

SD-WAN Manager is the single point of administration for the entire Cisco Catalyst SD-WAN fabric. This is the place where all management, monitoring, configuration, and troubleshooting are done for the entirety of the solution—including the configuration of all policies. Whereas this chapter primarily deals with the building blocks of policies with the CLI as an introduction, the following chapters walk through many different examples of policy configuration and activation using SD-WAN Manager, which is how most enterprises choose to manage their environments.

After a centralized policy is built in SD-WAN Manager, it is activated, and SD-WAN Manager writes that policy in its entirety into the configuration of SD-WAN Controller. This configuration transaction is accomplished through NETCONF—the same mechanism that is used to configure the WAN Edge configurations from SD-WAN Manager. As NETCONF is being used to modify the configuration of the SD-WAN Controllers, it is typical for the application process to take several seconds. As this process modifies the configuration of the SD-WAN Controllers, this means the policy changes are persistent. If an SD-WAN Controller reboots for any reason, when it reinitializes, it has a copy of the last policy that was configured from SD-WAN Manager.

A typical production deployment has two or more SD-WAN Controllers, depending on redundancy and scale needs, and it is the responsibility of SD-WAN Manager to ensure that the policy configuration on all of the SD-WAN Controllers remains synchronized. If, for some reason, the policy change is not applied successfully to all of the SD-WAN Controllers, SD-WAN Manager automatically rolls back the policy change from all SD-WAN Controllers.

NOTE Because activating a policy on SD-WAN Manager actually means manipulating the configuration of the SD-WAN Controller itself, the SD-WAN Controllers must be under the control of SD-WAN Manager (that is, in "Manager mode," also known as "vManage mode") and must have a template applied from SD-WAN Manager. This allows SD-WAN Manager to have authoritative control of the configuration of SD-WAN Controller. It does not matter whether the SD-WAN Controllers are running CLI templates or feature templates, but a template must be applied. It is very common for production deployments to use CLI templates for this use case, as they are quick, simple, and do not require administration beyond the initial deployment. Note that this is different from how most production deployments configure both the SD-WAN Validators (formerly vBond) and SD-WAN Manager itself; it is very common for no templates at all to be applied to SD-WAN Validator and SD-WAN Manager.

Key Topic

While all of the policies in the Cisco Catalyst SD-WAN fabric are administered in SD-WAN Manager, different types of policies are enforced at different locations in the network. Because Application-Aware Routing policies and data policies manipulate the forwarding of traffic in the data plane (and these policies are enforced on the WAN Edge routers), these policies need to be propagated all the way to the WAN Edge routers. With Cisco Catalyst SD-WAN, this is accomplished by configuring the policies in SD-WAN Manager and activating the policies to the SD-WAN Controllers. The SD-WAN Controller then encodes the necessary parts of the policies into an OMP update and advertises these policies to the WAN Edge routers. The left column in Figure 6-8 illustrates this process.

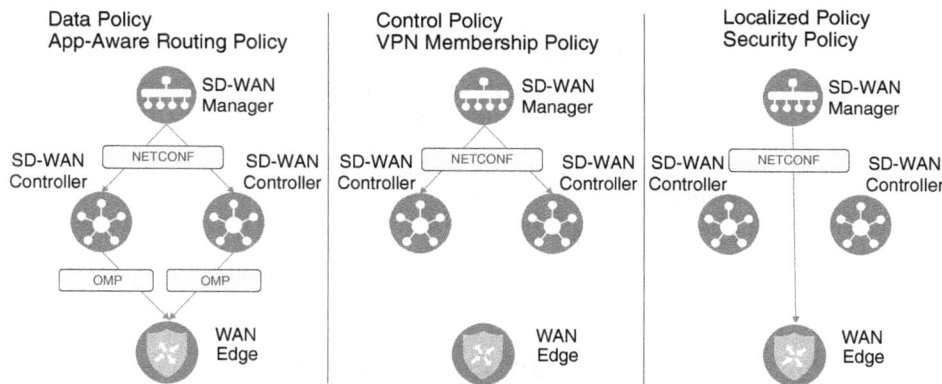

Figure 6-8   *Policy Administration, Activation, and Enforcement*

The architectural decision to encode centralized data policy updates in OMP rather than to encode them into the configuration of the WAN Edge with NETCONF has several important implications. Transmitting the centralized data policy as an OMP routing update allows for large-scale changes to be rolled out to the entire SD-WAN fabric very quickly rather than requiring individual NETCONF configuration transactions on potentially hundreds or thousands of devices (which could take minutes to tens of minutes).

Centralized data policy changes can be rolled out to the entirety of the fabric as quickly as any other routing update can be propagated and processed—typically, in a matter of seconds after the configuration is applied to the SD-WAN Controllers. In addition, because the policies are not stored in the configuration of the router, if the router reloads for any reason, the policy configuration is lost, and upon reinitialization, the router will have no effective policy. This is not considered a problem, as the WAN Edge will need to establish control connections with the SD-WAN Controllers in order to build fabric tunnels and forward traffic, and it will relearn the necessary policy information through OMP updates at that time.

Key Topic

As centralized control policies and VPN membership policies manipulate control plane updates, these policies are enforced on the SD-WAN Controllers. Fundamentally, these control policies manipulate or restrict the advertisement of control plane information. As all control plane information flows through the SD-WAN Controllers, enforcing control policies on the SD-WAN Controller provides an elegant, simple, and scalable solution. There is no need for these policies to be advertised to the individual WAN Edge routers. Instead, the effects of these policies are seen in the routing updates that are propagated from the SD-WAN Controllers to the WAN Edge routers. The center column of Figure 6-8 shows this relationship.

Key Topic

All localized policies, including traditional localized policies and security policies, are administered in SD-WAN Manager and configured directly to the WAN Edge routers via device template configuration. In this way, localized policies have much more in common with feature templates than do centralized policies. Localized policies and security policies do not directly interact with the SD-WAN Controllers. The rightmost column of Figure 6-8 illustrates this relationship.

Catalyst SD-WAN Version 20.12 introduced a new way to apply policies in SD-WAN Manager: via policy groups. With a policy group, you can build a logical grouping of different policies and deploy them to sites or devices that are managed by configuration groups. Policy groups are covered in more detail in Chapters 9 and 11.

NOTE   It is possible to manually configure policies directly onto the SD-WAN Controllers rather than administer and activate them through SD-WAN Manager. While this is technically feasible, the vast majority of networks are not administered this way, and this model of administration is outside the scope of this book.

Packet Forwarding Order of Operations

Because multiple types of policies can be applied to a given site and affect the forwarding of a single flow, it is important to understand the order in which these policies are applied and evaluated and how they work together. First, because control policies do not directly affect the data plane, they are processed independently of data plane policies. Control policies instead impact the routing information that the data plane is built on and, in this manner, they are able to impact the forwarding of traffic. Because control policies filter, manipulate, summarize, or restrict the advertisement of a specific routing prefix or TLOC, a WAN Edge device will have altered control plane information and will build its forwarding plane from this altered control plane information. Figure 6-9 shows the packet forwarding order of operations.

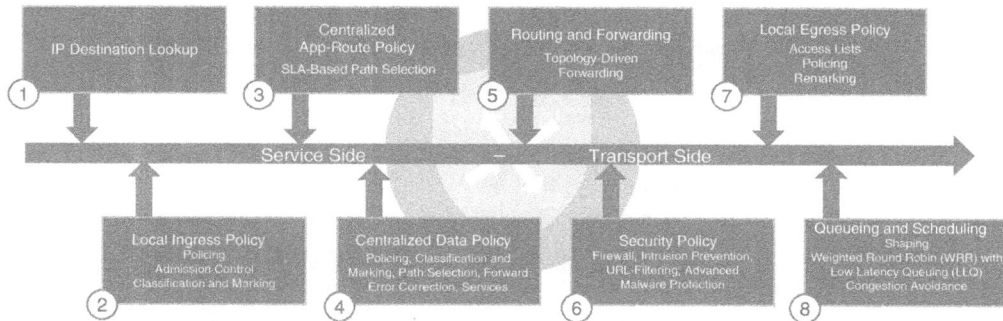

Figure 6-9 *Packet Forwarding Order of Operations*

The following steps are evaluated sequentially when forwarding a packet through a WAN Edge:

Step 1. **IP destination lookup:** The first step in the packet-forwarding process is to perform a routing lookup on the destination IP address of the packet in the routing table. This information is then used to inform the rest of the forwarding decisions that are made as the packet is processed through the WAN Edge.

Step 2. **Ingress interface ACL:** Localized policy can be used to create ACLs and tie them to interface templates. Interface ACLs can be used for packet filtering, policing, and QoS marking or remarking. If a packet is denied by the ingress ACL, it is dropped at this point and is not processed any further.

Step 3. **Application-Aware Routing (AAR):** The Application-Aware Routing policy is evaluated after the forwarding decision has been made based on the routing table. It is important to note that an Application-Aware Routing policy can only make distinctions between equal paths in the routing table. If the routes for a destination's multiple next-hop addresses are not equal-cost paths in the routing table, then the Application-Aware Routing policy will have no effect, and the flow will follow the most preferred path, based on the routing table. (This is explored further in Chapter 9.)

Step 4. **Centralized data policy:** The centralized data policy is evaluated after the Application-Aware Routing policy. If the data flow matches both Application-Aware Routing and the data policy, the following logic applies:

■ If the preferred colors in the AAR policy meet the SLA requirements, and some of those colors are present in the data policy, then the common preferred colors are chosen over others for forwarding.

■ If the preferred colors in the Application-Aware Routing policy do not meet the SLA, but there are other colors that are common with the data policy, and these colors meet the SLA in the AAR policy, then these colors take precedence and are chosen for forwarding.

■ If no tunnels or colors meet the SLA in the Application-Aware Routing policy, the data policy takes precedence and defines the colors to be used for forwarding.

Step 5.   **Routing and forwarding:** Routing lookups are performed to determine the correct output interfaces so that processing can be continued there.

Step 6.   **Security policy:** If security policies are configured, they are processed in the following order: firewall, Intrusion Prevention, URL filtering, and finally Advanced Malware Protection.

Step 7.   **Encapsulation and encryption:** As packets are prepared to be forwarded across the fabric, the necessary VPN labels and tunnel encapsulations are performed.

Step 8.   **Egress interface ACL:** As with ingress ACLs, local policy is able to create ACLs that are applied on egress as well. If traffic is denied or manipulated by the egress ACL, those changes will take effect before the packet is forwarded.

Summary

This chapter discusses the basics of building Cisco Catalyst SD-WAN policies. There are two main types of policies: centralized policies and localized policies. Policies are constructed from lists, which are used to identify groups of interest in both the control plane (such as prefix lists and site lists) and the data plane (such as application lists and data prefix lists).

Individual policies are structured sequences of **match** and **action** statements. The **match** statements are evaluated sequentially, and the first match wins. These component policies are then assembled into a single centralized policy that is activated on the SD-WAN Controller. The SD-WAN Controller enforces the control policies and encodes the necessary components of the data policies into OMP updates, which are advertised to the WAN Edge routers, where they are enforced in the data plane.

Review All Key Topics

Review the most important topics in the chapter, noted with the Key Topic icon in the outer margin of the page. Table 6-1 lists these key topics and the page number on which each is found.

Key Topic

Table 6-1   Key Topics

Key Topic Element	Description	Page
Paragraph	Policies using first-match logic	202
Paragraph	Structure of centralized policies	206
Paragraph/Figure 6-8	Centralized data policies	207
Paragraph/Figure 6-8	Centralized control policies	208
Paragraph/Figure 6-8	Localized policies	208

Define Key Terms

Define the following key terms from this chapter, and check your answers in the glossary:

centralized policy, control policy, data policy, localized policy

Chapter Review Questions

1. Which of the following are types of Cisco Catalyst SD-WAN policies? (Choose three.)

   a. Traffic engineering policy

   b. URL Filtering policy

   c. Application-Aware Routing policy

   d. Centralized data policy

2. True or false: Cisco Catalyst SD-WAN policies use a best-match (or most-specific-match) matching logic.

   a. True

   b. False

3. Which of the following are types of lists used in Cisco Catalyst SD-WAN policies? (Choose all that apply.)

   a. Prefix list

   b. SLA class

   c. Application list

   d. VPN list

   e. TLOC list

   f. Site list

4. True or false: A single IP Prefix list object can be used to match routes in the control plane and packets in the data plane.

   a. True

   b. False

5. Which of the following can only be configured as part of a local policy?

   a. Forwarding a specific type of traffic over a specific transport link

   b. Filtering specific routes from a BGP peer

   c. Dropping all YouTube traffic

   d. Forwarding voice calls over a link that has less than 150 ms of latency

6. Which types of policies are applied to and enforced on SD-WAN Controller (formerly vSmart)? (Choose all that apply.)

   a. VPN membership policies

   b. Topology (control) policies

   c. Zone-Based Firewall (ZBFW) policies

   d. Cflowd policies

7. Which types of policies are applied to and enforced on a WAN Edge? (Choose two.)

   a. Application-Aware Routing policies

   b. VPN membership policies

   c. Security policies

   d. Localized data policies

   e. Topology policies

8. Which types of policies are applied to SD-WAN Controllers (formerly vSmarts) and enforced on WAN Edge devices?

   a. Application-aware routing policies

   b. VPN membership policies

   c. Security policies

   d. Localized data policies

   e. Topology policies

9. In a typical Cisco Catalyst SD-WAN deployment, all policies are administered in which of the following?

   a. WAN Edge

   b. SD-WAN Controller (formerly vSmart)

   c. SD-WAN Validator (formerly vBond)

   d. SD-WAN Manager (formerly vManage)

   e. SD-WAN Policy (formerly vPolicy)

10. If a single flow matches sequences in both an Application-Aware Routing policy and a centralized data policy, and there are no tunnels or colors that meet the SLA in the AAR policy, the flow will be forwarded according to which policy?"

   a. Application-Aware Routing policy

   b. Centralized data policy

   c. Policy that was configured first

   d. Policy with the lower alphabetical order

CHAPTER 7

Centralized Control Policies

This chapter covers the following topics:

- **Centralized Control Policy Overview:** This section discusses the basics of centralized control policies and the directionality of policies when applied to an SD-WAN Controller.

- **Use Case 1: Isolating Remote Branches from Each Other:** This section covers the process of building a version of a hub-and-spoke network by applying a centralized control policy to limit the data plane tunnels that are built in the SD-WAN fabric.

- **Use Case 2: Enabling Branch-to-Branch Communication Through Data Centers:** This section covers the process of building another version of a hub-and-spoke network, using summarization and TLOC lists to enable sites that do not have direct data plane connectivity to communicate.

- **Use Case 3: Traffic Engineering at Sites with Multiple Routers:** This section covers the use of the TLOC Preference attribute to manipulate how traffic flows into sites with more than one WAN Edge router to influence symmetric routing.

- **Use Case 4: Preferring Regional Data Centers for Internet Access:** This section covers the use of the OMP Route Preference attribute to perform traffic engineering on a per-prefix basis.

- **Use Case 5: Regional Mesh Networks:** This section discusses how to create subsets of the fabric that have a full mesh of data plane connectivity, even while the whole fabric does not.

- **Use Case 6: Enforcing Security Perimeters with Service Insertion:** This section covers the use of service insertion to be able to direct a flow from anywhere in the fabric to a local or remote service.

- **Use Case 7: Isolating Guest Users from the Corporate WAN:** This section covers the use of VPN membership policies to be able to restrict which VPNs can join the overlay fabric.

- **Use Case 8: Creating Different Network Topologies for Each Segment:** This section covers the use of control policies to create multiple, arbitrary topologies that can be applied on a per-VPN basis.

- **Use Case 9: Creating Extranets and Access to Shared Services:** This section covers the construction of extranets to enable connectivity with business partners while still maximizing security posture.

Network administrators can use centralized control policies to manipulate the way traffic flows throughout the Cisco Catalyst SD-WAN fabric. Fundamentally, centralized control policies are the mechanism through which the control plane information that is advertised by Overlay Management Protocol (OMP) between the SD-WAN Controller (formerly vSmart) and WAN Edge routers is manipulated and/or filtered. By manipulating or filtering this information in the control plane, network administrators can influence the way that end-user traffic is forwarded in the data plane in order to accomplish their business objectives. This chapter explores several common business-relevant use cases, the network designs necessary to achieve them, and the centralized control policies used to implement them.

Centralized Control Policy Overview

Throughout the next several chapters, where we examine policies in Cisco Catalyst SD-WAN, we will be using the topology illustrated in Figure 7-1.

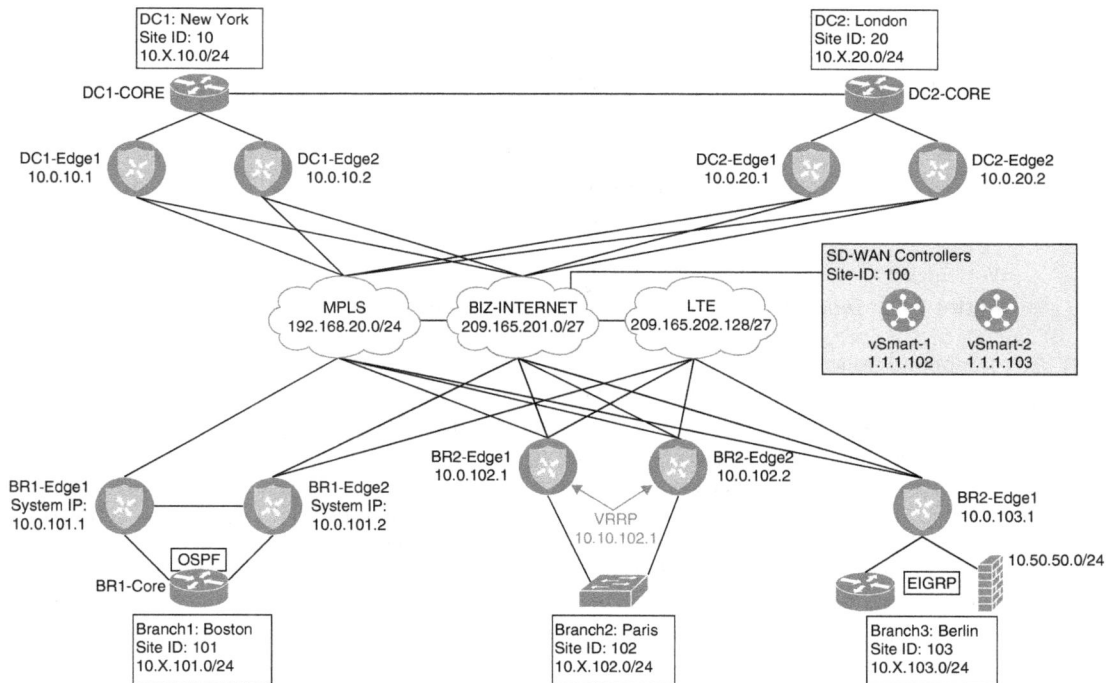

Figure 7-1 *Network Topology Overview*

This simple network topology features two different data centers (DCs) and three branch sites. Each data center has both an MPLS transport and an Internet transport. Each branch, in addition to having an MPLS transport and an Internet transport, also has an LTE transport. The hostnames, site IDs, router IDs, and network prefixes are also shown in this figure. The service-side addressing in this network follows the 10.X.Y.0/24 structure, where X signifies the service-side VPN, and Y signifies the site ID. For the first few use cases in this chapter, we will be focusing on VPN 10, but as we progress through the use cases, we will use additional VPNs 20 and 50. Therefore, all of the service-side addressing will be in the

10.X.Y.0/24 addressing blocks. The SD-WAN controllers and their system IP addresses are also indicated in this diagram. This topology will allow us to explore different types of policies, how they interact with the SD-WAN fabric, and how network administrators can apply these policies to solve business problems.

As discussed in Chapter 6, "Introduction to Cisco Catalyst SD-WAN Policies," each type of policy has a specific directionality to it. In the case of centralized control policies, policies can be applied in either the inbound or the outbound direction. This directionality is always from the perspective of the SD-WAN Controller, as shown in Figure 7-2.

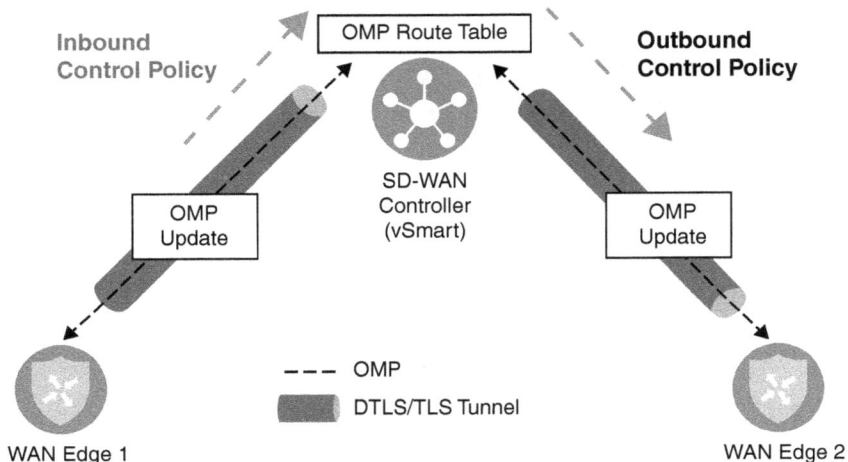

Figure 7-2 *Inbound and Outbound Control Policies*

Key Topic

Inbound policies are applied inbound on the SD-WAN Controllers on updates from the sites configured on the site list before the routes are processed through the best-path selection algorithm and before the routes are inserted into the OMP table on the SD-WAN Controllers. Therefore, any manipulation by inbound control policies will be evident in the SD-WAN Controller best-path selection process and, in turn, will be evident in the OMP advertisements made to all the other WAN Edge routers. Conversely, policies that are applied outbound apply after the SD-WAN Controller best-path selection process has been completed and are limited in scope to only those site IDs listed in the control policy application configuration. Centralized control policies that are applied inbound tend to be much more global in nature, whereas outbound control policies can be much more limited and targeted in scope and application.

In the following sections, we examine several different sets of business requirements and how network administrators can use centralized control policies to solve for these use cases. These use cases are meant to address common applications of centralized control policies as well as to provide an illustrative review of many of the building blocks of centralized control policies from which network administrators can build policies to accomplish their objectives.

NOTE This chapter is based on SD-WAN Version 20.12.

Use Case 1: Isolating Remote Branches from Each Other

The first use case we will be exploring involves turning the topology of the fabric from a full mesh into a hub-and-spoke design, with the data centers as hubs and the branch offices as spokes. Network designs like this are often used for several reasons: In many types of networks where security is a concern—like retail and finance, as well as a couple of market vertical examples—there is little need to be able to communicate from one branch directly to another branch. In such networks, the structure of the network can be changed to reflect the desired traffic flow, and the business intent can be encoded directly into the SD-WAN fabric. Furthermore, if this is a large network consisting of hundreds or thousands of spokes, the devices deployed at the branch sites may not have the capacity to build tunnels to all of the other branch offices. In this way, the devices at the branch offices do not need to be sized to handle hundreds or thousands of IPsec tunnels.

As discussed in Chapter 3, "Control Plane and Data Plane Operations," the default state of the Cisco Catalyst SD-WAN fabric with no policies applied is a full mesh. That is, every WAN Edge router builds an IPsec tunnel to every other router that it has reachability to. In our sample network, tunnels from the MPLS interfaces will only be built to the other MPLS interfaces. By contrast, tunnels from BIZ-INTERNET will be built to both BIZ-INTERNET and LTE interfaces on other routers. Tunnels from the LTE color will be built to both the BIZ-INTERNET and LTE interfaces on the other routers in the fabric. In this relatively simple network of only five sites and only nine routers, each of the WAN Edge devices at Branch 2 will build 24 different tunnels, as shown in the real-time output in Figure 7-3.

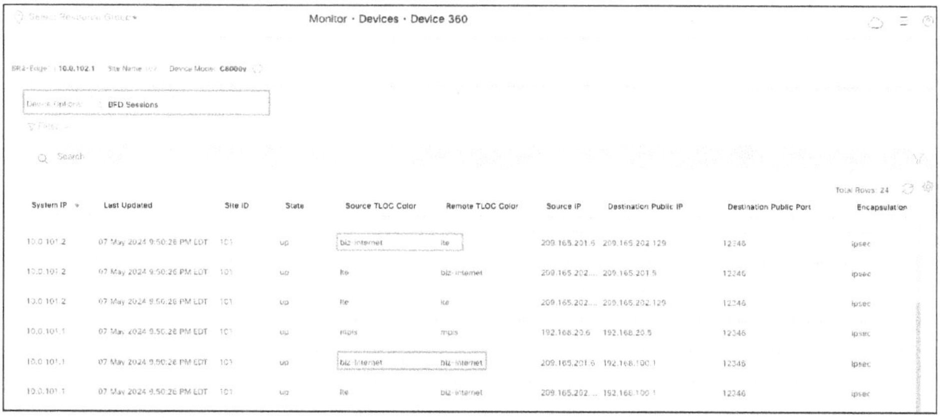

Figure 7-3 *BR2-Edge1 Tunnels with No Control Policy Applied*

NOTE The number of BFD sessions is directly influenced by the **restrict** attribute that is configured on the tunnel interfaces with the MPLS color. As outlined in the "Key Settings in Device Templates and Configuration Groups" section of Chapter 4, "Onboarding and Provisioning," this is a relevant setting for preventing session establishment between different types of transports.

You can access the real-time output, as shown in Figure 7-3, in SD-WAN Manager (formerly vManage) GUI by selecting Monitor > Devices > [*Device*]. You can use the Monitor > Devices display to track lots of information that administrators will find useful throughout the provisioning and operation of the Catalyst SD-WAN fabric. The Real Time option can be found at the very bottom of the list of elements. Once this option element is selected, the Device Options field at the top of the page can be used to query the device and display the output of a **show** command that would be used from the CLI interface. This feature is named Real Time because it queries the device *in real time* and does not rely on cached data, as do many of the other elements in the Monitor section of SD-WAN Manager. With this option selected, you might occasionally notice a slight delay as SD-WAN Manager queries the device for the requested real-time output.

Key Topic

As discussed in Chapter 3, the process of building data plane tunnels is controlled by the advertisement of Transport Location (TLOC) identifiers. If a WAN Edge device receives a TLOC route from the SD-WAN Controller, it will attempt to build a data plane tunnel to that TLOC and establish an encrypted Bidirectional Forwarding Detection (BFD) session, as long as the TLOC attributes such as **restrict** or **tunnel-group** are set to their default values. Monitoring BFD sessions, as shown in Figure 7-3, is a good way to understand whether tunnels are trying to be formed and whether they have been formed successfully. To change this behavior in the data plane, you must filter which TLOC routes are advertised from the SD-WAN Controller to the WAN Edge routers.

Key Topic

If the BFD session is working as expected, and there is bidirectional data plane connectivity, the BFD session will be listed in the "up" state. If the TLOC advertisement was received from the SD-WAN Controller, but the data plane tunnel is unable to form correctly, the BFD session will be listed in the "down" state. If the data plane tunnel does not appear in the list of BFD sessions, the WAN Edge device is not attempting to build the data plane tunnel. This behavior is generally caused for one of two reasons: Either the WAN Edge device has not received the TLOC advertisement from the SD-WAN Controller or the data plane tunnel is prohibited from being built by either the **restrict** or **tunnel-group** settings.

The current state of the network can also be examined in terms of the ways that traffic flows through the network. In Example 7-1, you can see that from Branch 2, the destination address 10.10.103.1 (which resides at Branch 3) is reached directly.

Example 7-1 *Tracing from BR2-Edge1 to BR3-Edge1*

```
! Traceroute from BR2-Edge1 to BR3-Edge1:
! The traceroute is successful, and shows that the path is direct
BR2-Edge1# traceroute vrf 10 10.10.103.1
<<<Output omitted for brevity>>>
  1 LTE-BR3-Edge1 (209.165.202.132) 32 msec 1 msec 0 msec
  2 BR3-Edge1-Core (172.16.103.2) 27 msec 1 msec *
```

```
! Traceroute from BR2-Edge1 to DC1 services:
! The traceroute is successful; resources in the DC are also direct
BR2-Edge1# traceroute vrf 10 10.10.10.100
<<<Output omitted for brevity>>>
  1 BIZ-INET-DC1-Edge1 (209.165.201.1) 37 msec 2 msec 0 msec
  2 DC1-Edge1-Core (172.16.10.2) 22 msec 1 msec 1 msec
  3 DC1-Service (10.10.10.100) 128 msec 1 msec 1 msec
```

In addition to the prefixes at Branch 3, Example 7-1 also shows that the prefixes in the data center are directly reachable. This is also reflected in the routing table, as shown with the real-time output, where the prefix 10.10.103.0/24 is reachable with the next-hop system IP address 10.0.103.1 (which is the system IP address of BR3-Edge1, as shown in Figure 7-1), and prefix 10.10.10.0/24 is reachable through the next-hop system IP address 10.0.10.2 (which is the system IP address of DC1-Edge2), as shown in Figure 7-4.

NOTE Remember that a TLOC identifier is composed of system IP address, color, encapsulation, and preference settings. The system IP address is independent of any IP address configured on device interfaces.

In order to implement the business intent to eliminate branch-to-branch communication and to reduce the number of tunnels that are established, a centralized policy can be created and applied so that the branches will only build tunnels with the data center WAN Edge devices. As each WAN Edge router will attempt to build tunnels to all of the TLOCs that it receives from the SD-WAN Controller, such a policy is architected to restrict the TLOC routes that are advertised to the branches to be only the TLOCs from the data centers (where the branches should still build their control connections).

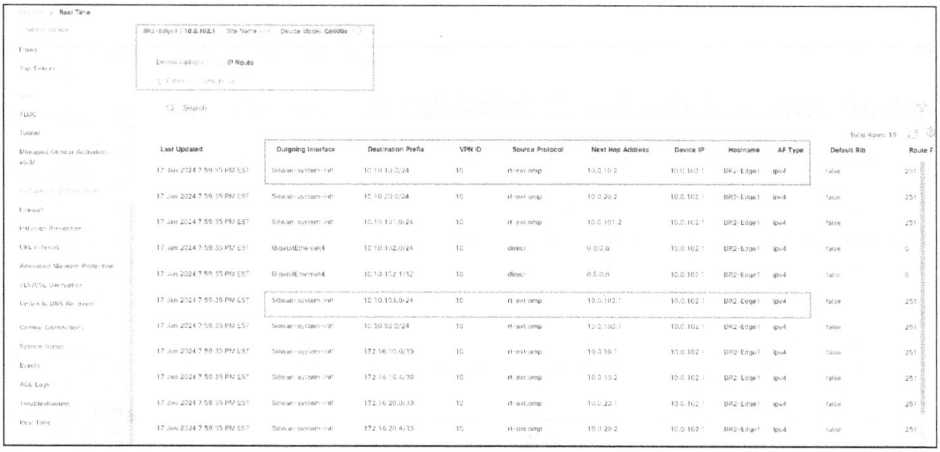

Figure 7-4   *Routing Table for VPN 10 on BR2-Edge1 with No Centralized Policy Applied*

The advertisement of TLOC routes is depicted in Figure 7-5 and involves the following steps:

Step 1.   All of the WAN Edge routers advertise their local TLOC routes to the SD-WAN Controllers.

Step 2.   The SD-WAN Controllers advertise all of the received TLOC routes back to all the WAN Edge devices. For the data center WAN Edge device, this means that the router receives all of the TLOC routes in the SD-WAN Controller table, including a copy of its own TLOCs. An outbound control policy is applied to SD-WAN Controllers that restricts the advertisement of the TLOC to only T1 and T2 (learned from the data center) to Branch 1 and Branch 2.

NOTE   The advertisements that the data center WAN Edge devices receive in step 2 contain all of the TLOCs in the network {T1, T2, T3, T4, T5, T6}, which is different from the TLOC routes received by the branches. The outbound control policy has limited the TLOCs that are advertised to the branches to only {T1, T2}, the TLOCs from the data center.

Step 3.   The effect of this policy can be seen when the data plane tunnels are built: All of the WAN Edge routers build data plane tunnels to all of the TLOCs they have received from the SD-WAN Controllers. For a data center WAN Edge device, this means that tunnels will be built to T3, T4, T5, and T6, the TLOCs of the branch routers. For the branches, tunnels will only be built to T1 and T2, the data center.

NOTE   There is no tunnel built from T3 to T5 or from T4 to T6 in Figure 7-5. Since the WAN Edge router at Branch 1 never received an advertisement for T5 and T6, it is unaware of those TLOCs and will not attempt to build those tunnels. Manipulating and restricting the advertised TLOCs, as shown in Figure 7-5, is the fundamental way to control which data plane tunnels are built in the SD-WAN fabric, and it is therefore the primary way that network administrators control the structure of the fabric.

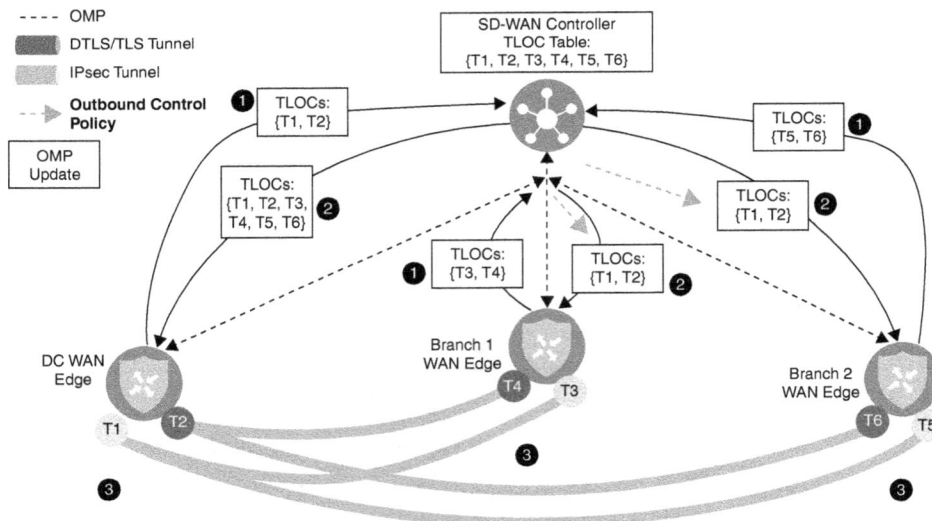

Figure 7-5   *Illustration of Control Policies Filter TLOCs*

NOTE   For the first two policy examples in this chapter, screenshots of the process to build and modify the necessary policies will be provided for both widely deployed traditional policies and a newly added topology approach. For brevity, the remaining policies in this chapter will be provided only with the CLI output to reflect the logic process, although the recommendation is to leverage the SD-WAN Manager GUI as it simplifies the process.

Custom Control Policy with a Traditional Workflow

The first step in constructing a custom control policy with a traditional workflow would be to open the Policy Wizard by clicking Add Policy from the Configuration > Policies screen in SD-WAN Manager, as shown in Figure 7-6.

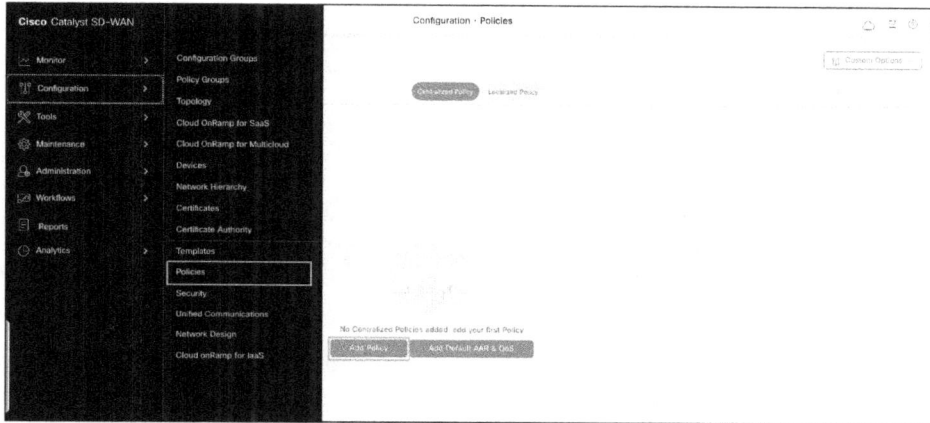

Figure 7-6 *Opening the Policy Wizard*

In the Policy Wizard, the first option is to configure all the criteria (lists) that will be used within this policy. For this first use case, you need to create two site lists: one that encompasses the site IDs of the data centers and a second that encompasses the site IDs of the branch offices. You create the site list by clicking on **New Site List** and typing in a friendly name and a specific site ID, a range of site IDs (separated with hyphens), or multiple site IDs (separated with commas). You can see these two lists in Figure 7-7. The ranges of site IDs configured in these lists reflect the ranges of site IDs identified in the network topology shown in Figure 7-1.

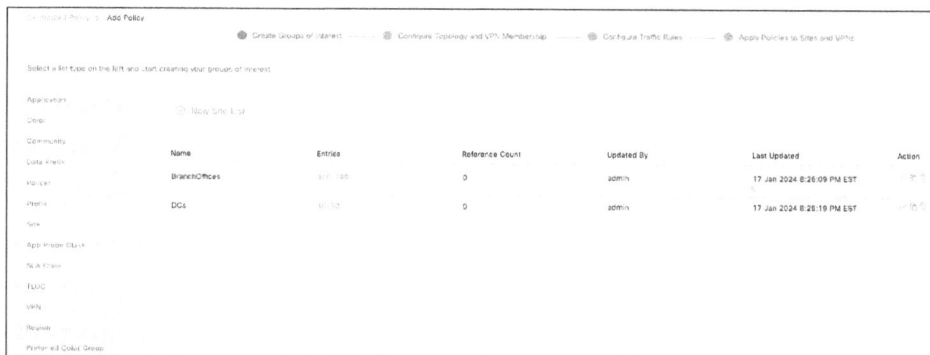

Figure 7-7 *Configuring Site Lists for Use in Centralized Policies*

After you click the Next button at the bottom of the Lists page, the wizard moves to the Configure Topology and VPN Membership page. On this page, click the Add Topology drop-down and select **Custom Control (Route & TLOC)** from the combo box, as shown in Figure 7-8.

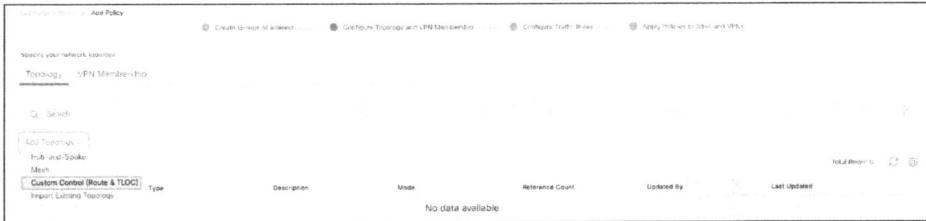

Figure 7-8   *Creating a Custom Control Policy*

NOTE   The SD-WAN Manager GUI includes wizards to build hub-and-spoke (where only hubs' routes are advertised) and mesh topologies, as shown in Figure 7-8. While some network administrators find these assisted workflows easier to use, this chapter focuses on custom control policies to better illustrate the construction of the policies and the principles behind their use.

The first pieces of configuration necessary for every control policy are the policy name and description, as shown in Figure 7-9.

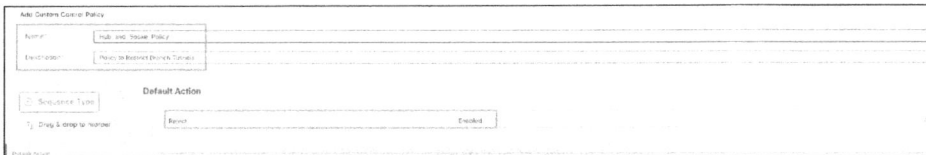

Figure 7-9   *Setting the Default Action in the Control Policy*

It is also important to notice in Figure 7-9 that the default action in custom route and TLOC policies is Reject, but this can be changed. If an OMP route or a TLOC is not matched by any other sequence in the policy and explicitly permitted, it will not be advertised from the SD-WAN Controller to the WAN Edge router.

Next, click the **Sequence Type** button and choose a TLOC sequence, as shown in Figure 7-10.

Next, create a new rule in the policy by selecting the + Sequence Rule option. In this sequence, specify a site list as the match criterion and match on the list called DCs, created previously. Finally, specify the action Accept with no further actions and then select **Save Match and Actions**, as shown in Figure 7-11.

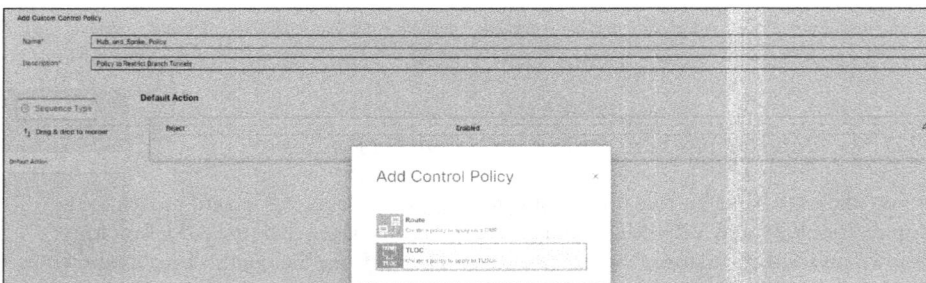

Figure 7-10   *Adding a TLOC Sequence to a Centralized Control Policy*

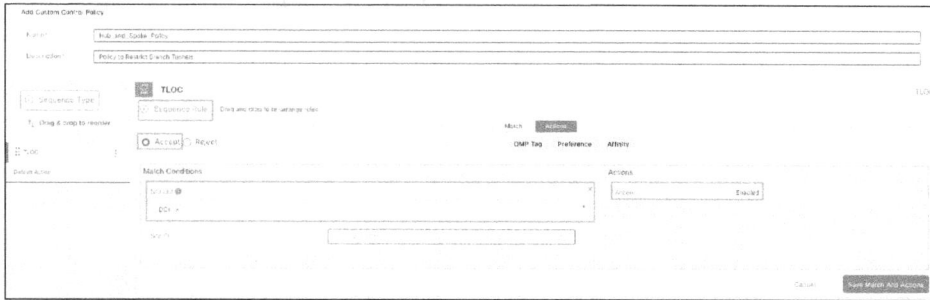

Figure 7-11   *Creating a TLOC Sequence Rule to Accept the DC TLOCs*

This TLOC sequence rule, in combination with the default rule that rejects anything that is not explicitly permitted, will result in only the DC TLOCs (that is, only the TLOCs from sites specified in the DCs site list) being advertised to the sites where this policy is applied. Once the TLOCs from the branch sites have been implicitly filtered, the network will have a topology analogous to that shown in Figure 7-5, and data plane tunnels will not form between the branch sites. However, as shown in Figure 7-4, the OMP routes for all the pre-fixes that exist at all the branch sites will still be reflected to all of the other branch sites. Without having received the necessary TLOC advertisements, these OMP routes will be unresolvable and unused, but bandwidth and compute resources will be wasted in transmit-ting these network updates.

Rather than continue to transmit routes that cannot be used, a better practice would be to filter out the routes from the branch sites in addition to the TLOCs. In order to accomplish this, select the **+ Sequence Type** button and choose Route, as shown in Figure 7-12.

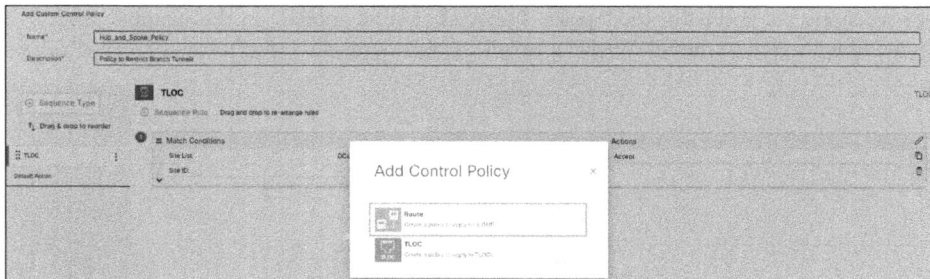

Figure 7-12   *Adding a Route Sequence to a Centralized Control Policy*

In a similar manner as was done for the TLOCs, the route sequence needs to be configured to match on the routes from the DCs site list and to accept them. No other sequences need to be configured at this time. You can see this configuration in Figure 7-13.

After the route sequence rule is saved by clicking the **Save Match and Actions** button, the entire policy can be saved by clicking the **Save Control Policy** button at the bottom.

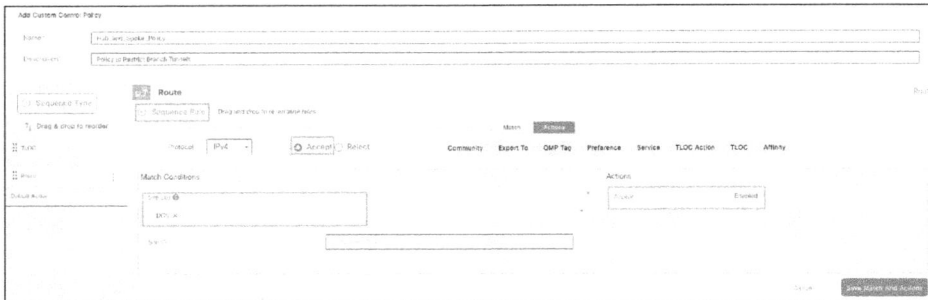

Figure 7-13   *Creating a Route Sequence Rule to Accept the DC Routes*

NOTE   Sequence types are a subset of sequences. As the policy engine converts the visual policy to command syntax, the *topmost* sequence is processed, with its associated sequence rules. The CLI sequences start with the number 1 and increment by 10. Once that sequence is complete, it moves to the next sequence and its associated rule sets and so forth until the default policy action is processed. You can rearrange the order of the sequence types and sequence rules by dragging and dropping them into the desired processing order.

Once the control policy is saved, you can progress through the SD-WAN Policy Wizard by clicking Next through the Configure Topology and VPN Membership and Configure Traffic Rules screens, until you arrive at the Apply Policies to Sites and VPNs screen, shown in Figure 7-14. On this last page of the wizard, you need to configure a name for the policy that consists of a maximum of 127 alphanumeric characters, a hyphen or an underscore, and a description. In addition, on the Topology tab, you must specify where and in what direction the recently created Hub_and_Spoke_Policy should be applied. In this example, the policy will be applied in the SD-WAN Controller's outbound direction to the branch offices.

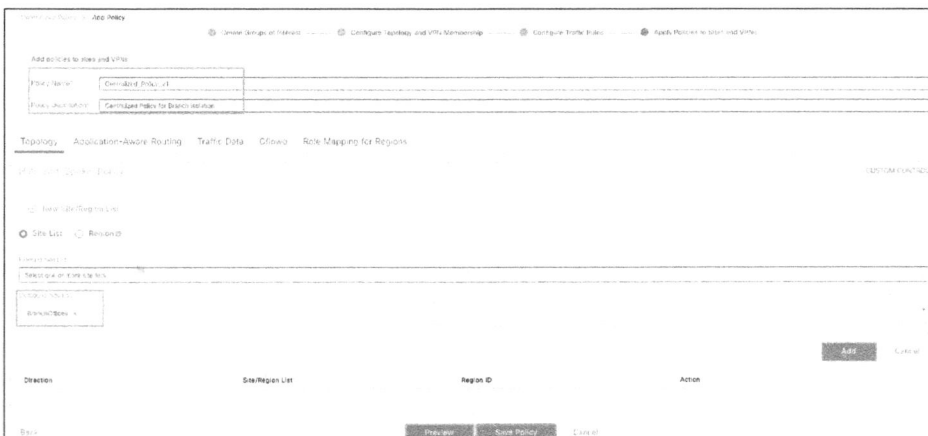

Figure 7-14   *Adding Policies to Sites and VPNs*

Only one global centralized policy can be applied at a time. This policy can contain different component policies, such as Topology, VPN membership, Application-Aware Routing (AAR),

Data policy, and cFlowd. The last page of the wizard is used to link these component policies to the sites and VPN, where they will influence behavior.

> **NOTE**   We recommend simply naming the centralized policies with intuitive names and version numbers, remembering to leave enough room to grow. In this case, the name Centralized_Policy_v1 was used as the policy name. As discussed in Chapter 6, there will only ever be a single centralized policy that is active at any point in time. From an operational view, it is easy to copy the existing centralized policy, increment the policy number, and then use the Policy Description field to list the changes from the previous version of the policy. In this way, you can create an archive of the policies on SD-WAN Manager. This way, should there ever be a need to roll back a change in the network, the process is as simple as activating a previous version of the policy.

Once the site list that the policy is to be applied to is saved by clicking the Add button, you can see the CLI of the entire policy by clicking the Preview button. Example 7-2 shows the full output of this policy.

Example 7-2   *Use Case 1: Complete Centralized Policy to Create Hub-and-Spoke Topology*

```
policy
 control-policy Hub_and_Spoke_Policy
    sequence 1
     match tloc
      site-list DCs
     !
     action accept
     !
    !
! The reference to the prefix list below was not configured,
! but instead was added automatically by SD-WAN Manager. The matching
! logic remains the same: Match all Routes.
    sequence 11
     match route
      site-list DCs
      prefix-list _AnyIpv4PrefixList
     !
     action accept
     !
    !
  default-action reject
 !
 lists
  site-list BranchOffices
   site-id 100-199
  !
```

```
! Only Routes and TLOCs that match this site list will be advertised
! by the policy above.
 site-list DCs
  site-id 10-50
 !
 prefix-list _AnyIpv4PrefixList
  ip-prefix 0.0.0.0/0 le 32
 !
!
!
! The policy is applied in the outbound direction to the sites that
! match the site list "BranchOffices".
apply-policy
 site-list BranchOffices
  control-policy Hub_and_Spoke_Policy out
 !
!
```

The policy can then be saved by clicking the Save Policy button at the bottom of the page
with the configuration preview. Once the policy is saved, it can be applied to the SD-WAN
fabric by selecting the **Activate** option from the policy menu, as shown in Figure 7-15. As
discussed in Chapter 6, in the process of activating a policy, SD-WAN Manager writes the
policy into the configuration of the SD-WAN Controllers.

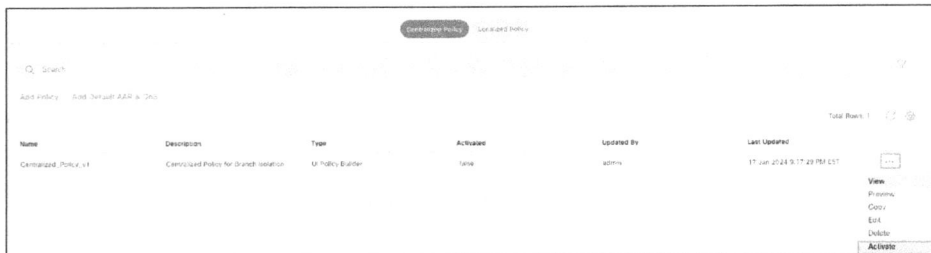

Figure 7-15   *Activating a Centralized Policy*

NOTE   Because configuring policy on a SD-WAN Controller from SD-WAN Manager is
actually manipulating the configuration of the SD-WAN Controller itself, the SD-WAN
Controllers must be in SD-WAN Manager (vManage) mode and have a template applied
from SD-WAN Manager. This allows SD-WAN Manager to have authoritative control of the
SD-WAN Controller configuration.

Topology Workflow Approach

The topology methodology of influencing a behavior at the SD-WAN Controller level is
available starting with SD-WAN Release 20.12. It allows you to provision mesh or hub-and-
spoke topologies with modular, reusable logic that is applied at one or more sites; this logic
can be added, edited, or removed easily based on site location, in contrast with the traditional approach that governs all sites. (You can find the prerequisites for this approach in the
official documentation "Policy Groups Configuration Guide.")

You can leverage this policy through a predefined topologies library that includes mesh and hub-and-spoke topologies, or you can create a custom topology, as in the traditional control policies case.

NOTE   Starting from SD-WAN Releases 20.12 and 17.12, the hub-and-spoke configuration approach also streamlines the setup of this type of topology, but it eliminates the need for a centralized control policy. Instead, it requires a simple configuration command at each SD-WAN Controller, hub router, and spoke router. For detailed information, refer to "Cisco Catalyst SD-WAN Routing Configuration Guide."

The initial step in constructing this policy through the first option is to open the Topology Wizard by clicking **Configuration > Topology** in SD-WAN Manager, as shown in Figure 7-16. (Notice that the following figures present both the guided workflow solution and a custom topology.)

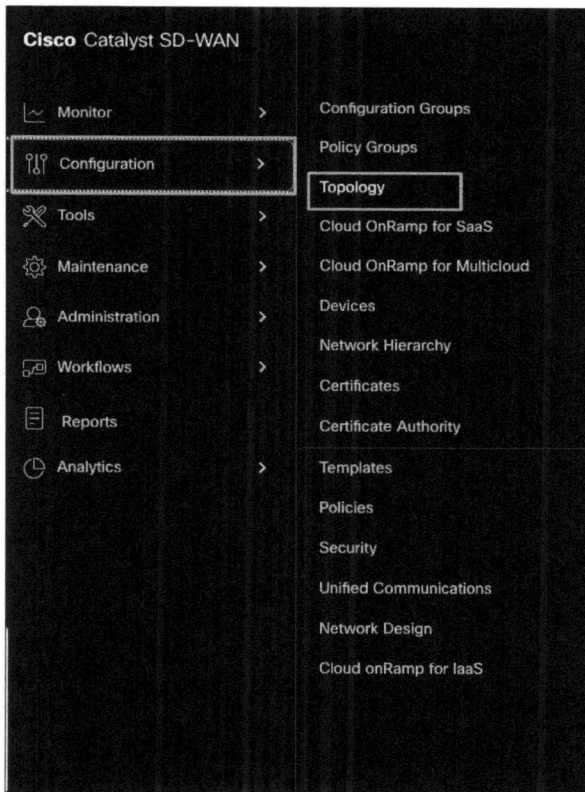

Figure 7-16   *Getting into the Topology Wizard*

In the Topology Wizard, you need to select **Create Topology**, as show in Figure 7-17, and provide a name and description for the topology policy, as shown in Figure 7-18. Then click Create.

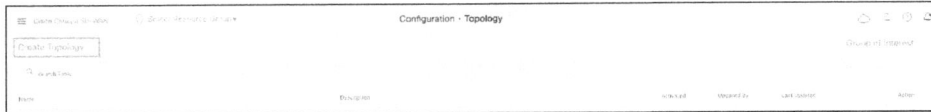

Figure 7-17   *Creating a Topology*

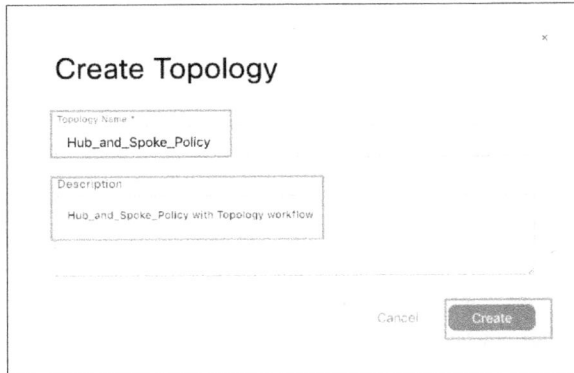

Figure 7-18   *Providing a Name and Description for the Topology*

After creating the topology, click **Add Topology** to reveal a drop-down menu, where **Hub and Spoke** is selected, to start creating the logic to isolate the communication between branches (see Figure 7-19).

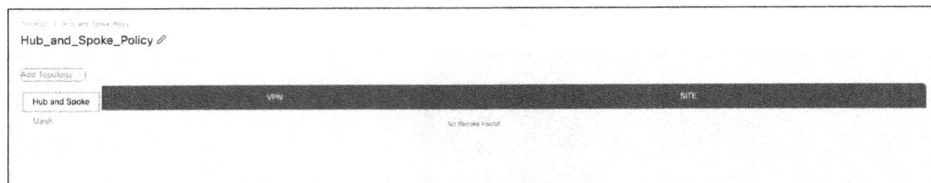

Figure 7-19   *Hub and Spoke Guided Workflow Selection*

Figure 7-20 shows that your next step is to provide a name for the policy (in this case, Hub_ and_Spoke_Policy) and select the data segment (VPN) that requires the topology enforcement.

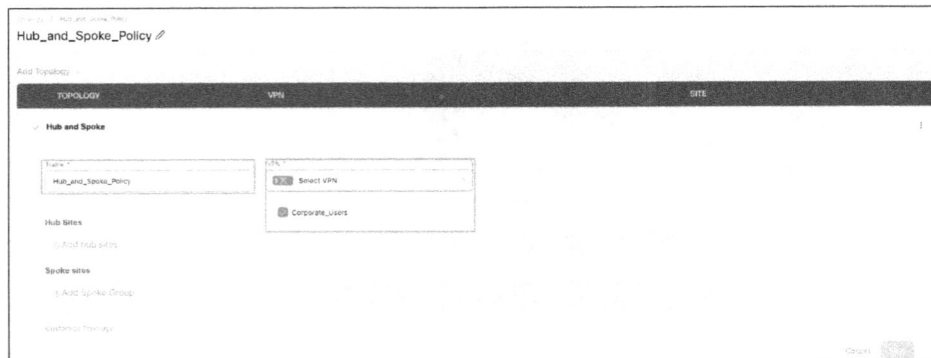

Figure 7-20   *Adding a Name and Selecting the Data Segment*

Select the appropriate site ID boxes of the sites to be used as Hubs and Spokes, respectively, in the lists shown in Figure 7-21 and Figure 7-22.

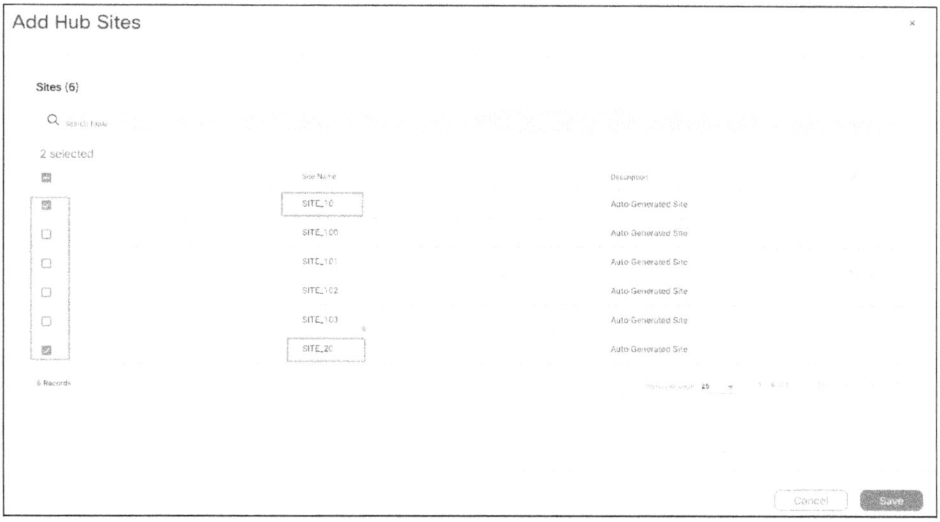

Figure 7-21   *Checking Site Boxes to Be Used as Hubs*

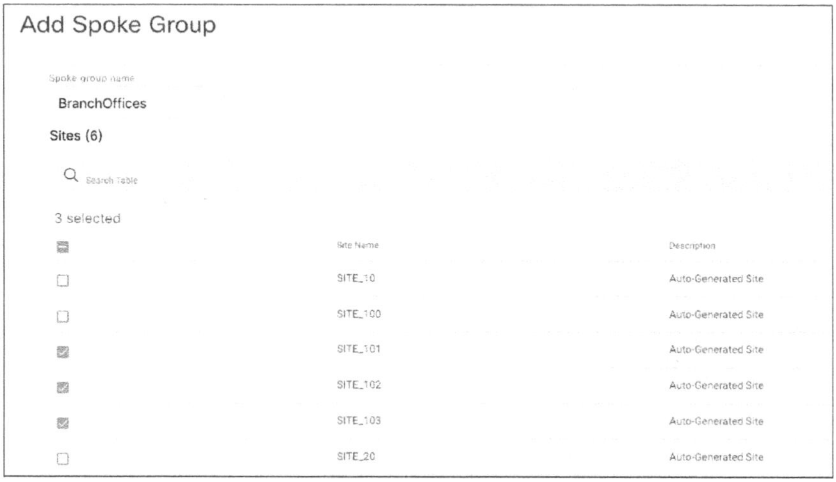

Figure 7-22   *Checking Site Boxes to Be Used as Spokes*

NOTE   Both data segments (VPNs) and site names available in this step are automatically created when the Configuration Groups workflow is used. Under Configuration > Network Hierarchy, you can manage SD-WAN fabric sites information such as name, description, and location parameters to simplify the overall experience. For more information, refer to the "System and Interfaces Configuration Guide."

In the Spoke Group selection screen, you can set a Hub Preference to specify the priority (see Figure 7-23). In this case, the data center sites are assigned the same priority, which means traffic will be load balanced. Click Save.

Figure 7-23 *Hub Sites Priority Setting*

As you can see in Figure 7-24, a summary screen shows the values previously populated through the guide workflow for the hub-and-spoke topology. Click Save to complete the configuration.

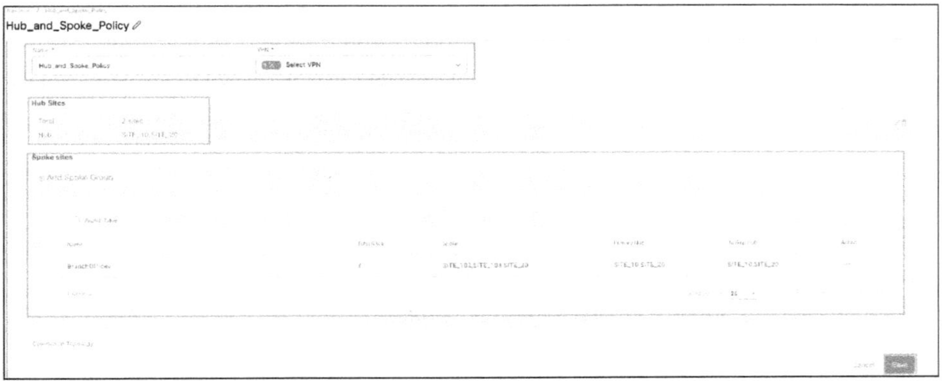

Figure 7-24 *Summary Screen for the Topology Group*

The previous workflow result is ready to influence the routing behavior when activated. This helps an organization quickly achieve the goal of applying a particular topology to the fabric, but you can see that there are not too many customizations available.

Figure 7-25 shows the policy activation procedure. Remember that an SD-WAN Controller needs to be attached to a template in order for SD-WAN Manager to have authoritative control of the configuration.

Figure 7-25 *Topology Activation*

When granular match-action pairings are required, using a custom topology is the best approach. You can start a topology from scratch or customize an existing one by selecting **Customize Topology,** as shown in Figure 7-26.

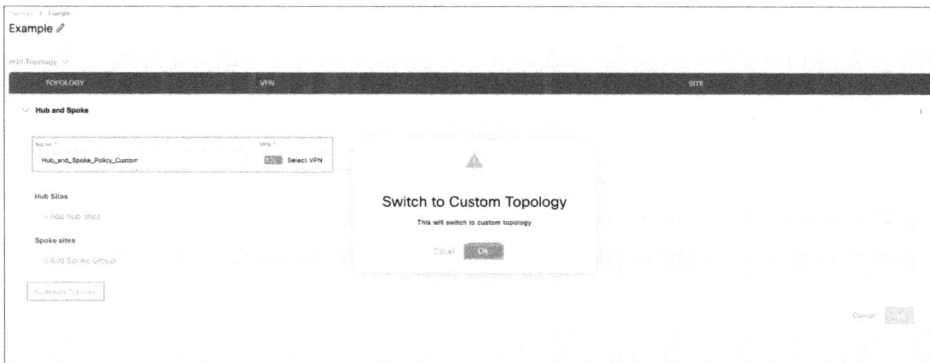

Figure 7-26 *Switching to a Custom Topology*

As shown in Figure 7-27, the first two parameters to provide for the custom topology are the name and VPN. As shown in Figure 7-28, the third parameter to specify is for Outbound Sites (which in traditional control policies means the outbound direction).

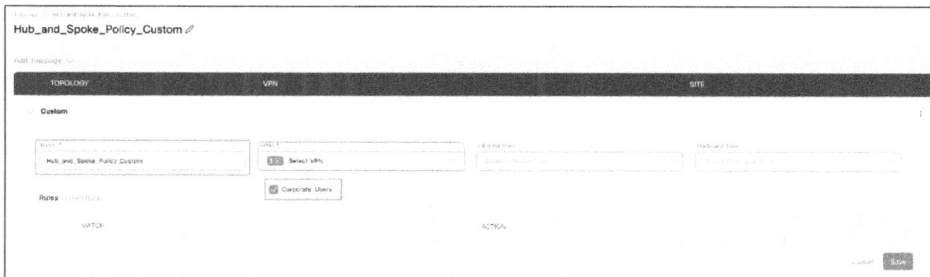

Figure 7-27 *Selecting the Name and Data Segment*

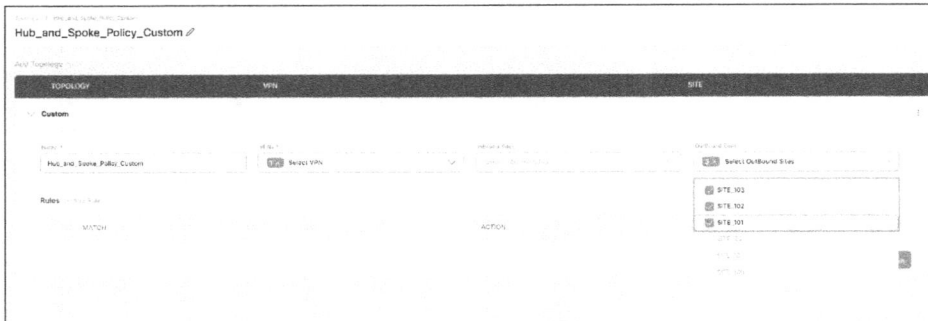

Figure 7-28   *Selecting Outbound Sites*

At this point, the policy direction and application are set, but the logic still needs to be set. Use the following steps to add match-action rules (see Figure 7-29 and Figure 7-30):

Step 1.   Click **Add Rules**. Sequence 1 is automatically populated.

Step 2.   Provide a name—in this case, **Match_and_Accept_DC_TLOCS**. Set the type to **TLOC**.

Step 3.   Select Add Conditions under Match, then select sites from the drop-down list and check the boxes for the DC1 and DC2 WAN Edge devices (site IDs 10 and 20).

Step 4.   Change Action to **Accept** and click **Save Match and Actions**.

Step 5.   Click **Add Rules**. Sequence 2 is automatically populated.

Step 6.   Provide a name—in this case, **Match_and_Accept_DC_Routes**. Set the type to **Route**.

Step 7.   Select **Add Conditions Sites** and check the boxes for the DC1 and DC2 WAN Edge devices (site IDs 10 and 20).

Step 8.   Change Action to **Accept** and click **Save Match and Actions**.

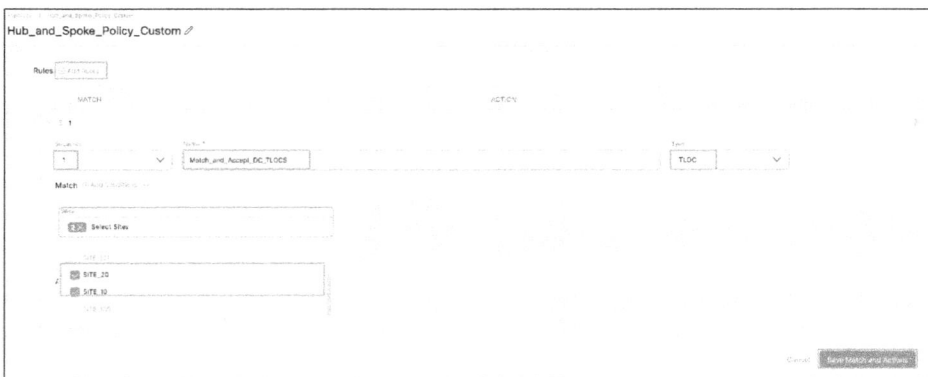

Figure 7-29   *TLOC Type Match-Action Configuration*

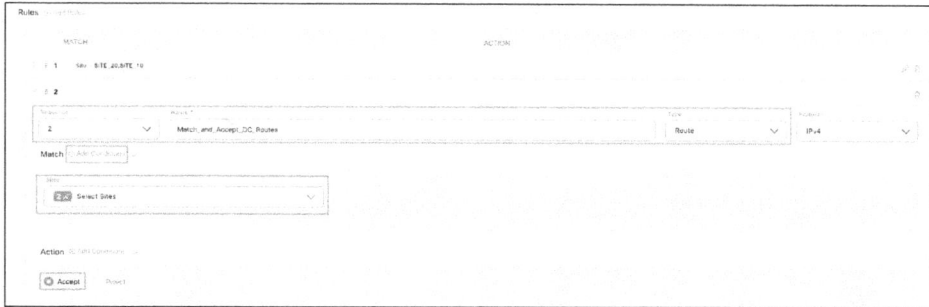

Figure 7-30   *Route Type Match-Action Configuration*

To complete the custom policy setup, click Save (see Figure 7-31). This screen provides a summary of the rules previously configured for the custom topology.

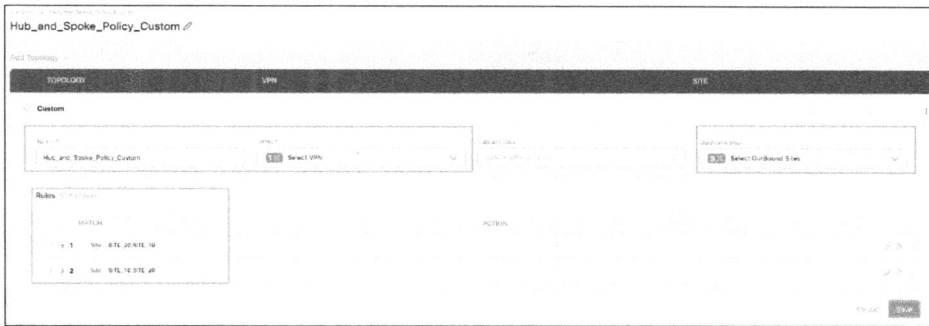

Figure 7-31   *Custom Topology Summary*

To activate a policy, select Activate next to the policy, as shown in Figure 7-32.

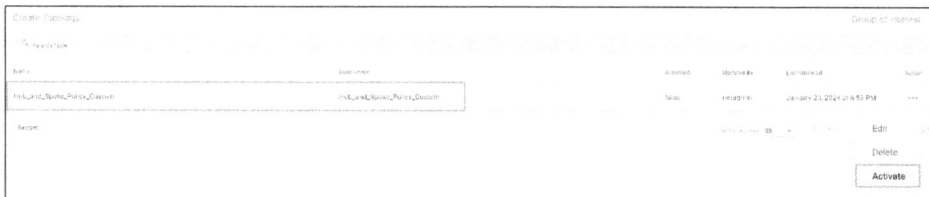

Figure 7-32   *Policy Activation*

Once the policy has been applied, you can see the effects of the policy by using the same monitoring techniques used before the policies were applied. From **Monitor > Devices > BR2-Edge1 > Real Time**, you can see the current list of BFD sessions (refer to Figure 7-16). When you compare Figure 7-33 to Figure 7-3, which shows the output before the policy was applied, you can see that the policy resulted in the number of BFD sessions (and IPsec tunnels) decreasing from 24 to 12. If you look closely at Figure 7-33, you also see that all the remaining BFD sessions come from routers with system IP addresses 10.0.10.1, 10.0.10.2, 10.0.20.1, or 10.0.20.2 (for routers in Data Center 1 or Data Center 2). All these tunnels are also established to sites with either Site ID 10 or 20.

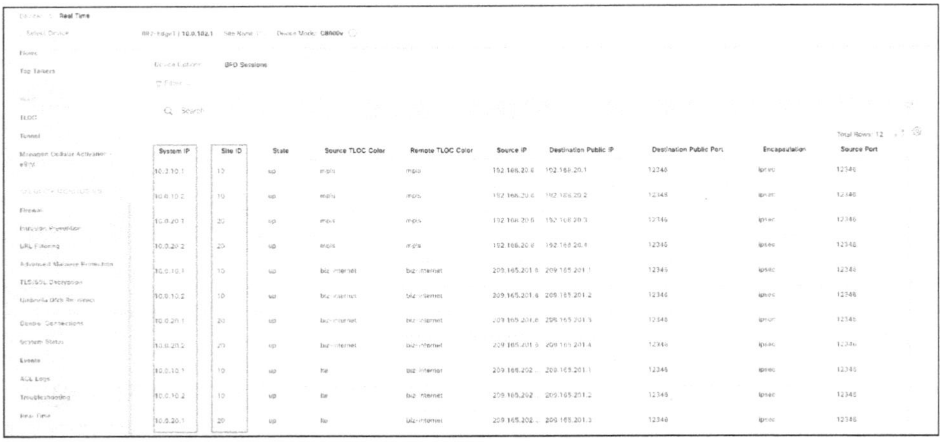

Figure 7-33   *BR2-Edge1 BFD Sessions After the Hub-and-Spoke Policy Is Applied*

Before the policy was applied, you were able to run a **traceroute** from Branch 2 to Branch 3 directly (refer to Example 7-1). Now, when the same **traceroute** is run from BR2-Edge1, you can see that the network is unreachable, as signified by the "* * *" response from the local host in Example 7-3.

Example 7-3   *The Network Is Unreachable When Tracing from BR2-Edge1 to BR3-Edge1*

```
! Traceroute from BR2-Edge1 to BR3-Edge1:
! The traceroute is unsuccessful based on the " * * *" (No response)
BR2-Edge1# traceroute vrf 10 10.10.103.1
<<<Output omitted for brevity>>>
  1  *  *  *
  2  *  *  *
```

```
! Traceroute from BR2-Edge1 to DC1-Edge1:
! The traceroute is successful; resources in the DC remain reachable
BR2-Edge1# traceroute vrf 10 10.10.10.100
<<<Output omitted for brevity>>>
  1 MPLS-DC1-Edge1 (192.168.20.1) 2 msec 1 msec 2 msec
  2 DC1-Edge1-Core (172.16.10.2) 1 msec 2 msec 1 msec
  3 DC1-Service (10.10.10.100) 2 msec
BR2-Edge1#
```

The second **traceroute** to the data center remains successful after the policy is applied. This behavior can be further explained by examining the IP routes table in the real-time output of BR2-Edge1. As shown in Figure 7-34, after filtering for routes only in VPN 10, you can see that the branch office no longer has a route for the 10.10.103.0/24 prefix, and therefore the network is listed as unreachable. The only routes that remain in the VPN 10 routing table on BR2-Edge1—other than the locally connected route 10.10.102.0/24—are the routes with prefixes 10.10.10.X and 10.10.20.X that originate in the data centers (Site ID 10 and Site ID 20).

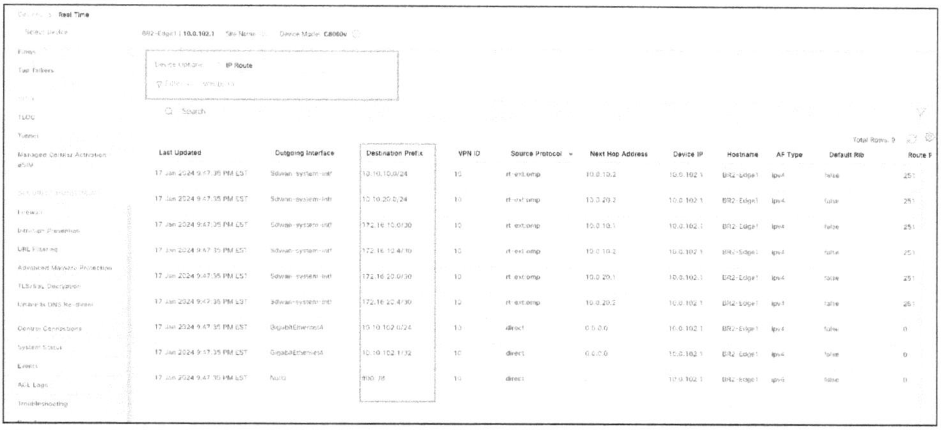

Figure 7-34 *The BR2-Edge1 Routing Table After the Policy Is Applied*

Use Case 1 Review

In this use case, you used centralized control policies to prohibit site-to-site communication between branch locations. By encoding the business intent into the structure of the SD-WAN fabric in this fashion, you can harden the security posture of the network by preventing unintended east–west traffic flows between branch sites. The use case explores the two existing methods to achieve this goal. We recommend selecting either traditional control policies contained in centralized policies or newer topology policies in order to avoid operational complexity.

Use Case 2: Enabling Branch-to-Branch Communication Through Data Centers

In the previous use case, you saw how centralized control policies can be used to completely isolate branch sites from each other. While this may be appropriate for some use cases where no communication is preferred, there are also use cases where organizations may want to enable site-to-site communication indirectly by proxying traffic through a data center or some other regional hub. This can have the benefits of reducing complexity and the scale of the control and data planes at the network edge while still maintaining full connectivity for the occasional traffic flows that may need to exist between branch locations. We will explore two different potential solutions for this use case: summarization and TLOC lists.

Enabling Branch-to-Branch Communication with Summarization

Summarization, in addition to the centralized control policy discussed in the previous use case, builds on the principle of longest-match routing and is not specific to any technology in Catalyst SD-WAN. If a network summary (such as 10.0.0.0/8) or the default route (0.0.0.0/0) were advertised from the data center routers, traffic would follow the path to the data center WAN Edge routers. The data center routers would then examine their routing tables and follow the route to the more specific match advertised from the branch sites. This is a common design mechanism that is used in hub-and-spoke WAN deployments such as with DMVPN Phase 1. Figure 7-35 illustrates this process.

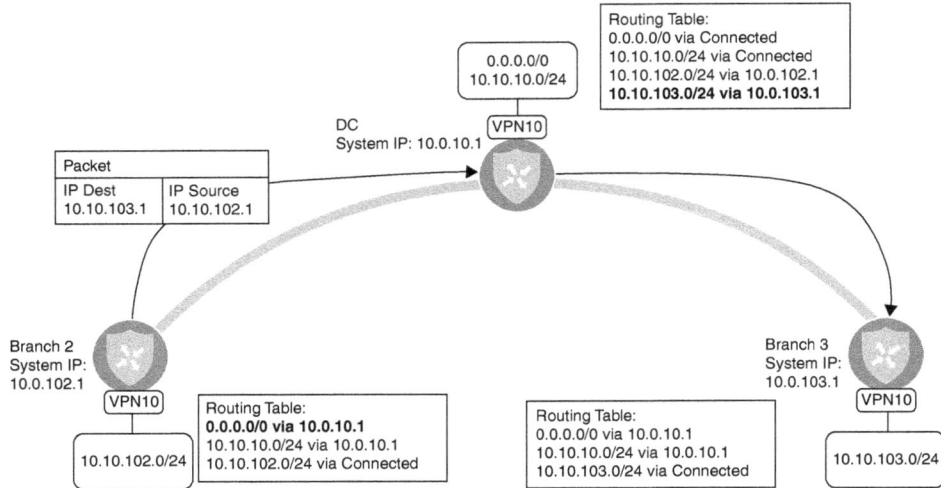

Figure 7-35   *Enabling Branch-to-Branch Communication with Summarization*

As shown in Figure 7-35, when the WAN Edge in Branch 2 does a routing lookup in order to forward a packet to the destination 10.10.103.1, the most specific match in the routing table is the default route. The default route is being advertised from the WAN Edge router in the data center with system IP address 10.0.10.1, so the packet is forwarded to that router. When the packet arrives at the data center router, it performs a lookup on the destination 10.10.103.1 in its own routing table. As the data center router has not had any routes or TLOC routes filtered, it has a more specific route to 10.10.103.1 via 10.0.103.1 and forwards the packet along to Branch 3. So you can establish communication through the data centers by injecting a default or summary route, without needing to change the SD-WAN fabric or any policies.

For this use case, say that you have injected a default route in Data Center 1 that is being advertised by DC1-Edge1 and DC1-Edge2. The specific method used to inject the default route is unimportant. If you have a default route in the routing protocol running in the data center, it can be advertised directly into OMP. Alternatively, you can configure a static default route and advertise that into OMP. Regardless of the method used, once the default route is advertised into OMP, it is then propagated to the branch offices, as shown in Figure 7-36.

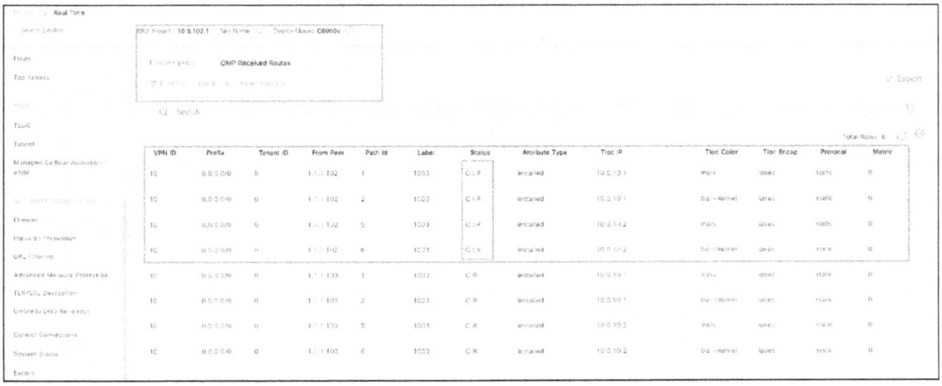

Figure 7-36   *BR2-Edge1 Routing Table with Default Route*

With the default routes in place, traffic can now be forwarded to the data center and then to a different branch site, as shown in Example 7-4.

Example 7-4 *Tracing from BR2-Edge1 to BR3-Edge1 Is Successful with the Difference of the Intermediate Hop*

```
! Traceroute from BR2-Edge1 to BR3-Edge1:
! The traceroute is successful, but requires an intermediate hop. The intermediary hop,
! identified by the system ip of 10.0.10.1, is the DC1-Edge1 router.
BR2-Edge1# traceroute vrf 10 10.10.103.1
<<<Omitted for brevity>>>
 1 MPLS-DC1-Edge1 (192.168.20.1) 1 msec 1 msec 1 msec
 2 BIZ-INET-BR3-Edge1 (209.165.201.8) 1 msec 1 msec 1 msec
 3 BR3-Edge1-Core (172.16.103.2) 2 msec 3 msec *


! Note that no changes have been made to the centralized control policy that was
! deployed for Use Case 1, and the number of data plane tunnels has not changed.
BR2-Edge1# show sdwan bfd summary
sessions-total 12
sessions-up      12
sessions-max     12
sessions-flap    0
poll-interval   120000
sessions-up-suspended 0
sessions-down-suspended 0
```

It is important to remember that no changes have been made to the centralized control policy applied for Use Case 1. The **show sdwan bfd summary** output in Example 7-4 indicates that there are still 12 BFD sessions (and 12 tunnels) established. This confirms that there are the same number of tunnels as displayed in Figure 7-33, and no new tunnels are established directly between the branches, but the default route is allowing the communication through the data center routers.

Enabling Branch-to-Branch Communication with TLOC Lists

Rather than injecting routes into the Cisco SD-WAN overlay to solve for the desired branch-to-branch communication pattern, it is possible to manipulate the routes that already exist in the overlay to accomplish the same objective.

As discussed in Chapter 3, a TLOC identifier uniquely identifies an SD-WAN tunnel interface in the SD-WAN fabric and also serves as the next-hop attribute that all OMP and network service routes use within the overlay. When routes are advertised by the WAN Edge routers to the SD-WAN Controller (and propagated by the SD-WAN Controller to the other WAN Edge routers), each OMP route is advertised with the local TLOCs as the next-hop values, as illustrated in Figure 7-37. In step 1, all of the WAN Edge routers advertise all of their locally reachable prefixes to the SD-WAN Controller with OMP updates. In step 2, the SD-WAN Controller reflects all these prefixes to all the other WAN Edge routers, using TLOC values as the next-hop addresses.

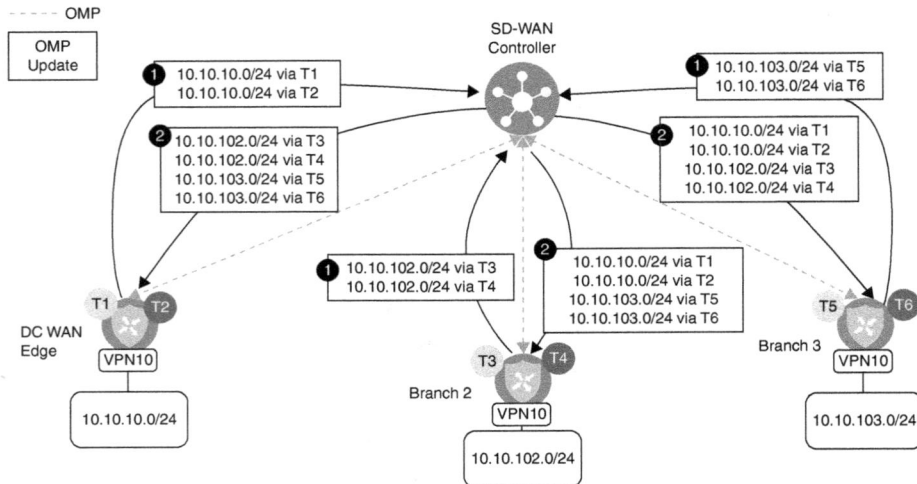

Figure 7-37   *OMP Routes with Next-Hop TLOCs Reflected Through the SD-WAN Controller*

Key Topic

A centralized control policy can be used to manipulate the TLOC attributes that are advertised as part of the OMP routes and, in effect, change the "next-hop address" that the OMP routes recurse to. Through this process, centralized control policies can be a very powerful tool to perform traffic engineering across the SD-WAN fabric. At the same time, this process maintains simplicity by requiring you to apply and execute the policy from only a single location: the SD-WAN Controller.

In order to permit the branch-to-branch communication via the data centers without the need for injecting a default route, in this use case you will slightly modify the policy from Use Case 1 (refer to Example 7-2) so that instead of dropping the routes from the other branches, the routes are instead advertised with new TLOC identifiers: the TLOC identifiers of the DC1 WAN Edge routers. Figure 7-38 illustrates the effect of this policy for the routes advertised from Branch 3.

Figure 7-38 builds on the route exchange process discussed with Figure 7-37. First, all of the WAN Edge routers advertise their locally connected prefixes to the SD-WAN Controllers. In the case of Branch 3, this means the prefix 10.10.103.0/24 in VPN 10 is advertised via OMP as being reachable via TLOCs T5 and T6. The result of this advertisement can be seen in the SD-WAN Controller OMP table. Next, this advertisement is reflected to the data center routers as is; no manipulation is performed on the advertisement. However, when the route is reflected to the Branch 2 WAN Edge router, an outbound centralized control policy is applied, and the TLOCs (next-hop addresses) are overwritten from the original values T5 and T6 (the TLOC identifiers of the WAN Edge at Branch 3) to T1 and T2 (the TLOC identifiers of the data center WAN Edge devices).

NOTE   Throughout the next several pages, we review the detailed process of modifying an existing centralized policy. This section shows the steps you need to take to create a copy of the policies created in the previous use case and then modify them to meet the requirements of this use case. This same process can be used to construct the policies used throughout the other use cases in this book, but configuration steps in the SD-WAN Manager GUI will not be covered to the same degree of detail used for Use Case 1 and Use Case 2.

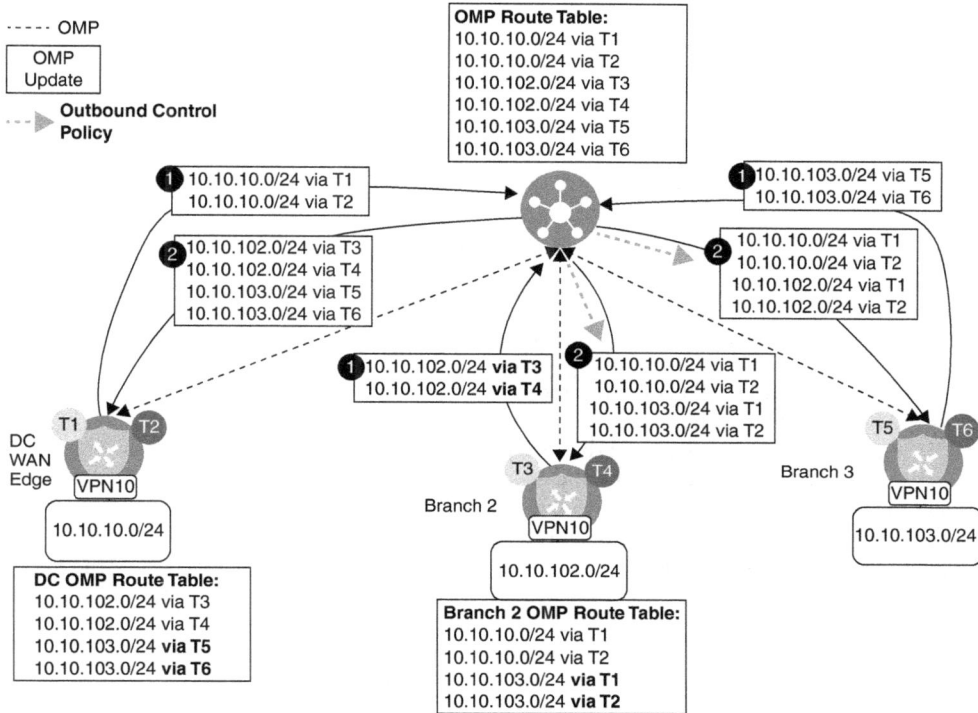

Figure 7-38 *Enabling Branch-to-Branch Communication with TLOC Manipulation*

To begin to construct this policy in the SD-WAN Manager GUI, the first step is to create the new list element that will be needed: a TLOC list. To start this configuration, select the Lists item from the Custom Options menu on the **Configuration > Policies** window, as shown in Figure 7-39.

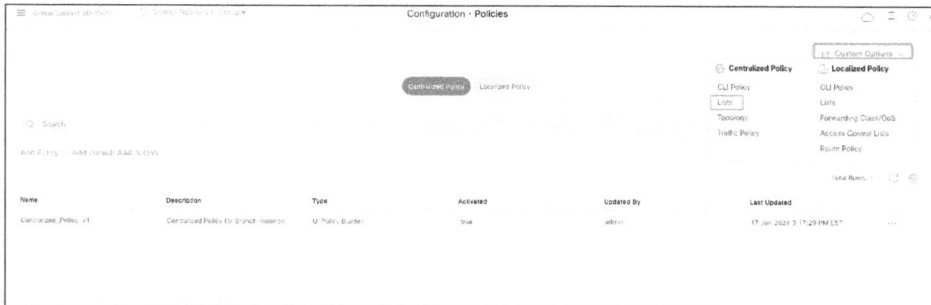

Figure 7-39 *Accessing the List Configuration for Centralized Policies*

To add a new TLOC list, select TLOC from the column of list types on the left and then click the **+New TLOC List** button, as shown in Figure 7-40.

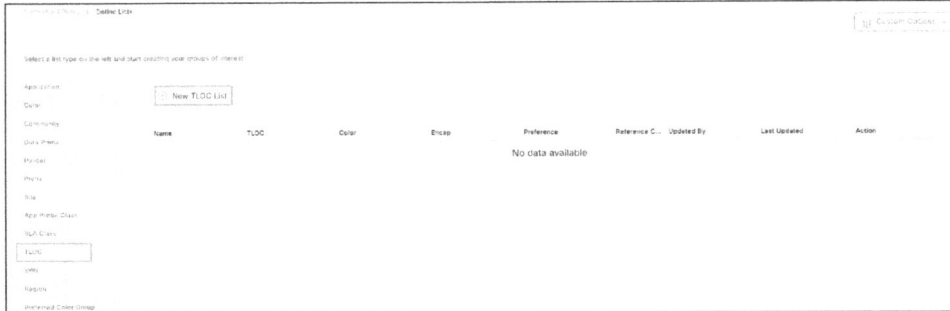

Figure 7-40   *Creating a New TLOC List*

Figure 7-41 shows a TLOC list configured with the name DC_TLOCs. There is a total of four TLOCs specified in the TLOC list: the mpls and biz-internet TLOC identifiers on both DC1-Edge1 and DC1-Edge2. Recall that each TLOC identifier is a unique combination of the system IP address, the color, and the encapsulation. In addition to specifying these three required values, an optional preference argument can be used to specify different TLOC preference values. (This optional attribute was not used in this example and will be discussed in later use cases.) Once the list is configured, you can save and close it by clicking the Save button.

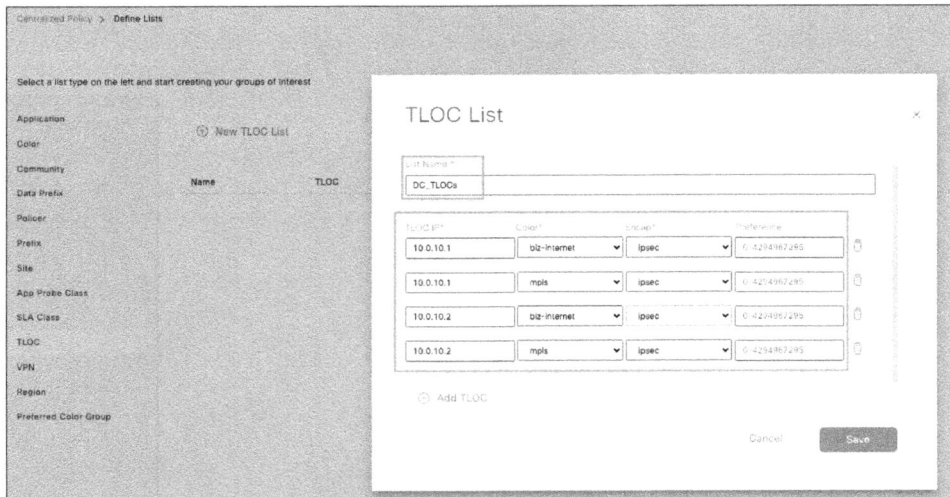

Figure 7-41   *Creating the TLOC List DC_TLOCs*

The next step in the configuration process is to create the necessary centralized control policy to use the TLOC list. In order to do this, select the Topology option from the Custom Options menu in the upper-right corner, as shown in Figure 7-42.

In order to copy the existing policy that was created in Use Case 1 so that it can be modified, click the three dots (…) menu next to the policy and select Copy, as shown in Figure 7-43.

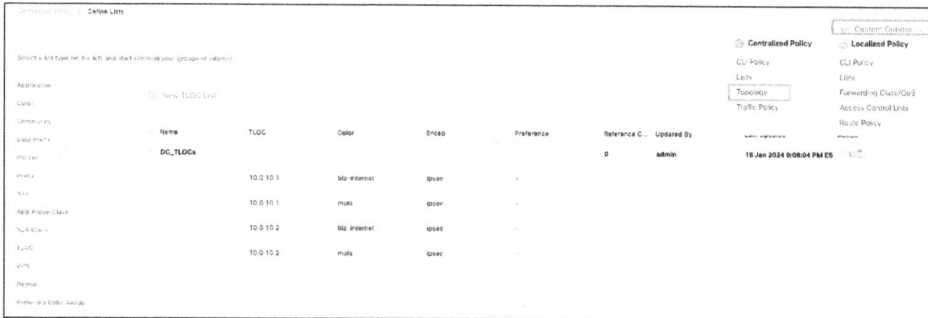

Figure 7-42 *Selecting Topology from the Custom Options Menu*

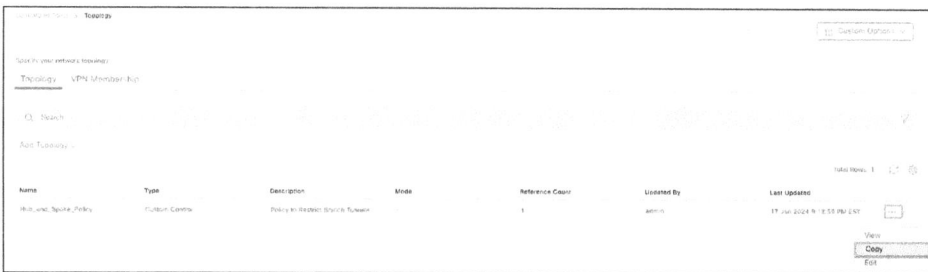

Figure 7-43 *Creating a Copy of an Existing Centralized Control Policy*

Every policy is required to be configured with a name and a description. In this case, the new centralized control policy is named Hub_and_Spoke_TLOC_Lists, as shown in Figure 7-44.

Now that the new copy of centralized control policy has been created from the original policy in Use Case 1, you can edit the policy by selecting the Edit option from the three dots menu, as shown in Figure 7-45.

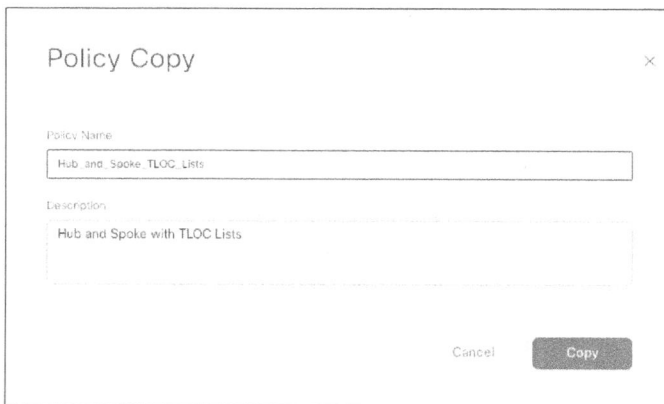

Figure 7-44 *Providing a Name and a Description for the Newly Copied Policy*

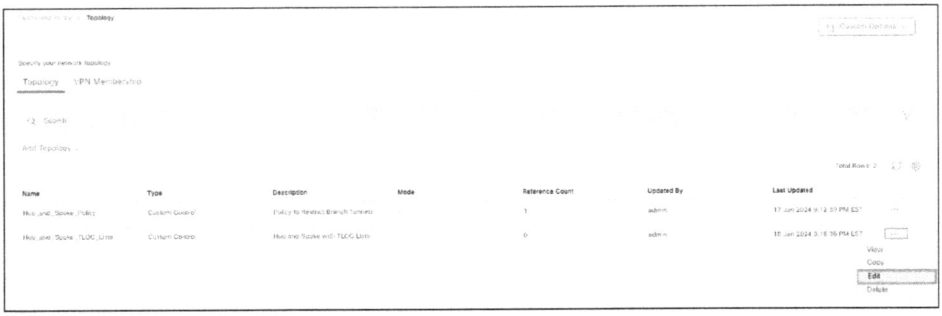

Figure 7-45 *Editing the Newly Copied Centralized Control Policy*

This policy needs to be altered so that the routes that are originating from the branch sites are rewritten to resolve to the new DC_TLOCs list that was previously created (see Figure 7-46). In order to accomplish this, you need to select the existing Route sequence type on the far left in the GUI. Then, click **+Sequence Rule** to add a new sequence rule. In this sequence rule, you configure the matching criterion as the BranchOffices site list that was created in the previous use case by clicking the **Match** sub-tab, selecting the Site criterion, and adding the necessary site list. Once the matching criterion is specified, select the Actions tab at the top of the sequence rule and select the **Accept** radio button. Once the routes are accepted, you can select the **TLOC** action and specify the previously created TLOC list DC_TLOCs. When the configuration is completed, select the blue **Save Match and Actions** button at the bottom of the sequence rule.

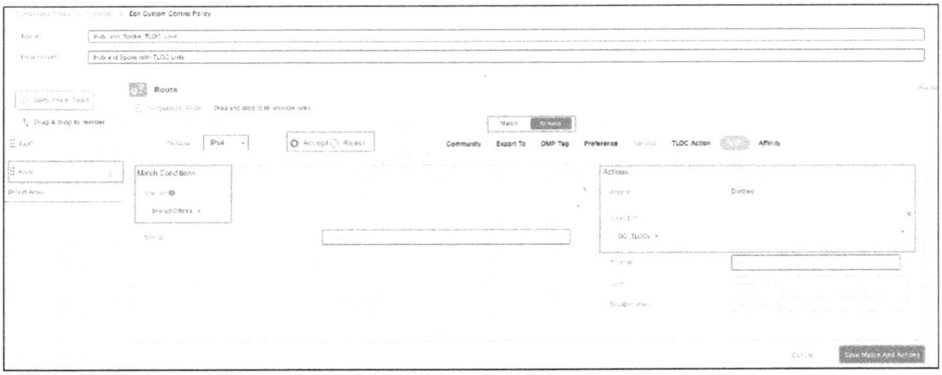

Figure 7-46 *Creating a New Sequence to Manipulate Routes Advertised from Branch Sites*

The completed policy with both the existing route sequence rule from the previous use case and the newly created route sequence rule are shown in Figure 7-47. In summary, the first sequence rule of this policy will match all the routes being advertised from the data centers and forward them on without any modifications. The second sequence will match all the routes being advertised from other branches and change their TLOC identifiers (or next-hop attributes) to be the TLOC identifiers of the data centers. You save the completed policy by clicking the blue **Save Control Policy** button at the bottom.

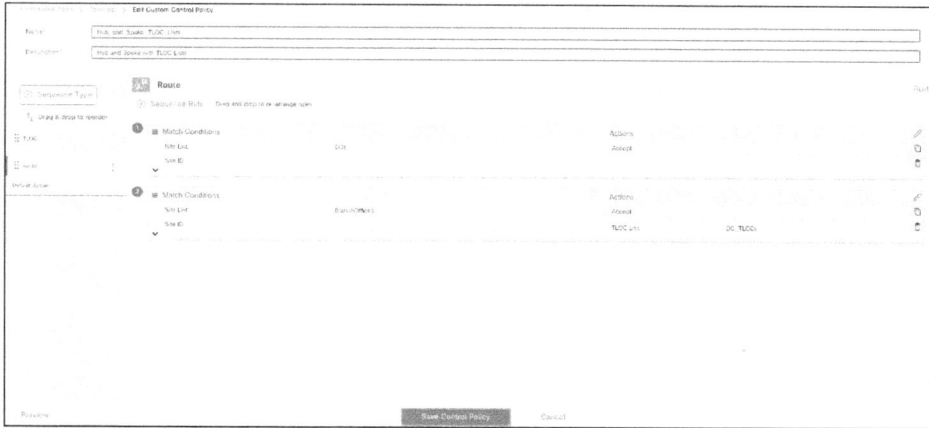

Figure 7-47   *Saving the Centralized Control Policy with Two Route Sequences*

Now that the centralized control policy has been created, it needs to be imported into a centralized policy. To do this, return to the main Centralized Policy Configuration screen by clicking Centralized Policy in the menu option at the top of the screen, as shown in Figure 7-48.

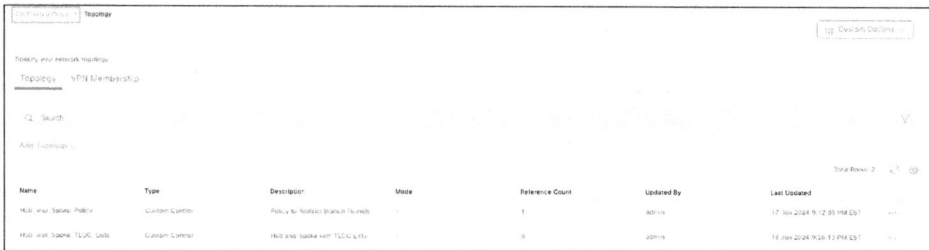

Figure 7-48   *Navigating Back to the Centralized Policy Configuration Screen Using the Breadcrumb Trail*

The next step in the configuration process is to create a copy of the centralized policy that was created in Use Case 1, which will then be modified. As shown in Figure 7-49, do this by clicking the three dots menu and selecting the Copy option.

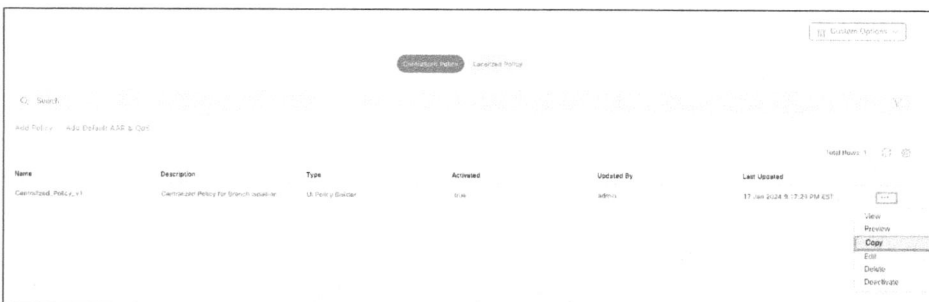

Figure 7-49   *Creating a Copy of a Centralized Policy Before Starting Modifications*

In order to copy the policy, you need to supply a name and description, as shown in Figure 7-50. Once these values are supplied, click the Copy button to complete the process.

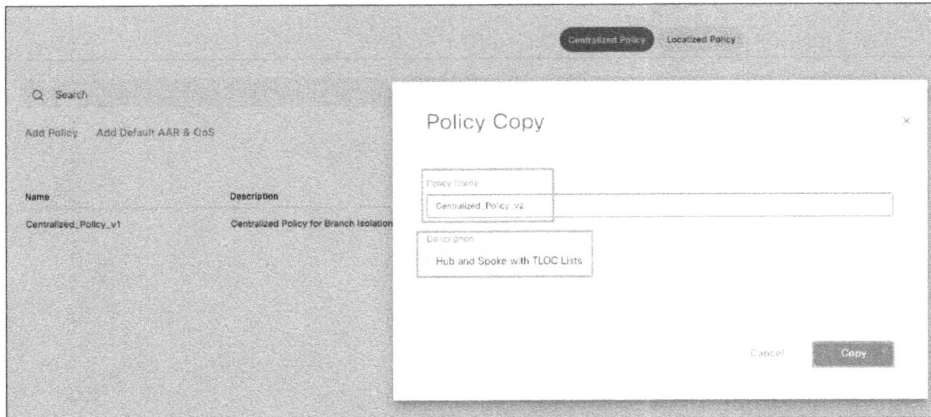

Figure 7-50   *Configuring a Name and Description for the Copied Centralized Policy*

Figures 7-49 and 7-50 show the rest of the process for copying the centralized policy, which is similar to the steps taken in Figures 7-43 and 7-44 for copying the centralized control policy. In both cases, it would have been possible to modify the existing policies rather than copy them and modify the copies. However, the process illustrated here is considered a best practice as it helps you avoid inadvertently applying a configuration to the network and aids in quickly rolling back any configuration changes should the need arise.

Now that you have created Centralized_Policy_v2, you can modify it to use the new control policy with the TLOC list by selecting the Edit option from the three dots menu, as shown in Figure 7-51.

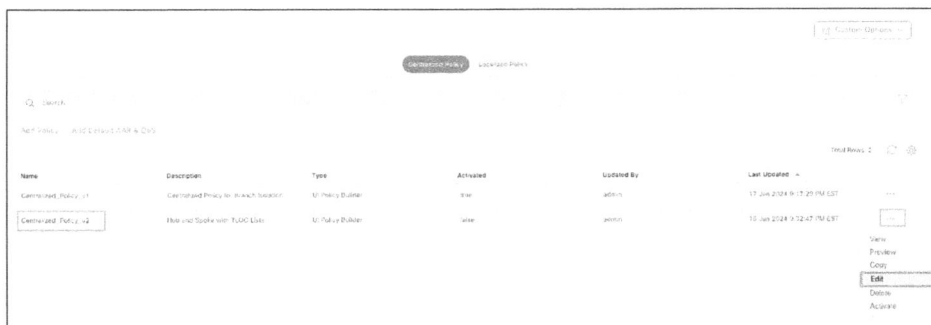

Figure 7-51   *Editing a Centralized Policy*

In order to modify this centralized policy for Use Case 2, you need to make several changes. The centralized control policy created in Use Case 1 needs to be separated from this policy, and the new centralized control policy that was created in Figures 7-43 through 7-47 needs to be imported into this centralized policy. Finally, that new policy has to be applied to the branch sites. In order to separate the old centralized control policy, click on the **Topology** tab at the top of the window, as shown in Figure 7-52. On the Topology tab, the Topology sub-tab is already selected, and the centralized control policies that are referenced by this centralized policy are listed. (Note that there is also a VPN Membership sub-tab that you will use in later use cases.) Select the **Detach** option from the three dots menu on the Hub_and_Spoke_Policy in order to separate this control policy from Use Case 1.

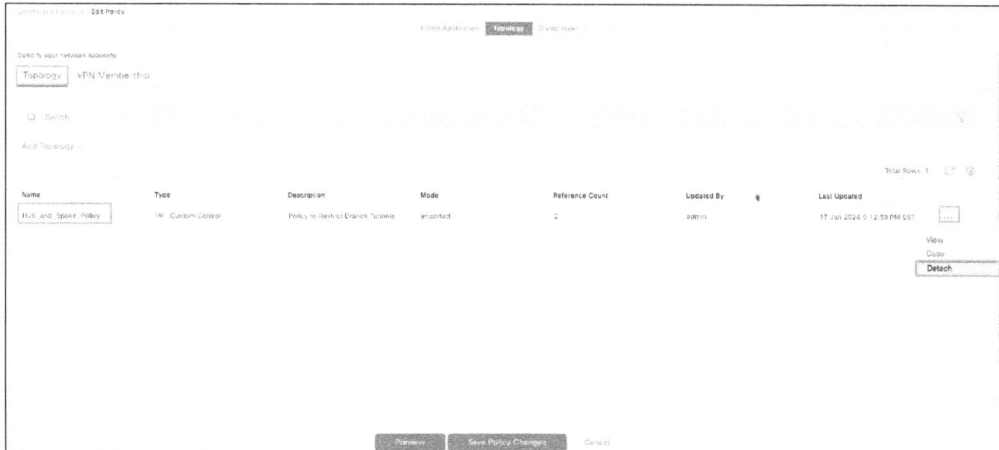

Figure 7-52 *Separating an Unnecessary Centralized Control Policy from a Centralized Policy*

Next, you need to attach the newly created centralized control policy to this policy by clicking the **+Add Topology** button and selecting the **Import Existing Topology** option, as shown in Figure 7-53.

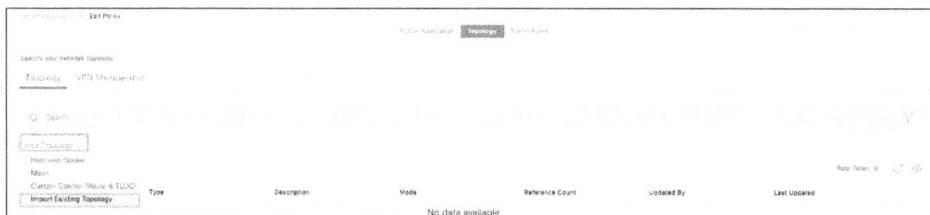

Figure 7-53 *Importing an Existing Control Policy into a Centralized Policy*

In the Import Existing Topology dialog box, select the radio button for **Custom Control (Route and TLOC)** under Policy Type and then select the name of the new centralized control policy Hub_and_Spoke_TLOC_Lists from the Policy drop-down. Complete the process by clicking the blue **Import** button, as shown in Figure 7-54.

Now that the new centralized control policy has been imported into the centralized policy, the last part of the configuration process is to specify where this policy should be applied. To start this process, move back to the Policy Application page by clicking that tab at the top of the window. The Topology sub-tab, which is selected by default, lists all the control policies in this centralized policy. (You will use the other sub-tabs in later chapters with application-aware routing and centralized data policies.)

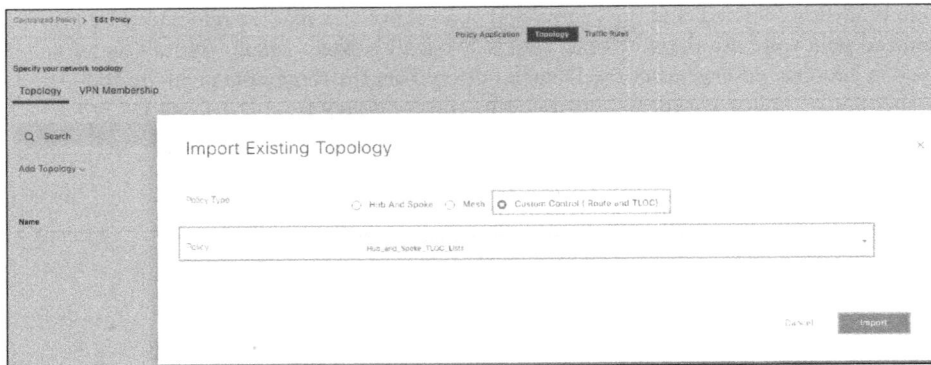

Figure 7-54 *Selecting the Existing Control Policy to Import into a Centralized Policy*

Under the Hub_and_Spoke_TLOC_Lists policy, click the blue +New Site/Region List button in order to specify the site lists that this policy should be applied to. Add the BranchOffices site list to the **Outbound Site List** field. The final step in saving the policy application configuration is to click the **Add** button on the right side and then click the **Save Policy Changes** button at the bottom, as shown in Figure 7-55.

The new centralized control policy has now been saved, and you can activate it by selecting the Activate option from the three dots menu, as shown in Figure 7-56. There is no need to deactivate Centralized_Policy_v1 before activating the new policy. Because there can only be a single centralized policy that is active at any point in time, activating the new policy automatically deactivates any other policy.

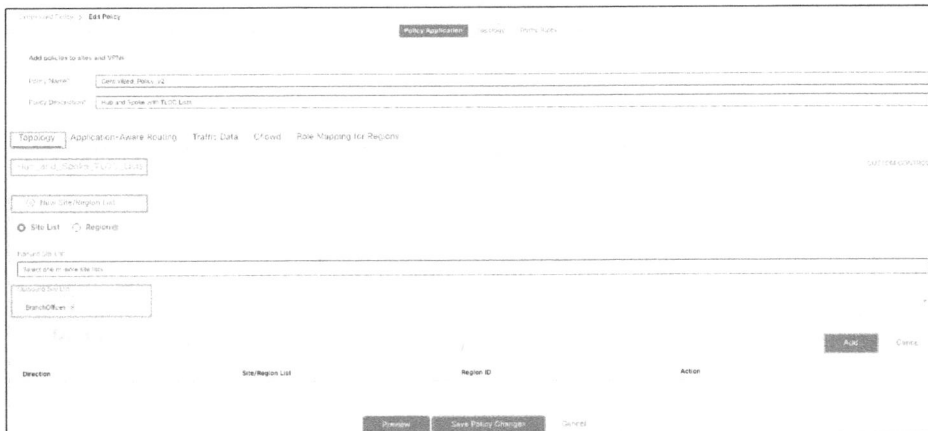

Figure 7-55 *Configuring the Policy Application for the Imported Control Policy in a Centralized Policy*

You can see the full CLI configuration of the policy by selecting the Preview option from the three dots menu (refer to Figure 7-56). The output of the policy preview displayed in Example 7-5 shows the complete centralized policy used to implement the objectives of this use case.

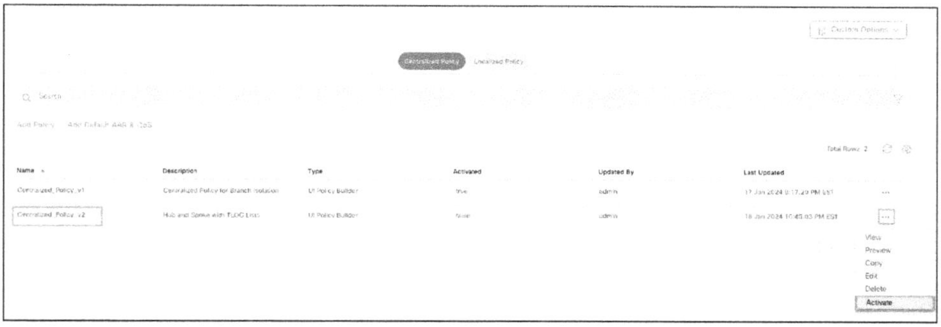

Figure 7-56   *Activating a Centralized Policy*

Example 7-5   *Use Case 2: Hub-and-Spoke Policy with TLOC Lists*

```
! Much of the centralized policy is unchanged from Example 7-2.
! The relevant changes in sequence 21 and the lists are highlighted below.
policy
 control-policy Hub_and_Spoke_TLOC_Lists
    sequence 1
     match tloc
      site-list DCs
     !
     action accept
     !
    !
    sequence 11
     match route
      site-list DCs
      prefix-list _AnyIpv4PrefixList
     !
     action accept
     !
    !
! The new sequence 21 has been added to permit the routes that are
! advertised from the branches, and advertise them with new TLOCs that are
! specified by the "DC_TLOCs" argument to the tloc-list command.
    sequence 21
     match route
      site-list BranchOffices
     prefix-list _AnyIpv4PrefixList
     !
     action accept
        set
         tloc-list DC_TLOCs
     !
     !
     !
```

```
   default-action reject
 !
 lists
  site-list BranchOffices
   site-id 100-199
  !
  site-list DCs
   site-id 10-50
  !
! A new list called "DC_TLOCs" is used to specify which TLOCs should be
! advertised as the next hop addresses of the routes.
  tloc-list DC_TLOCs
   tloc 10.0.10.1 color mpls encap ipsec
   tloc 10.0.10.1 color biz-internet encap ipsec
   tloc 10.0.10.2 color mpls encap ipsec
   tloc 10.0.10.2 color biz-internet encap ipsec
  !
  prefix-list _AnyIpv4PrefixList
   ip-prefix 0.0.0.0/0 le 32
  !
 !
 !
apply-policy
 site-list BranchOffices
  control-policy Hub_and_Spoke_TLOC_Lists out
 !
 !
```

Example 7-5 shows the command-line configuration for the TLOC list that configured in Figure 7-41. The TLOC list is established with the command **tloc-list** {*list-name*}. Once the list is created, each TLOC much be specified individually, using the following syntax:

tloc {*system-ip*} **color** {*color*} **encap** {**ipsec|gre**} [**preference** *preference*]

These configuration commands reflect the configuration performed in SD-WAN Manager in Figure 7-41. The TLOC list is then referenced in Sequence 21 of the control policy to overwrite the existing TLOC attributes that would have been advertised with the OMP routes from the branch sites. Finally, the last stanza in Example 7-5 shows that the policy is applied to the site list BranchOffices in the outbound (**out**) direction.

You can see the effect of applying this new centralized policy by looking at the routing table, as shown in Figure 7-57. In the IP routing table, you can see that you now have four different paths to the prefix 10.10.103.0/24. Careful inspection of those advertisements reveals that the TLOC IP address is not 10.0.103.1, as it was in Figure 7-4, with no control policy applied. Instead, it is now listed as 10.0.10.1 and 10.0.10.2, the TLOC IP addresses of the WAN Edge routers in DC1, as specified in the TLOC list.

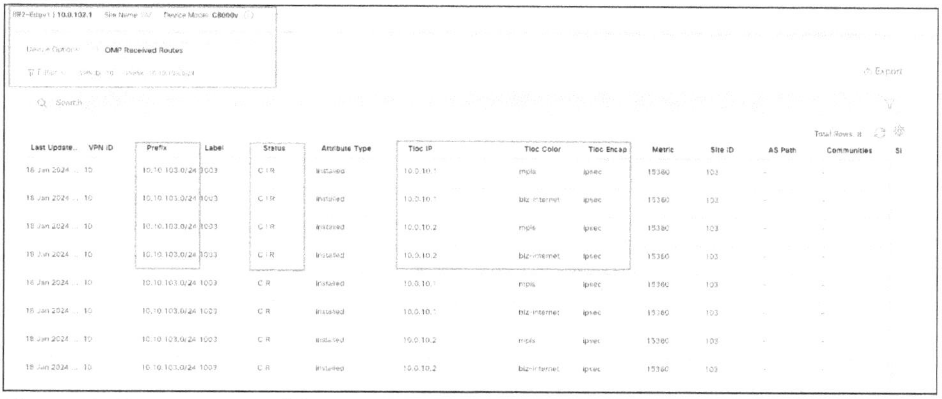

Figure 7-57 *Routing Table on BR2-Edge1*

It is also important to consider what effect the policy had on the routes that have been advertised to the data center. You can examine the OMP Received Routes output in the Real Time view, as shown in Figure 7-58, and see that the routes are received by the DC1-Edge1 router with all the original TLOC advertisements.

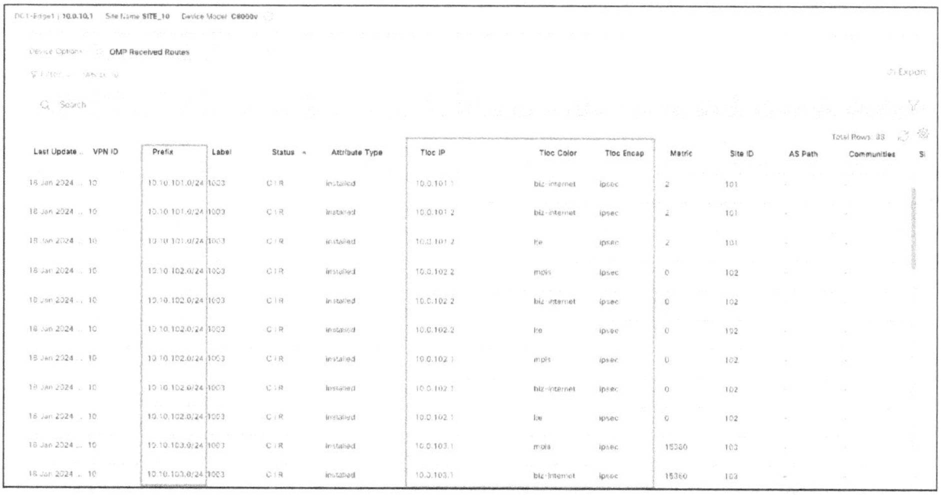

Figure 7-58 *Routing Table on DC1-Edge1*

As shown in Figure 7-58, the data center routing table entries for the prefixes from the branches are specified with the original TLOC IP addresses as the next-hop values. When you compare Figure 7-58 to Figure 7-57, you can clearly see that there are different TLOC IP addresses, or next-hop attributes, that are advertised to the branch WAN Edge devices than are advertised to the data center WAN Edge devices. This is expected because the route manipulation is happening *outbound* to the WAN Edges covered under the BranchOffices site list. There is no manipulation happening on the OMP advertisements being sent to the data center WAN Edge routers. Furthermore, a **traceroute** from the Branch 2 WAN Edge router is able to confirm that the data plane is working as expected, as shown in Example 7-6.

Example 7-6   *BR2-Edge1 Is Able to Access the Prefixes in Another Branch by Transiting the Data Center*

```
! BR2-Edge1 is able to reach the destination 10.10.103.1, but the path requires
! additional hops as it must transit through the DC WAN Edge Routers (System IP
10.0.10.2).
BR2-Edge1# traceroute vrf 10 10.10.103.1
<<<Output omitted for brevity>>>
  1 MPLS-DC1-Edge2 (192.168.20.2) 1 msec 2 msec 0 msec
  2 BIZ-INET-BR3-Edge1 (209.165.201.8) 1 msec 2 msec 1 msec
  3 BR3-Edge1-Core (172.16.103.2) 2 msec 3 msec *
BR2-Edge1#
```

Use Case 2 Review

This use case describes two different mechanisms to permit branch-to-branch communication in an SD-WAN fabric where TLOC routes were filtered to prohibit the establishment of direct branch-to-branch data plane tunnels. In the first mechanism, you advertised summary prefixes from the data center in order to draw branch-to-branch traffic, for which the branch routers did not have more specific routes, to the data centers. The data centers, in turn, could then use their more specific routing information to forward the traffic on to its final destination.

In the second mechanism, which is based on using a TLOC list, you used the **set tloc-list** action in the centralized control policy to manipulate the OMP routes so that the prefixes from remote branches were advertised with the TLOC identifiers of the data centers. Since the WAN Edge routers had already received the DC TLOC advertisements and had built tunnels to the data center WAN Edge routers, the OMP routes with these modified next-hop addresses could be used to forward traffic.

NOTE   A TLOC list is an incredibly powerful tool to create flexible policies in order to implement traffic engineering and meet the objectives of the network administrator. But remember that with great power comes great responsibility. Improper application of TLOC lists can cause unintended and unexpected forwarding behaviors. In addition, a TLOC list requires a static definition in the centralized control policy and is not updated automatically in the same manner as traditional OMP routing updates. For example, if (years after implementing this policy) an additional transport link is added to the data center and an additional tunnel interface is added to DC1-Edge1 and DC1-Edge2, the TLOC list used for this traffic engineering policy would not change automatically. The network administrator would need to remember to update the TLOC list if using all three transport networks is the desired behavior. In a more extreme example, if the WAN Edge routers at DC1 were to be assigned new system IP addresses, the addresses in the TLOC list would not automatically be updated. Traffic flows from branch to branch would then fail, even as the traffic flows from branch to DC would succeed.

Therefore, we recommend using TLOC lists only when they are the only tool able to accomplish the desired outcome. When considering the objective in this use case—that is, enabling branch-to-branch communication without building branch-to-branch tunnels—we strongly recommend using network summarization rather than the TLOC list method.

Use Case 3: Traffic Engineering at Sites with Multiple Routers

Currently in the sample network, three different sites are deployed with redundant active routers: Data Center 1, Data Center 2, and Branch 1. The default behavior when forwarding traffic across the fabric is to load-share across all equal paths, and in the case of these three sites, that could mean load-sharing across all of the paths from both routers, as shown in Figure 7-59.

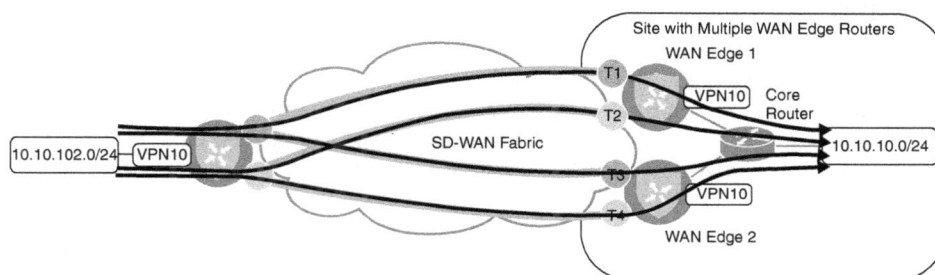

Figure 7-59 *Four Paths to 10.10.10.0/24*

In Figure 7-59, traffic that is destined to the prefix 10.10.10.0/24 may take any of the four established tunnels across the SD-WAN fabric. However, certain issues can arise if a device outside the SD-WAN fabric, such as the core router in Figure 7-60, forwards the return flow across a WAN Edge node other than the router on which the original flow was received. Because the SD-WAN fabric itself is stateless, there is no inherent problem with using multiple routers for flows to and from a specific destination. However, some advanced data plane services, such as deep packet inspection or the on-box security capabilities, require the ability to see both sides of a traffic flow in order to provide optimal application layer services.

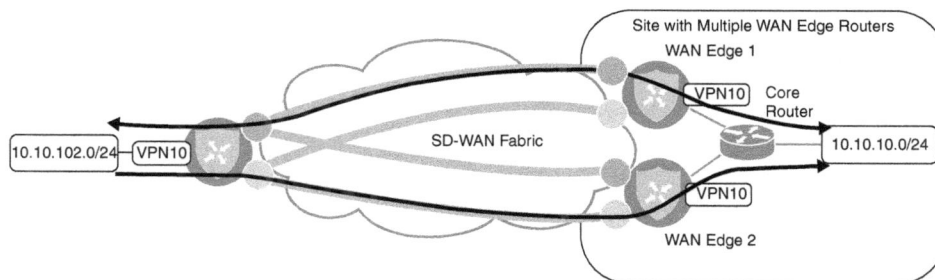

Figure 7-60 *Multipathing on the Fabric May Use Multiple WAN Edge Routers for a Single Flow*

In order to ensure that both halves of a flow are transiting the same WAN Edge router at a given site, it is common to configure the fabric so that all of the traffic traverses one of the routers in steady state, and the other router is not actively passing traffic until a failure occurs.

NOTE   Completing this configuration involves both how traffic is forwarded across the SD-WAN fabric to the WAN Edge devices and how traffic is forwarded back from the LAN switches to the WAN Edge devices. Chapter 6 discusses these separate and distinct policy domains.

This use case focuses on manipulating the SD-WAN fabric to prefer a single WAN Edge router when traffic is coming in from the fabric. The corresponding configuration for preferring a single WAN Edge router from the LAN side is discussed in detail in Chapter 10, "Localized Policies."

As discussed in Chapter 3, the Preference attribute for both TLOCs and OMP routes is evaluated in the OMP best-path selection process. Preference can therefore be altered to manipulate the OMP path selection. In many areas of networking, there is more than one way to accomplish any given objective. This use case explores two different methods for manipulating the TLOC Preference values in order to complete this traffic engineering use case. In the following sections, the manipulations at the data centers will be completed with a centralized control policy, and changes at Branch 1 will be made in the WAN Edge configurations locally.

Setting TLOC Preference with Centralized Policy

With the existing policy from Use Case 2 (refer to Example 7-5), both DC1-Edge1 and DC1-Edge2 are advertising equal-cost paths to the 10.10.10.0/24 prefix in DC1, as shown in Figure 7-61.

Last Update...	VPN ID	Prefix	Status	Tloc IP	Tloc Color	Tloc Encap	Site ID	OMP Tag	OMP Preference	Originator
02 Sep 2024 ...	10	10.10.10.0/24	C I R	13.0.10.2	mpls	ipsec	10	-	-	10.0.10.2
02 Sep 2024 ...	10	10.10.10.0/24	C I R	13.0.10.2	biz-internet	ipsec	10	-	-	10.0.10.2
02 Sep 2024 ...	10	10.10.10.0/24	C I R	10.0.10.1	mpls	ipsec	10	-	-	10.0.10.1
02 Sep 2024 ...	10	10.10.10.0/24	C I R	10.0.10.1	biz-internet	ipsec	10	-	-	10.0.10.1
02 Sep 2024 ...	10	10.10.10.0/24	C P	13.0.10.2	mpls	ipsec	10	-	-	10.0.10.2
02 Sep 2024 ...	10	10.10.10.0/24	C R	13.0.10.2	biz-internet	ipsec	10	-	-	10.0.10.2
02 Sep 2024 ...	10	10.10.10.0/24	C R	10.0.10.1	mpls	ipsec	10	-	-	10.0.10.1
02 Sep 2024 ...	10	10.10.10.0/24	C R	13.0.10.1	biz-internet	ipsec	10	-	-	10.0.10.1

Figure 7-61   *Four Paths to 10.10.10.0/24 Transiting Two Different WAN Edge Routers*

There is a total of four equal-cost paths for the prefix 10.10.10.0/24: two from DC1-Edge1 and two from DC1-Edge2. Each WAN Edge device is advertising a path with the colors mpls and biz-internet.

In the previous use cases, you have seen how to use centralized control policies applied in the outbound direction in order to filter and manipulate routes advertised from the SD-WAN Controller. Because the outbound manipulation does not affect the OMP routes and TLOCs in the SD-WAN Controller's own tables, they can be more limited in scope, making it easy to apply different changes in the advertisements to different sites. You saw this in the previous use case when the TLOC values for certain OMP routes from the branches were overwritten when advertised to some sites (branches) but not other sites (data centers). Conversely, when the intent is to make a global change to OMP routes or TLOC routes, it is often more appropriate to use an inbound centralized control policy. Inbound centralized control policies make manipulations before the SD-WAN Controller best-path selection algorithm is applied and before the routes are inserted into the SD-WAN Controller table. The manipulations made by inbound control policies are apparent in the advertisements to all other OMP peers unless overwritten by an additional outbound control policy.

Because the intention with this use case is to have all of the routers prefer to send their traffic to Edge1 over Edge2 in the data centers, you will use an inbound centralized policy to achieve this global change. Example 7-7 shows the changes to the centralized control policy that are required to achieve this objective.

NOTE   Parts of the policy in Example 7-7 that are either irrelevant to this use case or that are unchanged from the previous use case are omitted for clarity and brevity.

Example 7-7   *Use Case 3: Centralized Policy Setting TLOC Preference*

```
policy
 control-policy Hub_and_Spoke_TLOC_Lists
 ! <<<No changes made to this policy from Example 7-5, omitted for brevity>>>
 !
 ! A new control policy is created to set the TLOC preference values
 control-policy Set_DC_TLOC_Preference
    sequence 1
     match tloc
      originator 10.0.10.1
      !
     action accept
      set
       preference 500
      !
     !
    !
    sequence 11
     match tloc
      originator 10.0.10.2
      !
     action accept
      set
       preference 400
      !
     !
    !
    sequence 21
     match tloc
      originator 10.0.20.1
      !
```

```
      action accept
       set
        preference 500
       !
      !
     !
     sequence 31
      match tloc
       originator 10.0.20.2
       !
      action accept
       set
        preference 400
       !
      !
     !
   default-action accept
  !
  lists
  ! <<<No changes made to the lists from Example 7-5, omitted for brevity>>>
   !
  !
  ! The apply-policy statement has been modified to reflect that the new policy
  ! should be applied inbound on advertisements received from the datacenters
  apply-policy
  site-list DCs
   control-policy Set_DC_TLOC_Preference in
   !
  ! The existing policy for the branches remains unchanged
  site-list BranchOffices
   control-policy Hub_and_Spoke_TLOC_Lists out
   !
  !
```

Example 7-7 introduces a new control policy to add Preference values to the TLOCs that are being advertised from WAN Edge routers in the data centers. In Sequence 1, a new matching criterion is configured: **originator**. The originator syntax is **originator** {*originator-ip*}, where *originator-ip* is the system IP address of the WAN Edge device you are looking to match against. In this particular policy example, because the objective is to set different values for WAN Edge devices at the same site ID, matching with site lists would be ineffective. Once the TLOCs have been matched, the desired preference value is specified in the action statement with the syntax **preference** {*value*}. The acceptable range for Preference values is 0 through 4294967295 ($2^{32} - 1$). In Example 7-7, the Preference values 500 and 400 are used. As discussed in Chapter 4, under default conditions, the load is equally shared across available transports. The TLOC Preference attribute permits you to influence traffic outbound and inbound direction preference, with higher values being the most preferred.

You can see the effect of this policy in Figure 7-62, where the output is the result of the IP Route real-time query, which shows only one available next hop, the DC1-Edge1 router.

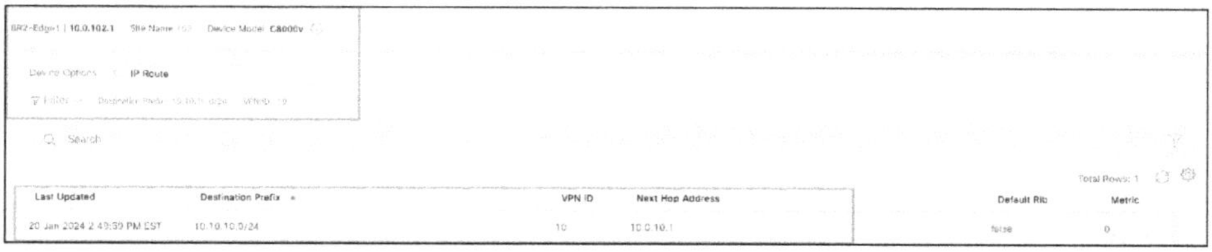

Figure 7-62   *10.0.10.1 [DC1-Edge1] as the Only Next Hop for 10.10.10.0/24*

Figure 7-63 is an updated display of the same output from Figure 7-61 that was taken after the policy in Example 7-7 was applied to the SD-WAN network. In this output, only four paths have been installed in the routing table on BR2-Edge1: the MPLS path and the BIZ-INTERNET path from both 10.0.10.1(DC1-Edge1) and 10.0.20.1(DC2-Edge1). The output shows all of the routes that have been received from OMP peers in a similar fashion to how the outputs of the Cisco IOS command **show ip bgp** would display all of the routes received from BGP neighbors (even if they are not the best BGP routes or actually installed in the routing table).

> **NOTE**   In Figure 7-63, in the Search Options field, there is a search for 1.1.1.102, which is the system IP address of SD-WAN Controller-1. This search has the functional effect of removing all the duplicate advertisements that would have been received from SD-WAN Controller-2 (with system IP address 1.1.1.103), making it easier for network administrators to understand the table. Because the same policy should always be applied to all of the SD-WAN Controllers, the same route advertisements should come from both SD-WAN Controllers, and it is safe to filter one set of them from this view.

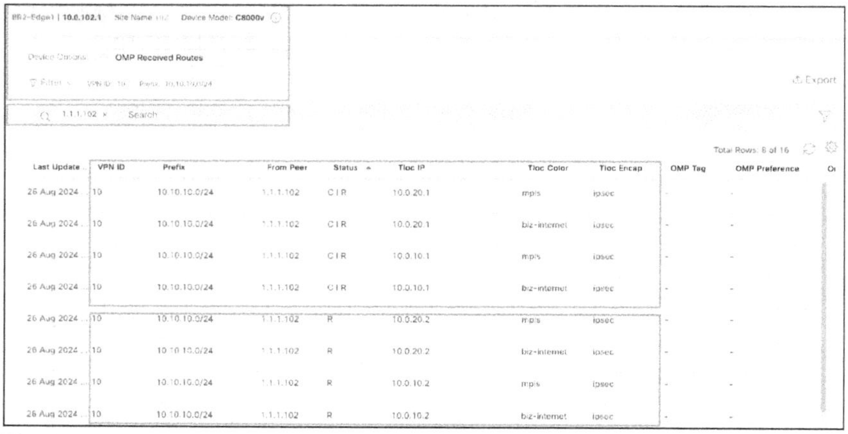

Figure 7-63   *OMP Route Table on BR2-Edge1, Showing Four Paths to 10.10.10.0/24*

It is clear from the OMP table that the WAN Edge device is still receiving the OMP route advertisements from DC1-Edge2 and DC2-Edge2. These advertisements are the fifth to eighth entries in the table, with TLOC IP address 10.0.10.2 and 10.0.20.2. The Status column for these routes displays R, and the Status column for OMP routes from 10.0.10.1 and

10.0.20.1 (the first to fourth rows) is displayed with the status C I R. The key code can be found in the output of **show sdwan omp routes** from the CLI, as shown in Example 7-8.

Example 7-8   *OMP Status Code Key*

```
BR1-Edge1# show sdwan omp routes
Code:
C -> chosen
I -> installed
Red -> redistributed
Rej -> rejected
L -> looped
R -> resolved
S -> stale
Ext -> extranet
Inv -> invalid
Stg -> staged
IA  -> On-demand inactive
U   -> TLOC unresolved
BR-R -> Border-Router reoriginated
TGW-R -> Transport-Gateway reoriginated
R-TGW-R -> Reoriginated Transport-Gateway reoriginated
<<<omitted for brevity>>>
```

Key Topic

While the full explanation of these values can be found in the Cisco documentation, a few values are reviewed in Table 7-1.

Table 7-1   OMP Status Codes

Status Code	Status Meaning	Explanation
C	Chosen	This route is the successor of the OMP best-path selection process.
I	Installed	The OMP route has been installed into the IP routing table.
R	Resolved	The TLOC referenced in the OMP route is present and operational.

The status code C I R means that the OMP route has been successfully installed in the routing table and is being used for forwarding. The fifth to eighth OMP routes from 10.0.10.2 and 10.0.20.2 have the status code R, which means these routes are resolved, but they have not been chosen as the best OMP routes, and they will not be used for forwarding. The reason that these routes have not been chosen can be seen in the output of the OMP TLOCs table, shown in Figure 7-64.

Since the TLOCs from 10.0.10.1 and 10.0.20.1 have a higher Preference value than the TLOCs from 10.0.10.2 and 10.0.20.2, the OMP routes that resolved to the TLOCs from 10.0.10.1 and 10.0.20.1 have won the best-path selection process. At this point, the lowest origin System IP is used as a tiebreaker, leading to the selection of routes from 10.0.10.1 as the best, which will subsequently be installed in the routing table.

IP	Color	Encap	From Peer	Site Id	Preference	Originator	Last Updated
10.0.10.1	mpls	ipsec	1.1.1.102	10	500	10.0.10.1	26 Aug 2024 9:23:29 PM.
10.0.10.1	biz-internet	ipsec	1.1.1.102	10	500	10.0.10.1	26 Aug 2024 9:23:29 PM.
10.0.20.1	mpls	ipsec	1.1.1.102	20	500	10.0.20.1	26 Aug 2024 9:23:29 PM.
10.0.20.1	biz-internet	ipsec	1.1.1.102	20	500	10.0.20.1	26 Aug 2024 9:23:29 PM.
10.0.10.2	mpls	ipsec	1.1.1.102	10	400	10.0.10.2	26 Aug 2024 9:23:29 PM.
10.0.10.2	biz-internet	ipsec	1.1.1.102	10	400	10.0.10.2	26 Aug 2024 9:23:29 PM.
10.0.20.2	mpls	ipsec	1.1.1.102	20	400	10.0.20.2	26 Aug 2024 9:23:29 PM.
10.0.20.2	biz-internet	ipsec	1.1.1.102	20	400	10.0.20.2	26 Aug 2024 9:23:29 PM.

Figure 7-64 *OMP TLOC Table on BR2-Edge1, Showing TLOCs with Different Preference Values*

Figure 7-65 shows the result of this effect, with the TLOCs from 1 and 2 received on WAN Edge 3 with two different TLOC Preference values. As the higher Preference value is received for the TLOCs that are advertised from WAN Edge 1, only the tunnels to WAN Edge 1 will be used for forwarding traffic. If WAN Edge 1 fails, or if both TLOCs are removed from WAN Edge 3, WAN Edge 3 would subsequently use the next available preferred path, in this case 10.0.20.1 (DC2-Edge1). Just in the case both of the highest preference TLOCs are unavailable, the traffic would fail over to the bottom set of tunnels (WAN Edge 2 - DC1-Edge2 or even DC2-Edge2).

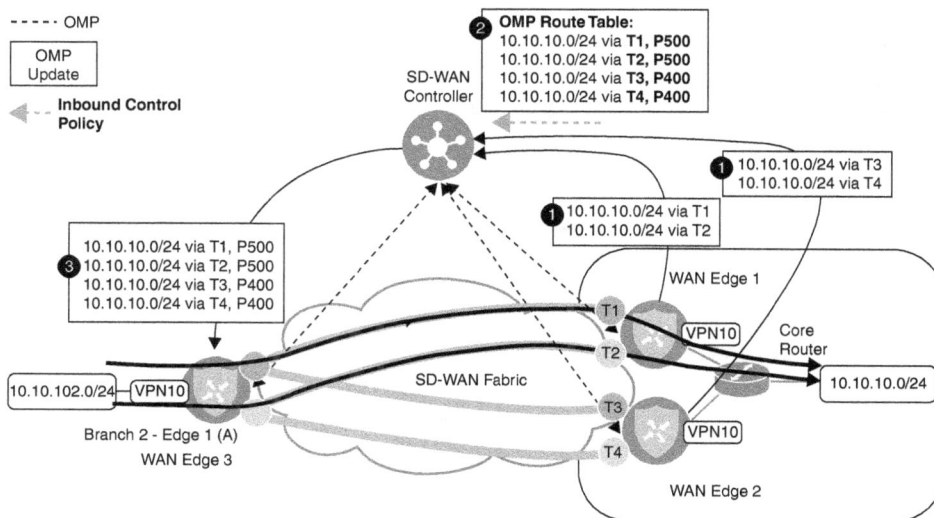

Figure 7-65 *Illustration of the Effects of Different Preference Values on the Forwarding Plane*

Setting TLOC Preference with Device Templates and Configuration Groups

The previous example reviewed the purpose of setting the TLOC Preference value and how to set that value using centralized control policies. In addition to using centralized control policies to set the TLOC Preference value, you can also configure it directly on the tunnel interface. Typically, WAN Edge router configurations are centrally managed using a combination of feature templates and device templates, as discussed in Chapter 4. While Weight and Preference are configurable on the tunnel interfaces with feature templates, they can also be configured with a CLI add-on template on the tunnel interface directly with the command **encapsulation** {**ipsec**|**gre**} [**preference** *preference*] [**weight** *weight*]. Example 7-9 reviews the CLI configuration used to accomplish these objectives. Starting from SD-WAN Releases 20.9 and 17.9, you can use Configuration Groups to achieve the same purpose by editing the desired TLOC under the Transport and Management profile.

Example 7-9   *Tunnel Interface Configuration with Weight and Preference*

```
! The following configuration excerpts from BR1-Edge1 and BR1-Edge2 that
! indicate the preference and weight settings that have been configured
! on the tunnel interfaces
!
BR1-Edge1# show sdwan running-config sdwan | inc interface
GigabitEthernet|color|encapsulation
 interface GigabitEthernet1
  tunnel-interface
   encapsulation ipsec preference 50 weight 5
   color mpls restrict
 interface GigabitEthernet2
  tunnel-interface
   encapsulation ipsec preference 50 weight 20
   color biz-internet
```

```
BR1-Edge2# show sdwan running-config sdwan | inc interface
GigabitEthernet|color|encapsulation
 interface GigabitEthernet1
  tunnel-interface
   encapsulation ipsec preference 40 weight 20
   color biz-internet
 interface GigabitEthernet2
  tunnel-interface
   encapsulation ipsec preference 4
   color lte
BR1-Edge2#
```

Key Topic

Example 7-9 shows the Preference attribute, whose values and their purposes we discussed in depth in the previous section. Example 7-9 also includes the use of the Weight attribute, which is used to determine the proportional load-sharing among TLOCs with equal preferences. Weight is not part of the best-path selection algorithm but is instead used after the best paths are determined to forward proportionally among the paths selected through the best-path process. The Weight attribute can range from a value of 1 (default) to 255. Weight is generally configured in proportion to the bandwidths of the links at a single site. In this example, the Weight settings 20 and 5 could represent links with speeds of 20 and 5 Mbps, respectively. Remember that there is no absolute reference value for Weight; it is only proportional among the transports at the local site.

In Example 7-9, the preferences on the BIZ-INTERNET and MPLS links of BR1-Edge1 are configured as 50 and 50 respectively. The preferences on BR1-Edge2 for the BIZ-INTER-NET and LTE links are configured as 40 and 4, respectively. As a result of this configuration, in steady-state operation, where all routers and all links are operational, inbound traffic to Branch 1 will be sent over the BIZ-INTERNET and MPLS links of BR1-Edge1. These links are configured with the highest Preference values and have won the best-path selection process. Furthermore, traffic will be load-shared on a per-flow basis of 20:5, or 4:1, based on the configured Weight values. If the MPLS and BIZ-INTERNET links on BR1-Edge1 become inoperable, and the TLOCs are no longer resolvable by other routers in the fabric, the TLOC advertisement from BR1-Edge2's BIZ-INTERNET links, configured with a TLOC preference of 40, will win the best-path selection process and will be used by other routers to send traffic to Branch 1. Only if all MPLS and BIZ-INTERNET TLOCs are unresolvable will the LTE TLOC on BR1-Edge2 win the best-path selection process with a preference of 4.

You can see the results of these configurations in the TLOCs that have been advertised to DC1-Edge1 in Figure 7-66.

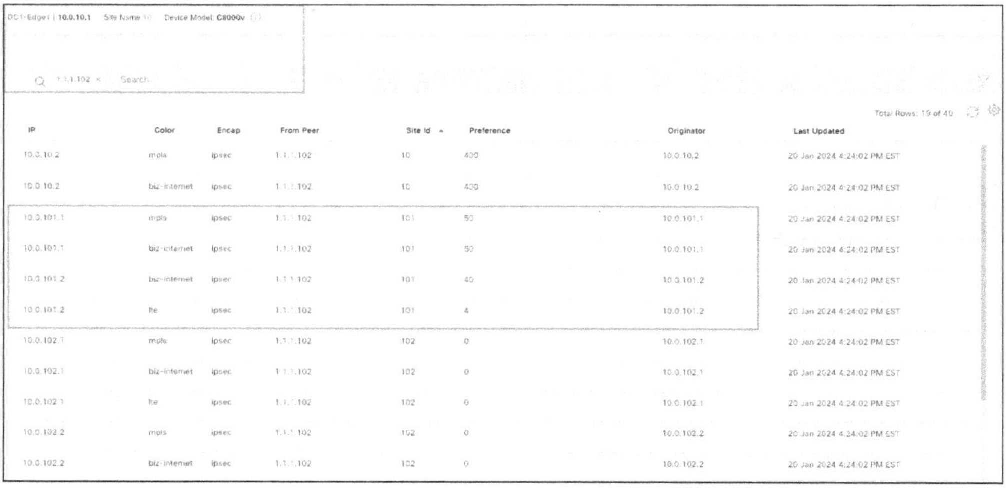

IP	Color	Encap	From Peer	Site Id	Preference	Originator	Last Updated
10.0.10.2	mpls	ipsec	1.1.1.102	10	400	10.0.10.2	20 Jan 2024 4:24:02 PM EST
10.0.10.2	biz-internet	ipsec	1.1.1.102	10	400	10.0.10.2	20 Jan 2024 4:24:02 PM EST
10.0.101.1	mpls	ipsec	1.1.1.102	101	50	10.0.101.1	20 Jan 2024 4:24:02 PM EST
10.0.101.1	biz-internet	ipsec	1.1.1.102	101	50	10.0.101.1	20 Jan 2024 4:24:02 PM EST
10.0.101.2	biz-internet	ipsec	1.1.1.102	101	40	10.0.101.2	20 Jan 2024 4:24:02 PM EST
10.0.101.2	lte	ipsec	1.1.1.102	101	4	10.0.101.2	20 Jan 2024 4:24:02 PM EST
10.0.102.1	mpls	ipsec	1.1.1.102	102	0	10.0.102.1	20 Jan 2024 4:24:02 PM EST
10.0.102.1	biz-internet	ipsec	1.1.1.102	102	0	10.0.102.1	20 Jan 2024 4:24:02 PM EST
10.0.102.1	lte	ipsec	1.1.1.102	102	0	10.0.102.1	20 Jan 2024 4:24:02 PM EST
10.0.102.2	mpls	ipsec	1.1.1.102	102	0	10.0.102.2	20 Jan 2024 4:24:02 PM EST
10.0.102.2	biz-internet	ipsec	1.1.1.102	102	0	10.0.102.2	20 Jan 2024 4:24:02 PM EST

Figure 7-66 *Branch 1 TLOCs Are Received in the DC with the Configured Preference and Weight Values*

Use Case 3 Review

This use case describes two different mechanisms to configure TLOC Preference values and how those Preference values can be used to manipulate how traffic flows across the network. You also saw how to use the **weight** command to perform unequal-cost load-sharing, which is commonly used when network administrators want to use multiple links of different speeds.

NOTE   Use Case 3 shows two different ways to set the TLOC Preference values. While the ability to write a centralized control policy to override the preferences that are configured on an interface is useful, the primary use of this policy is for *overriding* the values that were configured on the tunnel interface, not for configuring the values in the first place. We recommend configuring the TLOC Preference values on the WAN Edge tunnel interfaces directly through feature templates or feature parcels and manipulating them with centralized control policies only when necessary.

NOTE   You may have observed that the choices for Preference values for the data center routers were 500 and 400, while the values used for the Branch 1 location were 50, 40, and 4. While the Preference values have no absolute significance, the decision to use values that were an order of magnitude greater for the data centers than for the branches was by intention. When you configure the data centers with values of 500 and 400 and the branches with lower values, if a prefix (or a default route) that belongs to a data center is ever inadvertently advertised or redistributed from the branch office, the rest of the WAN Edge devices in the fabric will still prefer the advertisements from the data centers because of their higher TLOC preference values. This design choice helps protect the fabric from mistaken or malicious network updates.

Use Case 4: Preferring Regional Data Centers for Internet Access

A common business objective that network administrators need to account for is the desire to have geographically dispersed users access an instance of a shared resource that is close to the users. For example, if a service is accessible from the data centers in New York and London, the users in Boston should generally use the service in New York, whereas the users in Paris and Berlin should generally use the service in London. The definition of a service can be anything—an enterprise ERP application, a video conferencing server, or (as in this use case) a default route to provide Internet access. Figure 7-67 shows the topology for this use case with the configuration objective.

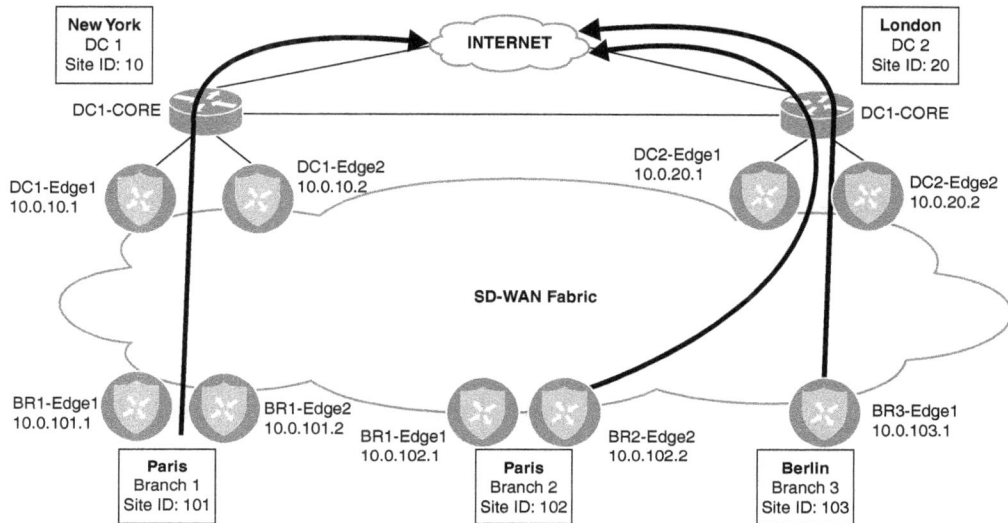

Figure 7-67   *Regionalizing Access to a Service, such as Internet Egress*

Before we proceed through this use case, it is once more necessary to inject default routes into the VPN 10 routing table from the data centers. As with Use Case 2, the specific method used to inject the default routes is inconsequential. With the default routes advertised from the data centers and the old policy applied, you can see in Figure 7-68 that there are four default routes installed in the VPN 10 routing table on BR2-Edge1.

NOTE   The number of paths you can observe for a single prefix at any given time is derived from the best path selection process. This process is influenced by the number of paths WAN Edge routers advertise to SD-WAN Controllers and vice versa. In the current use case, there are more than four routes per prefix, which is also common in Catalyst SD-WAN deployments. OMP configuration settings are available both at the WAN Edge router and the SD-WAN Controller to handle these types of situations. One such setting, **send-backup-paths**, allows the SD-WAN Controller to advertise the first set of non-best routes along with the best routes to WAN Edge devices, which helps to accelerate convergence during brown-out situations; this setting directly depends on the total limit path configured at the SD-WAN Controller. Another setting, **send-path-limit**, can be configured on WAN Edge routers to control the maximum number of equal-cost routes sent to SD-WAN Controllers and vice versa. In addition, the **ecmp-limit** setting is useful when it is necessary to control the total number of OMP paths installed in the WAN Edge route table. For more details, refer to the Cisco Catalyst SD-WAN Command Reference.

The first two of these four routes have the TLOC IP address 10.0.10.1, which is the system IP address of DC1-Edge1. The third and fourth routes have the TLOC IP address 10.0.20.1, which is advertised from DC2-Edge1. This implies that, in this example, the traffic from the Paris branch will egress at the London data center and will be inflicted with the additional latency caused by being routed out the New York data center.

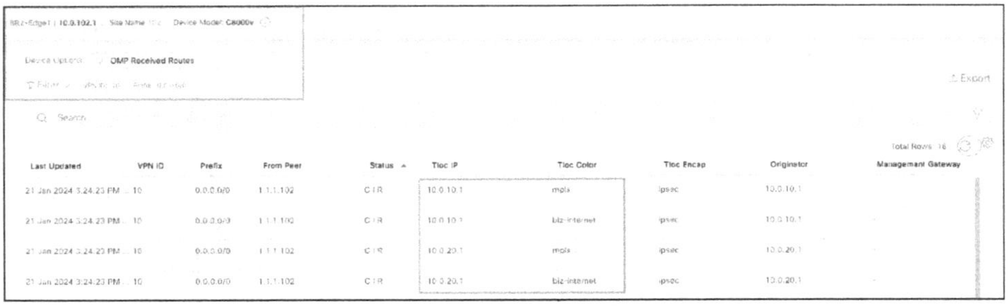

Figure 7-68   *BR2-Edge1 (Paris Branch) Has Installed Four Default Routes in the OMP Routing Table*

Similarly, for users in the Boston (Branch 1) and Berlin (Branch 3) branches, half of the traffic will egress from the geographically local data center, and half of the traffic will be sent all the way across the Atlantic Ocean. This is confirmed by the Simulate Flows output from the Boston branch, shown in Figure 7-69.

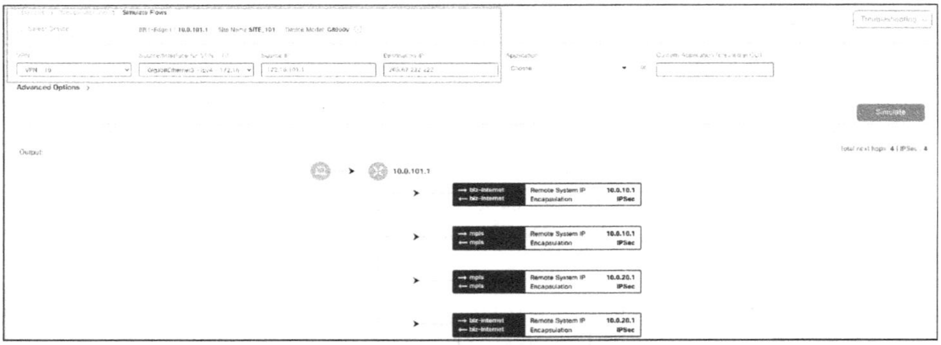

Figure 7-69   *Simulate Flows Output for Destination 208.67.222.222 Confirms That Branch 1 (Boston) Has Four Paths*

NOTE   The Simulate Flows tool can be found in the Troubleshooting section of Monitor > Devices > {*WAN Edge*}. The Simulate Flows tool can provide the expected forwarding path of a flow given the current state of the WAN Edge device. This output considers the routes in the routing table, the centralized and localized policies that have been applied, and the current performance of the transport links. This can be a very useful tool for seeing if the policies that have been applied will have the intended effect. The Simulate Flows tool does not actually generate and forward any traffic in the data plane; instead, it indicates the path that would be taken if a flow existed to be forwarded.

In order to ensure that users always use the Internet egress closest to their geographic location, you can configure the centralized control policy in Example 7-10 on the network. This policy builds on the policies that were configured for the previous use cases and creates separate outbound control policies such that the European branches will prefer the default routes from the European data centers, and the U.S. branches will prefer the default routes from the U.S. data centers.

Example 7-10   *Use Case 4: Policy for Regionalizing Internet Access*

```
! The control-policy "Hub_and_Spoke_TLOC_Lists" that was configured in
! Example 7-5 has been changed into two separate centralized
! control policies: Europe_Hub_and_Spoke_TLOC and North_America_Hub_and_Spoke_TLOC.
policy
 control-policy Europe_Hub_and_Spoke_TLOC
    sequence 1
     match tloc
      site-list DCs
     !
     action accept
     !
    !
! A new sequence was added to this policy to match the default route from
! the London DC (combination of prefix-list and site-list as matching criteria),
! and set a preference of 100.
!
    sequence 11
     match route
      prefix-list Default_Route
      site-list Europe_DC
!
     action accept
      set
       preference 100
      !
     !
    !
    sequence 21
     match route
      site-list DCs
      prefix-list _AnyIpv4PrefixList
     !
     action accept
     !
    !
    sequence 31
     match route
      site-list BranchOffices
      prefix-list _AnyIpv4PrefixList
     !
     action accept
      set
```

```
      tloc-list DC_TLOCs
     !
    !
   !
 default-action reject
 !
! Similar to the previous control policy, the following policy matches
! the default route specifically from the New York datacenter and
! sets a preference.  The rest of the policy is unchanged.
!
control-policy North_America_Hub_and_Spoke_TLOC
   sequence 1
    match tloc
     site-list DCs
    !
    action accept
    !
   !
   sequence 11
    match route
     prefix-list Default_Route
     site-list North_America_DC
    !
    action accept
     set
      preference 100
     !
    !
   !
   sequence 21
    match route
     site-list DCs
     prefix-list _AnyIpv4PrefixList
    !
    action accept
    !
   !
   sequence 31
    match route
     site-list BranchOffices
     prefix-list _AnyIpv4PrefixList      !
    action accept
     set
      tloc-list DC_TLOCs
     !
    !
   !
```

```
   default-action reject
 !
 control-policy Set_DC_TLOC_Preference
 ! <<<No changes made to this policy from Example 7-7, omitted for brevity>>>
 !
 lists
  ! <<<Some lists without changes from Example 7-5 are omitted for brevity>>>
  !
  ! A new prefix-list is created to match the default route
  !
  prefix-list Default_Route
   ip-prefix 0.0.0.0/0
  !
  site-list BranchOffices
   site-id 100-199
  !
  site-list DCs
   site-id 10-50
  !
  ! New site lists are created to allow for more specific matching criteria
  ! (Europe_DC and North_America_DC) and more targeted policy application scopes
  ! (Europe_Branches and North_America_Branches).
  !
  site-list Europe_Branches
   site-id 102-103
  !
  site-list Europe_DC
   site-id 20
  !
  site-list North_America_Branches
   site-id 101
  !
  site-list North_America_DC
   site-id 10
  !
 !
!
! Lastly, the policy that prefers the London DC is applied to the European
! branches, and the policy that prefers the American DC is applied to the
! American Branches.
!
!
apply-policy
 site-list Europe_Branches
  control-policy Europe_Hub_and_Spoke_TLOC out
 !
```

```
site-list North_America_Branches
 control-policy North_America_Hub_and_Spoke_TLOC out
 !
site-list DCs
 control-policy Set_DC_TLOC_Preference in
 !
!
```

With this new centralized policy applied to the SD-WAN fabric, the same outputs from the Paris and Boston offices can be evaluated to further understand the policy's effect. In Figure 7-70, you can see that there are now only two routes installed in the routing table on BR2-Edge1 (in contrast to the four routes present before the policy was applied; refer to Figure 7-68).

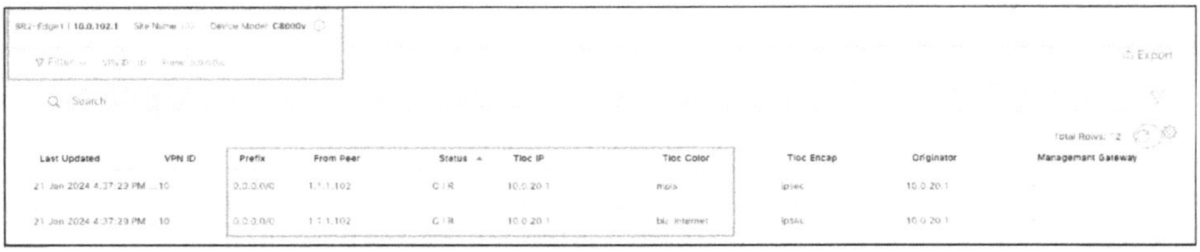

Figure 7-70   *BR2-Edge1 (Paris Branch) Has Two Default Routes Installed in the Routing Table*

The default routes installed on BR2-Edge1 (Paris branch) have the TLOC IP address 10.0.20.1, and they originate from the DC2-Edge1 router (London data center). Further inspection of the OMP Routes table on BR2-Edge1 in Figure 7-71 shows that all eight default routes have been received by the WAN Edge device, but only the two with Route Preference 100 have been selected as the best path and have been inserted into the VPN 10 routing table with the status C I R.

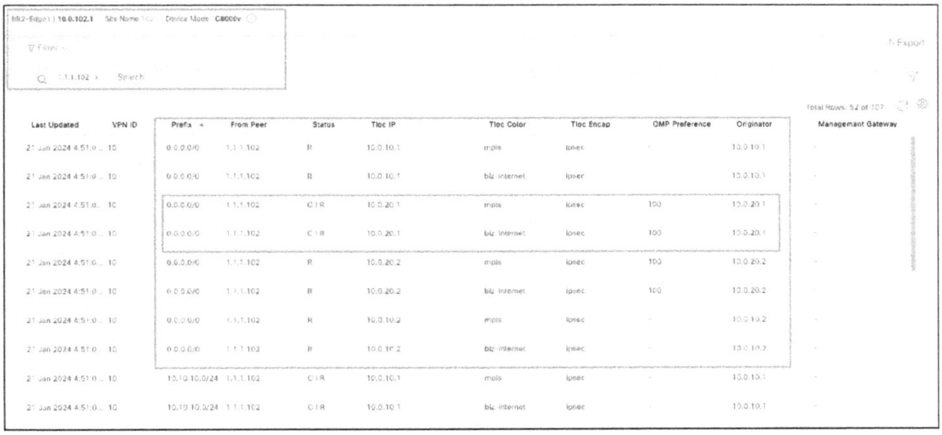

Figure 7-71   *BR2-Edge1 (Paris Branch) Has Installed Eight Default Routes in the OMP Table*

Figure 7-71 shows that BR2-Edge1 has received all eight default routes (four data center WAN Edge routers, each with MPLS and BIZ-INTERNET TLOCs). Of these eight routes, the four that are being advertised from the London data center (site ID 20) have OMP Route Preference 100. Of those four, the two that resolve to the 10.0.20.1 TLOC IP addresses have a TLOC Preference of 500 and will be preferred over the TLOC Preference of 400 for the TLOCs from 10.0.20.2 (from the policy created in Use Case 3). These two preferred routes are being installed into the routing table with of the status C I R.

The Boston branch has selected two different paths that it will use to forward its traffic toward the Internet, as shown in Figure 7-72.

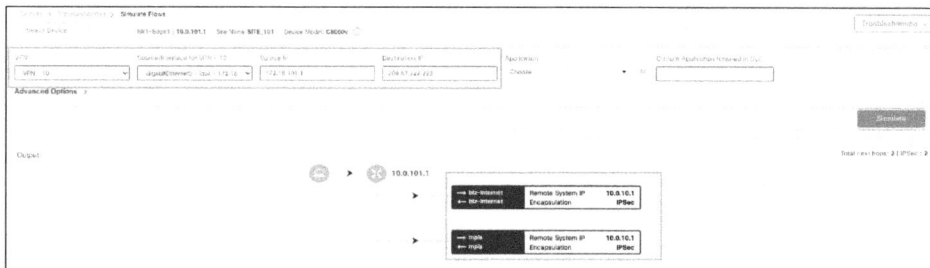

Figure 7-72   *Simulate Flows Output Confirms That Branch 1 (Boston) Will Egress via the New York Data Center (System IP Address 10.0.10.1)*

The Boston branch (BR1-Edge1) will use the two paths from DC1-Edge1 (system IP address 10.0.10.1) that have both a Route Preference of 100 and a TLOC Preference of 500.

Use Case 4 Review

This use case describes how to solve a traffic engineering problem that often plagues network administrators: how to choose the closest instance of a shared resource. While the configurations reviewed in this section may seem overwhelming for a simple network of just five sites, network administrators should consider that the only configuration that would be necessary to expand this design to a network of 500 or 5000 sites would be to update the definitions of the Europe_Branches and North_America_Branches site lists. This ability to have a single, centralized place to manage the WAN fabric is a fundamental part of the power of Cisco SD-WAN.

While the examples in the previous use case focused on TLOC Preference, this use case highlights the OMP Route Preference field, and it demonstrates how these two values can be used together. In the best-path selection algorithm, Route Preference is evaluated before TLOC Preference, and it can therefore be used to override the selection that would have been made based on TLOC Preference values for a specific prefix or group of prefixes. This type of flexibility allows network administrators the extremely fine control necessary to solve the business's traffic engineering objectives.

Use Case 5: Regional Mesh Networks

In Use Case 1, we explored turning the network from the default state of a full-mesh topology into a hub-and-spoke network. While a hub-and-spoke design may meet the needs of some organizations, it may be too rigid for many enterprises. Many times, there are legitimate business purposes for some branch office sites to be in communication with other branch office sites. This communication should be permitted without requiring traversal of a corporate data center. Sometimes organizations implement this type of network because they have sites that share geographic proximity; other times, organizations choose to implement this type of network based on the business function of a site (such as R&D, manufacturing, sales, and so on). Figure 7-73 shows an existing topology altered to form a regional mesh of the European offices.

Building on the policies that were created in the previous use cases, in this use case we look at building regional mesh networks in order to permit the sites in Europe to communicate directly with other sites in Europe without needing to transit a data center to do so. The new data plane tunnel that will need to be created is highlighted in Figure 7-73. A corresponding policy for North America will also be built, but because there is currently only a single branch site in North America, the policy will not have an effect on the network. Transiting the data centers will still be required in order for a branch office in North America to communicate with a branch office in Europe.

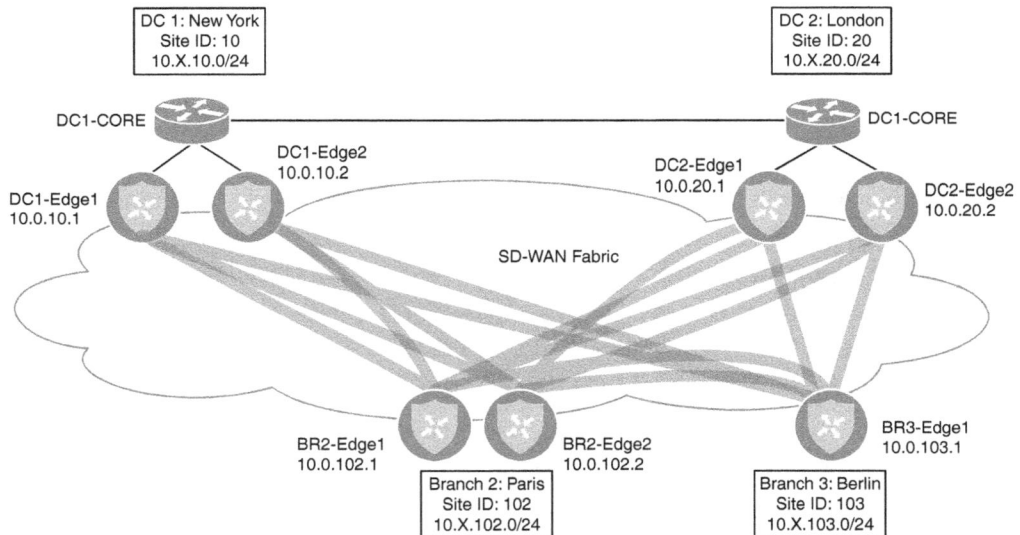

Figure 7-73 *Network Topology with Regional Meshes*

Before the new policy is applied, you can see that there is no direct data plane connection between BR2-Edge1 and BR3-Edge1 when you look at the real-time BFD Sessions output shown in Figure 7-74. All the BFD sessions terminate at data center WAN Edges, as indicated by the system IP addresses 10.0.10.X and 10.0.20.X.

The **traceroute** output in Example 7-11 confirms that while Branch 2 has connectivity to Branch 1 and Branch 3, the data plane must currently transit the data center, taking a total of two hops to reach both branch offices.

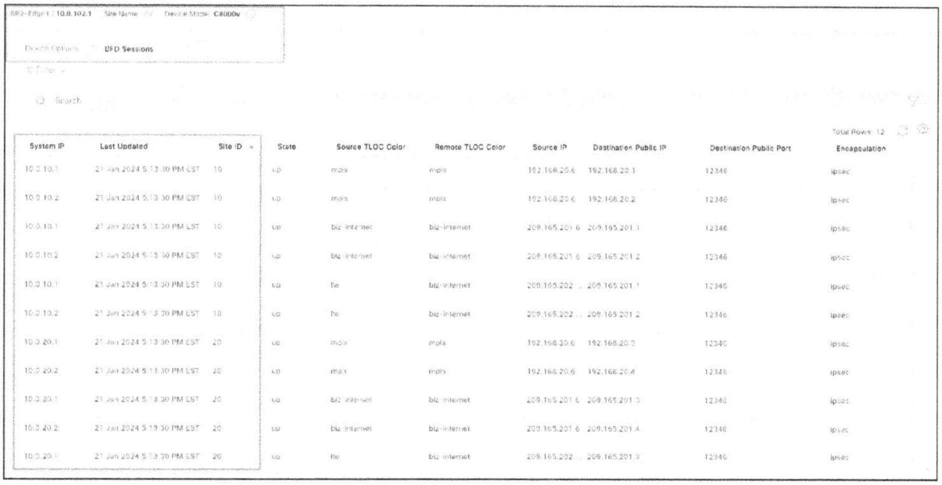

Figure 7-74 *BR2-Edge1 Does Not Currently Have Any Data Plane Tunnels to 10.0.103.1/ Site 103*

Example 7-11 *Tracing the Path from 10.10.102.1 to Other Branches via the Data Center*

```
! Tracing a path from BR2 to BR3 is successful, but the data path is indirect
! and transits a datacenter
!
BR2-Edge1# traceroute vrf 10 10.10.103.1
<<<Output omitted for brevity>>>
  1 BIZ-INET-DC1-Edge1 (209.165.201.1) 2 msec 1 msec 1 msec
  2 MPLS-BR3-Edge1 (192.168.20.8) 1 msec 2 msec 0 msec
  3 BR3-Edge1-Core (172.16.103.2) 2 msec 2 msec *
BR2-Edge1#
!
! Tracing a path from BR2 to BR1 is successful, but the data path is indirect
! and transits a datacenter
!
BR2-Edge1# traceroute vrf 10 10.10.101.1
<<<Output omitted for brevity>>>
  1 BIZ-INET-DC1-Edge1 (209.165.201.1) 1 msec 1 msec 1 msec
  2 BIZ-INET-BR1-Edge1 (192.168.100.1) 2 msec 2 msec 1 msec
  3 BR1-Edge1-Core (172.16.101.2) 14 msec 3 msec *
BR2-Edge1#
```

In order to enable a regional mesh for the European locations, the policy in Example 7-12 is applied. In order to form regional meshes, the SD-WAN Controllers will need to advertise the TLOC routes and the routes for the other sites within the mesh with which connectivity should be established. For sites that are outside the regional mesh, the TLOCs will not be advertised, and the OMP routes will be advertised with the data center TLOCs.

Example 7-12   *Use Case 5: Policy for Establishing Regional Mesh Data Planes*

```
! In the "To_Europe_Branches_Regional_Mesh" control policy, sequence 11 and sequence 41 were
! added to permit the advertisements of the TLOCs and Routes (respectively) from
! other sites in the Site List "Europe_Branches". Additionally, sequence 51 has
! been updated so that only the sites in the "North_America_Branches" site list
! now have their TLOCs updated with the TLOC list.
!

policy
 control-policy To_Europe_Branches_Regional_Mesh
    sequence 1
     match tloc
      site-list DCs


      !
     action accept
     !
    !
    sequence 11
     match tloc
      site-list Europe_Branches
      !
     action accept
     !
    !
    sequence 21
     match route
      prefix-list Default_Route
      site-list Europe_DC
     !
     action accept
      set
       preference 100
      !
     !
    !
    sequence 31
     match route
      site-list DCs
      prefix-list _AnyIpv4PrefixList
     !
     action accept
     !
    !
```

```
   sequence 41
    match route
     site-list Europe_Branches
     prefix-list _AnyIpv4PrefixList
     !
    action accept
     !
    !
   sequence 51
    match route
     site-list North_America_Branches
     prefix-list _AnyIpv4PrefixList
     !
    action accept
     set
      tloc-list DC_TLOCs
      !
     !
    !
  default-action reject
 !
! Similar to the previous control policy, the following policy permits the TLOCs
! and Routes from the "North_America_Branches" site list to be advertised.
! Additionally, sequence 51 has been updated to only apply to the European
! Branches.
!
control-policy To_North_America_Branches_Regional_Mesh
   sequence 1
    match tloc
     site-list DCs
     !
    action accept
     !
    !
   sequence 11
    match tloc
     site-list North_America_Branches
     !
    action accept
     !
    !
   sequence 21
    match route
     prefix-list Default_Route
     site-list North_America_DC
     !
```

```
      action accept
       set
        preference 100
       !
      !
     !
     sequence 31
      match route
       site-list DCs
       prefix-list _AnyIpv4PrefixList
!      action accept
       !
      !
     sequence 41
      match route
       site-list North_America_Branches
       prefix-list _AnyIpv4PrefixList
       !
      action accept
       !
      !
     sequence 51
      match route
       site-list Europe_Branches
       prefix-list _AnyIpv4PrefixList
       !
      action accept
       set
        tloc-list DC_TLOCs
        !
       !
      !
  default-action reject
  !
control-policy Set_DC_TLOC_Preference
! <<<No changes made to this policy from Example 7-7, omitted for brevity>>>
  !
lists
! <<<No changes made to the lists from Example 7-10, omitted for brevity>>>
  !
!
! Lastly, the new policies are applied to the site lists.
  !
```

```
apply-policy
 site-list Europe_Branches
  control-policy To_Europe_Branches_Regional_Mesh out
 !
 site-list North_America_Branches
  control-policy To_North_America_Branches_Regional_Mesh out
 !
 site-list DCs
  control-policy Set_DC_TLOC_Preference in
 !
```

After the policy in Example 7-12 is applied to the network, the necessary TLOC routes are exchanged between BR2-Edge1 (Paris) and BR3-Edge1 (Berlin) in order to form data plane tunnels. You can see these five additional tunnels between the two sites in the BFD Sessions output from BR2-Edge1 (see Figure 7-75).

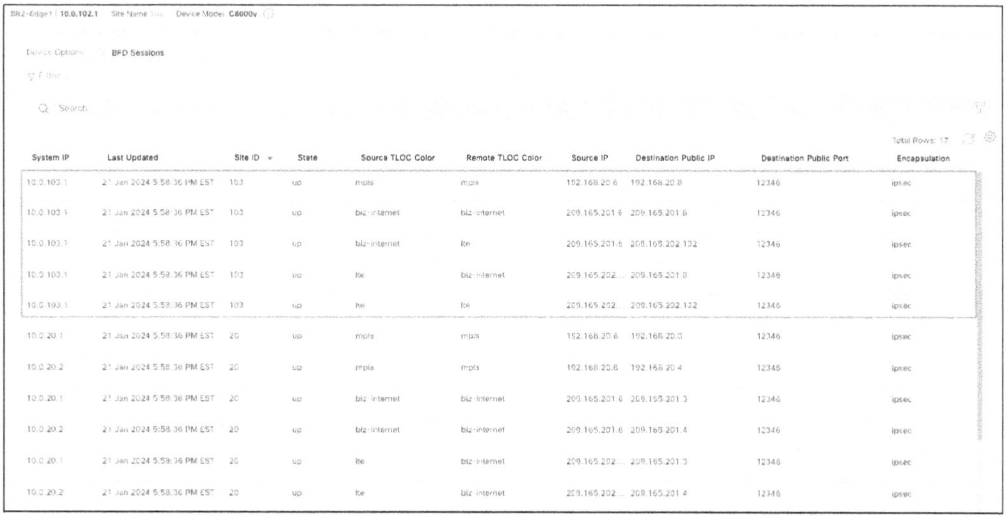

Figure 7-75   *BR2-Edge Has New Data Plane Tunnels to 10.0.103.1/Site 103*

The data plane connectivity can be validated by testing with **traceroute**, as shown in Example 7-13. The first trace shows that there is now a direct path established between Paris and Berlin as part of the European regional mesh. There is no longer a need to transit a data center router to facilitate that connectivity, and the path is now only a single hop. However, as the second **traceroute** output indicates, there is no direct data plane path from Paris to Boston. Traffic that is going from Branch 2 (Paris) or Branch 3 (Berlin) to Branch 1 (Boston) must still transit the data center.

Example 7-13 *Tracing the Path from 10.10.102.1 to Other Branches After the Regional Mesh Is Established*

```
! Tracing a path from BR2 to BR3 is successful and the path is now direct
!
BR2-Edge1# traceroute vrf 10 10.10.103.1
<<<Output omitted for brevity>>>
  1 BIZ-INET-BR3-Edge1 (209.165.201.8) 2 msec 1 msec 1 msec
  2 BR3-Edge1-Core (172.16.103.2) 1 msec 2 msec *
BR2-Edge1#
!
! Tracing a path from BR2 to BR1 is successful, but the data path is still
! indirect and transits a datacenter
!
BR2-Edge1# traceroute vrf 10 10.10.101.1
<<<Output omitted for brevity>>>
  1 BIZ-INET-DC1-Edge1 (209.165.201.1) 1 msec 1 msec 1 msec
  2 BIZ-INET-BR1-Edge1 (192.168.100.1) 1 msec 1 msec 2 msec
  3 BR1-Edge1-Core (172.16.101.2) 2 msec 2 msec *
BR2-Edge1#
```

Use Case 5 Review

This use case shows how to alter the structure of the SD-WAN fabric so that it is not purely a hub-and-spoke network and instead consists of multiple distinct regional mesh networks. Network administrators may deploy regional meshes to permit offices that are in close proximity to each other or offices that serve the same business function to communicate without the need for a data center to proxy the communication.

This use case also continues to highlight how trivial it is to create increasingly complex topologies through a single, centrally administered control policy. The only thing necessary to turn the hub-and-spoke network into a regional mesh network was to advertise the TLOC routes and OMP routes to the sites that need to be able to communicate with each other.

Use Case 6: Enforcing Security Perimeters with Service Insertion

Enterprises often have a need to inject services into the traffic path of the WAN environment. One of the most frequently used services is a security device such as a firewall. Other potential services include IPSs/IDSs, network sniffers, web proxies, caching engines, and WAN optimization appliances. Regardless of the specific type of service, Cisco SD-WAN can natively advertise the availability of the service across the WAN environment and direct traffic flows to that service.

In this use case, there is a need to ensure that users at branch sites in Europe cannot communicate directly with branch sites in North America without first having their traffic inspected by a firewall and vice versa. We are going to continue to build on the policies created for the previous use cases and modify them to meet this objective.

The first step in service insertion is the configuration of the service itself. For this use case, we are going to provision a firewall attached to DC1-Edge1 as a network service, as shown in Figure 7-76. Traffic flows that originate at a European branch site, such as the example in the diagram, must be inspected by this firewall before being forwarded to a branch location in North America.

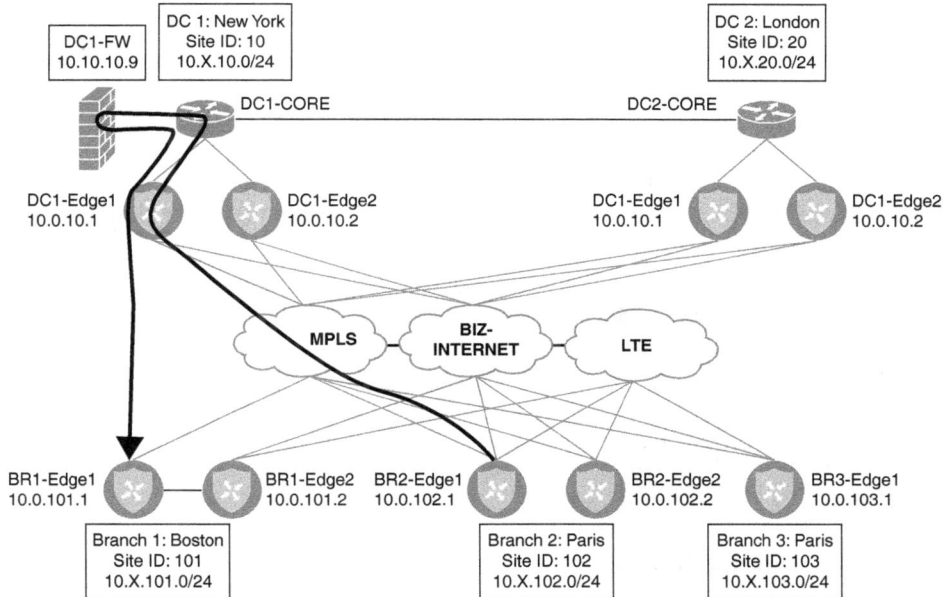

Figure 7-76 *Using a Firewall at the Data Center to Inspect Flows Transiting Between Two Branch Sites*

Example 7-14 shows the configuration needed to create the service in DC1-Edge1 and the advertisements on the SD-WAN Controller as soon as the service is provisioned on the WAN Edge device. Once the service has been provisioned, a new label is assigned to indicate which traffic received by this WAN Edge device should be forwarded to the service. As Example 7-14 shows, the label in this case is 1004.

Example 7-14 *Firewall Service Configuration on DC1-Edge1*

```
! The minimum configuration necessary for a service is a single line that
! specifies where the service is reachable.
!
DC1-Edge1# show sdwan running-config sdwan
sdwan
 service firewall vrf 10
  no track-enable
  ipv4 address 10.10.10.9
!
! Output omitted for brevity
!
```

```
! As soon as the service is configured, it is advertised to the SD-WAN Controller
and
! ready to be reflected to the entire fabric. Other WAN Edges that want to
! send traffic to this service should use label 1004.
!
DC1-Edge1# show sdwan omp services
ADDRESS                                          PATH  REGION  GROUP
FAMILY  TENANT  VPN  SERVICE  ORIGINATOR  FROM PEER  ID    ID      NUMBER  LABEL  STATUS   VRF
----------------------------------------------------------------------------------
ipv4    0       10   FW       10.0.10.1   0.0.0.0   66    None    None    1004   C,Red,R  10
                                          0.0.0.0   68    None    None    1004   C,Red,R  10
```

A locally attached service, such as the firewall in this example, is configured with the syntax **service** {*service-name*} **vrf** {*vrf-number*} **ipv4 address** {*ip address*}.

Before the policy is applied to the SD-WAN fabric, Branch 2 is able to reach Branch 1 in two hops, as indicated in Example 7-15. Furthermore, this traffic is being forwarded with the label 1003, which represents VPN 10.

Example 7-15   *Tracing the Path from 10.10.102.1 to Branch 1 Before Service Insertion Is Activated*

```
! Tracing a path from BR2 to BR1 is successful, but the data path transits
! a datacenter.
!
BR2-Edge1# traceroute vrf 10 10.10.101.100
Type escape sequence to abort.
Tracing the route to 10.10.101.100
VRF info: (vrf in name/id, vrf out name/id)
  1 MPLS-DC1-Edge1 (192.168.20.1) 2 msec 1 msec 1 msec
  2 BIZ-INET-BR1-Edge1 (192.168.100.1) 2 msec 3 msec 1 msec
  3 BR1-Edge1-Core (172.16.101.2) 1 msec 2 msec 2 msec
  4 BR1-PC1 (10.10.101.100) 1 msec 3 msec 2 msec
BR2-Edge1#
!
! The OMP Route table indicates that the label that is used to reach
! 10.10.101.0/24 without the service insertion policy is 1003.
!
BR2-Edge1# show sdwan omp routes 10.10.101.0/24 detail

---------------------------------------------------
omp route entries for tenant-id 0 vpn 10 route 10.10.101.0/24
---------------------------------------------------
            RECEIVED FROM:
peer            1.1.1.102
path-id         3
```

```
label               1003
status              C,I,R
loss-reason     not set
lost-to-peer    not set
lost-to-path-id not set
    Attributes:
      originator      10.0.101.1
      type            installed
      tloc            10.0.10.1, mpls, ipsec
<<Output omitted for brevity>>>
            RECEIVED FROM:
peer            1.1.1.102
path-id         67108867
label               1003
status              C,I,R
loss-reason     not set
lost-to-peer    not set
lost-to-path-id not set
    Attributes:
      originator      10.0.101.1
      type            installed
      tloc            10.0.10.1, biz-internet, ipsec
<<Output omitted for brevity>>>
```

Once the firewall service is configured on the WAN Edge router, only a single line of the centralized control policy needs to be changed in order to direct the branch sites to use the service, as shown in Example 7-16.

Example 7-16   *Use Case 6: Service Insertion for Firewalling Branch-to-Branch Transatlantic Traffic*

```
! The only change that has been made is to change the action in sequence
! 51 from referencing the TLOC Lists to now reference the FW service.
!
policy
 control-policy To_Europe_Branches_Reg_Mesh_with_FW
    sequence 1
     match tloc
      site-list DCs
     !
     action accept
     !
    !
   sequence 11
     match tloc
      site-list Europe_Branches
     !
```

```
     action accept
      !
     !
    sequence 21
     match route
      prefix-list Default_Route
      site-list Europe_DC
      !
     action accept
      set
       preference 100
       !
      !
     !
    sequence 31
     match route
      site-list DCs
      prefix-list _AnyIpv4PrefixList
      !
     action accept
     !
     !
    sequence 41
     match route
      site-list Europe_Branches
      prefix-list _AnyIpv4PrefixList
      !
     action accept
      !
     !
    sequence 51
     match route
      site-list North_America_Branches
      prefix-list _AnyIpv4PrefixList
      !
     action accept
      set
       service  FW
      !
     !
     !
   default-action reject
  !
 control-policy To_North_America_Branches_Reg_Mesh_with_FW
```

```
! The change in this policy mirrors the change made in the
! To_Europe_Branches_Reg_Mesh_with_FW policy, and was omitted for brevity
!
control-policy Set_DC_TLOC_Preference
! No changes made to this policy from Example 7-7, omitted for brevity
!
lists
! No changes made to the lists from Example 7-10, omitted for brevity
!
!
!
apply-policy
 site-list Europe_Branches
  control-policy To_Europe_Branches_Reg_Mesh_with_FW out
 !
 site-list North_America_Branches
  control-policy To_North_America_Branches_Reg_Mesh_with_FW out
 !
 site-list DCs
  control-policy Set_DC_TLOC_Preference in
 !
!
```

Once the service insertion policy has been activated, the OMP route table is updated to reflect the new label that will be used to forward traffic from BR2-Edge1 to 10.10.101.0/24. Note that the new label in Example 7-17 is 1004, which is the same label associated with the firewall service in Example 7-14.

The additional hops in the path from Branch 2 to Branch 1 are related to the firewall that the policy requires these transatlantic flows to transit. At the same time, flows between Branch 2 and Branch 3, both part of the European mesh, go directly between the WAN Edge devices and are not required to be filtered through the firewall.

Example 7-17 *Tracing the Path from 10.10.102.1 to Branch 1 After Service Insertion Is Activated*

```
! The OMP Route table indicates that the label that is used to reach
! 10.10.101.0/24 with the service insertion policy is 1004.
!
BR2-Edge1# show sdwan omp routes 10.10.101.0/24 detail
---------------------------------------------------
omp route entries for tenant-id 0 vpn 10 route 10.10.101.0/24
---------------------------------------------------
            RECEIVED FROM:
peer             1.1.1.102
path-id          268435459
label            1004
```

```
status          C,I,R
loss-reason     not set
lost-to-peer    not set
lost-to-path-id not set
    Attributes:
     originator       10.0.101.1
     type             installed
     tloc             10.0.10.1, mpls, ipsec
<<omitted for brevity>>>
          RECEIVED FROM:
peer            1.1.1.102
path-id         335544323
label           1004
status          C,I,R
loss-reason     not set
lost-to-peer    not set
lost-to-path-id not set
    Attributes:
     originator       10.0.101.1
     type             installed
     tloc             10.0.10.1, biz-internet, ipsec
<<omitted for brevity>>>
!
! Tracing a path from BR2 to BR1 is successful, but the data path now
! has additional hops for the Firewall Service in the datacenter.
!
BR2-Edge1# traceroute vrf 10 10.10.101.100
<<<Output omitted for brevity>>>
  1 MPLS-DC1-Edge1 (192.168.20.1) 2 msec 1 msec 0 msec
  2 DC1-Edge1-Core (172.16.10.2) 2 msec 1 msec 0 msec
  3 DC1-FW-SVC (10.10.10.9) 2 msec 1 msec 1 msec
  4 DC1-Edge1-Core-Self (172.16.10.1) 2 msec 1 msec 1 msec
  5 BIZ-INET-BR1-Edge1 (192.168.100.1) 3 msec 3 msec 3 msec
  6 BR1-Edge1-Core (172.16.101.2) 1 msec 2 msec 3 msec
  7 BR1-PC1 (10.10.101.100) 1 msec 3 msec 2 msec
```

```
BR2-Edge1# traceroute vrf 10 10.10.103.1
Type escape sequence to abort.
Tracing the route to 10.10.103.1
VRF info: (vrf in name/id, vrf out name/id)
  1 BIZ-INET-BR3-Edge1 (209.165.201.8) 1 msec 1 msec 1 msec
  2 BR3-Edge1-Core (172.16.103.2) 2 msec 1 msec *
BR2-Edge1#
```

Use Case 6 Review

This use case reviews how to provision a network service and manipulate the control policy so that traffic flows are directed to that service. This example uses a single firewall that is advertised throughout the fabric. In the real world, it is much more common to see redundant sets of network services distributed throughout the WAN fabric. In those cases, the lessons from the previous use cases can be combined with network service insertion to ensure that users have reliable, fast access to the services they need and that the services fail over in a predictable manner.

The traffic engineering completed in this use case is all based on the control plane; the policy is keyed off a specific set of source and destination sites and prefixes. In Chapter 8, "Centralized Data Policies," we will explore how to continue to enhance this policy so that specific applications can be directed through network services rather than through just an entire site or subnet.

Use Case 7: Isolating Guest Users from the Corporate WAN

Many organizations have sites where guests are permitted onto the network. Basic security can be provided by confining guest users to their own VPN. However, the default behavior of the SD-WAN fabric is such that connectivity within a single VPN is automatically established between different sites through the exchange of TLOC routes and OMP routes. While this automatic behavior is desired for the corporate network segments, most organizations do not want to permit guest users to communicate with other guest users across the WAN fabric. In this use case, we will explore the use of VPN membership policies to prohibit the exchange of control plane information from VPN 50 (the guest user VPN) to the SD-WAN Controllers.

Before any policy is applied to the network, users in the guest VPN (VPN 50) are able to reach other guest users at different sites, as shown in Example 7-18.

Example 7-18 *Guest VPN Connectivity Between Different Sites*

```
! BR2-Edge1 is able to reach BR3-Edge1 in the guest VPN
!
BR2-Edge1# ping vrf 50 10.50.103.1
Type escape sequence to abort.
Sending 5, 100-byte ICMP Echos to 10.50.103.1, timeout is 2 seconds:
!!!!!
```

In order to prohibit this type of site-to-site connectivity in the guest VPN, we can add a VPN membership policy to the centralized control policy. Example 7-19 shows the centralized control policy to implement this change.

Example 7-19   *Use Case 7: VPN Membership Policy to Prohibit Guest VPN Connectivity Between Different Sites*

```
! The new piece of this policy is the VPN Membership policy. This VPN membership
! policy permits the VPNs for Corporate (VPN 10), and PCI (VPN 20). All other
! VPNs will be subject to the default action (reject).
policy
 vpn-membership vpnMembership_-950781881
    sequence 10
     match
      vpn-list Corporate_Segment
      !
     action accept
      !
     !
    sequence 20
     match
      vpn-list PCI_VPN
      !
     action accept
      !
     !
  default-action reject
 !
 control-policy Set_DC_TLOC_Preference
  ! <<<No changes made to this policy from Example 7-7, omitted for brevity>>>
  !
 control-policy To_Europe_Branches_Reg_Mesh_with_FW
  ! <<<No changes made to this policy from Example 7-16, omitted for brevity>>>
  !
 control-policy To_North_America_Branches_Reg_Mesh_with_FW
  ! <<<No changes made to this policy from Example 7-16, omitted for brevity>>>
  !
 lists
  ! <<<Some lists without changes from Example 7-5 are omitted for brevity>>>
  !
  ! Two new VPN lists were created to work with the VPN membership policy.
  !
  vpn-list Corporate_Segment
   vpn 10
   !
  vpn-list PCI_VPN
   vpn 20
   !
  !
 !
```

```
! Lastly, the VPN Membership policy is applied to the Branch Offices
!
apply-policy
 site-list Europe_Branches
  control-policy To_Europe_Branches_Reg_Mesh_with_FW out
 !
 site-list North_America_Branches
  control-policy To_North_America_Branches_Reg_Mesh_with_FW out
 !
 site-list DCs
  control-policy Set_DC_TLOC_Preference in
 !
 site-list BranchOffices
  vpn-membership vpnMembership_950781881
 !
!
```

As Example 7-19 shows, VPN membership policies follow a similar structure and syntax to the other centralized control policies that we have been working with throughout this chapter. In the most basic sense, a VPN membership policy specifies which VPNs will be permitted to join the fabric from a specific site. The remaining VPNs are rejected by the default action.

You can clearly see the effect of the VPN membership policy by looking at the OMP services output on the SD-WAN Controller, as shown in Example 7-20. The command **show omp services** for VPN 50 lists the service as rejected. In this state, the SD-WAN Controller will not propagate any incoming updates from VPN 50 to other OMP peers, and the SD-WAN Controller will not forward updates about VPN 50 from other WAN Edge routers to these locations that have been rejected. Functionally, this isolates VPN 50 from a control plane perspective. This is proven out in Example 7-20 when users in the guest segment at Branch 2 are no longer able to reach the guest segments at other locations.

Example 7-20   *Use Case 7: Effects of the VPN Membership Policy*

```
vSmart-1# show omp services family ipv4 vpn 50
C    -> chosen
I    -> installed
Red -> redistributed
Rej -> rejected
L    -> looped
R    -> resolved
S    -> stale
Ext -> extranet
Inv -> invalid
Stg -> staged
IA   -> On-demand inactive
U    -> TLOC unresolved
```

```
                                            PATH   REGION
     VPN    SERVICE  ORIGINATOR  FROM PEER   ID     ID    LABEL   STATUS

     ---------------------------------------------------------------------

     50     VPN      10.0.102.1  10.0.102.1   66    None   1004   Rej,R,Inv
                                 10.0.102.1   68    None   1004   Rej,R,Inv
                                 10.0.102.1   70    None   1004   Rej,R,Inv
     50     VPN      10.0.102.2  10.0.102.2   66    None   1004   Rej,R,Inv
                                 10.0.102.2   68    None   1004   Rej,R,Inv
                                 10.0.102.2   70    None   1004   Rej,R,Inv
     50     VPN      10.0.103.1  10.0.103.1   66    None   1005   Rej,R,Inv
                                 10.0.103.1   68    None   1005   Rej,R,Inv
                                 10.0.103.1   70    None   1005   Rej,R,Inv
     !
     !
     ! BR2-Edge1 is unable to reach BR3-Edge1 in the Guest VPN
     !
     BR2-Edge1# ping vrf 50 10.50.103.1
     Type escape sequence to abort.
     Sending 5, 100-byte ICMP Echos to 10.50.103.1, timeout is 2 seconds:
     U.U.U
     Success rate is 0 percent (0/5)
     BR2-Edge1#
     !
     ! Guest Users at BR2-Edge1 are still able to access the public internet via
     ! local internet egress even though they can no longer reach other branch sites.
     !
     BR2-Edge1# ping vrf 50  208.67.222.222
     Sending 5, 100-byte ICMP Echos to 208.67.222.222, timeout is 2 seconds:
     !!!!!
     Success rate is 100 percent (5/5), round-trip min/avg/max = 1/1/2 ms
     BR2-Edge1#
```

Use Case 7 Review

This use case shows how to use a VPN membership policy to prohibit the guest VPN from exchanging control plane information with the SD-WAN Controllers and in turn prohibit the guest VPN from forwarding traffic across the SD-WAN fabric. While a VPN membership policy can be used to prohibit a VPN from being used at all over the SD-WAN fabric, it can also be used to protect and secure VPNs by prohibiting a WAN Edge device that is provisioned either mistakenly or maliciously with a sensitive VPN from being able to exchange control plane information and access the data plane.

Use Case 8: Creating Different Network Topologies for Each Segment

In this use case, we will continue to revise and combine some of the earlier policies that we have discussed and apply them to different network segments at the same time. Currently, there is a European regional mesh that connects Branch 2 and Branch 3. In this use case, we will keep that forwarding path available for the corporate users in VPN 10, but we will revert the PCI VPN (VPN 20) back to a hub-and-spoke topology.

Before the policy is activated, the output in Example 7-21 confirms that currently both VPN 10 and VPN 20 have direct data plane connections from Branch 2 to Branch 3.

Example 7-21   *All VPNs Are Directly Connected Between Branch 2 and Branch 3*

```
!
! BR2-Edge1 is one hop away from Branch 3 in VPN 10
!
BR2-Edge1# traceroute vrf 10 10.10.103.1
<<<Output omitted for brevity>>>
  1 BIZ-INET-BR3-Edge1 (209.165.201.8) 2 msec 1 msec 1 msec
  2 BR3-Edge1-Core (172.16.103.2) 1 msec 2 msec *
BR2-Edge1#
!
! BR2-Edge1 is one hop away from Branch 3 in VPN 20
!
BR2-Edge1# traceroute vrf 20 10.20.103.1
<<<Output omitted for brevity>>>
  1 BIZ-INET-BR3-Edge1 (209.165.201.8) 2 msec 1 msec 1 msec
  2 BR3-Edge1-Core (172.20.103.2) 2 msec 2 msec *
BR2-Edge1#
```

Example 7-22 highlights the necessary changes to the centralized control policy. In order to enact this policy, a new criterion was added to sequence 41 so that it only applies to routes from the corporate VPN. Now sequence 41 will match all routes from European branches in VPN 10 and accept them without any modifications. In addition, sequence 51 is added to match the routes from European branches in the PCI VPN. These routes have their TLOCs (next-hop attributes) altered so that the prefixes are advertised as being reachable from the European data centers.

Example 7-22   *Use Case 8: Multi-Topology Policy*

```
!
! In order to create different logical topologies on a per-VPN basis, the
! routes need to be manipulated on a per-VPN basis. In this policy, this is
! done in sequence 41, which matches and accepts the routes in the corporate
! VPN, and in sequence 51, which matches routes in the PCI VPN and sets a
! TLOC list with the TLOCs of DC2.
!
policy
 control-policy Euro_Reg_Mesh_with_FW_MultiTopo
    sequence 1
     match tloc
      site-list DCs
     !
     action accept
     !
     !
```

7

```
sequence 11
 match tloc
  site-list Europe_Branches
 !
 action accept
 !
!
sequence 21
 match route
  prefix-list Default_Route
  site-list Europe_DC
 !
 action accept
  set
   preference 100
  !
 !
!
sequence 31
 match route
  site-list DCs
  prefix-list _AnyIpv4PrefixList
 !
 action accept
 !
!
sequence 41
 match route
  site-list Europe_Branches
 vpn-list Corporate_Segment
  prefix-list _AnyIpv4PrefixList
 !
 action accept
 !
!
sequence 51
 match route
  site-list Europe_Branches
 vpn-list PCI_VPN
  prefix-list _AnyIpv4PrefixList
 !
 action accept
  set
  tloc-list Europe_DC_TLOCs
  !
 !
!
```

```
   sequence 61
    match route
     site-list North_America_Branches
     prefix-list _AnyIpv4PrefixList
     !
    action accept
     set
      service  FW
     !
     !
    !
 default-action reject
 !
control-policy North_America_Reg_Mesh_with_FW
 ! <<<No changes made to this policy from Example 7-16, omitted for brevity>>>
 !
vpn-membership vpnMembership_950781881
 ! <<<No changes made to this policy from Example 7-19, omitted for brevity>>>
 !
control-policy Set_DC_TLOC_Preference
 ! <<<No changes made to this policy from Example 7-7, omitted for brevity>>>
 !
lists
 ! <<<Some lists without changes from Example 7-5 are omitted for brevity>>>
  !
 ! A new TLOC List is created for the TLOCs in DC2
  !
 tloc-list Europe_DC_TLOCs
  tloc 10.0.20.1 color mpls encap ipsec
  tloc 10.0.20.1 color biz-internet encap ipsec
  tloc 10.0.20.2 color mpls encap ipsec
  tloc 10.0.20.2 color biz-internet encap ipsec
  !
 !
 !
apply-policy
 site-list Europe_Branches
  control-policy Euro_Reg_Mesh_with_FW_MultiTopo out
  !
 site-list DCs
  control-policy Set_DC_TLOC_Preference in
  !
 site-list North_America_Branches
  control-policy North_America_Reg_Mesh_with_FW out
  !
```

```
site-list BranchOffices
 vpn-membership vpnMembership_950781881
 !
 !
```

As the multi-topology policy in Example 7-22 shows, creating different logical topologies on a per-VPN basis involves manipulating the routes on a per-VPN basis. The centralized policy in this use case creates a new TLOC list with the TLOCs from the London data center and applies the TLOC list as the next hop for the routes in VPN 20, the PCI segment. The effect of this policy is that, while the connectivity in VPN 10 will continue to be direct, the communication in VPN 20 will be proxied through the data centers. You can see the effects of this policy in Example 7-23.

Example 7-23   *VPN 10 Has a Direct Data Plane; VPN 20 Must Transit the Data Center When Passing Traffic from Branch 2 to Branch 3*

```
!
! BR2-Edge1 is one hop away from Branch 3 in VPN 10
BR2-Edge1# traceroute vrf 10 10.10.103.1
<<<Output omitted for brevity>>>
  1 BIZ-INET-BR3-Edge1 (209.165.201.8) 2 msec 1 msec 1 msec
  2 BR3-Edge1-Core (172.16.103.2) 1 msec 2 msec *

BR2-Edge1#
!
! BR2-Edge1 is additional hops away from Branch 3 in VPN 20
!
BR2-Edge1# traceroute vrf 20 10.20.103.1
<<<Output omitted for brevity>>>
  1 BIZ-INET-DC2-Edge1 (209.165.201.3) 2 msec 1 msec 1 msec
  2 BIZ-INET-BR3-Edge1 (209.165.201.8) 2 msec 2 msec 0 msec
  3 BR3-Edge1-Core (172.20.103.2) 2 msec 2 msec *
BR2-Edge1#
```

Use Case 8 Review

This use case shows how to create a multi-topology policy by combining the elements of prior use cases. This use case demonstrates how network administrators can create different data plane topologies on a per-segment basis to meet their business needs by using the VPN criterion in addition to other criteria to select, filter, and manipulate the control plane updates.

Use Case 9: Creating Extranets and Access to Shared Services

In the final centralized control policy use case, we will explore building an extranet. Enterprises commonly use extranets to provide multiple business partners with access to a shared resource, such as an ERP solution, while at the same time ensuring that the partners cannot directly access each other. In this use case, we are going to use VPNs 101 and 102, at Sites 101 and 102, respectively, to represent the business partners. The shared resource that these partners need to access will be in VPN 100 at DC1. Figure 7-77 shows the extranet that will be built on top of the existing policies from the previous examples.

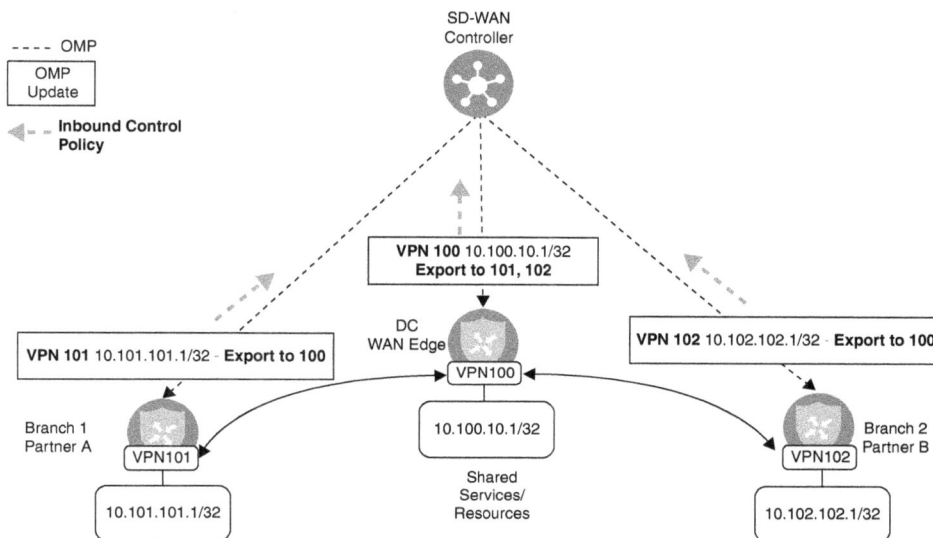

Figure 7-77   *Building an Extranet to Enable Partner Connectivity*

In order to build the necessary connectivity to accomplish this design, there are several key parts of the centralized policy that need to be either adjusted or created from scratch. The VPN membership policy created in Use Case 7 needs to be adjusted to account for the new VPNs being used for the extranet. In addition, the inbound route policies need to be either edited (in the case of the data centers) or created (in the case of the branches) so that the route leaking via the **export-to** command can take effect. The Set_DC_TLOC_Preference policy has to be rewritten to include the statements for route leaking. Because there can be only a single control policy for a specific site ID applied in a single direction, the functions of setting the TLOC preferences and leaking the routes from VPN 100 to VPN 101 and 102 need to be combined into a single policy. We will rename this new policy DC_Inbound_Control_Policy to reflect the fact that its purpose is broader than just manipulating the data center TLOCs.

The policy in Example 7-24 implements the necessary changes to completely deploy this extranet. This example presents the policy in its entirety so that you can use it as a reference.

Example 7-24   *Use Case 9: Extranet*

```
policy
!
! The VPN membership policy is extended to account for the additional VPNs
! that need to be advertised to form the extranet connectivity. Specifically,
! these are grouped into the CLIENT_VPNS (VPNs 101 and 102), and the
! SERVICE_VPN (VPN 100).
!
vpn-membership vpnMembership_-1376283532
```

```
    sequence 10
     match
      vpn-list CLIENT_VPNS
      !
     action accept
      !
     !
    sequence 20
     match
      vpn-list Corporate_Segment
      !
     action accept
      !
     !
    sequence 30
     match
      vpn-list SERVICE_VPN
      !
     action accept
      !
     !
    sequence 40
     match
      vpn-list PCI_VPN
      !
     action accept
      !
     !
   default-action reject
  !
 !
 ! The former "Set_DC_TLOC_Preference" policy has been renamed to
 ! "DC_Inbound_Control_Policy" and has had sequence 41 inserted in order to perform
 ! the route leaking from VPN 100 to VPN 101 and 102.
 !
 control-policy DC_Inbound_Control_Policy
    sequence 1
     match tloc
      originator 10.0.10.1
      !
     action accept
      set
       preference 500
      !
     !
     !
```

```
sequence 11
 match tloc
  originator 10.0.10.2
  !
 action accept
  set
   preference 400
  !
 !
!
sequence 21
 match tloc
  originator 10.0.20.1
  !
 action accept
  set
   preference 500
  !
 !
!
sequence 31
 match tloc
  originator 10.0.20.2
  !
 action accept
  set
   preference 400
  !
 !
!
sequence 41
match route
 vpn-list SERVICE_VPN
  prefix-list _AnyIpv4PrefixList
  !
action accept
 export-to vpn-list CLIENT_VPNS
  set
  !
  ! An OMP TAG is similar to a route tag that can be found in other
  ! routing protocols.  While it is not strictly necessary to set an OMP TAG
  ! during redistribution, it may become useful in the future to assist with
  ! tracking how routes are propagating as well as creating additional
  ! criteria to filter on.
  !
```

```
      omp-tag 100
     !
    !
   !
  default-action accept
 !
!
!
! The "North_America_Reg_Mesh_with_FW" policy remains unchanged from previous
! versions.
!
control-policy North_America_Reg_Mesh_with_FW
    sequence 1
     match tloc
      site-list DCs
     !
     action accept
     !
    !
    sequence 11
     match tloc
      site-list North_America_Branches
     !
     action accept
     !
    !
    sequence 21
     match route
      prefix-list Default_Route
      site-list North_America_DC
     !
     action accept
      set
       preference 100
      !
     !
    !
    sequence 31
     match route
      site-list DCs
      prefix-list _AnyIpv4PrefixList
     !
     action accept
     !
    !
```

```
   sequence 41
    match route
     site-list North_America_Branches
     prefix-list _AnyIpv4PrefixList
     !
    action accept
     !
    !
   sequence 51
    match route
     site-list Europe_Branches
     prefix-list _AnyIpv4PrefixList
     !
    action accept
     set
      service  FW
     !
     !
    !
  default-action reject
 !
 !
 ! The "Euro_Reg_Mesh_with_FW_MultiTopo" policy remains unchanged from previous
 ! versions.
 !
control-policy Euro_Reg_Mesh_with_FW_MultiTopo
   sequence 1
    match tloc
     site-list DCs
     !
    action accept
     !
    !
   sequence 11
    match tloc
     site-list Europe_Branches
     !
    action accept
     !
    !
   sequence 21
    match route
     prefix-list Default_Route
     site-list Europe_DC
     !
```

7

```
  action accept
   set
    preference 100
    !
   !
  !
 sequence 31
  match route
   site-list DCs
   prefix-list _AnyIpv4PrefixList
   !
  action accept
   !
  !
 sequence 41
  match route
   site-list Europe_Branches
   vpn-list Corporate_Segment
   prefix-list _AnyIpv4PrefixList
   !
  action accept
   !
  !
 sequence 51
  match route
   site-list Europe_Branches
   vpn-list PCI_VPN
   prefix-list _AnyIpv4PrefixList
   !
  action accept
   set
    tloc-list Europe_DC_TLOCs
    !
   !
  !
 sequence 61
  match route
   site-list North_America_Branches
   prefix-list _AnyIpv4PrefixList
   !
  action accept
   set
    service  FW
    !
   !
  !
```

```
 default-action reject
!
!
! A new control policy is created in order to be applied inbound from the
! branch sites and export the routes from VPN 101 and VPN 102 to VPN 100.
! An OMP tag is again added during the route leaking, and while not strictly
! required, it is highly recommended to do so.
!
control-policy Branch_Extranet_Route_Leaking
   sequence 1
    match route
     vpn 101
     prefix-list _AnyIpv4PrefixList
    !
    action accept
       export-to vpn-list SERVICE_VPN
      set
       omp-tag 101
     !
    !
   !
   sequence 11
     match route
      vpn 102
     prefix-list _AnyIpv4PrefixList
    !
    action accept
       export-to vpn-list SERVICE_VPN
      set
        omp-tag 102
      !
    !
   !
 default-action accept
!
lists
 prefix-list Default_Route
  ip-prefix 0.0.0.0/0
  !
 site-list BranchOffices
  site-id 100-199
  !
 site-list DCs
  site-id 10-50
  !
```

```
  site-list Europe_Branches
   site-id 102-103
  !
  site-list Europe_DC
   site-id 20
  !
  site-list North_America_Branches
   site-id 101
  !
  site-list North_America_DC
   site-id 10
!
  tloc-list Europe_DC_TLOCs
   tloc 10.0.20.1 color mpls encap ipsec
   tloc 10.0.20.1 color biz-internet encap ipsec
   tloc 10.0.20.2 color mpls encap ipsec
   tloc 10.0.20.2 color biz-internet encap ipsec
  !
  vpn-list CLIENT_VPNS
   vpn 101
   vpn 102
  !
  vpn-list Corporate_Segment
   vpn 10
  !
  vpn-list PCI_VPN
   vpn 20
  !
  vpn-list Guest_Segment
   vpn 50
  !
  vpn-list SERVICE_VPN
   vpn 100
  !
  prefix-list _AnyIpv4PrefixList
   ip-prefix 0.0.0.0/0 le 32
  !
 !
 !
 !
 ! Lastly, all of the policies are applied.  Note, the policies that perform
 ! route leaking must be applied inbound.
 !
```

```
apply-policy
 site-list Europe_Branches
  control-policy Euro_Reg_Mesh_with_FW_MultiTopo out
 !
 site-list DCs
  control-policy DC_Inbound_Control_Policy in
 !
 site-list BranchOffices
  control-policy Branch_Extranet_Route_Leaking in
  vpn-membership vpnMembership_-1376283532
 !
 site-list North_America_Branches
  control-policy North_America_Reg_Mesh_with_FW out
 !
!
```

In Example 7-24, route leaking is configured in both the Branch_Extranet_Route_Leaking and the DC_Inbound_Control_Policy policies with the **export-to** action. The **export-to** action allows the matching routes to be copied from the existing VPN and injected into a different VPN or VPN list, using the syntax **export-to** {**vpn** *vpn-id* | **vpn-list** *vpn-list*}.

Route leaking is a powerful and flexible tool that network administrators have at their disposal. However, there are some considerations with how the **export-to** command must be used. First, the **export-to** action must be applied on an inbound control policy. If the **export-to** action is applied in the outbound direction, the action will have no effect. Second, the **export-to** command only works to leak routes from a service-side VPN into a different service-side VPN. The **export-to** command cannot be used to leak routes into or out of VPN 0 or VPN 512. The isolation of these VPNs is intentional and, specifically with VPN 0, has significant security implications and needs to be executed carefully. There is some discussion in Chapter 5, "Cisco Catalyst SD-WAN Design and Migration," about different design concepts that aim to solve these challenges.

NOTE The method described here is effective for service VPN-to-service VPN route leaking. You can achieve bidirectional route leaking between a service VPN and a global VPN by using the **route-replicate** and **redistribute** commands in conjunction; together, these commands allow you to share common services that multiple data segments need to access. For more comprehensive information, consult the Cisco Catalyst SD-WAN Routing Configuration Guide.

When the policy in Example 7-24 is applied, the results of the route leaking can be seen in the routing tables on BR1-Edge1 and BR2-Edge1, as shown in Figure 7-78 and Figure 7-79, respectively. The BR1-Edge1 and BR2-Edge1 routing tables have installed the two routes for the services VPN. These routes are also displayed with the tag 100 as a reminder that they originated in VPN 100.

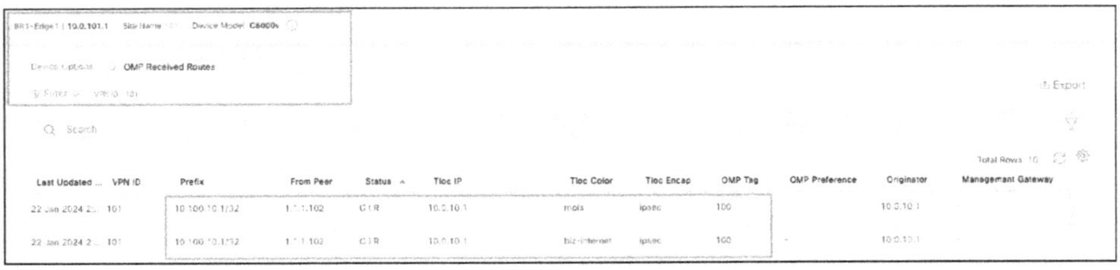

Figure 7-78 *Service Routes from VPN 100 Have Been Imported into VPN 101*

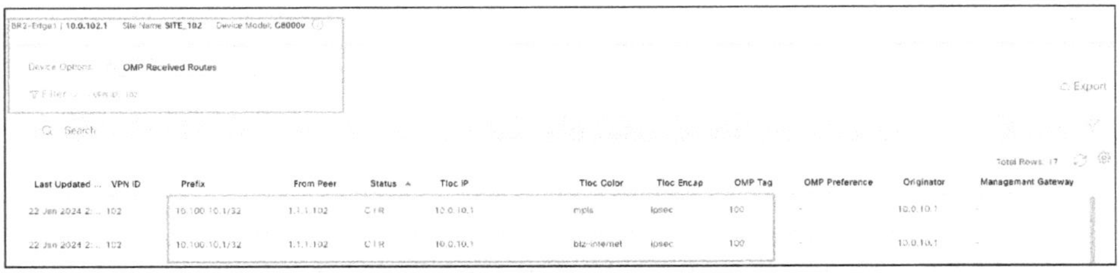

Figure 7-79 *Service Routes from VPN 100 Have Been Imported into VPN 102*

Finally, the data plane of the extranet can be validated by ensuring that VPN 101 and VPN 102 both have access to the shared services hosted in VPN 100 but that VPN 101 cannot communicate directly with VPN 102. Example 7-25 shows the results from the pings to test the data plane of the extranet.

Example 7-25 *Validating the Data Plane Connectivity of the Extranet Connections*

```
!
! BR2-Edge1 is able to reach the shared services in VPN 100
!
BR2-Edge1#
BR2-Edge1# ping vrf 102 10.100.10.1
Type escape sequence to abort.
Sending 5, 100-byte ICMP Echos to 10.100.10.1, timeout is 2 seconds:
!!!!!
Success rate is 100 percent (5/5), round-trip min/avg/max = 1/1/2 ms
!
! BR2-Edge1 is not able to directly reach hosts in VPN 101
!
BR2-Edge1# ping vrf 102 10.101.101.1
Type escape sequence to abort.
Sending 5, 100-byte ICMP Echos to 10.101.101.1, timeout is 2 seconds:
.....
Success rate is 0 percent (0/5)
!
!
! BR1-Edge1 is able to reach the shared services in VPN 100
!
```

```
BR1-Edge1# ping vrf 101 10.100.10.1
Type escape sequence to abort.
Sending 5, 100-byte ICMP Echos to 10.100.10.1, timeout is 2 seconds:
!!!!!
Success rate is 100 percent (5/5), round-trip min/avg/max = 1/1/1 ms
!
! BR1-Edge1 is not able to directly reach hosts in VPN 102
!
BR1-Edge1# ping vrf 101 10.102.102.1
Type escape sequence to abort.
Sending 5, 100-byte ICMP Echos to 10.102.102.1, timeout is 2 seconds:
.....
Success rate is 0 percent (0/5)
BR1-Edge1#
```

The output in Example 7-25 confirms that the extranet is working as expected. VPNs 101 and 102 have access to the shared resource that exists in VPN 100, but VPNs 101 and 102 are not able to communicate between themselves.

Use Case 9 Review

This use case shows how to create an extranet to allow business partners to communicate while still maintaining security and isolation across the SD-WAN fabric. This extranet is configured by establishing a unique VPN for each of the different entities and then leaking routes from the client VPNs (101 and 102) into the service VPN (100) and vice versa. Route leaking with centralized control policies is a technique that can be used for many different purposes. In addition to creating extranets for shared services access, as was done in this use case, another common use case that requires VPN leaking is using the SD-WAN security feature set, particularly the zone-based firewall. Cisco SD-WAN security is covered in Chapter 11, "Cisco Catalyst SD-WAN Security."

Summary

This chapter discusses one of the key types of SD-WAN policies: centralized control policies applied using a traditional approach as well as topology groups. It includes several use cases using centralized control policies and shows how policies can be used to manipulate the structure of the SD-WAN data plane fabric, turning an SD-WAN fabric from a full-mesh deployment to a strict hub-and-spoke deployment or a regional mesh. In addition, this chapter provides several traffic engineering use cases that show how to use TLOC lists to manipulate the next-hop information of an OMP route, as well as network service insertion. Finally, this chapter shows how to use centralized control policies to harden the security posture of the network, including using VPN membership policies and building extranets with route leaking.

This chapter shows how various kinds of policies can be combined and used together to create the architecture necessary to meet any business objective in an easy and intuitive but powerful way. Administrators are advised to select either the new topology approach or use centralized control policies to avoid unnecessary complexity. Using the topology approach can enhance configuration reusability and provide a more structured approach, potentially simplifying network operations.

Review All Key Topics

Review the most important topics in the chapter, noted with the Key Topic icon in the outer margin of the page. Table 7-2 lists these key topics and the page number on which each is found.

Table 7-2   Key Topics

Key Topic Element	Description	Page
Paragraph	Data plane tunnels	216
Paragraph	BFD session status and data plane tunnel status	218
Paragraph	TLOC attribute in OMP routes	218
Paragraph, Example 7-8	OMP route status codes	238
Table 7-1	OMP status codes	255
Paragraph, Figure 7-65	TLOC Preference value	257
Paragraph	Weight attribute for configuring unequal-cost load-sharing	258
Figure 7-71, Paragraph	Routes with greatest OMP Preference values	266
Paragraph	VPN membership policies	283
Paragraph	Route leaking	297

Define Key Terms

Define the following key terms from this chapter and check your answers in the glossary:

extranet, inbound control policy, multi-topology, originator, outbound control policy, service insertion, TLOC list, topology group

Chapter Review Questions

1. What is the default setting of the default action in a centralized control policy?

   a. Accept

   b. Permit

   c. Reject

   d. Deny

   e. There is no default action; an action must be configured manually.

2. Which of the following are configuration options for a TLOC list? Choose four.

   a. Site ID

   b. System IP address

   c. Color

   d. Encapsulation

   e. Preference

    f. Weight

    g. VPN

    h. Prefix

3. The TLOC attribute Weight is used _____.

    a. as the first and most important criterion in the OMP best-path selection process.

    b. as the final tie-breaker in the OMP best-path selection process.

    c. for determining the ratio of flows for load-sharing on the TLOCs that have been selected as the best paths.

    d. for turning off the anti-gravity machine.

4. True or false: OMP Route Preference values can be configured via feature templates and device templates.

    a. True

    b. False

5. What is the status of an OMP process that has been inserted into the IP routing table?

    a. C I R

    b. C R

    c. R

    d. Rej, R, Inv

6. Preference is an OMP attribute associated with which of the following?

    a. TLOCs

    b. OMP routes

    c. Both TLOCs and OMP routes

    d. Neither TLOCs nor OMP routes

7. What are VPN membership policies used to do?

    a. Determine which users belong to which VPNs.

    b. Determine which routes belong to which VPNs.

    c. Determine which WAN Edge routers belong to which SD-WAN fabrics.

    d. Determine which VPNs will be permitted to join the overlay fabric on a WAN Edge router.

    e. Determine the ratio of flows for load-sharing on the TLOCs that have been selected as the best paths.

8. True or false: Centralized control policies that leak routes must always be applied in the outbound direction.

    a. True

    b. False

9. True or false: A centralized control policy can be used to leak routes between service-side VPNs and VPN 0.

    a. True

    b. False

10. Which type of policy is used to export OMP routes from one VPN to another VPN?

    a. Route import/export policies

    b. VPN membership policies

    c. Centralized control policies

    d. Localized control policies

    e. No policy; it is not possible to have the same route in more than one VPN.

11. True or false: Topology groups help to achieve the same behavior as centralized control policies.

    a. True

    b. False

References

"Cisco Catalyst SD-WAN Command Reference," https://www.cisco.com/c/en/us/td/docs/routers/sdwan/command/sdwan-cr-book.html.

"Policy Groups Configuration Guide, Cisco IOS XE Catalyst SD-WAN Release 17.x," https://www.cisco.com/c/en/us/td/docs/routers/sdwan/configuration/Policy-Groups/policy-groups/m-topology.html.

"Hub-and-Spoke Configuration, Cisco Catalyst SD-WAN Routing Configuration Guide,"

https://www.cisco.com/c/en/us/td/docs/routers/sdwan/configuration/routing/ios-xe-17/routing-book-xe/hub-and-spoke.html.

"Network Hierarchy and Resource Management, Systems and Interfaces Configuration Guide," https://www.cisco.com/c/en/us/td/docs/routers/sdwan/configuration/system-interface/ios-xe-17/systems-interfaces-book-xe-sdwan/network-hierarchy-and-resource-management.html.

"Route Leaking between VPNS, Cisco Catalyst SD-WAN Routing Configuration Guide," https://www.cisco.com/c/en/us/td/docs/routers/sdwan/configuration/routing/ios-xe-17/routing-book-xe/m-routing-leaking-for-service-sharing.html.

CHAPTER 8

Centralized Data Policies

This chapter covers the following topics:

■ **Centralized Data Policy Overview:** This section reviews the basics of centralized data policies and the directionality of policies when applied to a WAN Edge router.

■ **Use Case 10: Direct Internet Access for Guest Users:** This section covers a simple data policy to ensure that only publicly routable packets are forwarded to the Internet. This section also discusses how to build a centralized data policy with the SD-WAN Manager GUI.

■ **Use Case 11: Direct Cloud Access for Trusted Applications:** This section covers the use of a centralized data policy to change the forwarding path for a specific application and provide direct Internet egress.

■ **Use Case 12: Application-Based Traffic Engineering:** This section reviews different methods for performing traffic engineering of flows that traverse the SD-WAN fabric.

■ **Use Case 13: Protecting Corporate Users with a Secure Internet Gateway:** This section reviews how to redirect traffic to Cisco Umbrella Secure Internet Gateway.

■ **Use Case 14: Protecting Applications from Packet Loss:** This section covers two different methodologies for reconstructing data flows that have been affected by lossy transport networks.

Building on the examples in Chapter 7, "Centralized Control Policies," this chapter focuses on centralized data policies. Unlike centralized control policies, which manipulate the routing information in the data plane, centralized data policies are used to override the forwarding decisions that would normally be made by a router and instead tell the router to follow a specific set of forwarding instructions. Such a policy can be implemented for a specific flow or application or for all of the traffic at a site. Because of the incredible control they provide to network administrators, centralized data policies are often referred to as "policy-based routing on steroids." However, centralized data policies are much easier to administer than traditional policy-based routing because, as their name indicates, they are all configured and applied centrally.

Centralized Data Policy Overview

A centralized data policy is a powerful tool that allows administrators to override the normal forwarding actions that would occur in the data plane and specify a different set of actions that should be taken instead. As the use cases in this chapter show, those new actions could be as simple as dropping a packet, redirecting a flow down a specific path or to a specific service, providing additional data plane services to accelerate data transfers and protect against packet loss, or any combination of these actions.

As discussed in Chapter 6, "Introduction to Cisco Catalyst SD-WAN Policies," each type of policy has a specific directionality. Centralized data policies can either be applied to traffic that is originating "from tunnel," traffic that is originating "from service," or traffic that is traversing a WAN Edge router in both directions. Figure 8-1 illustrates these directions.

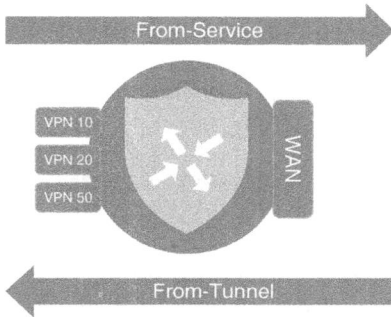

Figure 8-1 *Data Policy Directionality*

The following sections examine several different sets of common business requirements and explore how network administrators can use centralized data policies to handle them. These use cases highlight common applications of centralized data policies and identify many of the building blocks of centralized data policies from which network administrators can build their own policies to accomplish business objectives. The examples in this chapter build on the network and the examples provided in Chapter 7. Figure 8-2 shows the topology used with all the use cases throughout this chapter, and Example 7-24 at the end of Chapter 7 provides the centralized policy that is used as a starting point.

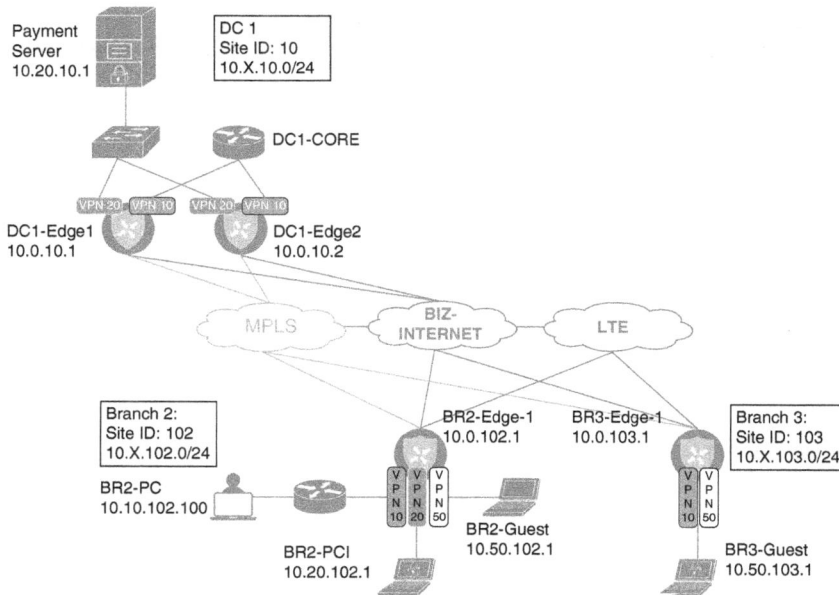

Figure 8-2 *Network Topology for Chapter 8*

Although the network featured in Figure 8-2 is identical to the network used in Chapter 7, there are several changes in this diagram that accompany some elements that are used throughout this chapter. Specifically, Branch 2 is drawn in greater detail to illustrate the end hosts that reside in the Corporate, PCI, and Guest data segments (that is, the service VPNs). Also note that the payment processing server is located in Data Center 1, in the PCI VPN. As noted in Chapter 7, the service-side addressing in this network follows the 10.X.Y.0/24 structure, where X signifies the service-side VPN, and Y signifies the site ID. The first few use cases in this chapter focus on VPN 10 and VPN 50, and service-side addressing is in the 10.10.Y.0/24 and 10.50.Y.0/24 address blocks. This topology will allow us to explore different types of policies, how they interact with the SD-WAN fabric, and how network administrators can apply these policies to solve business problems.

Use Case 10: Direct Internet Access for Guest Users

This use case builds on the VPN membership policy we explored in Chapter 7 to provide Internet access to guest users. In Chapter 7, Example 7-20 shows that users in the Guest VPN on BR2-Edge1 are able to reach the Internet but are not able to reach the other branches. But this is not the complete story, as all the traffic in the VPN is following the default route. Even traffic that is destined to addresses that are not reachable across the public Internet, such as traffic using private (RFC 1918) addresses, is being forwarded out onto the public Internet, where it is eventually dropped, as shown in Example 8-1.

Example 8-1 *Connectivity from the Guest VPN on BR2-Edge1*

```
! BR2-Edge1 is able to reach the public internet from the Guest VPN
BR2-Edge1# ping vrf 50 208.67.222.222
Type escape sequence to abort.
Sending 5, 100-byte ICMP Echos to 208.67.222.222, timeout is 2 seconds:
!!!!!
Success rate is 100 percent (5/5), round-trip min/avg/max = 9/9/10 ms

! BR2-Edge1 is unable to reach BR3-Edge1 in the Guest VPN as expected

BR2-Edge1# ping vrf 50 10.50.103.1
Type escape sequence to abort.
Sending 5, 100-byte ICMP Echos to 10.50.103.1, timeout is 2 seconds:
.....
Success rate is 0 percent (0/5)
!
! Looking at the traceroute to 10.50.103.1 and the routing table, it is clear
! that BR2-Edge1 is using the default route to the internet to forward this
! packet, rather than dropping the traffic.
!
BR2-Edge1# traceroute vrf 50 10.50.103.1
Type escape sequence to abort.
```

```
Tracing the route to 10.50.103.1
VRF info: (vrf in name/id, vrf out name/id)
  1 209.165.201.30 1 msec 1 msec 0 msec
  2 198.18.128.1 2 msec 2 msec 1 msec
  3 10.255.0.3 1 msec 1 msec 1 msec
  4 10.1.27.9 1 msec 2 msec 1 msec
  5 64.100.12.36 2 msec 2 msec 2 msec
  6 64.102.244.193 3 msec 3 msec 3 msec
  7 64.102.244.177 2 msec 2 msec 2 msec
  8 64.102.254.210 1 msec 2 msec 2 msec
  9 * * *
 10 * * *
! Output omitted for brevity
29 * * *
30 * * *
!
! The output indicates that this traffic is being sent out
! to the transit interfaces in VPN 0 straight to the internet
!
BR2-Edge1# show sdwan policy service-path vpn 50 interface Loopback 251 source-ip
10.50.102.1 dest-ip 10.50.103.1  protocol 1 all
Next Hop: IPsec
  Source: 192.168.20.6 12346 Destination: 192.168.20.1 12386 Local Color: mpls
Remote Color: mpls Remote System IP: 10.0.10.1
Next Hop: IPsec
  Source: 209.165.201.6 12346 Destination: 209.165.201.1 12346 Local Color: biz-
internet Remote Color: biz-internet Remote System IP: 10.0.10.1
Next Hop: IPsec
  Source: 209.165.202.130 12346 Destination: 209.165.201.1 12346 Local Color: lte
Remote Color: biz-internet Remote System IP: 10.0.10.1
```

NOTE   Public transport interfaces are commonly used not only to establish IPsec tunnels but also for providing Direct Internet Access breakout. If default routes from data centers are not present, other methods of providing Internet access, such as selective Direct Internet Access policy, are available. This approach is explained later in this chapter.

As Example 8-1 shows, bandwidth is being wasted because packets are being forwarded out the Internet interfaces that are destined to private, internal addresses and therefore cannot possibly reach their destinations across the Internet. Rather than uselessly forwarding these packets out to the Internet, we could construct a centralized data policy to drop them.

The first step in the process of creating a centralized data policy is to create the data prefix lists that are necessary. The Custom Options menu for creating lists is in the upper-right corner of the Configuration > Policies screen (see Figure 8-3).

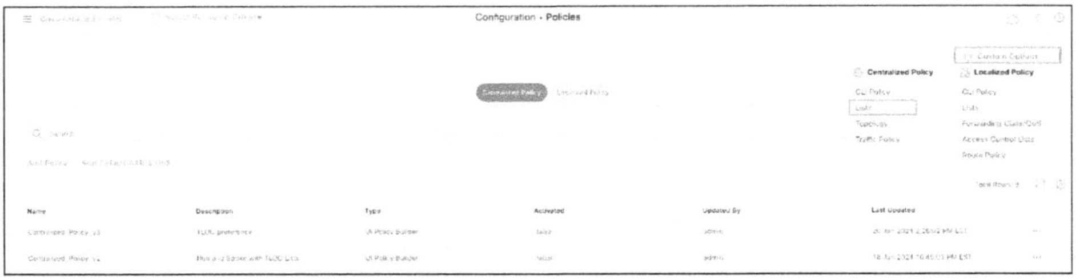

Figure 8-3   *Creating Required Lists in a Centralized Policy*

The first list that is needed for this centralized data policy is a data prefix list of bogon addresses. The following definition is from RFC 3871:

> A "bogon" (plural: "bogons") is a packet with an IP source address in an address block not yet allocated by IANA or the Regional Internet Registries (ARIN, RIPE, APNIC…) as well as all addresses reserved for private or special use by RFCs. See [RFC3330] and [RFC1918].

Filtering out packets that are destined to networks that cannot exist on the public Internet will help save resources by avoiding forwarding unnecessary packets. You can create a data prefix list to accomplish this filtering by selecting the **Data Prefix** list type and clicking the blue +New Data Prefix List button. In the Data Prefix List configuration window that appears, you configure a list name and the necessary data prefixes, as shown in Figure 8-4.

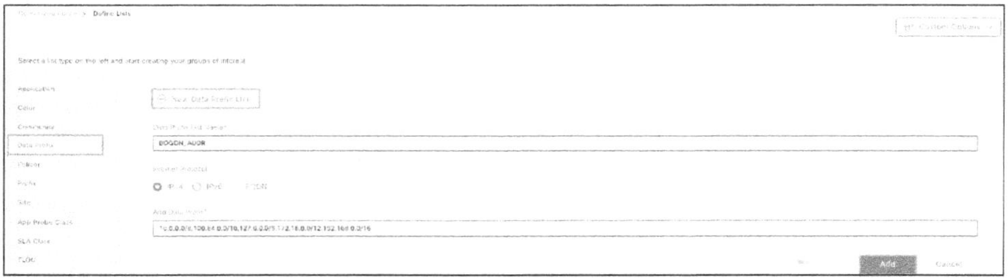

Figure 8-4   *Configuring a Data Prefix List*

As Figure 8-4 indicates, this data prefix list includes RFC 1918 ranges, the 127.0.0.0/8 localhost range, and the 100.64.0.0/10 carrier-grade NAT range. None of these ranges are publicly routable, and therefore traffic that is destined to any of these destinations should not be forwarded to the Internet. To build a centralized policy to accomplish this filtering, the next step would be to build the data policy itself. Start by selecting **Traffic Policy** from the Custom Options drop-down menu (refer to Figure 8-3). In the Traffic Policy screen, you see three tabs across the top: Application Aware Routing, Traffic Data, and Cflowd. To create a new traffic data policy, select the **Traffic Data** tab and then select the **Create New** option under the **Add Policy** menu (see Figure 8-5).

Next, you need to add a sequence type to the new policy by clicking the **+Sequence Type** button. As shown in Figure 8-6, there are a number of different sequence types available in a centralized data policy, including Application Firewall, QoS, Service Chaining, and Traffic Engineering. These different sequence types expose a limited subset of the actions available to an administrator and highlight the different actions that may be used to address some of these use cases. The Custom sequence type provides access to all of the action options in the GUI, and many administrators prefer to use this sequence type for all use cases. For this example, select the **Custom** sequence type, as indicated in Figure 8-6.

Figure 8-5 *Creating a New Centralized Data Policy*

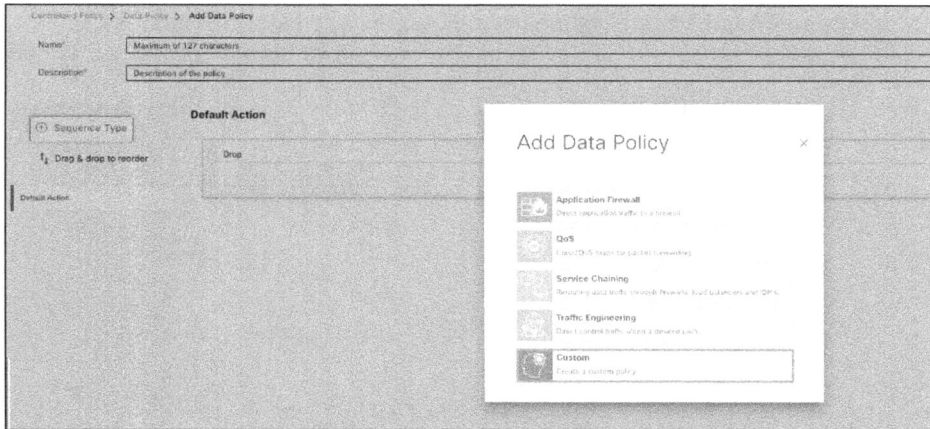

Figure 8-6 *Adding a New Sequence Type to the Data Policy*

This new policy needs to consist of two different sequence rules, as shown in Figure 8-7. The first sequence rule will match the packets destined to the addresses in the bogon data prefix list and drop them. There is an additional Counter action that is applied to this sequence rule as well. A counter named GUEST_DROPPED_PKTS is then specified to track the number of packets that match this sequence. While counters in and of themselves don't provide any impact to how traffic is forwarded, they do provide a useful tool when evaluating and troubleshooting policies.

The second sequence rule will send all other packets out the VPN 0 interfaces to the underlay. Matching all other packets is accomplished by not specifying any matching criteria at all in this sequence rule. There are three actions specified in the second sequence rule: NAT VPN, Local TLOC, and Counter. The NAT VPN action allows you to specify traffic that should be leaked to VPN 0 and forwarded out a NAT-enabled interface. The VPN argument for this action is always VPN 0. You cannot use the NAT VPN action to leak between service-side VPNs; the NAT VPN action can only be used to leak between a service VPN and VPN 0 for the purpose of allowing Direct Internet Access. The local TLOC action allows you to selectively route traffic to specific TLOCs, such as the NAT-enabled interfaces like the biz-internet TLOC in this case.

For ease of visibility, a counter called GUEST_DIA_PKTS is added to the **action** statements in this sequence that will count the number of packets forwarded by the second sequence.

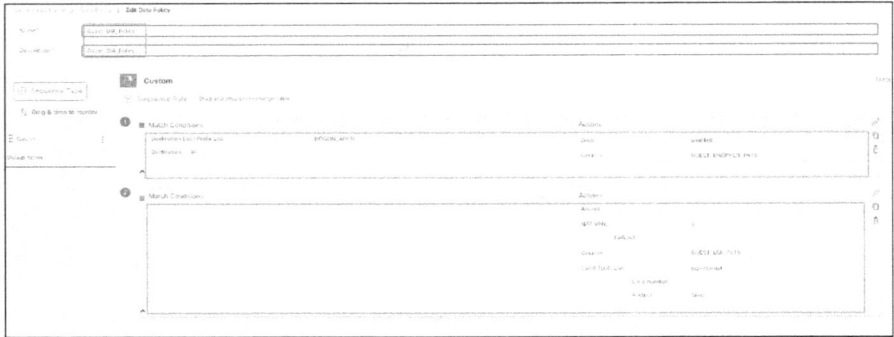

Figure 8-7   *Guest Internet Access Data Policy*

Once the necessary sequences have been added and a name and description have been added, the centralized data policy can be saved. The next step in the configuration process is to add this data policy to the existing centralized policy from Chapter 7. The easiest way to do so is to select the centralized policy and create a copy of it by selecting that option from the drop-down menu on the right side of the screen (see Figure 8-8).

Figure 8-8   *Creating a Copy of a Centralized Policy*

Once the new policy is created, you can edit it by selecting the **Edit** option from the same drop-down menu on the newly copied policy. As shown in Figure 8-9, the Edit Policy screen has three main tabs at the very top: Policy Application, Topology, and Traffic Rules. You can select the Traffic Rules tab to reveal three sub-tabs: Application Aware Routing, Traffic Data, and Cflowd (the same tabs you saw when the data policy was initially created). After selecting the **Traffic Data** sub-tab, select the **Add Policy** menu in order to import the existing policy, as indicated in Figure 8-9.

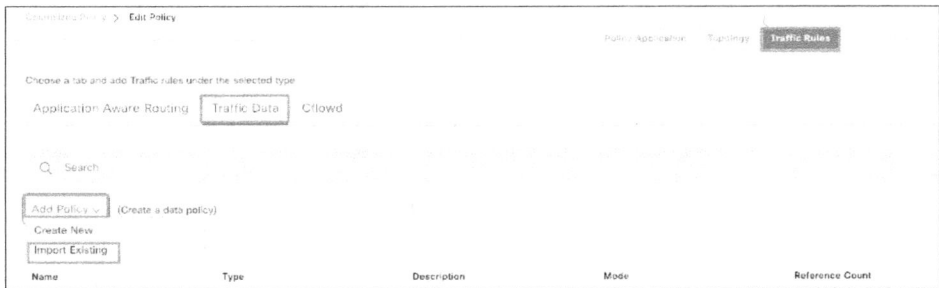

Figure 8-9   *The Edit Policy Screen*

When prompted, select the previously created Guest_DIA_Policy, as shown in Figure 8-10, and click the **Import** button.

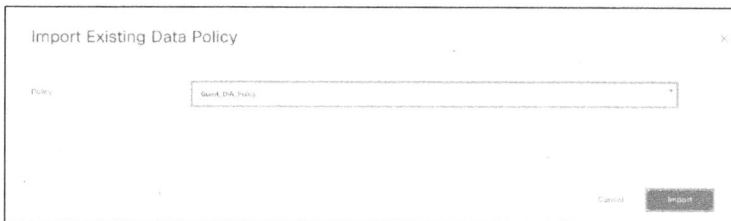

Figure 8-10 *Importing the Guest_DIA_Policy into the Centralized Policy*

Once the Guest DIA policy is referenced in the centralized policy, the last step in creating the centralized policy is to specify where the data policy should be applied by clicking the **New Site/Region List and VPN List** button. This policy is applied to the site ID list (BranchOffices), the VPN list (GUEST_ACCESS_VPN), and the direction (From Service), as shown in Figure 8-11.

Figure 8-11 *Applying the New Data Policy*

Save these configurations by clicking the **Add** button. The policy should now be saved and activated on the SD-WAN fabric. Example 8-2 shows the new policy, highlighting relevant changes to the configuration from the full policy displayed in Example 7-24.

Example 8-2 *Guest Internet Access Policy*

```
policy
 ! No changes were made to the control policies or VPN membership policies,
 ! and they are omitted for brevity. The full configuration of those policies
 ! can be found in Example 7-24.
 !
 ! The newly created data policy is specified below. Note that the vpn-list
 ! the policy is applied to is specified in the policy definition, not in the
 ! apply-policy section at the end.
 !
```

```
data-policy _Guest_Segment_Guest_DIA_Policy
 vpn-list Guest_Segment
    sequence 1
     match
     destination-data-prefix-list BOGON_ADDR
     !
     action drop
      !
       ! The count action and counter are specified here, and are used for
       ! monitoring and troubleshooting.
       count GUEST_DROPPED_PKTS_2067976837
      !
     !

     ! In the second sequence, all other packets are forwarded using the
     ! "nat use-vpn 0" syntax and also counted. Note that the matching criteria
     ! of any source address were automatically inserted by SD-WAN Manager (vManage).

    sequence 11
      match
       source-ip 0.0.0.0/0
      !
     action accept
       nat use-vpn 0
       count GUEST_DIA_PKTS_2067976837
       set
        local-tloc-list
         color biz-internet
      !
     !
 default-action drop
 !
lists
 ! Some lists without changes from Example 7-24 are omitted for brevity
 !
 data-prefix-list BOGON_ADDR
   ip-prefix 10.0.0.0/8
   ip-prefix 100.64.0.0/10
   ip-prefix 127.0.0.0/8
   ip-prefix 172.16.0.0/12
   ip-prefix 192.168.0.0/16
 !
 site-list BranchOffices
   site-id 100-199
```

```
   !
  vpn-list Guest_Segment
   vpn 50
   !
 !
apply-policy
 site-list Europe_Branches
  control-policy Euro_Reg_Mesh_with_FW_MultiTopo out
 !
 ! The newly created policy is applied to the Site List "BranchOffices"
 ! with the direction "from-service".
 !
 site-list BranchOffices
  data-policy _Guest_Segment_Guest_DIA_Policy from-service
  control-policy Branch_Extranet_Route_Leaking in
  vpn-membership vpnMembership_1710051916
 !
 site-list DCs
  control-policy DC_Inbound_Control_Policy in
 !
 site-list North_America_Branches
  control-policy North_America_Reg_Mesh_with_FW out
 !
 !
```

The structure of the data policy shown in Example 8-2 is very similar to the structure of the control policies discussed in Chapter 7. Each policy is a structured sequence of **match** statements that specify the criteria and a list of actions to take—that is, sequence types and sequence rules. In this policy, the first sequence rule is matching packets destined to the addresses in the BOGON_ADDR list. These packets are dropped and counted with the counter GUEST_DROPPED_PKTS. The second sequence matches all other traffic and forwards it out the VPN 0 interfaces to the Internet, using the **nat use-vpn 0** command. This traffic is also being tracked with the counter GUEST_DIA_PKTS. In this particular policy, the setting of the default action is irrelevant because all traffic that wasn't matched by sequence 1 will be matched by sequence 11.

Example 8-3 shows the effects of this policy: Users can still access the same resources on the public Internet, but traffic that should not be forwarded to the Internet is dropped instead of consuming that bandwidth.

Example 8-3   *Effects of the Data Policy on Users in the Guest VPN*

```
! As the centralized data policy is enforced on the WAN-Edge router, the policy
! is encoded as an OMP update by the SD-WAN controller (vSmart) and
advertised to the
! WAN-Edge. The policy is viewable with the "show sdwan policy from-vsmart" command.
!
```

```
BR2-Edge1# show sdwan policy from-vsmart
from-vsmart data-policy _Guest_Segment_Gues_DIA_Policy
 direction from-service
 vpn-list Guest_Segment
  sequence 1
   match
    destination-data-prefix-list BOGON_ADDR
   action drop
    count GUEST_DROPPED_PKTS_2067976837
  sequence 11
   match
    source-ip 0.0.0.0/0
   action accept
    count GUEST_DIA_PKTS_2067976837
    nat use-vpn 0
    no nat fallback
    set
     local-tloc-list
     color biz-internet
  default-action drop
from-vsmart lists vpn-list Guest_Segment
 vpn 50
from-vsmart lists data-prefix-list BOGON_ADDR
 ip-prefix 10.0.0.0/8
 ip-prefix 100.64.0.0/10
 ip-prefix 127.0.0.0/8
 ip-prefix 172.16.0.0/12
 ip-prefix 192.168.0.0/16
BR2-Edge1#
!
! The counters that are configured in the policy can be seen with the "show
sdwan policy
! data-policy-filter" command. Before any traffic is sent, both counters are 0.
!
BR2-Edge1# show sdwan policy data-policy-filter
data-policy-filter _Guest_Segment_Guest_DIA_Policy
 data-policy-vpnlist Guest_Segment
  data-policy-counter default_action_count
   packets 0
   bytes   0
  data-policy-counter GUEST_DIA_PKTS_2067976837
   packets 0
   bytes   0
```

```
   data-policy-counter GUEST_DROPPED_PKTS_2067976837
    packets 0
    bytes   0
!
! After sending four packets to 208.67.222.222, the GUEST_DIA_PKTS counter
! has incremented to 5.
BR2-Edge1# ping vrf 50 208.67.222.222
Type escape sequence to abort.
Sending 5, 100-byte ICMP Echos to 208.67.222.222, timeout is 2 seconds:
!!!!!
Success rate is 100 percent (5/5), round-trip min/avg/max = 10/10/10 ms
BR2-Edge1# show sdwan policy data-policy-filter
data-policy-filter _Guest_Segment_Guest_DIA_Policy
 data-policy-vpnlist Guest_Segment
  data-policy-counter default_action_count
    packets 0
    bytes   0
  data-policy-counter GUEST_DIA_PKTS_2067976837
    packets 5
    bytes   500
  data-policy-counter GUEST_DROPPED_PKTS_2067976837
    packets 0
    bytes   0
! After sending five packets to 10.50.103.1, the GUEST_DROPPED_PKTS counter has
! incremented to 5.
!
BR2-Edge1# ping vrf 50 10.50.103.1
Type escape sequence to abort.
Sending 5, 100-byte ICMP Echos to 10.50.103.1, timeout is 2 seconds:
.....
Success rate is 0 percent (0/5)
BR2-Edge1# show sdwan policy data-policy-filter
data-policy-filter _Guest_Segment_Guest_DIA_Policy
 data-policy-vpnlist Guest_Segment
  data-policy-counter default_action_count
    packets 0
    bytes   0
  data-policy-counter GUEST_DIA_PKTS_2067976837
    packets 5
    bytes   500
  data-policy-counter GUEST_DROPPED_PKTS_2067976837
    packets 5
    bytes   500
```

8

Key Topic

As shown in Example 8-3, the relevant portion of the data policy has been sent to the WAN Edge devices from the SD-WAN Controllers (formerly vSmarts). Note that this is different from the behavior for centralized control policies. Example 8-2 shows that there is a centralized control policy and a VPN membership policy that has also been applied to the site list BranchOffices; however, only the data policy is visible in the output of **show sdwan policy from-vsmart**. This is because the control policies are configured and executed on the SD-WAN Controllers directly and therefore have no reason to be advertised to the WAN Edge devices. The data policies, however, are configured and applied centrally on the SD-WAN Controller and therefore need to be advertised to the WAN Edge devices for enforcement at the data plane.

Network administrators can use the **show sdwan policy data-policy-filter** command to use counters to monitor how flows are being forwarded across the network (refer to Example 8-3). The first time the command is run, all the counters display zeros, as there have been no packets matched by the policy yet. After pinging a destination on the Internet with five packets, the GUEST_DIA_PKTS counter indicated that four packets were forwarded. Finally, the five pings sent to a bogon address are reflected in the GUEST_DROPPED_PKTS counter.

You can also see these effects by using the Simulate Flows tool, which can be found under the Troubleshooting menu on the **Monitor > Devices > [Device]** page discussed in Chapter 7. When simulating flows that are destined to 208.67.222.222, as shown in Figure 8-12, there are only a next-hop address and an interface specified for the flow. The output is lacking the remote system IP address, encapsulation, and color, which indicates that the flow is not going to be forwarded across the SD-WAN fabric but is instead going to egress from the GigabitEthernet2 interface.

Figure 8-12 *Simulate Flows Output to 208.67.222.222 from VPN 50 Shows That Traffic Is Forwarded to the Internet*

On the other hand, when Simulate Flows is performed for traffic going to 10.50.103.1, it shows the unambiguous results displayed in Figure 8-13.

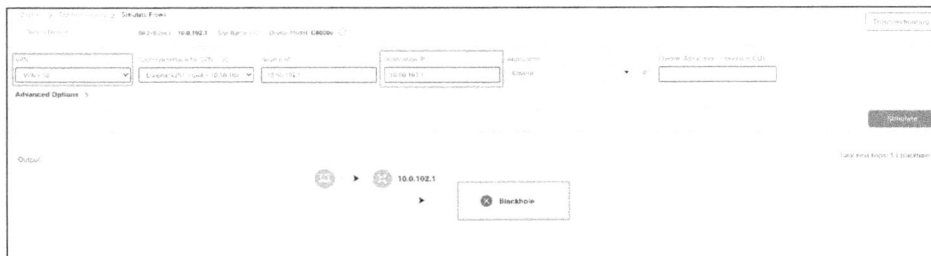

Figure 8-13 *Simulate Flows Output to 10.50.103.1 from VPN 50 Shows That Traffic Is Blackholed*

Direct Internet Access for the Guest VPN Using Policy Groups

Starting in release 20.12, a simpler, reusable, and more structured approach for configuring policies in Catalyst SD-WAN Manager is available: policy groups. Chapter 7 covers topology groups as the equivalent to centralized control policies. The equivalent to centralized data policies is policy groups. Using policy groups involves using different policy profiles, such as application priority and SLA, embedded security, secure Internet gateway, and DNS security profiles. This use case shows how guest Internet access can be provided and assumes that VPN membership equivalent configuration is in place.

There are some prerequisites to using Policy Groups, such as ensuring the minimum software version for WAN Edge devices and configuring them to leverage configuration groups. For details, see the "Policy Groups Configuration Guide" on the Cisco website.

To begin working with policy groups, choose **Configuration > Policy Groups**, as shown in Figure 8-14.

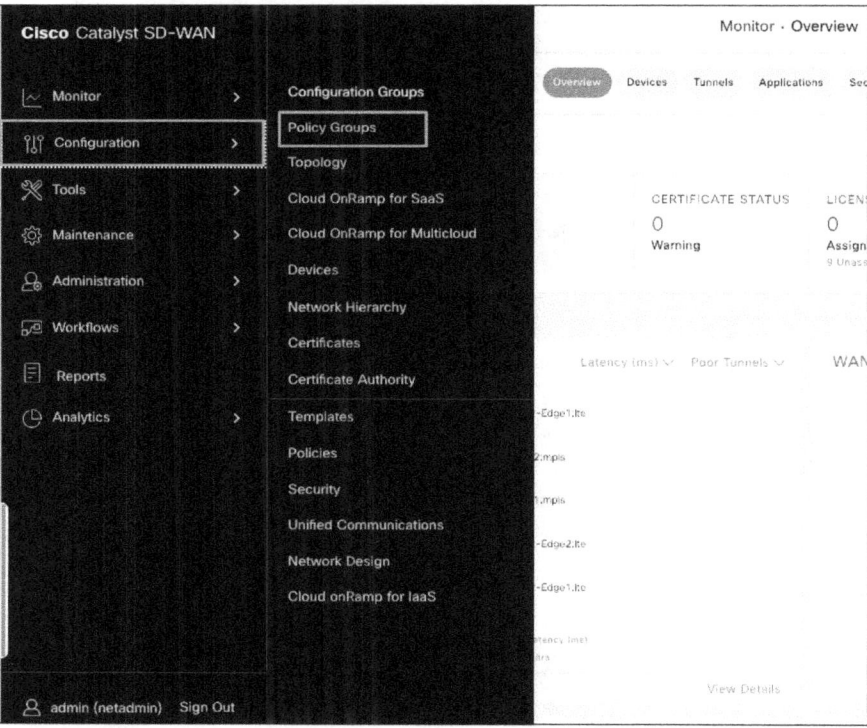

Figure 8-14   *Opening the Policy Groups Screen*

At this point, an Application Priority & SLA policy profile is selected, as shown in Figure 8-15. When you select **Add Application Priority Policy**, a window will pop up requesting a policy name and description, as shown in Figure 8-16.

Figure 8-15 *Creating an Application Priority Policy*

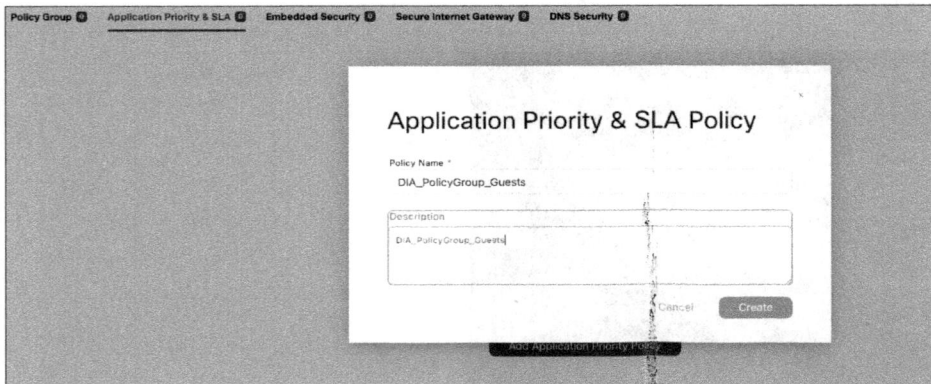

Figure 8-16 *Providing a Name and Description for the Newly Created Policy*

In the Application Priority & SLA Policy window, you can see that smart defaults are provided to make it easier to create policies. Click Create. To proceed, select **Advanced Layout**, as shown in Figure 8-17. This allows you to use a blank canvas, as in the previous data policy model.

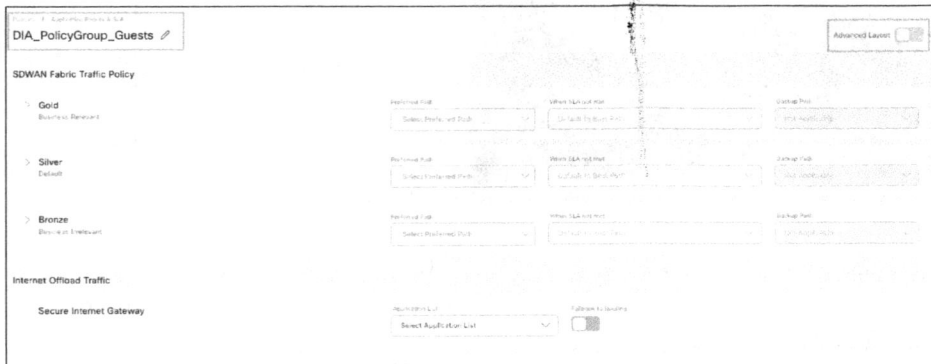

Figure 8-17 *Selecting Advanced Layout*

Click **Add Traffic Policy**, and the Add Traffic Policy List window appears. Fill in the name, select **VPN 50—Guest Users**, and select **Service** Direction, as shown in Figure 8-18, and then click Add.

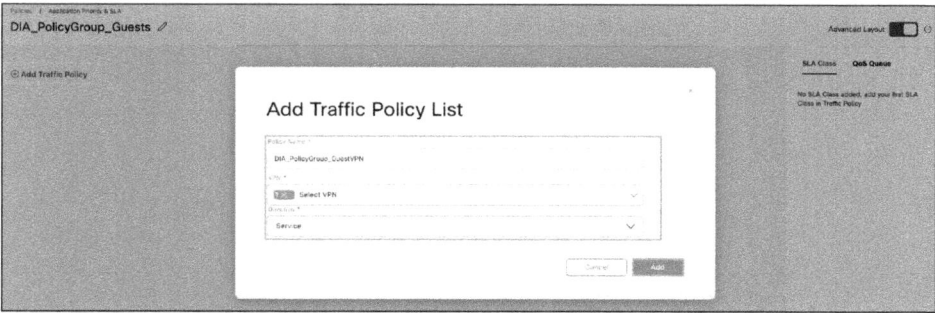

Figure 8-18 *Add Traffic Policy List Window*

Inside the recently created policy, you need to click **Add Rules** and provide a name for the sequence (in this case, BOGON_ADDR). You need to select **Add Match**, then select **Destination** and an option to enter a value or create an object pop up as shown in Figure 8-19.

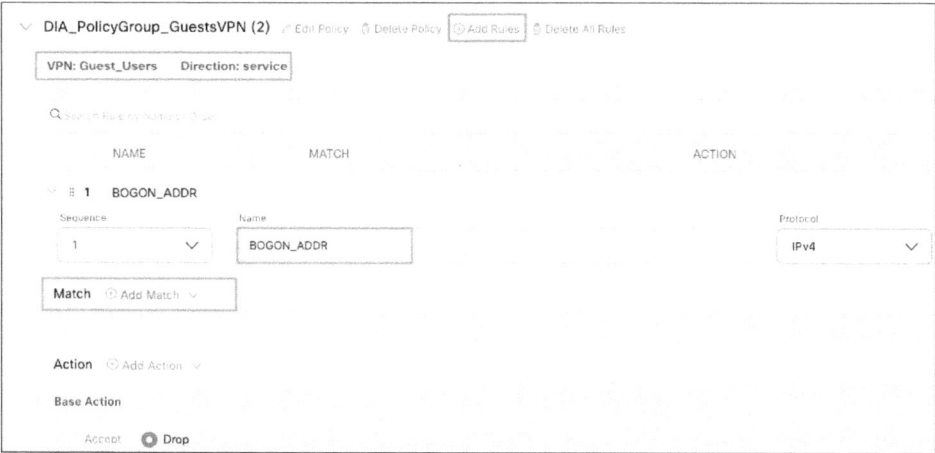

Figure 8-19 *Advanced Layout BOGON Sequence Rule*

Select **Create New** for Destination Data Prefix (IPv4), and a Data Prefix List window pops up. Enter a name for the list and prefix values, separated by commas (see Figure 8-20). Then click **Save**.

Once the data prefix list is created, select it from the Destination Data Prefix (IPv4) drop-down list to use it as a **match** statement. Figure 8-21 shows the selections you need to make for the **match** statement as well as for the base action (Drop) and the counter name (GUEST_DROPPED_PKTS). Click Save Match and Actions.

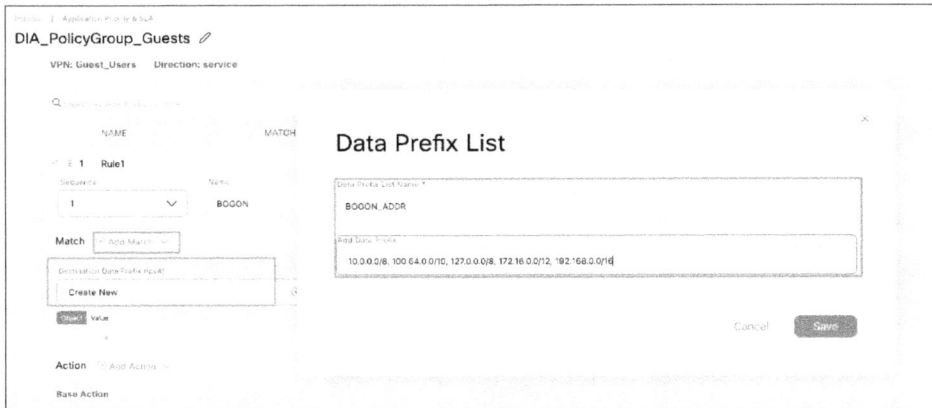

Figure 8-20   *Creating a Data Prefix List Inside a Policy Group Profile*

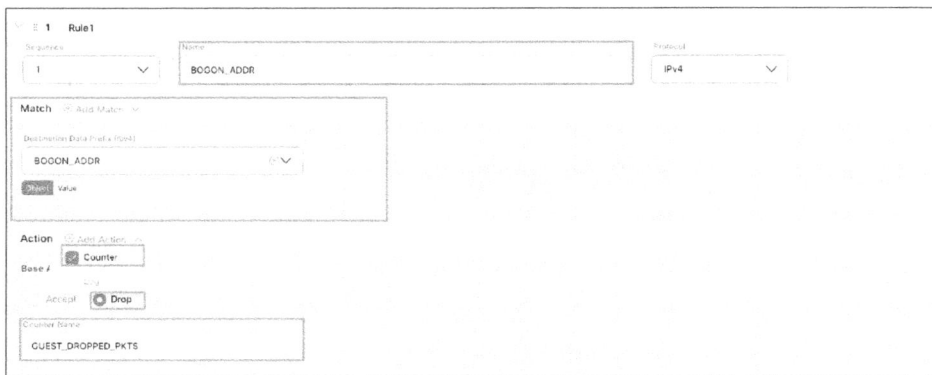

Figure 8-21   *Completing the Match and Actions for the BOGON Sequence*

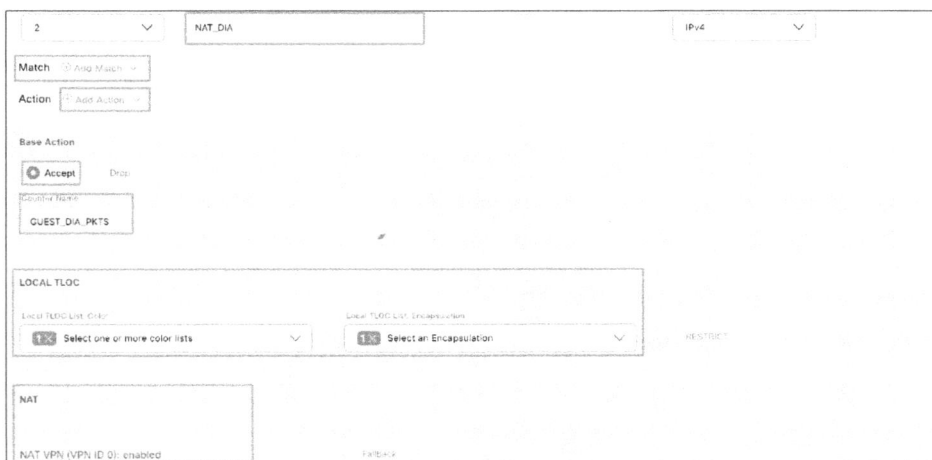

Figure 8-22   *Completing the Match and Actions for the NAT VPN*

Because direct Internet access is needed, you need to add a second rule to the policy. Figure 8-22 shows the selections you need to make. Leave **Match** empty in order to match any and set Base **Action** to **Accept**. Click **+Add Action** and configure **Local TLOC** by selecting biz-internet color along with IPsec encapsulation and VPN ID 0 as the NAT VPN. Then click **Save Match and Actions**.

The result is two sequence rules in the Policy Group profile, as shown in Figure 8-23. Make sure the rules are correct and click **Save**.

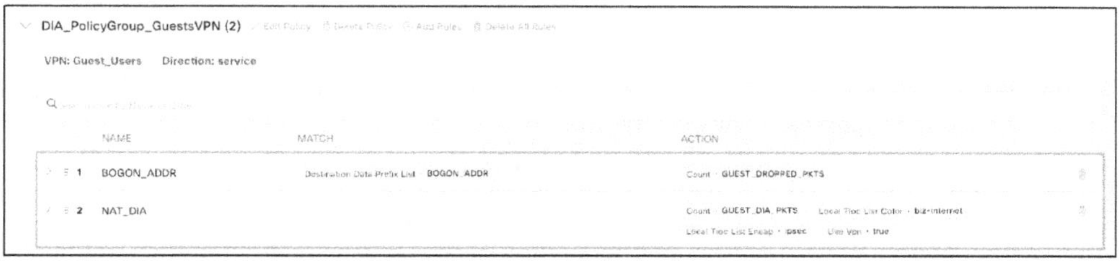

Figure 8-23 *Policy Profile Result*

Once the Application Priority & SLA profile is created, it is associated to a Policy Group, which will group different sets of policy profiles. Figure 8-24 shows how to create a policy group by providing a name and a description. Then click Create.

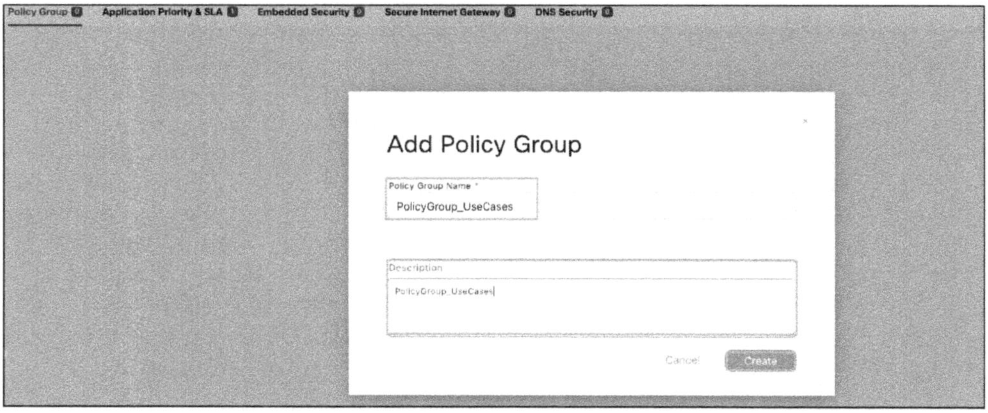

Figure 8-24 *Creating a Policy Group*

In the Policy Group screen, as shown in Figure 8-25, you can select the drop-downs for the policy profile options. In this case, you associate the newly created application priority profile DIA_PolicyGroup_Guests. An intermediate step is required to associate this policy group to devices; only devices associated with a Configuration Group are available. Once the desired devices are associated, click **Deploy**.

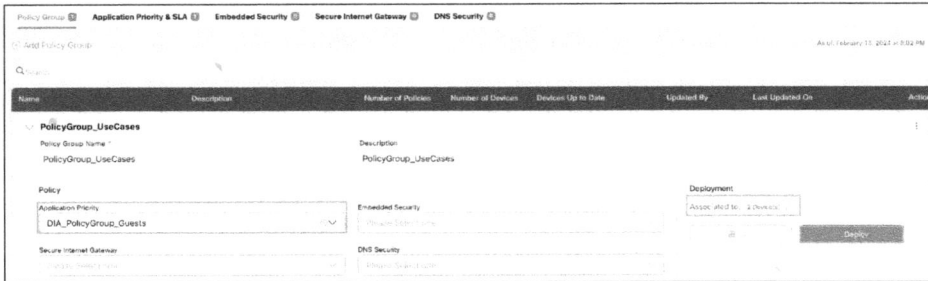

Figure 8-25 *Associating the Application Priority with the Policy Group and the Device*

Use Case 10 Review

This use case shows how to create a simple data policy and Application Priority & SLA profile and applied them to VPN 50. In this example, you have seen how data policies and policy groups can be used to manipulate the forwarding path of traffic. The two simple examples for the guest user VPN illustrate that the structure of this type of policy, consisting of **match** and **action** sequence rules, is very similar to the structure of control policies (refer to Chapter 7). While the purpose of this policy—dropping packets destined to a specific destination—is relatively straightforward, it is easy to see how other policies could be used for much more intricate tasks. For example, it would be trivial to drop traffic destined to a specific port while permitting traffic to other ports with a data policy—and it would be impossible to do so with a control policy.

Use Case 11: Direct Cloud Access for Trusted Applications

In addition to providing Internet access for guest users, many organizations leverage local Internet breakout for employees as well. However, there are significant security implications involved with permitting direct Internet access from every branch office to the entirety of the Internet. (You can find detailed discussions of the security features that are built in to the WAN Edge routers in Chapter 11, "Cisco Catalyst SD-WAN Security.") One of the ways that organizations can choose to limit the security implications of these choices is to restrict direct access to the Internet from the branch to certain applications or destinations that are deemed to be trusted or lower risk. Such applications may include enterprise services such as Microsoft 365, Google apps, and Salesforce.com. The terms *direct cloud access* and *direct Internet access* are often used interchangeably throughout this chapter to refer to policies that selectively permit access to destinations on the Internet.

In this use case, you will see how to build a data policy that allows users to access a specific trusted application, Cisco Webex, directly from the local branch, while still requiring all other Internet traffic to traverse the main security perimeter through the data centers. Figure 8-26 illustrates this traffic pattern for corporate users.

Before the policy is applied, all the traffic from the corporate users behind BR2-Edge1 traverses through DC1 to reach the public Internet. You can see this with Simulate Flows tool results in Figure 8-27. The remote system IP address of the device to which the traffic is going to be forwarded is listed as 10.0.10.1 in this output, and the application webex-meeting is specified in the flow criteria.

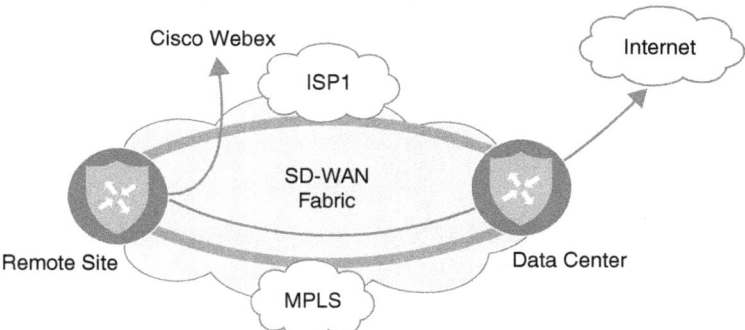

Figure 8-26 *Desired Forwarding Paths Are Different for Each Application*

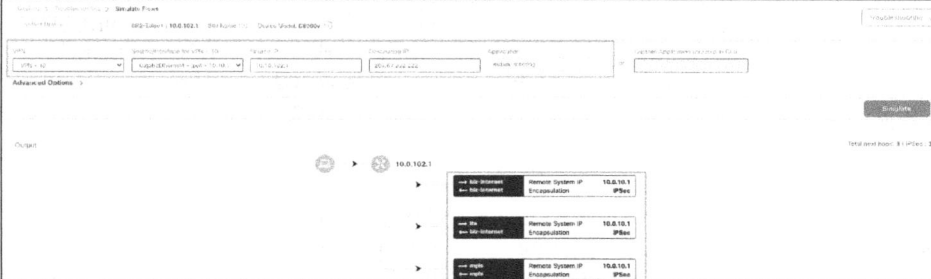

Figure 8-27 *Webex Traffic from Users in VPN 10 Would Be Forwarded to DC1 WAN Edge Routers*

NOTE In Figure 8-27 and Figure 8-28, different applications are specified, and an Internet-routable address is used as the destination (a Cisco Umbrella DNS address). By specifying a combination of different applications, DSCP markings, addresses, ports, and/or protocols, the Simulate Flows tool is a particularly powerful tool that helps network administrators understand how traffic is flowing through the network.

In Figure 8-27 and Figure 8-28, both Webex traffic and YouTube traffic are forwarded across the SD-WAN fabric to DC1-Edge1 or any site that is advertising a default route, as indicated by the remote system IP address 10.0.10.1. These application flows would be load-shared across the MPLS, LTE, and BIZ-INTERNET paths, as indicated by the multiple paths in the output. These outputs, taken before the updated policy is applied, show that the forwarding path for the two applications is the same.

NOTE As discussed in Chapter 7, the best-path selection algorithm picks the best route to a destination and advertises it through Overlay Management Protocol (OMP) to WAN Edge devices. For this case, the only available path is through remote system IP 10.0.0.1 because the control policy to influence symmetry and prefer DC1-Edge1 (preference 500) is still in place. Under normal conditions, all available paths would be present in the output. Remember that settings such as ecmp-limit or send-path-limit also influence the number of paths WAN Edge devices will use to forward traffic to its destination. For simplicity in this use case, only DC1 is advertising a default route.

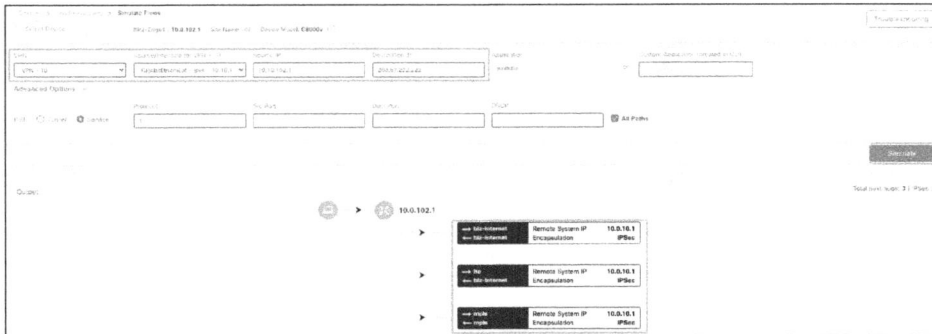

Figure 8-28 *YouTube Traffic from Users in VPN 10 Would Be Forwarded to DC1 WAN Edge Routers*

In order to meet the requirements of this use case and forward the Webex traffic directly out to the Internet while continuing to backhaul all other traffic, including YouTube traffic, across to the data centers, the centralized policy from Example 8-2 is modified to include a new data policy that matches the Webex application and forwards it out the local interface, as shown in Example 8-4.

NOTE SD-WAN Application Intelligence Engine (SAIE) provides the ability to look into a packet beyond the basic header information. It relies on the Network-Based Application Recognition (NBAR) and Software Defined-Application Visibility Control (SD-AVC) engines to achieve tasks like application recognition and classification based on the characteristics of the traffic flow to set an action to it through policies. This setting configuration is explained in Chapter 10, "Localized Policies."

Example 8-4 *A Corporate Direct Cloud Access Policy*

```
policy
 ! No changes were made to the control policies or VPN membership policies,
 ! and they are omitted for brevity. The full configuration of those policies
 ! can be found in Example 7-24.
 !
 ! The data policy below specifies two different VPNs, and each VPN has an
 ! individual set of sequences with different rules. However, the entire policy
 ! is applied to the site list.
 !
 data-policy
 Corporate_Segment_Corporate_DCA_Guest_Segment_Guest_DIA_Policy
  vpn-list Corporate_Segment
    sequence 1
      ! In the new sequence for the Corporate_Segment, we are matching a specific
app-list
```

```
    ! for the TRUSTED_APPS. The action (nat use-vpn 0) is the same action that was
    ! used for guest internet access. A new counter was also created and applied
    ! for monitoring.
  match
   app-list TRUSTED_APPS
    source-ip 0.0.0.0/0
    !
      ! The nat fallback configuration specifies the forwarding behavior in the event
      ! that the NAT enabled interface, biz-internet TLOC, is not operational
   action accept
    nat use-vpn 0
     nat fallback
    !
    count CORP_DCA_-1626632101
    !
   !
  ! All non-webex traffic will be matched by the default action and forwarded as
  ! normal across the fabric.
  !
 default-action accept
!
! The Guest_DIA_Policy that was configured as part of Use Case 10 is unchanged.
!
 vpn-list Guest_Segment
  sequence 1
   match
    destination-data-prefix-list BOGON_ADDR
    !
   action drop
    count GUEST_DROPPED_PKTS_-1626632101
    !
   !
  sequence 11
   match
    source-ip 0.0.0.0/0
    !
   action accept
    nat use-vpn 0

    count GUEST_DIA_PKTS_-1626632101
    set
      local-tloc-list
```

```
        color biz-internet
    !
    !
 default-action drop
 !
 lists
 ! <<<Some lists without changes are omitted for brevity>>>
 !
  app-list TRUSTED_APPS
   app webex
   app webex-app-sharing
   app webex-meeting
   app webex_weboffice
   app webex-audio
   app webex-media
   app webex-control
  !
  vpn-list Corporate_Segment
   vpn 10
  !
  vpn-list Guest_Segment
   vpn 50
  !
 !
!
apply-policy
 site-list Europe_Branches
  control-policy Euro_Reg_Mesh_with_FW_MultiTopo out
 !
 site-list BranchOffices
  data-policy _Corporate_Segment_Corporate_DCA_Guest_Segment_Guest_DIA_Policy
from-service
  vpn-membership vpnMembership_1718052183
 !
 site-list DCs
  control-policy DC_Inbound_Control_Policy in
 !
 site-list North_America_Branches
  control-policy North_America_Reg_Mesh_with_FW out
 !
!
```

Example 8-4 highlights the modifications to the data policy that were made in order to implement the direct cloud access functionality for corporate users. This policy builds on the policy that was created in Use Case 10 and adds support for corporate users in a second VPN (VPN 10) with an entirely different set of rules. It is important to understand that these two sets of sequences for the two different VPNs have been concatenated into a single data policy when activated on the SD-WAN Controller (formerly vSmart), even though they are administered in SD-WAN Manager (formerly vManage) as two separate data policies (as shown in Figure 8-29). In this case, the policy _Corporate_Segment_Corporate_DCA_ Guest_Segment_Guest_DIA_Policy affects the VPNs specified by both the Corporate_ Segment and Guest_Segment lists, albeit with different policies specified in their respective sequence sets. Furthermore, there is no reference to the VPNs that the data policy is applied to in the apply-policy stanza at the end of the centralized policy; this is configured by the VPN lists referenced in the data policies.

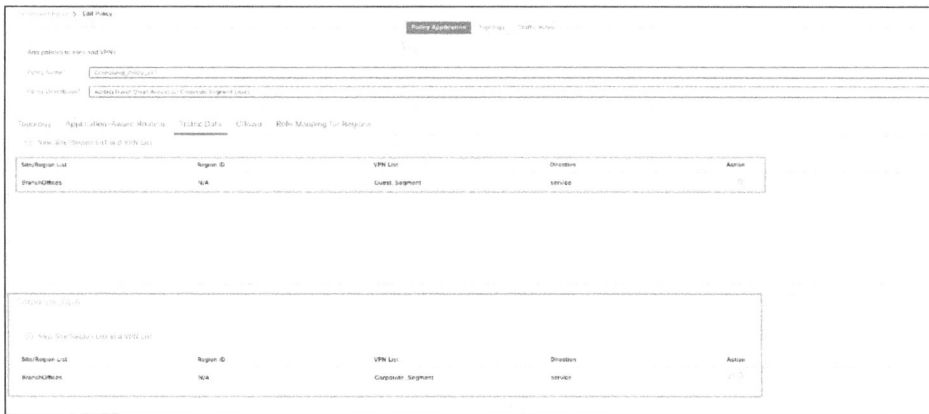

Figure 8-29 *Applying a Policy Configuration Showing That Corporate and Guest Data Policies Are Separate Policies*

Once the policy is activated, the results can be validated using the Simulate Flows tool. As shown in Figure 8-30, Webex traffic now egresses directly to the Internet. This flow pattern is different from what was observed for Webex traffic before the policy was applied, in Figure 8-27, and it's similar to what was seen for traffic in the Guest VPN in Figure 8-12.

Conversely, the forwarding pattern for YouTube traffic, as shown in Figure 8-31 after the policy is activated, is the same as in Figure 8-28 before the policy was activated. All the YouTube traffic is going to be forwarded across the fabric to the data center and will be inspected by the traditional security perimeter there.

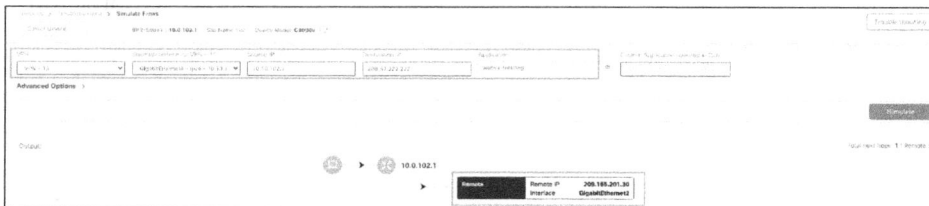

Figure 8-30 *Webex Traffic from Users in VPN 10 Would Egress Directly to the Internet*

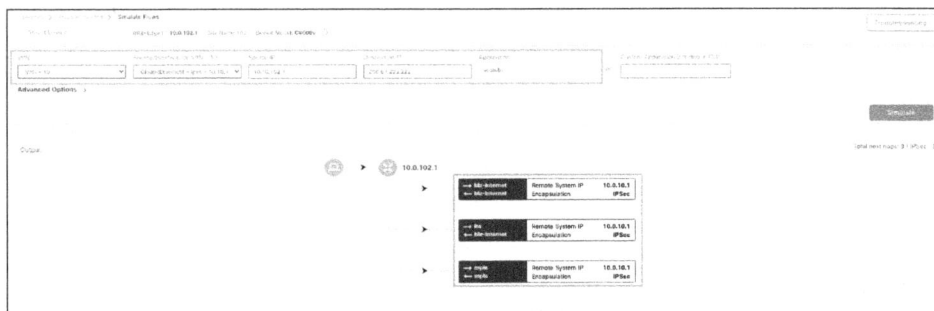

Figure 8-31 *YouTube Traffic from Users in VPN 10 Would Continue to Be Forwarded to the DC1 WAN Edge Routers*

As highlighted in Figure 8-7 and Example 8-4, the **nat use-vpn 0** action has the optional configuration argument **nat fallback**. This argument allows the administrator to specify the desired behavior in the event of a failure. With **nat fallback** enabled, in the event that all the NAT-enabled VPN 0 interfaces on the local edge were in a non-operational state, the traffic would follow the forwarding path determined by the routing table. This would typically mean that the traffic traverses the fabric and egresses at a different site (such as a data center). Figure 8-32 illustrates this traffic pattern.

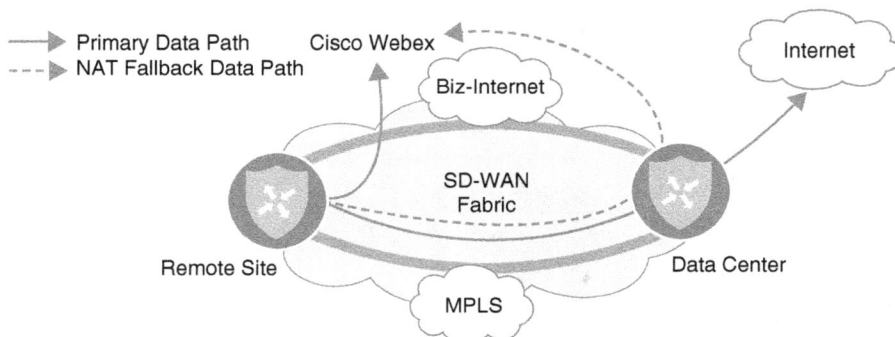

Figure 8-32 *Illustrated nat fallback Data Path*

NOTE   A non-operational state for a NAT-enabled interface can occur in two main ways: a hard failure, where the interface goes down completely, or a soft failure, where a NAT DIA tracker associated with the interface changes status to down.

In Use Case 10, the **nat use-vpn 0** action is configured for guest Internet access traffic without **nat fallback** enabled. If all of the local interfaces with NAT configured were to go down, guest traffic would not fall back and would not be forwarded across the SD-WAN fabric and would instead be blackholed. In this use case, the data policy for the corporate VPN does have the **nat fallback** option configured, and this allows for the Webex traffic to be backhauled through the data center in the event of a failure of the local Internet connection. Example 8-5 shows both traffic patterns.

Example 8-5 also introduces a new tool for monitoring the forwarding decision of flows from the CLI: **show sdwan policy service-path**. This **show** command is the CLI equivalent of the Simulate Flows tool that has been shown inside the SD-WAN Manager GUI.

NOTE   For direct Internet access forwarding scenarios, NAT Direct Internet Access tracking is used to determine if the Internet or external network is unavailable and hence the Internet-bound traffic needs to be routed through an alternate path.

Example 8-5   *Webex Traffic with Failure of the Local Internet Connection*

```
! When all of the transport interfaces as well as interface tracker are up / up:
!
BR2-Edge1# show ip interfaces brief
Interface              IP-Address      OK? Method Status            Protocol
GigabitEthernet1       192.168.20.6    YES other  up                up
GigabitEthernet2       209.165.201.6   YES other  up                up


BR2-Edge1#sh endpoint-tracker interface  GigabitEthernet 2
Interface                    Record Name            Status
Address Family   RTT in msecs    Probe ID   Next Hop
GigabitEthernet2             Tracker_Biz_Internet   Up          IPv4
9               1        209.165.201.30
!
! With all of the transports up / up, Webex traffic from VPN 10 will egress
! locally. This output matches Figure 8-30.
!
BR2-Edge1# show sdwan policy service-path vpn 10 interface GigabitEthernet 4 source-
ip 10.10.102.1 dest-ip 208.67.222.222 protocol 1 app webex-meeting all
Number of possible next hops: 1
Next Hop: Remote
  Remote IP: 209.165.201.30, Interface GigabitEthernet2 Index: 8
BR2-Edge1#
!
! VPN 50 has connectivity to resources on the internet.
!
BR2-Edge1# ping vrf 50 208.67.222.222
Type escape sequence to abort.
Sending 5, 100-byte ICMP Echos to 208.67.222.222, timeout is 2 seconds:
!!!!!
Success rate is 100 percent (5/5), round-trip min/avg/max = 9/9/10 ms
BR2-Edge1#
!
! Turning GigabitEthernet2 to a down state (hard failure), simulating the failure of
the local internet link:
```

8

```
!
BR2-Edge1#show ip interface brief
Interface              IP-Address      OK? Method Status              Protocol
GigabitEthernet1       192.168.20.6    YES other   up                  up
GigabitEthernet2       209.165.201.6   YES other   administratively down down
<<<Output omitted for brevity>>>
BR2-Edge1#
BR2-Edge1#sh endpoint-tracker
Interface                       Record Name             Status           Address
Family    RTT in msecs     Probe ID    Next Hop
GigabitEthernet2                Tracker_Biz_Internet    Down             IPv4
25                 0            209.165.201.30
!
! With the local internet connection down, Webex traffic will be forwarded across
! the fabric to destinations 209.165.201.1 and 192.168.20.1. From the OMP TLOCs
table,
! we can see that this is DC1-Edge1 (System IP 10.0.10.1).
BR2-Edge1# show sdwan policy service-path vpn 10 interface GigabitEthernet 4 source-
ip 10.10.102.1 dest-ip 208.67.222.222 protocol 1 app webex-meeting all
Number of possible next hops: 2
Next Hop: IPsec
   Source: 209.165.202.130 12346 Destination: 209.165.201.1 12346 Local Color: lte
Remote Color: biz-internet Remote System IP: 10.0.10.1
Next Hop: IPsec
   Source: 192.168.20.6 12346 Destination: 192.168.20.1 12346 Local Color: mpls
Remote Color: mpls Remote System IP: 10.0.10.1


!
! On the other hand, guest traffic originating in VPN 50 does not fallback across
! the fabric and now blackholed:
!
BR2-Edge1# ping vrf 50 208.67.222.222
Type escape sequence to abort.
Sending 5, 100-byte ICMP Echos to 208.67.222.222, timeout is 2 seconds:
.....
Success rate is 0 percent (0/5)
BR2-Edge1# show sdwan policy service-path vpn 50 interface GigabitEthernet6 source-
ip 10.50.102.1 dest-ip 208.67.222.222 protocol 1 app webex-meeting all
Number of possible next hops: 1
Next Hop: Blackhole
```

Use Case 11 Review

In this use case, you are beginning to see the true power of centralized data policies: They enable you to specify different forwarding behaviors on an app-by-app basis. While the forwarding decisions in this policy were made on the basis of a Layer 7 application definition, centralized data policies can match on a number of different Layer 3, Layer 4, and/or Layer 7 criteria. For example, this policy could be extended to match on a combination of the Webex application and a source data prefix, such that the rule would only apply to users residing in certain subnets. Users outside those specific source ranges would follow the traditional forwarding pattern.

This use case also continues to build on the **nat use-vpn 0** action with the **nat fallback** action. With this combination of actions, network administrators can create dynamic policies to meet business needs, while at the same time being able to create predictable behavior in the event of a failure. If network administrators are concerned about conserving limited site-to-site bandwidth, the configurations in this policy can easily be extended to provide access for many different applications using local Internet egress points. These administrators could then be very selective about which applications would be permitted to fall back to the limited site-to-site tunnels, and NAT DIA tracker could be configured on the NAT-enabled interface. For example, a cloud-hosted payroll application might be considered business critical and permitted to fall back to the site-to-site path. At the same time, Internet radio may be permitted to use the local Internet egress path, but in the event of a failure, it would not be considered business critical and would not be permitted to fall back to the site-to-site path.

Use Case 12: Application-Based Traffic Engineering

Enterprise WANs are becoming increasingly important to business and are constantly being tasked with providing faster and more reliable connectivity, all while using less expensive transport networks and cutting overall costs. Traditionally, organizations used expensive leased-line transports with small bandwidth but guaranteed service-level agreements (SLAs) in order to connect their diffuse sites. As organizations transition to hybrid transport environments (where they may still have expensive small links that are being augmented with substantially larger circuits without guaranteed SLAs), there is an ever-growing need for new and powerful tools to be able to dictate which paths applications take as they flow across the WAN.

As Figure 8-31 from Use Case 11 shows, the currently configured policy has both critical and noncritical business traffic, such as Microsoft 365 or Facebook traffic, indistinctly load-shared across the MPLS and BIZ-INTERNET paths. Wasting the limited and expensive MPLS bandwidth on noncritical traffic is not desired, so in this use case, the centralized data policy will continue to be refined so that certain classes of traffic are forwarded across the BIZ-INTERNET path only. This policy will consider two different classes of traffic, Microsoft 365 and Facebook traffic, and set different forwarding rules for each. Microsoft 365 traffic will be preferred across the BIZ-INTERNET SD-WAN tunnels. In the event that the BIZ-INTERNET tunnels are not available, the Microsoft 365 traffic will move to any of the other transports available. Traffic for the second application, Facebook, will be required to use the BIZ-INTERNET tunnels to reach the data centers. In the event that the BIZ-INTERNET tunnels are not available, this application will be unavailable. These traffic patterns are illustrated in Figure 8-33.

Before the policy from Example 8-4 has been modified, the forwarding behavior shown in Example 8-6 can be observed.

8

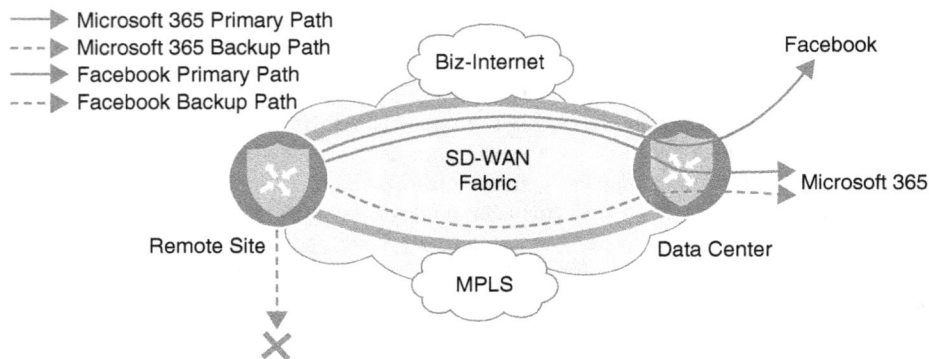

Figure 8-33 *Desired Forwarding Behavior for Facebook and Microsoft 365 Traffic*

Example 8-6 *Application Forwarding Behavior Without Policy Changes*

```
!
! Before modifications are made to the policy, both Facebook and Microsoft 365
traffic is
! forwarded across both links.
!
BR2-Edge1# sh sdwan policy service-path vpn 10 int GigabitEthernet 4 source-ip
10.10.102.1 dest-ip 208.67.222.222 protocol 1 app facebook all
Number of possible next hops: 3
Next Hop: IPsec
  Source: 209.165.201.6 12346 Destination: 209.165.201.1 12346 Local Color:
biz-internet Remote Color: biz-internet Remote System IP: 10.0.10.1
Next Hop: IPsec
  Source: 209.165.202.130 12346 Destination: 209.165.201.1 12346 Local Color:
lte Remote Color: biz-internet Remote System IP: 10.0.10.1
Next Hop: IPsec
  Source: 192.168.20.6 12346 Destination: 192.168.20.1 12346 Local Color: mpls
Remote Color: mpls Remote System IP: 10.0.10.1
BR2-Edge1# sh sdwan policy service-path vpn 10 int GigabitEthernet 4 source-ip
10.10.102.1 dest-ip 208.67.222.222 protocol 1 app ms-office-365 all
Number of possible next hops: 3
Next Hop: IPsec
  Source: 209.165.201.6 12346 Destination: 209.165.201.1 12346 Local Color:
biz-internet Remote Color: biz-internet Remote System IP: 10.0.10.1
Next Hop: IPsec
  Source: 209.165.202.130 12346 Destination: 209.165.201.1 12346 Local Color:
lte Remote Color: biz-internet Remote System IP: 10.0.10.1
Next Hop: IPsec
  Source: 192.168.20.6 12346 Destination: 192.168.20.1 12346 Local Color:
mpls Remote Color: mpls Remote System IP: 10.0.10.1
BR2-Edge1#
```

Example 8-6 again uses the **show sdwan policy service-path** command to determine the path or paths that particular flows would take through a WAN Edge router. This example shows the outputs for the application facebook and the application ms-office-365, indicating that flows from both applications would be load-shared across the MPLS, LTE, and BIZ-INTERNET tunnels to DC1-Edge1. In order to change this behavior, the policy configured in Example 8-7 uses the **local-tloc** action and the **tloc-list** action.

The **local-tloc** action is configured with this syntax:

```
set local-tloc color {color} [encap {ipsec|gre}]
```

where *color* is any one of the supported TLOC colors. This action directs packets to be forwarded out the local TLOC that is specified in the **color** argument. If this TLOC is not available (because, for example, it is not configured or the tunnel is down), the traffic is forwarded out any valid TLOC, as indicated by the routing table. In addition, the configuration command **set local-tloc-list** allows for the selection of one or more colors. SD-WAN Manager defaults to using this syntax when policies are configured through the GUI.

Similar to what **set local-tloc-list** offers when listing more than one preferred transport, the command **set preferred-color-group** {*color-group-name*} not only helps select the egress local TLOC but provides up to three levels of color preference.

The **tloc-list** action in a centralized data policy is similar in structure and function to the centralized control policy **tloc-list** action that we explored in Use Case 2 (refer to Chapter 7). By using the **tloc-list** action, a network administrator is statically specifying the fabric tunnel endpoints toward which the flow will be forwarded. This functionality is roughly equivalent to the **set next-hop-address** functionality in a traditional policy-based-routing route map. With the **tloc-list** action, if the TLOCs specified in the list are not available, then the traffic is blackholed, even though there may be a different path available.

To summarize, the **local-tloc** action selects the *preferred* egress TLOC on the *local* WAN Edge router, the **preferred-color-group** action provides tiered preference for local egress TLOCs, and the **tloc-list** action *mandates* the TLOCs on the *receiving* WAN Edge that the traffic will be forwarded to. The modified policy in Example 8-7 shows these two different configurations.

Example 8-7   *Application-Based Traffic Engineering Policy*

```
policy
 ! <<<No changes were made to the control policies, VPN membership policies, or
 ! the Guest VPN data policies, and they are omitted for brevity.>>>
 !
! <<<No changes were made to the control policies, VPN membership policies, or
 ! the Guest VPN data policies, and they are omitted for brevity.>>>
 !
data-policy _Corporate_Segment_Branch_AppTrafficEng
  vpn-list Corporate_Segment
    sequence 1
```

```
    match
     app-list TRUSTED_APPS
     source-ip 0.0.0.0/0
     !
    action accept
     nat use-vpn 0
     nat fallback
     count CORP_DCA_-1766920491
     !
    !
    !
    ! Sequence 11 uses the local-tloc-list command to indicate the color or colors
    ! on the local WAN Edge that are PREFERRED to be used for forwarding this flow.
    !
   sequence 11
    match
     app-list office365_apps
     source-ip 0.0.0.0/0
     !
    action accept
     count CORP_M365_-1766920491
     set
     local-tloc-list
      color biz-internet
      encap ipsec
      !
     !
    !
    !
    ! Sequence 21 uses the tloc-list command to specify the TLOCs that this traffic
    ! MUST be forwarded to. If the TLOCs are unavailable, the traffic will be
    ! dropped.
    !
   sequence 21
    match
     app-list Facebook
     source-ip 0.0.0.0/0
     !
    action accept
     count CORP_FACEBOOK_-1766920491
     set
     vpn 10
     tloc-list DC_INET_TLOCS
```

```
      !
     !
    !
 default-action accept
 !
 vpn-list Guest_Segment
<<<Output omitted for brevity>>>
 !
lists
! <<<Some lists without changes are omitted for brevity>>>
 !
 app-list Facebook
  app facebook
  app facebook-audio
  app facebook_apps
  app facebook-video
  app facebook_messenger
  app facebook_mail
  app facebook_live
  app facebook_video
  app fbcdn
  app facebook-media

 !
 app-list office365_apps
  <<<Output omitted for brevity>>>
  app sharepoint
  app ms-office-365
  app outlook-web-service
  app skydrive
<<<Output omitted for brevity>>>
 !
 site-list BranchOffices
  site-id 100-199
 !
 tloc-list DC_INET_TLOCS
  tloc 10.0.10.1 color biz-internet encap ipsec preference 500
  tloc 10.0.10.2 color biz-internet encap ipsec preference 400
 !
 !
 !
apply-policy
 site-list Europe_Branches
```

```
    control-policy Euro_Reg_Mesh_with_FW_MultiTopo out
 !
 site-list BranchOffices
  data-policy _Corporate_Segment_Branch_AppBasedEng from-service
  control-policy Branch_Extranet_Route_Leaking in
  vpn-membership vpnMembership_373293275
 !
 site-list DCs
  control-policy DC_Inbound_Control_Policy in
 !
 site-list North_America_Branches
  control-policy North_America_Reg_Mesh_with_FW out
 !
 !
```

NOTE   Keep in mind that Cisco Catalyst SD-WAN often provides multiple ways to achieve the same result. For example, if administrators want to send traffic such as Microsoft 365 traffic directly to the Internet, but need a failover path in case direct Internet access fails, previously covered options like using the NAT VPN in conjunction with **nat fallback** can fulfill the requirement. On the other hand, if noncritical traffic, like Facebook traffic in the current use case, does not need an alternative path due to its lower business priority, the **restrict** action makes it possible to drop undesired traffic.

In sequence 11 in Example 8-7, Microsoft 365 application traffic is being matched, and then the **local-tloc-list** action is configured to preferably forward this traffic out the BIZ-INTERNET TLOC, if the TLOC is available. In sequence 21, Facebook traffic is being matched and is being forwarded to BIZ-INTERNET TLOCs on DC1-Edge1 and DC1-Edge2, as specified with the **tloc-list** action. The effects of these two different configuration options can be seen in Example 8-8, where the results are shown in both a steady state and a state where the Internet connection of both WAN Edge devices at DC1 has failed.

Key Topic

Example 8-8   *Application Traffic Engineering Behavior with Policy in Steady State and Failed State*

```
! When all of the Biz-Internet BFD Sessions to Site 10 are operational:
!
BR2-Edge1#sh sdwan bfd sessions table | include biz-internet
                                       SRC    DST            SITE   DETECT
TX
SRC IP          DST IP        PROTO  PORT   PORT    SYSTEM IP   ID   LOCAL COLOR
COLOR           STATE MULTIPLIER  INTERVAL  UPTIME        TRANSITIONS
-------------------------------------------------------------------------------
-----------------------------------------------------------------
```

```
209.165.201.6    209.165.201.1    ipsec  12346  12346  10.0.10.1   10    biz-
internet  biz-internet  up    7          1000      1:20:16:12  3
209.165.202.130 209.165.201.1    ipsec  12346  12346  10.0.10.1   10    lte
biz-internet  up    7        1000      1:20:16:04  3
209.165.201.6    209.165.201.2    ipsec  12346  12346  10.0.10.2   10    biz-
internet  biz-internet  up    7          1000      0:00:04:07  5
209.165.202.130 209.165.201.2    ipsec  12346  12346  10.0.10.2   10    lte
biz-internet  up    7        1000      0:00:04:04  5
!
! In steady state, when all of the links are operational, the two configurations
! have the same effect:  Traffic matching the Microsoft 365 app-list and traffic
matching
! the Facebook app-list are both forwarded across biz-internet tunnel to
! 209.165.201.1    (DC1-Edge1).
BR2-Edge1# show sdwan policy service-path vpn 10 interface GigabitEthernet 4
source-ip 10.10.102.1 dest-ip 208.67.222.222 protocol 1 app ms-office-365 all
Next Hop: IPsec
  Source: 209.165.201.6 12346 Destination: 209.165.201.1 12346 Local Color:
biz-internet Remote Color: biz-internet Remote System IP: 10.0.10.1
BR2-Edge1# show sdwan policy service-path vpn 10 interface GigabitEthernet4
source-ip 10.10.102.1 dest-ip 208.67.222.222 protocol 1 app facebook all
 Number of possible next hops: 1
Next Hop: IPsec
  Source: 209.165.201.6 12346 Destination: 209.165.201.1 12346 Local Color:
biz-internet Remote Color: biz-internet Remote System IP: 10.0.10.1
!
! After an internet failure at DC1, all of the Biz-Internet BFD Sessions to
! Site 10 are down:
!
BR2-Edge1#sh sdwan bfd sessions table | include biz-internet
                                      SRC    DST              SITE
DETECT      TX
SRC IP          DST IP          PROTO  PORT   PORT   SYSTEM IP  ID    LOCAL COLOR
COLOR           STATE  MULTIPLIER  INTERVAL  UPTIME       TRANSITIONS
----------------------------------------------------------------------------------
------------------------------------------------------------------
209.165.201.6    209.165.201.1    ipsec  12346  12346  10.0.10.1   10    biz-
internet  biz-internet  down    7          1000      1:20:16:12  5
209.165.202.130 209.165.201.1    ipsec  12346  12346  10.0.10.1   10    lte
biz-internet  down    7        1000      1:20:16:04  5
209.165.201.6    209.165.201.2    ipsec  12346  12346  10.0.10.2   10    biz-
internet  biz-internet  down    7          1000      0:00:04:07  7
209.165.202.130 209.165.201.2    ipsec  12346  12346  10.0.10.2   10    lte
biz-internet  down    7        1000      0:00:04:04  7
!
! In a failed state, where there is no longer a path to DC1 via the Biz-Internet
color,
```

```
! the Microsoft 365 traffic will be forwarded across the MPLS path.
!
BR2-Edge1#show sdwan policy service-path vpn 10 interface GigabitEthernet 4
source-ip 10.10.102.1 dest-ip 208.67.222.222 protocol 1 app ms-office-365 all
Number of possible next hops: 1
Next Hop: IPsec
  Source: 192.168.20.6 12346 Destination: 192.168.20.1 12346 Local Color: mpls
Remote Color: mpls Remote System IP: 10.0.10.1
! The Facebook application, will not failover to the MPLS path. The tloc-list
! action statically specifies the next-hop tunnel endpoints.  If those
! endpoints are not available, the traffic is blackholed.
!
BR2-Edge1#show sdwan policy service-path vpn 10 interface GigabitEthernet 4
source-ip 10.10.102.1 dest-ip 208.67.222.222 protocol 1 app facebook all
Number of possible next hops: 1
Next Hop: Blackhole
BR2-Edge1#
```

When the network is in a state where all of BIZ-INTERNET tunnels are operating as expected, Example 8-8 shows that the forwarding behavior for these two configurations is the same: Both the Microsoft 365 and Facebook flows are forwarded across the BIZ-INTER-NET tunnel to 209.165.201.1, the Internet interface IP address of DC1-Edge1. The difference between these two configurations becomes apparent when the network is in a failed state, as would occur if the BIZ-INTERNET transport to DC1 were severed by a fiber-seeking backhoe. Example 8-8 shows that the Microsoft 365 application, configured with the **local-tloc-list** action, fails over to the MPLS TLOC and continues to operate. The Facebook application, on the other hand, which was configured with the **tloc-list** action, where the next hops were statically specified, does not fail over, and the traffic is instead blackholed.

Application-Based Traffic Engineering with Policy Groups

Let's look at an example of the same traffic engineering scenario we've been working with but now leveraging policy groups. Create a policy group by going to **Configuration > Policy Groups > +Add Policy Group** and providing a name and description, as shown in Figure 8-34.

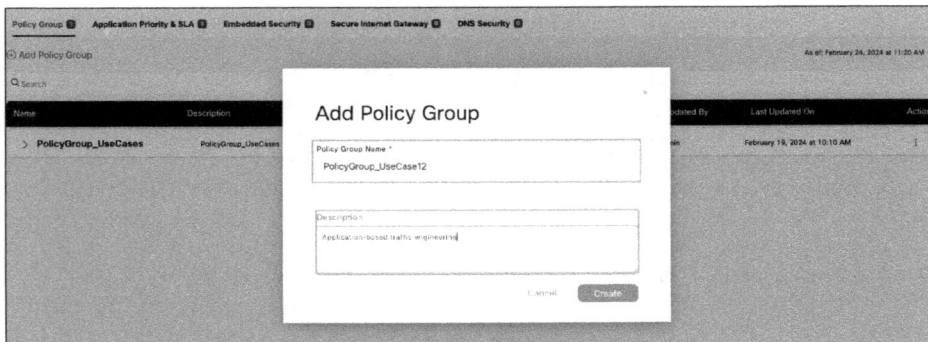

Figure 8-34 *Creating a Policy Group*

Next, create an Application Priority profile, by clicking **Create New** and providing a name and description, as shown in Figure 8-35.

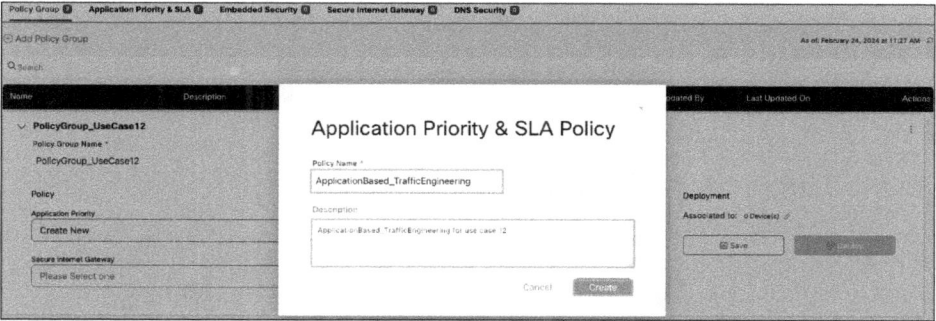

Figure 8-35 *Creating an Application Priority & SLA Policy*

In the Application Priority profile you just created, click **Advanced Layout**, then select **Add Traffic Policy** and specify the name, the VPN (Corporate_Segment), and the direction of the policy (Service), as shown in Figure 8-36.

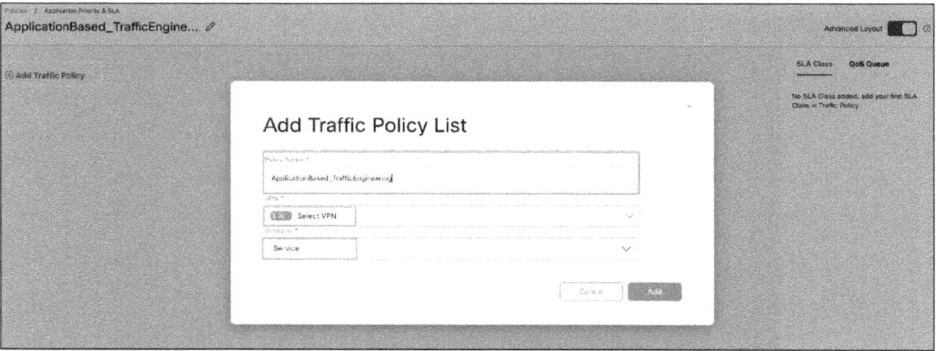

Figure 8-36 *Creating a Traffic Policy for VPN 10*

Just as with the conventional policy methodology, two sequence rules are created, one for each of the applications discussed. Click **+Add Rules** and use this first rule for Microsoft 365 traffic that is matched based on the **Application / Traffic Class** criteria, and then click **Create New** and select the desired applications under **Application-Family** to create the list. Next, select **Accept** under Base Action. Under **LOCAL TLOC**, select biz-internet as the color and IPsec as the encapsulation to be used for the preferred path (see Figure 8-37). Then click **Save Match and Actions**.

Next, click **+Add Rules** to add a second sequence for Facebook traffic, which is matched based on the application list with facebook as the value. Then select **Accept** under Base Action. Under **TLOC List**, select the BIZ-INTERNET TLOCs at DC1-Edge1 and DC1-Edge2 as the preferred paths (see Figure 8-38). (This rule differs from the previous rule in that unavailability of these paths will drop the traffic.) Click **Save Match and Actions** again.

Figure 8-37   *Defining a Rule for Microsoft 365 Traffic*

Figure 8-38   *Defining a Rule for Facebook Traffic*

After the rules specifying the actions for the different types of traffic are set, click Save, as shown in Figure 8-39.

Finally, deploy the policy group to the desired devices. The workflow guides you through the required steps to define the devices that will be subject to one or more policy profiles contained in the policy group. In this case, only the newly created Application Priority & SLA policy is sent to the devices (see Figure 8-40).

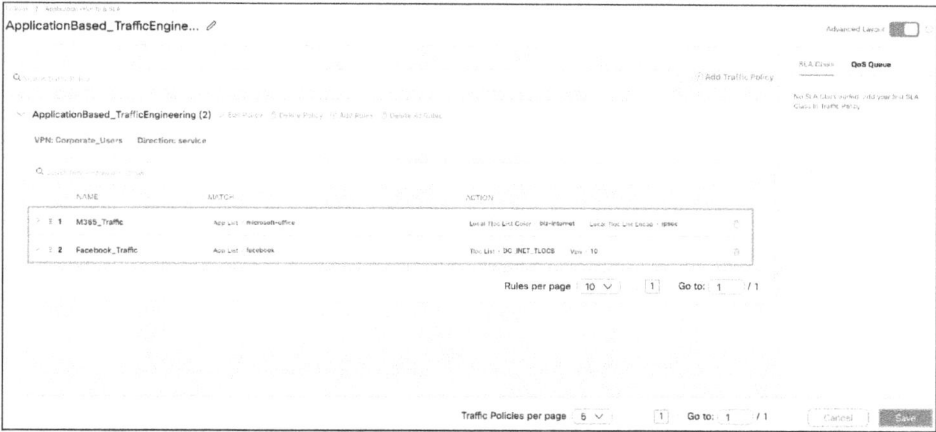

Figure 8-39 *Application Priority Policy Profile Preview*

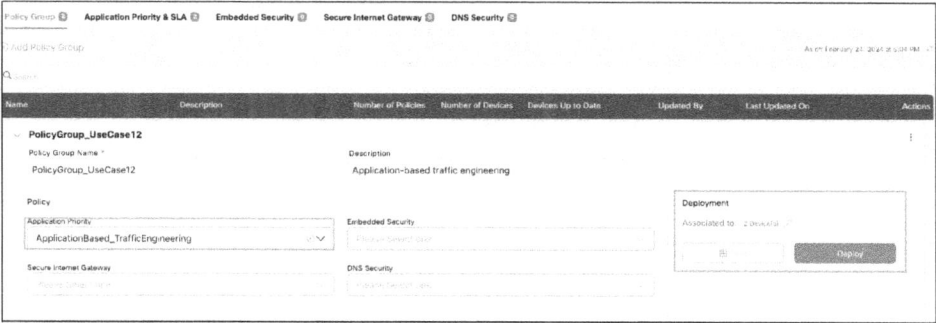

Figure 8-40 *Deploying a Policy Group*

Use Case 12 Review

This use case again illustrates that there are often several different design and configuration choices that can be used to accomplish any specific task. It is important for administrators to not only consider the forwarding behavior that is desired but also to think through the possible outcomes and effects of different failure scenarios and the effects of design choices on the eventual outcomes. As Example 8-8 shows, TLOC lists are powerful but unforgiving tools; use them with caution.

This example uses Facebook and Microsoft 365 as two sample applications for illustration purposes, but these placeholders can easily be replaced with applications that are important to the business: thin clients, enterprise resource planning (ERP) systems, file servers, email, collaboration software, and so on. Network administrators can apply the lessons learned here to solve the challenges facing their organizations.

Use Case 13: Protecting Corporate Users with a Secure Internet Gateway

Throughout this chapter, we have explored use cases where users were accessing the Internet by egressing directly from the WAN Edge, such as the Webex application in Use Case 11. In Use Case 12, you saw examples of traffic engineering policies that allowed users to access Internet-based applications by backhauling the traffic through a data center. This use case explores a third option: integrating a cloud-delivered firewall (CDFW), such as Cisco Umbrella Secure Internet Gateway (SIG), to the SD-WAN fabric and redirecting traffic flows to Cisco Umbrella SIG. This use case focuses on the integration of Umbrella SIG with the SD-WAN fabric and the centralized data policies that are necessary to redirect traffic to Umbrella SIG.

NOTE   For more information about Cisco Umbrella SIG and the specific configurations for integrating Umbrella with Cisco SD-WAN, see the references listed at the end of this chapter and visit https://umbrella.cisco.com.

In Chapter 7, you saw a firewall inside one of the sites configured and advertised as a service in the SD-WAN fabric. All the traffic that was passing between sites was forwarded through the service based on manipulation of the routing table with a centralized control policy. In this use case, rather than manipulating the routing table to send all traffic through the CDFW, a centralized data policy will be created to send only a specific set of applications through the firewall—specifically, a variety of Google apps. Figure 8-41 illustrates this traffic flow.

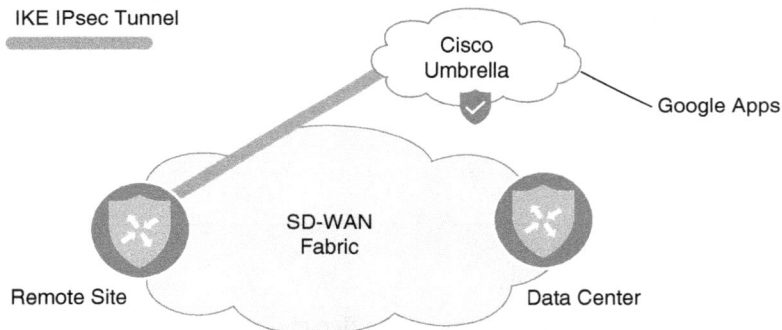

Figure 8-41   *Redirecting Google Apps Traffic to Cisco Umbrella SIG*

The first step in the process is to establish the tunnel for connectivity to the Secure Internet Gateway solution, as shown in Example 8-9. While this example uses Cisco Umbrella, this integration would also work with another SIG provider that uses IPsec or GRE tunnels to establish connectivity.

Example 8-9   *SD-WAN Router Configuration for a Secure Internet Gateway Tunnel*

```
!
! An IPSec tunnel to Cisco Umbrella is configured in VPN0.
!
BR2-Edge1#sh sdwan running-config   | section Tunnel100001
interface Tunnel100001
 no shutdown
```

```
  ip unnumbered         GigabitEthernet2
  no ip clear-dont-fragment
  ip mtu                1400
  tunnel source GigabitEthernet2
  tunnel destination dynamic
  tunnel mode ipsec ipv4
  tunnel protection ipsec profile if-ipsec1-ipsec-profile
  tunnel vrf multiplexing
  tunnel route-via GigabitEthernet2 mandatory
    interface-pair Tunnel100001 active-interface-weight 1 None backup-interface-
weight 1
  interface Tunnel100001
   tunnel-options tunnel-set secure-internet-gateway-umbrella tunnel-dc-preference
primary-dc source-interface GigabitEthernet2
BR2-Edge1#
BR2-Edge1#sh sdwan running-config | section sig
 service sig vrf global
  ha-pairs
   interface-pair Tunnel100001 active-interface-weight 1 None backup-interface-
weight 1
  !
BR2-Edge1#show sdwan secure-internet-gateway  tunnels
TUNNEL IF                                                    HA      DEVICE  SIG
TRACKER   SITE   DESTINATION            TUNNEL
NAME            TUNNEL ID  TUNNEL NAME                       PAIR    STATE   STATE
STATE    ID     DATA CENTER   PROVIDER  TYPE    TIMESTAMP
--------------------------------------------------------------------------------
--------------------------------------------------------------------------------
Tunnel100001  622182010  SITE102SYS10x0x102x1IFTunnel100001  Active   Up      UP
Enabled  102    CoreSite NY2  Umbrella  IPsec   2024-02-25T01:21:45.486565236Z  !
BR2-Edge1#
```

In Example 8-9, the status of the SIG tunnels is also validated. The same verification is available at **Monitor > Tunnels > SIG Tunnels** in SD-WAN Manager (see Figure 8-42). The details for establishing these tunnels are typically provided by the SIG provider. After the SIG tunnel is configured, a centralized data policy needs to be created to redirect the traffic of interest to the security service.

Centralized control policies are enforced centrally on the SD-WAN Controller and are only evaluated when sending or receiving control plane updates with OMP. Therefore, there is limited impact from the control policies on the SD-WAN Controllers, and there is no performance impact on the WAN Edge routers. Centralized data policies, however, are forwarded to the WAN Edge routers from the SD-WAN Controller through OMP, where each flow is then evaluated against the policy. Hence, the structure of the policy can have significant performance implications. It is beneficial to structure a policy such that as few of the sequences as necessary are evaluated for each flow. For example, if you have a data policy that is only concerned with external applications, you can create the first sequence of the data policy to match all the internal traffic and eliminate it from consideration for the rest of the sequences in the policy (rather than relying on the default action at the end of the data policy).

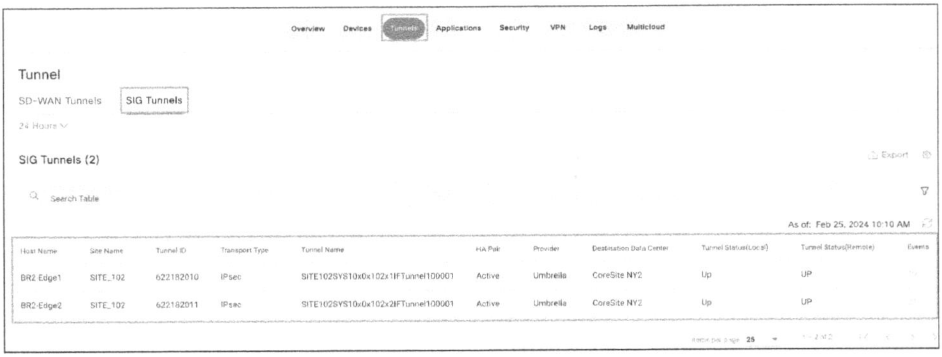

Figure 8-42   *Monitoring the SIG Tunnel from SD-WAN Manager*

While not strictly necessary for this policy in a lab environment, this best practice has been implemented in the policy in Example 8-10 by the first sequence in the policy.

Example 8-10   *SIG Policy*

```
policy
! <<<No changes were made to the control policies, VPN membership policies, or
! the Guest VPN data policies, and they are omitted for brevity.>>>
!
data-policy
_Corporate_Segment_Corporate_DCA_SIG_Guest_Segment_Guest_DIA_Policy
    ! Sequence 1 stops any traffic that is being routed across the fabric from
    ! needing to be processed by any of the rules that are for internet bound
    ! applications.
    sequence 1
     match
      destination-data-prefix-list INTERNAL_ADDRESSES
     !
     action accept
      count INTERNAL_PCKTS_1774762089
     !
    !
    sequence 11
     match
      app-list TRUSTED_APPS
      source-ip 0.0.0.0/0
     !
     action accept
      nat use-vpn 0
      nat fallback
      count CORP_DCA_1774762089
```

```
  !
  !
 sequence 21
  match
   app-list office365_apps
   source-ip 0.0.0.0/0
  !
  action accept
   count CORP_M365_1774762089
   set
    local-tloc-list
     color biz-internet
     encap ipsec
   !
  !
 !
 sequence 31
  match
   app-list Facebook
   source-ip 0.0.0.0/0
  !
  action accept
   count CORP_FACEBOOK_1774762089
   set
    vpn 10
    tloc-list DC_INET_TLOCS
   !
  !
 !
 !
 ! Sequence 41 redirects applications matching the "Google_Apps" list to the SIG
tunnel
 !
 sequence 41
  match
   app-list Google_Apps
   source-ip 0.0.0.0/0
  !
  action accept
   count UMBRELLA_PCKTS_1041684049
   sig
   !
  !
```

```
     !
  default-action accept
 !
 vpn-list Guest_Segment
  ! <<<Output omitted for brevity>>>
  !
 lists
 ! <<<Some lists without changes are omitted for brevity>>>
  !
  !
 ! At SD-WAN Manager some smart default lists are offered,
 ! office365_apps and Google_Apps for example. These two lists contain a myriad of
different applications that are
 ! produced by the two organizations. Custom app-lists can be created to match
 ! only a subset of apps, but the default app-list is used in this example. The
 ! entire list is not displayed for brevity.
  !
  app-list Google_Apps
   app gmail
   app google
   app google_translate
   app gmail_drive
   app gtalk
   app youtube
   app youtube_hd
 ! <<< Omitted for brevity >>>
   !
  app-list TRUSTED_APPS
   app webex-meeting
   app webex_weboffice
   app webex
   !
  app-list office365_apps
 ! <<< Omitted for brevity>>>
   app word_online
   app excel_online
   app onedrive
   app yammer
   app sharepoint
   app ms-office-365
   !
  data-prefix-list INTERNAL_ADDRESSES
   ip-prefix 10.0.0.0/8
```

```
     ip-prefix 172.16.0.0/12
     ip-prefix 192.168.0.0/16


   !
  !
 !
apply-policy
 site-list Europe_Branches
  control-policy Euro_Reg_Mesh_with_FW_MultiTopo out
 !
 site-list BranchOffices
  data-policy
_Corporate_Segment_Corporate_DCA_SIG_Guest_Segment_Guest_DIA_Policy
from-service
  control-policy Branch_Extranet_Route_Leaking in
  vpn-membership vpnMembership_1718052183
 !
 site-list DCs
  control-policy DC_Inbound_Control_Policy in
 !
 site-list North_America_Branches
  control-policy North_America_Reg_Mesh_with_FW out
 !
!
```

Key Topic

Example 8-10 shows the changes that were made to the policy in order to accomplish the objectives of this use case. In sequence 41, packets that match the Google_Apps app list are forwarded to the CDFW with the action **sig**, which enables the service to redirect the specific traffic through the previously established IPsec tunnel. Much as with **nat fallback** in Use Case 11, when SIG integration is used, the Fallback to Routing setting is available, and it specifies that if the local paths to the SIG provider are unavailable, the traffic should not be dropped but should instead follow the routing table forwarding decisions. For additional details and prerequisites, refer to "Cisco Catalyst SD-WAN Security Configuration Guide."

With the policy changes in Example 8-10 applied to the network, you see the results shown in Example 8-11.

Example 8-11 *Validating Redirection to the Secure Internet Gateway Service*

```
BR2-Edge1# show sdwan policy data-policy-filter
data-policy-filter
_Corporate_Segment_Corporate_DCA_SIG_Guest_Segment_Guest_DIA_Policy
 data-policy-vpnlist Guest_Segment
  data-policy-counter default_action_count
```

```
                 packets 0
                 bytes   0
              data-policy-counter GUEST_DIA_PKTS_-1942050084
                 packets 0
                 bytes   0
              data-policy-counter GUEST_DROPPED_PKTS_-1942050084
                 packets 0
                 bytes   0
           data-policy-vpnlist Corporate_Segment
            data-policy-counter CORP_DCA_1774762089
              packets 0
              bytes   0
            data-policy-counter CORP_M365_1774762089
              packets 129941
              bytes   33472283
            data-policy-counter default_action_count
              packets 23303
              bytes   1587839
            data-policy-counter CORP_FACEBOOK_1774762089
              packets 631
              bytes   64413
            data-policy-counter INTERNAL_PCKTS_1774762089
              packets 50
              bytes   5494!
    ! The counters indicate that traffic is being forwarded to the Cisco Umbrella SIG.
    !
    data-policy-counter UMBRELLA_SIG_PCKTS_1774762089
        packets 3086
        bytes   360261
    BR2-Edge1#
```

Example 8-11 shows the use of **show sdwan policy data-policy-filter** to validate that the policy is successfully redirecting traffic to the Cisco Umbrella SIG service.

Key Topic

Figure 8-43 and Figure 8-44 show another good way to get deep insights into the network. These figures show Network Wide Path Insights (NWPI) being leveraged to visualize how traffic from Google apps is forwarded through a SIG tunnel. NWPI provides end-to-end path tracing from SD-WAN Manager, with detailed information from the network level to packet level. For more details, see Chapter 14, "Cisco Catalyst SD-WAN Monitoring and Operations."

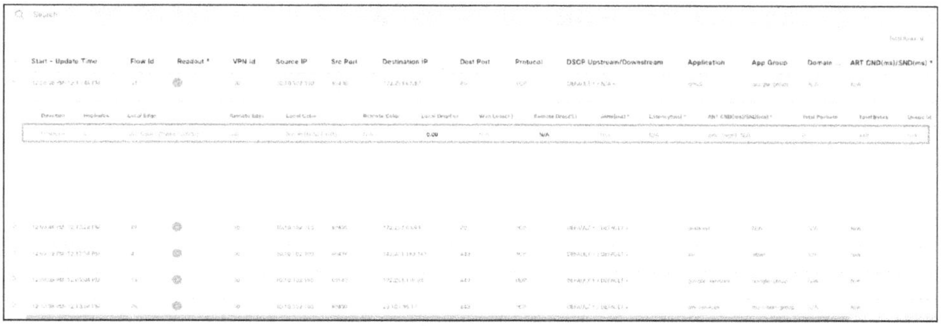

Figure 8-43   *Insight for Gmail from SD-WAN Manager*

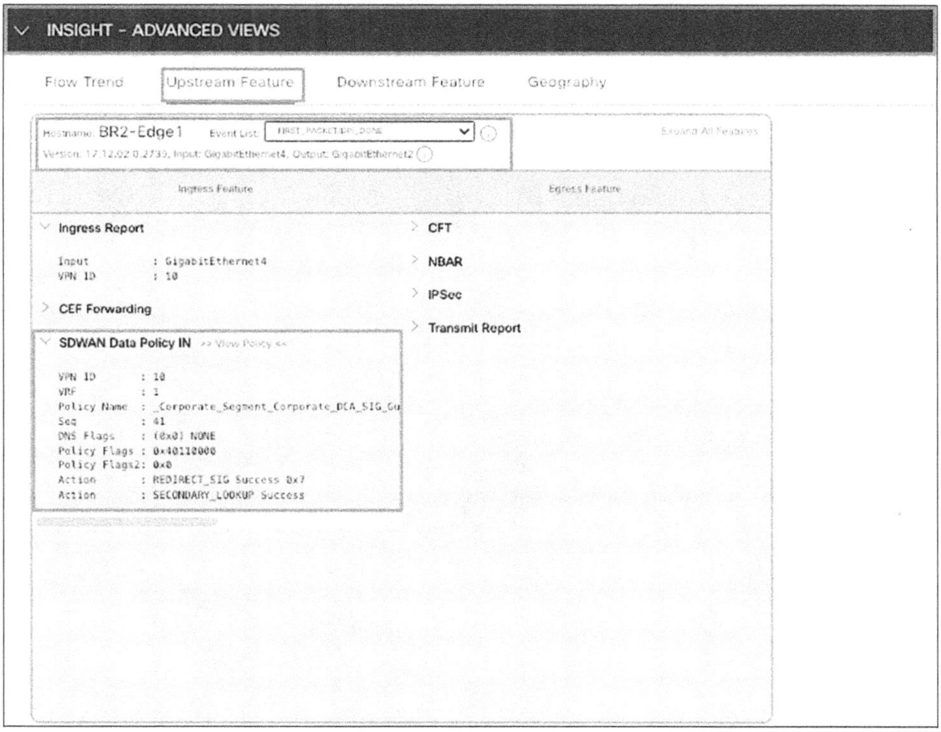

Figure 8-44   *Advanced View Showing a SIG Action for Google Apps*

Protecting Corporate Users with a Secure Internet Gateway Using Policy Groups

As previously discussed, Policy Groups offer a simpler way to implement different traffic policies. In this case, we look at using them to create a tunnel to Cisco Umbrella SIG. This first step in this configuration is adding a name and description for the Secure Internet Gateway policy profile, as shown in Figure 8-45.

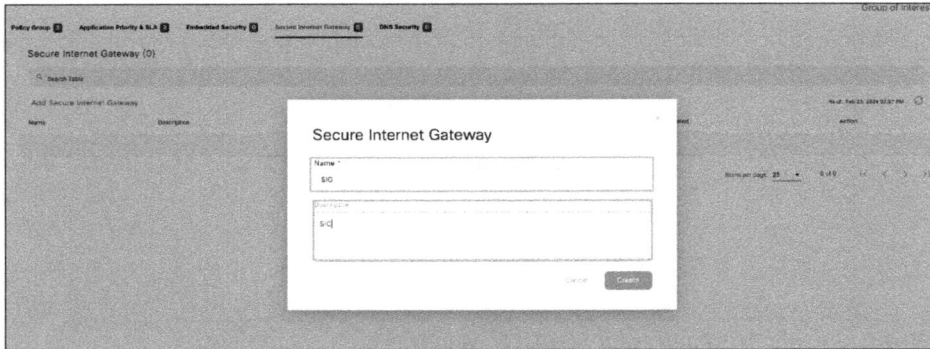

Figure 8-45 *Creating a Secure Internet Gateway Policy Profile*

The next step is to select the SIG provider and provide either the credentials if this is a fresh deployment or the tunnel number and the physical or logical interface where the IPsec tunnel will source from if credentials have been provided before (see Figure 8-46).

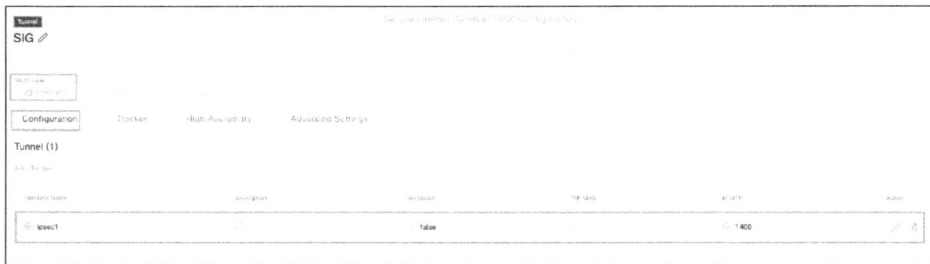

Figure 8-46 *SIG Tunnel Configuration Screen*

A tracker is added by default if the workflow automates the tunnel's creation. An unused private address is requested for this step, but customized trackers can be leveraged as well, as shown in Figure 8-47.

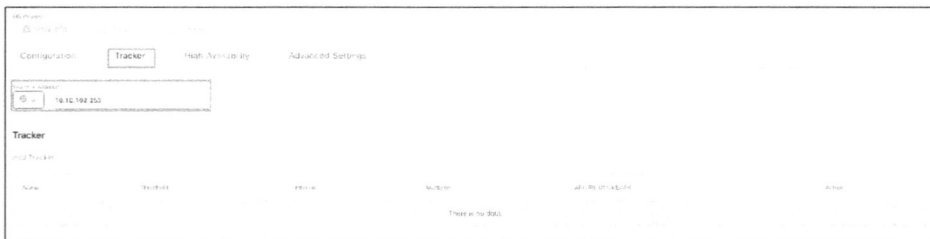

Figure 8-47 *SIG Tunnel Tracker Configuration*

Figure 8-48 shows how active and backup tunnels as well as the weight for each of them can be set. In this case, a single tunnel is configured.

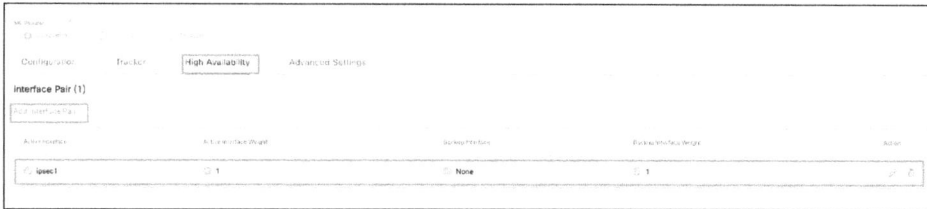

Figure 8-48 *SIG Tunnel Interface Pair Configuration*

Figure 8-49 shows how to allow the user to configure the primary and secondary data centers to send the traffic to. This step is only necessary when location compliance rules apply to an organization or simply when an administrator is seeking predictable behavior.

Figure 8-49 *Advanced Settings for a SIG Tunnel*

As discussed earlier in this chapter, the selection of the policy type, such as SIG, and subsequent deployment to the associated devices is the final step (see Figure 8-50). This configuration deals with tunnel establishment.

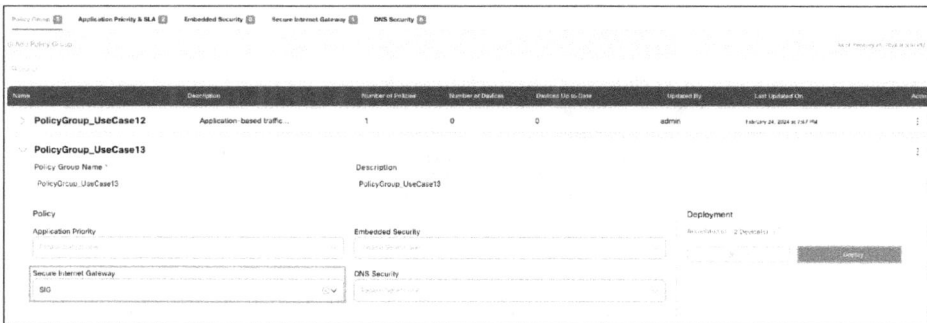

Figure 8-50 *Secure Internet Gateway Policy Deployment*

To complete the configuration, you can add a new sequence to any existing Application Priority & SLA policy associated with the desired WAN Edge devices or create a new policy profile. Figure 8-51 shows Google_Apps also matched and the SIG set to Action so that the traffic is redirected to the SIG provider.

Finally, append both of the components created—the Application Priority & SLA policy and the SIG policy—to the Policy Group and click Deploy to deploy the changes to the associated devices (see Figure 8-52).

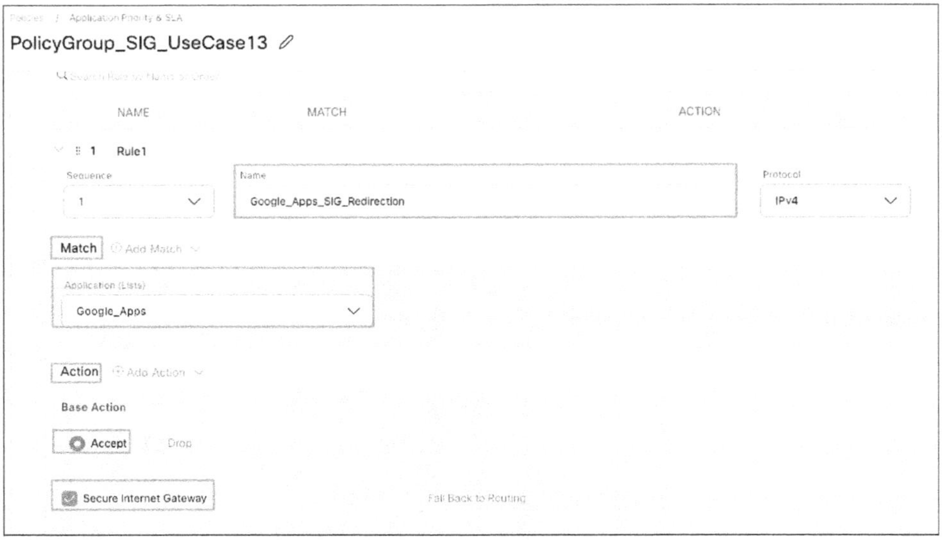

Figure 8-51 *Sequence Rule to Match Google Apps Applications and Redirect Traffic to the SIG Provider*

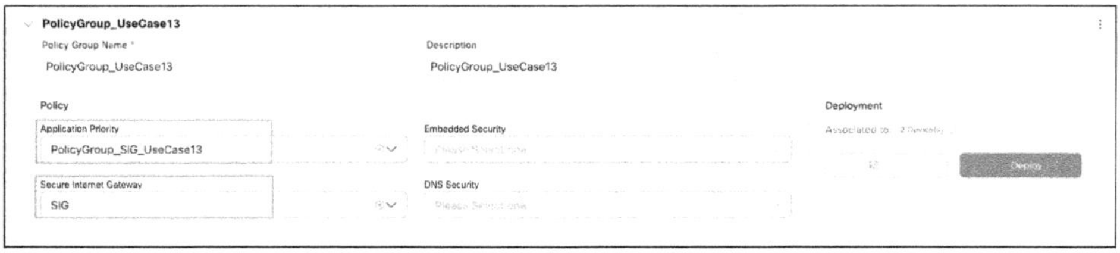

Figure 8-52 *Selecting the Application Priority and SIG Policy Profiles in the Policy Group*

NOTE Both Use Case 12 and Use Case 13 demonstrate methods for directing traffic to the Internet by using the **nat use-vpn 0** and **sig** actions. Cloud OnRamp for SaaS provides a more intelligent and dynamic approach to automating the best-path selection for custom and standard applications requiring Internet access. This functionality is detailed in Chapter 12, "Cisco Catalyst SD-WAN Cloud OnRamp."

Use Case 13 Review

This use case shows traditional as well as policy group approaches to redirecting specific traffic flows to Cisco Umbrella SIG. In environments where direct Internet access is leveraged, security and network administrators prefer some set of threat mitigation mechanisms, and SD-WAN Manager makes it possible to execute such mechanisms in a simple way. Chapter 11 provides detailed information about the configuration of these functions.

Use Case 14: Protecting Applications from Packet Loss

This final use case of the chapter covers several tools that can be used to protect applications from the effects of lossy transport links. IP-based networks, by definition, operate at a best-effort level of packet delivery. There is no mechanism at the IP layer to ensure successful delivery of the packet, regardless of whether the underlying transport is a directly connected cable, a service such as MPLS with a contractually guaranteed SLA, or the public Internet. It is typical for all networks to experience some degree of packet loss, and most applications designed to operate on IP networks are engineered to tolerate some degree of packet loss.

One of the most effective ways to counter the effects of packet loss on underlying transport networks is simply to move sensitive applications off transports that are currently experiencing packet loss. In the Cisco SD-WAN fabric, this function is achieved through application-aware routing policies and is discussed in greater detail in Chapter 9, "Application-Aware Routing Policies." However, there are often circumstances (such as when there is only a single transport link available or when all transport links are currently experiencing some degree of packet loss) when simply moving an application off a lossy transport link is not a viable option. In this use case, you can use two different tools to mitigate the effects of loss: Forward Error Correction and packet duplication.

Forward Error Correction for Audio and Video

Forward Error Correction (FEC) is not a new or novel technology. Different FEC methods have been used with different implementations for decades. The principle behind FEC is that additional information (parity) is transmitted along with the original message so that if a portion of the original message is compromised, the entirety of the original message can be reconstructed. Many commonly used protocols implement some form of FEC at different layers of the networking stack: 40GBASE-T and 100GE Ethernet standards use FEC at Layer 2, and most voice over IP (VoIP) protocols implement some form of FEC at Layer 7. With Catalyst SD-WAN, you can also add FEC to Layer 3 (the network layer).

Figure 8-53 shows the current state of the MPLS transport network on BR2-Edge1. The output indicates that the MPLS network between BR2 and DC1 is currently experiencing 5% to 10% packet loss. This use case shows how to implement FEC in order to mitigate the impact of this lossy transport network on the audio and video applications that the employees are using for collaboration.

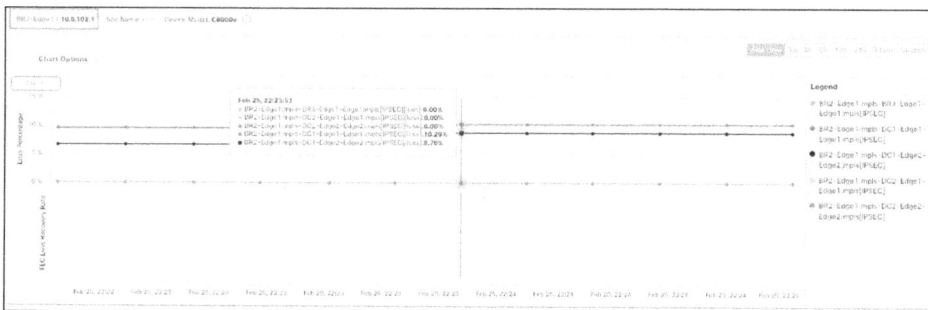

Figure 8-53 *Monitor > Devices > WAN Tunnel Shows the Current Packet Loss Rates*

Key Topic

With Cisco SD-WAN, FEC operates on sets of four packets called a FEC block, as illustrated in Figure 8-54. In the first step, the four packets in an FEC block are processed with a mathematical operation called XOR. The result of this operation is transmitted in the fifth packet, called a parity packet. Each of the packets is encoded with a new FEC header and transmitted to the receiver. If any one of the original four packets is lost in transit to the receiver, as indicated in step 2, but the parity packet is received with the three remaining original packets, the XOR operation is reversed so the lost packet can be reconstructed from the three packets that were received and the parity information that is stored in the fifth packet, as indicated in step 3. If two or more of the five transmitted packets (four data packets and one parity packet) are corrupted or lost, the lost packets cannot be reconstructed, and only the correctly received packets will be forwarded on to the end host. In this circumstance, the end hosts will notice that packet loss has occurred.

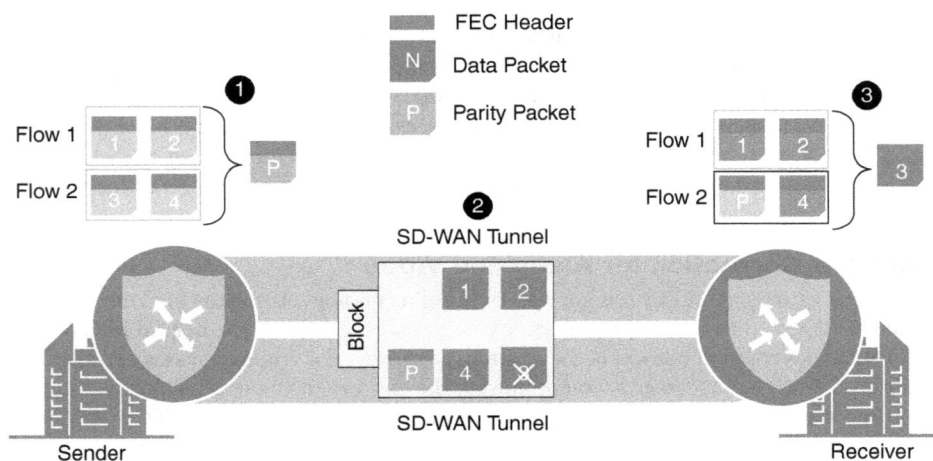

Figure 8-54 *FEC Operation*

The process of sending five packets (four data packets and one parity packet) for every four packets of data being transmitted across the WAN would result in an increase of bandwidth consumption of at least 25% (as the parity packet is as large as the largest data packet out of the set of four in the FEC block). While this increase in bandwidth consumption can be beneficial during times of packet loss on the transport links, it may also be unnecessary during a large portion of the time. In order to optimize this, there are two different FEC configuration modes: FEC-always and FEC-adaptive. FEC-always operates exactly as it sounds like it does: The FEC process takes place unconditionally. FEC-adaptive, on the other hand, operates only when the loss percentage on the transport link is detected to be more than 1%. As of SD-WAN Version 20.12, this threshold value can be configured to anywhere between 1% and 5%.

In order to implement this packet loss minimization policy, you need a new sequence to match on the audio/video application family. Then, we need to enable adaptive FEC in order to provide FEC when the transport packet losses are above 1%. In addition to configuring this on the data policy that is applied to the branch routers, you need to configure a corresponding policy on the data center routers so that the traffic that is being forwarded from the data center to the branch sites is also protected by FEC. This policy also needs to configure the **local-tloc** action in order to pin the traffic to the MPLS transport to better illustrate what is happening with the FEC policy. Example 8-12 shows these configurations.

Example 8-12 *FEC Policy*

```
policy
! <<<No changes were made to the control policies, VPN membership policies, or
! the Guest VPN data policies, and they are omitted for brevity.>>>
!
! Branch Data Policy
!
data-policy _Corporate_Segment_Guest_DIA_FECEnabled_Branch
  vpn-list Corporate_Segment
  ! Sequence 1 matches all of the applications in the Audio / Video App family
  ! and turns on fec-adaptive.
  !
    sequence 1
     match
      app-list AUDIO_VIDEO_APPS
      source-ip 0.0.0.0/0
     !
     action accept
      count CORP_AUDIO_VIDEO_-548650615
      loss-protect fec-adaptive
      loss-protection forward-error-correction adaptive
      set
       local-tloc-list
        color mpls
      !
     !
    !
    sequence 11
     match
      destination-data-prefix-list INTERNAL_ADDRESSES
     !
     action accept
      count INTERNAL_PCKTS_-548650615
     !
    !
    !<<<remaining sequences are unchanged and omitted for brevity>>>
    !
  default-action accept
  !
  vpn-list Guest_Segment
```

```
! <<<Output omitted for brevity>>>
!
! A corresponding policy is also configured on the datacenter routers in order
! to apply the FEC policy to traffic that is being sent from the DC to the Branch
!
data-policy _Corporate_Segment_Guest_DIA_FECEnabled_DC
 vpn-list Corporate_Segment
   sequence 1
    match
     app-list AUDIO_VIDEO_APPS
     source-ip 0.0.0.0/0
     !
     action accept
      count CORP_AUDIO_VIDEO_-431671793
     loss-protect fec-adaptive
     loss-protection forward-error-correction adaptive
      set
       local-tloc-list
        color mpls
      !
     !
    !
  default-action accept
 !
 lists
 ! <<<Some lists without changes are omitted for brevity>>>
 !
  app-list AUDIO_VIDEO_APPS
   app-family audio-video
   app-family audio_video
  !
  !
 !
!
apply-policy
 site-list Europe_Branches
  control-policy Euro_Reg_Mesh_with_FW_MultiTopo out
 !
 site-list BranchOffices
  data-policy _Corporate_Segment_Guest_DIA_FECEnabled_Branch from-service
  control-policy Branch_Extranet_Route_Leaking in
 vpn-membership vpnMembership_373293275
 !
```

```
site-list DCs
 data-policy _Corporate_Segment_Guest_DIA_FECEnabled_DC from-service
 control-policy DC_Inbound_Control_Policy in
 !
site-list North_America_Branches
 control-policy North_America_Reg_Mesh_with_FW out
 !
!
```

Example 8-12 includes the new sequence that was added to the data policy for the branch sites as well as the new policy that was created and applied to the data center sites. You can see the effects of this policy by using the **show sdwan tunnel statistics fec** command, as shown in Example 8-13.

Example 8-13 *Validating FEC Policy from the Command Line*

```
DC1-Edge1# show sdwan tunnel statistics fec | sec 192.168.20.6
tunnel stats ipsec 192.168.20.1 192.168.20.6 12346 12346
 fec-rx-data-pkts      212615
 fec-rx-parity-pkts    52913
 fec-tx-data-pkts      198605
 fec-tx-parity-pkts    49651
 fec-reconstruct-pkts 15496
 fec-capable           true
 fec-dynamic           true
DC1-Edge1#
```

Example 8-13 shows the output from DC1-Edge1, the recipient of the flows from BR2-Edge1. The fec-rx-data-pkts and fec-rx-parity-pkts values are the number of data packets and parity packets, respectively, that have been received by this router. Allowing for slight discrepancies due to the packets that may have been lost in transit, it is notable that approximately 212,615 data packets have been received, which is approximately four times the number of parity packets received (52,913). This is as would be expected since there are four data packets and a single parity packet in each FEC block. The **fec-reconstruct-pkts** value specifies how many packets were able to be recovered based on the received parity packets. The output indicates that there were 15,496 times when at least three, but not four, of the data packets in the FEC block were received by DC1-Edge1. Using the received parity packet, the router was able to reconstruct the missing packets for these blocks, and the end hosts were unaware that any packet loss occurred during the transmission. The ratio of FEC blocks that were able to be reconstructed to the total number of missing packets can also be seen in the SD-WAN Manager GUI at Monitor > Devices > [Device] > WAN - Tunnel. The fec-tx-data-pkts and fec-tx-parity-pkts values specify how many data packets and parity packets, respectively, have been sent to BR2-Edge1.

Packet Duplication for Credit Card Transactions

As Figure 8-55 indicates, while FEC can be effective at dramatically reducing the number of packets that are lost by the end applications, even in the preceding example, there are

8

many times when the loss recovery rate is not 100%. For circumstances in which the utmost effort needs to be made to have zero packet loss, packet duplication may be the appropriate solution.

Key Topic

Figure 8-56 shows WAN Edge devices forwarding traffic flows with a packet duplication policy enabled. For each packet that is forwarded across a tunnel, a duplicate packet is forwarded across a different tunnel between the same pair of WAN Edge routers. The tunnel that is selected to forward the duplicate packet is the tunnel that currently has the lowest rate of packet loss of any of the tunnels between the pair of WAN Edge devices (excluding the tunnel that was used to forward the original packet).

Figure 8-55   *The Current FEC Reconstructs Packets*

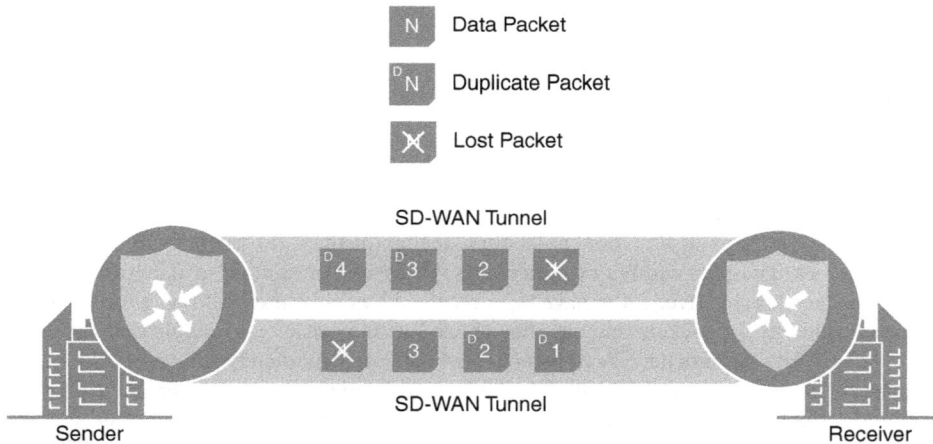

Figure 8-56   *Packet Duplication*

This type of policy is commonly used in retail environments and applied to credit card transactions. Credit card transactions are typically very small flows, but if a packet is lost in transit and is required to be retransmitted, the end-user experience can be slowed down dramatically. For this reason, network administrators find that it may be worth the "price" of transmitting every packet twice in order to ensure that the latency penalty caused by a packet needing to be retransmitted is avoided.

Example 8-14 demonstrates the forwarding conditions between the credit card reader in Branch 2 and the payment server in the data center through the use of Internet Control Message Protocol (ICMP). The current path between these two sites is experiencing more than 3% packet loss.

Example 8-14 *Packet Loss on the PCI Segment Resulting in Slow Credit Card Processing*

```
C:\Users\BR2-PC> ping 10.20.10.1 -1 10000
Pinging 10.20.10.1 with 10000 bytes of data:
Reply from 10.20.10.1: bytes=10000 time=2ms TTL=125
Reply from 10.20.10.1: bytes=10000 time=4ms TTL=125
Request timed out.Request timed out.
Request timed out.Request timed out.

Ping statistics for 10.20.10.1:
    Packets: Sent = 4, Received = 2, Lost = 2 (50% loss),
Approximate round trip times in milli-seconds:
    Minimum = 2ms, Maximum = 4ms, Average = 3ms
C:\Users\BR2-PC>
```

Example 8-15 shows the data policies that are configured on the PCI VPNs in order to perform packet duplication and protect this loss-sensitive traffic. Note that two sequences are configured in both the policy applied to the data center and the policy applied to the branches. One sequence matches traffic with a source address of the payment servers; the other sequence matches the return traffic (traffic with a destination address of the payment servers). Structuring the policy this way enables the policy to be used for both the data center and branch locations simultaneously.

Example 8-15 *Packet Duplication Policy*

```
policy
! <<<No changes were made to the control policies, VPN membership policies,
 ! the Guest VPN or the Corporate VPN data policies, and they are omitted for
 ! brevity.>>>
 !
 data-policy _Corporate_Segment_Guest_DIA_PacketDupEnabled_Branch
 vpn-list Corporate_Segment
  !  <<<Output omitted for brevity>>>
  !
 vpn-list PCI_Segment
   sequence 1
    match
     source-data-prefix-list PAYMENT_SERVERS
    !
    action accept
     count PCI_PCKTS_-1041354892
     set
      local-tloc-list
       color mpls
```

```
        !
      loss-protect pkt-dup
      loss-protection packet-duplication
      !
    !
    sequence 11
     match
      destination-data-prefix-list PAYMENT_SERVERS
      !
     action accept
      count PCI_PCKTS_-1041354892
      set
       local-tloc-list
        color mpls
       !
       loss-protect pkt-dup
       loss-protection packet-duplication
      !
    !
   default-action accept
  !
  vpn-list Guest_Segment
   !  <<<Output omitted for brevity>>>
  !
 data-policy
 _Corporate_Segment_Guest_DIA_PacketDupEnabled_DC vpn-list Corporate_Segment
  !  <<<Output omitted for brevity>>>
  !
  vpn-list PCI_Segment
    sequence 1
     match
        source-data-prefix-list PAYMENT_SERVERS
      !
     action accept
      count PCI_PCKTS_-1041354892
      set
       local-tloc-list
        color mpls
       !
       loss-protect pkt-dup
       loss-protection packet-duplication
      !
```

```
      !
    sequence 11
     match
      destination-data-prefix-list PAYMENT_SERVERS
      !
     action accept
      count PCI_PCKTS_-1041354892
      set
       local-tloc-list
        color mpls
       !
       loss-protect pkt-dup
       loss-protection packet-duplication
      !
     !
  default-action accept
 !
 lists
 ! <<<Some lists without changes are omitted for brevity>>>
  !
  data-prefix-list PAYMENT_SERVERS
   ip-prefix 10.20.10.0/24
   !
  vpn-list PCI_Segment
   vpn 20
   !
  !
 !
apply-policy
 site-list Europe_Branches
  control-policy Euro_Reg_Mesh_with_FW_MultiTopo out
 !
 site-list BranchOffices
  data-policy _Corporate_Segment_Guest_DIA_PacketDupEnabled_Branch from-service
  control-policy Branch_Extranet_Route_Leaking in
  vpn-membership vpnMembership_373293275
 !
 site-list DCs
  data-policy _Corporate_Segment_Guest_DIA_PacketDupEnabled_DC from-service
  control-policy DC_Inbound_Control_Policy in
 !
 site-list North_America_Branches
  control-policy North_America_Reg_Mesh_with_FW out
 !
!
```

8

After the policy in Example 8-15 is applied, the same test is performed again on the credit card reader as was performed in Example 8-14. As Example 8-16 shows, the packet loss has been completely eliminated from the perspective of the end hosts.

Example 8-16 *Results After Packet Duplication Is Applied to the Network*

```
C:\Users\BR2-PC> ping 10.20.10.1 -1 10000
Pinging 10.20.10.1 with 10000 bytes of data:
Reply from 10.20.10.1: bytes=10000 time=2ms TTL=125
Reply from 10.20.10.1: bytes=10000 time=4ms TTL=125
Reply from 10.20.10.1: bytes=10000 time=2ms TTL=125
Reply from 10.20.10.1: bytes=10000 time=4ms TTL=125

Ping statistics for 10.20.10.1:
    Packets: Sent = 4, Received = 4, Lost = 0 (0% loss),
Approximate round trip times in milli-seconds:
    Minimum = 2ms, Maximum = 4ms, Average = 3ms
```

Using the tunnel packet duplication statistics output from the Real Time display on DC1-Edge1, Figure 8-57 shows in the PKTDUP RX column that only 856 of the original 1074 packets were received on the MPLS tunnel. However, because all 1074 duplicated packets were received on the Internet tunnel, as indicated by the output in the PKTDUP RX OTHER column, the value in the PKTDUP RX THIS column is 1074. The PKTDUP RX THIS column reflects the total number of original packets that the WAN Edge router was able to receive from a combination of the primary tunnel and the tunnel forwarding the duplicate packets.

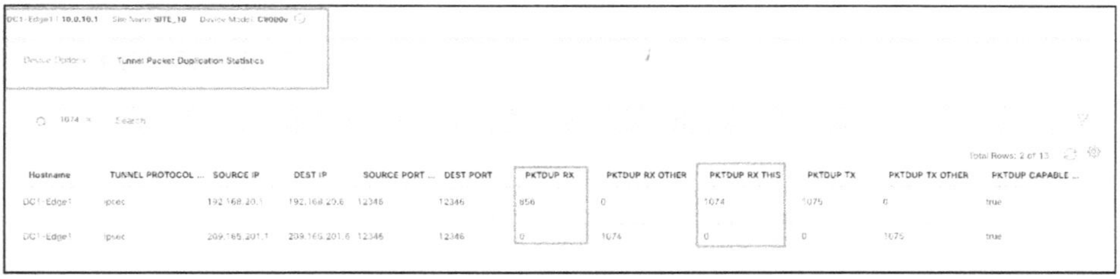

Figure 8-57 *Real-Time Output Showing the Packet Duplication Statistics on DC1-Edge1*

Output in PKTDUP TX and PKTDUP TX OTHER in Figure 8-57 indicates that the 1075 reply packets were also transmitted down the MPLS tunnel and duplicated down the BIZ-INTERNET tunnel. Figure 8-58 shows that packet duplication is doing its job because 1076 packets are being received on both paths. Just as with the DC1-Edge1 router, the 1076 value in PKTDUP RX THIS, which represents the number of original packets received across any transport tunnel and ready to be forwarded to the local end hosts, indicates that no packets were lost in transit for which a duplicate did not successfully arrive.

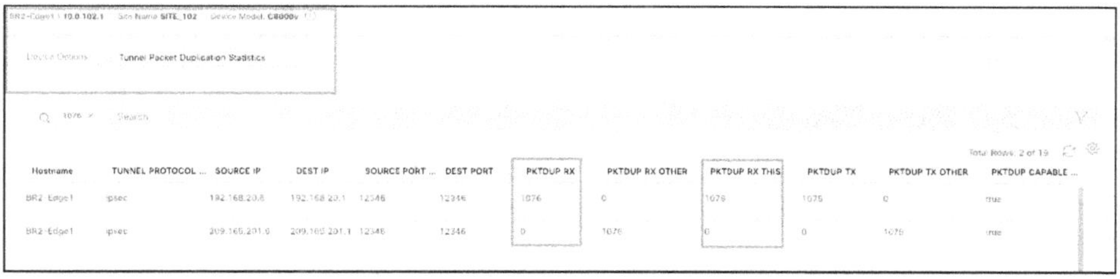

Figure 8-58   *Real-Time Output Showing Packet Duplication Statistics on BR2-Edge1*

The use case makes extensive use of two different data plane features that are designed to protect against packet loss: packet duplication and Forward Error Correction. Other functionalities, such as TCP optimization (TCP-Opt) and Data Redundancy Elimination (DRE), are part of AppQoE and fundamentally address application performance challenges for data packets as they are forwarded through the router.

Network administrators need to keep prerequisites and minimum requirements in mind when planning and designing their AppQoE deployments, and they should always check the release notes for the latest information about which features are supported on which platforms due to resource requirements. For more information, refer to the "Cisco Catalyst SD-WAN AppQoE Configuration Guide."

Use Case 14 Review

This use case explores two different methods for reducing the impact of lossy underlying transport networks on business applications: Forward Error Correction and packet duplication. Chapter 9 discusses another method, Application-Aware Routing, in great detail. Application-Aware routing can also be used to solve similar challenges by moving affected traffic classes off transports that are currently exhibiting packet loss.

Summary

This chapter discusses one of the key types of SD-WAN policies, traditional centralized data policies. It includes several different use cases, focusing on using centralized data policies to make per-application forwarding decisions as well as for direct cloud access, redirecting traffic on a per-application basis toward a Secure Internet Gateway, and mitigating the effects of using lossy transport networks with Forward Error Correction and packet duplication. Some of these use cases look at both the traditional policy approach and using policy groups.

The use cases reviewed in this chapter represent a large cross-section of what centralized data policies can accomplish. There are a plethora of actions not included in the use cases in this chapter, however. Some additional topics that network engineers may be interested in learning more about include quality of service (specifically DSCP marking and remarking), setting the forwarding class on a flow to be matched in a localized policy (for queuing and scheduling purposes, as discussed in Chapter 10), and using traffic policers. Centralized data policies can also be used to generate Cflowd and NetFlow records that can be exported to an external flow collector for monitoring and reporting purposes. More information and configuration examples for all of these topics can be found in the Cisco documentation.

While these use cases represent some of the most common challenges that network engineers need to solve in order to meet business objectives, the tools and techniques discussed throughout this chapter can also be applied and extended in novel ways to solve practically any set of requirements.

Review All Key Topics

Review the most important topics in the chapter, noted with the Key Topic icon in the outer margin of the page. Table 8-1 provides a reference for these key topics and the page numbers on which each is found.

Table 8-1   Key Topics

Key Topic Element	Description	Page
Paragraph, Figure 8-1	Data policy directionality	305
Paragraph	Control policies versus data policies enforced on WAN Edge devices	316
Paragraph	Concatenating data policies	327
Example 8-8	Application traffic engineering behavior with policy in steady state and failed state	336
Paragraph	Centralized control policy enforcement behaviors	343
Paragraph	Behavior of the **sig** and **nat fallback** policy actions	347
Paragraph	Network Wide Path Insights (NWPI) as a tool to gain deep insights into traffic matching in a data policy.	348
Paragraph	FEC block operations	354
Paragraph	WAN Edge forwarding of traffic flows with a packet duplication policy enabled	358
Paragraph	Deployment concerns for the data plane features Forward Error Correction, packet duplication, and APPQOE	363

Define Key Terms

Define the following key terms from this chapter and check your answers in the glossary:

Forward Error Correction, NAT fallback, packet duplication

Chapter Review Questions

1. In a centralized data policy, how do you match all flows?

   a. By using the **match-all** criteria

   b. By not specifying any matching criteria and only configuring the action statements

   c. By using only the default action

2. When the **nat use-vpn** configuration command is used, which VPN is the traffic going to be set to by NAT?

   a. VPN 0

   b. VPN 1

   c. VPN 65535

   d. The VPN specified in the configuration

3. What is the purpose of the **nat fallback** configuration command?

   a. Provides a backup forwarding path in the event that all of the WAN tunnels go down

   b. Provides a backup forwarding path in the event that all of the local interfaces configured with NAT go down

   c. Provides a backup forwarding path in the event that the destination is not reachable via NAT

4. In an SD-WAN Controller configuration, how many data policies can be applied per site?

   a. Zero. Data policies are not applied in an SD-WAN Controller configuration.

   b. One. Each site gets only one data policy.

   c. Two. Each site gets one data policy that is applied to traffic that is originating from the LAN and a second policy that is applied to the traffic that originates from the WAN.

   d. As many as necessary but never more than two per VPN per site.

5. True or false: When the TLOC specified in the **local-tloc** action is not available, the traffic that was matched in the data policy sequence is blackholed.

   a. True

   b. False

6. How many packets are in a single FEC block?

   a. One data packet and one parity packet

   b. One data packet and four parity packets

   c. Two data packets and one parity packet

   d. Four data packets and one parity packet

   e. The value is configurable in the policy.

7. When adaptive FEC data policies are used, what is the loss threshold at which FEC begins to operate?

   a. 0%

   b. 1%

   c. 2%

   d. 5%

   e. The value is configurable in the policy.

8. When packet duplication is configured, which tunnel is used to send the duplicated packets?

   a. The tunnel that is configured in the policy

   b. The least utilized tunnel to the same destination

    c. The same tunnel that the original packets were sent down

    d. The tunnel that is currently experiencing the least amount of packet loss

9. When packet duplication is used, which field indicates the total number of unique packets that have been received?

    a. PKTDUP RX

    b. PKTDUP RX OTHER

    c. PKTDUP RX THIS

    d. PKTDUP TX

    e. PKTDUP TX OTHER

10. True or false: In order to use policy groups, it is a prerequisite to use configuration groups.

    a. True

    b. False

11. When redirecting traffic to a secure Internet gateway, what does the action Fallback to Routing mean?

    a. Drop the traffic when the tunnels are down.

    b. Block the traffic if the tunnels are up.

    c. Follow the routing table to find an alternate path.

12. True or false: AppQoE functions such as TCP optimization and Data Redundancy Elimination (DRE) are available through data policies.

    a. True

    b. False

References

RFC 3871, "Operational Security Requirements for Large Internet Service Provider (ISP) IP Network Infrastructure," https://tools.ietf.org/html/rfc3871.

"Cisco Catalyst SD-WAN Command Reference," https://www.cisco.com/c/en/us/td/docs/routers/sdwan/command/sdwan-cr-book.html.

"Centralized Policy," https://www.cisco.com/c/en/us/td/docs/routers/sdwan/configuration/policies/ios-xe-17/policies-book-xe/centralized-policy.html.

"Configure NAT," https://www.cisco.com/c/en/us/td/docs/routers/sdwan/configuration/nat/nat-book-xe-sdwan/configure-nat.html#nat-dia-tracker.

"Policy Groups Configuration Guide," https://www.cisco.com/c/en/us/td/docs/routers/sdwan/configuration/Policy-Groups/policy-groups/m-policy-groups.html

"Cisco Catalyst SD-WAN Security Configuration Guide," https://www.cisco.com/c/en/us/td/docs/routers/sdwan/configuration/security/ios-xe-17/security-book-xe/m-secure-internet-gateway.html.

"Cisco Catalyst SD-WAN AppQoE Configuration Guide," https://www.cisco.com/c/en/us/td/docs/routers/sdwan/configuration/AppQoE/ios-xe-17/AppQoE-book-xe/m-support-for-multiple-AppQoE-service-nodes.html.

CHAPTER 9

Application-Aware Routing Policies

This chapter covers the following topics:

- **The Business Imperative for Application-Aware Routing:** This section covers the reasons customers choose to use Application-Aware Routing policies.

- **The Mechanics of Traditional App-Route Policies:** This section covers the steps that must be completed in order to use app-route policies.

- **Constructing an App-Route Policy:** This section covers the building blocks of an app-route policy and the process of constructing a simple app-route policy through the SD-WAN Manager GUI.

- **Monitoring Tunnel Performance:** This section covers the process of using BFD to monitor tunnel performance and how tunnel statistics are calculated.

- **Mapping Traffic Flows to a Transport Tunnel:** This section covers the configuration options inside of app-route policy and how those options interact with different transport conditions.

- **Constructing an Application Priority Policy with Policy Groups:** This section describes the use of policy groups to achieve the same purpose as using traditional application-aware routing policies.

- **Enhanced Application-Aware Routing:** This section covers the improvements to application priority policies that EAAR brings.

Building on the discussion of centralized data policies in Chapter 8, "Centralized Data Policies," this chapter focuses on a special type of data policy, the App-Route policy. It is important to note that throughout this chapter, the terms *App-Route* and *Application-Aware Routing (AAR)* are used interchangeably. Application-aware routing enables an organization to move away from high-cost, guaranteed performance transport links such as MPLS and move to commodity Internet circuits while not sacrificing application performance; it also allows organizations to easily diversify the type of transport by mixing transports by monitoring the characteristics of the transport links in real time and then incorporating that information into the routing decision process. Network administrators can use AAR to ensure that their applications are always being forwarded down a path that meets or exceeds the requirements of the application.

The Business Imperative for Application-Aware Routing

One of the key business drivers for many organizations to move to SD-WAN is the ability to replace their existing, expensive legacy transport networks with higher-capacity and less-expensive Internet circuits or simply gain more efficient usage while still using existing transports or a mix of current private transport plus another type, such as broadband, enterprise Direct Internet Access, or cellular. This transition is enabled in part by Cisco Catalyst SD-WAN's capability to continue to provide an assured application experience over transports without an underlying SLA commitment.

By moving away from existing legacy transport networks and toward using the Internet as a transport, many organizations are finding that they can dramatically increase their available bandwidth while at the same time reducing their transport costs. However, there are no guaranteed service levels or service-level agreements (SLAs) on the Internet. Many organizations have relied on their leased-line and MPLS transport providers for assured levels of service. While no solution can guarantee an assured level of service over the Internet, Cisco Catalyst SD-WAN can leverage the benefits of low-cost Internet transports while at the same time using Application-Aware Routing and packet-loss mitigation technologies to bring leased-line benefits to organizations.

By using Application-Aware Routing, network administrators can identify business-critical traffic and specify the required SLA for that traffic class.

When replacing or augmenting existing MPLS transport circuits with Internet-as-a-transport, an organization can establish multiple connectivity paths between its locations. The ability to move to the Internet as a transport while still being able to provide for the required end-user experience enables an enterprise to realize cost savings by using all of its bandwidth in an active/active fashion rather than needing to continue to invest in upgrading circuits.

The Mechanics of Traditional App-Route Policies

There are three key parts to the Application-Aware Routing process:

- **Constructing an App-Route policy:** With the default configuration, traffic is equally load balanced based on tunnel availability, as no app-route policy is in place. Although tunnel performance measurement is enabled by default, these metrics are not yet considered. The first step in Application-Aware Routing is to build an app-route policy, which is a specific type of centralized data policy that has many similarities with the data policies explored in Chapter 8. Constructing such a policy involves defining the necessary lists, building the policy from a sequence of **match** and **action** statements, and activating the policy.

- **Measuring and monitoring the performance of the transport links:** The process of monitoring the performance of the SD-WAN tunnels in real time begins once the WAN Edge router successfully establishes tunnels. When an app-route policy is activated, the WAN Edge device can determine which tunnels are in compliance with the required SLAs. This performance information is gathered from Bidirectional Forwarding Detection (BFD) packets, which are sent automatically across each of the different tunnels created as part of the SD-WAN fabric.

- **Mapping application traffic to a specific transport link:** After the tunnel performance has been determined by BFD packets, these metrics are then evaluated against the configured SLA classes to determine which tunnels are in compliance. Forwarding decisions are then made with respect to these SLA compliance states.

The sections that follow explain each of these steps in more detail.

Constructing an App-Route Policy

The first step in building an app-route policy, just as with the control policies and data policies described in Chapters 7, "Centralized Control Policies," and 8, "Centralized Data Policies," is to define all the lists. As you saw with data policies in Chapter 8, a number of criteria can be used to identify traffic of interest. These include traditional Layer 3 and Layer 4 headers, such as IP addresses, protocols, port numbers, and DSCP markings. Administrators can also match traffic based on the Layer 7 application definitions defined as an application list. To start the configuration, go to **Configuration > Policies** in SD-WAN Manager (formerly vManage). From the **Custom Options** button in the upper-right corner, select **Lists**, as shown in Figure 9-1.

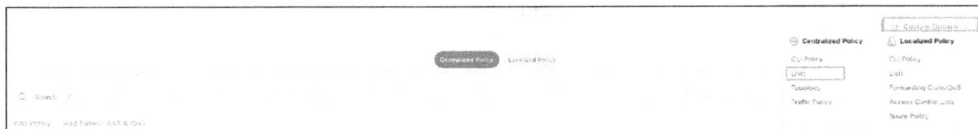

Figure 9-1 *Creating Lists to Use in Policies*

There is a type of list used specifically for app-route policies, called an *SLA class list*. Network administrators use an SLA class list to define the *maximum* permitted latency, loss, or jitter (or a combination of the three values) at a minimum that an application class can tolerate while still maintaining the desired end-user experience. (Other available settings are covered later in this chapter.) If any one of the loss, latency, or jitter values exceeds the configured threshold in the SLA class list, the transport is deemed noncompliant, and the application flow is moved to a different, compliant transport tunnel. In order to be in a compliant state, all three values must be below the configured thresholds. Because some types of traffic, such as real-time voice and video, have much stricter network requirements than other types of traffic, it is common for network administrators to configure multiple SLA class lists. Figure 9-2 shows an example of an SLA class list called CUSTOM_REALTIME_SLA that has been configured for unified communications traffic with a maximum packet loss of 2%, a maximum latency of 100 ms, and a maximum jitter of 30 ms. (The CLI configuration for this and subsequent configuration steps is shown later in the chapter, in Example 9-1.)

NOTE SD-WAN Manager contains a set of smart defaults, including SLA class lists that can simplify SLA definitions. When an organization has special requirements, it can create customized objects.

Once the lists have been defined, the next step in building an app-route policy is to construct the policy from a sequence of **match** and **action** statements. Because an app-route policy is a type of data policy, you configure it by selecting the **Traffic Policy** submenu from **Custom Options**, as shown in Figure 9-3.

Once you are on the **Traffic Policy** Configuration tab, where the **Application-Aware Routing** subtab is selected by default, you can create a new app-route policy by clicking the **Add Policy** button and selecting **Create New**, as shown in Figure 9-4.

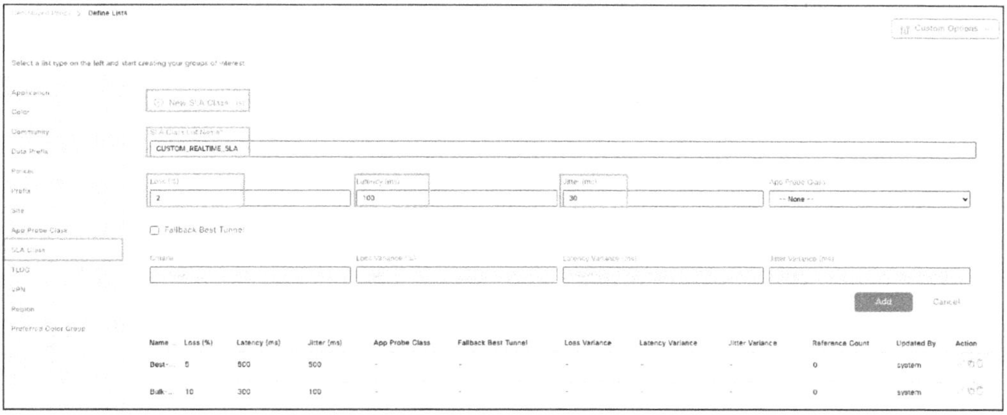

Figure 9-2 *Creating a New SLA Class List*

Figure 9-3 *Opening the Traffic Policy Configuration Menu*

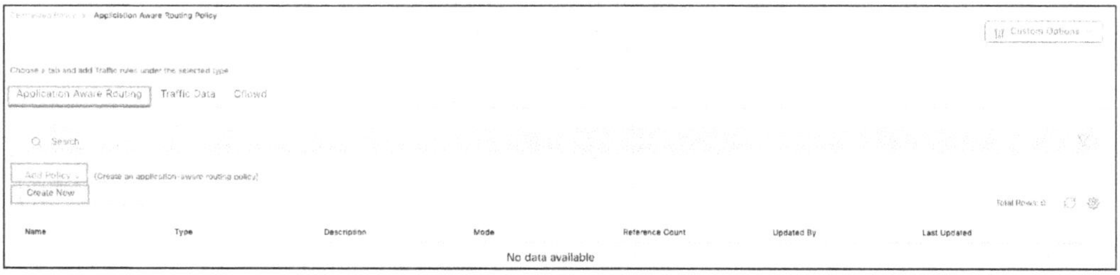

Figure 9-4 *Creating a New Application-Aware Routing Policy*

The process of building an app-route policy is identical to the process used with data policies in Chapter 8. The only notable difference is that different actions are used in an app-route policy. Figure 9-5 shows an app-route policy example with a single sequence rule that matches on traffic marked with DSCP 46 (expedited forwarding). A common approach for administrators when designing AAR policies is to prioritize the most critical applications first and then address the remaining traffic that requires special treatment.

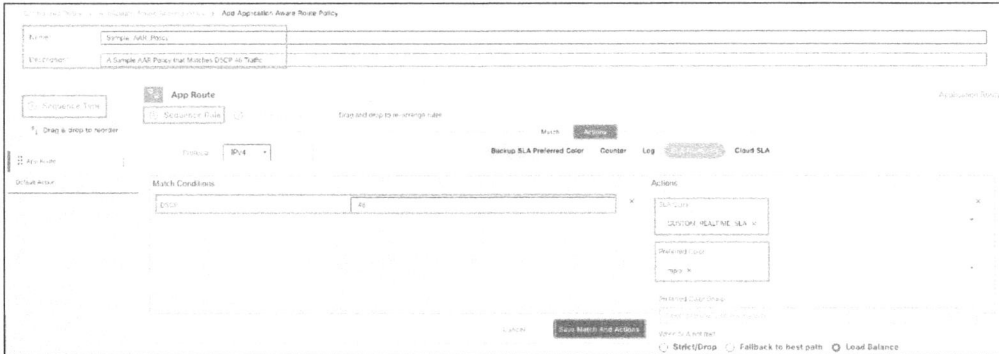

Figure 9-5   *Sample Application-Aware Routing Policy Sequence Rule*

As shown in Figure 9-5, an app-route policy needs to be configured with a name and a description. App-route policies use the same structures of sequence type and sequence rule that are used with centralized control policies and centralized data policies. In the sample policy shown in Figure 9-5, the matching criterion of a DSCP value of 46 is specified. Two fields have been configured in this action: SLA Class and Preferred Color. The primary action taken in an app-route policy sequence is called SLA class in SD-WAN Manager. The SLA Class field references an SLA class list that was previously configured, specifying the maximum permitted loss, latency, and jitter. The Preferred Color field contains the color or colors that the network administrator desires to forward this application class across, as long as the specified color or colors are in compliance with the SLA class.

In this example, the network is configured such that DSCP 46 traffic should be forwarded through the tunnel with the color value mpls, as long as that tunnel is in compliance with the CUSTOM_REALTIME_SLA class. (A further discussion of logic can be found in the following section, "Mapping Traffic Flows to a Transport Tunnel.") Once the configuration is complete, you save the sequence rule by clicking the Save Match and Actions button and save the policy by clicking the Save Application-Aware Routing Policy button.

Finally, all app-route policies need to be applied through a centralized policy. A new centralized policy can be created by selecting **Add Policy** on the Centralized Policy page, as shown in Figure 9-6. You could also import the app-route policy into an existing policy by copying and then editing the policy as described in Chapters 7 and 8. (That process is not reviewed in this chapter.)

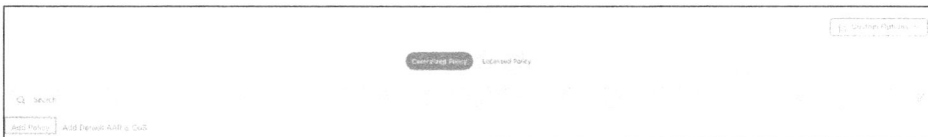

Figure 9-6   *Creating a New Policy with the Centralized Policy Wizard*

Because no additional lists or control policies need to be created for this example, click the **Next** button twice to skip the **Create Groups of Interest** as well **as Configure Topology** and **VPN Membership** tabs and move to the **Configure Traffic Rules** tab, shown in Figure 9-7.

Figure 9-7 *Advancing the Centralized Policy Wizard Through Lists and Control Policies*

On the **Configure Traffic Rules** tab, on the **Application-Aware Routing** subtab, click **Add Policy** and select the **Import Existing** option, as shown in Figure 9-8.

Figure 9-8 *Importing an Application-Aware Routing Policy into a Centralized Policy*

Select the app-route policy that was created previously and click Import in the window. Click the Next button at the bottom of the page to proceed. Figure 9-9 shows these steps.

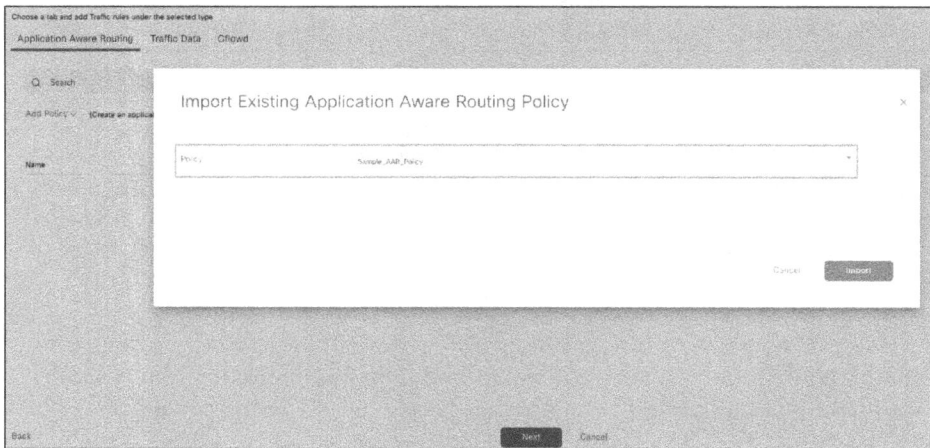

Figure 9-9 *Selecting the App-Route Policy to Import*

The final step in creating the centralized policy is to apply the component policies. First, a name and description must be provided for this policy, as shown in Figure 9-10. In order to apply the app-route policy, select the Application-Aware Routing tab and click the New Site/Region List and VPN List button under the Sample_AAR_Policy policy. You apply this policy to all the data centers and all the branch offices by referencing the site lists created in the previous chapters. Next, specify the VPN or VPNs that the policy is to be applied to. In this case, specify Corporate_Segment, VPN 10 (see Figure 9-10). Finally, click Add to save the policy application for this policy and then click Save Policy, as shown in Figure 9-10, to complete the centralized policy configuration.

Figure 9-10   *Applying an Application-Aware Routing Policy in a Centralized Policy*

NOTE   Because an app-route policy is a type of centralized data policy, it is applied on the SD-WAN Controllers, encoded into an Overlay Management Protocol (OMP) update, and advertised down to the WAN Edge routers where the policies are enforced. Chapter 6, "Introduction to Cisco Catalyst SD-WAN Policies," provides additional details on this process.

As discussed in Chapter 8, data policies can be applied in a specific direction—either from service or from tunnel. App-route policies do not have a direction specified when they are applied. App-route policies are always applied to traffic from service destined to the fabric, as an app-route policy determines which site-to-site tunnel traffic is forwarded across when it is sent out across the WAN. It is important to note that each WAN Edge device independently monitors conditions and performs flow mapping based on the data it gathers. Always ensure that the app-route policy is properly configured for the intended set of devices to avoid traffic asymmetry.

Example 9-1 provides the annotated configuration of the entire sample app-route policy. Just as with the policy examples in Chapters 7 and 8, the full CLI configuration for a policy created from SD-WAN Manager is available by selecting Preview in the Centralized Policy page.

For the remainder of this chapter, AAR policy examples are presented as configuration snippets for brevity and for illustration. As with all other Cisco Catalyst SD-WAN policies, the configuration can be performed either via the SD-WAN Manager GUI or from the command line. As stated in earlier chapters, to set up centralized policies, SD-WAN Controllers must be managed by SD-WAN Manager (that is, they must have a template attached). The GUI is generally the preferred method for ease of use.

Example 9-1 *Sample App-Route Policy*

```
policy
! The SLA Class that specifies the required tunnel performance
  sla-class CUSTOM_REALTIME_SLA
   latency 100
   loss 2
   jitter 30
  !
! The AAR policy that is composed of 'match' and 'action' sequence rules
app-route-policy _Corporate_Segment_Sample_AAR_Policy
 vpn-list Corporate_Segment
   sequence 1
     match
      dscp 46
       source-ip 0.0.0.0/0
      !
! The sla-class action specifies the SLA Class and the preferred colors
     action
      sla-class CUSTOM_REALTIME_SLA  preferred-color mpls
     !
    !
  !
! Additional lists used within the policy. In this case, these lists are used
! when the policy is applied.
 lists
  site-list BranchOffices
   site-id 100-199
  !
  site-list DCs
   site-id 10-50
  !
  vpn-list Corporate_Segment
   vpn 10
  !
 !
!
! The AAR policy is applied to selected Site Lists and VPN Lists.
! Note: There is no directionality to this policy.
apply-policy
 site-list DCs
 app-route-policy _Corporate_Segment_Sample_AAR_Policy
 !
 site-list BranchOffices
 app-route-policy _Corporate_Segment_Sample_AAR_Policy
 !
!
```

9

Monitoring Tunnel Performance

The Bidirectional Forwarding Detection (BFD) protocol is used to monitor the real-time condition of the underlying transport network. BFD packets are initiated by each router across every tunnel that is brought up as part of the Cisco Catalyst SD-WAN fabric and serve two different purposes: liveliness detection and path quality monitoring. BFD packets are echoed bidirectionally across each tunnel and, therefore, active BFD neighbors are not formed across the SD-WAN fabric. Figure 9-11 illustrates this process.

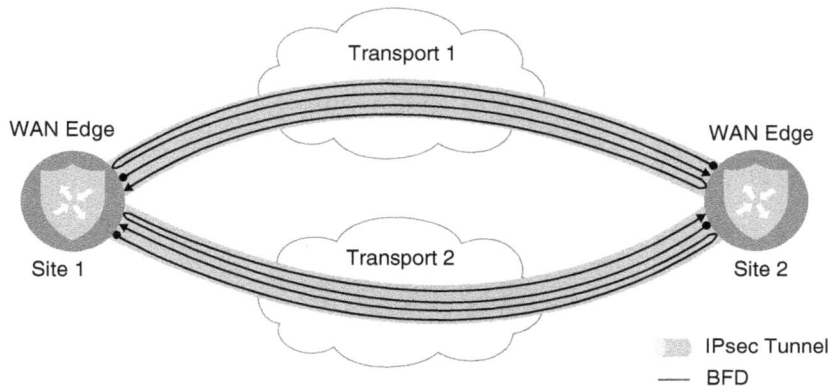

Figure 9-11 *BFD Packets in the SD-WAN Fabric*

As shown in Figure 9-11, each router initiates a BFD packet on each tunnel. When the packet is received by the router at the far end of the tunnel, it is echoed back to the originating router. The configuration parameters for BFD probes are set in the BFD feature template and are referenced in the individual device templates. In this way, different routers can have different BFD settings.

Liveliness Detection

There are several configurable options inside the BFD feature template, as shown in Figure 9-12.

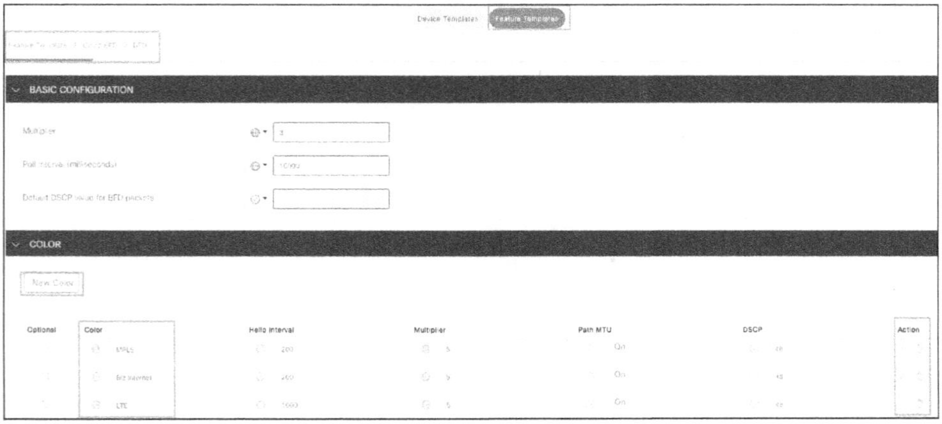

Figure 9-12 *BFD Feature Template*

The two sections of the BFD template are the Basic Configuration section and the Color section. The Basic Configuration section has the configuration elements related to application-aware routing and is discussed later in this chapter. The Color section contains four settings: per-color Hello Interval, Multiplier, Path MTU, and DSCP. As shown in Figure 9-12, these settings allow you to have different values for different colors, which means you can configure different settings for different transport links. A common design choice is to have more aggressive BFD timers on wired connections and more conservative timers on metered ones.

Hello Interval

The hello interval specifies how frequently a BFD probe will be sent across a given tunnel. The default value for this timer is once per second, and the value is specified in milliseconds (ms). In Figure 9-12, the hello interval for the MPLS and Biz-Internet colors is set to 200 ms. The hello interval for the LTE color is set to 1000 ms.

When different devices have different BFD timers configured for the same tunnel, BFD negotiates to use the greater of the two values. Figure 9-13 shows one example where this negotiation behavior is beneficial. Many times, WAN Edge routers use different colors at each end of an SD-WAN tunnel. This commonly occurs when transports such as LTE are used to connect to the Biz-Internet TLOCs at other branches or the Biz-Internet TLOCs at the data center, where the LTE TLOC may not be configured at all. In these circumstances, having the tunnels that use the LTE TLOCs (at either end of the tunnel) use the slower timers would help to conserve LTE bandwidth, and at the same time it would ensure that the tunnels that are running completely on the wireline TLOCs continue to use the more aggressive timers.

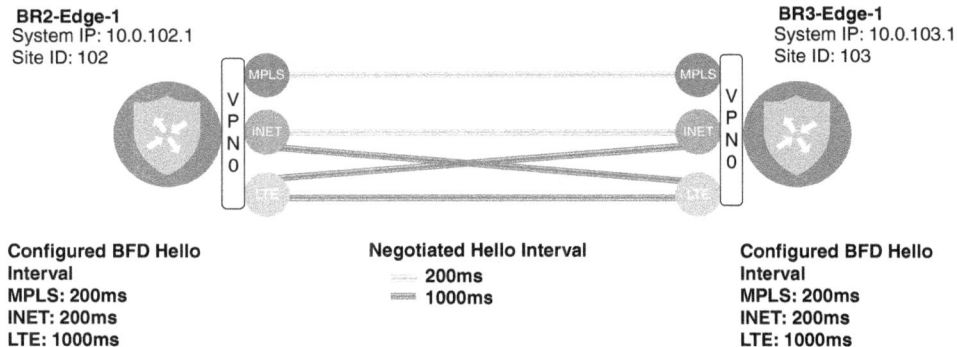

BR2-Edge-1
System IP: 10.0.102.1
Site ID: 102

BR3-Edge-1
System IP: 10.0.103.1
Site ID: 103

Configured BFD Hello
Interval
MPLS: 200ms
INET: 200ms
LTE: 1000ms

Negotiated Hello Interval
  200ms
  1000ms

Configured BFD Hello
Interval
MPLS: 200ms
INET: 200ms
LTE: 1000ms

Figure 9-13 *BFD Hello Interval Negotiation*

Figure 9-13 shows a scenario where the WAN Edges negotiate to use the greater of the two configured BFD hello intervals for an SD-WAN tunnel. After the configuration shown in the BFD feature template in Figure 9-12 is applied, this effect can be seen by using the real-time output of BR2-Edge1, as shown in Figure 9-14.

Figure 9-14 shows that the BFD sessions between these two WAN Edge routers are being negotiated to the greater of the two configured values. In the first row in the table, the tunnel that originates on the Biz-Internet TLOC (configured with a hello interval of 200 ms), destined to the remote router's Biz-Internet TLOC, is operating with a Tx interval (the negotiated hello interval) of 200 ms. In the second row in the table, the tunnel that originates from the same TLOC but that is destined for the LTE TLOC at the far end of the tunnel has a Tx interval of 1000 ms.

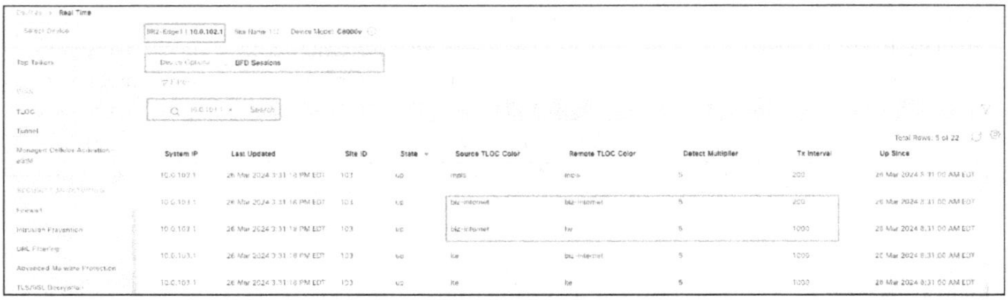

Figure 9-14   *Effects of BFD Hello Interval Negotiation*

Multiplier

The multiplier value specifies how many consecutive BFD probes can be lost before the tunnel is declared to be down. This feature forms the basis of liveliness detection and is useful for detecting things such as indirect fiber cuts, where the physical interface remains in an up state but no traffic can be sent across a link. In circumstances where the transport interface state changes from up to down, there is no need to wait for the multiplier to expire because the tunnel is immediately set to down, and the corresponding routes are withdrawn. The default multiplier value is 7, and in Figure 9-12, the value has been changed to 5.

Figure 9-15 illustrates the relationships between the hello interval, the hello multiplier, and the amount of time it takes to detect a circuit failure for the values configured for the MPLS color in Figure 9-12.

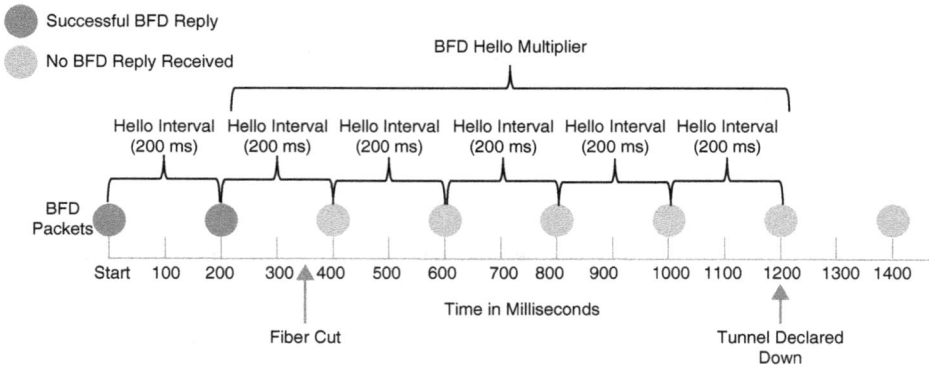

Figure 9-15   *BFD Path Liveliness Detection*

As Figure 9-15 illustrates, with a configured hello interval of 200 ms and a configured hello multiplier of 5, it would take approximately 1000 ms to detect an indirect circuit failure. With the default Hello Interval of 1 second (1000 ms) and the default multiplier of 7, it is possible that it would take the SD-WAN solution 7 seconds (1 packet per second × 7 packets) to detect an indirect circuit failure. (Later in this section, you will learn more information about and recommendations for setting these timers.)

Two additional settings are available on the Color tab. The first is Path MTU Discovery (PMTUD), which is enabled by default and helps a device negotiate MTU on the transport connection. The second is the DSCP decimal value of control traffic (48), which BFD packets have by default, but if there is a requirement to set a different value to match the service provider scheme or simply determine the quality of service (QoS) queue the BFD echo request will be queued in, this decimal value can be adjusted.

Path Quality Monitoring

In addition to being used for liveliness detection, BFD packets are used to monitor the performance and quality of each of the transport paths. These settings, including the app-route multiplier and the app-route poll interval, are shown in the Basic Configuration section of Figure 9-12. As indicated in Figure 9-12, the poll interval and the multiplier are per-device settings; there is only one app-route polling interval and only one app-route multiplier setting for each WAN Edge router.

App-Route Poll Interval

The app-route poll interval is a period of time for which the WAN Edge router will calculate the loss, latency, and jitter for each tunnel, using the BFD packets sent during that interval. App-route poll intervals are occasionally referred to as "buckets" because they represent the statistics from a collection of individual BFD packets. The WAN Edge routers calculate or recalculate each tunnel's SLA compliance and proceed to forward packets in accordance with the configured app-route policies until the end of the next app-route poll interval, when the cycle repeats.

Figure 9-16 illustrates a sample poll interval with a duration of 10 seconds, where BFD packets are sent every 1 second.

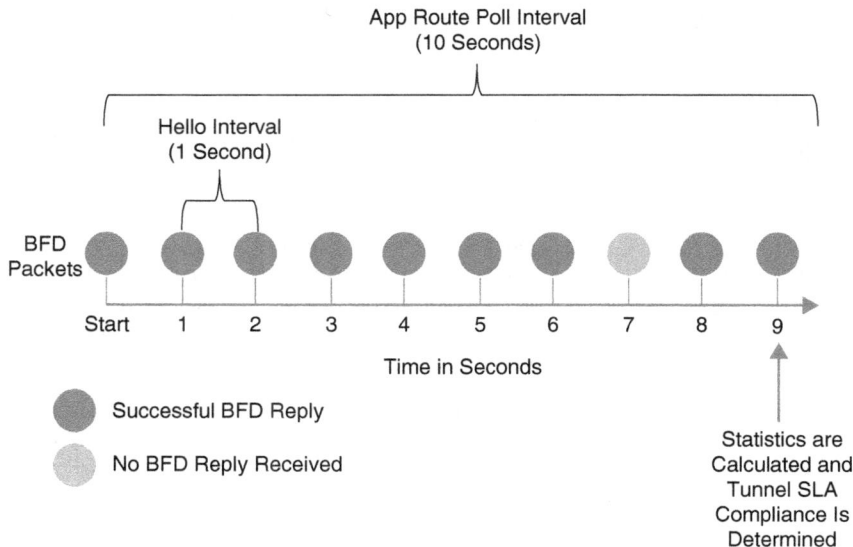

Figure 9-16 *App-Route Poll Interval Illustration*

As shown in Figure 9-16, the app-route poll interval is the period of time for which statistics are calculated from the BFD packets sent during that window. The number of BFD packets and, thus, the sample size for that statistical calculation are not explicitly configured but instead are derived from the combination of the length of the hello interval and the length of the app-route poll interval.

Expanding the example shown in Figure 9-16 further, we can use the data in Table 9-1 to calculate the loss, latency, and jitter during the app-route poll interval.

Table 9-1 Individual BFD Packets During an App-Route Poll Interval

BFD Packet	Received/Lost	Round-Trip Time
1	Received	10 ms
2	Received	11 ms
3	Received	13 ms
4	Received	11 ms
5	Received	10 ms
6	Received	11 ms
7	Received	10 ms
8	Lost	N/A
9	Received	12 ms
10	Received	11 ms

At the end of each app-route poll interval, the app-route statistics are calculated from the BFD packets sent during that interval. Using the data in Table 9-1, the packet loss percentage is calculated from the percentage of BFD packets successfully echoed back to the originating router. The latency is calculated to be 11 ms via the arithmetic mean of the round-trip time for all of the samples where a reply was received ((10 + 11 + 13 + 11 + 10 + 11 + 10 + 12 + 11) / 9). The jitter is calculated to be 1 ms by finding the mean of the absolute value of the difference in the round-trip time ((1 + 2 + 2 + 1 + 1 + 1 + 2 + 1) / 8) (see Table 9-2).

Table 9-2 BFD Statistics Calculated After an App-Route Poll Interval

App-Route Poll Interval	Loss Percentage	Latency	Jitter
0	10%	11 ms	1 ms

Key Topic

Figure 9-16 and Table 9-2 illustrate a key concept about the app-route poll interval and BFD hello interval: It is important to ensure that there are enough BFD probes in a particular poll interval to generate statistically significant results. In this particular example, there might have been only 0.05% packet loss, but because a single BFD probe was lost, and that probe represented 10% of all of the probes, the packet loss is recorded as 10%.

When the values in Table 9-2 are compared against the CUSTOM_REALTIME_SLA class list that was configured in Figure 9-2 and Example 9-1, it is clear that the current loss percentage, 10%, exceeds the configured threshold of 2%. Therefore, the determination would be made at the end of the app-route poll interval that this path would be out of compliance with the CUSTOM_REALTIME_SLA class list at this point in time. Traffic is not rerouted based on a single app-route poll interval; the total number of app-route multipliers must be completed before a determination can be made.

App-Route Multiplier

The app-route multiplier specifies how many polling intervals of previously collected BFD probes to consider when calculating tunnel SLA compliance. This can be thought of as how many different "buckets" are evaluated when looking at circuit performance. The maximum configuration value and the default value of the app-route multiplier are 6. The configuration shown in Figure 9-10 uses an app-route multiplier of 3. In other words, the statistics from a maximum of three different buckets will be considered when calculating tunnel performance. Continuing on with the previous example, Table 9-3 illustrates the app-route statistics after the completion of a second app-route poll interval.

Table 9-3   BFD Statistics from Multiple App-Route Poll Intervals

App-Route Poll Interval	Loss Percentage	Latency	Jitter
0	0%	10 ms	1 ms
1	10%	11 ms	1 ms

The original statistics from the first app-route poll interval, Interval 0, are moved down the table to the second row (Interval 1). The new values for tunnel performance are calculated by averaging the values from each of the app-route poll intervals in Table 9-3:

- Packet loss = 5%

- Latency = 10 ms

- Jitter = 1 ms

Figure 9-17 illustrates these app-route poll intervals and the subsequent calculations to determine compliance with the SLA class that occurs at the end of each app-route poll interval. As discussed previously, at time A, the circuit would be out of compliance with the SLA class because it experienced 10% packet loss. Because only a single app-route poll interval had elapsed, the statistics gathered during this interval are the only statistics available.

At time B, two different app-route poll intervals have elapsed. While there was no packet loss in the second interval, the 10% loss from the first interval caused the average packet loss to be 5% and, thus, the circuit still exceeded the SLA class requirement of 2%.

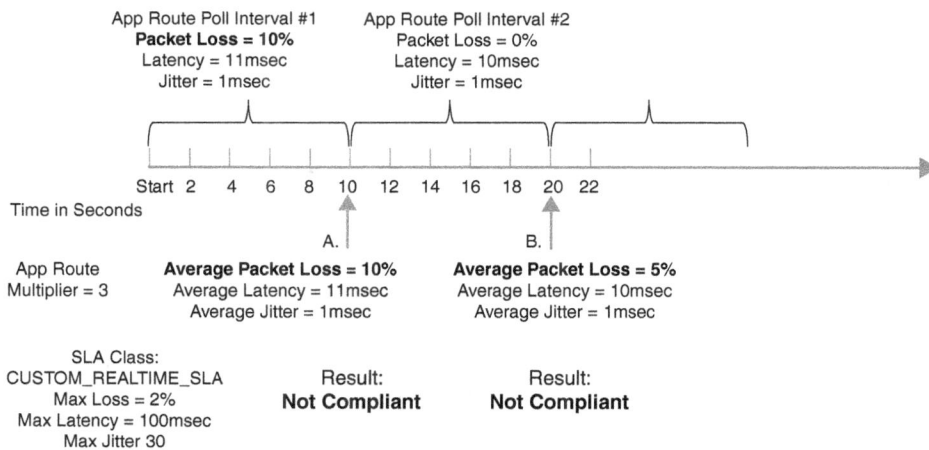

Figure 9-17   *SLA Calculations with Two App-Route Poll Intervals*

After two more app-route poll interval periods have elapsed, the data in Table 9-4 is used to calculate the SLA statistics.

Table 9-4   BFD Statistics from Four App-Route Poll Intervals

App-Route Poll Interval	Loss Percentage	Latency	Jitter
0	0%	200 ms	25 ms
1	0%	11 ms	0 ms
2	0%	10 ms	1 ms
3 (Aged out values)	10%	11 ms	1 ms

Note in Figure 9-17 that the original statistics from the first example gathered in Table 9-2 are now shaded. Because the configured app-route multiplier value is 3, only statistics from the three most recent buckets will be considered for the tunnel performance calculation, but these initial values have aged out of the table and are no longer considered. From the remaining three values, the following averages are calculated:

- Packet loss = 0%

- Latency = 73 ms

- Jitter = 8 ms

Building on Figure 9-17, Figure 9-18 illustrates what happens after the conclusion of the next two app-route poll intervals, at times C and D.

At time C, three intervals have elapsed. Even though there has been no additional packet loss, the average packet loss across all three app-route poll intervals is 3% and remains out of compliance. If only the three first intervals were present at this point in time, the decision to move traffic is made because three poll intervals have happened, which is equal to the multiplier number.

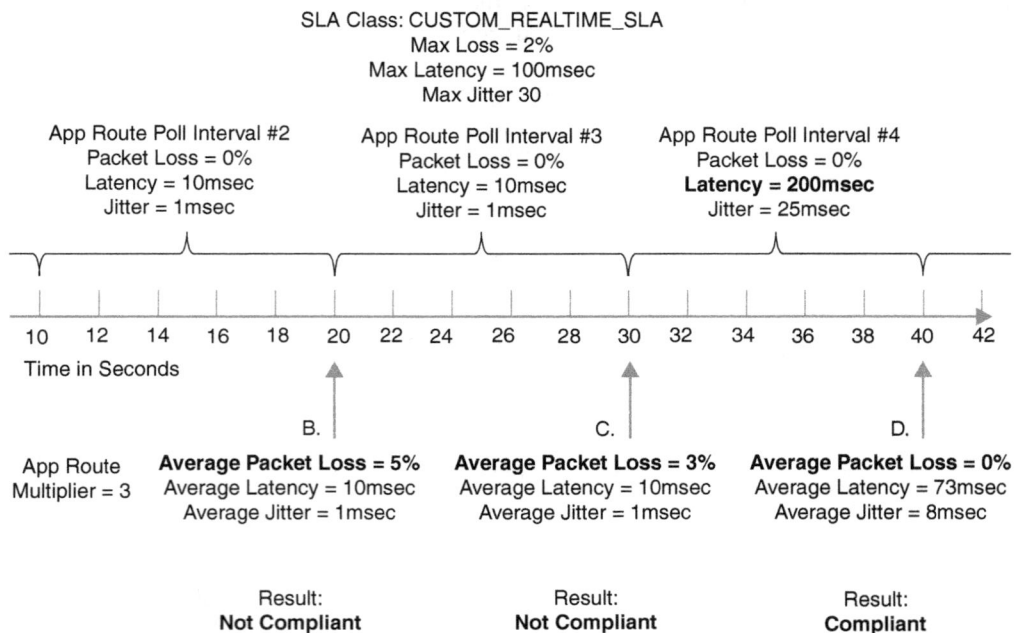

Figure 9-18   *SLA Calculations with Multiple App-Route Poll Intervals*

At time D, the first app-route poll interval is no longer taken into account because the app-route multiplier is configured as 3. Therefore, the first interval where the packet loss was experienced is not included in the average, and the packet loss average is now calculated as 0%.

If the app-route multiplier had been configured to 1 instead of the current value of 3, then only the statistics from Poll Interval #2 would have been taken into account at time B, and the transport would have been compliant with the SLA class because the packet loss during Poll Interval #2 was 0%. The same is true at time C: If the only poll interval considered had been Poll Interval #3, the transport would have been considered compliant. In this way, the app-route multiplier functions as a hold-down timer and prevents excessive flapping of application flows between SD-WAN paths that would otherwise be caused by transient events in the underlying transport network.

Greater app-route multipliers allow for more poll intervals and, therefore, longer periods of time to be considered when calculating compliance with SLA classes. At the same time, the opposite effect can also happen: When the latency in Poll Interval #4 spikes to 200 ms, while this value is above the threshold of 100 ms stated in the SLA class, the value is averaged with the values from the two previous app-route poll intervals. The average value of these three intervals (73 ms) is below the 100 ms threshold; therefore, this circuit will be treated as compliant for the time being. Network administrators can configure both the length of the app-route poll interval and the app-route multiplier to tune the amount of historical performance to consider when evaluating SLA compliance. Those BFD packets are marked as control traffic (DSCP 48), as mentioned earlier, and there is an option to change this value at the global level.

NOTE   SLA metrics based on the high-priority DSCP 48 (CS6), traveling in the low-latency queue, may not reflect the priority that will be received by the actual data that flows through the edge device. Depending on the application class, data can potentially go out with different DSCP values and receive a different treatment from the underlying network (MPLS). In such scenarios, the app-probe class is valuable for determining the QoS queue where the BFD echo request will be queued at the egress tunnel port, providing more accurate health measurements from the local queue.

You configure the app-probe class under **Configuration > Policies > Custom Options > Lists > App Probe Class** and can refer to this class in the sla-class construct.

Key Topic

SLA compliance is only reevaluated at the end of the app-route poll interval. Other than moving a tunnel to the down state because of an interface state change or a failure to receive a hello packet within the hello multiplier, changes to the condition of a circuit will only be evaluated at the end of the app-route poll interval. Hello intervals, app-route poll intervals, and app-route multipliers need to be configured to ensure that the network is responsive enough to changes in network conditions while also having enough BFD data to gather statistically meaningful metrics. While faster BFD hellos and more aggressive timers may make the network react to brownouts more quickly, they can increase the susceptibility to false positives. This results in traffic moving from tunnel to tunnel unnecessarily, device scalability degradation and, thus, a potentially higher administrative burden for the team operating the network. Enhanced Application-Aware Routing (EAAR) has been developed to address the issues presented by traditional AAR's inappropriate timer settings. This function is analyzed later in this chapter.

9

NOTE   While the specific design objectives and topologies for an SD-WAN deployment are unique to each individual enterprise, the following settings are a reasonable starting place for many organizations:

- App-route polling interval: 120,000 ms (2 min)
- App-route multiplier: 5
- Hello interval: 1000 ms (1 s)
- Hello multiplier: 7

When these values are considered together, the WAN Edge routers will be able to detect and respond to indirect transport interruptions after 7 seconds (1000 ms per BFD hello interval × 7 packets). Individual tunnels will be evaluated for compliance with the SLA classes once every 2 minutes, and that compliance will be based on the last 10 minutes of data (2 minutes per polling interval × 5 intervals). Each polling interval will have data from 120 BFD packets (120,000 ms polling interval / 1000 ms hello interval). The higher the number of BFD packets in each polling interval, the better the loss, latency, and jitter statistics will be at truly representing the performance of the underlying transport.

Mapping Traffic Flows to a Transport Tunnel

So far, we have examined the calculation of packet loss, latency, and jitter on a per-tunnel basis. The ultimate goal of the Application-Aware Routing process is to map a network data flow to a specific transport tunnel. However, determining which tunnel should forward a specific flow is initially done by performing the necessary lookup in the traditional routing table. If and only if there are multiple equal-cost matches in the routing table, the app-route policy is evaluated to make a forwarding decision.

Packet Forwarding with Application-Aware Routing Policies

This section continues to use the sample network that was used throughout Chapters 7 and 8. Specifically, in this chapter, we will be looking at flows that are originating in Branch 2 (10.10.102.0/24) and destined to Branch 3 (10.10.103.0/24). The validation work and **show** commands that will be undertaken will occur on BR2-Edge1. Figure 9-19 shows the relevant excerpt of this topology.

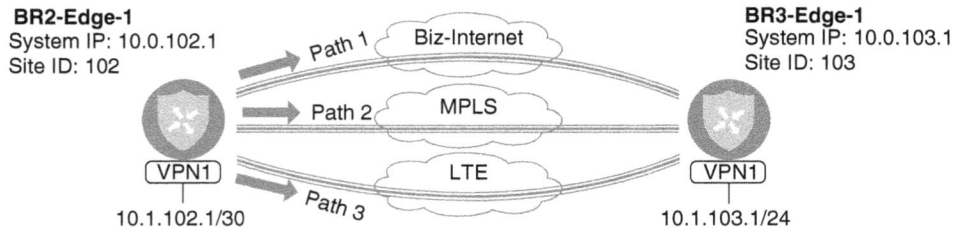

BR2-Edge-1
System IP: 10.0.102.1
Site ID: 102

Path 1   Biz-Internet
Path 2   MPLS
Path 3   LTE

BR3-Edge-1
System IP: 10.0.103.1
Site ID: 103

VPN1
10.1.102.1/30

VPN1
10.1.103.1/24

Figure 9-19   *Application-Aware Routing Network Topology*

Traditional Lookup in the Routing Table

Using the topology in Figure 9-19, we can now consider how app-route policies affect how flows are mapped to transport tunnels. The first step in the process is to perform a normal routing lookup in the routing table.

The routing table is always considered prior to the evaluation of any app-route policies. If there is more than one equal-cost route for the destination in the routing table, the app-route policy will be evaluated in order to potentially select one or more paths from the paths in the table. If there is only one OMP best path installed in the table, and there are not multiple equal-cost routes, the traffic will be forwarded according to the only route in the routing table, and the app-route policy will not be considered. Application-aware routing policies are only used to choose between multiple equal best paths in the routing table.

As shown in Example 9-2, the WAN Edge router has three different paths to the 10.10.103.0/24 segment at Branch 3 installed in the routing table. Note that each of the routes has the status set to C,I,R, indicating that these routes have been selected and installed into the forwarding information base (FIB). In addition, this output displays the TLOC color for each of the routes. In Figure 9-19, you can see that there is one route across the MPLS connection, one across the Biz-Internet connection, and one across the LTE connection.

Example 9-2 *Equal-Cost Paths Installed in the Routing Table*

```
BR2-Edge1# sh sdwan omp routes vpn 10 10.10.103.0/24 detail

<<<Output omitted for brevity>>>
          RECEIVED FROM:
peer              1.1.1.102
path-id           1
label             1003
status            C,I,R
loss-reason       not set
lost-to-peer      not set
lost-to-path-id   not set
   Attributes:
    originator        10.0.103.1
    type              installed
    tloc              10.0.103.1, mpls, ipsec
<<<Output omitted for brevity>>>
          RECEIVED FROM:
peer              1.1.1.102
path-id           2
label             1003
status            C,I,R
loss-reason       not set
lost-to-peer      not set
lost-to-path-id   not set
```

```
      Attributes:
       originator      10.0.103.1
       type            installed
       tloc            10.0.103.1, biz-internet, ipsec
      <<<Output omitted for brevity>>>
            RECEIVED FROM:
peer            1.1.1.102
path-id         3
label           1003
status          C,I,R
loss-reason     not set
lost-to-peer    not set
lost-to-path-id not set
      Attributes:
       originator      10.0.103.1
       type            installed
       tloc            10.0.103.1, lte, ipsec
<<<Output omitted for brevity>>>
```

SLA Class Action

If a prefix has multiple equal-cost matches in the routing table and an application-aware routing policy has been created that matches the specific traffic class, the SLA class action is evaluated. Next, we are using an extended version of the policy from Example 9-1. The full policy can be displayed on the SD-WAN Controller using the **show running-config policy** command, as shown in Example 9-3.

Example 9-3 *Expanded Application-Aware Routing Policy*

```
vSmart-1# show running-config policy
policy
 sla-class Bulk-Data
  jitter 100
  latency 300
  loss 10
 !
sla-class CUSTOM_REALTIME_SLA
  latency 100
  loss 2
  jitter 30
 !
sla-class Voice-And-Video
  jitter 30
  latency 45
  loss 2
```

```
 !
 app-route-policy _Corporate_Segment_Sample_AAR_Expanded
  vpn-list Corporate_Segment
   sequence 1
    match
     source-ip 0.0.0.0/0
     dscp      46
     !
     action
      sla-class CUSTOM_REALTIME_SLA preferred-color mpls
      backup-sla-preferred-color mpls
     !
    !
   sequence 11
    match
     source-ip 0.0.0.0/0
     app-list  REAL_TIME_APPS
     !
     action
      sla-class CUSTOM_REALTIME_SLA strict preferred-color mpls
     !
    !
   sequence 21
    match
     source-ip 0.0.0.0/0
     app-list  TRUSTED_APPS
     !
     action
      sla-class Voice-And-Video preferred-color biz-internet mpls
     !
    !
   sequence 31
    match
source-ip 0.0.0.0/0
     dscp 8

 !
     action
      sla-class Bulk-Data preferred-color biz-internet
     !
    !
  !
lists
  vpn-list Corporate_Segment
   vpn 10
   !
```

9

```
      app-list REAL_TIME_APPS
       app rtp
       app sccp
       app sip
       app sip_soap
       app skinny
       app uaudp_rtp
      !
      app-list TRUSTED_APPS
       app webex
       app webex-app-sharing
       app webex-audio
       app webex-control
       app webex-media
       app webex-meeting
       app webex_weboffice
      !
      site-list BranchOffices
       site-id 100-199
      !
      site-list DCs
       site-id 10-50
      !
     !
    !
   apply-policy
    site-list BranchOffices
     app-route-policy _Corporate_Segment_Sample_AAR_Policy_Expanded
    !
    site-list DCs
     app-route-policy _Corporate_Segment_Sample_AAR_Policy_Expanded
    !
   !
   vSmart-1#
```

Two new SLA class lists have been added to the configuration of this policy: the Voice-And-Video and Bulk-Data Class lists.

Key Topic

Reevaluating every tunnel on the WAN Edge router after every poll interval is a CPU- and memory-intensive task. Therefore, WAN Edge router models can scale from 6 to a maximum of 15 different user-configurable SLA class lists, starting from SD-WAN Release 17.6. Refer to the "Cisco Catalyst SD-WAN Policies Configuration Guide" for further details on hardware resource requirements.

Several additional sequences have also been added to this app-route policy. Each of them is a structured sequence of **match** and **action** statements. These sequence rules are configured with the **sla-class** action. Each **sla-class** action references one of the configured sla-class lists (in this example, CUSTOM_REALTIME_SLA, CRITICAL_DATA_SLA, or BULK_DATA_SLA), and it lists the preferred TLOC color(s). The tunnels matching the preferred color(s), as specified in the SLA class action, are evaluated against the requirements of the SLA class. If one or more of the preferred colors are in compliance with the SLA class, then that is the color(s) that will be used to forward traffic.

In sequence 1 of the aforementioned policies, the traffic marked with a DSCP value of 46 is configured with the action sla-class CUSTOM_REALTIME_SLA preferred color **mpls**. This configuration should be interpreted to mean that the traffic class, DSCP 46, needs a transport that meets the requirements of the CUSTOM_REALTIME_SLA list. If a tunnel with the color **mpls** can meet that requirement, it will be used to forward the traffic. You can see the process at the CLI by using the commands shown in Example 9-4.

Example 9-4 *Observing Tunnel Compliance with Configured SLA Classes*

```
BR2-Edge1# show sdwan app-route sla-class
                                                     APP PROBE
INDEX NAME              LOSS  LATENCY  JITTER  CLASS ID  APP PROBE CLASS   FALLBACK BEST TUNNEL
-----------------------------------------------------------------------------------------------
0     __all_tunnels__    0     0        0       0         None              None
1     Bulk-Data          10    300      100     0         None              None
2     CUSTOM_REALTIME_SLA 2    100      30      0         None              None
3     Voice-And-Video    2     45       30      0         None              None

BR2-Edge1# show sdwan app-route stats local-color mpls remote-system-ip 10.0.103.1
app-route statistics 192.168.20.6 192.168.20.8 ipsec 12346 12426
 remote-system-ip          10.0.103.1
 local-color               mpls
 remote-color              mpls
 sla-class-index           0,1,2,3
 fallback-sla-class-index None
 enhanced-app-route        Disabled
 sla-dampening-index       None
<<<output omitted for brevity>>>
!Within device dashboard, under Realtime 'App Routes Statistics' command could offer
the same information from GUI
BR2-Edge1#
```

As shown in Example 9-4, the sla-class-index for the CUSTOM_REALTIME_SLA class is 2. You can use the **show sdwan app-route stats** command to see which SLA classes a particular tunnel is compliant with. Because the MPLS tunnel is compliant with the SLA class, and the **mpls** color is configured in the app-route policy as the preferred color, traffic marked with DSCP 46 will be forwarded across this tunnel.

This can also be validated with the Simulate Flows troubleshooting tool in SD-WAN Manager (see Figure 9-20).

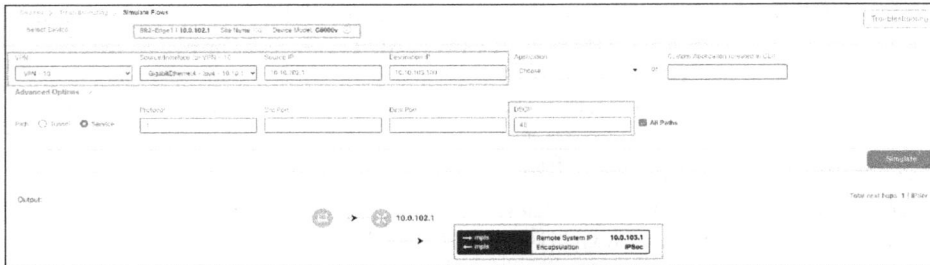

Figure 9-20   *Validating MPLS TLOC in Compliance Status Using Simulate Flows Tool*

Continuing on with the **sla-class CUSTOM_REALTIME_SLA preferred-color mpls** command and sequence 1 from the policy in Example 9-3, if the **mpls** color is out of compliance and other colors are in compliance, the traffic will be forwarded over those tunnels. You can see this at the CLI by using the **show sdwan app-route stats** command (see Example 9-5).

Example 9-5   *Observing Tunnel Compliance with the Preferred Color Out of Compliance*

```
BR2-Edge1# show sdwan app-route stats remote-system-ip 10.0.103.1
app-route statistics 192.168.20.6 192.168.20.8 ipsec 12346 12426
 remote-system-ip        10.0.103.1
 local-color             mpls
 remote-color            mpls
 sla-class-index         0
fallback-sla-class-index None
 enhanced-app-route      Disabled
 sla-dampening-index     None
 app-probe-class-list None
  mean-loss     20.000
  mean-latency 400
  mean-jitter   0
  interval 0
   total-packets     661
   loss              149
   average-latency   400
   average-jitter    0
   tx-data-pkts      0
   rx-data-pkts      0
   ipv6-tx-data-pkts 0
   ipv6-rx-data-pkts 0
  interval 1
   total-packets     661
   loss              133
   average-latency   400
   average-jitter    0
   tx-data-pkts      0
   rx-data-pkts      0
```

```
    ipv6-tx-data-pkts 0
    ipv6-rx-data-pkts 0
!... Intervals 2 to 5 are removed for brevity
<<<Output omitted for brevity>>>

app-route statistics 209.165.201.6 209.165.201.8 ipsec 12346 12426
 remote-system-ip 10.0.103.1
 local-color      biz-internet
 remote-color     biz-internet
 sla-class-index  0,1,2,3
<<<Output omitted for brevity>>>

app-route statistics 209.165.202.130 209.165.201.8 ipsec 12346 12426
 remote-system-ip 10.0.103.1
 local-color      lte
 remote-color     lte
   sla-class-index     0,1,2,3
<<<Output omitted for brevity>>>
BR2-Edge1#
```

As Example 9-5 shows, the Biz-Internet and LTE tunnels are still listed as being in compliance with SLA class index 3 (CUSTOM_REALTIME_SLA), but the MPLS tunnel is only compliant with the DEFAULT SLA class, index 0 (__all_tunnels__). This is caused by the 20% mean packet loss and 400 ms mean latency on the MPLS tunnel. In this situation, DSCP 46 traffic will be forwarded across the Biz-Internet and LTE tunnels, as shown in Figure 9-21.

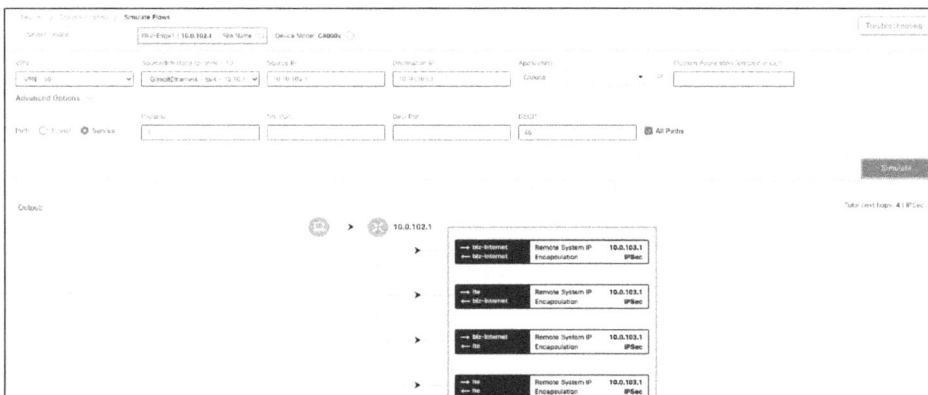

Figure 9-21   *Validating MPLS TLOC Out of Compliance Status Using Simulate Flows Tool*

Figure 9-21, which was created using the same criteria as Figure 9-20, illustrates that when the preferred color is not in compliance with the configured SLA class, all the available equal-cost tunnels that are in compliance with the SLA class will be used. In this case, there are four different tunnels. (The LTE TLOC is also building a tunnel to the receiving router's Biz-Internet TLOC and vice versa.)

In the examples up to this point, the **preferred-color [color]** command has only specified a single color as the preferred color. However, administrators are able to configure multiple colors as arguments to this command. This functionality is demonstrated in sequence 21 of the app-route policy shown in Example 9-3: **sla-class Voice-And-Video preferred-color biz-internet mpls**. In the case of multiple preferred colors, where multiple colors are in compliance, the traffic will be load-shared on a per-flow basis. In the case that multiple preferred colors are specified but only a single color is compliant, the traffic class will be forwarded across that color.

Key Topic

In instances where more than one color is needed to adhere to a specific order due to the administrator's preference to prioritize based on reliability or other criteria, the preferred-color-group feature is highly beneficial. This feature provides up to three tiers of preference. Initially, the creation of a preferred color group is necessary, and this can be achieved by navigating to **Configuration > Policies** and selecting **Preferred Color Group** under **Custom Options**. Preferred color group list creation is illustrated in Figure 9-22. In this configuration, the three designated colors are defined for primary, secondary, and tertiary transports. The only mandatory color value in a group is the primary color.

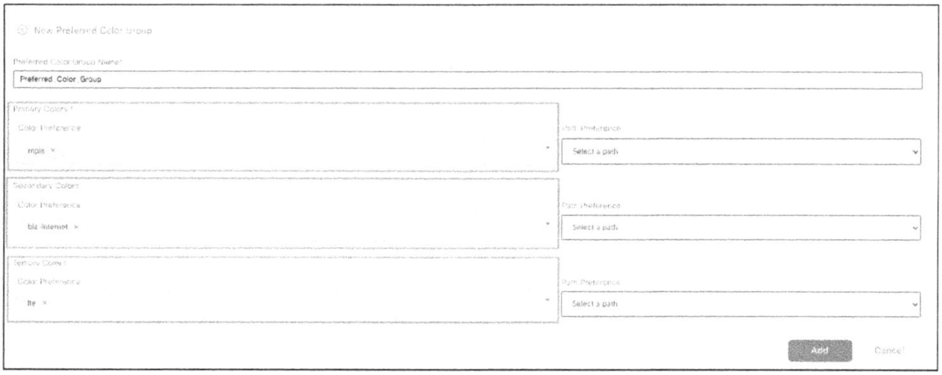

Figure 9-22   *Preferred Color Group List with **mpls**, **biz-internet**, and **lte** Colors*

The second step is the selection of the preferred color group within the policy sequence, as shown in Figure 9-23.

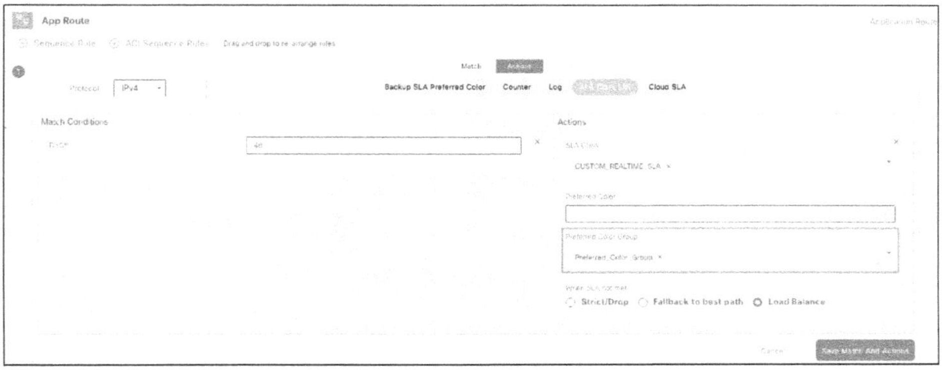

Figure 9-23   *Preferred Color Group Setting in the Policy Sequence*

As with Example 9-5, when none of the preferred colors is compliant with the SLA require-ments, the traffic is forwarded across any of the nonpreferred colors that are compliant with the SLA class. Another variation of this configuration is where the SLA class action is speci-fied but no preferred color is specified. In this case, the traffic is load-shared per flow among all the colors that meet the required SLA.

The last permutation to consider is the behavior of the **sla-class** command when none of the TLOCs meet the required SLA, as demonstrated in Example 9-6.

Example 9-6 *Observing Tunnel Compliance with All Colors Out of Compliance*

```
BR2-Edge1# show sdwan app-route stats remote-system-ip 10.0.103.1 | i app|sla|col
app-route statistics 192.168.20.6 192.168.20.8 ipsec 12346 12426
  local-color               mpls
  remote-color              mpls
  sla-class-index           0
<<<Output omitted for brevity>>>
app-route statistics 209.165.201.6 209.165.201.8 ipsec 12346 12426
  local-color               biz-internet
  remote-color              biz-internet
  sla-class-index           0
<<<Output omitted for brevity>>>
app-route statistics 209.165.201.6 209.165.202.132 ipsec 12346 12426
  local-color               biz-internet
  remote-color              lte
  sla-class-index           0
<<<Output omitted for brevity>>>
app-route statistics 209.165.202.130 209.165.201.8 ipsec 12346 12426
  local-color               lte
  remote-color              biz-internet
  sla-class-index           0
<<<Output omitted for brevity>>>
app-route statistics 209.165.202.130 209.165.202.132 ipsec 12346 12426
  local-color               lte
  remote-color              lte
  sla-class-index           0
<<<Output omitted for brevity>>>
BR2-Edge1#
```

When all of the tunnels are out of compliance with the configured SLA class, as in Example 9-6, several different configuration options dictate the forwarding behavior. In the simplest use case, shown in sequence 31 of Example 9-7, when there are no further configured actions beyond the sla-class action, the traffic is load-shared across all available transports.

Example 9-7   *Configuration Options When SLA Class Cannot Be Honored*

```
vSmart-1# show running-config policy
<<< Omitted for Brevity>>>
app-route-policy Corporate_Segment_Sample_AAR_Expanded
  vpn-list Corporate_Segment
    sequence 1
     match
      source-ip 0.0.0.0/0
      dscp     46
     !
     action
! When the backup-sla-preferred-color command is supplied, traffic is forwarded
! across that color or colors if no colors can meet the required SLA
      sla-class CUSTOM_REALTIME_SLA preferred-color mpls
       backup-sla-preferred-color mpls
    !
   !
    sequence 11
     match
      source-ip 0.0.0.0/0
      app-list  REAL_TIME_APPS
     !
     action
! When the strict command is supplied, traffic is forwarded across the
! preferred color if the preferred color is able to meet the SLA.  If the
! preferred color does not meet the SLA, but any other color does, the
! traffic will be forwarded on that tunnel.  If there are no colors that
! meet the required SLA, the traffic is dropped.
      sla-class CUSTOM_REALTIME_SLA strict preferred-color mpls
     !
<<< Omitted for Brevity>>>
   !
    sequence 31
     match
      dscp     8
      source-ip 0.0.0.0/0
     !
     action
! When no other arguments are configured, and no colors meet the SLA, then the
! traffic is load shared per flow across all available paths.  This functionality
! is equivalent to not having an app-route policy configured.
      sla-class Bulk-Data preferred-color biz-internet
  !
```

Some alternative configurations can be used in the event that none of the tunnels is able to meet the configured SLA: **backup-sla-preferred-color**, **strict**, and **fallback-to-best-path**.

One option when SLA is not met is the **backup-sla-preferred-color** action, which specifies the color that the traffic should be forwarded across in the event that none of the colors is able to support the required SLA class. Sequence 1 in Example 9-7 illustrates the use of the **backup-sla-preferred-color** configuration option. While it might look strange at first glance to have the **mpls** color specified as both **preferred-color** and **backup-sla-preferred-color**, this is a rational and commonly used configuration choice. This configuration should be understood as follows:

- If the MPLS tunnel meets the required SLA, then forward the traffic on the MPLS tunnel.

- If the MPLS tunnel does not meet the required SLA but some other tunnels do, then forward the traffic on the tunnels that meet the SLA.

- If no tunnels meet the required SLA, then forward the traffic on the MPLS tunnel.

Sequence 1 in Example 9-7 allows for the transmission of sensitive, real-time communications flows over the MPLS path, where there is an SLA agreement with the carrier, as long as that transport is performing to the required SLA. If the MPLS path is failing to meet the SLA but some other transport is able to meet the SLA, this sensitive traffic class is forwarded over that path. In the event that no transports are able to meet the required SLAs (and the network administrators are having a *really bad day*), the sensitive traffic classes are transported over the MPLS path where there is a contractual SLA with the carrier, and hopefully service will be restored soon.

Another option when SLA is not met is the **strict** command, as shown in sequence 11 of Example 9-7. The **strict** option specifies that if no colors are available that meet the required SLA class, the traffic should be dropped instead of forwarded. The **backup-preferred-color** and **strict** options are mutually exclusive and cannot be used in the same sequence rule.

NOTE   Although **strict** may be useful for specific applications, such as SCADA networks, where timely delivery of monitoring traffic is critical, its nature of dropping traffic makes it an uncommon option among customers.

Although you might want to pin traffic to specific transport even when no tunnels meet the required SLA, as explained with the use of **backup-sla-preferred-color**, or simply drop the traffic, as discussed with **strict** setting, certain applications can benefit from selecting the least noncompliant alternative; for these cases, **fallback-to-best-path** is a great option. Two steps are required to use this mechanism:

Step 1.   Enable the **Fallback Best Tunnel** parameter in the SLA Class List(s) under **Configuration > Policies > Custom Options**. Figure 9-24 shows the Latency Variance set to 5 ms in CUSTOM_REALTIME_SLA.

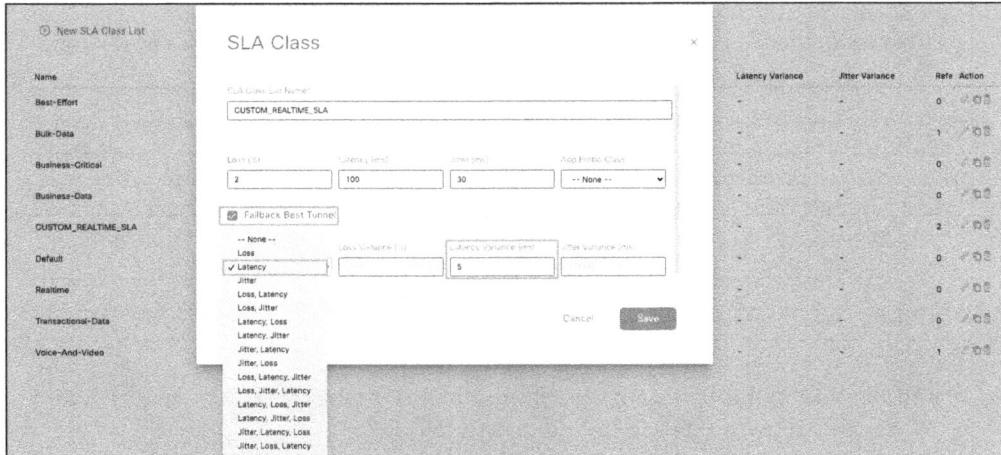

Figure 9-24 *Setting Fallback Best Tunnel with Latency Variance*

NOTE This chapter was written using Cisco SD-WAN Release 20.12, and with this version, 16 possible options are available as variance criteria for the Fallback Best Tunnel function (see Figure 9-24).

Variance denotes the extent of deviation in loss, latency, jitter, or a combination of these metrics that a tunnel can tolerate to still qualify as the superior tunnel among those that do not meet the SLA class.

Step 2. Enable the **Fallback to Best Path** setting inside the policy sequence rule, as shown in Figure 9-25.

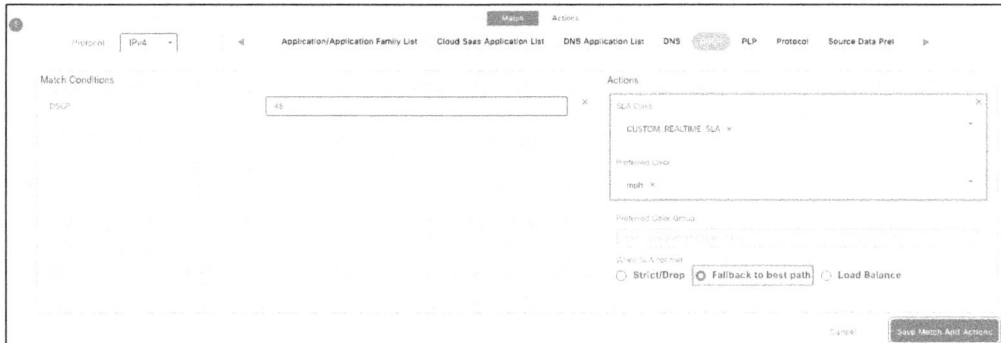

Figure 9-25 *Setting Fallback to Best Path in the Action Policy Sequence*

The best of worst logic described here is leveraged to find the healthiest tunnel from among the noncompliant tunnels for the SLA class requirements. Some examples are shown in sequences 1 and 21 of Example 9-8.

Example 9-8 *Configuration Options When the SLA Class Cannot Be Honored*

```
vSmart-1# show running-config policy
<<<Output omitted for brevity>>>
sla-class CUSTOM_REALTIME_SLA
  loss     2
  latency 100
  jitter  30
  fallback-best-tunnel
   criteria           latency
   latency-variance 5
  !
 !
! SLA Class indicating latency as a fall-back criteria
 sla-class Voice-And-Video
  loss     2
  latency 45
  jitter  30
  fallback-best-tunnel
   criteria latency
app-route-policy Corporate_Segment_Sample_AAR_Expanded
  vpn-list Corporate_Segment
   sequence 1
    match
     source-ip 0.0.0.0/0
     dscp      46
    !
    action
   ! When non-compliant SLA tunnels are available, the MPLS tunnels will
   !satisfy requirements allowing the additional number of milliseconds specified
as variance
     sla-class CUSTOM_REALTIME_SLA preferred-color mpls fallback-to-best-path
<<< Omitted for Brevity>>>
sequence 11
    match
     source-ip 0.0.0.0/0
     app-list  TRUSTED_APPS
    !
    action
! In contrast  to sequence 1, when no variance is specified, the fallback will occur
to the lowest latency available tunnel as criteria.
      sla-class Voice-And-Video preferred-color biz-internet fallback-to-best-path
<<< Omitted for Brevity>>>
```

Consider the measurements from the three available tunnels shown in Table 9-5.

Table 9-5   Measurements from Tunnels with Latency Variance

Tunnel	Latency	Loss	Jitter
T1	105 ms	0	20 ms
T2	107 ms	0	20 ms
T3	115 ms	0	20 ms

Taking sequence 1 as an example, we can determine that a latency variance of 5 ms would cause a pair of tunnels with latency measurement of 105 ms (the lowest measurement) up to 110 ms to be treated as being the same with respect to latency variance in sla-class, so T1 and T2 would be the best of the worst tunnels. The range of tolerated latency from 105 to 110 ms is obtained with the following formula:

(best_metric_measurement, best_metric_measurement +
metric_accepted_variance) = (105, 105 + 5)

In sequence 11, the Voice-And-Video sla-class value is referenced, and measurements from tunnels are displayed in Table 9-6. A latency variance is not set, and so T1 is the best of the worst available tunnels.

Table 9-6   Measurements from Tunnels Without Latency Variance

Tunnel	Latency	Loss	Jitter
T1	50 ms	1	25 ms
T2	55 ms	1	25 ms
T3	58 ms	1	25 ms

As shown in Example 9-8 and explained in the previous examples, variance criteria are used to dampen a small deviation in the selected criteria, to ensure that no data path reprogramming is needed. This prevents the generation of excessive path changes and hence network instability. **fallback-to-best-path** is a solid option when dropping traffic is not desired in out-of-compliance SLA scenarios. It is important to design your policy considering both SLA in compliance and out of compliance scenarios, as well as the possible SLA action combinations. Table 9-7 lists the possible combinations.

Table 9-7   Primary and Secondary AAR Action Combinations

SLA Class Action	Tunnel Meeting SLA Action	Tunnel Not Meeting SLA Action
SLA class configured	Preferred color(s) or preferred color group	load-balance, load-balance + backup-sla-preferred-color, strict, or **fallback-to-best-path**
	No preferred color(s) or preferred color group	load-balance, load-balance + backup-sla-preferred-color, strict, or **fallback-to-best-path**
SLA class not configured	—	backup-sla-preferred-color

Constructing an Application Priority Policy with Policy Groups

As discussed in previous chapters, using policy groups is a newer and simpler method to configure policies. When it comes to creating a policy where SLAs are needed, Application Priority & SLA policies offer the same possibilities as Application-Aware Routing policies. The following steps show how to create an Application Priority & SLA policy profile:

Step 1.   Create a policy profile by selecting **Configuration > Policy Groups**. The dialog box shown in Figure 9-26 appears.

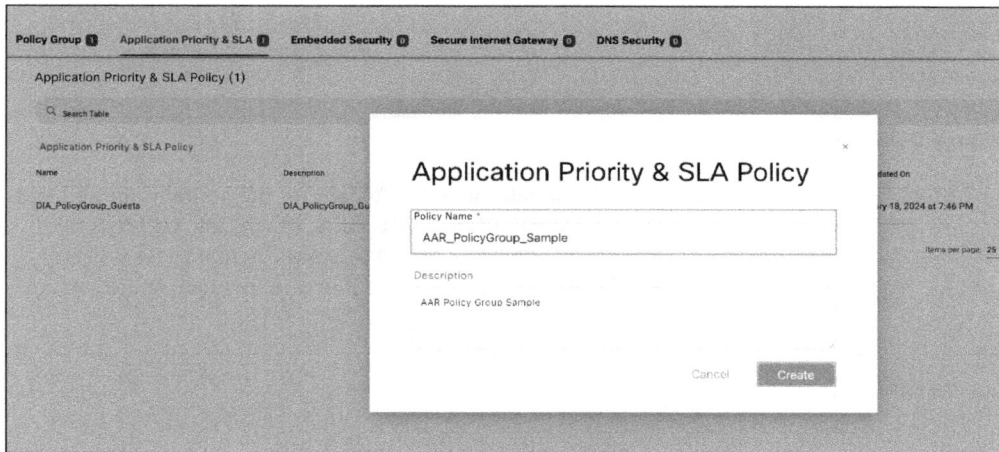

Figure 9-26   *Application Priority & SLA Policy Dialog Box*

Step 2.   Based on the required customization, decide whether you need a predefined **Gold (Business-relevant)**, **Silver (Default)**, or **Bronze (Business-irrelevant)** application group or select **Advanced Layout** (see Figure 9-27). If you were to select a predefined business-relevance application group, your next step would be the policy application to the specific sites. In this case, select **Advanced Layout**.

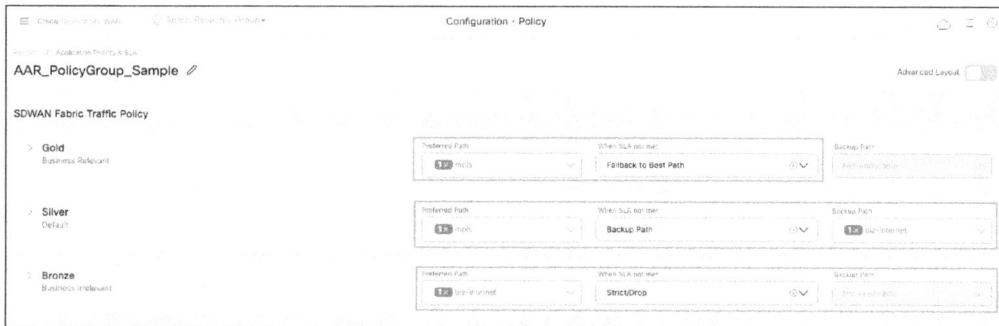

Figure 9-27   *Predefined Application Priority Policy Options*

Step 3.   Specify policy name, a VPN or VPNs, and a direction, as shown in Figure 9-28.

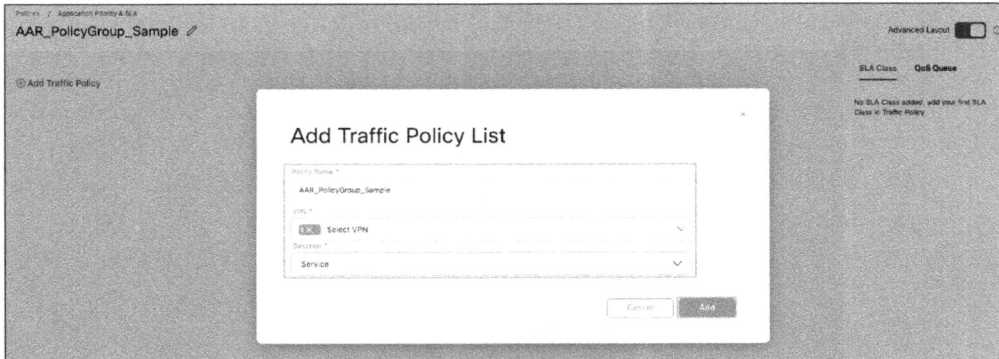

Figure 9-28   *Adding a Traffic Policy List*

Step 4.   Specify **DSCP 46** for the **match** value and **Accept** for the **action** value and add an SLA Class named **CUSTOM_REALTIME_SLA**, specifying **MPLS** as the preferred color, and select **Fallback to Best Path** as the action to take when the SLA is not met. These settings are part of Rule 1, with name DSCP_46 in Figure 9-29.

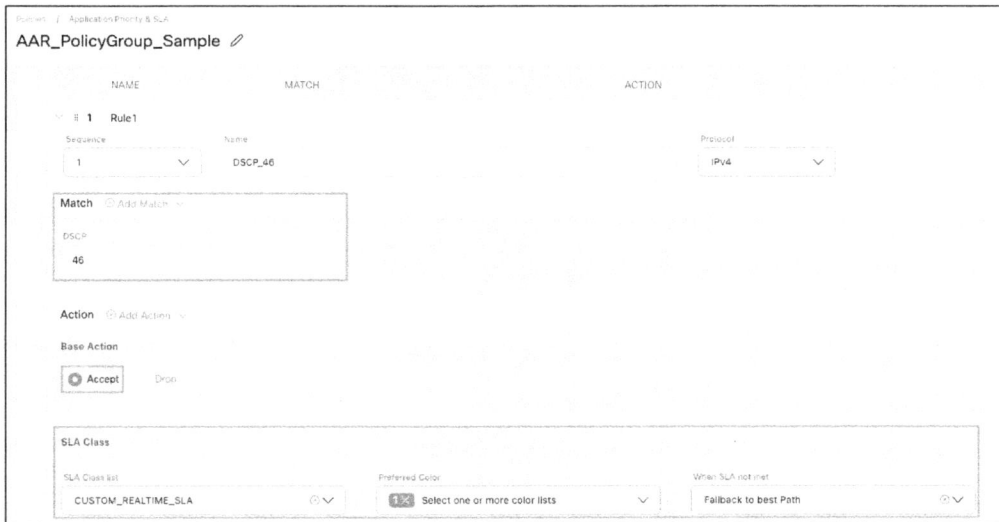

Figure 9-29   *Creating an Application Priority Policy Rule to Match DSCP 46*

Step 5.   Specify the Application List named REALTIME_TRUSTED_APPS for the **match** value and **Accept** for the **action** value and add the SLA Class named CUSTOM_REALTIME_SLA, specifying a Preferred Color group with name Preferred_Color_Group. These settings are part of Rule 2, with name REALTIME_TRUSTEDAPPS in Figure 9-30.

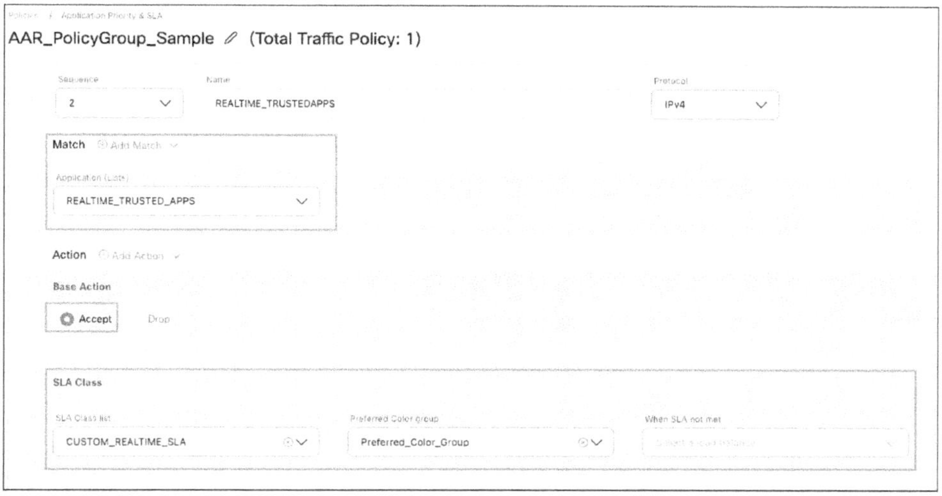

Figure 9-30   *Creating an Application Priority Policy Rule to Match an Applications List*

NOTE   If you select **Configuration > Policy Groups** and then select **Group of Interest** in the top right, you can create objects for various policy profile types, such as SLA class, TLOC lists, or security functions such as Zones or Advanced Inspection Profiles. When creating a Group of Interest, you follow the same principles as with lists in the traditional policy approach.

Figure 9-31 shows the summary you get now, which is similar to the one in Figure 9-27. In this case, you see two rules. The first rule matches DSCP 46, sets MPLS as the preferred color, sets the CUSTOM_REALTIME_SLA as the SLA class and uses the Fallback to Best Path parameter when no tunnels are in compliance with SLA requirements.

The second rule shown in Figure 9-31 matches the application group of interest (list) named REALTIME_TRUSTED_APPS. The **action** sets an SLA Class Preferred Color Group named *Preferred_Color_Group* where MPLS, BIZ-INTERNET, and LTE will be primary, secondary, and tertiary transports, respectively, with CUSTOM_REALTIME_SLA as the SLA class.

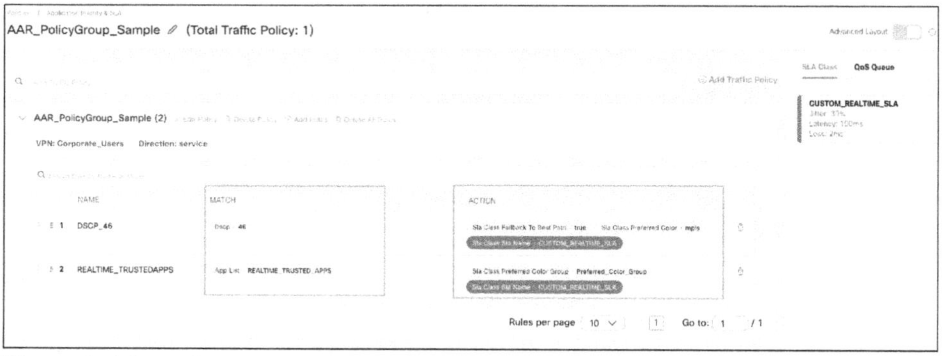

Figure 9-31   *Policy Summary View*

The final action after creating the logic behind the policy is to apply the policy, which you do by selecting the recently created policy profile under Policy Group, as shown in Figure 9-32, so that you can later deploy it to the desired devices in the environment. Remember that only devices leveraging Configuration Groups can benefit from the Policy Groups workflow.

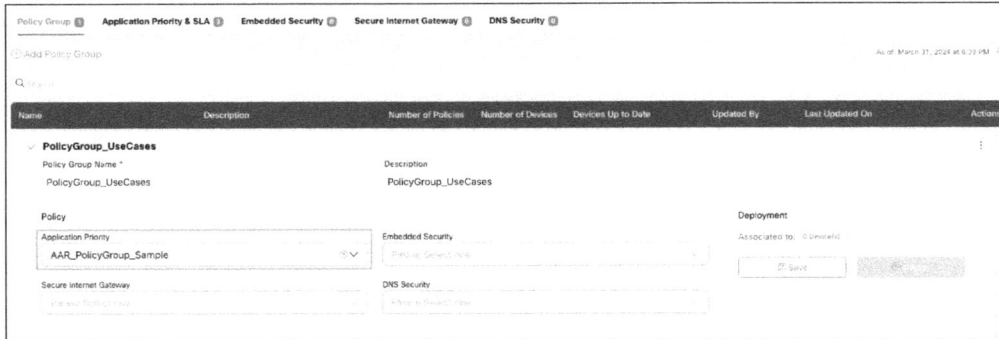

Figure 9-32   *Selecting the Application Priority Policy*

Enhanced Application-Aware Routing

Devices may take several minutes to determine that traffic needs to be switched from one transport to another because the tunnels are not complying with the required loss, latency, and jitter requirements, as explained earlier in this chapter. By default, the BFD hello interval is 1 second and the app-route poll interval is 10 minutes, with a multiplier of 6. With default timers, tunnel degradation detection and switchover can take up to an hour. Administrators tend to adjust poll-interval and multiplier values to improve detection, but this can lead to false positives, depending on the number of samples collected, the number of buckets, and the amount of data.

SD-WAN Release 20.12 introduced Enhanced Application-Aware Routing to help achieve faster detection of tunnel performance issues. These are some of the main benefits available with EAAR:

■ Performance routing metrics (loss, latency, and jitter) can be measured more accurately with inline data insertion, which means actual user and application data traffic metrics are used in real time, which helps increase accuracy and improves degradation detection (down to 10 to 60 seconds). In addition, unidirectional measurements for metrics such as loss and jitter are possible.

■ The app-route poll interval can be set to a minimum of 10 seconds, which means the SLA switchover can occur more quickly. When a tunnel is out of compliance with the SLA, it is swiftly removed from the forwarding to ensure required network performance and reliability.

■ The SLA dampening process is available to prevent instability in the network. This process introduces a waiting window before returning to SLA forwarding after an out-of-compliance state.

Three modes of operation are predefined with EAAR: Aggressive, Moderate, and Conservative (see Table 9-8).

Table 9-8   EAAR Predefined Modes

Mode	EAAR Poll Interval	EAAR Poll Multiplier	EAAR Poll Window	SLA Dampening Multiplier	SLA Dampening Window
Aggressive	10 s	6	10–60 s	120	20 min
Moderate	60 s	5	60–300 s	40	40 min
Conservative	300 s	6	300–1800 s	12	60 min

Figure 9-33 shows how to enable EAAR predefined modes by using the feature template for System settings. You can use a CLI add-on feature template if you need different values.

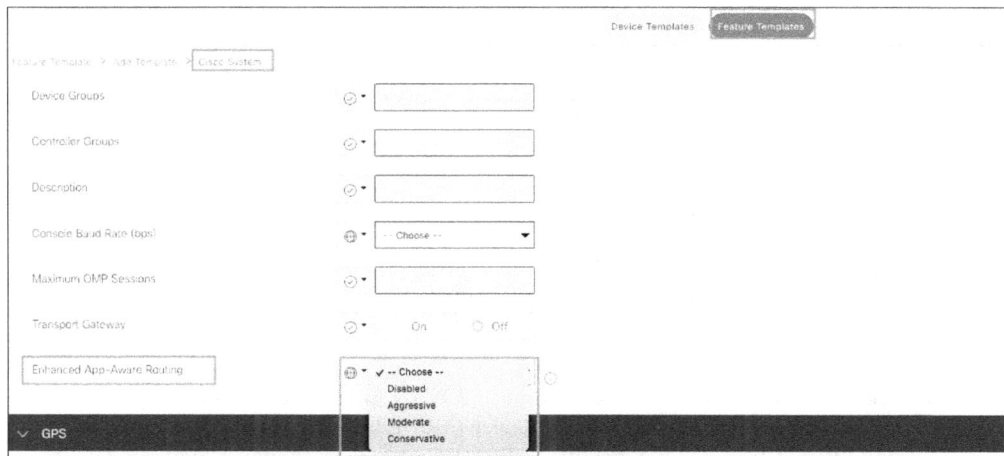

Figure 9-33   *EAAR Settings Under Feature Template*

On the other hand, when Configuration Groups are used for configuration, the EAAR setting can be adjusted under the System Profile configuration (see Figure 9-34). When different values are needed, a CLI Add-on Profile can be used.

9

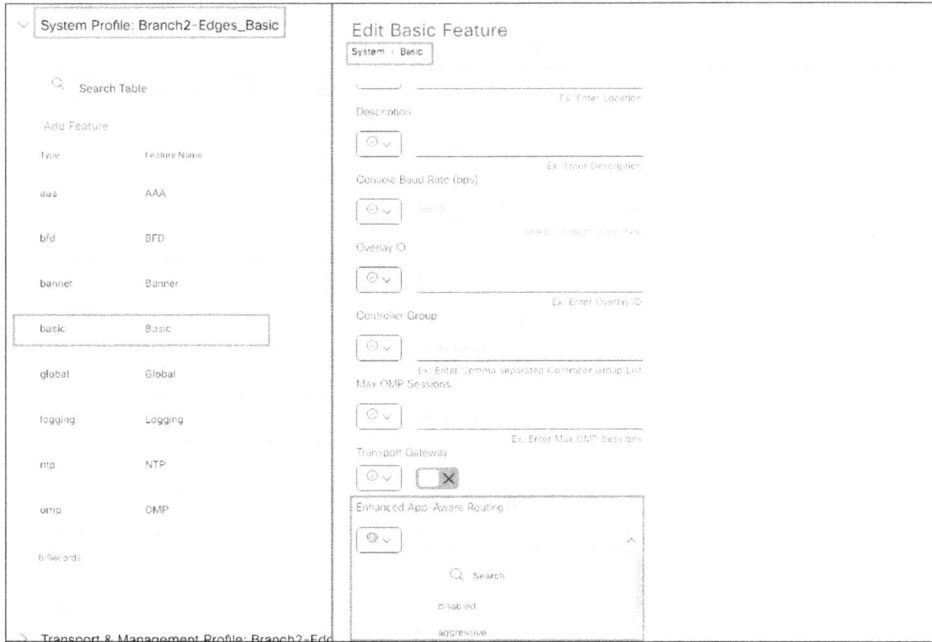

Figure 9-34   *EAAR Using Configuration Groups*

NOTE   In order to use EAAR, it must be enabled on both sides where the communication takes place; that is, the sender and receiver routers need to negotiate whether they are using the enhanced mechanism when turned on or falling back to the traditional BFD approach. For more details, see the "Cisco Catalyst SD-WAN Policies Configuration Guide" at the Cisco website.

Prior to enabling the functionality in the Branch 2 WAN Edge devices (BR2-Edge1, BR2-Edge2) and the Branch 3 WAN Edge device (BR3-Edge1), the EAAR status and SLA dampening settings from the perspective of BR2-Edge1 look as shown in Figure 9-35.

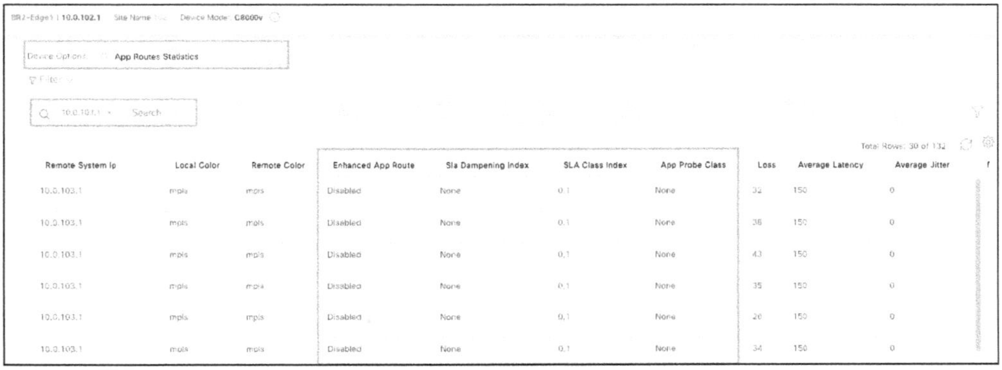

Figure 9-35   *Enhanced App Route and SLA Dampening Are Disabled by Default*

Example 9-9 shows how to verify whether EAAR is enabled as well as the new settings in the device configuration, such as **bfd enhanced-app-route pfr-poll-interval**, **bfd enhanced-app-route pfr-multiplier**, and **bfd sla-dampening multiplier**.

Example 9-9   *Verifying EAAR via the CLI*

```
BR2-Edge1# show sdwan running-config bfd
<<<Output omitted for brevity>>>
!Configuration changes after turning on the function. SD-WAN
!Manager provides these options values by default, if !different ones are needed,
CLI Add-On is supported.
bfd default-dscp 48
bfd app-route multiplier 6
bfd app-route poll-interval 600000
bfd enhanced-app-route enable
bfd enhanced-app-route pfr-poll-interval 10000
bfd enhanced-app-route pfr-multiplier 6
bfd sla-dampening enable
bfd sla-dampening multiplier 120
BR2-Edge1# show sdwan app-route params
Enhanced Application-Aware routing
    Config:                  :Enabled
    Poll interval:           :10000
    Poll multiplier:         :6
App route
    Poll interval:           :600000
    Poll multiplier:         :6
SLA dampening
    Config:                  :Enabled
    Multiplier:              :120
BR2-Edge1# sh sdwan app-route stats remote-system-ip 10.0.103.1
<<<Output omitted for brevity>>>
app-route statistics 192.168.20.6 192.168.20.8 ipsec 12346 12346
 remote-system-ip        10.0.103.1
 local-color             mpls
 remote-color            mpls
 sla-class-index         0,1
 fallback-sla-class-index 2,3
 enhanced-app-route      Enabled
 sla-dampening-index     None
 app-probe-class-list None
  mean-loss     0.911
  mean-latency 150
 mean-jitter  0
<<<Output omitted for brevity>>>
```

As you can see in Example 9-9, once EAAR has been set on the devices, the new configuration settings appear as follows:

- The **bfd enhanced-app-route pfr-poll-interval** setting, which is equivalent to the app-route poll interval timer, indicates that the collection of data (bucket) will last 10,000 ms.

- The next new setting present in the configuration is **bfd enhanced-app-route pfr-multiplier**, which indicates that a total of six measurement buckets will be collected.

- The third value that appears in the configuration, **bfd sla-dampening multiplier**, works in conjunction with the EAAR poll interval. In this case, the Aggressive mode contains a poll interval of 10 s and SLA dampening multiplier of 120. The total time the SLA dampening window will be in place before a tunnel is determined to be in compliance and back to SLA forwarding is (120 × 10) = 1200 s (20 min). The goal of dampening is to avoid the instability that occurs with excessive switchover.

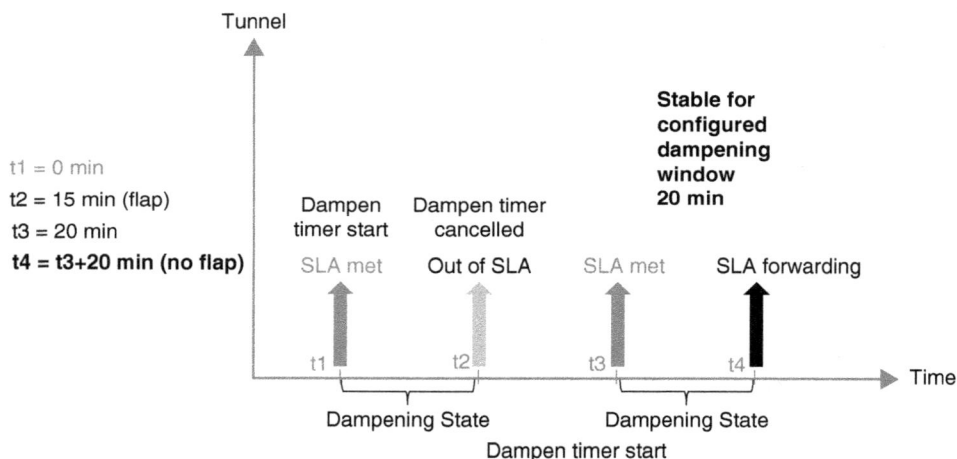

Figure 9-36 *SLA Dampening Operation with EAAR Aggressive Mode*

Figure 9-36 shows that SLA dampening involves the following steps:

Step 1. At t1, the tunnel SLA is in compliance, and the dampening state is triggered.

Step 2. After 15 minutes, at t2, the tunnel changes to out of compliance, and the dampening timer is canceled.

Step 3. After 5 more minutes, the SLA is met again, and the dampening timer restarts.

Step 4. For the next 20 minutes after t3, the transport measurements stabilize, and no SLA changes occur. At this point, tunnels are put back into SLA forwarding.

NOTE In this example, app-probe class is not used, but it is recommended to combine it with the SLA class when crafting AAR policies. This combination improves the accuracy of measurements for each local queue where the BFD echo request is sent. For more details, see the "Cisco Catalyst SD-WAN Policies Configuration Guide."

A similar view to validate EAAR settings is available in the SD-WAN Manager GUI. If you select **Monitor > Devices > [*Device*] > Realtime** and select **App Route Statistics,** you get the screen shown in Figure 9-37. Here you can see that the output in Example 9-9 matches the configuration for EAAR settings shown in the current screen (see Figure 9-37) such as Enhanced App Route (**bfd enhanced-app-route enable**) and SLA Dampening Index. You can also see that MPLS tunnels are dampened, which means these tunnels will not be selected as part of the SLA forwarding until the dampening window completes.

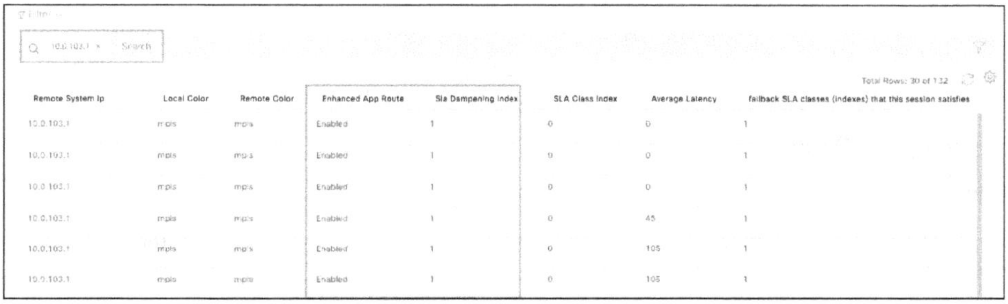

Figure 9-37   *EAAR and SLA Dampening Verification via SD-WAN Manager*

EAAR introduces more precise measurements by using unidirectional measurement and inline data insertion into live traffic streams. This enables quicker traffic switchover during noncompliant conditions and stabilizes the network through integrated SLA dampening.

Summary

This chapter discusses the basics of building app-route policies with Cisco Catalyst SD-WAN. Every SD-WAN tunnel that is established in the data plane automatically starts to send BFD probes. These BFD probes serve two purposes: They detect whether the forwarding path between two WAN Edge routers is still valid, and they determine the loss, latency, and jitter conditions of the forwarding path. The information about the real-time condition of the transport paths can then be used to inform the forwarding process and ensure that business-critical applications are sent over paths that are able to meet the required service-level agreements. As you have seen, EAAR is a new method that can be used for faster switchover, more accurate measurements, and network stability. Both traditional and EAAR methods, with traditional policies or policy groups, enable organizations to move away from their expensive, legacy transport providers and adopt commodity Internet circuits or simply diversify the transport options mix while not having to compromise on application performance.

Review All Key Topics

Review the most important topics in the chapter, noted with the Key Topic icon in the outer margin of the page. Table 9-9 lists these key topics and the page number on which each is found.

Key Topic

Table 9-9 Key Topics

Key Topic Element	Description	Page
Paragraph	Ensuring that there are enough BFD probes in a poll interval	380
Paragraph	Evaluating path condition	383
Paragraph	App-route policy forwarding decisions	385
Paragraph	SLA compliance verification	388
Paragraph	Preferred color groups and AAR policies	392
Section	Enhanced Application-Aware Routing	402

Define Key Terms

Define the following key terms from this chapter and check your answers in the glossary:

app-probe class, app-route multiplier, app-route poll interval, backup-sla-preferred-color, BFD hello interval, enhanced application-aware routing (EAAR), fallback-to-best-path, preferred color, preferred color group, SLA class list, SLA dampening, strict

Chapter Review Questions

1. What is the scope of an application-aware routing policy?

   a. Per site

   b. Per VPN

   c. Per direction

   d. Per site, per VPN

   e. Per site, per direction

   f. Per site, per VPN, per direction

2. Where are app-route policies applied and enforced?

   a. Applied on an SD-WAN Controller; enforced on an SD-WAN Controller

   b. Applied on an SD-WAN Controller; enforced on a WAN Edge device

   c. Applied on a WAN Edge device; enforced on an SD-WAN Controller

   d. Applied on a WAN Edge device; enforced on a WAN Edge device

3. Which administratively configured options affect the calculation of the loss, latency, and jitter statistics used for application-aware routing? (Choose all that apply.)

   a. BFD hello interval

   b. BFD hello multiplier

   c. Number of SLA classes

   d. App-route poll interval

   e. Number of tunnels

   f. Number of colors

   g. App-route multiplier

4. What is the maximum number of app-route poll intervals that can be used for tunnel performance calculations?

   a. 2

   b. 4

   c. 6

   d. 8

   e. 16

5. When are tunnels evaluated/reevaluated for compliance with the SLA classes?

   a. After every BFD packet is received by the WAN Edge router

   b. After every hello interval

   c. After every hello multiplier

   d. After every app-route poll interval

6. How many different SLA classes can be applied to a single WAN Edge router?

   a. 16

   b. 4

   c. 8

   d. 256

   e. Unlimited

7. How many different SLA classes can be configured in a Catalyst SD-WAN Controller policy?

   a. 256

   b. 4

   c. 8

   d. 16

   e. Unlimited

8. When is traffic forwarded across the backup SLA preferred color?

   a. When no tunnels are configured or active with the preferred SLA color(s)

   b. When none of the preferred SLA color(s) are currently meeting the required SLA class

   c. When no colors are currently meeting the required SLA class

9. True or false: When the **strict** option is configured in an AAR policy, the policy drops the traffic if the preferred color(s) fails to meet the SLA class requirements.

   a. True

   b. False

10. True or false: In order for an application-aware routing policy to have any effect, there must be multiple equal-cost routes in the routing table.

   a. True

   b. False

11. True or false: Policy groups can be used to configure policies that need to take SLA into consideration.

   a. True

   b. False

12. What are the available modes that enhanced application-aware routing permits by default? (Choose all that apply.)

   a. Fast mode

   b. Aggressive mode

   c. Conservative mode

   d. Slow mode

   e. Moderate mode

13. True or false: SLA dampening provides a waiting window that prevents path reprogramming changes and hence network instability when the transport is not fully recovered.

   a. True

   b. False

References

"Centralized Policy," https://www.cisco.com/c/en/us/td/docs/routers/sdwan/configuration/policies/ios-xe-17/policies-book-xe/centralized-policy.html.

"Cisco Catalyst SD-WAN Policies Configuration Guide, Application Aware Routing," "https://www.cisco.com/c/en/us/td/docs/routers/sdwan/configuration/policies/ios-xe-17/policies-book-xe/application-aware-routing.html

"Policy Groups Configuration Guide," https://www.cisco.com/c/en/us/td/docs/routers/sdwan/configuration/Policy-Groups/policy-groups/m-policy-groups.html

"Enhanced Application-Aware Routing," https://www.cisco.com/c/en/us/td/docs/routers/sdwan/configuration/policies/ios-xe-17/policies-book-xe/m-enhanced-application-aware-routing.html

CHAPTER 10

Localized Policies

This chapter covers the following topics:

- **Introduction to Localized Policies:** This section covers the different types of localized policies and how these policies relate to other types of policies used by Catalyst SD-WAN with both Device Templates and Configuration Groups.

- **Localized Control Policies:** This section covers localized control policies and how they can be used to manipulate routing advertisements to network elements outside the SD-WAN fabric.

- **Localized Data Policies:** This section covers the construction and use of localized data policies, particularly access control lists.

- **Quality of Service Policies:** This section covers the construction and application of quality of service with localized policies, including traffic classification, queuing and scheduling, and congestion management.

As discussed in Chapter 6, "Introduction to Cisco Catalyst SD-WAN Policies," two main types of policies are used in the Cisco SD-WAN solution: centralized policies and localized policies. Chapters 7, "Centralized Control Policies," 8, "Centralized Data Policies," and 9, "Application-Aware Routing Policies," focus on the different types of centralized policies; this chapter discusses localized policies. Just as there are two main classifications of centralized policies (centralized control policies and centralized data policies), there are also localized control policies and localized data policies. This chapter discusses the different types of localized policies, how they are configured and applied, and common use cases for different types of localized policies.

Introduction to Localized Policies

The two main types of localized policies are localized control policies and localized data policies.

Just as centralized control policies are used to manipulate the control plane and routing advertisements inside the Cisco SD-WAN fabric, localized control policies are used to manipulate routing advertisements that happen at the perimeter of the SD-WAN fabric, when the WAN Edge router is communicating with other routers via BGP, OSPF, or EIGRP. Localized control policies can be used to filter routes or manipulate routing attributes such as OSPF cost, BGP local preference, and EIGRP delay. Localized data policies are used to manipulate individual packets or flows transiting the data plane of the WAN Edge router.

There are two main types of localized data policies: access control lists (ACLs) and quality of service (QoS) policies. ACLs can be used to filter, rewrite, or apply additional services to a packet or flow as it transits the router. Network administrators use QoS for marking, queuing, and scheduling in order to allow to prioritize certain classes of traffic.

While centralized policies and localized policies share many similarities in their structure, because centralized policies are activated on the SD-WAN Controller (formerly vSmart) and localized policies are applied as part of the WAN Edge configuration templates, there are no common configuration elements or lists that can be shared between the two different types of policies. Figure 10-1 illustrates the relationships between these different types of policies.

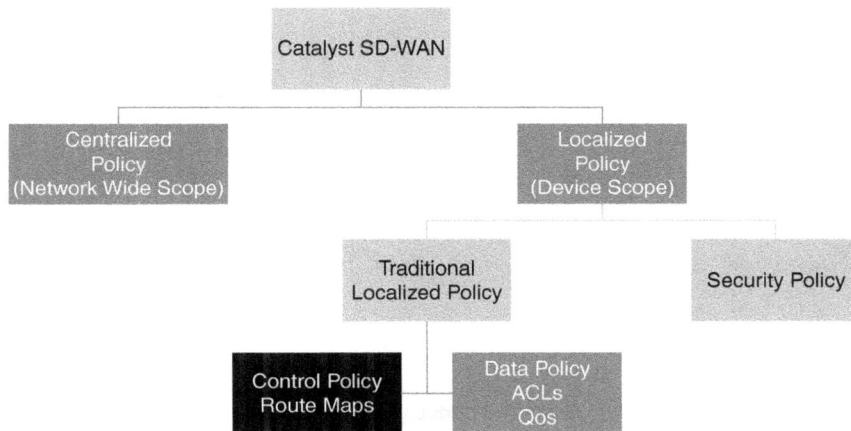

Figure 10-1 *Localized Policy Overview*

In addition to localized control policies and localized data policies, there is a special type of localized policy called a security policy. Security policies are discussed in detail in Chapter 11, "Cisco Catalyst SD-WAN Security."

NOTE With Device Templates, network administrators create localized policies separately and attach them to device templates. In contrast, Configuration Groups simplify configuration, permitting network administrators to create route policies or ACLs inside feature profiles.

Localized Control Policies

The purpose of localized control policies is to manipulate route attributes or filter out routes completely as they are advertised from the WAN Edge routers to the rest of the routing domain via traditional routing protocols. Using localized control policies makes it possible to differentially prefer one WAN Edge router over another on the LAN side for a site that is configured with dual routers for high availability. While Cisco Catalyst SD-WAN deploys an active/active high-availability design, and there is no concept of a "standby" router (each router is always capable of forwarding any received traffic at all times during operation), there are some advantages to deploying a network in a way that ensures that particular flows always transit particular routers.

Use Case 3 in Chapter 7 looks at the details involved in ensuring that a network always moves particular flows via particular routers. Whereas Chapter 7 covers the traffic engineering steps required to accomplish this on the WAN side of the router using the TLOC Preference attribute, the following example shows how to complete this design using different routing policies on the LAN side of the WAN Edge routers.

Figure 10-2 shows the topology of Data Center 1. There are two WAN Edge routers that connect to a traditional core switch. With the default configuration at WAN Edge routers, the core switch with Maximum-Paths set to 2, will load-share traffic across the two WAN Edge routers.

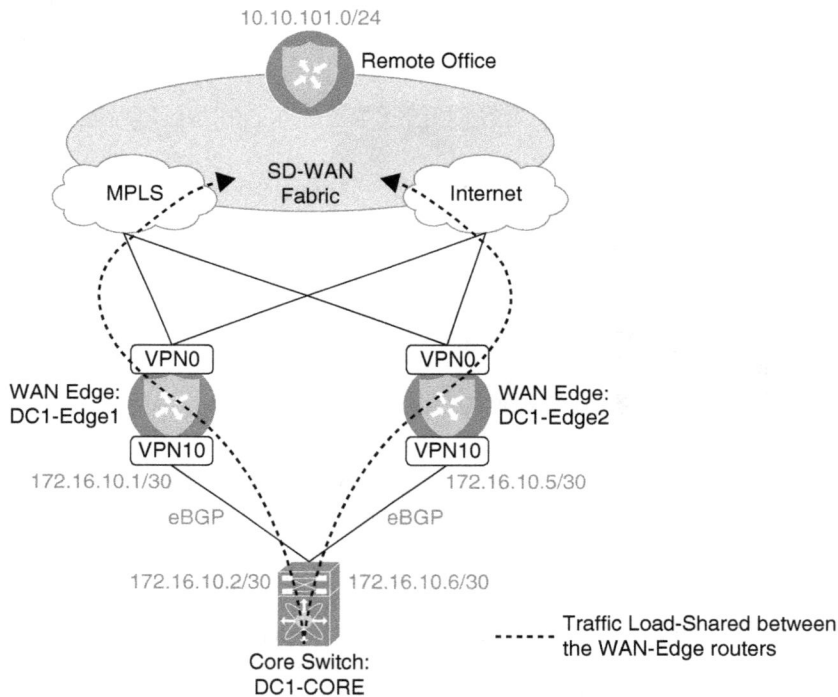

Figure 10-2 *Data Center Topology*

In order to prefer one WAN Edge router and create the desired symmetric flow patterns, we can adjust the routing advertisements from DC1-Edge1 and DC1-Edge2 so that the routes being advertised from DC1-Edge1 are more preferred. That is, traffic flowing from the data center across the WAN will prefer DC1-Edge1 in steady-state operation. In this case, because the network is using eBGP as the routing protocol between the WAN Edge routers and the data center core, we need to manipulate route preferences with BGP attributes. While different attributes could be used, such as AS_Path Prepending, this example uses Multi-Exit Discriminator (also called MED or Metric). Because lower MED values are always preferred, we will set the MED value on the routes advertised from DC1-Edge1 to 100 and on the DC1-Edge2 to 1000.

Before any policy is applied, DC1-CORE has equal-cost paths from each of the WAN Edge
routers, indicated by the two next hops for each route (172.16.10.1 and 172.16.10.5). With
this default state, DC1-CORE would use ECMP to load-share flows between the two routers,
as shown in Example 10-1.

Example 10-1 *DC1-CORE Routing Table*

```
DC1-CORE#show ip route bgp
Codes: L - local, C - connected, S - static, R - RIP, M - mobile, B - BGP
       D - EIGRP, EX - EIGRP external, O - OSPF, IA - OSPF inter area
       N1 - OSPF NSSA external type 1, N2 - OSPF NSSA external type 2
       E1 - OSPF external type 1, E2 - OSPF external type 2
       i - IS-IS, su - IS-IS summary, L1 - IS-IS level-1, L2 - IS-IS level-2
       ia - IS-IS inter area, * - candidate default, U - per-user static route
       o - ODR, P - periodic downloaded static route, H - NHRP, l - LISP
       a - application route
       + - replicated route, % - next hop override, p - overrides from PfR
Gateway of last resort is not set

      10.0.0.0/8 is variably subnetted, 6 subnets, 2 masks
B        10.10.20.0/24 [20/1000] via 172.16.10.5, 00:12:33
                       [20/1000] via 172.16.10.1, 00:12:33
B        10.10.101.0/24 [20/1000] via 172.16.10.5, 00:12:33
                        [20/1000] via 172.16.10.1, 00:12:33
B        10.10.102.0/24 [20/1000] via 172.16.10.5, 00:12:33
                        [20/1000] via 172.16.10.1, 00:12:33
B        10.10.103.0/24 [20/1000] via 172.16.10.5, 00:12:33
                        [20/1000] via 172.16.10.1, 00:12:33
      172.16.0.0/16 is variably subnetted, 11 subnets, 2 masks
B        172.16.20.0/30 [20/1000] via 172.16.10.5, 00:12:33
                        [20/1000] via 172.16.10.1, 00:12:33
B        172.16.20.4/30 [20/1000] via 172.16.10.5, 00:12:33
                        [20/1000] via 172.16.10.1, 00:12:33
B        172.16.101.0/30 [20/1000] via 172.16.10.5, 00:12:33
                         [20/1000] via 172.16.10.1, 00:12:33
B        172.16.101.4/30 [20/1000] via 172.16.10.5, 00:12:33
                         [20/1000] via 172.16.10.1, 00:12:33
B        172.16.103.0/30 [20/1000] via 172.16.10.5, 00:12:33
                         [20/1000] via 172.16.10.1, 00:12:33
DC1-CORE#
```

The process of building a traditional localized control policy is similar to the process of
building centralized policies covered in previous chapters. However, the process of applying
a localized control policy is slightly different. In this first example, we will work through the

process of configuring the policy in the SD-WAN Manager GUI (formerly vManage); for all other examples in this chapter, we will simply review the CLI configuration.

The first step in the configuration process is to create the route policies. The route policies that are used for configuring localized control policies are similar in structure to the centralized control policies reviewed in Chapter 7. For this particular example with traditional localized policies, we will be creating two different route policies: one that sets a MED value of 100, and one that sets a MED value of 1000. These route policies can be configured in SD-WAN Manager from the **Configuration > Policies** menu, followed by selecting **Route Policy** from the **Custom Options** menu in the upper corner, as shown in Figure 10-3.

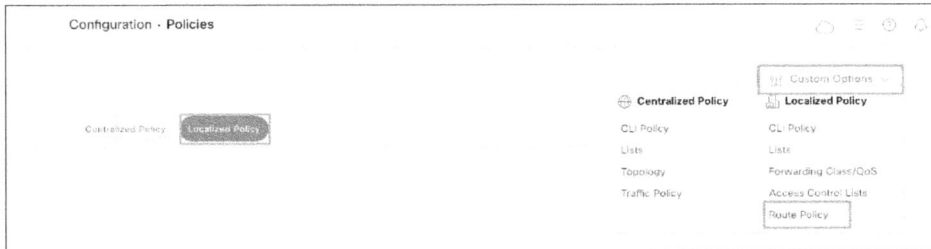

Figure 10-3   *Accessing the Route Policy Configurations*

Select the **Create New** option from the **Add Route Policy** menu, as shown in Figure 10-4.

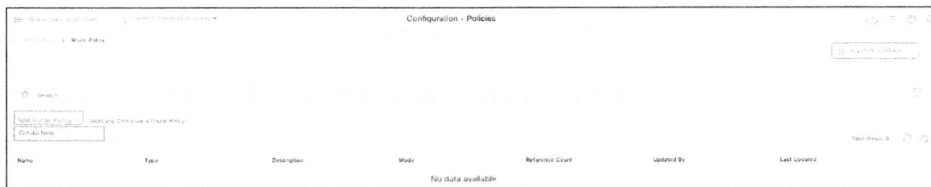

Figure 10-4   *Creating a New Route Policy*

The route policy needs to be configured with a name and a description. The next step is to add a new sequence type by clicking the **+Sequence Type** button on the left, as shown in Figure 10-5. In a localized control policy, the only applicable sequence type is a route sequence, so this button automatically adds a new route sequence, as highlighted on the left. In the new route sequence, add a new sequence rule by clicking **+Sequence Rule**. Because this MED value will apply to all of the routes being advertised by the WAN Edge device, there will be no matching criteria specified. In order to have all the routes permitted by this first sequence rule, click the Actions tab and click the Accept radio button. From the list of available actions, select the Metric action and then specify the MED value 100. Finally, select Save Match and Actions under the individual sequence and then click Save Route Policy at the very bottom of the page to complete the configuration of the route policy.

You can see the CLI rendering of the policy by clicking the Preview button in the lower-left corner. Example 10-2 shows the CLI display for this policy.

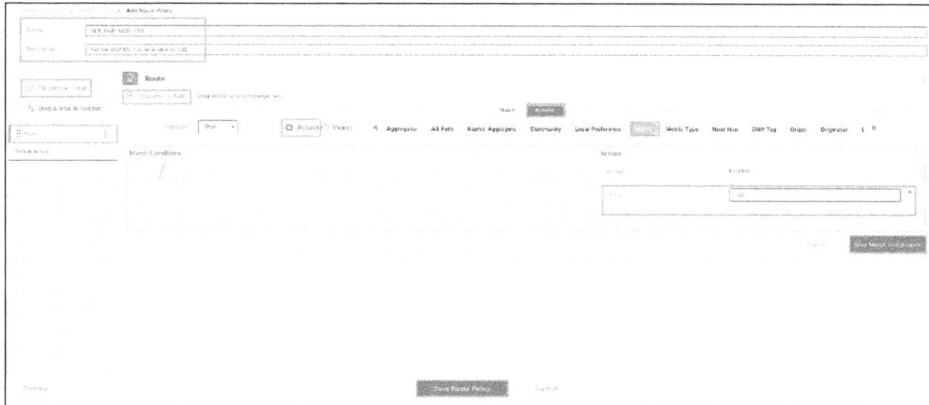

Figure 10-5 *Configuring a Route Policy to Set the BGP MED Value to 100*

Example 10-2 *Route Policy to Set the BGP MED Value*

```
route-policy SET_BGP_MED_100
 sequence 1
   action accept
     set
       metric 100
     !
   !
  !
default-action reject
 !
```

NOTE The default-action step in this policy has no effect because all the routes are matched in sequence 1. Ordinarily, network administrators need to pay special attention to the default-action statements in route policy configurations.

A second route policy is then created for the second WAN Edge router in order to set MED to 1000 by repeating all the steps used to create the first policy. Figure 10-6 shows this second policy.

Once the route policies have been created, a localized policy needs to be created. A single centralized policy could contain many different component parts, and a localized policy has a similar structure. There is a single localized policy that is applied to any router, but that localized policy can include multiple localized control policies and multiple localized data policies that are applied to different parts of the local router's configuration. In order to create the local policy, select the Add Policy option from the localized policy screen at **Configuration > Policies** to start the Localized Policy Wizard (see Figure 10-7).

10

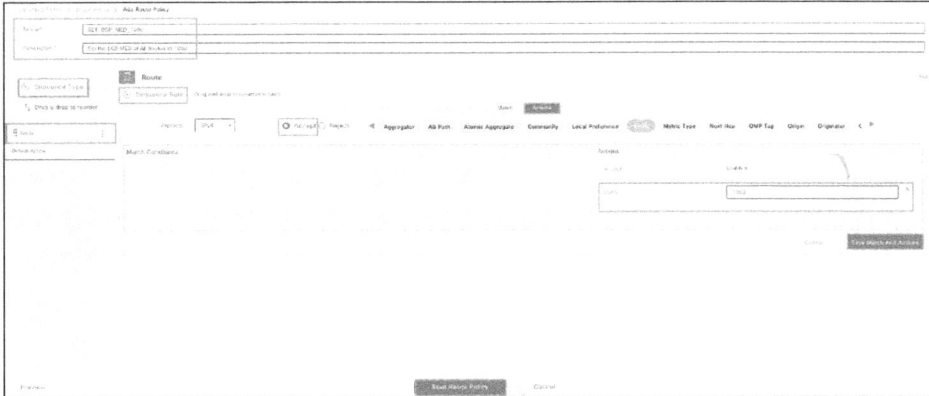

Figure 10-6   *Configuring a Second Route Policy to Set the BGP MED Value*

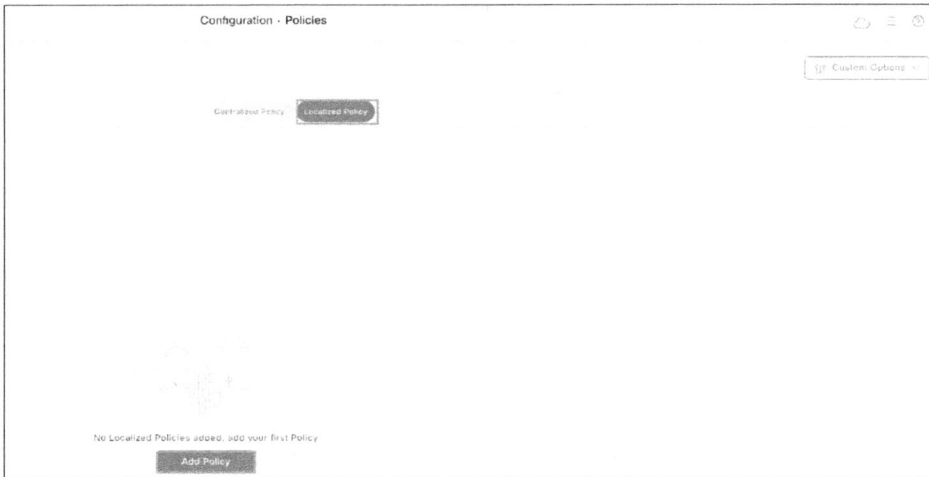

Figure 10-7   *Creating a New Localized Policy*

Click Next in the first several steps of the Local Policy Wizard until you arrive at the **Configure Route Policy** option. On this screen, import the two route policies that were previously created and attach them to this localized policy by clicking on the **+Add Route Policy** button and then selecting the policies, as shown in Figure 10-8 and Figure 10-9.

Figure 10-8   *Importing Existing Route Policies into the Localized Policy Wizard*

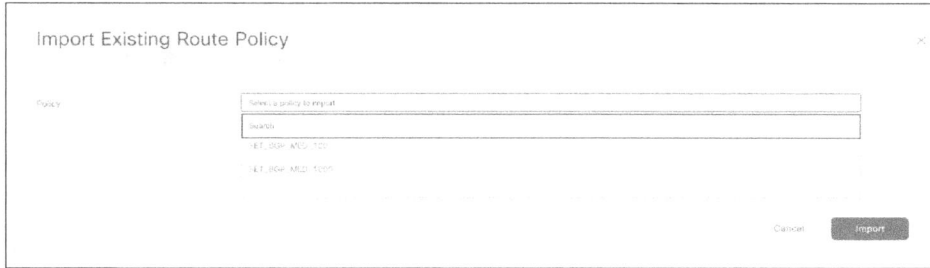

Figure 10-9 *Selecting the Route Policies to Be Imported into the Localized Policy*

Finally, the local policy needs to have a name and description configured, as shown in Figure 10-10, and then you can save it by clicking the Save Policy button at the bottom of the screen.

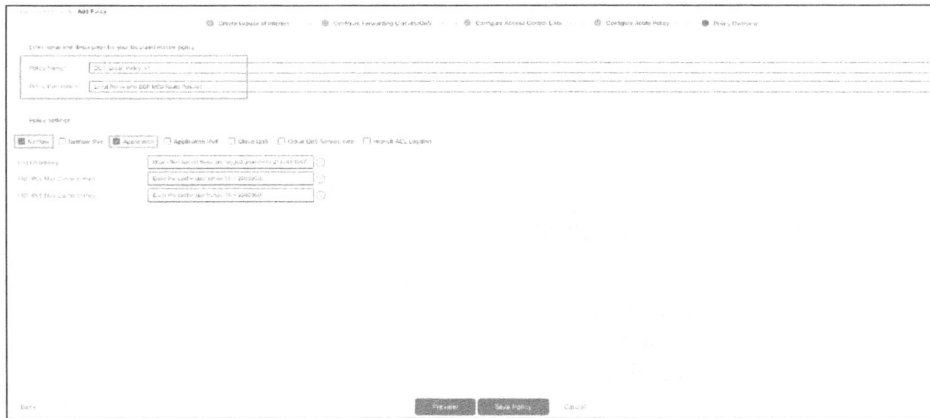

Figure 10-10 *Saving the Localized Policy*

NOTE Notice that additional parameters have been selected under **Policy Settings** (Netflow and Application). Although these parameters are not necessarily required for the current use case, they are used to get visibility into network traffic when leveraging device templates. Specifically, the Application setting enables the SD-WAN Application Intelligence Engine (SAIE) (formerly Deep Packet Inspection [DPI]), which allows a device to recognize applications for further use inside traffic policies like application-aware routing policies. For additional details, refer to the Localized Policy section in "Cisco Catalyst SD-WAN Policies Configuration Guide."

The first step in using the localized policy just created is to attach it to the device template. To do so, you need to edit the appropriate device template and then select the localized policy to be applied from the drop-down in the **Additional Templates** section, as shown in Figure 10-11.

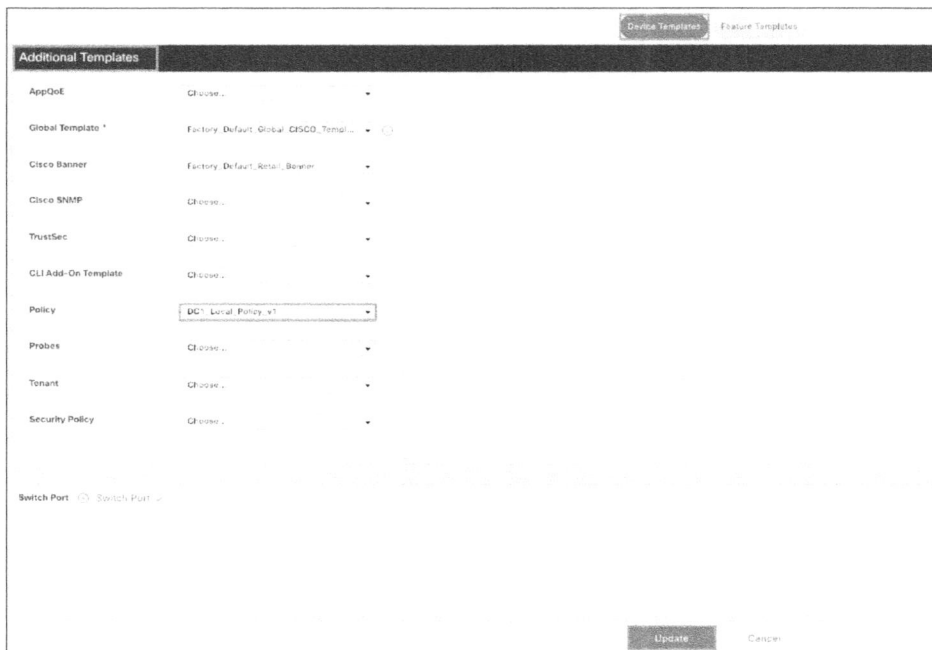

Figure 10-11 *Adding the Localized Policy to the Device Template*

Once the localized policy has been added to the device template, you can click Update to immediately push a configuration change to all of the devices that are attached to this device template. If more than one device is attached to the device template, you will receive a warning that you are changing multiple devices.

NOTE   One of the biggest differences between centralized policies and localized policies is in where the policies are applied. Centralized policies are applied to the SD-WAN Controller configurations; localized policies are applied as part of each individual WAN Edge router's configuration.

Once the localized policy has been created and attached to the device template, the route map itself can then be referenced by the feature template for the interface where it will ultimately be used. The process of creating a route map does not in and of itself configure the router to use the created route map. The route policy still has to be referenced in the configuration in order to have any effect. You can see this by examining the configuration of the WAN Edge router from the CLI, as shown in Example 10-3. Here you can see that the route policies are in the running configuration but are not referenced by the BGP configuration; they will therefore not have any effect.

Example 10-3 *Viewing the Route Policies in the Device Configuration*

```
! Route-Policies are visible in the configuration of the WAN Edge router.
DC1-Edge1# show running-config | section route-map
route-map SET_BGP_MED_100 permit 1
 set metric 100
route-map SET_BGP_MED_100 deny 65535
route-map SET_BGP_MED_1000 permit 1
 set metric 1000
route-map SET_BGP_MED_1000 deny 65535
! The route polices are not yet applied to any routing protocol.
DC1-Edge1# show run | section router bgp
router bgp 65001
 bgp log-neighbor-changes
 !
 address-family ipv4 vrf 10
  bgp router-id 10.0.10.1
  redistribute omp
  propagate-aspath
  neighbor 172.16.10.2 remote-as 65010
  neighbor 172.16.10.2 activate
  neighbor 172.16.10.2 send-community both
  distance bgp 20 200 20
 exit-address-family
DC1-Edge1#
```

NOTE From an order of operations perspective, the localized policy must be tied to the device template before the individual component policies can be referenced anywhere else in the device configuration. This may be a counterintuitive process for engineers who are unfamiliar with it. If the opposite were done—that is, if the route maps were referenced by the BGP configuration before the localized policy was attached to the device template—SD-WAN Manager would display a syntax error, indicating that a route map was referenced but was not found in the localized policy configuration. Therefore, it is important to always update the localized policy tied to the device template prior to referencing any component parts of that localized policy. Multiple route policies and ACLs can exist within the same localized policy and can be referenced by specific components in the Feature Templates.

Once the localized policy has been successfully attached to the device template, you can then go back and update the BGP feature template so that the configured BGP neighbors will use the new route map. In order to configure this, select **Neighbor**, set the **Address Family** radio button to **On**, set the Address Family combo box to **ipv4-unicast**, check the **Route Policy Out** radio button, and add a variable as a name for the policy, as shown in Figure 10-12.

10

By using a variable for the name of the route policy, you can use the same configuration across both routers and reference the two different route maps that you created and configured with the local policy. This structure allows for maximum template reuse. Once this configuration is saved, you are prompted to provide the names of the route policies—in this case, SET_BGP_MED_100 for DC1-Edge1 and SET_BGP_MED_1000 for DC1-Edge2.

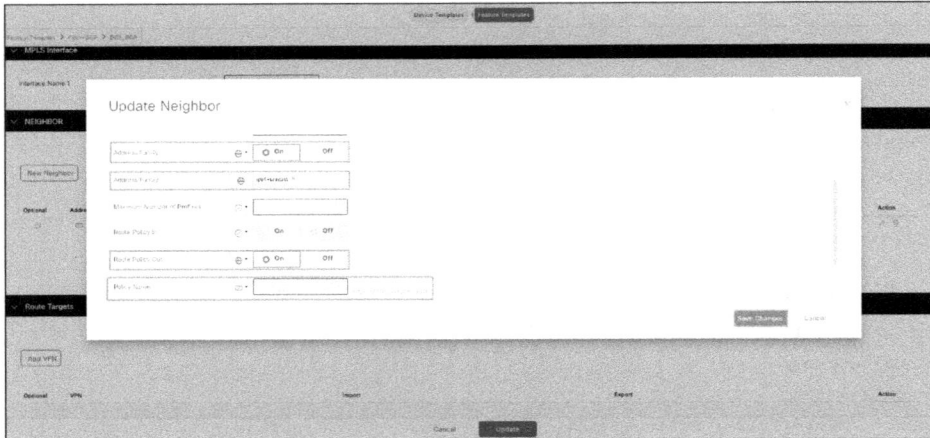

Figure 10-12   *Adding the Local Policy to the Device Template*

Once the changes are applied, you can see this configuration by looking at the CLI configuration for BGP in VPN 10 on both of the DC WAN Edge routers, as shown in Example 10-4.

Example 10-4   *Viewing the Route Policies Applied in the Device Configuration*

```
! Each WAN Edge router is applying a different route-policy.
DC1-Edge1# show run | section router bgp
router bgp 65001
 bgp log-neighbor-changes
 !
 address-family ipv4 vrf 10
  bgp router-id 10.0.10.1
  redistribute omp
  propagate-aspath
  neighbor 172.16.10.2 remote-as 65010
  neighbor 172.16.10.2 activate
  neighbor 172.16.10.2 send-community both
  neighbor 172.16.10.2 route-map SET_BGP_MED_100 out
  distance bgp 20 200 20
 exit-address-family

DC1-Edge1# show run interface gigabitEthernet3 | i interface|ip address|vrf
interface GigabitEthernet3
```

```
   vrf forwarding 10
   ip address 172.16.10.1 255.255.255.252
```

```
DC1-Edge2# show run | section router bgp
router bgp 65001
 bgp log-neighbor-changes
 !
 address-family ipv4 vrf 10
  bgp router-id 10.0.10.2
  redistribute omp
  propagate-aspath
  neighbor 172.16.10.6 remote-as 65010
  neighbor 172.16.10.6 activate
  neighbor 172.16.10.6 send-community both
  neighbor 172.16.10.6 route-map SET_BGP_MED_1000 out
  distance bgp 20 200 20
 exit-address-family
DC1-Edge2# show run interface gigabitEthernet3 | i interface|ip address|vrf
interface GigabitEthernet3
 vrf forwarding 10
 ip address 172.16.10.5 255.255.255.252
```

After applying the configuration in Example 10-4, you can return to the data center core device in Example 10-5 and see that the switch still receives both sets of BGP advertisements: one from DC1-Edge1 and one from DC1-Edge2. However, only the routing advertisements from DC1-Edge1 are selected as best paths, and only the routes from DC1-Edge1 are inserted into the routing table. In this way, you can be assured that the core switch will send all traffic to the DC1-Edge1 router in a steady state.

Example 10-5   *Viewing the Effects of the Route Policies on Neighboring Routers*

```
! Routes from both WAN Edge routers are present in the BGP table, but the
! different MED (metric) values influence the BGP path selection algorithm to
! select only the routes from DC1-Edge1.
DC1-CORE#sho ip bgp
BGP table version is 92, local router ID is 10.10.10.1
Status codes: s suppressed, d damped, h history, * valid, > best, i - internal,
              r RIB-failure, S Stale, m multipath, b backup-path, f RT-Filter,
              x best-external, a additional-path, c RIB-compressed,
              t secondary path, L long-lived-stale,
Origin codes: i - IGP, e - EGP, ? - incomplete
RPKI validation codes: V valid, I invalid, N Not found

     Network          Next Hop            Metric LocPrf Weight Path
 *>   10.10.10.0/24    0.0.0.0                  0          32768 i
```

```
*>    10.10.20.0/24     172.16.10.1         100          0 65001 ?
*                       172.16.10.5        1000          0 65001 ?
*>    10.10.101.0/24    172.16.10.1         100          0 65001 ?
*                       172.16.10.5        1000          0 65001 ?
*>    10.10.102.0/24    172.16.10.1         100          0 65001 ?
*                       172.16.10.5        1000          0 65001 ?
*>    10.10.103.0/24    172.16.10.1         100          0 65001 ?
*                       172.16.10.5        1000          0 65001 ?
*>    172.16.20.0/30    172.16.10.1         100          0 65001 ?
*                       172.16.10.5        1000          0 65001 ?
*>    172.16.20.4/30    172.16.10.1         100          0 65001 ?
*                       172.16.10.5        1000          0 65001 ?
*>    172.16.101.0/30   172.16.10.1         100          0 65001 ?
*                       172.16.10.5        1000          0 65001 ?
*>    172.16.101.4/30   172.16.10.1         100          0 65001 ?
*                       172.16.10.5        1000          0 65001 ?
*>    172.16.103.0/30   172.16.10.1         100          0 65001 ?
*                       172.16.10.5        1000          0 65001 ?
! The routing table on the DC1-Core device now only lists routes from DC1-Edge1.
! This is indicated by the next hop address of 172.16.10.1.
!
DC1-CORE#sho ip route bgp
Codes: L - local, C - connected, S - static, R - RIP, M - mobile, B - BGP
       D - EIGRP, EX - EIGRP external, O - OSPF, IA - OSPF inter area
       N1 - OSPF NSSA external type 1, N2 - OSPF NSSA external type 2
       E1 - OSPF external type 1, E2 - OSPF external type 2
       i - IS-IS, su - IS-IS summary, L1 - IS-IS level-1, L2 - IS-IS level-2
       ia - IS-IS inter area, * - candidate default, U - per-user static route
       o - ODR, P - periodic downloaded static route, H - NHRP, l - LISP
       a - application route
       + - replicated route, % - next hop override, p - overrides from PfR
Gateway of last resort is not set


      10.0.0.0/8 is variably subnetted, 6 subnets, 2 masks
B        10.10.20.0/24 [20/100] via 172.16.10.1, 00:13:08
B        10.10.101.0/24 [20/100] via 172.16.10.1, 00:13:08
B        10.10.102.0/24 [20/100] via 172.16.10.1, 00:13:08
B        10.10.103.0/24 [20/100] via 172.16.10.1, 00:13:08
      172.16.0.0/16 is variably subnetted, 11 subnets, 2 masks
B        172.16.20.0/30 [20/100] via 172.16.10.1, 00:13:08
B        172.16.20.4/30 [20/100] via 172.16.10.1, 00:13:08
B        172.16.101.0/30 [20/100] via 172.16.10.1, 00:13:08
B        172.16.101.4/30 [20/100] via 172.16.10.1, 00:13:08
B        172.16.103.0/30 [20/100] via 172.16.10.1, 00:13:08
DC1-CORE#
```

As Example 10-5 shows, localized control policies can be used to manipulate the routing advertisements into or out of the WAN Edges in order to perform traffic engineering at the local site.

As mentioned earlier in the chapter, when using the traditional configuration approach (Device Templates), localized policies are created separately and attached to specific Device Templates as needed. In contrast, the Configuration Groups method allows an administrator to add required features as route policies or ACLs inside Feature Profiles, minimizing cross-navigation in SD-WAN Manager. Select Edit for the desired Configuration Group in the list at **Configuration > Configuration Groups**. Then, in the screen for editing Configuration Groups, under either Transport & Management Profile or Service Profile, click Add Feature and then select Route Policy from the drop-down list, as shown in Figure 10-13, where a route policy for one of the routers (DC1-Edge1) is used as an example.

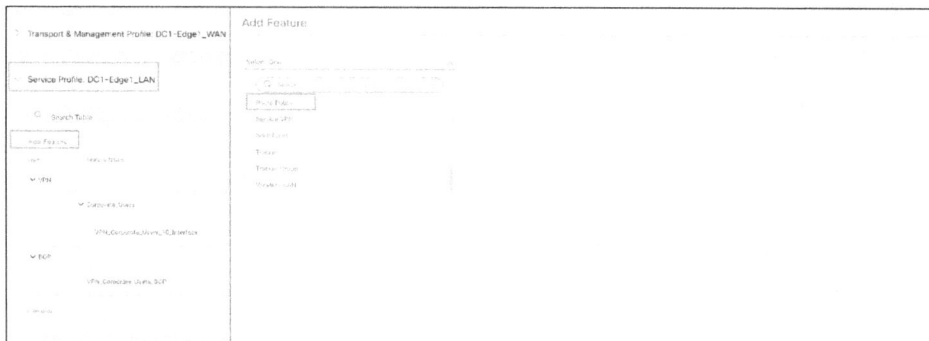

Figure 10-13   *Creating a New Route Policy in a Feature Profile*

Provide a name and description to the route policy. Next, click **Add Routing Sequence** and provide a name for it. Then, configure a match any by leaving Condition empty; from Action Type drop-down list select **Accept** and from **Accept Condition** drop-down list select **Metric** and set a metric to 100, just as you did earlier (see Figure 10-14).

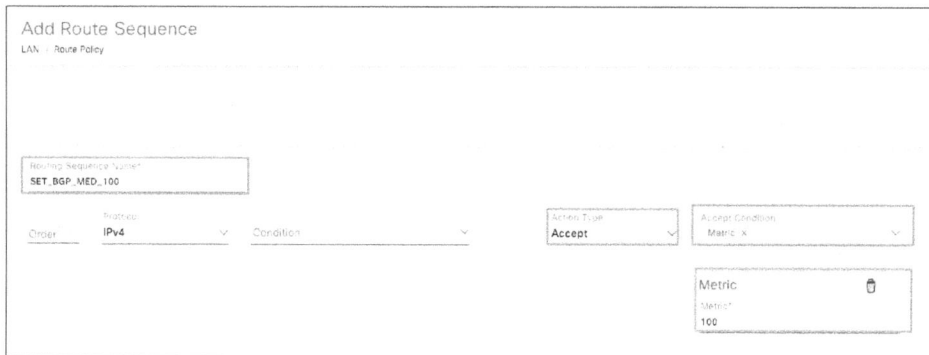

Figure 10-14   *Configuring a Route Policy to Set the BGP MED Value to 100*

Much as in traditional templates, in your Configuration Group you set an address family with the value ipv4-unicast under Neighbor in the BGP feature parcel, and from **Select Out**

Route Policy drop-down list select the policy with name SET_BGP_MED_100 to apply the policy in outbound direction, as shown in Figure 10-15. Then, click Update and proceed to deploy the changes to the DC1-Edge1 WAN Edge device.

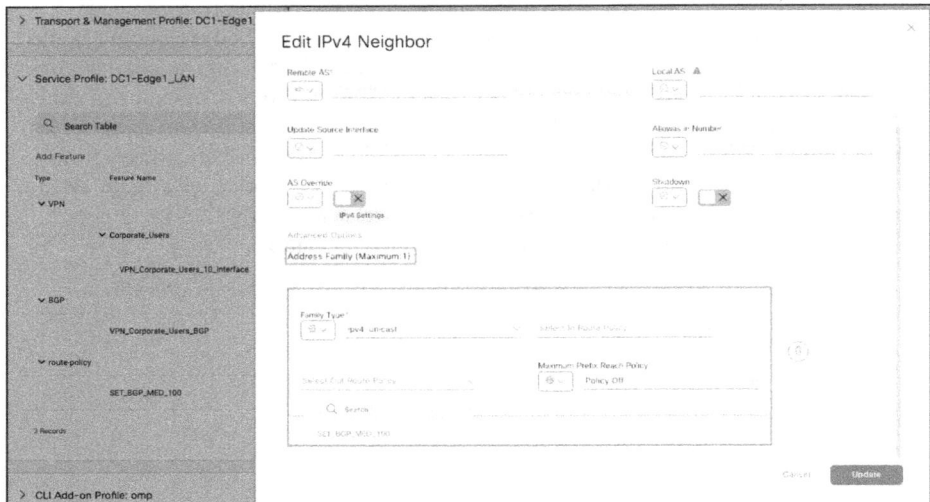

Figure 10-15 *Adding a Route Policy to the BGP Feature Parcel*

Keep in mind that the configuration described in this section is only half of the configuration necessary to get all of the traffic at a site to flow through a particular WAN Edge device and the second half can be achieved leveraging another type of policies as in Use Case 3 in Chapter 7, "Centralized Control Policies." These two configuration methods (Route Policy through traditional Localized Policy and Configuration Groups) handle how network elements attached to the service VPNs will forward traffic to the WAN Edge device when using traditional localized policies. To see how to manipulate how other SD-WAN routers will forward traffic to this site across the SD-WAN fabric, refer to Use Case 3 in Chapter 7.

Localized Data Policies

The second main use of localized policies is to configure data policies (specifically access control lists) used for filtering, classifying, and marking traffic at the interface level. This section continues to expand on the previously configured local policy and adds an interface ACL to prohibit SSH sessions through the service-side interface. Example 10-6 shows that, before any policy is configured, it is possible to connect into the DC1-Edge1 router from DC1-Core with the SSH protocol.

Example 10-6 *Establishing an SSH Session from DC1-Core to DC1-Edge1*

```
! DC1-Core is able to successfully establish an SSH session to DC1-Edge1
DC1-CORE#ssh -l admin 172.16.10.1
Password:
DC1-Edge1#
```

In order to filter this data plane traffic with a local policy, a new ACL needs to be configured from the **Custom Options** menu, as shown in Figure 10-16.

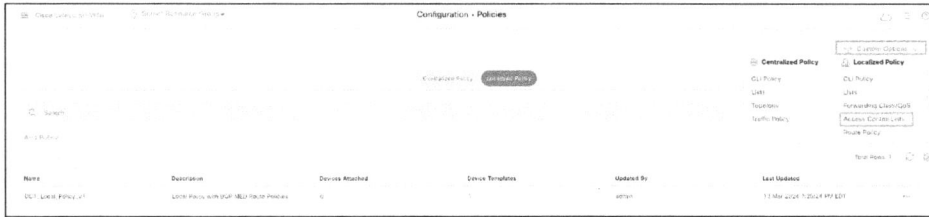

Figure 10-16 *Creating a New Access Control List*

The objective of dropping SSH traffic can be achieved by matching on source port 22 or destination port 22 and dropping the traffic, as shown in Figure 10-17. In order to test that the policy is working, you can configure a counter on the ACL sequence. Keep in mind that when you configure a policy to drop selected traffic like this, it is necessary to change the default action to accept in order to permit any other traffic to be forwarded.

Figure 10-17 *Configuring an ACL to Drop Traffic on Port 22*

You can then add this new ACL to the previously configured local policy by editing that policy and importing this ACL into it. (This is similar to other policy examples throughout the book.) Example 10-7 shows the full localized policy.

Example 10-7 *Previewing the Localized Policy with Route Policies and ACLs*

```
policy
! Existing route-policies are still contained in the localize policy
<<<Output omitted for brevity>>>
! New ACL "DENY_SSH" added
access-list DENY_SSH
    sequence 1
      match
```

```
      source-port 22
   !
   action drop
    count SSH_DROP_COUNTER
   !
  !
   sequence 11
   match
    destination-port 22
   !
   action drop
    count SSH_DROP_COUNTER
   !
  !
 default-action accept
!
app-visibility
flow-visibility
```

Key Topic

Just as there can be only a single centralized SD-WAN Controller policy that is activated at any point in time (although that policy can have many different component parts), there can be only a single localized policy that is activated at any point in time. Each router can have only a single localized policy attached to it at any given point in time, and that single local-ized policy can have as many component route policies and/or ACLs as necessary.

NOTE   Because the policy in this example is currently in use by one or more routers, sav-ing changes to the localized policy will result in configuration changes to all the routers that currently reference this policy. If you would prefer to configure a change to the local policy but apply that change at a later point in time, you can achieve this by copying the current localized policy and then editing the copy of that policy. When you are ready to apply the necessary changes at some point in the future, you can do so by changing which localized policy (LocalizedPolicy_v1 or LocalizedPolicy_v2) is applied in the device template.

Once the ACL has been configured as part of the localized policy, the last step is to refer-ence the ACL as part of the interface configuration template. This can be achieved by setting the **ingress ACL–IPv4** option on the interface template to On and then specifying the name of the ACL in the IPv4 Ingress Access List field, as shown in Figure 10-18.

You can see the effect of this policy by attempting to establish an SSH session again from the DC Core to the WAN Edge router, as shown in Example 10-8. It is clear from the example that the SSH session no longer opens correctly. In addition, the ACL counter is incrementing on DC1-Edge1 to reflect that the packets are being matched and dropped by the ACL.

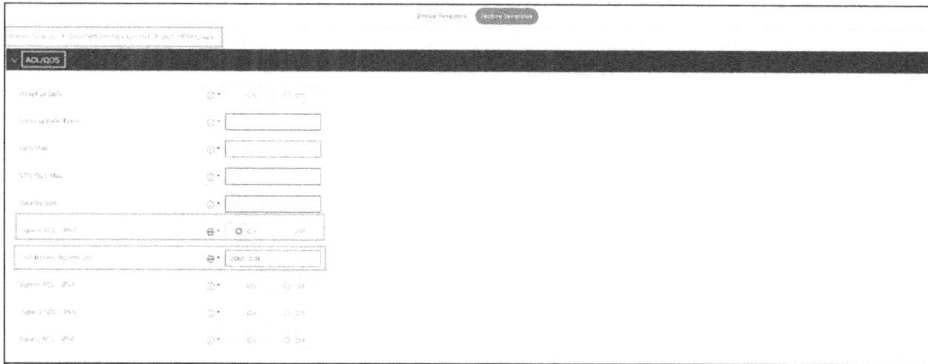

Figure 10-18   *Configuring the Interface Template to Reference the ACL in the Localized Policy*

Example 10-8   *Effects of Applying an Access Control List*

```
! The DC1-CORE device is no longer able to SSH into DC1-Edge1.
DC1-CORE#ssh -l admin 172.16.10.1
% Connection timed out; remote host not responding
DC1-CORE#
```

```
! DC1-Edge1 shows the blocked packets in the ACL counter
DC1-Edge1# show sdwan policy access-list-counters
NAME        COUNTER NAME                        PACKETS        BYTES
-------------------------------------------------------------------------
DENY_SSH    SSH_DROP_COUNTER                    7              390
            default_action_count               0              0
```

As this example shows, interface ACLs are useful for filtering traffic flows transiting the router. Traffic rules specific to SSH and SNMP could be addressed by common ACLs like the one leveraged here or through device access lists. (Using Device Access Lists is the preferred way to control access to a device.) Both options are available within **Configuration > Policies > Localized Policy**, as shown in Figure 10-19.

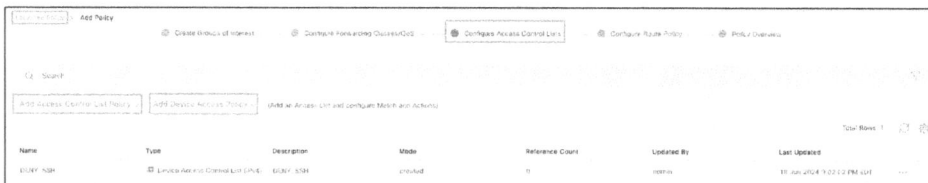

Figure 10-19   *Access Control List and Device Access Policy Under Localized Policy*

This specific example provides a way to protect device CPU to avoid malicious or undesired traffic. ACLs can also be used for a number of other actions, including mirroring traffic to an additional destination, manipulating the forwarding path by setting an alternative next-hop address, policing the data rate of a type of traffic, and remarking the traffic by setting a different DSCP value. While these use cases are beyond the scope of this book, additional information on these topics can be found in Cisco Catalyst SD-WAN Forwarding and QoS Configuration Guide and Cisco Catalyst SD-WAN Policies QoS Configuration Guide Localized Policy and Device Access Policy sections.

NOTE Tunnel interfaces have default implicit ACLs applied to them to permit or deny different traffic to enter these interfaces and enhance network security. You can apply an explicit ACL or explicitly allow services to override this default behavior. Further information about the behavior when explicit ACLs are configured on tunnel interfaces can be found in the Cisco Catalyst SD-WAN Policies Configuration Guide.

Quality of Service Policies

In the traditional policies approach, aspects of quality of service (QoS) such as classification can be configured from both centralized policies and localized policies. As discussed in Chapters 8 and 9, centralized data and app-route policies can be used to make forwarding decisions in the Cisco SD-WAN fabric. While those two technologies are used to determine which path a specific packet or flow should take, the QoS configuration in the localized data policy is used to perform scheduling and queuing functions. Network administrators often use QoS to minimize delay and jitter for business-critical applications such as VoIP and video conferencing by prioritizing the queuing and forwarding of specific traffic classes. They also use QoS to manage buffer allocation across different types of traffic, as well as to determine the congestion management behavior when the buffers are full. A detailed discussion of generic QoS theory and each of these features is beyond the scope of this book, but there are additional resources available in the Cisco documentation and through Cisco Press. This section focuses on the high-level structure needed to implement QoS with Cisco Catalyst SD-WAN.

Although it may be overwhelming at first glance, configuring a QoS policy on a WAN Edge router is a simple process. It consists of the following steps:

Step 1. Define the forwarding classes and map them to hardware queues.

Step 2. Configure the scheduling parameters for each queue and group them into a single QoS map.

Step 3. Configure the transport interfaces with the QoS map.

Step 4. Classify traffic to forwarding classes.

The following sections walk through these steps to show the entire process of building a sample QoS policy. The sample policy will have different classes of traffic: a class for voice and video traffic that is placed in the priority queue, a class for business-critical traffic, and a class for everything else.

Step 1: Define the Forwarding Classes and Map Them to Hardware Queues

The very first step in the QoS configuration is to define the forwarding classes and assign them to their respective hardware queues. You accomplish this configuration in the GUI by creating a new type of localized policy list called a *class map*. The class map list can be found at **Configuration > Policies** under **Custom Options** (see Figure 10-20).

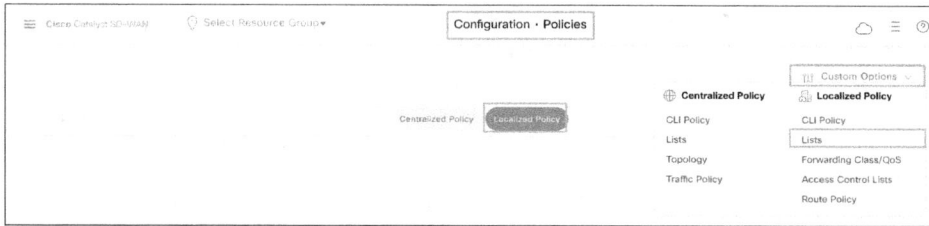

Figure 10-20 *Navigating to the Class Map Lists in the Localized Policy*

From the Localized Policy lists screen, select **Class Map** from the list type and create the required forwarding classes by clicking **New Class List** and then providing a name for each class and the hardware queue it will forward traffic through, as shown in Figure 10-21.

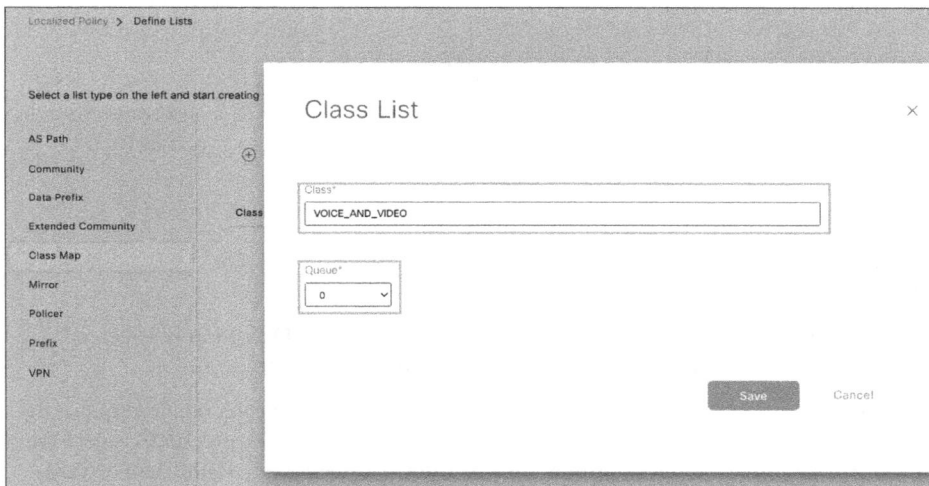

Figure 10-21 *Creating Forwarding Classes*

In this example, the VOICE_AND_VIDEO class is mapped to queue 0, the CRITICAL_DATA traffic is mapped to queue 1, and the BEST_EFFORT traffic is mapped to queue 7 (see Figure 10-22).

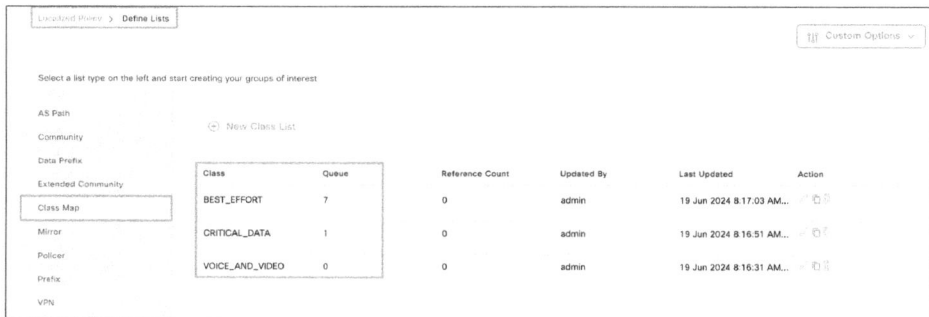

Figure 10-22 *Recently Created Class Maps/Forwarding Classes*

Step 2: Configure the Scheduling Parameters for Each Queue and Group Them into a Single QoS Map

When using traditional localized policies to deploy QoS configurations, the second step in the process of configuring a QoS policy is to configure the scheduling parameters for each individual queue. Each scheduler will contain a reference to the traffic class, the maximum bandwidth to be used during congestion, the percentage of the buffer that is allocated, the scheduling mechanism (low-latency queuing or weighted round robin), and the congestion management technique (tail drop or random early detection). When QoS configurations are generated in the SD-WAN Manager GUI, additional classes called Queue0, Queue1, Queue2, and so on are created, and the schedulers are tied to these classes.

To create the required schedulers and group them into a QoS map, navigate to **Configuration > Policies** and then click the **Custom Options** button and select **Forwarding Class/ QoS**, as shown in Figure 10-23.

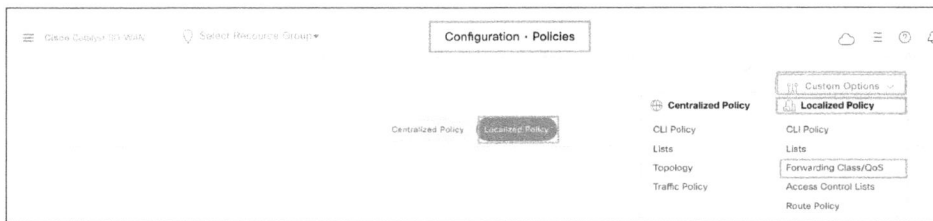

Figure 10-23   *Navigating to the QoS Map and Schedulers*

When you reach the **Forwarding Class/QoS** screen, you see that **QoS Map** is selected by default. Click **Add QoS Map** and select **Create New**, as shown in Figure 10-24.

In the QoS Map screen, add a name and a description. You can add each required queue by clicking **Add Queue**. Then, in the Add Queue dialog box, shown in Figure 10-25, select the queue number from the Queue drop-down list. SD-WAN Manager populates the Forwarding Class value according to the class map/forwarding classes created in step 1. Then set the bandwidth and buffer percentages as well as the queuing method (at the Drops setting). Create each of the different queues by following this procedure.

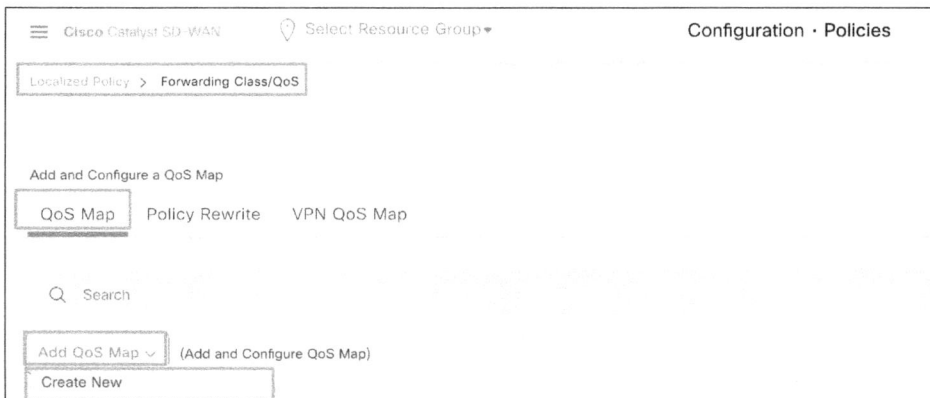

Figure 10-24   *Creating a New QoS Map*

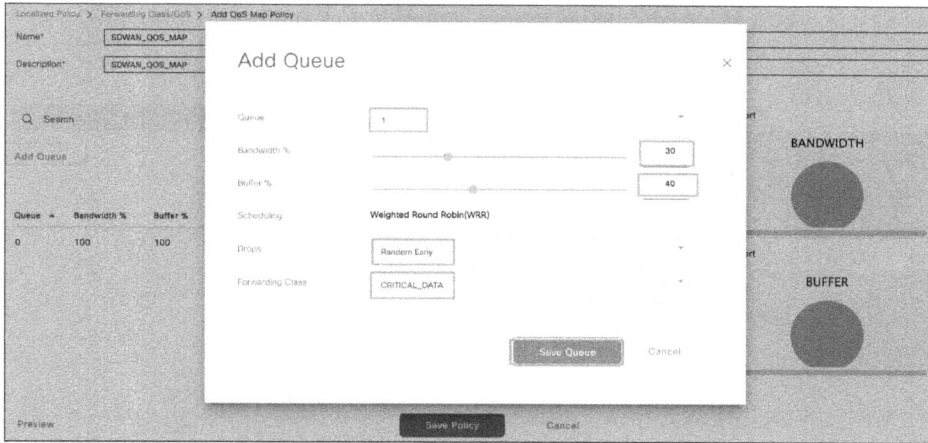

Figure 10-25   *Adding Queue 1 for Critical Data*

Cisco WAN Edge routers support a total of eight queues, numbered 0 through 7. Queue 0 is always configured as a low-latency queue and is the only queue that supports low-latency queuing. In addition, all control traffic that is originated by the WAN Edge router, including DTLS/TLS, BFD probes, and routing protocol traffic, is automatically mapped to queue 0. Any user-defined traffic classes that are mapped to queue 0, such as the VOICE_AND_VIDEO class, must also be configured for low-latency queuing. Queues 1 through 7 support weighted round robin forwarding, where the weighting is proportional to the configured bandwidth percentage.

Figure 10-26 shows the end result, including a QoS map preview. You can group schedulers together with a single QoS map that can be referenced under the interface configuration. Example 10-9 show the preview output. To conclude the configuration, click Save.

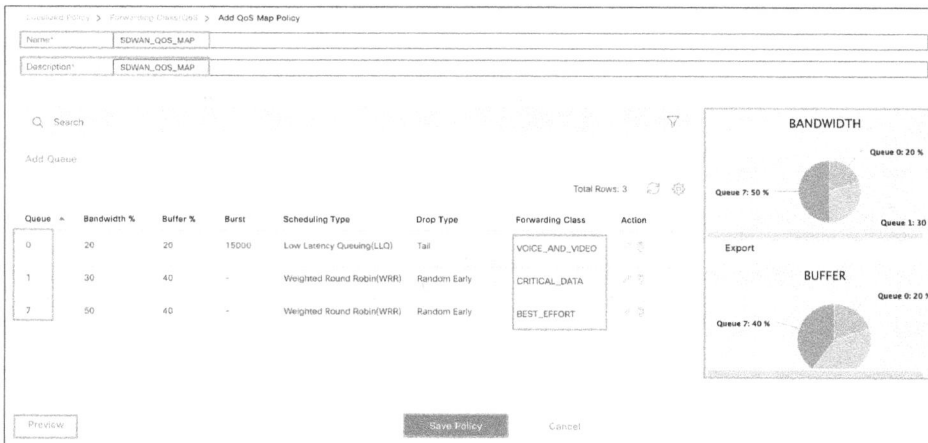

Figure 10-26   *QoS Map Grouping Schedulers*

Example 10-9   *QoS Schedulers Grouped into QoS Map Configuration*

```
qos-scheduler SDWAN_QOS_MAP_0
  class Queue0
  bandwidth-percent 20
  buffer-percent 20
  scheduling llq
  drops tail-drop
  burst 15000
  !
 qos-scheduler SDWAN_QOS_MAP_1
  class Queue1
  bandwidth-percent 30
  buffer-percent 40
  scheduling wrr
  drops red-drop
  !
qos-scheduler SDWAN_QOS_MAP_7
  class Queue7
  bandwidth-percent 50
  buffer-percent 40
  scheduling wrr
  drops red-drop
  !
qos-map SDWAN_QOS_MAP
  qos-scheduler SDWAN_QOS_MAP_0
  qos-scheduler SDWAN_QOS_MAP_1
  qos-scheduler SDWAN_QOS_MAP_7
```

At this stage, the recently created QoS map must be imported into the existing localized policy and pushed to the device configuration as part of the device template. You can accomplish this by attaching the policy under **Additional Templates** for the desired devices, as shown in Figure 10-27.

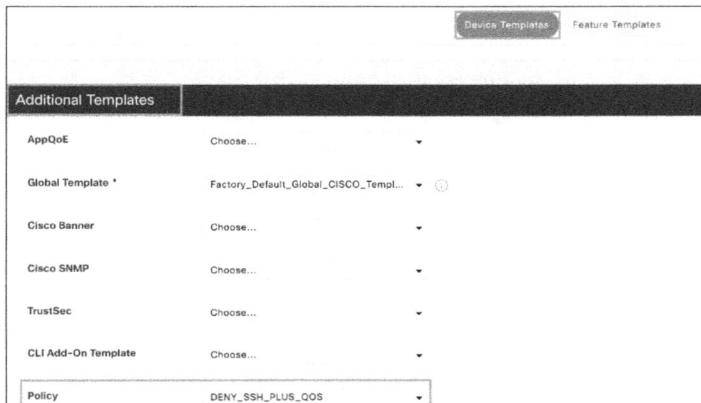

Figure 10-27   *Attaching a Localized Policy to a Device Template*

Step 3: Configure the Transport Interfaces with the QoS Map

The third step in the process of configuring a QoS policy is to configure the interface to use the QoS map that was created in step 2. A QoS map can be applied to any interface to affect the scheduling and queuing of outbound traffic. However, because the available WAN bandwidth is typically lower than LAN bandwidth and, therefore, congestion is most likely to occur on the WAN, QoS maps are most commonly configured outbound on the transport (WAN) interfaces.

If device and feature templates are used, the QoS map is associated to the transport interface feature template in the ACL/QOS section, as shown in Figure 10-28.

On the other hand, when Configuration Groups and Policy Groups are used, the recommended approach for QoS configuration is to use the Queuing Model section under Application Priority & SLA (see Figure 10-29), opting between smart default values or an Advanced Layout. To get there, navigate to **Configuration > Policy Groups >Application Priority & SLA**, and then, under **QoS Queue** from **Advanced Layout** in this case, click **Add QoS Policy**. Notice that the target interface is requested here.

Regardless of which method is used, the end goal is to configure the QoS map in the interface. Example 10-10 shows the QoS map applied to transport interfaces.

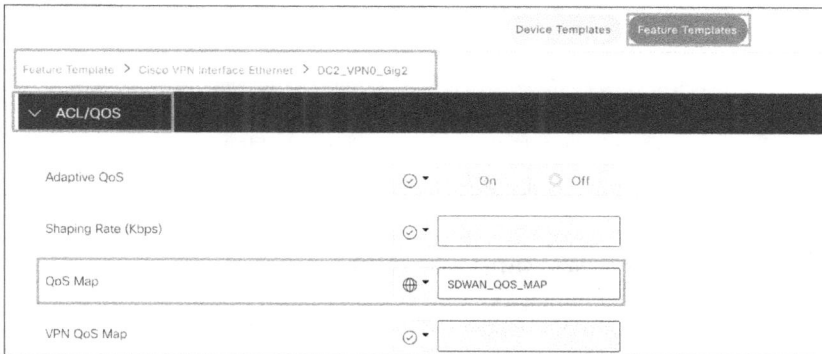

Figure 10-28   *Assigning a QoS Map to the MPLS Interface Feature Template*

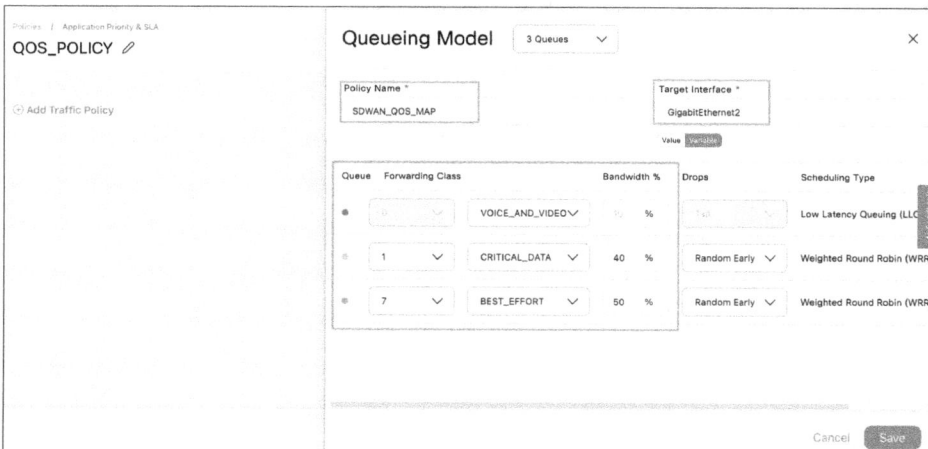

Figure 10-29   *The Queueing Model with Policy Groups*

Example 10-10   *Applying QoS Maps to Transport Interfaces*

```
! QoS Maps applied to transport interfaces in VPN 0.
DC1-Edge1# show running-config interface GigabitEthernet1
interface GigabitEthernet1
 ip address 209.165.201.1 255.255.255.224
 <<<output omitted for brevity>>>
 service-policy output SDWAN_QOS_MAP
end
DC1-Edge1# show running-config interface GigabitEthernet2
interface GigabitEthernet2
 ip address 192.168.20.1 255.255.255.0
 <<<output omitted for brevity>>>
 service-policy output SDWAN_QOS_MAP
end
! Sample show commands to validate that the QOS Map is applied
! Outbound on the transport interfaces (WAN).
!
DC1-Edge1#sh policy-map interface brief
Service-policy output: SDWAN_QOS_MAP
 GigabitEthernet1
 GigabitEthernet2
<<<Output omitted for brevity>>>
! Sample known show command to validate that the QOS Map is configured
! with the correct QoS Schedulers.
```

Step 4: Classify Traffic to Forwarding Classes

The final step in the process of configuring a QoS policy is to assign traffic flows to different forwarding classes. You can perform this step with either a centralized data policy or an ACL from a localized data policy by specifying the class action. This section continues to expand on the existing localized policy shown in Example 10-7. You will see how to add more sequences in order to classify traffic into the appropriate forwarding classes (see Figure 10-30).

Figure 10-30   *QoS Classification ACL Sequence Rules*

NOTE   In this scenario, QoS for a single VPN is configured, but other variations of QoS settings, such as per-tunnel QoS, per-VPN QoS, or adaptive QoS, are available in some SD-WAN versions. For details, refer to the "Cisco Catalyst SD-WAN Forwarding and QoS Configuration Guide."

Now the classification ACL needs to be applied in any desired service-side interface to match traffic coming from the LAN.

Example 10-11 shows the QoS configuration that is done through localized policies. Additional verification commands demonstrate service-side interfaces where the classification ACL is applied and the transport interfaces where the QoS map has been configured.

Example 10-11   *QoS Configuration and Policy Verification*

```
DC1-Edge1#sh sdwan running-config | sec class-map|policy-map
! Class-maps are used to map forwarding classes to Hardware queues
class-map match-any BEST_EFFORT
 match qos-group 7
class-map match-any CRITICAL_DATA
 match qos-group 1
class-map match-any Queue0
 match qos-group 0
class-map match-any Queue1
 match qos-group 1
class-map match-any Queue7
 match qos-group 7
class-map match-any VOICE_AND_VIDEO
 match qos-group 0
! A QoS Map groups the QoS schedulers used to configure the forwarding
! parameters of each traffic class
policy-map SDWAN_QOS_MAP
 class Queue0
  police rate percent 20
  !
  priority level 1
 !
 class Queue1
  bandwidth remaining ratio 30
  random-detect precedence-based
 !
 class Queue7
  bandwidth remaining ratio 50
```

10

```
      random-detect precedence-based
   !
```

```
DC1-Edge1#sh policy-map interface brief
! QoS Map is applied to the outbound transport interfaces
Service-policy output: SDWAN_QOS_MAP
 GigabitEthernet1
 GigabitEthernet2
DC1-Edge1#sh sdwan policy access-list-associations
! ACL is applied at ingress direction on service side interfaces
                                      INTERFACE
NAME                 INTERFACE NAME   DIRECTION
DENY_SSH_PLUS_QOS  GigabitEthernet3  in
DC1-Edge1#show sdwan running-config | sec policy
<<<Output omitted for brevity>>>
policy
<<<Output omitted for brevity>>>
lists
  data-prefix-list CRITICAL_SERVERS
   ip-prefix 10.10.250.0/24
  !
 !
 class-map
  class Queue0 queue 0
  class VOICE_AND_VIDEO queue 0
  class CRITICAL_DATA queue 1
  class Queue1 queue 1
  class BEST_EFFORT queue 7
  class Queue7 queue 7
 !
! ACL is used to assign traffic to forwarding classes
access-list DENY_SSH_PLUS_QOS
 <<<Output omitted for brevity>>>
 ! Sequences 21, 31, and 41 match permitted traffic and set the 'class' action
 ! to specify the forwarding class.
   sequence 21
    match
     dscp 40 46
    !
    action accept
     class VOICE_AND_VIDEO
    !
    !
```

```
   sequence 31
    match
     source-data-prefix-list CRITICAL_SERVERS
    !
    action accept
     class CRITICAL_DATA
   !
   !

   sequence 41
    action accept
     class BEST_EFFORT
    !
   !
 default-action accept
```

As shown in Example 10-11, traffic is matched to the VOICE_AND_VIDEO class based on the DSCP markings of the traffic. In Cisco Catalyst SD-WAN policies, DSCP is always specified in decimal values. Traffic is matched to the CRITICAL_DATA class by matching the data prefix list CRITICAL_SERVERS. Any traffic that is not matched to either the VOICE_AND_VIDEO or CRITICAL_DATA class will be placed into the BEST_EFFORT class. While this example matches on DSCP values and IP addresses, any criteria that can be matched in an ACL or a centralized data policy can be used to match traffic and set the class action.

NOTE   Network administrators might find it familiar to use ACLs to assign types of traffic to forwarding classes, but traditional Centralized Data Policies and Policy Groups make this task easy, too. Because Centralized Data Policies and Policy Groups use Layer 7 attributes as match parameters too and offer ease of configuration and more granular classification, administrators commonly prefer these two methods.

Summary

This chapter discusses localized policies and how they are used with Cisco SD-WAN. There are two main types of localized policies, localized control policies and localized data policies, both of which are configured in a single policy section of the WAN Edge router configuration and are device specific in scope when leveraging device templates or configuration groups/policy groups.

This chapter provides examples of how localized control policies are used to manipulate routing advertisements outside the SD-WAN fabric and how this functionality can be used to achieve certain traffic engineering and outcomes. Localized data policies can be used to create access control lists and manipulate traffic flowing in the data plane through the router. Localized data policies can also be used to configure quality of service on WAN Edge routers, including queuing and congestion management, in order to prioritize certain classes of traffic over others. Although traditional localized policies are widely used, we recommend using Policy Groups, which can leverage configurations executed at the device level, such as ACLs, route policies, or QoS, contributing to a simplified overall configuration process.

10

Review All Key Topics

Review the most important topics in the chapter, noted with the Key Topic icon in the outer margin of the page. Table 10-1 lists these key topics and the page number on which each is found.

Table 10-1   Key Topics

Key Topic Element	Description	Page
Paragraph	Where centralized policies and localized policies are applied	420
Paragraph	Attaching only a single localized policy to a router at a time	428
Paragraph	The queues supported by Cisco WAN Edge routers	433

Chapter Review Questions

1. Localized policies are configured on which element of the Catalyst SD-WAN fabric?

   a. SD-WAN Validator

   b. SD-WAN Controller

   c. WAN Edge routers

   d. Policy

2. True or false: A single list object can be used in both a centralized policy and a localized policy.

   a. True

   b. False

3. What is the scope of localized policy?

   a. Device specific

   b. Site specific

   c. VPN specific

   d. The entire network

4. Which of the following actions can be taken in a localized control policy? (Choose two that apply.)

   a. Accept

   b. Reject

   c. Drop

   d. Inspect

   e. Pass

5. True or false: Ensuring symmetric flows through a single WAN Edge router is preferable to using equal-cost multipathing because it ensures that flows will not be blocked by a firewall or NAT state mismatches.

   a. True

   b. False

6. Which of the following actions can be taken in a localized data policy? (Choose two that apply.)

a. Accept

b. Reject

c. Drop

d. Inspect

e. Pass

7. How many queues are supported on a WAN Edge router interface?

a. 0

b. 2

c. 4

d. 8

e. 256

8. Which queues support low-latency queuing and priority queueing on WAN Edge router platforms?

a. Queue 0

b. Queue 1

c. Queue 7

d. Queue 8

e. Queues 0 and 1

f. All queues

9. Which queue is control plane traffic automatically mapped to?

a. Queue 0

b. Queue 1

c. Queue 7

d. Queue 8

10. Which of the following are part of the localized policy QoS configuration on a WAN Edge router? (Choose three that apply.)

a. class-map

b. qos-map

c. shaper

d. qos-scheduler

11. True or false: When configuring QoS, assignment of traffic types to forwarding classes is exclusively done through ACLs in localized policies.

a. True

b. False

12. True or false: Configuration groups help reduce cross-navigation within SD-WAN Manager, making it possible to configure route policies and ACLs from feature profiles.

a. True

b. False

10

References

"Cisco Catalyst SD-WAN Policies Configuration Guide, Localized Policy," https://www.cisco.com/c/en/us/td/docs/routers/sdwan/configuration/policies/ios-xe-17/policies-book-xe/localized-policy.html

"Cisco Catalyst SD-WAN Forwarding and QoS Configuration Guide," https://www.cisco.com/c/en/us/td/docs/routers/sdwan/configuration/qos/ios-xe-17/qos-book-xe/forwarding-qos.html

"Policy Groups Configuration Guide," https://www.cisco.com/c/en/us/td/docs/routers/sdwan/configuration/Policy-Groups/policy-groups/m-policy-groups.html

CHAPTER 11

Cisco Catalyst SD-WAN Security

This chapter covers the following topics:

- **Cisco Catalyst SD-WAN Security: Why and What:** This section discusses what SD-WAN security is and why it is relevant to an organization.

- **Cisco Catalyst SD-WAN Security Policies:** This section explains the main security features embedded in Cisco Catalyst SD-WAN. It includes, in particular, application-aware enterprise firewall, intrusion detection and prevention, URL filtering, Advanced Malware Protection, DNS security, and TLS/SSL decryption.

- **Unified Security Policies:** This section covers a new method of configuring a single unified security policy that combines firewall, DNS security, and threat defense features in one place.

- **Secure Internet Gateway (SIG):** This section covers concepts related to and configuration of cloud-based security for enterprise data traffic using Cisco Umbrella or a third-party SIG provider.

- **Policy Groups:** This section explains how to deploy security policies using Policy Groups.

- **Secure Segmentation:** This section covers the basics of network microsegmentation in a Cisco Catalyst SD-WAN solution built based on Cisco TrustSec.

- **SD-WAN Manager Authentication and Authorization:** This section covers concepts related to and configuration of SD-WAN Manager role-based access control.

Modern business processes significantly rely on the underlying IT infrastructure. Because of that, cybersecurity is not considered a convenient addition to the network anymore. Security has become a critical mandatory part of any networking solution. This chapter introduces the main security functions and tools integrated in Cisco Catalyst SD-WAN.

Cisco Catalyst SD-WAN Security: Why and What

As organizations are migrating many business-critical applications to the cloud and rapidly adopting Internet circuits as business-grade transports, a new and better way to consume applications is being leveraged. Direct Internet access allows end users to reach cloud applications and resources in a more optimal fashion by connecting to the closest and highest-performing point of presence. Most cloud application providers highly recommend not backhauling this traffic through a remote data center or hub but suggest instead using direct Internet access—going directly from the branch to the application, and leveraging DNS and geolocation services for the best possible performance. In addition, organizations are realizing that they can leverage these same Internet circuits as a way to offload guest traffic to the Internet directly instead of using up WAN and data center resources that would be better used for business-critical applications. Direct Internet Access coupled with Cisco Catalyst SD-WAN application-aware routing and visibility provides a solution that makes sense for the majority of organizations across most verticals.

Realistically, however, we cannot ignore the security implications of moving the Internet edge to the branch. In addition, with the common trend of moving infrastructure to the cloud, the network perimeter that needs protection has expanded. The direct Internet access model—where Internet access is distributed across many branches, unsecured guest users are allowed Internet access directly, and payment card infrastructure is exposed to these new access models—increases the attack surface of the network. The proliferation of highly publicized massive data breaches has made security compliance, particularly for organizations that are subject to PCI DSS (Payment Card Industry Data Security Standard), a critical task for almost every organization. The threat landscape is wide and includes cyber warfare, ransomware, and targeted attacks. These threats may manifest as security bugs and vulnerabilities, malware, denial of service attacks, botnets, and so on.

It is important to note that security threats can come from both inside a network and outside it, and all attack vectors must be considered. Figure 11-1 illustrates the ever-growing threat surface. As you can see, outside-in threats are originated externally; common examples include unauthorized access to internal resources and denial-of-service attacks (DoS/DDoS attacks). Inside-out threats, which emerge inside the network and then spread externally, can lead to the business-critical data loss or further spread of malware infection, phishing, and so on. Finally, internal threats remain inside the network, where they can produce untrusted access to the internal resources, on-path attacks, and so on.

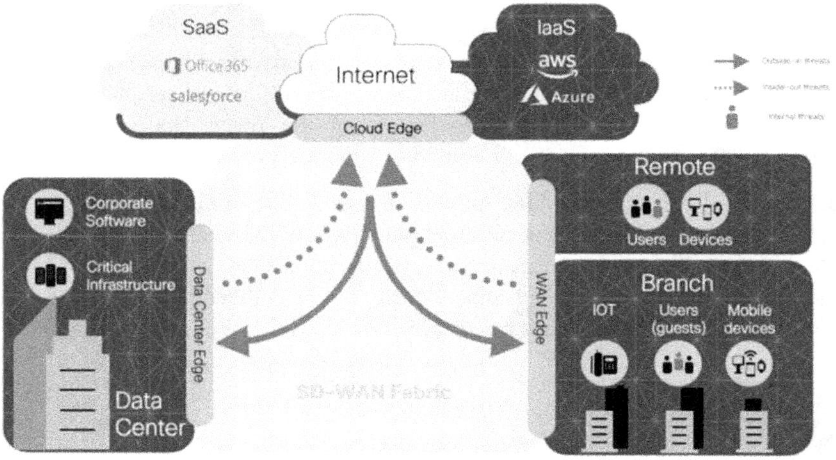

Figure 11-1 *Threat Surface*

It is critical for a branch to leverage the appropriate security mechanisms, such as firewalling, intrusion prevention, URL filtering, and malware protection, in order to protect the network by preventing and detecting all types of threats. Network architects need to consider how security services should be consumed by the branches. One way to consume Cisco Catalyst SD-WAN security is by leveraging Cisco's integrated security applications within a rich portfolio of powerful WAN Edge routers, such as Catalyst 8000 series devices. On top of the native application-aware stateful firewall, these WAN Edge routers are capable of dedicating compute resources to application service containers running within IOS XE to enable inline IDS/IPS, URL filtering, and Advanced Malware Protection. Cisco Catalyst SD-WAN Manager is the unified management console that provides visibility into and reporting for these integrated security applications.

While this chapter focuses mainly on integrated security at the branch, Cisco Catalyst SD-WAN security can also be consumed through cloud services or through regional hubs where virtual network functions (VNF) based security chains may be leveraged or robust security stacks may already exist. In the end, the appropriate security architecture depends on the organization's technical and business requirements.

Figure 11-2 illustrates some of the security deployment models that organizations can choose to deploy:

- **Integrated (embedded) security:** This model leverages the embedded security features that are present on IOS XE WAN Edge routers. It includes features like zone-based firewall, IPS/IDS, URL filtering, AMP, TLS/SSL proxy, and DNS security (which requires Cisco Umbrella integration). While the embedded security features provide comprehensive protection from both internal and external threats, enabling these features can impact the performance and forwarding rates of WAN Edge routers. Thus, careful planning is recommended when choosing the branch router platforms and deploying the required security features. (For more details and technical tips, refer to the "Cisco SD-WAN Security Sensitive Branch Design Case Study" document referenced at the end of this chapter.)

- **Secure Internet Gateway (SIG):** When using the SIG model, a WAN Edge router redirects user traffic to a secure Internet gateway provider (such as Cisco Umbrella or a third-party provider). The SIG provider is responsible for all security inspections of the traffic, which allows the organization to reduce the load on the WAN Edge routers and use less powerful router models in the small branches. The SIG model protects data traffic against external threats but does not provide any visibility or control over the internal traffic.

- **Hybrid: Integrated security with SIG:** A hybrid model combines the benefits of both previous models and allows a network administrator to balance and adjust the SD-WAN security policies to the organization's needs. In particular, the administrator can decide which traffic should be examined locally by the embedded security mechanisms and which traffic should be redirected to the SIG.

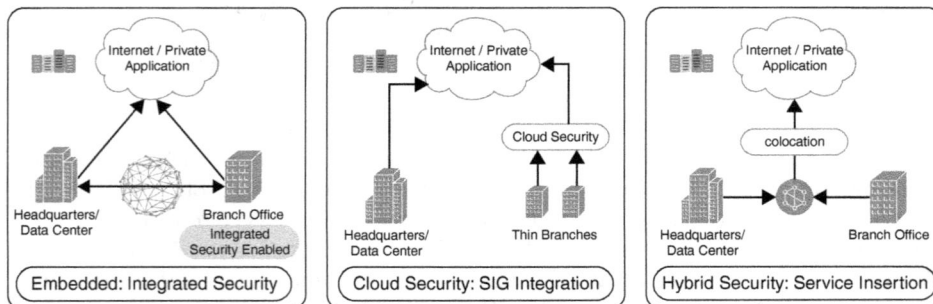

Figure 11-2 *Security Deployment Models*

Here are some benefits of the Cisco Catalyst SD-WAN security suite:

- **Simple and automated security solution:** The intent-based workflow is designed for ease of configuration and deployment of the SD-WAN security solution. The workflow allows you to leverage templates or Policy Groups in order to include all the relevant security capabilities and deploy the policy to multiple devices at the same time.

- **Comprehensive SD-WAN security:** With security capabilities such as an application-aware enterprise firewall and IPS enabled on a WAN Edge device, you can do the following:

  - Restrict access to certain Internet destinations for remote employees and guests, with improved application experience.

  - Protect the internal network from malware and/or malicious content in real time.

  - Incur no additional hardware costs, as deploying the Cisco Catalyst SD-WAN security solution eliminates the need to deploy any additional equipment within your SD-WAN network to enable security features.

- **Centralized management:** You can deploy, troubleshoot, and monitor an SD-WAN overlay solution with security capabilities across the WAN Edge devices centrally via the SD-WAN Manager GUI.

As briefly mentioned previously, Cisco Catalyst SD-WAN security features are centrally configured via SD-WAN Manager. In Cisco Catalyst SD-WAN Release 20.12 and above, there are three ways to configure security features. First, the *traditional security policy* provides a guided workflow that can assist a network operator in building security policy based on well-known use cases or based on a custom use case. Second, the *unified policy* allows you to create a single policy that includes all next-generation firewall and threat defense security features in one place. Finally, *Policy Groups* provide a reusable and structured approach to building policies that can be applied to the devices managed by Configuration Groups.

NOTE This book is focused on the latest Cisco Catalyst SD-WAN versions and IOS XE WAN Edge devices as of May 2024. Thus, most of the security features described in this chapter are supported only on Cisco IOS XE based routers running SD-WAN code. Please refer to the Cisco Catalyst SD-WAN Security Configuration Guide published on the Cisco documentation site for additional deployment details.

Figure 11-3 shows the security policies configuration page in SD-WAN Manager. Once a security policy is configured, it can be assigned to the desired branch through the attached device template. We will start with a detailed discussion of Cisco Catalyst SD-WAN security features as a part of traditional security policy. Later in this chapter, we will also cover the other approaches to configuring policies that were just mentioned: using the unified security policy (which is the recommended way to configure policies at this writing) and using policy groups (which is a new method that can be used in conjunction with configuration groups).

11

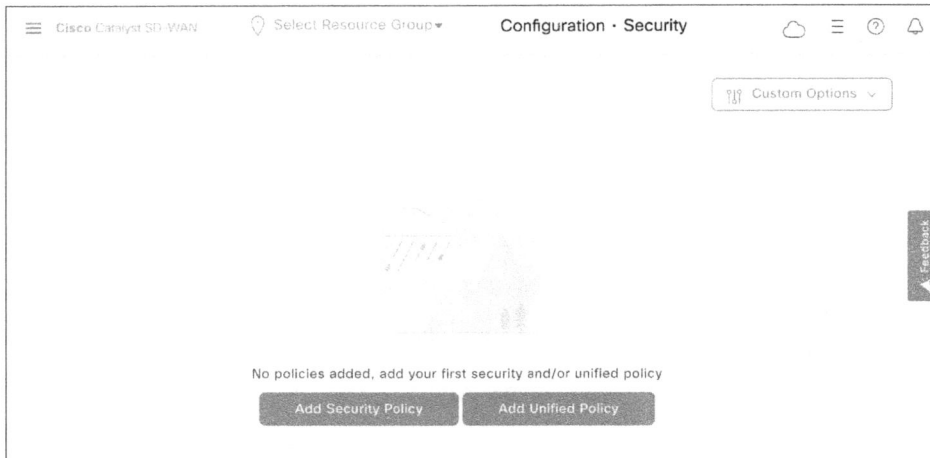

Figure 11-3 *Security Policy Configuration*

NOTE All screenshots throughout this chapter were taken from SD-WAN Manager release 20.12. Other versions of the software may have slightly different appearances, but the basic functionality remains the same.

NOTE For an end user, the main difference between traditional and unified policies is in the way security features are configured and put together. From the WAN Edge router's perspective, unified policies can be more efficient in terms of device performance due to how the traffic classification and inspection works. However, the basics of the SD-WAN security features operation remain the same regardless of the configuration method, as you'll see in the next section. Other configuration methods are covered in later sections of this chapter.

Cisco Catalyst SD-WAN Security Policies

The security policy workflow in SD-WAN Manager allows a network administrator to select from a list of predefined policies, including Compliance, Guest Access, Direct Cloud Access, Direct Internet Access, or Application Quality of Experience. Figure 11-4 shows the available policies and the security features included in each of them. If none of the preconfigured policies satisfies the business requirements, the administrator can create their own custom policy and combine the security features as needed for the specific use case requirements.

Application-Aware Enterprise Firewall

Key Topic

One of the most basic yet crucial forms of security at a branch is firewalling. A proper firewall provides protection for stateful TCP sessions, enables logging, and ensures that a zero-trust domain is implemented between segments in the network. Traditional branch firewall design involves deploying a firewall appliance in either inline Layer 3 mode or transparent Layer 2 mode behind (or ahead of) the WAN Edge router. This adds complexity to the enterprise branch and creates needless additional administrative overhead in managing the added firewalls.

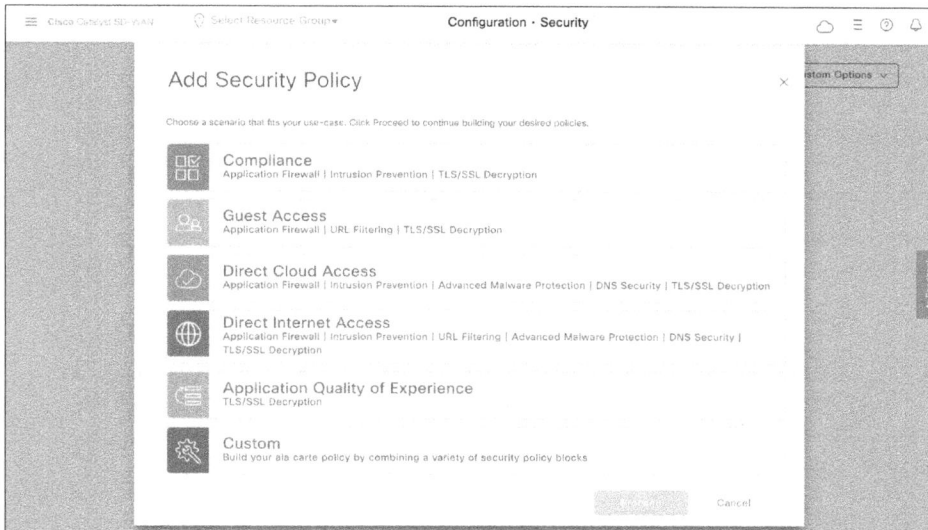

Figure 11-4 *Security Policy Workflow*

Cisco Catalyst SD-WAN takes an integrated approach and has implemented a robust application-aware enterprise firewall directly in the SD-WAN code. The Cisco Catalyst SD-WAN Enterprise Firewall with Application Awareness provides stateful inspection, zone-based policies, and segment awareness. Also, through network-based application recognition, it can classify more than 1400 Layer 7 applications for granular policy control. These applications can be secured based on category or on an individual basis, depending on how the feature is leveraged in the security policy. Because these policies are VPN aware, they can be applied within a zone, between zones on the same WAN Edge router, or between zones across the Cisco Catalyst SD-WAN fabric. Depending on its type (VPN or interface), a *zone* can be a grouping of one or more VPNs or a grouping of interfaces. Creating zones allows you to establish security boundaries in your overlay network so that you can control the flow of all data traffic that passes between these zones.

NOTE Interface-based firewall policies can be configured only for unified security policies, as discussed later in this chapter.

Zone-based firewall configuration consists of the following components:

- The *source zone* is a grouping of VPNs where the data traffic flows originate.

- The *destination zone* is a grouping of VPNs where the data traffic flows terminate.

- The *firewall policy* is a localized security policy that defines the conditions that the originating data traffic flow must match to allow the flow to continue to the destination zone.

- A *zone pair* is a container that associates a source zone with a destination zone and that applies a firewall policy to the traffic that flows between the two zones.

11

In addition, there is a self-zone policy for inspecting traffic destined to the WAN Edge router itself in order to protect against inbound threats, DDoS attacks, and unauthorized access to the WAN Edge router. When combined with other Cisco Catalyst SD-WAN security features, Enterprise Firewall with Application Awareness is an important component of the solution for an organization looking to meet PCI DSS compliance across the enterprise branch footprint. Figure 11-5 provides an overview of the typical zones and traffic flows for an application-aware firewall.

Firewall events and logs can be exported to security information and event management systems through traditional syslog or, for more advanced implementations, via NetFlow Version 9 to support high-speed logging requirements.

NOTE   Support for application recognition through a firewall policy is only available on Cisco IOS XE SD-WAN software and not Viptela OS. Cisco vEdge and ISR appliances running Viptela OS can still enjoy the benefits of a firewall but must use Layer 3 and Layer 4 criteria to identify traffic.

With the help of Cisco SD-WAN Manager, implementing a firewall policy at the branch is relatively straightforward. As with all other security features available in Cisco Catalyst SD-WAN, the first place to start is by navigating to the **Security** section and either building a new security policy (and following the simple workflow to build a firewall policy) or directly navigating to the **Firewall Policy** subsection under **Custom Options**. No matter how the firewall policy is configured, it must eventually be tied to an overall security policy, which is then attached to the branch WAN Edge device template.

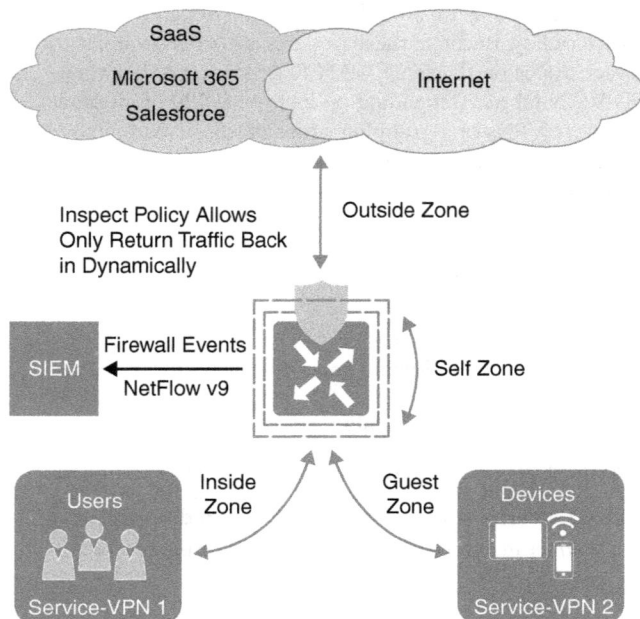

Figure 11-5   *Application-Aware Enterprise Firewall*

Enterprise Firewall with Application Awareness is a localized security policy that allows stateful inspection of data traffic flows that are matched based on six different criteria available within the SD-WAN Manager security policy dashboard. The match criteria are source data prefix, destination data prefix, source port, destination port, protocol, and application/application family. Traffic flows that originate in a given zone are allowed to proceed to another zone based on the policy match and action criteria set between the two zones.

Within a given firewall policy, accepted matching flows can be subjected to the following three actions:

- **Inspect:** When the action is set to *Inspect*, Enterprise Firewall with Application Awareness tracks the state of the flows and creates sessions. Because it maintains the state of the flows, return traffic is allowed, and there is no need to configure a separate policy to allow the response traffic.

- **Pass:** This action allows the router to forward the traffic from one zone to another zone. The *Pass* action does not track the state of the flows. In other words, the firewall does not create sessions when the action is set to Pass. The Pass action allows the traffic to flow in only one direction. You must have a corresponding policy to allow the response traffic.

- **Drop:** When the action is set to *Drop* and packets match against the set match parameters, the packets are dropped.

NOTE   When leveraging application recognition for match criteria in traditional security policies, the Inspect action is equivalent to the Drop action. *Application List to Drop* criteria can be used only in firewall rules with an Inspect action, and the configured application(s) will be always dropped, while the traffic matching other criteria in the same firewall rule will be inspected. This behavior was changed in the unified policies, and we will discuss it later in this chapter.

Based on the flow of traffic between zones, Enterprise Firewall with Application Awareness is further divided into *intra-zone-based security* and *inter-zone-based security*.

Figure 11-6 illustrates an intra-zone security use case where hosts within the same zone on the same WAN Edge router can be secured with a firewall policy, while the same policy can also secure hosts across the fabric in the same zone. For the firewall policy rule to have an impact, traffic must ingress and egress the WAN Edge router and should not be bypassed via a downstream Layer 3 device.

Figure 11-7 illustrates an inter-zone security use case where hosts on different zones within the same WAN Edge router can be secured with a firewall policy, while the same policy can also secure hosts across the fabric on different zones. For inter-zone connectivity to occur, an SD-WAN Controller policy that leaks routes between VPNs must first be configured and applied. This is called an *extranet policy*, and it leverages the "Export to" route-based control policy sequence.

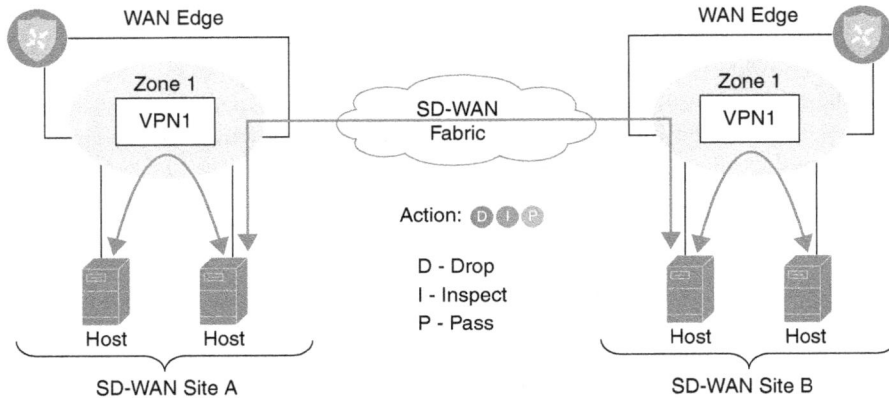

Figure 11-6 *Intra-Zone Firewall Application*

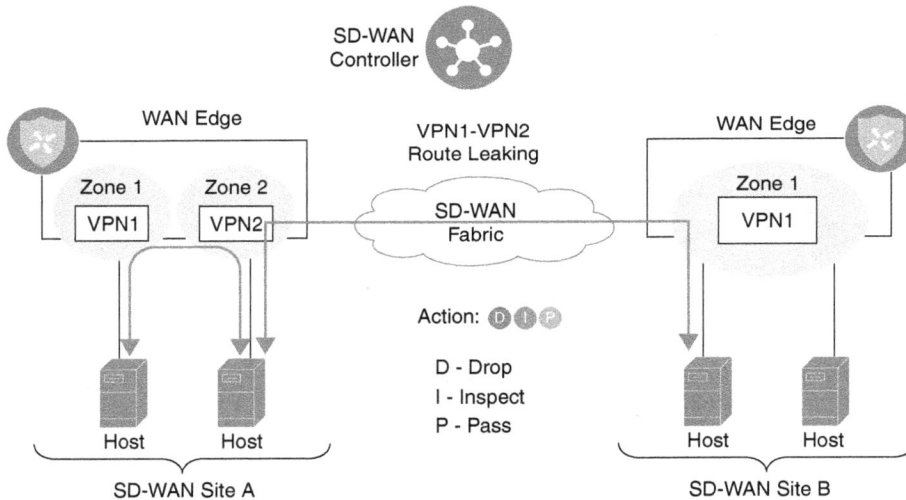

Figure 11-7 *Inter-Zone Firewall Application*

Configuring a firewall policy in Cisco SD-WAN Manager involves the following steps:

Step 1. **Create a new firewall policy.** Name and describe the policy.

Step 2. **Configure zones.** Create your source and destination zones. Zones can be defined either based on a VPN list or based on the WAN Edge interface(s) through which the data traffic flows.

Step 3. **Apply zone pairs.** Group the source and destination zones into a zone pair to define the traffic direction. The policy sequences will be applied to this zone pair.

Step 4. **Configure a default action.** This is the action that will take place if a sequence match is not found. Drop and Pass are valid options.

Step 5. **Configure sequence rules.** Match traffic using Layer 3 or 4 information (such as source data prefix lists, source ports, destination data prefix lists, and so on) or by matching on application category or name.

To start the configuration, navigate to **Configuration > Security > Add Security Policy > Custom.** Figure 11-8 shows the first step, creating a firewall policy in SD-WAN Manager.

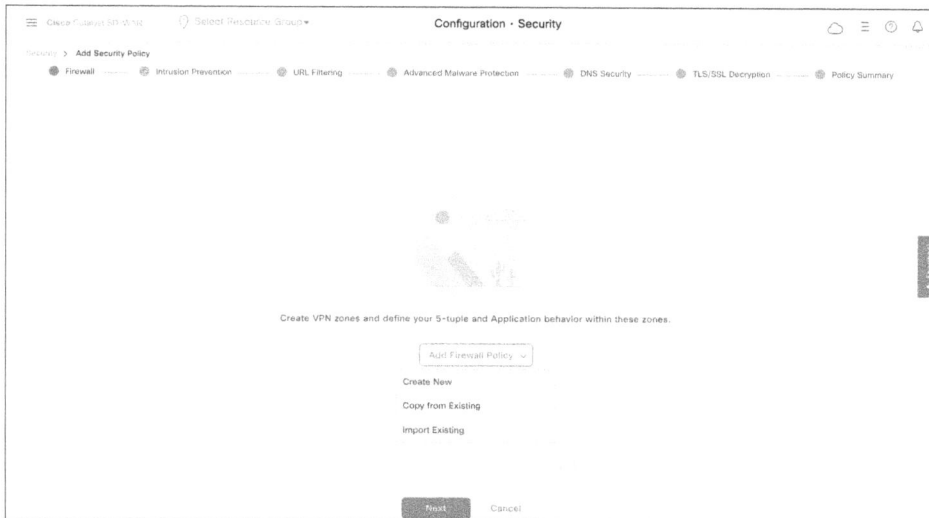

Figure 11-8   *Building a Firewall Policy*

Once a firewall policy is created, the zones and zone pairs are then created and applied. Keep in mind that a new zone list can be defined during the firewall policy configuration, as shown in Figure 11-9. Alternatively, you can create and manage Zones under **Configuration > Security > Custom Options > Lists.**

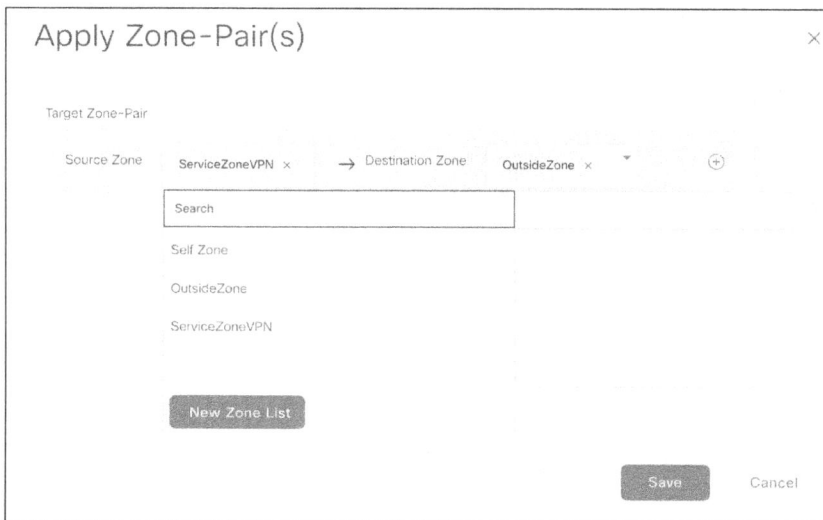

Figure 11-9   *Zone Lists and Zone-Pair Configuration*

After the zones and zone pairs are configured, you need to build the sequence rules. You can also specify a default action in the sequence rule configuration, as shown in Figure 11-10.

Figure 11-10   *Sequence Rule Configuration*

Once all the desired sequence rules are configured, the firewall policy can be saved and other security functions, such as IPS/IDS, can be enabled through additional workflow tasks. Advanced firewall features such as high-speed logging, policy bypass for direct Internet access, TCP SYN flood limiting, and audit trails for inspection logging can be enabled at the end of the workflow in the **Policy Summary** section, as shown in Figure 11-11.

Figure 11-11   *Advanced Firewall Features*

NOTE   You can add multiple firewall policies to the same security policy, as long as they have a unique combination of source and destination zones. However, you can add only one policy of any other type, such as intrusion prevention, URL filtering, and so on.

The security policy that has the newly built firewall policy can then be referenced in a template that is attached to a branch WAN Edge router in the **Additional Templates** section. Figure 11-12 shows a summary of how a firewall policy is built, attached to a security policy, and applied to a device template for activation.

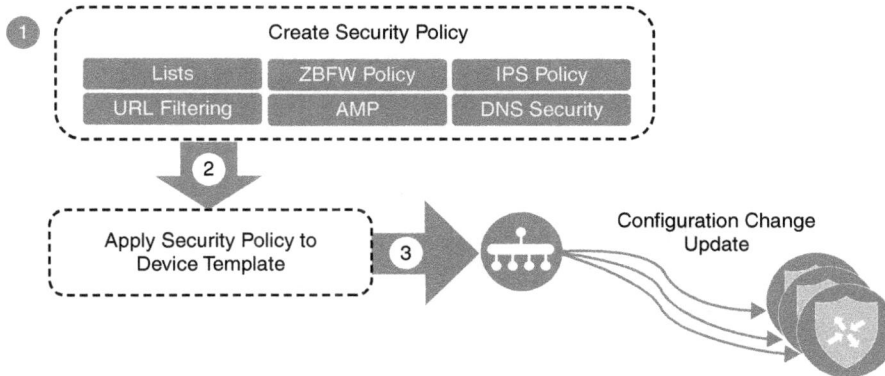

Figure 11-12 *Security Policy Application*

Figure 11-13 demonstrates how to attach a security policy to a device template in the **Additional Templates** section.

NOTE If your security policy contains features that require additional configuration, such as security app hosting, you will be asked to provide an additional profile template along with your security policy. However, no additional templates are required for firewall-only policy, as Cisco Enterprise Firewall with Application Awareness does not use application service containers.

Figure 11-13 *Security Policy in a Device Template*

You can monitor Enterprise Firewall with Application Awareness statistics through the main security dashboard or, for more complete details, through the Firewall section of the Device Dashboard. Both screens are able to show a historical view of inspected/dropped sessions, though the dashboard view can display the actual firewall policy sequence being hit for more granular reporting (see Figure 11-14).

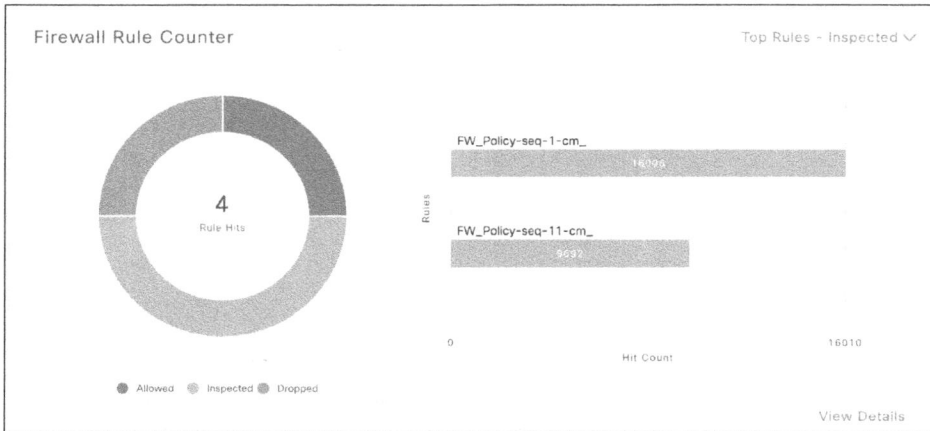

Figure 11-14 *Security Dashboard*

You can use the Firewall section in the Device 360 dashboard to monitor traffic statistics and view what policies are applied (and their associated zones). Figure 11-15 shows the Firewall Policy Monitor page of this dashboard in SD-WAN Manager.

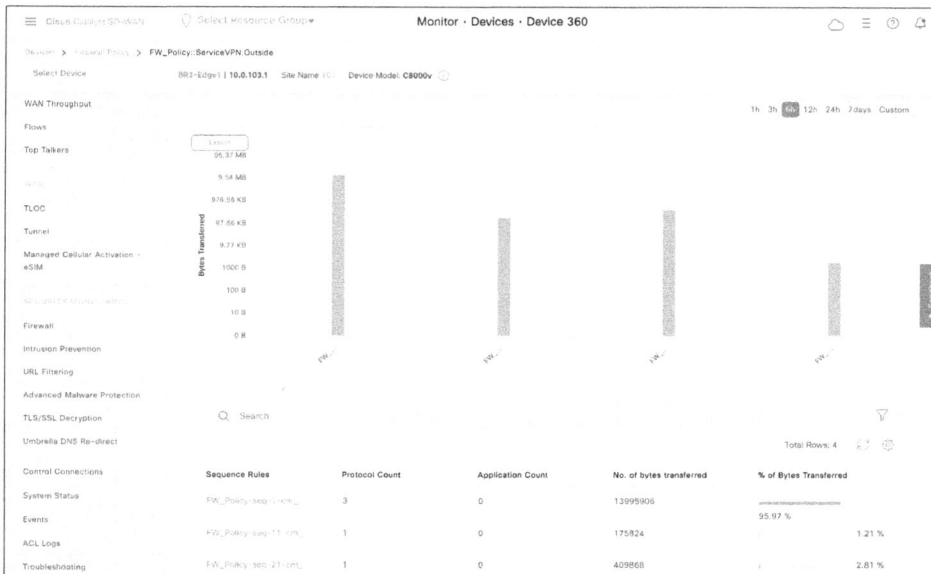

Figure 11-15 *Firewall Page in Device 360 Dashboard*

NOTE   Refer to the Cisco Catalyst SD-WAN Security Configuration Guide published on the Cisco documentation site for additional deployment details.

NOTE   You can gather more detailed firewall statistics in the **Real Time** section of the Device 360 dashboard or via the CLI **show** command set.

Intrusion Detection and Prevention

Intrusion detection and prevention is another important key to branch security and a component of the Cisco Catalyst SD-WAN security suite. An Intrusion Detection System/Intrusion Prevention System (IDS/IPS) can inspect traffic in real time in order to detect and prevent cyberattacks by comparing the application behavior against a known database of threat signatures. When an IDS/IPS detects a problem, it can notify the network operator through syslog events and dashboard alerts, and an IPS can even stop the attack by blocking the threatening traffic flow. An IDS/IPS can be enabled through the use of IOS XE application service container technology. Application service containers allow the network operator to leverage CPU cores and memory on a Cisco router to host virtual machines directly in IOS XE and redirect application flows through the container for processing.

The two VM technologies used by service containers are called Kernel-based Virtual Machine (KVM) and Linux Virtual Containers (LXC). These two technologies differ mainly in how tightly they are coupled to the Linux kernel used in most network operating systems, such as IOS XE. An LXC container uses many of the kernel resources of the host, while a KVM container has its own independent kernel. This means that a KVM container can be slightly more portable than an LXC container, while an LXC container might have a slight performance edge over a KVM container. To the end user, however, the container type is completely invisible because all of this is determined by the service container developer. Cisco Catalyst SD-WAN security leverages LXC containers.

Figure 11-16 shows an example of the application service container architecture in IOS XE.

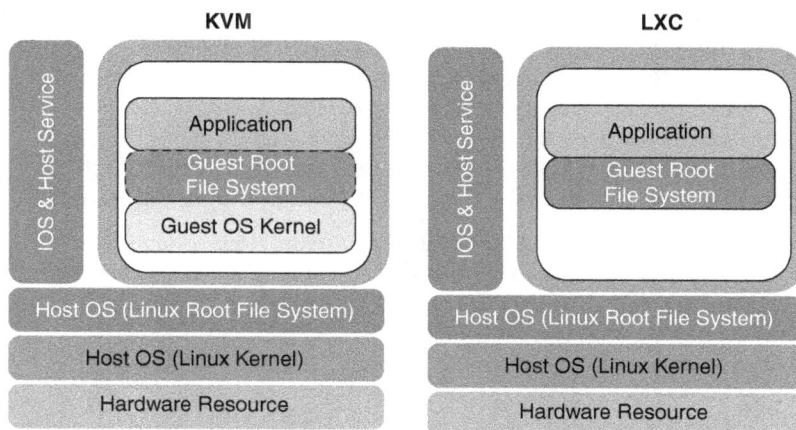

Figure 11-16 *Application Service Container Architecture*

The Cisco Catalyst SD-WAN IDS/IPS runs Snort, the most widely deployed intrusion prevention engine in the world, and leverages dynamic signature updates published by Cisco Talos. The Cisco Talos Intelligence Group, which is one of the largest commercial threat intelligence teams in the world, is composed of world-class researchers, analysts, and engineers. Talos team members are supported by unrivaled telemetry and sophisticated systems to create accurate, rapid, and actionable threat intelligence for Cisco customers, products, and services. Thanks to Talos, the IDS/IPS can provide real-time traffic analysis to reliably protect the branch from thousands of threats on a daily basis. Cisco SD-WAN Manager connects to the Talos signature database and downloads the signatures on a configurable periodic or on an on-demand basis and pushes them down into the branch WAN Edge routers without user intervention. A signature is a set of rules that an IDS/IPS uses to detect typical intrusive activity.

The two methods of updating signatures are centralized IPS signature updates via SD-WAN Manager and manual IPS signature updates using CLI commands available on WAN Edge devices. When a new signature package is updated, the Snort engine restarts, and traffic may be interrupted or may bypass inspection for a short period (depending on the data plane fail-open/fail-close configuration). Cisco SD-WAN Manager allows an administrator to configure automatic IPS signature downloads from the Cisco website or from the company-managed server via FTP, HTTP, or SCP, as well as upload signature packages manually. Automatic regular updates are recommended for better network protection.

As with all other security features available in Cisco Catalyst SD-WAN, the first place to start with a security policy is to navigate to the Security section. There, you can either build a new security policy (and follow the simple workflow to build an IDS/IPS policy) or directly navigate to the **Intrusion Prevention Policy** subsection under **Custom Options**. No matter how the IDS/IPS policy is configured, it must eventually be tied to an overall security policy (which is then attached to the branch WAN Edge router template).

NOTE   To support IDS/IPS functionality, a router must be configured with a minimum of 8 GB of DRAM and 8 GB of system flash.

Before configuring an IDS/IPS policy, the network operator must upload a security virtual image to SD-WAN Manager. The security virtual image is Unified Threat Defense engine software that can be found at Cisco Software Central, under the corresponding router platform images. As discussed previously, this is the LXC container that will host Snort. It is packaged in *.TAR* format. In addition, the network operator's Cisco CCO username and password must be configured in SD-WAN Manager for automatic signature updates to succeed. This is done under **Administration > Settings > UTD Snort Subscriber Signature.**

To upload a new virtual image, navigate to **Maintenance > Software Repository > Virtual Images > Add New Virtual Image.** Figure 11-17 shows the process of uploading a security virtual image to SD-WAN Manager. The same virtual image will be required for many threat defense security features, such as IDS/IPS, URL filtering, and Advanced Malware Protection.

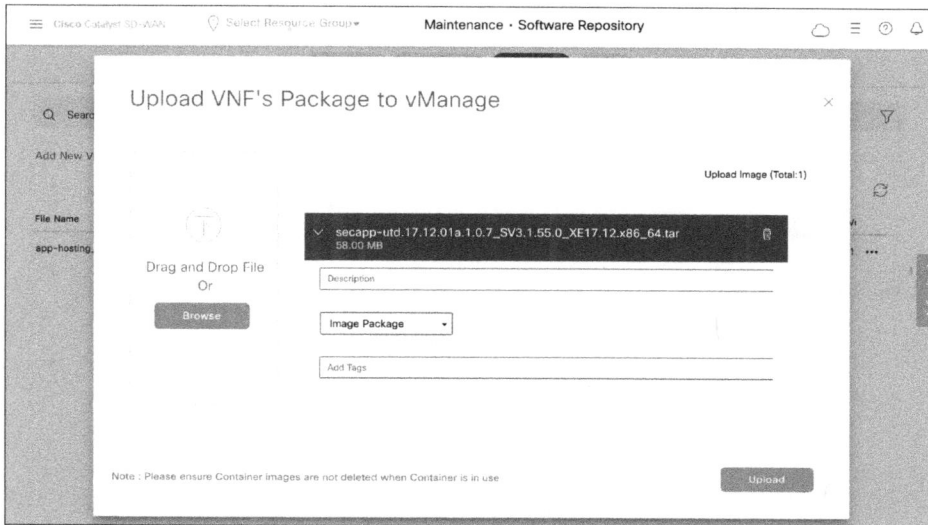

Figure 11-17 *Security Virtual Image Upload*

The following is a summary of steps required to configure an IDS/IPS policy in Cisco Catalyst SD-WAN:

Step 1. (Prerequisite) Upload a Security App Hosting Image File. A security app hosting image is required to support IDS/IPS functionality on WAN Edge routers. The procedure for uploading a virtual image into SD-WAN Manager is described previously.

Step 2. Create a new IDS/IPS policy. Name the policy.

Step 3. Select an Inspection Mode. Choose between Detection (IDS) and Protection (IPS) modes.

Step 4. Configure the signature set. Specify the desired signature set: Balanced, Connectivity, or Security.

Step 5. Configure the signature whitelist (optional). Specify an allowlist (called *whitelist* in SD-WAN Manager GUI) of signature IDs.

Step 6. Configure the alerts log level (optional): Specify the alerts log level, from Debug to Emergency.

Step 7. Configure target VPNs. Specify the VPNs to be inspected.

NOTE Remember that every WAN Edge router can have only one security policy attached to it, and a single security policy can have only one IDS/IPS sub-policy. As you build your IDS/IPS policy, consider that it will be applied to all VPNs you choose as targets.

Figure 11-18 shows the configuration of an IDS/IPS policy in SD-WAN Manager.

11

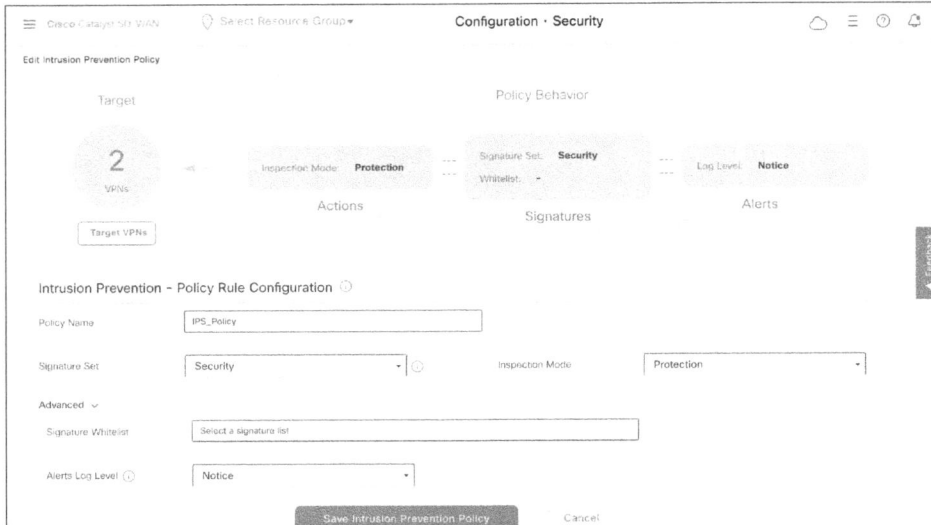

Figure 11-18 *IDS/IPS Policy Configuration*

The IDS/IPS engine allows for the network operator to configure three different signature sets: Balanced, Connectivity, and Security. Each of the signature levels contains a list of security vulnerabilities categorized based on the score assigned using the Common Vulnerability Scoring System (CVSS). (CVSS is a free and open industry standard for assessing the severity of security vulnerabilities.)

Here are the three signature levels available within the SD-WAN Manager IPS:

■ **Balanced:** This is the default signature set, which contains rules published within the past 2 years. The Balanced signature set is designed to provide protection without a significant effect on system performance.

This signature set is for vulnerabilities with a CVSS score of 9 or greater, and its categories include the ones listed in Table 11-1.

Table 11-1 Balanced Signature Set

Category	Definition
Blacklist	Rules for URIs, user agents, DNS hostnames, and IP addresses that have been determined to be indicators of malicious activity
Exploit-kit	Rules that are designed to detect exploit kit activity
Malware-CNC	Rules for known malicious command and control activities for identified botnet traffic, including call home activities, downloading of dropped files, and exfiltration of data
SQL injection	Rules that are designed to detect SQL injection attempts

■ **Connectivity:** This signature set contains rules published within the past 2 years for vulnerabilities with a CVSS score of 10. The Connectivity signature set is less restrictive than the Balanced set, with better performance, as there are fewer rules attached to this signature level.

- **Security:** This signature set contains rules from the past 3 years. With more added rules than the previous two sets, this signature level offers more protection, but overall performance of your WAN Edge device may be lower.

The Security signature set is for vulnerabilities with a CVSS score of 8 or greater, and its categories include those listed in Table 11-2.

Table 11-2 Security Signature Set

Category	Definition
App-detect	Rules that look for and control the traffic of certain applications that generate network activity
Blacklist	Rules for URIs, user agents, DNS hostnames, and IP addresses that have been determined to be indicators of malicious activity
Exploit-kit	Rules that are designed to detect exploit kit activity
Malware-CNC	Rules for known malicious command and control activities for identified botnet traffic, including call home activities, downloading of dropped files, and exfiltration of data
SQL injection	Rules that are designed to detect SQL injection attempts

The network operator can also configure a signature whitelist, which provides the opportunity to define a list of signature IDs using the format *GeneratorID:SignatureID*. Any application flow that matches a signature ID defined in the list is ignored and passed through the IDS/IPS engine without action. This is useful for suppressing false indications of an attack with legitimate network traffic.

The Snort engine can operate in either Detection mode, where threats are only detected and logged, or Protection mode, where the engine detects and drops the threat while also providing a log of the event. SD-WAN Manager also provides a multitude of configurable IDS/IPS alert log levels to fit the security requirements of the organization.

Once the IDS/IPS policy options are configured, a target VPN or VPNs must be defined in order for the engine to know which segments on the branch WAN Edge router need application flows redirected through the Snort engine for processing.

The **Policy Summary** section of the workflow allows the network operator to configure the failure mode of the Snort engine. The Fail-close option drops all IDS/IPS traffic when there is an engine failure or engine reboot. The Fail-open option allows all IDS/IPS traffic when there is an engine failure or engine reboot. The default option is Fail-open.

Figure 11-19 provides a high-level view of how application flows are passed through the Snort engine in a Cisco router.

NOTE   If an application service-based security feature has never been enabled on a particular router before, a container installation task will automatically begin after the security policy is attached to the branch template. Once this installation is complete, the security policy will be enabled. You can monitor this task for successful completion by navigating to the Active Task pane at the top right of the Cisco SD-WAN Manager dashboard.

11

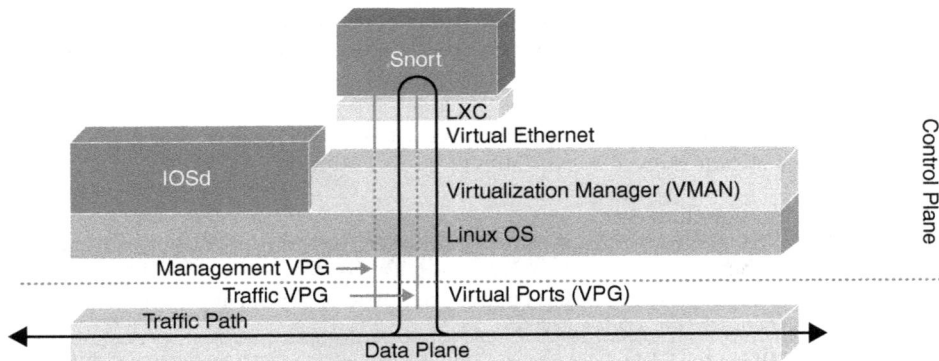

Figure 11-19   *Snort Traffic Engine*

If needed, other security sub-policies, such as a firewall policy, URL filtering, and Advanced Malware Protection, can be added to the final security policy. The last step would be to attach the overall security policy to a branch device template. (This process is identical to the process illustrated in Figure 11-13.)

NOTE   If a security policy contains sub-policies that require a Unified Threat Defense engine virtual image (such as an IDS/IPS policy), you will be asked to select a corresponding container profile in the Additional Templates section, under Device Template. It is a best practice to configure a custom security app hosting template that contains the default settings and is referenced under Device Template.

You can monitor IDS/IPS statistics through the main security dashboard under **Monitor > Security** (see Figure 11-20). To get more complete details, you can monitor IDS/IPS statistics through the Intrusion Prevention section of the device dashboard (**Monitor > Devices > <*specific device*> > Intrusion Prevention**). The security dashboard screen can show historical top signature hits by count or by severity, and it can provide details about a particular IPS event and the affected devices. In addition, this view can provide details around which source and destination IP addresses and VPNs are involved with the signature hits.

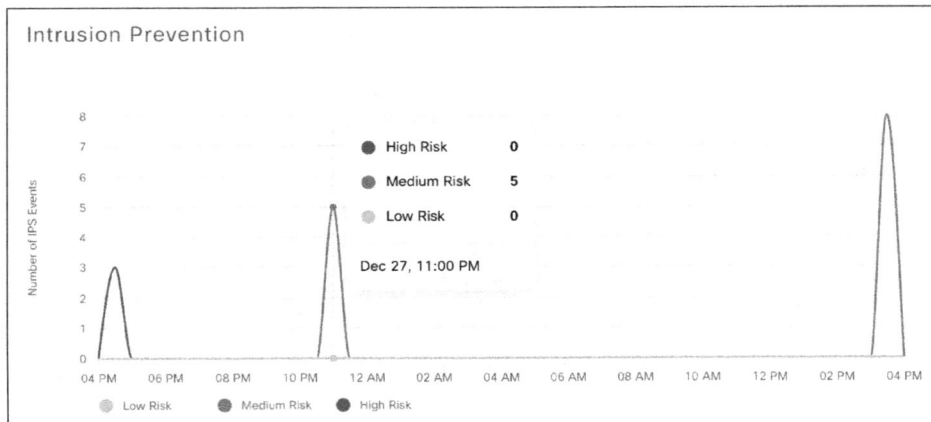

Figure 11-20   *Intrusion Prevention Security Dashboard View*

The Intrusion Prevention device dashboard screen also provides a view of signature hits by severity or count, but with more granularity and historical resolution, as shown in Figure 11-21. In addition, this view can provide the IPS version, when the signatures were last updated, and descriptions of the signatures being hit. On this screen, the network operator can access a hyperlink to learn more about the specific signature being hit in the environment.

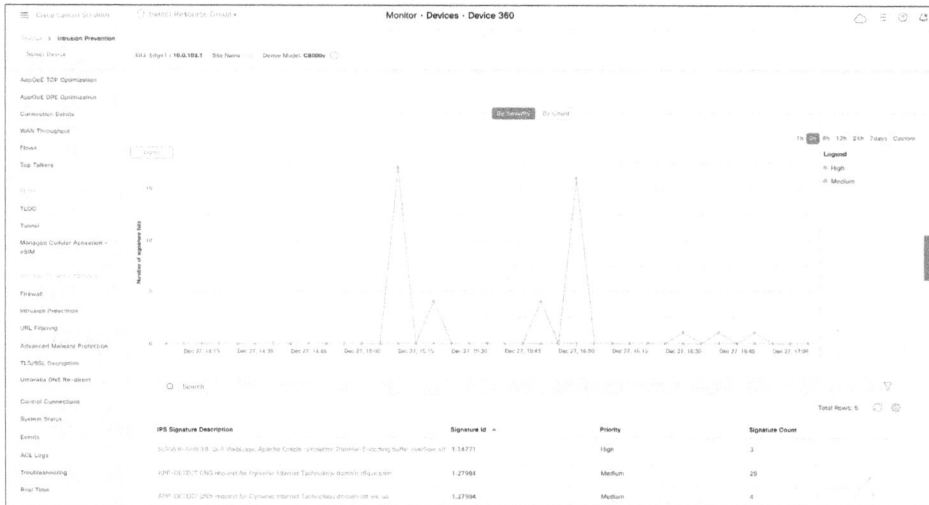

Figure 11-21 *IDS/IPS Device Dashboard View*

NOTE You can gather more detailed IDS/IPS statistics from the **Real Time** section of the device dashboard or via the CLI **show** commands.

URL Filtering

URL filtering is a Cisco Catalyst SD-WAN security function that leverages the Snort engine to control access to Internet websites accessible via HTTP or HTTPS. The URL filtering engine enforces acceptable use controls to block or allow websites. An administrator can choose to permit or deny websites based on 82 different categories, the site's web reputation score, and a dynamically updated URL database. Custom blacklists and whitelists can also be created to deny or accept website access and bypass the URL filtering engine.

When an end user requests access to a particular website through their web browser, the URL Filtering engine inspects the web traffic and first queries any custom URL lists. If the URL matches an entry in the whitelist, access is granted, with no further inspection or processing. If the URL matches an entry in the blacklist, access is denied, with no further inspection. When access is denied, the user can be redirected to a block page with a cus-tomizable message or can be redirected to a custom URL (if an internal block page already exists and the organization wants to leverage it). If the URL is not on either list, it is subject to inspection and will then be compared against the blocked or allowed categories policy. If allowed through the category inspection, the web reputation will then be considered and, based on the strictness of the policy, the page will either be allowed or blocked. As a final

11

step, the URL filtering database is consulted. This process can either use a cloud-hosted database or locally hosted one. If cloud based, the lookup result is cached in memory so that the next identical lookup match can happen more efficiently. Figure 11-22 illustrates the URL Filtering process and how risky domain requests are handled.

NOTE   To support URL Filtering functionality, a router must be configured with a minimum of 8 GB of DRAM and 8 GB of system flash if doing cloud lookups. A minimum of 16 GB of DRAM and 16 GB of system flash is required if doing on-box database lookups.

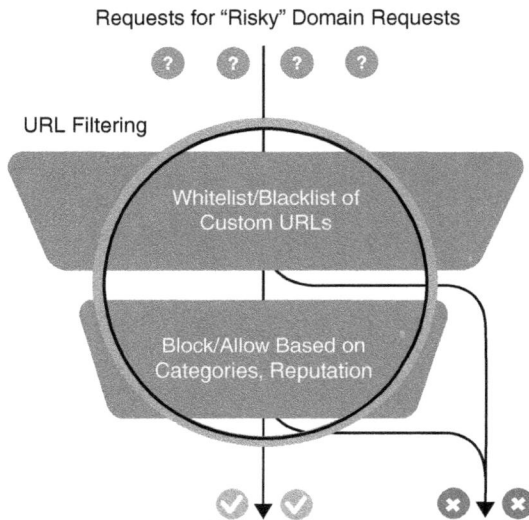

Requests for "Risky" Domain Requests

URL Filtering

Whitelist/Blacklist of
Custom URLs

Block/Allow Based on
Categories, Reputation

Figure 11-22   *URL Filtering Process*

Before a URL Filtering policy can be configured, the network operator must upload a security virtual image to SD-WAN Manager under the Software Repository section (**Maintenance > Software Repository > Virtual Images**). Note that all threat defense security features require the same Unified Threat Defense software virtual image, so if it was previously uploaded for another SD-WAN security functionality, no additional image is required. (The "Intrusion Detection and Prevention" section of this chapter discusses this process and illustrates it in Figure 11-17.) The security virtual image can be downloaded from the Cisco software portal and is packaged in *.TAR* format.

Like all other security features available in Cisco Catalyst SD-WAN, the first place to start is by navigating to the security section and either building a new security policy (following the simple workflow to build a URL filtering policy) or directly navigating to the **URL Filtering policy** subsection under **Custom Options**. No matter how the URL Filtering policy is configured, it must eventually be tied to an overall security policy, which is then attached to the branch WAN Edge router template.

These are the basic steps required to configure a URL filtering policy in Cisco Catalyst SD-WAN:

Step 1. **Create a new URL Filtering policy.** Name the policy.

Step 2. **Configure web categories.** Specify the blocked or allowed web category list.

Step 3. **Configure the web reputation.** Specify the web reputation for allowed websites.

Step 4. **Configure the whitelist URL list (optional).** Specify the URLs that should always be allowed.

Step 5. **Configure the blacklist URL list (optional).** Specify the URLs that should always be blocked.

Step 6. **Configure a block page or redirect URL (optional).** Specify what should be displayed to a user if the original URL was blocked: the custom locally created block page or another web resource.

Step 7. **Configure the alerts and logs (optional).** Specify which alerts should be generated.

Step 8. **Configure target VPNs.** Specify the VPNs to be inspected.

NOTE Remember that every WAN Edge router can have only one security policy attached to it, and a single security policy can have only one URL Filtering sub-policy. As you build your URL filtering policy, keep in mind that it will be applied to all VPNs you choose as targets.

The URL filtering engine allows the network operator to select from a list of five reputation levels. The website's reputation will be considered if it does not match any custom lists and was allowed through the configured web categories. The URL filtering web reputation engine will allow sites based on a numeric value (between −10 and 10) assigned to the site by Cisco Talos. Sites that either meet the configured reputation level or are of a lower risk level will be allowed. Administrators can approve websites using preconfigured reputation levels (that is, Trustworthy or High Risk). It is also possible to specify a whitelist and blacklist that leverage regular expression entries for more flexibility. Figure 11-23 shows the policy behavior as well as the configuration options available.

For blocked websites, the network operator can select between a built-in block page (with customizable content) and a redirect URL. URL Filtering alerts are user definable and can provide insight into blacklist, whitelist, and reputation/category hits.

Once the URL Filtering policy options are configured, a target VPN or VPNs must be defined in order for the engine to know which segments on the branch WAN Edge router need to be inspected by the URL Filtering engine.

Finally, the security policy containing the URL Filtering policy must be attached to a branch template for deployment.

11

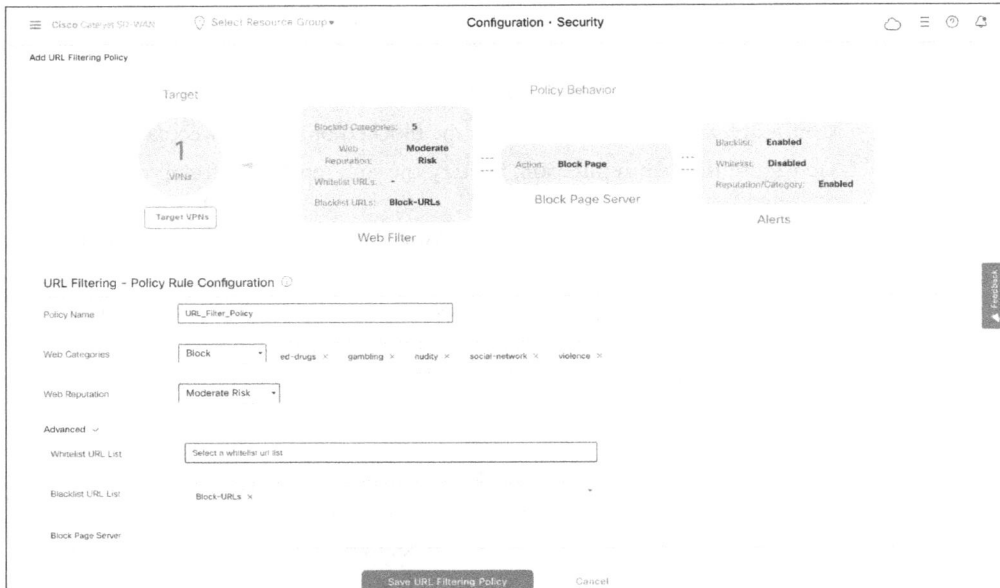

Figure 11-23   *URL Filtering Configuration*

NOTE   It is a best practice to configure a security app hosting template to be referenced in the Container Profile section. The template can retain default settings. If the WAN Edge router is equipped with 16 GB flash and 16 GB memory and an on-box URL Filtering database is required, select high for the Resource Profile option in the template.

NOTE   If an application service-based security feature has never been enabled on a particular router before, a container installation task will automatically begin after the security policy is attached to the branch template. Once this installation is complete, the security policy will be enabled. This task can be monitored for successful completion by navigating to the Active Task pane at the top right of the Cisco SD-WAN Manager dashboard.

You can monitor the URL Filtering statistics through the main security dashboard or, for more complete details, through the URL Filtering section of the device dashboard. The security dashboard screen can show the top-hitting blocked and allowed URL categories by percentage as well as the amount of times the category was hit, as shown in Figure 11-24. In addition, this view can provide details around which WAN Edge router in the Cisco Catalyst SD-WAN fabric is contributing to the category hits.

The device dashboard URL Filtering screen, shown in Figure 11-25, presents the same data in a bar graph format with more historical resolution and includes reputation block counts.

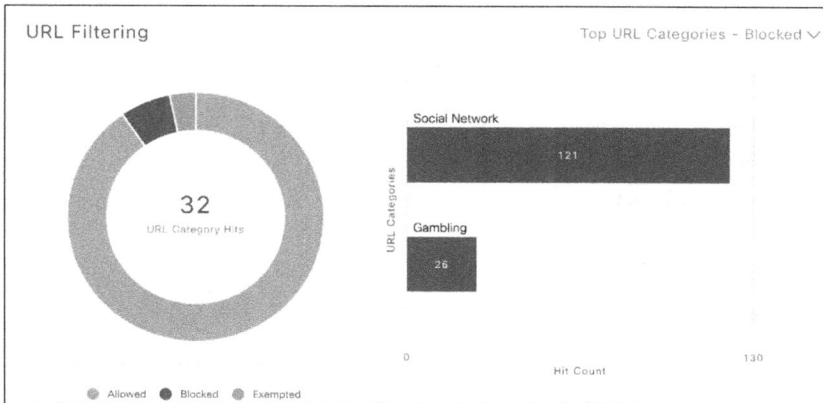

Figure 11-24 *URL Filtering Security Dashboard View*

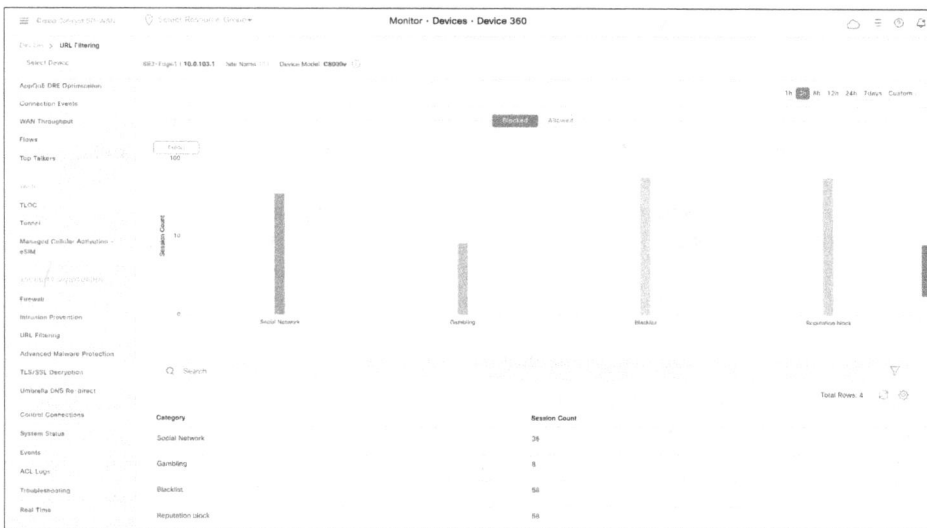

Figure 11-25 *URL Filtering Device Dashboard View*

NOTE You can gather more detailed URL Filtering statistics in the **Real Time** section of the device dashboard or via the CLI **show** commands.

Advanced Malware Protection and Threat Grid

Advanced Malware Protection (AMP) and Threat Grid are Cisco security technologies that provide protection and visibility for all stages of the malware lifecycle. As with URL filtering, both AMP and Threat Grid leverage the Snort engine and Talos for inspection of file downloads and detection of malware in real time. AMP can block malware trying to enter your network using antivirus detection engines, one-to-one signature matching, machine learning, and fuzzy fingerprinting. Figure 11-26 provides a high-level overview of this process.

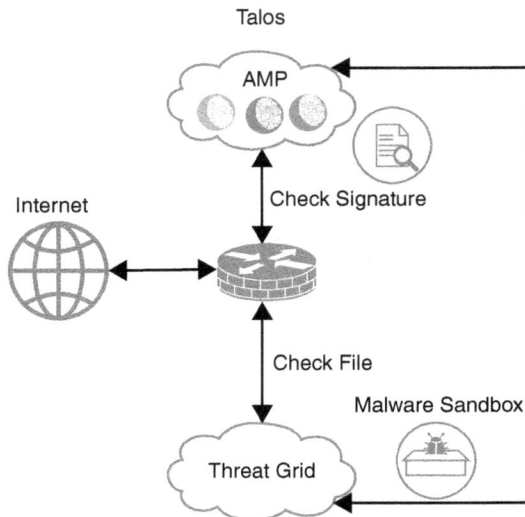

Figure 11-26 *Advanced Malware Protection Process*

Cisco Talos experts analyze millions of malware samples and terabytes of data each day and push that intelligence to AMP. AMP then correlates files, telemetry data, and file behavior against this context-rich knowledge base to proactively defend against known and engaging threats. If the AMP cloud is unable to determine if the file being inspected is good or bad, advanced sandboxing through Threat Grid can be leveraged, and retrospective analysis can be performed. Threat Grid combines advanced sandboxing with threat intelligence in one unified solution to protect organizations from malware. With a robust, context-rich malware knowledge base, the network operator can understand what malware is doing (or attempting to do), the threat it poses, and how to defend against it.

When a file is downloaded, the Snort file preprocessor on the WAN Edge router identifies the file download, computes the SHA256 hash for the file, and looks it up in the local cache to learn if it is a known good or bad hash. If no match is found in the local database, the hash is sent to the AMP cloud for identification. The AMP cloud can then respond with one of three responses:

- **Clean:** If the file is clean, the file download is allowed to complete.

- **Malicious:** If the file is malicious, the file download is interrupted and stopped.

- **Unknown:** If the character of the file is unknown (provided that Threat Grid is enabled) and active content is found, the WAN Edge router sends the file to Threat Grid for sandboxing. The WAN Edge router queries Threat Grid for a period of time and then queries AMP for retrospection. Threat Grid then updates the new status of the hash in the AMP cloud once it is known.

NOTE   As of this writing, the current SD-WAN code supports a maximum exportable file size of 10 MB.

These are the basic steps required to configure an AMP and Threat Grid policy in Cisco Catalyst SD-WAN:

Step 1.   **Create a new AMP policy.** Name the policy.

Step 2.   **Configure the AMP cloud region.** Specify the region to use for the AMP cloud: North America (NAM), Europe (EU), or Asia Pacific (APJC).

Step 3.   **Configure the AMP alerts log level.** Specify which alerts level should be considered.

Step 4.   **Configure file types.** Specify, from a list, the file types to be inspected.

Step 5.   **Enable Threat Grid file analysis (optional).** Enable Threat Grid file analysis, if applicable.

Step 6.   **Configure the Threat Grid region.** Choose Threat Grid cloud region from a drop-down list.

Step 7.   **Configure the Threat Grid API key.** Specify the Threat Grid API key. This step is required only if the file analysis is enabled.

Step 8.   **Configure the Threat Grid alerts log level.** Specify which alerts level should be considered.

Step 9.   **Configure target VPNs.** Specify the VPNs to be inspected.

NOTE   To support AMP functionality, a router must be configured with a minimum of 8 GB of DRAM and 8 GB of system flash.

Before an AMP policy can be attached to the device template, the network operator must upload a security virtual image to SD-WAN Manager, under the Software Repository section, as described in the "Intrusion Detection and Prevention" section, earlier in this chapter. The security virtual image can be downloaded from the Cisco software portal and is packaged in *.TAR* format.

As with all other security features available in Cisco Catalyst SD-WAN, the first place to start when configuring an AMP and Threat Grid policy in Cisco Catalyst SD-WAN is by navigating to the Security section and either building a new security policy (following the simple workflow to build an AMP policy) or directly navigating to the **AMP Policy** subsection, under **Custom Options.** No matter how the AMP policy is configured, it must eventually be tied to an overall security policy, which must then be attached to the branch WAN Edge router template.

The AMP engine allows for the network operator to configure the AMP cloud region in order to have the most optimal experience, based on the location of the branch site. Cisco supports AMP clouds in North America, Europe, and Asia. Three levels of alert logging can also be configured: Info, Warning, and Critical. If your organization's SD-WAN license includes Threat Grid, you can also enable file analysis. You will be asked to select the Threat Grid cloud region (either North America or Europe) and provide the Threat Grid API key before you can use this feature.

11

Figure 11-27 shows the workflow in SD-WAN Manager. Once the AMP and Threat Grid policy options are configured, a target VPN or VPNs must be defined in order for the engine to know which segments on the branch WAN Edge router need to be inspected by the AMP engine.

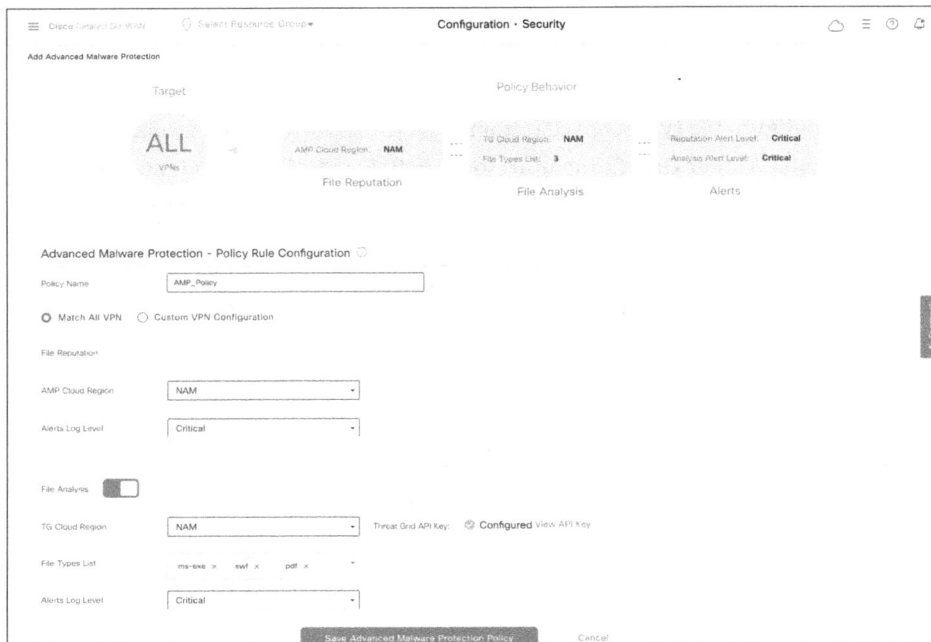

Figure 11-27   *AMP Policy Configuration*

Finally, the security policy containing the AMP policy must be attached to a branch template for deployment.

NOTE   It is a best practice to configure a security app hosting template in the Container Profile section. The template can retain the default settings. If the WAN Edge router is equipped with 16 GB flash and 16 GB memory and Threat Grid is being leveraged in the policy, select high for the Resource Profile option in the template.

NOTE   If an application service-based security feature has never been enabled on a particular router before, a container installation task will automatically begin after the security policy is attached to the branch template. Once this installation is complete, the security policy will be enabled. You can monitor this task for successful completion by navigating to the Active Task pane at the top right of the Cisco SD-WAN Manager dashboard.

You can monitor the AMP statistics through the main security dashboard or, for more complete details, through the AMP section of the device dashboard. The security dashboard screen, shown in Figure 11-28, can show historical information on the number of malicious files being detected via AMP and the number of files being exported to Threat Grid for analysis. This view can also provide details around which WAN Edge router is contributing to the most AMP cloud reputation hits.

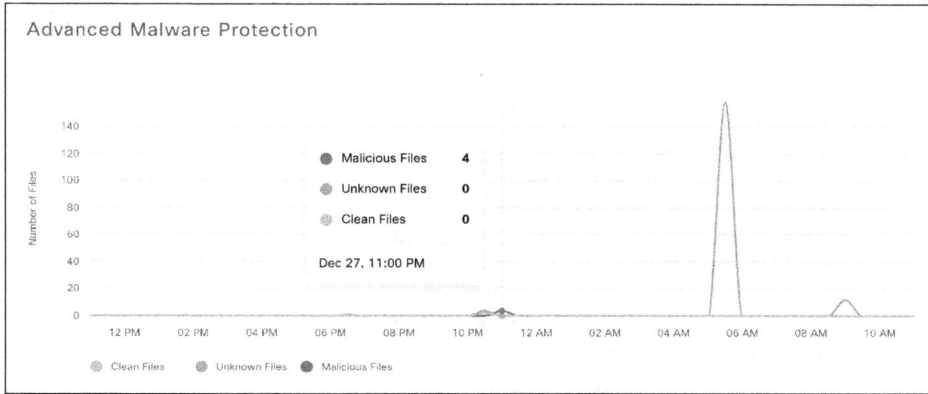

Figure 11-28 *AMP Security Dashboard View*

The AMP device dashboard provides a historical view of the number of file hashes the AMP cloud has registered as well as the AMP cloud responses of those file hashes. In addition, this view details the filename, the hash value, the file type, the disposition, the timestamp, the VPN, and the action the WAN Edge router took for the file. Figure 11-29 shows the AMP device dashboard.

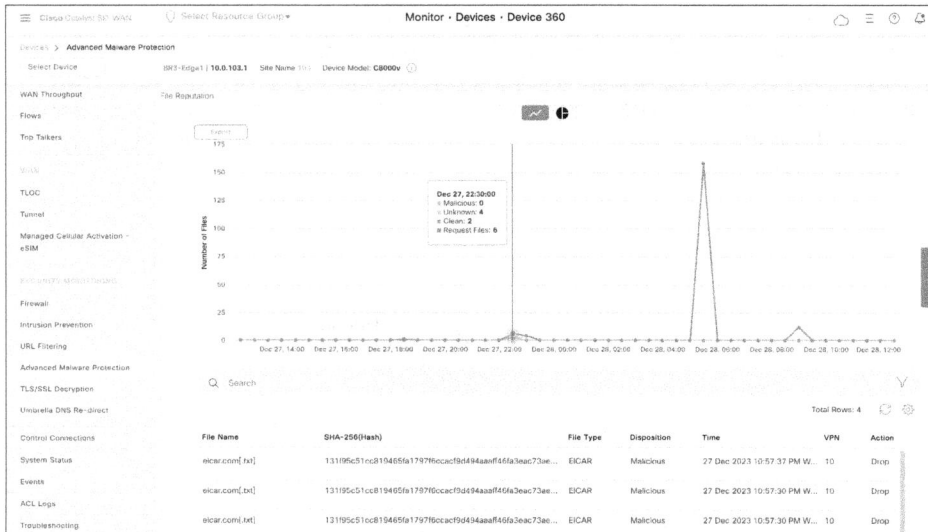

Figure 11-29 *Advanced Malware Protection Device Dashboard View*

NOTE You can gather more detailed AMP statistics in the **Real Time** section of the device dashboard or via the CLI **show** commands.

11

DNS Web Layer Security

Key Topic

Cisco Catalyst SD-WAN security leverages the Cisco Umbrella cloud in order to bring a comprehensive, VPN-aware suite of web security tools and enhanced cloud application visibility to the branch. DNS web layer security integration prevents enterprise branch users and guests from accessing inappropriate content or malicious sites that might contain malware, phishing attacks, and other security risks. Once registered with the Umbrella cloud, the WAN Edge router intercepts DNS requests from the LAN and redirects them to Umbrella resolvers. If the requested page is a known malicious site or is not allowed (based on the policies configured in the Umbrella portal), the DNS response will contain the IP address for an Umbrella-hosted block page. The DNS response will contain the IP address of the destination website if the site is considered to have a good reputation, is not malicious, and is allowed by the policy configured on the Umbrella portal. If Umbrella is not completely certain that the page being requested is safe, Intelligent Proxy can be enabled so that the Umbrella cloud acts as an intermediary. In this way, Umbrella can inspect the page data as it loads to avoid compromising the security of the end user.

DNS web layer security supports DNSCrypt, EDNS, and TLS decryption as well. Just as SSL turns HTTP web traffic into HTTPS encrypted web traffic, DNSCrypt turns regular DNS traffic into encrypted DNS traffic that is secure from eavesdropping and on-path attacks. It does not require any changes to domain names or how they work; it simply provides a method for securely encrypting communication between the end user and the DNS servers in the Umbrella cloud. Extension mechanisms for DNS (EDNS) is a specification for expanding the sizes of several parameters of the DNS protocol in order to carry metadata (such as VPN ID) for additional context that can be leveraged in an Umbrella cloud policy.

In some scenarios, it may be important not to intercept DNS requests for internal resources and pass them on to an internal or alternate DNS resolver. To meet this requirement, the WAN Edge router can leverage local domain bypass functionality, where a list of internal domains is defined and referenced during the DNS request interception process. Any domain defined in the list is ignored, and no interception or redirection occurs. Figure 11-30 provides a high-level overview of the DNS web layer security process.

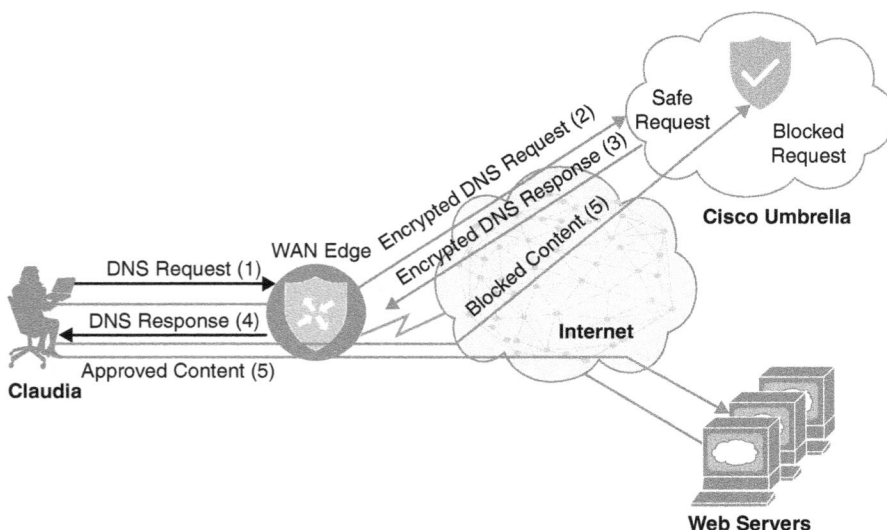

Figure 11-30 *DNS Web Layer Security Process*

These are the basic steps required to configure DNS web layer security with Cisco Umbrella:

Step 1. **Create a new DNS Security policy.** Name the policy.

Step 2. **Generate and register the Umbrella organization.** Possible options are to retrieve the Umbrella credentials automatically from the Smart Account, provide the credentials manually, or use an Umbrella registration token for the legacy devices.

Step 3. **Configure the local domain bypass list (optional).** Define the list of local domains that should bypass inspection.

Step 4. **Configure the DNS server IP address.** Specify the DNS server to use for redirection: the Umbrella default server or a custom DNS server.

Step 5. **Configure DNSCrypt.** Enable or disable DNSCrypt.

Step 6. **Configure target VPNs.** Specify the VPNs to be inspected. You can choose to match all VPNs or provide a custom list of target VPNs.

NOTE DNS web layer security enforcement through the Umbrella cloud requires a specific SD-WAN license tier. Cloud application visibility through the Umbrella cloud portal is available in all SD-WAN license tiers.

Before a DNS security policy can be configured, the network operator must register SD-WAN Manager with the Umbrella cloud portal. This is done in SD-WAN Manager under **Configuration > Security > Custom Options**; you then choose **Umbrella Registration** from the drop-down list in the upper-right corner. If you previously configured SD-WAN Manager with your Cisco Smart Account credentials, it can automatically retrieve Umbrella credentials (such as organization ID, registration key, and secret). Alternatively, you can obtain those credentials manually from the Umbrella cloud portal and configure them in SD-WAN Manager. For legacy devices, you can also use a 40-digit Umbrella registration token that is also obtained in the Umbrella portal.

Once the WAN Edge router is successfully registered in the Umbrella cloud, the intercepted DNS requests are authorized and can be processed by Cisco Umbrella. Refer to the Umbrella cloud portal documentation in order to learn how to generate Umbrella API keys or tokens.

NOTE You can verify the status of the device registration in the WAN Edge CLI by using the command **show sdwan umbrella device-registration.** If the registration fails, this command will provide the error details.

As with all other security features available in Cisco Catalyst SD-WAN, the first place to start when configuring DNS web layer security with Cisco Umbrella is by navigating to the Security section and either building a new security policy (following the simple workflow to build a DNS security policy) or directly navigating to the **DNS Security Policy** subsection, under **Custom Options.** No matter how the DNS security policy is configured, it must eventually be tied to an overall security policy, which must then be attached to the branch WAN Edge router template.

The DNS security policy allows the network operator to verify that the Umbrella registration status is configured. If the registration status is not configured, tooltips are provided to direct the network operator on how to configure SD-WAN Manager with API keys or a token. A local domain bypass list can also be configured and can support * for wildcard matching, but an entry cannot be more than 240 characters in length. The default DNS server IP address of Umbrella can be used in the policy or, alternatively, a custom DNS server IP address can be set. DNSCrypt can be enabled or disabled in the DNS security policy as well. Figure 11-31 shows these available options and settings.

Once the DNS security policy options are configured, a target VPN or VPNs must be defined in order for the engine to know which segments on the branch WAN Edge router are candidates for DNS interception and redirection. By default, the *Match All VPN* option is selected.

Finally, the security policy containing the DNS security policy must be attached to a device template for deployment.

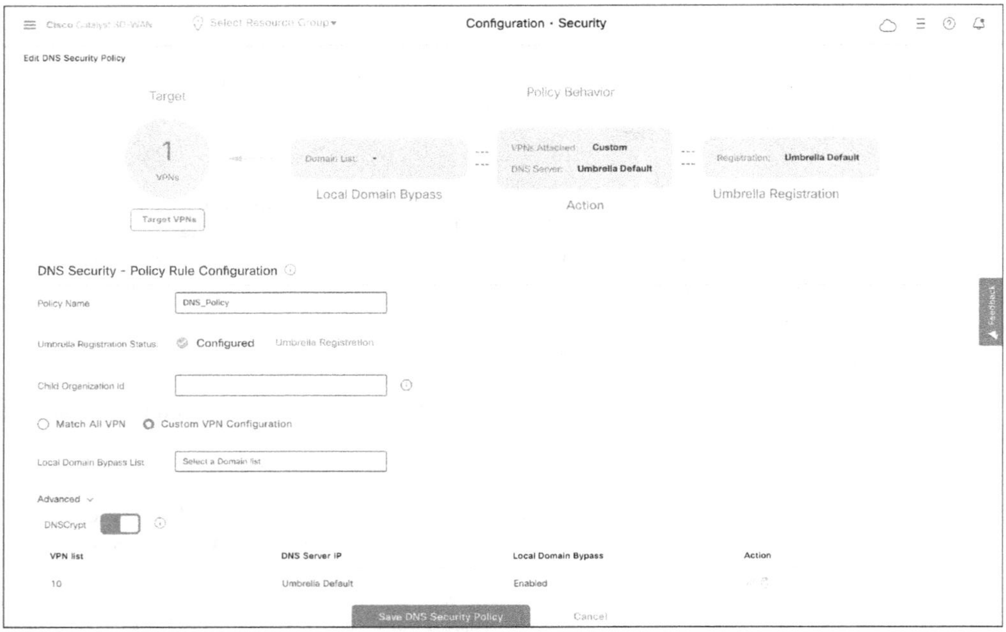

Figure 11-31 *DNS Security Configuration*

SD-WAN Manager provides only basic monitoring of DNS security interception and redirection, as shown in Figure 11-32. Detailed monitoring around policy enforcement, cloud app visibility, and other Umbrella cloud–specific information should be consumed through the Umbrella cloud portal. The **Umbrella DNS Re-direct** section of the SD-WAN Manager device dashboard provides a historical overview of DNS requests that were redirected to Umbrella, DNS requests that were bypassed using Local Domain Bypass, timestamps, a count of Umbrella registered VPNs, and the status of DNSCrypt.

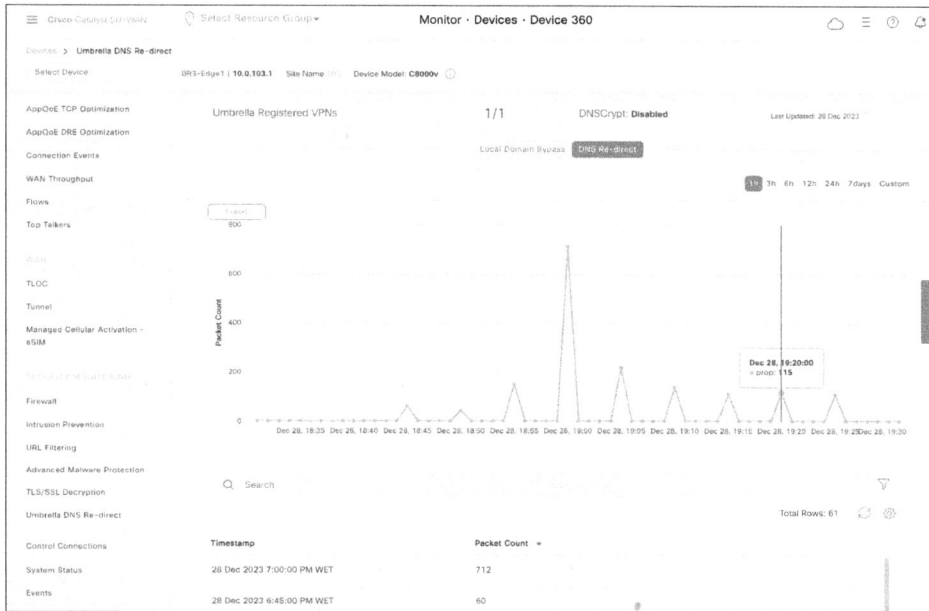

Figure 11-32 *DNS Security Device Dashboard View*

> **NOTE** As of this writing, only IOS XE SD-WAN supports DNS web layer security with Umbrella configuration through a security policy. Viptela OS supports interception and redirection, but only through the use of a data policy, which is beyond the scope of this chapter.

TLS/SSL Decryption

With the ever-growing concerns about data security and privacy, more and more applications are using encryption mechanisms to establish secure and authenticated communication channels between two parties for the traffic exchange. An example of such communication is HTTPS, which is the secure version of HTTP. HTTPS uses Transport Layer Security (TLS)—and formerly used Secure Sockets Layer (SSL)—to encrypt the traffic.

In 2023, the total percentage of encrypted traffic in the worldwide Internet was around 95%—which is good from the security point of view. Traffic encryption provides an additional layer of data protection by preventing attackers from reading Internet communication and getting unauthorized access to confidential information. Also, the encryption mechanisms allow clients to verify the identity of the server (or even perform mutual authentication) and confirm the authenticity of the remote site.

At the same time, encryption makes it more difficult for security teams to inspect the traffic flowing through their networks. Malicious activity can be hidden inside the encrypted channel and remain invisible from corporate security systems. The solution to this challenge is to use a TLS/SSL proxy, which is a security device that acts as a legitimate intermediary and decrypts the TLS traffic so it can be inspected by other security solutions. After the inspection, the TLS/SSL proxy re-encrypts the traffic before sending it to the original destination.

11

In Cisco Catalyst SD-WAN, a WAN Edge router can act as a TLS/SSL proxy, decrypt the data traffic, and send it to the Unified Threat Defense engine for further inspection. TLS/SSL decryption itself does not provide any security functions, but it can add extra benefits when combined with other Unified Threat Defense features. Therefore, a TLS/SSL proxy cannot be configured as a standalone security policy in SD-WAN Manager; it must be accompanied by at least one intrusion prevention, URL filtering, or Advanced Malware Protection policy.

In order for a TLS/SSL proxy to successfully decrypt the data traffic, it must participate in the traffic exchange from the beginning—that is, from the initial establishment of the secure channel (see Figure 11-33). The communication between the client and the proxy is secured with the proxy certificate rather than with the original server certificate. So for seamless operation, the client must trust the proxy certificate.

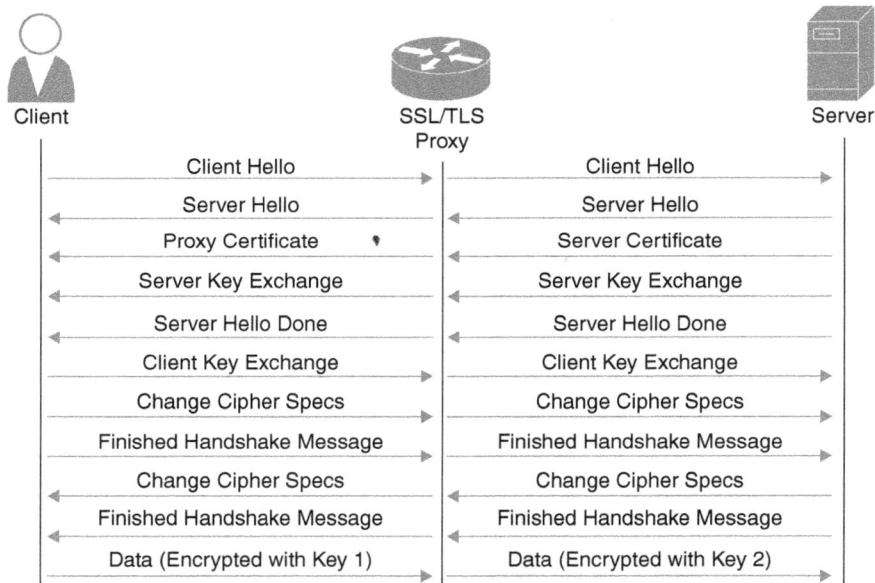

Figure 11-33   *TLS/SSL Proxy Operation*

When a WAN Edge router is configured to be a TLS/SSL proxy, it needs to get its X.509 certificate with certificate-signing capabilities. When working as a TLS/SSL proxy, a WAN Edge router acts as a subordinate certification authority (CA) and dynamically generates and signs the proxy certificates.

Cisco Catalyst SD-WAN supports the following CA options for TLS/SSL proxies:

- **Enterprise CA:** The TLS/SSL proxy certificate is signed by the Enterprise CA with either manual certificate enrollment or dynamic provisioning using Simple Certificate Enrollment Protocol (SCEP).

- **Cisco SD-WAN Manager as CA:** The TLS/SSL proxy certificate is signed by SD-WAN Manager acting as a root CA.

- **Cisco SD-WAN Manager as intermediate CA:** The TLS/SSL proxy certificate is signed by SD-WAN Manager acting as an intermediate (or subordinate) CA. In such deployments, the SD-WAN Manager certificate can be a part of the global enterprise certificate chain.

Key Topic

No matter what deployment option is chosen, the network administrator must ensure that the root CA certificate is distributed to the client endpoints and added to the corresponding certificate trusted store. This will make the TLS/SSL decryption smooth and fully transparent for the end users.

NOTE Internet X.509 public key infrastructure (PKI) certificates and X.509 PKI path building are described in RFC 5280 and RFC 4158, respectively.

As with all other security features available in Cisco Catalyst SD-WAN, the first place to start when creating a TLS/SSL decryption policy is to navigate to the Security section and either build a new security policy (and follow the simple workflow to build a TLS/SSL decryption policy) or directly navigate to the **TLS/SSL Decryption Policy** subsection, under **Custom Options.** No matter how the TLS/SSL decryption policy is configured, it must eventually be tied to an overall security policy, which must then be attached to the branch WAN Edge router template. Note that before the TLS/SSL decryption policy is added to the overall security policy, at least one of the Unified Threat Defense policies must be configured (an IDS/IPS, URL filtering, or AMP policy).

These basic steps are required to configure a TLS/SSL decryption policy in Cisco Catalyst SD-WAN:

Step 1. **Configure the Certification Authority.** Specify whether you want to use an enterprise CA or SD-WAN Manager as CA and create or upload the required certificates.

Step 2. **Create a new TLS/SSL Decryption policy.** Name the policy.

Step 3. **Configure the TLS/SSL decryption rules.** Possible options are network-based rules and URL-based rules.

Step 4. **Configure the Default Action for network rules.** Choose between the Decrypt, No Decrypt, and Pass Through options.

NOTE To support TLS/SSL proxy functionality, a router must be configured with a minimum of 8 GB of DRAM and 8 GB of system flash.

Cisco SD-WAN Manager allows you to configure the traffic decryption policy based on network rules or URL-based rules.

Network rules define whether the traffic should or should not be decrypted based on source or destination VPNs, networks, or ports, as well as application types.

Figure 11-34 illustrates the configuration process of the TLS/SSL decryption policy based on the network rules. The possible traffic actions are Decrypt, No Decrypt, and Pass

11

Through. The Decrypt action means the traffic can be processed further by the Unified Threat Defense engine, that is, intrusion prevention, URL filtering, or Advanced Malware Protection. The Pass Through action means that Unified Threat Defense does not require traffic decryption, but this traffic can be decrypted and analyzed by other features, if needed. The No Decrypt action means that neither Unified Threat Defense nor other features can decrypt the matched traffic.

NOTE Another feature besides Unified Threat Defense can request that traffic be decrypted: Application Quality of Experience (AppQoE).

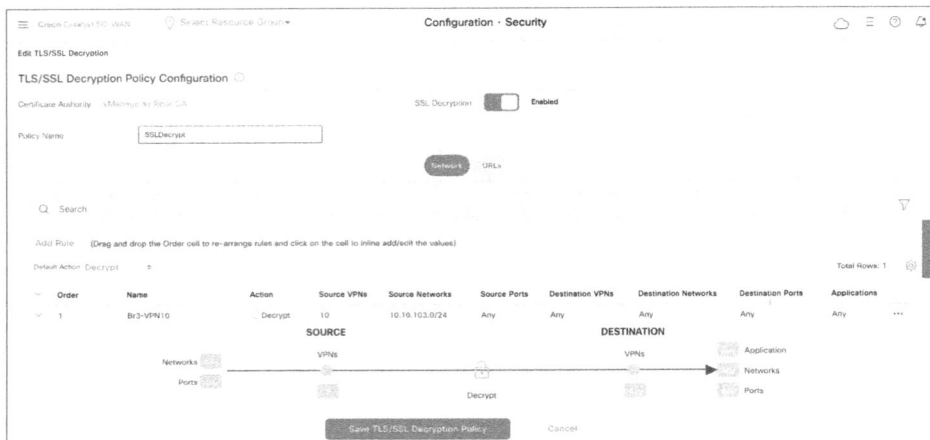

Figure 11-34   *TLS/SSL Decryption Policy Configuration*

URL-based rules define traffic actions based on the URL category or reputation of the URL. You can also set the explicit Decrypt and No-Decrypt lists that will overwrite the category or reputation rules and force the URLs to be always decrypted or never decrypted, respectively. If a URL lookup to the cloud takes too long, the administrator can set an action to decrypt the traffic or skip decryption for this traffic temporarily.

NOTE The decision about what URL categories should be decrypted is usually based on a combination of the company security requirements and the local laws (for example, General Data Protection Regulation in the European Union or any country-specific legal regulations). Most companies usually do not decrypt sensitive information such as financial or medical websites.

SD-WAN Manager provides the monitoring of TLS/SSL decryption activity as a part of device monitoring, as shown in Figure 11-35. The TLS/SSL Decryption dashboard provides a historical overview and shows the amount of matched traffic per policy rule. The dashboard also allows the network operator to switch between the Network Policy and URL Policy views.

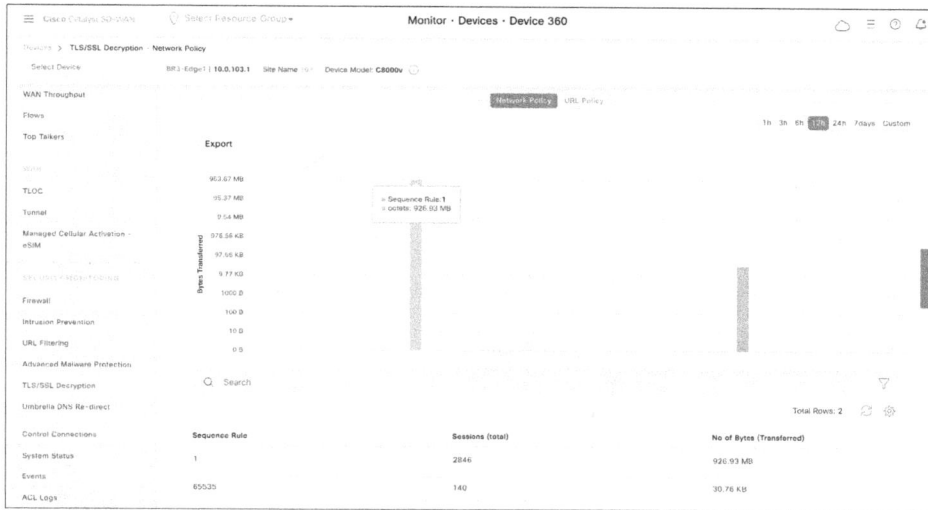

Figure 11-35   *TLS/SSL Decryption Device Dashboard View*

NOTE   You can gather more detailed TLS/SSL decryption statistics in the **Real Time** section of the device dashboard or via the CLI **show sslproxy** command.

Unified Security Policies

In addition to the traditional security policies discussed earlier in this chapter, Cisco SD-WAN Manager provides another method to configure security features: using a unified security policy. A unified security policy can combine firewall and Unified Threat Defense security features (such as next-generation firewall, intrusion prevention, URL filtering, Advanced Malware Protection, and TLS/SSL decryption) in a single policy.

Combining different security features in one policy has benefits. From a configuration perspective, SD-WAN Manager provides a simplified way for an administrator to configure it only once, without a need to create multiple policies, one for each security feature. From a device performance perspective, unified policies are also more efficient because they do not require reclassification of traffic for each security feature.

Unified policies are also configured from the Security configuration section of SD-WAN Manager. If you plan to use any Unified Threat Defense inspection of the traffic (for example, intrusion prevention, Advanced Malware Protection, URL filtering), you must pre-create those policy elements under **Custom Options**. It is not possible to configure individual inspection policies from the Unified Policy window. Once you switch the policy mode to Unified, the individual policies won't have traffic matching criteria, such as target VPNs, network rules, and so on (see Figure 11-36 as an example). Those criteria are not needed because the sub-policies do not perform traffic classification individually; rather, traffic classification will be done only once as a part of the unified policy rule. Once a unified policy is configured, it must be attached to the branch WAN Edge device template.

11

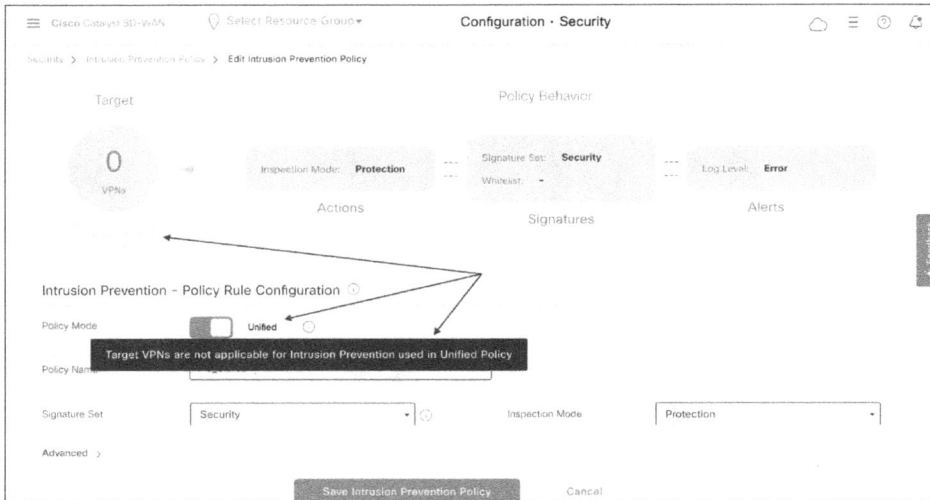

Figure 11-36   *Intrusion Prevention Policy in the Unified Mode*

These are the basic steps required to configure a unified security policy in Cisco Catalyst SD-WAN:

Step 1.   **Configure the next-generation firewall (NGFW) policy.** Specify the required firewall and Unified Threat Defense features together with the desired application behavior. Assign the VPN zones.

Step 2.   **Add the DNS security policy (optional).** Configure DNS traffic redirection to the Cisco Umbrella cloud for real-time inspection.

Step 3.   **Create a policy summary.** Provide the policy name and description and save the policy.

As you can see, it takes fewer steps to create a unified policy than it takes to create individual policies. However, if you want to use any Unified Threat Defense inspection policies, you need to configure them under **Security Custom Options** as a prerequisite step. Make sure Policy Mode is set to *Unified* (refer to Figure 11-36).

Note that the NGFW policy configuration step is a complex task. It includes the following sub-steps:

Step 1.   **Define criteria to match the traffic.** The data traffic can be matched based on its source or destination, and based on the protocol or the application list. There are several ways to define the traffic that should be matched by a particular firewall rule:

■   **Object group:** A set of filters can be created to identify the traffic. An object group can be preconfigured under Security Custom Options in advance, or it can be created at the same time as a new firewall rule. Once an object group is created, it can be reused in multiple NGFW policies.

- **Individual filters:** A custom list of filters can be applied directly to a firewall rule. Combining object groups with individual filters is not possible for the same traffic criterion (for example, source). But you can use both approaches within the same NGFW rule (for example, define the source with an object group and define the destination with individual filters, as shown later in this chapter).

Figure 11-37 shows an example of object group configuration. The possible object group elements are IP prefix, fully qualified domain name (FQDN), geographic location, and port(s). Those values can be set explicitly or referred to in predefined lists.

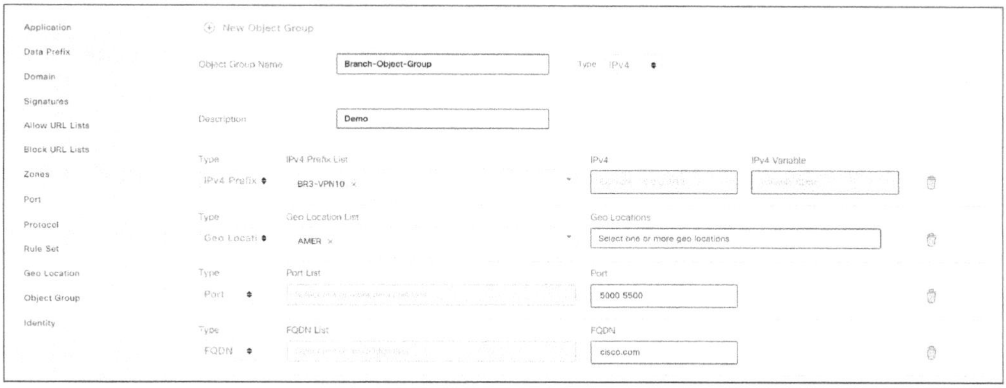

Figure 11-37 *Object Group Configuration Example*

Step 2. **Configure traffic actions.** Specify what should be done with the matched traffic. The possible options are Inspect, Pass, and Drop. With unified policies, the traffic is categorized using Network Based Application Recognition (NBAR). You can also configure the default action for the whole NGFW policy, and this action will be applied to all traffic that was not matched by any of the rules.

Step 3. **Add the Advanced Inspection Profile.** If the traffic action inside the firewall rule is set to Inspect, you can additionally set the advanced inspection profile and enable logging. Unlike in traditional security policies (where the Inspect action is equivalent to Drop), in the Unified Policies, the Inspect action means the traffic will be passed, and the advanced security features can be applied to it. Figure 11-38 shows an advanced inspection profile configuration. The profile includes the Unified Threat Defense inspection policies, such as intrusion prevention, URL filtering, Advanced Malware Protection, and TLS/SSL decryption.

Figure 11-39 shows an example of a complete NGFW rule based on all the configuration described in this section. You can create multiple rules within an NGFW policy, with different traffic actions and advanced inspection profiles.

11

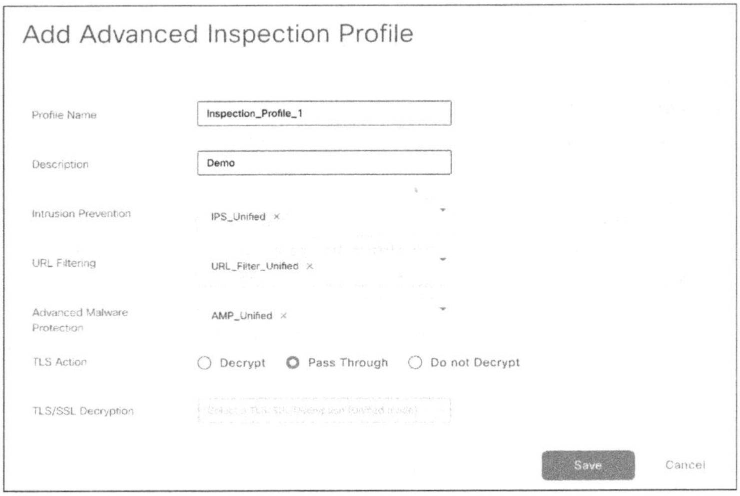

Figure 11-38 *Advanced Inspection Profile Configuration*

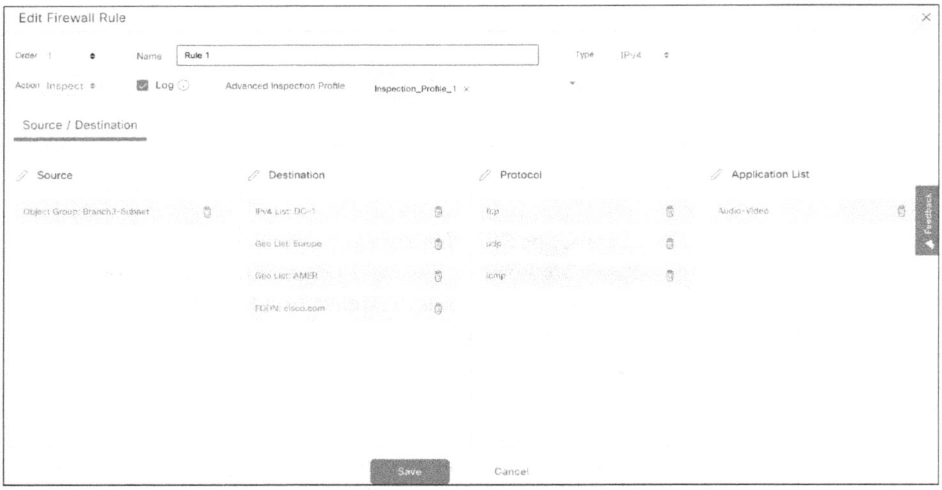

Figure 11-39 *NGFW Rule Configuration Example*

Step 4.   **Assign zone pairs.** After the NGFW policy is configured, you need to assign the zone pair(s) to apply the policy to the traffic that flows in the specified direction. Similarly to the traditional firewall policies discussed earlier in this chapter (refer to Figure 11-9), a zone pair is a combination of a source zone and a destination zone between which the data traffic flows.

In addition to the NGFW sub-policy, a unified security policy can also contain a DNS security policy. DNS inspection requires Cisco Umbrella integration, and it works in the same way as in the traditional security policies discussed earlier in this chapter. Also, the same DNS security policy can be used in both traditional and unified policies at the same time.

The final unified policy summary page allows you to define the advanced firewall settings, such as the TCP SYN flood limit, half-opened sessions limits, and advanced logging settings (see Figure 11-40). Also, if you assign an advanced inspection profile with TLS/SSL decryption to the individual NGFW rules or to the whole unified security policy, you must assign the TLS/SSL decryption policy in the Policy Summary page shown in Figure 11-40.

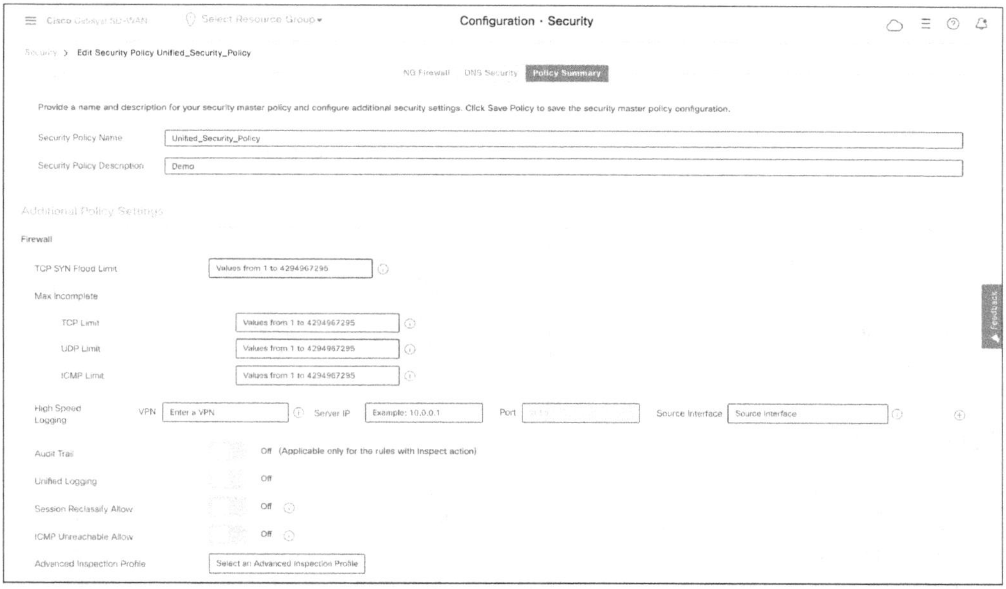

Figure 11-40 *Unified Security Policy Summary*

Monitoring the security features configured via unified policies is no different from the monitoring of traditional security policies. It can be done using the security dashboard or using the appropriate section of the device dashboard.

Secure Internet Gateway (SIG)

While integrated security provides a convenient and efficient way to consume and manage security at a branch, it can also place a compute burden on the WAN Edge router, effectively lowering its forwarding performance. This is not usually a problem at bigger branches with properly selected high-end WAN Edge devices. However, high performance is not always required in small branches, where lower-end devices may be used. Enabling multiple security features on such WAN Edge routers can cause significant performance degradation.

A great alternative to running all security inspections locally is a Secure Internet Gateway (SIG) solution. SIG can be compared to cloud-delivered firewalls. WAN Edge routers establish secure IPsec or GRE tunnels with the cloud security provider and redirect the user data traffic to the SIG for security inspection.

11

Figure 11-41 illustrates some of the common cloud security connectivity options. On the left side, there is a small remote site with the local Internet exit (Direct Internet Access). The branch does not have any local security policies, and the user traffic destined for the Internet is sent through the SIG point of presence (POP) and inspected by the cloud security provider. On the right side of the figure, the cloud security provider inspects the data traffic between two SD-WAN branches (using a hub-and-spoke topology with additional security policies).

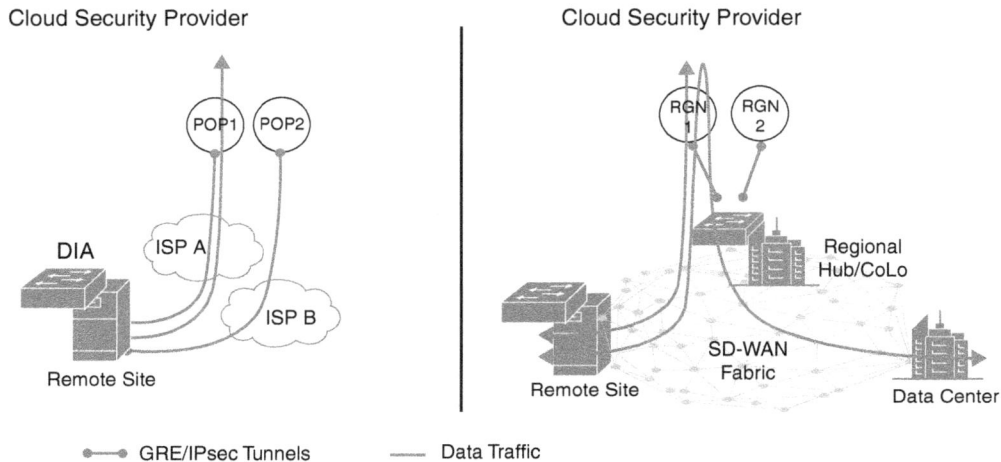

Figure 11-41 *Cloud Security Connectivity*

As of this writing, Cisco Catalyst SD-WAN supports automatic IPsec tunnels with Cisco Umbrella SIG, automatic GRE or IPsec tunnels with Zscaler SIG, and manual IPsec or GRE tunnels with any generic third-party SIG. Because Cisco Catalyst SD-WAN supports the configuration and connectivity of standards-based IPsec and GRE tunnels, virtually any cloud-delivered firewall solution can be seamlessly integrated into a WAN Edge router.

Secure Internet Gateway integration is configured in the SIG feature template in SD-WAN Manager. To configure automatic tunnels with Cisco Umbrella or Zscaler, you need to provide SIG credentials and API keys that allow you to manage the remote SIG configuration.

Cisco Catalyst SD-WAN supports multiple tunnels to the SIG provider for high availability and load-balancing purposes. You can have up to four active tunnels to the primary data center and the same number of backup tunnels to the secondary data center (optional). Depending on your business requirements, you can configure an active/active or active/backup setup with SIG. Tunnel-specific configurations like IP MTU, IKE, or IPsec timers are preconfigured in SD-WAN Manager templates and can be customized if needed. Figure 11-42 shows the configuration of automatic tunnels with the Cisco Umbrella SIG.

Configuration of manual tunnels with a third-party SIG provider is similar to the configuration of automatic tunnels. However, you need to provide all the information required to establish an IPsec or GRE tunnel, including the tunnel destination address(es) and authentication parameters. Also, you need to configure the remote site yourself, whereas with automatic tunnels, SD-WAN Manager takes care of the remote site configuration.

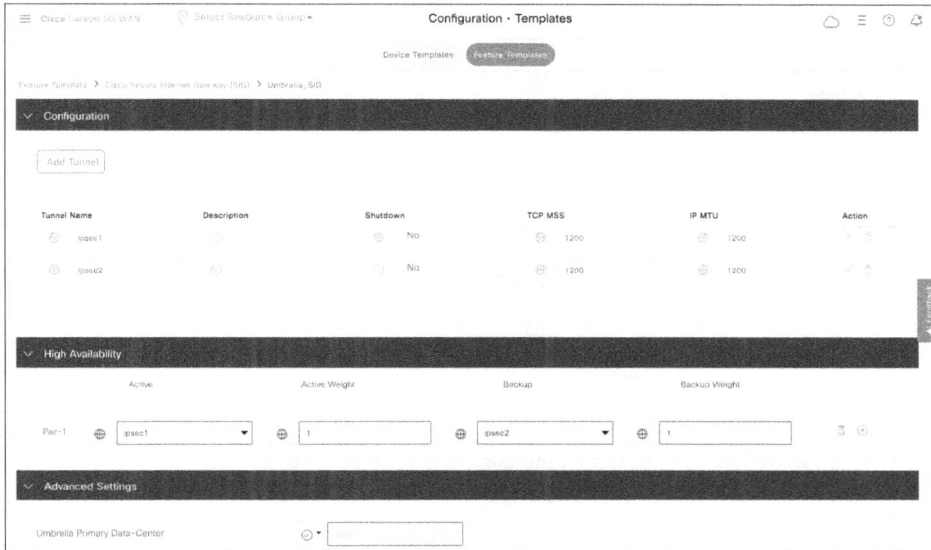

Figure 11-42 *Cisco Umbrella SIG Configuration Template*

You can verify the status of the automatic SIG tunnels in the main security dashboard or on the **Tunnels Monitoring** page (see Figure 11-43).

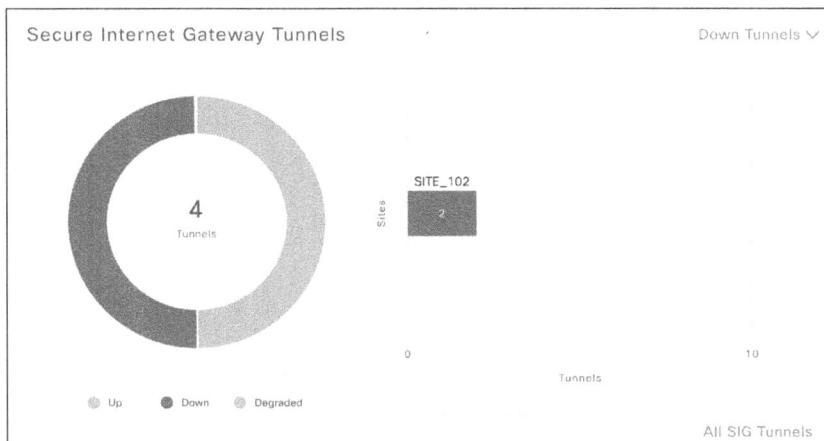

Figure 11-43 *Security Dashboard: Automatic SIG Tunnels Monitoring*

Configuring and bringing up the SIG tunnels is a mandatory but not sufficient set. The next important step is to configure the traffic redirection to SIG. This can be done either through the centralized data policy (by setting an action to redirect traffic to the SIG) or by using the service route to the SIG.

The actual configuration of the cloud-based security policies is done in the SIG provider itself and is beyond the scope of this book.

11

NOTE   You can gather more detailed statistics in the **Real Time** section of the device dashboard or via the CLI **show sdwan secure-internet-gateway** command.

Policy Groups

As discussed in previous chapters, the main methods of configuring WAN Edge routers from SD-WAN Manager are either by assigning device templates or by using configuration groups. As explained previously, when a device is managed by device templates, a required traditional or unified security policy, as well as a SIG feature template, are attached inside the corresponding device template.

Starting from Cisco SD-WAN Release 20.12, the security policies can be also configured via policy groups. This method is used to assign security policies to WAN Edge devices managed by the configuration groups.

At this writing, a single policy group can include any combination of Application Priority and SLA, embedded security, SIG, and DNS security policies. Chapter 9, "Application-Aware Routing Policies," covers Application Priority and SLAs in policy groups. In this chapter, we focus on security policies.

To start configuring Policy Groups, navigate to **Configuration > Policy Groups**. Figure 11-44 shows the initial configuration screen.

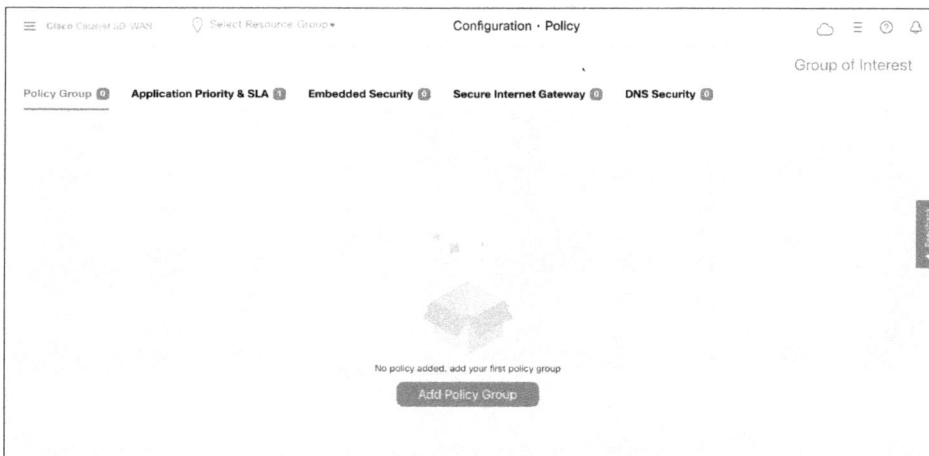

Figure 11-44   *Adding a Policy Group*

The process of creating a Policy Group includes the following steps:

Step 1.   **Pre-create Groups of Interest (optional).** Groups of interest include the elements required to build a security policy. They are discussed in more detail later in this section.

Step 2.   **Create the policies.** Create the required policies, such as application priority and SLA, embedded security, Secure Internet Gateway, or DNS security policies.

Step 3. **Create a Policy Group.** Combine the separate policies created in step 2 into one Policy Group. Any combination of policies is supported within a Policy Group. However, only one policy of each type can be added to a particular Policy Group.

Step 4. **Associate and provision devices.** Much as with configuration groups, a policy group must be associated to devices, and then the devices must be provisioned. Remember that you can apply policy groups only to the devices managed by configuration groups.

You can start building a policy group or its policy components immediately and then create missing groups of interest as you go, or you can pre-create a group of interest first by clicking the **Group of Interest** button in the upper-right corner of the screen shown in Figure 11-44.

The Group of Interest window provides a list of related policy objects that can be used in the *match* or *action* components of a policy. A security group of interest contains components of two types: objects and profiles. Objects are very similar to lists in traditional security policies. They can include elements such as data prefixes, allowed or blocked URLs, security zones, and lists of protocols and ports. Figure 11-45 shows an example of configuring objects by creating security zones.

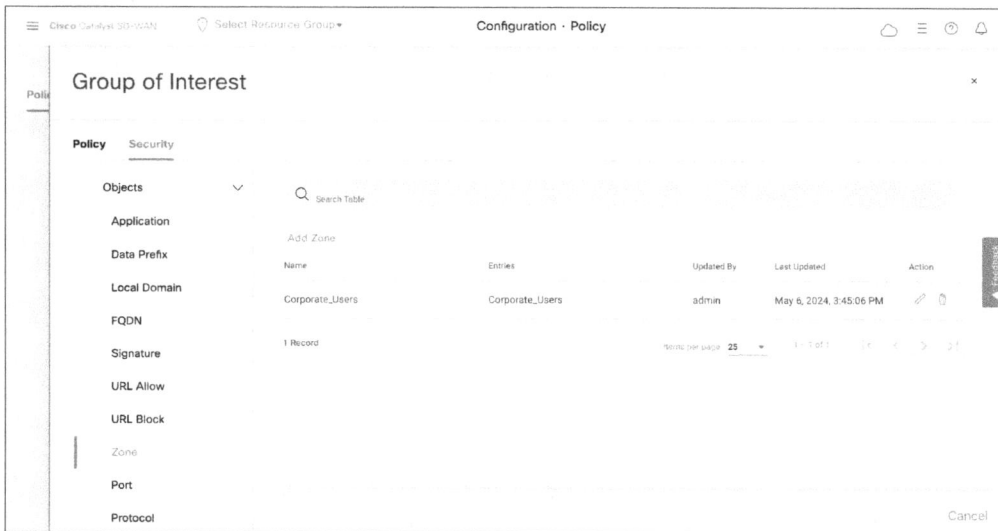

Figure 11-45 *Security Group of Interest: Configuring Objects*

Profiles include individual inspection profiles, such as intrusion prevention, URL filtering, Advanced Malware Protection, and TLS/SSL decryption. Individual profiles can be combined into a bigger advanced inspection profile (as discussed earlier in this chapter, in the section "Unified Security Policies"). Figure 11-46 shows the URL Filtering profile configuration page.

11

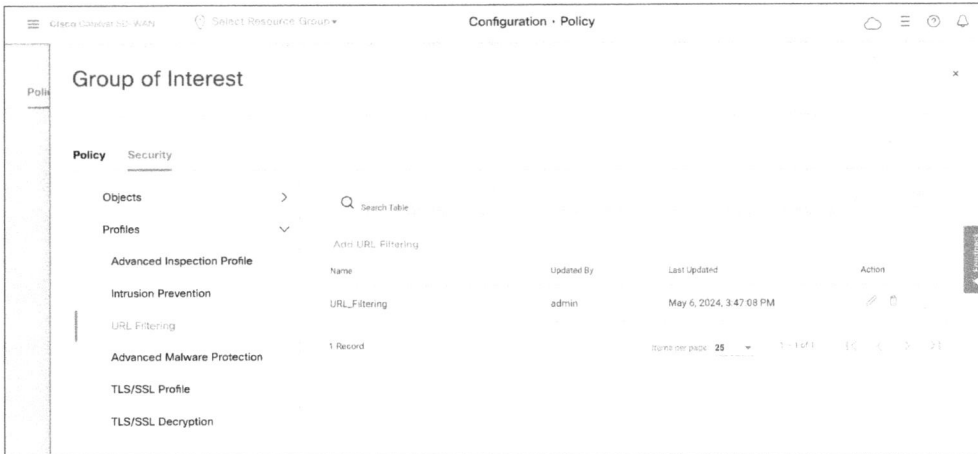

Figure 11-46   *Security Group of Interest: URL Filtering Profile*

Figure 11-47 shows how to create an advanced security profile. It can be also found under **Group of Interest > Profiles.** This advanced security profile is a combination of IPS, URL filtering, Advanced Malware Protection, and TLS/SSL decryption profiles.

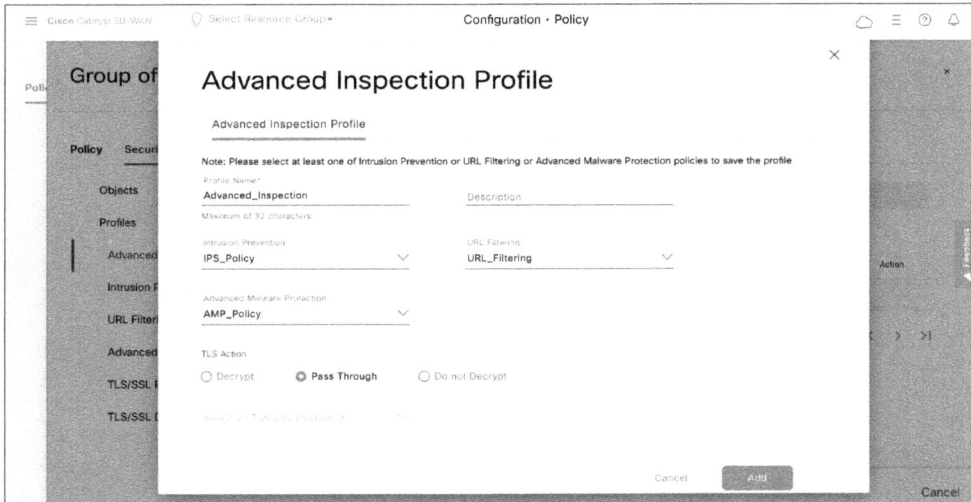

Figure 11-47   *Security Group of Interest: Advanced Inspection Profile*

The next step would be to create an embedded security policy. Go to **Configuration > Policy Groups,** select the **Embedded Security** tab, and then click **Add Security Policy** (see Figure 11-48). Alternatively, you can access the same configuration page by navigating to **Workflows > Create Security Policy.**

An embedded security policy is similar to the next-generation firewall policy that we discussed earlier in this chapter, in the "Unified Security Policies" section. It includes multiple firewall sub-policies combined with the advanced inspection profiles.

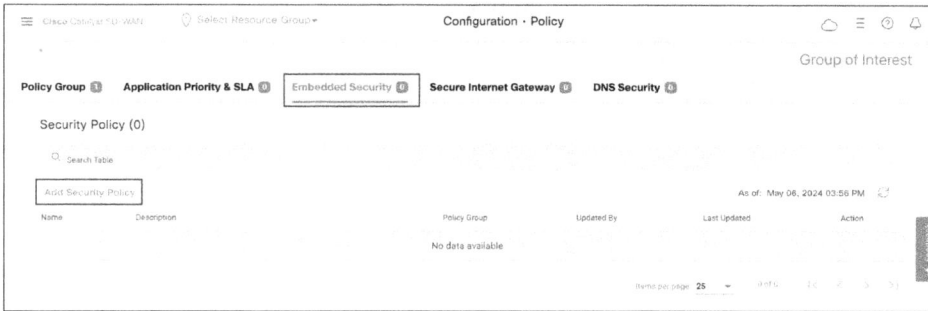

Figure 11-48 *Adding an Embedded Security Policy*

Creating an embedded security policy is a five-step process. The first step is shown in Figure 11-49, which shows the initial steps required to create a policy.

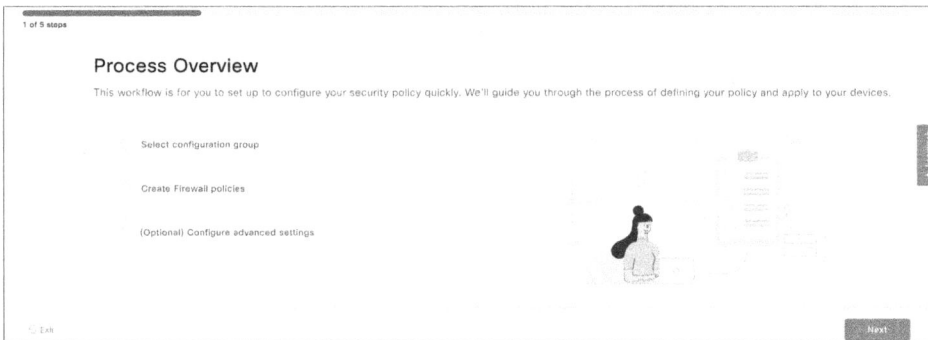

Figure 11-49 *Creating an Embedded Security Policy: Step 1 of 5*

Figure 11-50 shows the second step, where you need to provide a policy name and, optionally, a description.

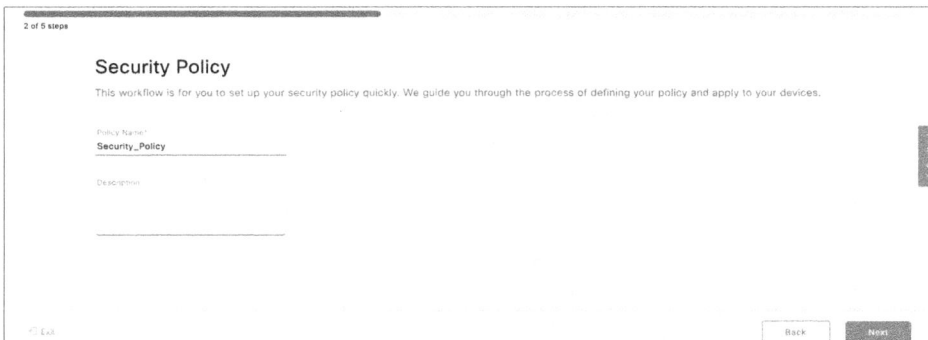

Figure 11-50 *Creating an Embedded Security Policy: Step 2 of 5*

In the third step, shown in Figure 11-51, you need to select the configuration group that will be used in conjunction with the current security policy.

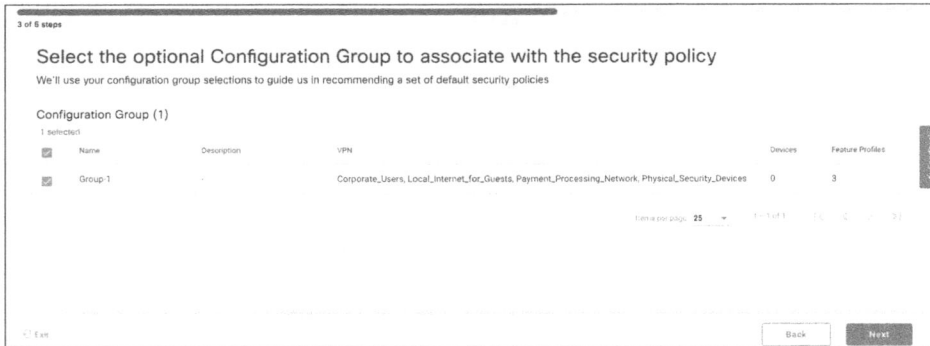

Figure 11-51   *Creating an Embedded Security Policy: Step 3 of 5*

Figure 11-52 shows the security policy configuration. If you selected the existing configuration group at the previous step, SD-WAN Manager pre-creates the firewall sub-policies by using every VPN as a source zone. You can also create them manually or delete the unnecessary sub-policies, if needed. At this step, you add sequential firewall rules for the combination of a source zone and one or several destination zones.

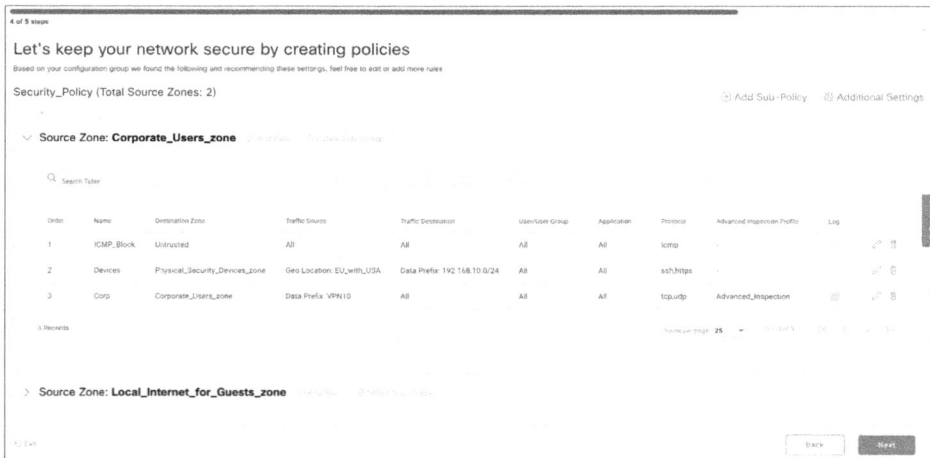

Figure 11-52   *Creating an Embedded Security Policy: Step 4 of 5*

In addition to the zone pairs, every firewall rule can have additional match conditions, as shown in Figure 11-53. The match conditions can be a combination of a source or destination data prefix list, geographic location, VPN, protocol, port, application list, and so on. You can specify a condition by selecting an object from a group of interest (refer to Figure 11-45), by providing an explicit value, or by choosing names from the predefined list (for example, select the standard protocol names, such as TCP, UDP, ICMP, and so on). You can also configure what action must be applied to the matched traffic. Possible options are Pass, Drop, and Inspect. If the Inspect action is chosen, you can also select the required advanced inspection profile. Note that with the current approach, different advanced inspection profiles can be applied to different rules within the same firewall policy.

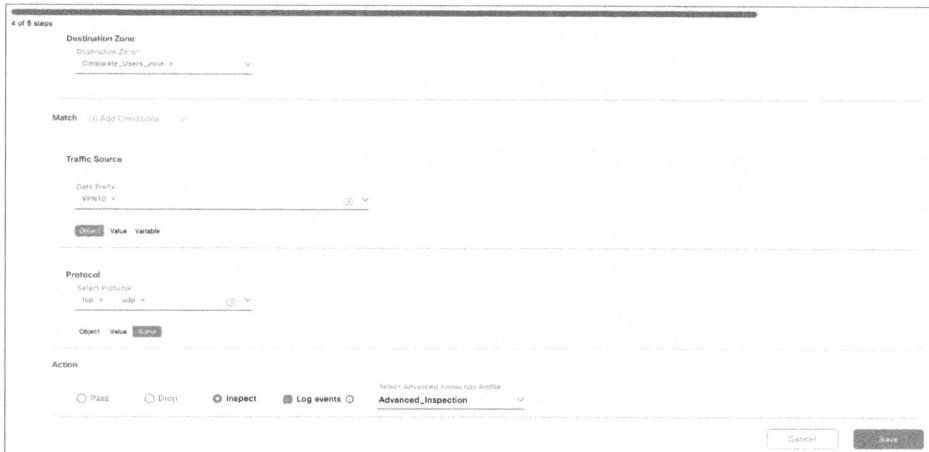

Figure 11-53 *Creating an Embedded Security Policy: Editing the NGFW Rule*

The **Additional Settings** dialog (accessible in the upper right corner) allows you to set the parameters like TCP SYN flood limit, maximum number of incomplete connections, and logging details (see Figure 11-54). You can also set the advanced inspection profile that will be globally applied to the whole security policy.

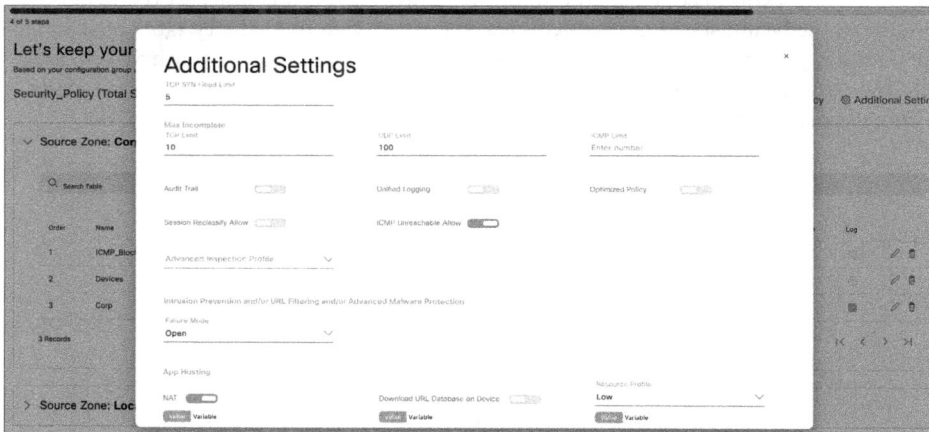

Figure 11-54 *Creating an Embedded Security Policy: Additional Settings*

The last step of the policy configuration is to review the summary and submit the changes (see Figure 11-55).

In addition to creating an embedded security policy, you can add a SIG policy. To do so, switch to the Secure Internet Gateway tab from the policy group configuration page shown in Figure 11-44. We discussed the general concepts and operation of SIG earlier in this chapter. Here we cover only the difference in the policy configuration.

11

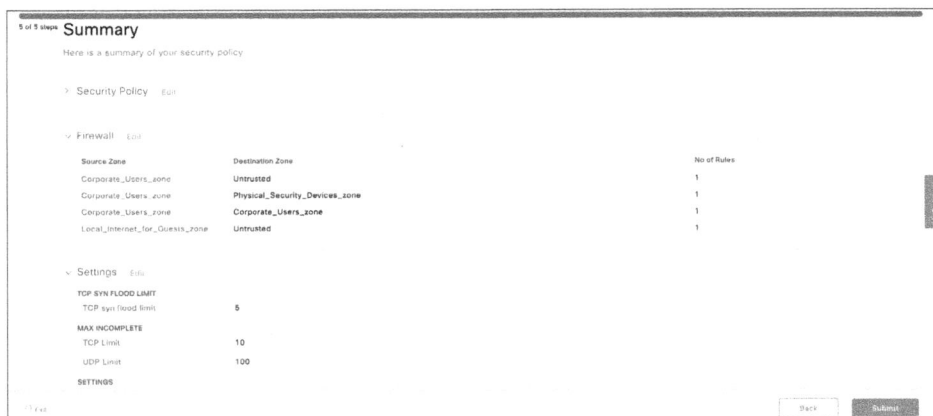

Figure 11-55   *Creating an Embedded Security Policy: Step 5 of 5*

You need to enter the SIG provider credentials under **Administration Settings > Cloud Provider Credentials.** Note that if you want to use the Umbrella SIG, you need to obtain API keys of type *Umbrella Management* from the Umbrella administration portal.

SIG policy configuration with Umbrella as a SIG provider is shown in Figure 11-56. On the **Configuration** tab, you can add automatic tunnels and customize the tunnel settings. The **Tracker** tab allows you to configure the source IP address and enable trackers that will be used to track the health status of the SIG tunnels. On the **High Availability** tab, you can configure interface pairs that will be used in the active/backup manner to establish SIG tunnels. Finally, the **Advanced Settings** tab allows you to choose the preferred primary and secondary Umbrella data centers (which, by default, are both set to Auto).

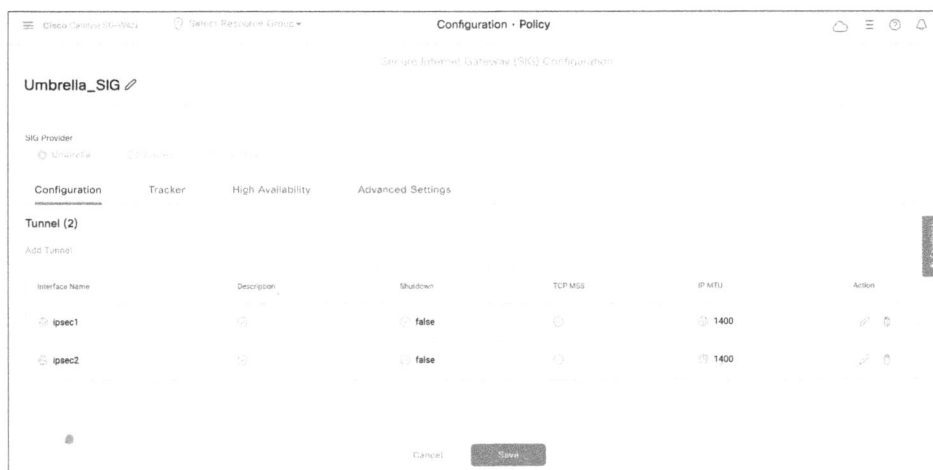

Figure 11-56   *Creating a Secure Internet Gateway Policy*

Figure 11-57 shows how you add a SIG tunnel. The mandatory configuration parameters are the interface name and the tunnel source interface. In addition, you can specify advanced configuration options, such as IP MTU, TCP MSS, IKE, and IPsec parameters.

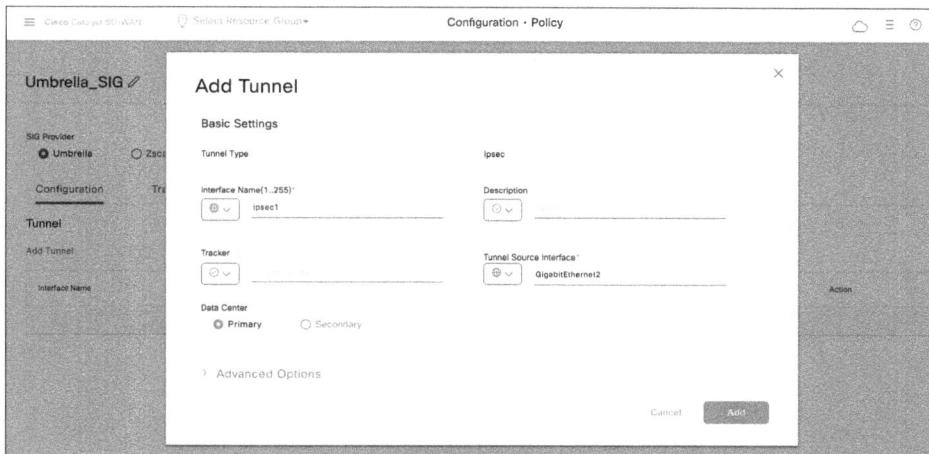

Figure 11-57   *Creating a SIG Policy: Adding a Tunnel*

To add a DNS security policy, switch to the last tab, DNS Security, from the policy group configuration page shown in Figure 11-44. To add a DNS security policy, you need to enter Umbrella credentials under **Administration Settings > Cloud Provider Credentials**. However, DNS security requires a different type of API keys than Umbrella SIG; for this feature, you use an *Umbrella Network Devices* key, which you can obtain from the Umbrella administration portal. Note that SD-WAN Manager allows you to add both types of credentials at the same time because they are used for different purposes.

Figure 11-58 shows the screen for configuring a DNS security policy. Here you can configure the DNS server settings, target VPNs, and other parameters (all of which are discussed earlier in this chapter).

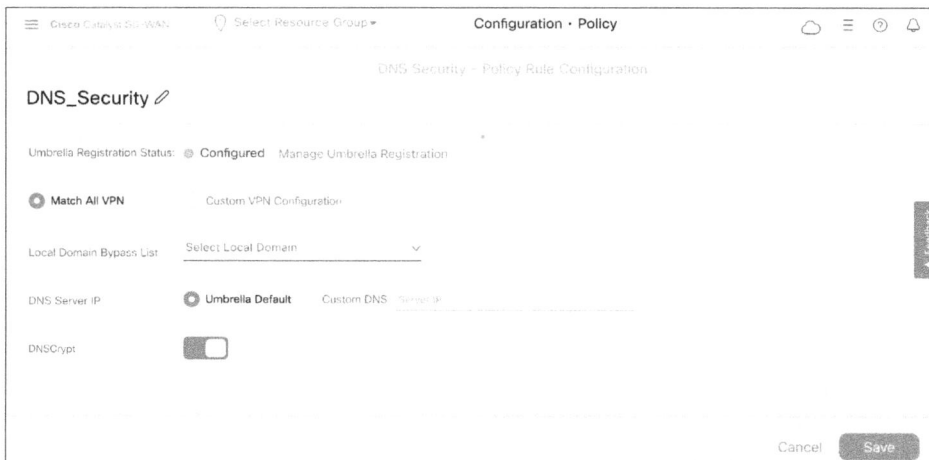

Figure 11-58   *Creating a DNS Security Policy*

The next step is to combine the individual policies into one policy group. You do this by selecting **Configuration > Policy Groups** and going to the **Policy Groups** tab. As you can see in Figure 11-59, a single policy group can include up to one policy of each type (that is, application priority, embedded security, SIG, and DNS security). After you build the policy group, you need to associate it with and deploy it to WAN Edge devices; you can see the buttons for this on the right side of Figure 11-59.

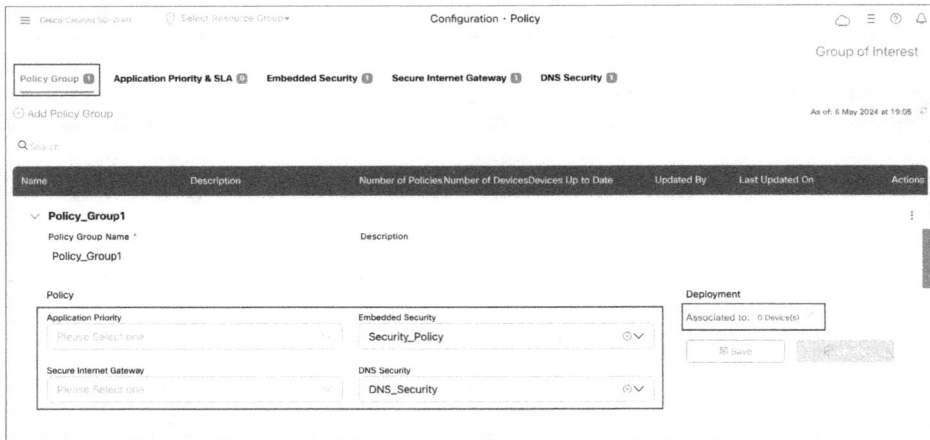

Figure 11-59 *Building a Policy Group*

The process of assigning a policy group is very similar to the process of deploying a configuration group. First, you need to choose the devices, as shown in Figure 11-60. This screen shows only WAN Edge devices that are managed by configuration groups. After that, you have to complete the device provisioning, using the same process you use to deploy configuration groups.

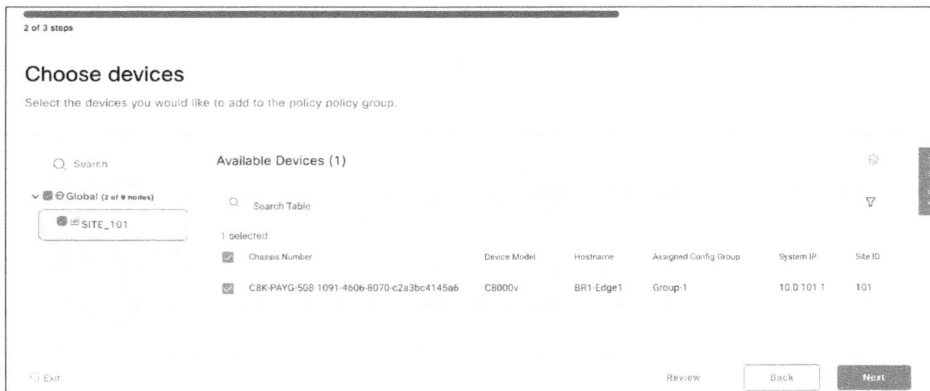

Figure 11-60 *Associating Devices with a Policy Group*

Secure Segmentation

Organizations today have high demands for network security due to the constantly growing cybersecurity risks. It is extremely important to understand who and what access your network and to perform strict access control to network-attached resources and services.

Network segmentation plays a significant role in cybersecurity defense because it provides a way to isolate logically independent parts of the network so users or devices from one network segment cannot access the resources in another segment. Segmentation allows you to provide access control to critical network assets and also allows you to reduce the scope of a possible cyberattack by limiting how far it can spread across the network.

Segmentation in Cisco Catalyst SD-WAN Overlay Networks

Cisco Catalyst SD-WAN provides two levels of network segmentation, often referred to as macrosegmentation and microsegmentation. Figure 11-61 illustrates the difference between them.

Segmentation at the macro level is done based on Virtual Routing and Forwarding (VRF) technology. As discussed in Chapter 3, "Control Plane and Data Plane Operations," VPNs in Cisco Catalyst SD-WAN are simply different VRF instances in traditional IP networks. This means every VPN (or every VRF instance) has its own instances of routing and forwarding tables that do not exchange information by default. It is safe to say that macrosegmentation is already achieved by deploying VPNs, without any additional configuration. However, if you need to provide connectivity between different VPNs in your network, you can do it by manually configuring inter-VPN route leaking.

Segmentation at the micro level is done based on Cisco TrustSec technology. It allows you to achieve more granular segmentation within the same VPN due to dynamic tagging and flexible policies that can be assigned to every user or device.

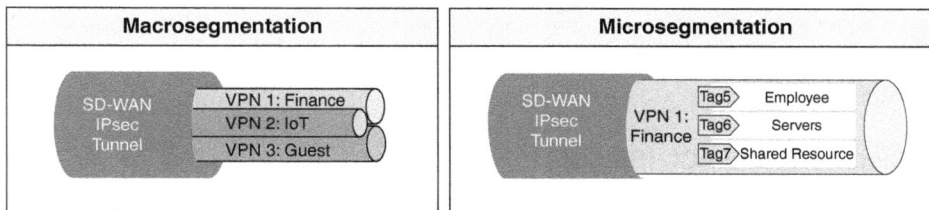

Figure 11-61   *Segmentation in Cisco Catalyst SD-WAN*

By adding microsegmentation to a Cisco Catalyst SD-WAN solution, you can get comprehensive end-to-end segmentation across an organization-wide network and apply granular role-based policies by considering the particular user identity or device role.

Cisco TrustSec Introduction

Cisco TrustSec (CTS) is a software-defined segmentation technology that allows you to abstract from traditional network attributes such as IP subnets or VLANs and implement logical grouping of devices based on their roles. As a network grows, managing traditional IP-based access lists can become a big challenge due to the size and complexity of these lists. In addition, managing these lists requires precise control over IP address and VLAN assignment. It can be relatively easy to carry out IP-based access control in static environments (such as a server infrastructure that is unlikely to change IP addresses often), but it is more difficult in dynamic environments where users can move around, connect to the network from different places, and get their IP addresses dynamically assigned via DHCP.

Cisco TrustSec uses a special tag—the *Security Group Tag (SGT)*—to represent logical group membership. Figure 11-62 shows an example of security group classification. As you

11

can see, SGTs are assigned exclusively based on the device or user role (such as employee, IT admin, phone, printer, and so on). Usually SGTs are defined by a number and a human-readable name, such as *SGT 5:Employees*. Security group membership is IP address agnostic, so even if the users are connected to the same subnet, they can have different types of access, based on their identity and the company role.

Another new concept in Cisco TrustSec is *Security Group Access Control Lists (SGACLs)*. When you define the access permissions, you can also do it at the logical level (for example, *IT Admins* group is allowed to access *Printers* group, *Employees* group does not have access to *Printers* or *Phones*, and so on). In addition, as with a regular access list, with an SGACL, you can specify the protocol and port to be allowed or denied.

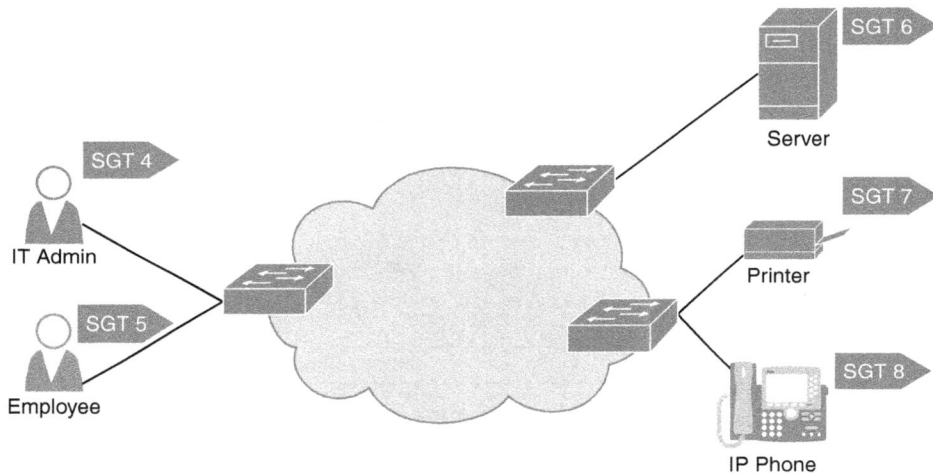

Security Group ACL (SGACL)

Source \ Destination	Printers	IP Phones	Servers
IT Admins	Allow HTTPS	Allow all	Allow RDP, HTTPS, SSH
Employees	Deny all	Deny all	Allow HTTPS

Figure 11-62 *Introduction to SGT and SGACL*

Cisco TrustSec operates in three phases:

- **Classification:** This phase involves assigning the SGT to a user or device when they connect to the network.

- **Propagation:** This phase involves distributing SGTs across the network, from the place where they were assigned to a place where the policy enforcement will happen.

- **Enforcement:** This phase involves applying the SGACL policies to allow or deny the traffic based on the source and destination SGTs.

Classification

When a user or a device connects to the network, they get an SGT tag assigned. This SGT assignment is called *classification*. The possible numeric SGT values range from 1 to 65,533. SGT 0 is used to mark the unknown (unclassified) traffic.

Cisco TrustSec supports both static and dynamic classification. *Static classification* involves the manual association of an SGT with an IP address, a VLAN, or a port profile. Although it is a legitimate method of assigning SGTs, static classification is used rarely—mostly when dynamic SGT assignment is not possible. On the other hand, *dynamic classification* allows you to assign SGTs based on the authentication result. It requires a RADIUS server that supports Cisco TrustSec and that can assign SGTs (such as Cisco ISE). Dynamic classification is the preferred method of assigning SGTs to user devices and endpoints because it is not tied to specific IP addresses or VLANs and allows you to abstract from the underlying network infrastructure.

A device can have only one SGT at a time. The SGT can be dynamically changed. For example, if some network security device has detected malicious behavior of the endpoint, Cisco ISE can mark it as non-compliant, trigger the Change of Authorization (CoA) event, place the endpoint into a new security group with limited access (that is, quarantine it), and reassign the SGT accordingly. In such a case, the endpoint device will lose its original SGT, and only the new *Quarantine* SGT will be used.

An endpoint device is not aware of its SGT. When the traffic is sent from the endpoint toward the network, the tag is assigned by the network device (such as an access-layer switch, wireless LAN controller, or wireless access point) and propagated further in the network. When the return traffic is sent back to the endpoint, the network device removes the SGT information from the data packet headers so the endpoint will never receive it.

Propagation

As we discussed previously, traffic classification occurs at the network entry point, where the user or device connects to the network. So initially only the network device that assigned an SGT is aware of it. After the traffic is classified, the SGT must be sent further— from where the classification took place to where the enforcement action is invoked. This process is called *propagation*, and it is required for other network devices to correlate the source or destination IP address with the assigned SGT.

Cisco TrustSec supports two types of SGT propagation: data plane propagation and control plane propagation.

Data plane propagation implies that a source SGT is attached to the data packets and propagated in the network as a part of a data packet header. In a traditional network (or a service-side VPN inside a branch) the SGTs are added to a special packet header field called Cisco Metadata (CMD), as shown in Figure 11-63. This method is called *inline tagging*.

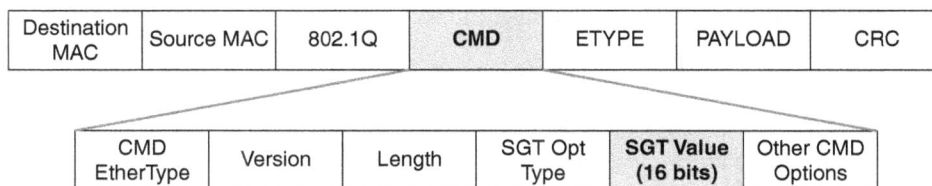

Destination MAC	Source MAC	802.1Q	**CMD**	ETYPE	PAYLOAD	CRC

CMD EtherType	Version	Length	SGT Opt Type	**SGT Value (16 bits)**	Other CMD Options

Figure 11-63 *SGT Propagation Using Inline Tagging*

On the WAN side, the source SGT can be propagated in the IPsec header. In Cisco Catalyst SD-WAN, SGTs are propagated over the data plane IPsec or GRE tunnels, as shown in Figure 11-64.

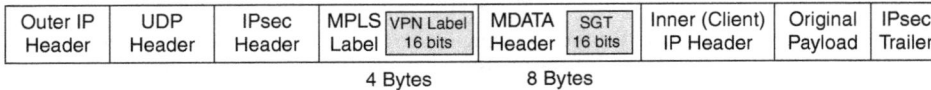

Outer IP Header	UDP Header	IPsec Header	MPLS Label	VPN Label 16 bits	MDATA Header	SGT 16 bits	Inner (Client) IP Header	Original Payload	IPsec Trailer

4 Bytes　　　　8 Bytes

Figure 11-64　*SGT Propagation in a Cisco Catalyst SD-WAN IPsec Tunnel*

NOTE　For inline tagging to work properly, all network devices that forward data traffic must support Cisco TrustSec at the hardware level. CMD is an additional field embedded in the MAC (Layer 2) header, and if a network device does not support Cisco TrustSec, the CMD field will be ignored and not propagated further.

In Cisco Catalyst SD-WAN, when you configure SGT propagation from LAN to WAN, you can instruct the WAN Edge router to propagate the received SGT without any changes or rewrite it with the explicitly configured value. In the opposite direction, you can define whether the received SGT is propagated from WAN to LAN or whether the SGT should not be included in the LAN packets. This configuration is done in the VPN 0 and service-side interface templates in SD-WAN Manager. (Refer to the "Cisco Catalyst SD-WAN Security Configuration Guide" for more details.)

If all branches have hardware devices that support TrustSec (called *TrustSec-enabled branches*), the end-to-end microsegmentation can be achieved with data plane propagation only. Inside the branches, the SGTs will be propagated in the CMD header, while on the WAN side, the tags will be carried inside an IPsec header. Figure 11-65 illustrates this scenario between the Branches 1 and 3.

With control plane propagation, IP-to-SGT mappings are propagated independently of the data traffic, using a separate out-of-band control connection. The most commonly used technologies are *SGT Exchange Protocol (SXP)* and the *Cisco pxGrid* framework. Cisco Catalyst WAN Edges support SXP for the control plane SGT propagation.

SXP is a TCP-based protocol that uses port 64999 for connection initiation. There are no special hardware requirements for the network devices because IP-to-SGT mappings are distributed over a standard IP protocol.

The devices that establish SXP connections can have different roles:

- **SXP speaker:** A device that advertises IP-to-SGT mappings over SXP

- **SXP listener:** A device that receives and learns IP-to-SGT mappings over SXP

- **Both:** A device that is both SXP speaker and SXP listener at the same time

SXP connections can be established directly between network devices (such as routers, switches, firewalls), or between a network device and Cisco ISE. In Cisco Catalyst SD-WAN, SXP is a good alternative to the inline tagging in the remote branches that do not have TrustSec-enabled network devices. Figure 11-65 illustrates this scenario in Branch 2.

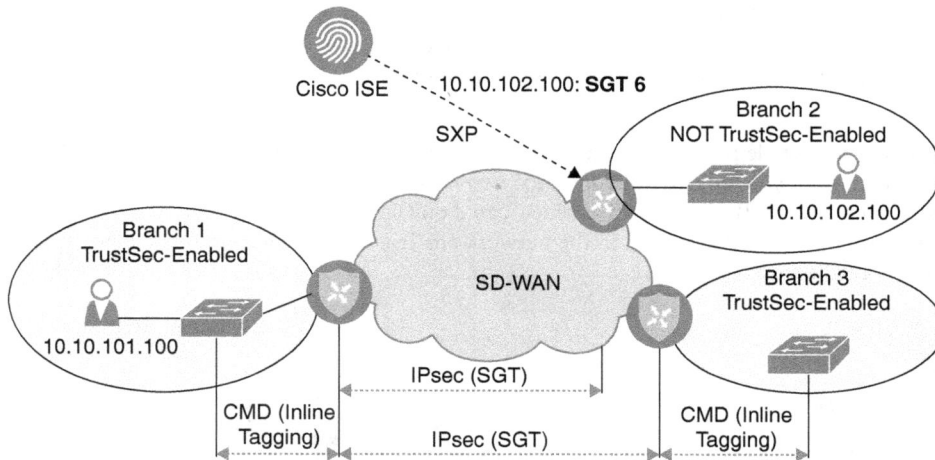

Figure 11-65 *End-to-End SGT Propagation in Cisco Catalyst SD-WAN*

There is one more SXP device role that is not mandatory but highly recommended in large SD-WAN networks: SXP reflector. Usually the SXP reflector is a non-SD-WAN router with high-performance compute resources that participates in SXP exchange between Cisco ISE and WAN Edge routers. SXP reflectors are required in several use cases. First, Cisco ISE has a limit on the number of SXP sessions it can handle, and SXP reflectors can help solve the scalability problem and facilitate multiple SXP connections between the network devices and Cisco ISE. Second, SXP reflectors can be configured with granular filtering rules so that only relevant IP-to-SGT bindings are pushed down to the Cisco Catalyst WAN Edge routers. Note that overlapping or remote entries coming through an SXP reflector can have an adverse effect on overlay routing or cause unnecessary resource utilization on the router, which is why it is recommended to filter them out.

NOTE Starting from Cisco IOS XE Release 17.12, the behavior of OMP was changed to support Cisco TrustSec. In the previous versions, the router's forwarding information base (FIB) did not contain OMP routes. In the latest releases, a new type of route, known as the *CTS route*, is added to the FIB. The CTS route contains the OMP prefix, the length, and the associated SGT value, and it allows you to enforce the overlay SGT-based security policies at any branch or at the headend.

Enforcement

The main goal of Cisco TrustSec is to apply security policies based on the source and destination SGTs. This process is called *enforcement*, and traditionally it is done as close to the destination as possible.

Security policies are defined as SGACLs, which are quite similar to the traditional IP access lists; the main difference is that SGACLs use SGTs instead of IP addresses. This means an SGACL consists of the source SGT, the destination SGT, and the action (permit or deny). An SGACL can be configured centrally on Cisco ISE and then downloaded to the network devices that do the policy enforcement (routers, switches, firewalls, and so on).

11

The network device doing enforcement downloads *only* SGACLs with the destination SGTs it knows about. This significantly decreases the devices' resource consumption because they need to process smaller numbers of SGACLs rather than everything that exists in the network.

Let's review the whole process of end-to-end Cisco TrustSec segmentation. Figure 11-66 shows the topology details. In this topology, two users (User A and User B) are connected to different switches. Both users are authenticated on Cisco ISE and get their SGTs assigned dynamically from ISE. All devices in the network are TrustSec enabled, and data plane propagation is configured everywhere.

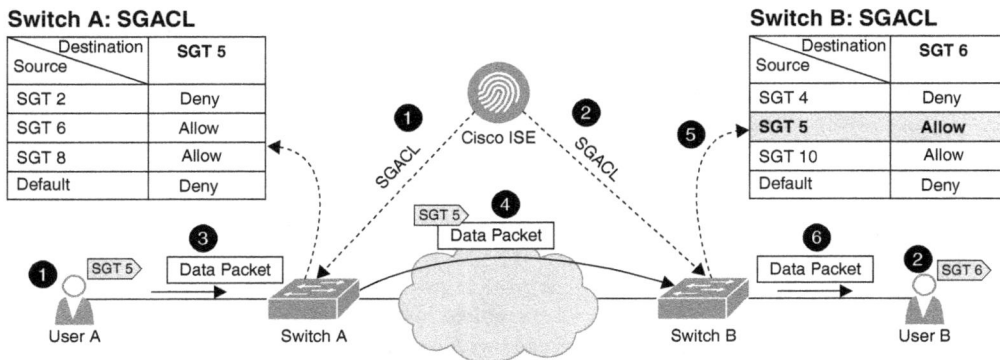

Switch A: SGACL

Source \ Destination	SGT 5
SGT 2	Deny
SGT 6	Allow
SGT 8	Allow
Default	Deny

Switch B: SGACL

Source \ Destination	SGT 6
SGT 4	Deny
SGT 5	Allow
SGT 10	Allow
Default	Deny

Figure 11-66 *End-to-End Cisco TrustSec Segmentation*

The communication between User A and User B happens in the following steps:

Step 1. User A connects to Switch A, authenticates, and gets SGT 5 assigned from Cisco ISE. Switch A downloads all SGACLs with destination SGT 5 from Cisco ISE. No other SGACLs are downloaded.

Step 2. User B connects to Switch B, authenticates, and gets SGT 6 assigned from Cisco ISE. Switch B downloads all SGACLs with destination SGT 6 from Cisco ISE. No other SGACLs are downloaded.

Step 3. User A sends a packet to User B. The endpoint devices are not aware of SGTs, so there is no SGT in the original packet between the user and the access-layer switch.

Step 4. Switch A adds a CMD header to the packet and updates the SGT value to 5 (which is always a source SGT). Switch A is not aware of the destination SGT, which is why it cannot do the policy enforcement.

Step 5. Switch B receives the packet and extracts the source SGT 5 from the CMD header. It already knows the destination SGT that was assigned to User B (SGT 6), and it has the SGACL that allows traffic from SGT 5 to SGT 6.

Step 6. Switch B removes the CMD header and forwards the original data packet to User B.

NOTE   If the traffic from SGT 5 to SGT 6 should be denied, the packet will also be dropped by Switch B. Even though it seems to create an additional load on the network due to the unnecessary traffic forwarding, in fact this helps to significantly decrease the load on all network devices. In large networks, the total number of network-attached devices and endpoints can become huge, and if every network device had to download and process all possible IP-to-SGT bindings and associated SGACLs, high-performance switches and routers would be needed everywhere in the network.

In Cisco Catalyst SD-WAN, the policy enforcement can be done either by the service-side routers/switches or by the egress WAN Edge router. If the destination branch is TrustSec aware, the source SGT can be propagated further into the branch, and the enforcement can be done by the network devices inside the branch, as close to the traffic destination as possible. This is the recommended approach, as it eliminates the need for out-of-band distribution of destination IP-to-SGT mappings to the device doing the enforcement.

In the legacy branches (those that are not TrustSec aware), the enforcement can be done by the WAN Edge device itself. In such a case, the control plane propagation of IP-to-SGT mappings is required to ensure that the WAN Edge router knows the destination SGT and downloads the required policies.

All TrustSec configuration related to SGT propagation and enforcement on SD-WAN devices is done inside the service-side interface template. Figure 11-67 shows the possible configuration options. To enable SGT enforcement on the current WAN Edge device, set the *Enable Enforcement* parameter to *On*.

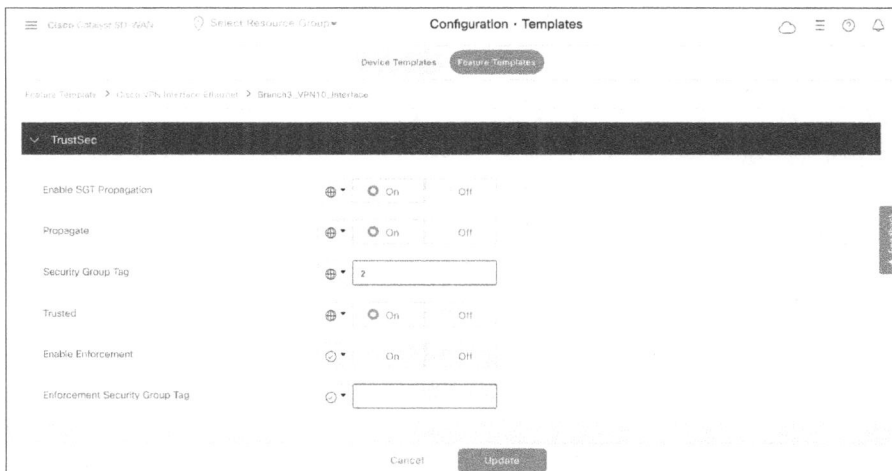

Figure 11-67   *TrustSec Configuration Inside the Interface Template*

From the WAN Edge perspective, an SGT tag can come either from the LAN side (that is, a service-side VPN interface) or from the WAN (that is, from SD-WAN tunnels). Depending on its configuration, the WAN Edge device can forward (propagate) the original SGT without any changes, overwrite an SGT with the preconfigured value, or not propagate an SGT at all. We will use the sample topology shown in Figure 11-68 to explore the possible behavior of the WAN Edge device.

11

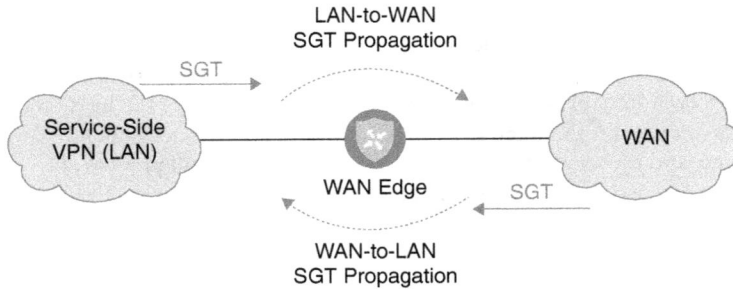

Figure 11-68 *SGT Propagation by a WAN Edge Router*

The first configuration parameter, *Enable SGT Propagation*, enables the propagation of SGT tags in the LAN-to-WAN direction. This option must be enabled to use TrustSec on the particular WAN Edge device. The SGT propagation behavior of a WAN Edge device is determined by the combination of configuration parameters illustrated in Figure 11-67. Table 11-3 summarizes the possible SGT Propagation options.

Table 11-3 SGT Propagation Options in Catalyst SD-WAN

Configuration	LAN to WAN	WAN to LAN
Enable SGT Propagation = On Propagate = On Security Group Tag = *<SGT_Value>* Trusted = On	SGT is propagated from LAN to WAN without any changes (because Trusted is set to On).	SGT is propagated from WAN to LAN without any changes.
Enable SGT Propagation = On Propagate = On Security Group Tag = *<SGT_Value>* Trusted = Off	SGT is propagated from LAN to WAN. SGT is overwritten with the configured value (*SGT_Value*).	SGT is propagated from WAN to LAN without any changes.
Enable SGT Propagation = On Propagate = Off Security Group Tag = *<SGT_Value>* Trusted = On	SGT is propagated from LAN to WAN without any changes (because Trusted is set to On).	SGT is not propagated from WAN to LAN.
Enable SGT Propagation = On Propagate = Off Security Group Tag = *<SGT_Value>* Trusted = Off	SGT is propagated from LAN to WAN. SGT is overwritten with the configured value (*SGT_Value*).	SGT is not propagated from WAN to LAN.
Enable SGT Propagation = On Propagate = On (Usually configured on the physical interface if there are existing subinterfaces)	SGT is propagated from LAN to WAN with SGT value 0.	SGT is propagated from from WAN to LAN with SGT value 0.
Enable SGT Propagation = Off (Other configuration options are not possible.)	SGT is not propagated from LAN to WAN.	SGT is not propagated from WAN to LAN.

NOTE   It is important to remember that SGT propagation can be enabled only on the Layer 3 (routed) interfaces of a WAN Edge device. Inline tagging is not supported on the Layer 2 (switch) ports of the router.

NOTE   Refer to "Cisco Catalyst SD-WAN Security Configuration Guide," published on the Cisco documentation site, for additional deployment details.

SD-WAN Manager Authentication and Authorization

The final component of Cisco Catalyst SD-WAN security is the hardening of the SD-WAN network management system itself. SD-WAN Manager plays a critical role in the overall security of the enterprise. For this reason, access to the SD-WAN Manager should be strictly controlled and secured. Cisco SD-WAN Manager supports a multitude of authentication and authorization methods and functionalities, and the best practice is to assign the network administrators and operators the minimum permissions required to complete their job functions.

Local Authentication with Role-Based Access Control (RBAC)

Users can be authenticated into SD-WAN Manager through a built-in local database that can be found in the **Administration** section. Users can then be tied to a user group to provide customized access to the solution.

There are several predefined user groups, including the following:

- **Netadmin:** Provides unfettered read and write access to the entirety of SD-WAN Manager.

- **Operator:** Provides read-only access to SD-WAN Manager.

- **Basic:** Provides read-only access to the interface and system sections of SD-WAN Manager.

- **Network_operations:** Provides read and write access to non-security operations on SD-WAN Manager (such as managing non-security policies, attaching device templates, and so on).

- **Security_operations:** Provides read and write access to security policies and security data monitoring on SD-WAN Manager.

NOTE   Different SD-WAN Manager versions can have different preconfigured user groups by default. Custom user groups can also be created, and a combination of read and write access to all components of SD-WAN Manager can be configured, as needed.

These are the basic steps required to configure a new local database user:

Step 1.   Add the user. In the **Manage Users** section under **Administration**, click **Add User** on the Users tab.

Step 2.   Configure the full name. Specify the user's full name.

11

Step 3.   **Configure the username.** Specify the user's desired username.

Step 4.   **Configure the password.** Specify and confirm the user's password, which can be changed at first login, if necessary.

Step 5.   **Select the user group.** Select from one of the three predefined user groups or a custom user group.

Figure 11-69 illustrates the process of adding new users to SD-WAN Manager.

Figure 11-69   *Adding a New Local User*

These are the basic steps required to configure a custom user group:

Step 1.   **Add the user group.** In the **Manage Users** section under **Administration**, click **Add User Group** on the User Groups tab.

Step 2.   **Configure the user group name.** Specify the user group name.

Step 3.   **Select read and write access.** Select the desired read and write access levels.

When you're creating a user group, read and write options are available for various features. Figure 11-70 shows the user group configuration pane in SD-WAN Manager.

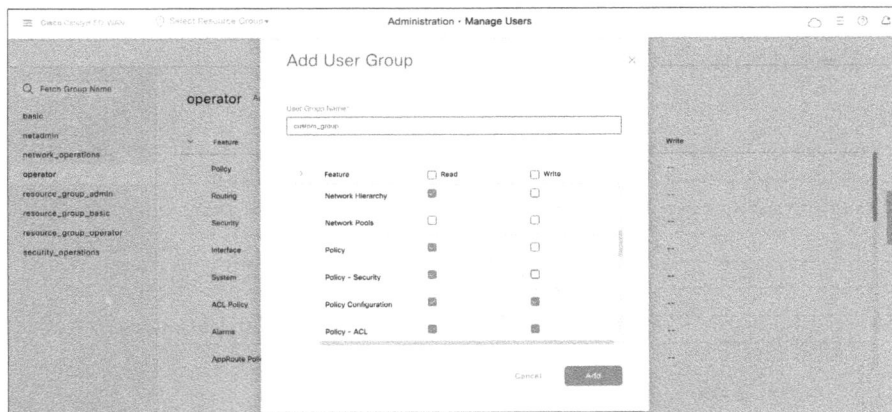

Figure 11-70   *Adding a Custom User Group*

You can make RBAC VPN aware. That is to say, you can tie a user to a specific user group that is assigned to an RBAC group that provides visibility into only a single VPN or a subset of VPNs.

The following basic steps are required to configure RBAC for a VPN:

Step 1.   **Configure VPN segments.** In the **VPN Segments** section under **Administration**, enter a segment name and VPN number. Figure 11-71 shows the screen for adding a VPN number to a VPN segment. This is a way for SD-WAN Manager to tie a VPN number to a name so that it can be referenced later on in a VPN group.

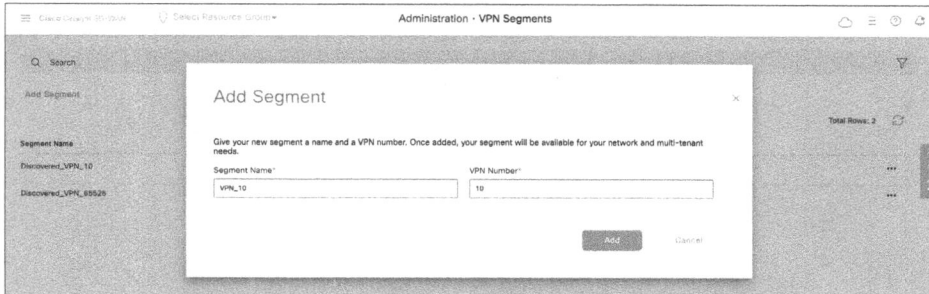

Figure 11-71   *Adding a VPN Segment*

Step 2.   **Configure a VPN group.** In the **VPN Segments** section under **Administration**, enter a VPN group name and description, create the RBAC user group, and assign a segment or multiple segments to the VPN group.

A VPN group enables SD-WAN Manager to tie a single segment or multiple segments to a group that can then be attached to a custom RBAC user group. This RBAC user group will appear in the User Group section of SD-WAN Manager and can then be tied to a user. Figure 11-72 shows the screen for creating a VPN group.

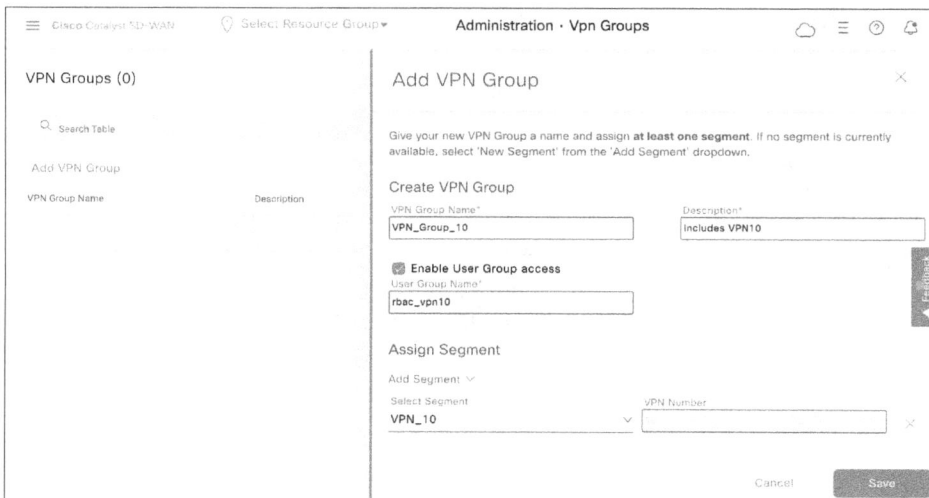

Figure 11-72   *Adding a VPN Group*

Step 3.   **Assign the user to the user group.** Select the newly created RBAC user group. Configure the user to be in the newly created RBAC user group so that, when the user logs in, only the information from the VPNs assigned to the VPN group is consumable. You can edit an existing user or create a new one (refer to Figure 11-69).

When a user who is assigned to a VPN-attached user group logs in, only information that is relevant to the VPNs allocated in the VPN group will be visible. This includes device health, site health, WAN Edge health, and top applications (see Figure 11-73).

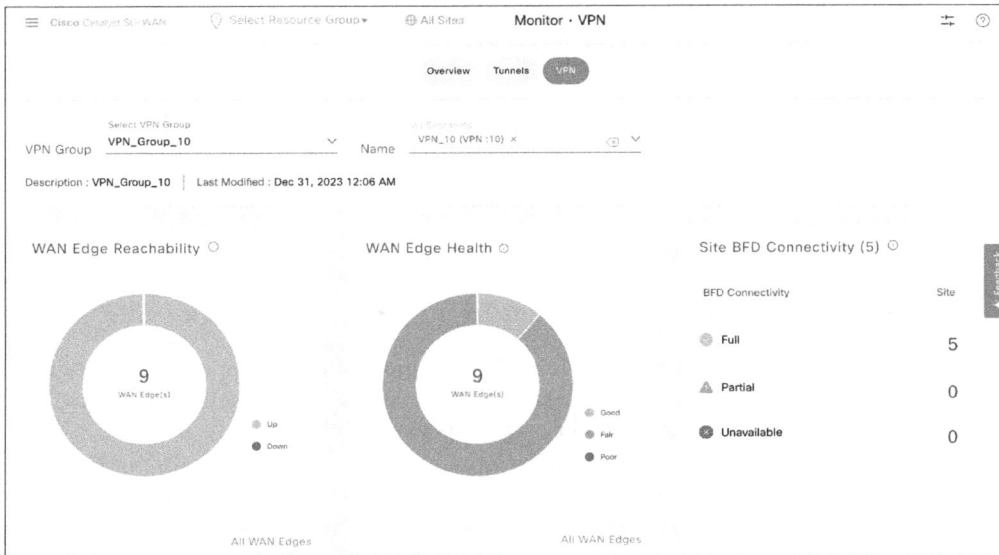

Figure 11-73   *RBAC by VPN Visibility*

Remote Authentication with Role-Based Access Control (RBAC)

SD-WAN Manager also supports remote authentication with role-based access control through the use of a RADIUS/TACACS or single sign-on (SSO) authentication server.

Figure 11-74 shows the RADIUS and TACACS configuration pane within SD-WAN Manager. To authenticate via RADIUS/TACACS, simply configure a AAA SD-WAN Manager feature template or manually configure the RADIUS/TACACS server information via the SD-WAN Manager CLI. User groups can be leveraged with remote authentication as long as the authentication server can pass the group name as a parameter to SD-WAN Manager.

To authenticate via SSO, upload a SAML 2.0–compliant metadata file to SD-WAN Manager by navigating to **Identity Provider Settings** in the SD-WAN Manager **Administration > Settings** section. Figure 11-75 shows how to enable the identity provider.

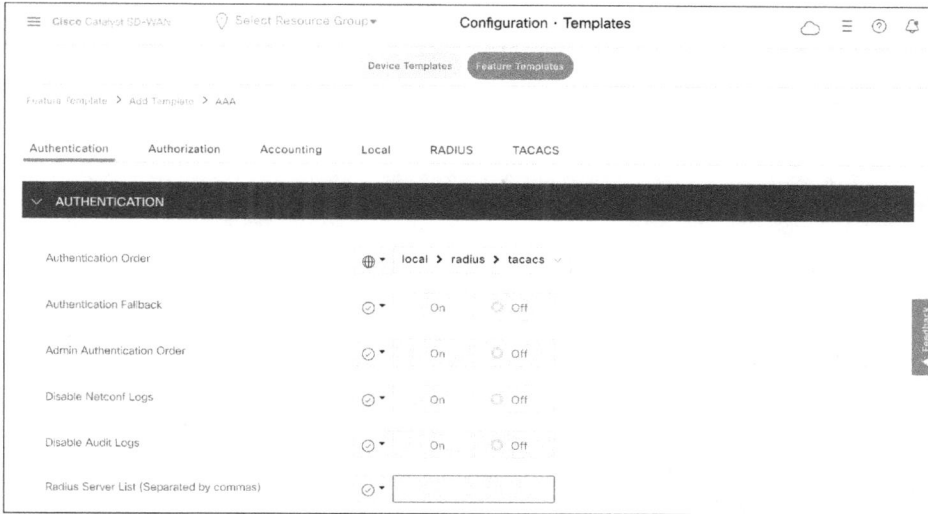

Figure 11-74 *RADIUS/TACACS Configuration*

Figure 11-75 *Identity Provider Configuration*

When creating a user who should authenticate using an external identity provider, you should configure this user to be remote and provide a user email address that belongs to the domain configured in the IDP settings. You still can assign the user groups on SD-WAN Manager, but there is no need to set the password locally. The user will be authenticated by the IDP, and only the authentication result will be sent to SD-WAN Manager. Figure 11-76 shows the screen for creating a remote user.

RBAC by Resource Groups

Another way to differentiate levels of access for users is to provide role-based access control based on resource groups. This method allows you to split the network management between multiple administrators, especially in big geographically distributed deployments.

A resource group is a list of sites. When a user is assigned to a specific resource group, they have access only to the resources in that resource group. At the same time, a global admin has access to all resources across the entire SD-WAN deployment.

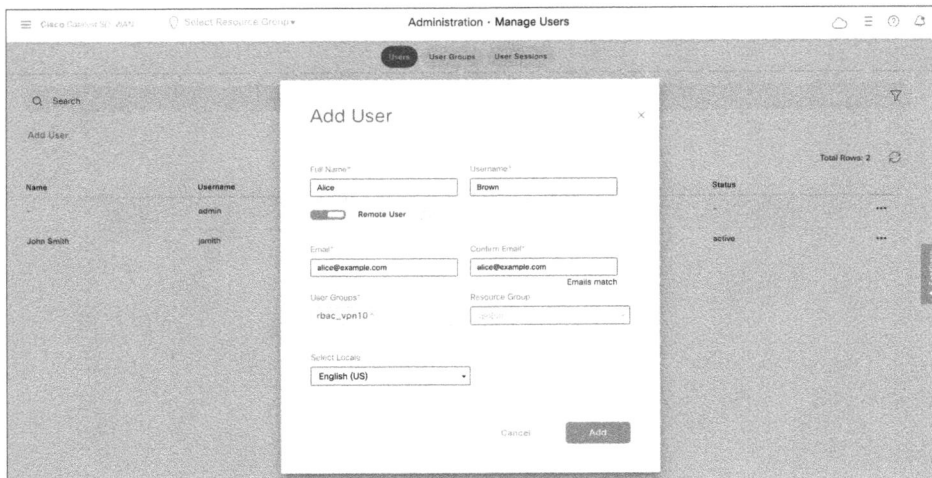

Figure 11-76   *Creating a Remote User*

Similarly to the global RBAC permissions we discussed before, a user within a resource group can have the following permissions:

- **Resource_group_admin:** The user has full read/write access to the devices within the corresponding resource group and can troubleshoot, monitor, attach, or detach templates for the WAN Edge devices in their group.

- **Resource_group_operator:** The user has read-only access to all devices in the specified resource group.

- **Resource_group_basic:** The user has read-only access to the interface and system resources in the assigned resource group.

To manage resource groups, go to **Administration > Resource Groups.** The system-defined *global* group is present there by default, and the admin user belongs to that group. All other groups are custom. Figure 11-77 shows this configuration page.

Figure 11-77   *Resource Group Management*

To create a new group, click the **Add Resource Group** button and provide the group details, as shown in Figure 11-78. This example shows the creation of a resource group named *dc_sites* that includes the data center sites with site IDs 10 and 20.

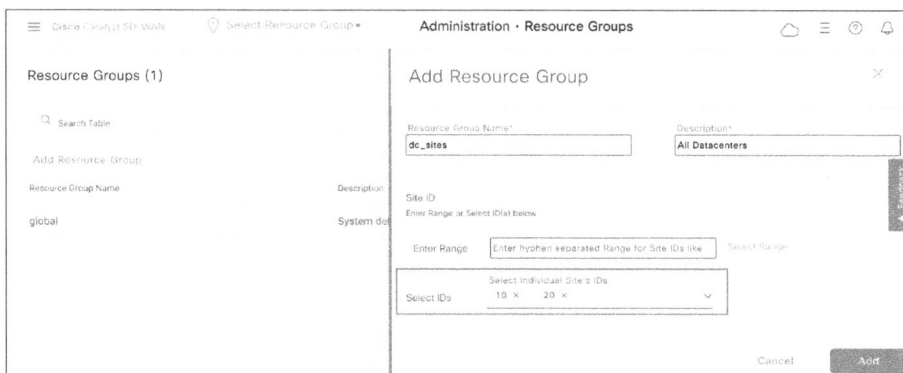

Figure 11-78 *Adding a Resource Group*

The next step is to create a new user or update the existing one. Figure 11-79 shows how to add the user *dc_admin*, place this user in the user group *resource_group_admin*, and assign the *dc_sites* resource group to the user.

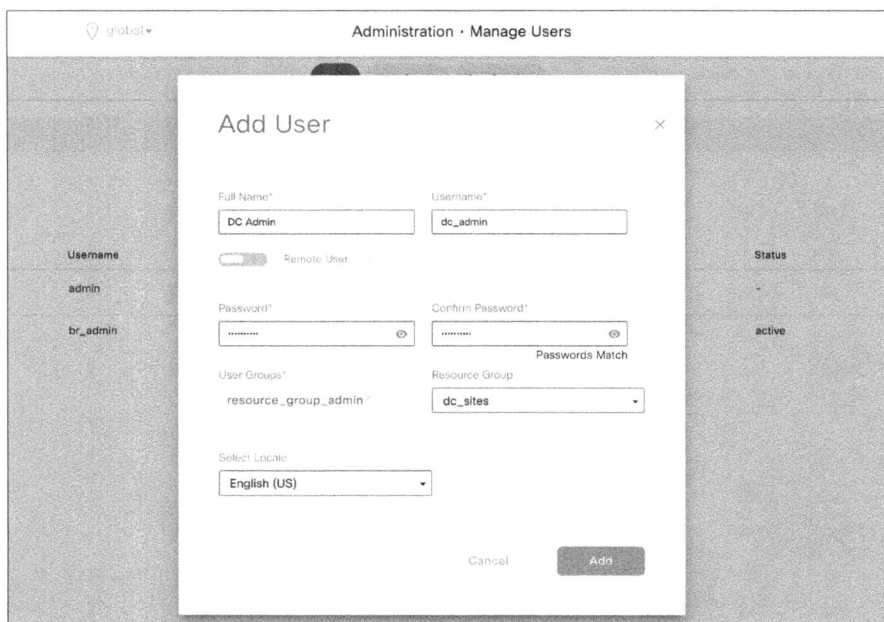

Figure 11-79 *Adding a User to the Resource Group*

When the *dc_admin* user (*resource_group_admin*) logs into SD-WAN Manager, they see only the devices that are associated with DC-1 (site ID 10) and DC-2 (site ID 20). Figure 11-80 shows the SD-WAN Manager interface of such a user. Notice that only four WAN Edge devices and two sites are displayed to the user.

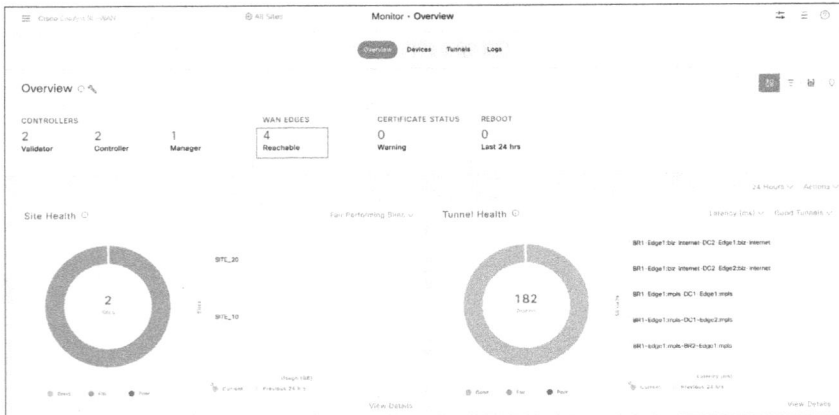

Figure 11-80   *Resource Group Admin View*

Meanwhile, a full admin user (from the *global* resource group) sees all configuration and monitoring options in SD-WAN Manager, as shown in Figure 11-81. Notice the difference in WAN Edge devices (the admin user can see all nine devices) and SD-WAN sites (the admin user can see all five sites). Also, if a user has access to several resource groups, they can choose *View* in the top-left corner and switch to the view of a custom resource group. In Figure 11-81, the view is set to Global.

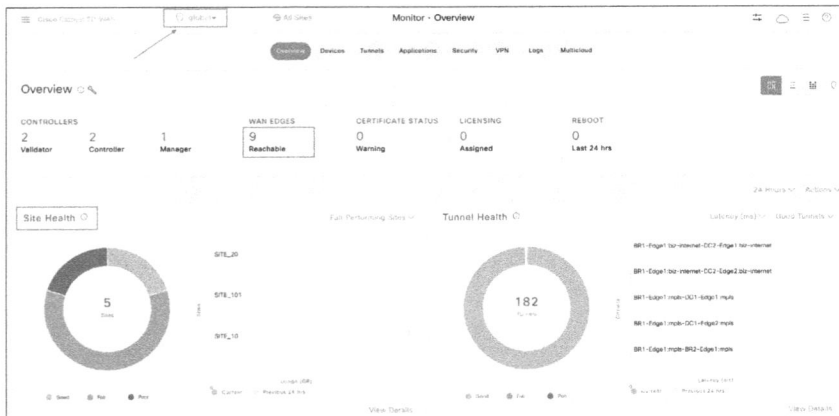

Figure 11-81   *Global Admin View*

Summary

This chapter covers all aspects of Cisco Catalyst SD-WAN security, including integrated functionality, such as application-aware enterprise firewalls, intrusion prevention, URL filtering, AMP, DNS security, and TLS/SSL decryption, as well as Secure Internet Gateway, secure segmentation, and SD-WAN Manager authentication and authorization. Cisco's goal with SD-WAN security is to ensure that no matter what your requirements may be at the branch, a viable option exists to ensure that the appropriate security posture can be attained, managed efficiently, and accessed securely.

Review All Key Topics

Review the most important topics in the chapter, noted with the Key Topic icon in the outer margin of the page. Table 11-4 lists these key topics and the page number on which each is found.

Table 11-4   Key Topics

Key Topic Element	Description	Page
Section	Application-aware enterprise firewall	448
Figure 11-12	Security policy application	455
Section	Intrusion detection and prevention	457
Section	URL filtering	463
Section	Advanced Malware Protection and Threat Grid	467
Section	DNS web layer security	472
Section	TLS/SSL decryption	475
Paragraph	Umbrella root certificate considerations	477
Section	Secure Internet Gateway (SIG)	483
Section	Policy Groups	486
Section	Secure segmentation	494
Section	SD-WAN Manager authentication and authorization	503

Define Key Terms

Define the following key terms from this chapter and check your answers in the glossary:

Direct Internet Access, IDS/IPS, RBAC, zone

Chapter Review Questions

1. True or false: The Cisco Catalyst SD-WAN Enterprise Firewall with Application Awareness is not VPN aware.

   a. True

   b. False

2. What actions can be set in a firewall policy? (Choose three.)

   a. Pass

   b. Inspect

   c. Redirect

   d. Export

   e. Drop

3. True or false: Logging is not available for Enterprise Firewall with Application Awareness policies.

   a. True

   b. False

11

4. What signature sets are available for selection in an IDS/IPS policy? (Choose three.)

   a. Strict

   b. Balanced

   c. Relaxed

   d. Connectivity

   e. Security

5. Which Snort engine modes are supported during an engine failure or engine reboot? (Choose two.)

   a. Fail-block

   b. Fail-close

   c. Fail-pass

   d. Fail-wide

   e. Fail-open

6. True or false: Before an IDS/IPS policy can be configured, the network operator must upload a security virtual image to SD-WAN Manager, in the Software Repository section.

   a. True

   b. False

7. True or false: URL filtering requires a minimum of 4 GB DRAM and 4 GB flash to be deployed.

   a. True

   b. False

8. What URL filtering feature can be leveraged to explicitly block certain websites?

   a. Categories

   b. Reputation

   c. URL blacklist

   d. URL whitelist

9. URL filtering visibility includes which of the following information? (Choose two.)

   a. URLs accessed

   b. Session count

   c. Website reputation

   d. Blocked and allowed categories by percentage

10. True or false: The maximum exportable file size for file analysis is 1000 MB.

    a. True

    b. False

11. Which tasks are involved in configuring file analysis for Advanced Malware Protection? (Choose three.)

    a. Configure the Threat Grid API key.

    b. Configure the file types list.

    c. Enable file analysis.

    d. Enable HTTPS inbound to the WAN Edge router.

    e. Configure a security rule for Threat Grid.

12. True or false: AMP visibility can display the malware filename.

    a. True

    b. False

13. How is the Cisco Umbrella API token generated?

    a. Automatically during SD-WAN Manager bootup

    b. Manually in the SD-WAN Manager Umbrella settings

    c. By the Cisco SE and provided to the customer by email

    d. In the Cisco Umbrella portal

14. If a customer wants the DNS web layer security redirection process to ignore a specific set of domains, what feature can be leveraged?

    a. Corporate domain bypass

    b. Domain filtering

    c. Local domain bypass

    d. Domain rules

15. Which privilege types can be assigned to a user group in SD-WAN Manager? (Choose two.)

    a. Read

    b. Erase

    c. Reboot

    d. Administer

    e. Write

16. True or false: RBAC by VPN allows some users to configure some VPN features but not others.

    a. True

    b. False

17. Which remote authentication types does SD-WAN Manager support? (Choose three.)

    a. Single sign-on (SSO)

    b. RADIUS

    c. Local

    d. TACACS

Reference

"Cisco SD-WAN Security Sensitive Branch Design Case Study," https://www.cisco.com/c/en/us/td/docs/solutions/CVD/SDWAN/Cisco_SDWAN_Case_Study_Security_Sensitive.html.

"Cisco Catalyst SD-WAN Security Configuration Guide," https://www.cisco.com/c/en/us/td/docs/routers/sdwan/configuration/security/ios-xe-17/security-book-xe.html

11

CHAPTER 12

Cisco Catalyst SD-WAN Cloud OnRamp

This chapter covers the following topics:

- **Cisco Catalyst SD-WAN Cloud OnRamp:** This section covers what Cisco Catalyst SD-WAN Cloud OnRamp is and why it is relevant to your organization.

- **Cloud OnRamp for SaaS:** This section covers the concepts and configuration of Cloud OnRamp for SaaS.

- **Cloud OnRamp for Multicloud:** This section explains how the enterprise WAN can be extended to the public cloud.

- **SD-WAN Cloud Interconnect:** This section explains how software-defined interconnects can link branch locations with each other by using a cloud-agnostic backbone and how they can connect to the cloud service providers via private links.

In recent years, not only has the industry seen applications migrating to the cloud on a massive scale, but "born in the cloud" has become the de facto standard for application development and delivery. In addition, the rapid adoption of business-critical cloud services by nearly all organizations across every vertical is fueling all things cloud and unveiling new challenges for network architects. These challenges include the following:

- **Providing reliable, flexible, and secure cloud connectivity models:** There are a multitude of ways to reach public or private cloud workloads and applications today. Network architects are now tasked with providing reliable, secure, and seamless connectivity from the branch, hub, or data center to workloads and applications.

- **Ensuring optimal cloud application performance and visibility:** Most networks have multiple egress points to the Internet, and it is important to ensure that the best path is utilized on a per-application basis and that performance of the path is collected and available for reporting.

- **Designing scalable multicloud architectures:** Organizations are starting to realize the benefits of a multicloud environment when it comes to private and public cloud workload placement. They need to ensure that these architectures are normalized, scalable, and easy to spin up and spin down, and they want them to stay operationally simple and cost-effective.

Cisco Catalyst SD-WAN Cloud OnRamp provides a set of features that allow network administrators to simplify and automate the process of connecting on-premises resources with the cloud, keep consistent end-to-end policies across the whole infrastructure, perform efficient path selection, and maintain an optimal application experience for the cloud-based services.

Figure 12-1 shows the different Cloud OnRamp options offered with Cisco Catalyst SD-WAN.

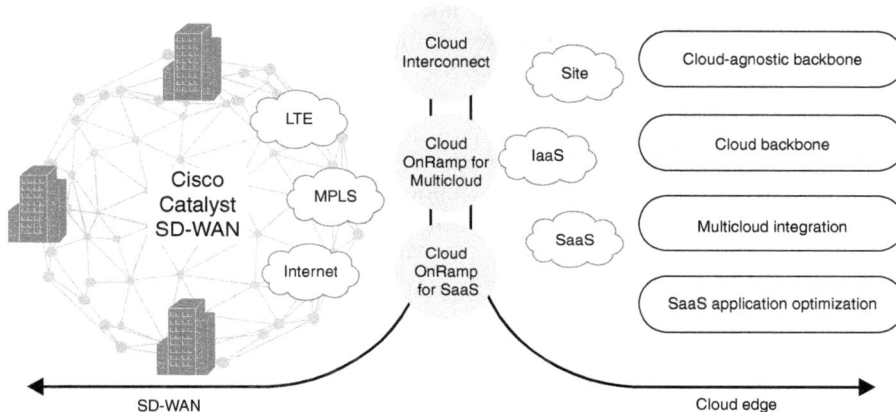

Figure 12-1 *Cisco Catalyst SD-WAN Cloud OnRamp Options*

At this writing, Cisco Catalyst SD-WAN Cloud OnRamp offerings include the following options:

■ **Cloud OnRamp for SaaS (site-to-application):** This option provides the most optimal path from SD-WAN sites to SaaS-based applications or to custom applications that are accessible via SaaS.

■ **Cloud OnRamp for Multicloud (site-to-cloud, region-to-region, site-to-site, cloud-to-cloud):** This option allows an organization to extend the enterprise infrastructure by connecting to public clouds, establish connectivity between enterprise sites and cloud-based applications, and handle on-demand provisioning of region-to-region connectivity to let an application talk to another application hosted in another region of the cloud. Cloud OnRamp can also use the cloud provider's backbone to build site-to-site connectivity over the public cloud infrastructure (such as Amazon Web Services TGW Peering/Cloud WAN, Microsoft Azure vWAN, and Google Cloud NCC).

■ **SD-WAN Cloud Interconnect (site-to-site, site-to-cloud):** This option automates the on-demand network edge creation to the nearest metro area using Megaport or Equinix POPs, allowing organizations to create on-demand direct connections to AWS, Express routes to Azure, and interconnections to Google Cloud to establish connectivity from the branches, hubs, and data centers to the public cloud providers. It also offers a cloud-agnostic backbone that allows organizations to build on-demand connectivity between remote sites.

SD-WAN Cloud OnRamp features are built on the principles of centralized management and automation, unified security across the whole deployment, and providing the best experience to end users. This chapter covers a variety of Cloud OnRamp use cases in detail.

NOTE   Earlier releases of Catalyst SD-WAN included Cloud OnRamp for IaaS (Infrastructure-as-a-Service). It allowed an organization to integrate the SD-WAN fabric with public cloud infrastructure, such as virtual machines, networks, and other resources. In the latest versions of Catalyst SD-WAN, Cloud OnRamp for IaaS has been combined with many additional features, and now all cloud-related configuration is done under the Cloud OnRamp for Multicloud section in SD-WAN Manager.

Cloud OnRamp for SaaS

Key Topic

In today's cloud-centric world, where SaaS consumption reigns supreme and SD-WAN is a necessity, the outdated practice of funneling traffic through costly and inefficient WAN routes to centralized hubs undermines the user experience.

Many SaaS applications depend on fast, secure, and reliable network connectivity to provide a seamless user experience. SD-WAN Cloud OnRamp for SaaS can significantly improve the user experience through continuous monitoring of all possible paths to the SaaS application and automatic selection of the best path for routing user traffic.

The benefits of Cloud OnRamp for SaaS include the following:

■ Improved branch office user experience for SaaS applications due to automatic path selection and use of the best-performing network path

■ Increased SaaS application resiliency with multiple network path selections and active monitoring

■ Visibility into SaaS application performance through the visibility of real-time and historical metrics

■ Operational simplicity and consistency through centralized control and management of SaaS application policies

Figure 12-2 provides an overview of SD-WAN Cloud OnRamp for SaaS. Cisco Catalyst SD-WAN continuously measures the performance of a designated SaaS application, such as Microsoft 365 or Google Apps, through all available paths from a branch, including designated backhaul paths. For each path, the fabric computes a quality of experience score ranging from 0 to 10, with 10 being the best performance. This score gives network administrators visibility into application performance that has never before been available. Most importantly, the fabric automatically makes real-time decisions to choose the best-performing path between the end users at a remote branch and the cloud SaaS application. Enterprises have the flexibility to deploy this capability in several ways, according to their business needs and security requirements.

Network administrators can configure different behaviors for the SaaS application traffic based on their organizational requirements and needs.

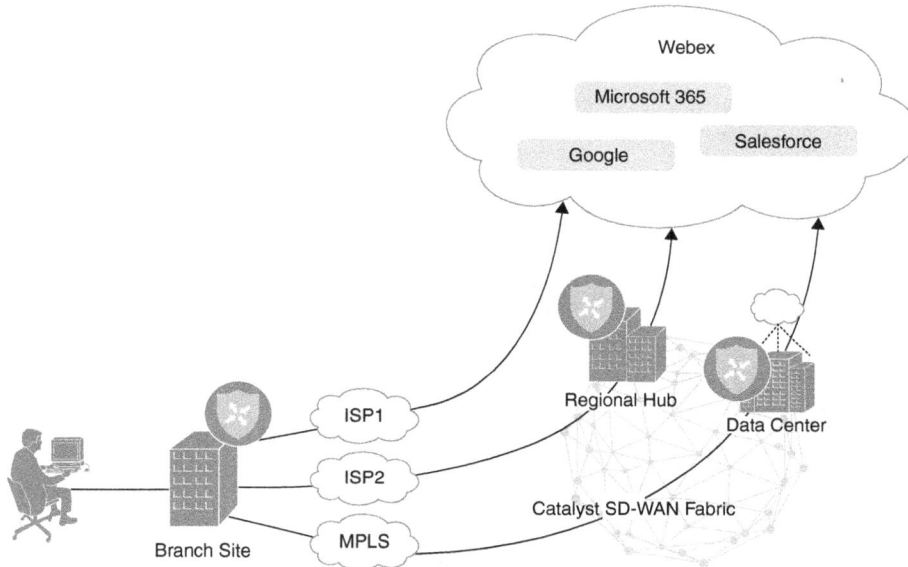

Figure 12-2 *Cloud OnRamp for SaaS*

One common use case is Direct Cloud Access (DCA) from a remote site. This feature is based on Direct Internet Access (DIA), but it allows an administrator to select the designated SaaS applications that should be routed from the remote branch directly to the Internet, while all other Internet-bound traffic takes the usual path, which could be through a regional hub, a data center, or a carrier-neutral facility. This feature allows the remote site to bypass the latency of tunneling Internet-bound traffic to a central site, subsequently improving the connectivity to the prioritized SaaS application. The WAN Edge router chooses the most optimal path to access these SaaS applications. Different applications could traverse different paths because the path selection is calculated on a per-application basis.

If any SaaS application path becomes unreachable or its performance score falls below an unacceptable level, the path is removed from a candidate path list. If all paths cannot be path candidates due to reachability or performance issues, traffic to the SaaS application follows the normal, routed path.

Figure 12-3 shows a remote site using DIA to access SaaS applications.

Another common use case is cloud access through a gateway. Many enterprises do not use DIA at the branch office because either their sites are connected by only private transports or centralized policy or security requirements don't permit it. They may use data centers, regional hubs, or even carrier-neutral facilities to enable Internet connectivity. In this case, SaaS traffic is tunneled to the best-performing gateway site, where it is subsequently routed to the Internet to reach the requested SaaS application service. Note that different remote sites and different applications may use different gateway sites and paths, depending on the application and measured application performance. Remote sites that use gateway sites for Internet access are referred to as client sites.

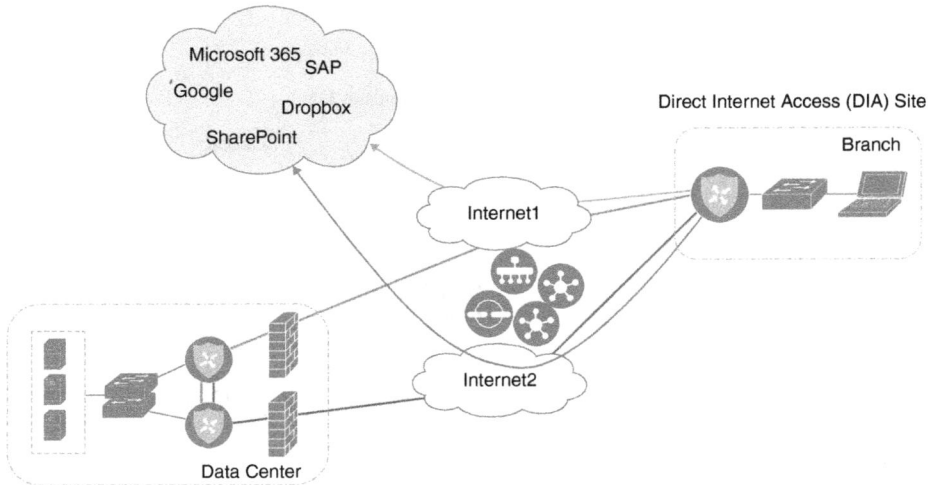

Figure 12-3   *Direct Cloud Access/Direct Internet Access*

Figure 12-4 illustrates cloud access through a gateway.

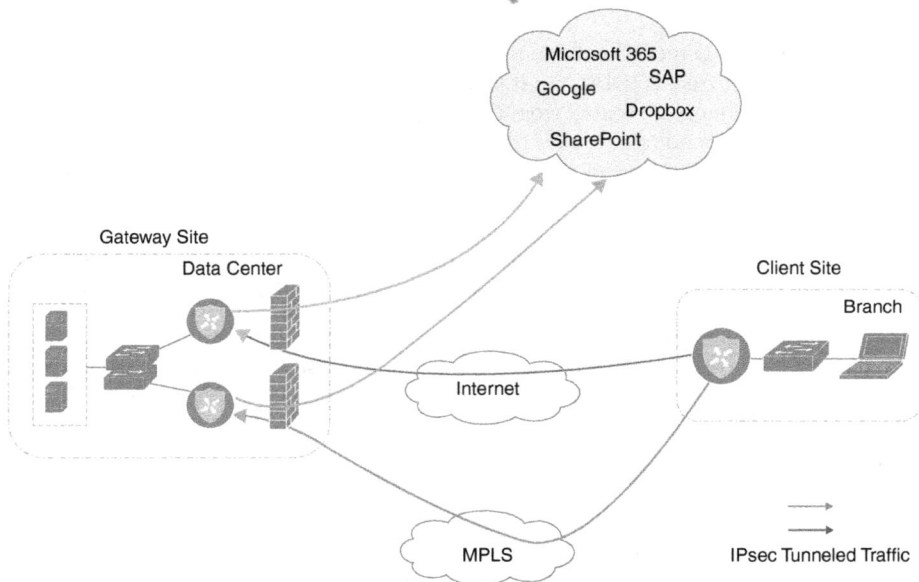

Figure 12-4   *Cloud Access Through a Gateway*

A third deployment model, the hybrid approach, makes it possible to have a combination of DIA sites and client/gateway sites. When you define both DIA sites and gateway sites, SaaS applications can use either local DIA exits or the gateway sites for any given application, depending on which path provides the best performance.

Cisco SD-WAN Cloud OnRamp for SaaS supports multiple business applications, including Webex, Microsoft 365, AWS, Google Apps, Salesforce, Dropbox, SAP Concur, Intuit, Box,

Oracle, Zendesk, Zoho, SugarCRM, and GoToMeeting. You can also use NBAR (Network Based Application Recognition) and enable Cloud OnRamp for SaaS capabilities for the standard or custom applications of your choice.

The Cloud OnRamp for SaaS feature actively monitors SaaS application performance from each site over multiple paths. A WAN Edge router views performance statistics differently, depending on whether it is part of a DIA, gateway, or client site. A DIA or gateway site calculates performance statistics of the SaaS application directly, but a client site does not. SaaS performance from a client site depends on the SaaS application performance from a gateway site, plus the performance of the path from the client site to that gateway site.

In the case of a DIA or gateway site, the WAN Edge router issues numerous probes to constantly measure the reachability and performance of the SaaS application over all available paths. To detect possible DNS failures, the WAN Edge router sends duplicated DNS requests toward all possible Internet egress points or gateway sites.

To assess the path quality, the WAN Edge sends HTTP requests to each SaaS application over every available path to that application. Over a 2-minute sliding window, the router determines the average loss and latency for each application and path pair, and then uses this data to calculate a quality of experience (vQoE) score. Figure 12-5 illustrates the detailed process of vQoE measurement.

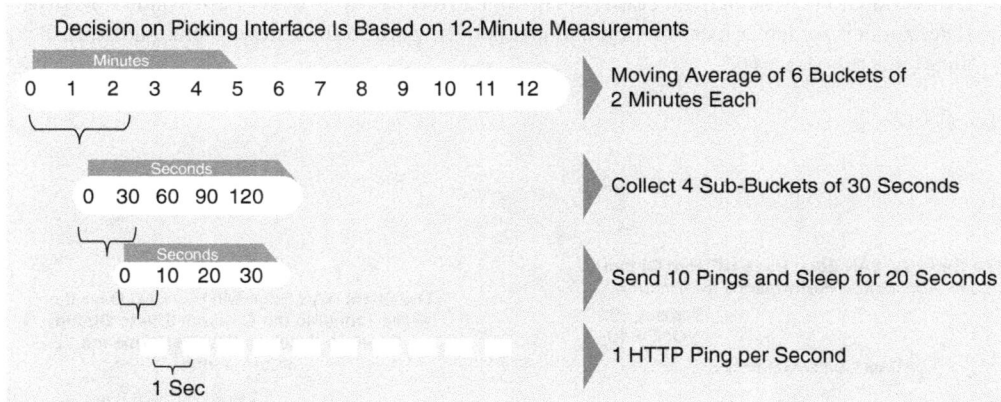

Figure 12-5 *Measuring vQoE*

To get the vQoE score, the WAN Edge router accounts for average loss and latency. SD-WAN Manager (formerly vManage) then collects this data and keeps a record of expected average loss and latency values for all of the SaaS applications. If the actual measured loss and latency are less than the expected loss and latency, a vQoE score of 10 is given. If actual loss and latency are more than the expected loss and latency, a vQoE score that reflects a percentage of the baseline performance on a 10-point scale is assigned.

SD-WAN Manager assigns a color and vQoE status to each application and path. A vQoE score of 8 to 10 is green or good, a score of 5 to 8 is yellow or average, and a score of 0 to 5 is red or bad. Figure 12-6 illustrates how the vQoE scores are calculated.

For any application, the WAN Edge router takes a moving average over several 2-minute time periods and then picks the path with the highest vQoE score.

vQoE Calculation

The vQoE Value Ranges from 0 to 10,
with 0 Being the Worst Quality
and 10 Being the Best.

vQoE = Avg(vQoE(Loss) + vQoE(Latency))

vQoE (Loss) = Baseline Loss / Actual Loss * 100
Actual Loss = Loss % Over Last 12 Minutes

vQoE (Latency) = Baseline Latency / Actual Latency * 100
Actual Latency = Average Latency Over Last 12 Minutes

	8-10	Green	5-8	Yellow	0-5	Red

SaaS Apps	DIA1	DIA2
O365	3	9
Salesforce	2	6
Zendesk	5	6

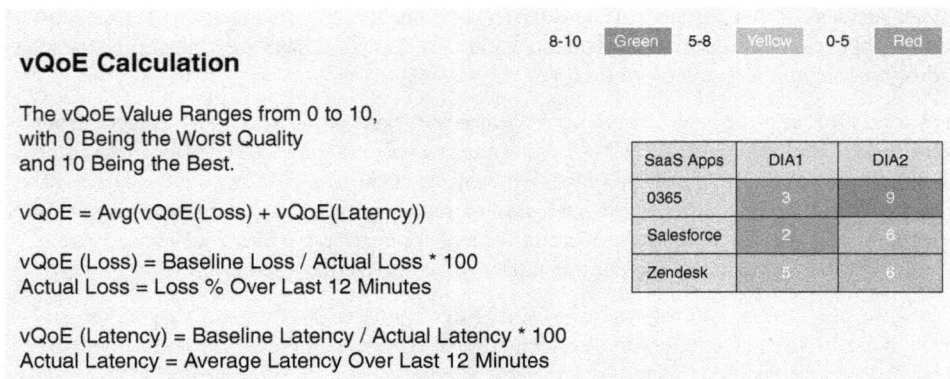

Figure 12-6   *Calculating a vQoE Score*

As discussed earlier in this chapter, the gateway site issues HTTP requests directly to the SaaS application and calculates loss and latency of the application along each of the Internet exit paths. It relays this information back to the client sites via Overlay Management Protocol (OMP), which runs between the WAN Edge routers and SD-WAN Controllers and establishes and maintains the control plane in the overlay network. The client site uses Bidirectional Forwarding Detection (BFD), which runs between WAN Edge routers over the IPsec tunnels to detect loss, latency, and jitter on the path to the gateway site. Figure 12-7 illustrates this process.

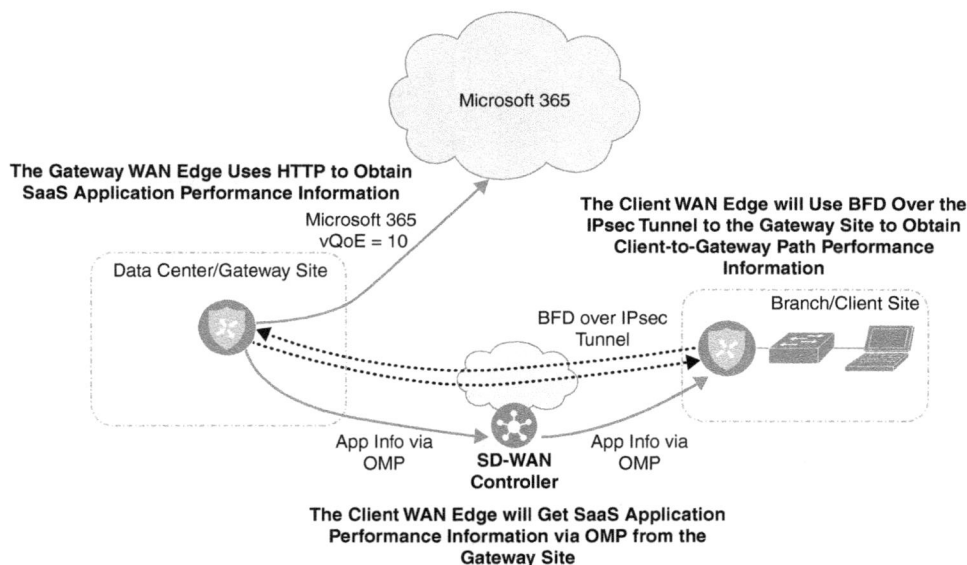

**The Gateway WAN Edge Uses HTTP to Obtain
SaaS Application Performance Information**

Microsoft 365
vQoE = 10

Data Center/Gateway Site

Microsoft 365

**The Client WAN Edge will Use BFD Over the
IPsec Tunnel to the Gateway Site to Obtain
Client-to-Gateway Path Performance
Information**

Branch/Client Site

BFD over IPsec
Tunnel

App Info via
OMP

**SD-WAN
Controller**

App Info via
OMP

**The Client WAN Edge will Get SaaS Application
Performance Information via OMP from the
Gateway Site**

Figure 12-7   *Obtaining Performance Metrics for Client/Gateway Sites*

DIA sites execute the same probing process for their locally connected Internet circuits in addition to leveraging probe information to and from gateway sites. Figure 12-8 illustrates this process.

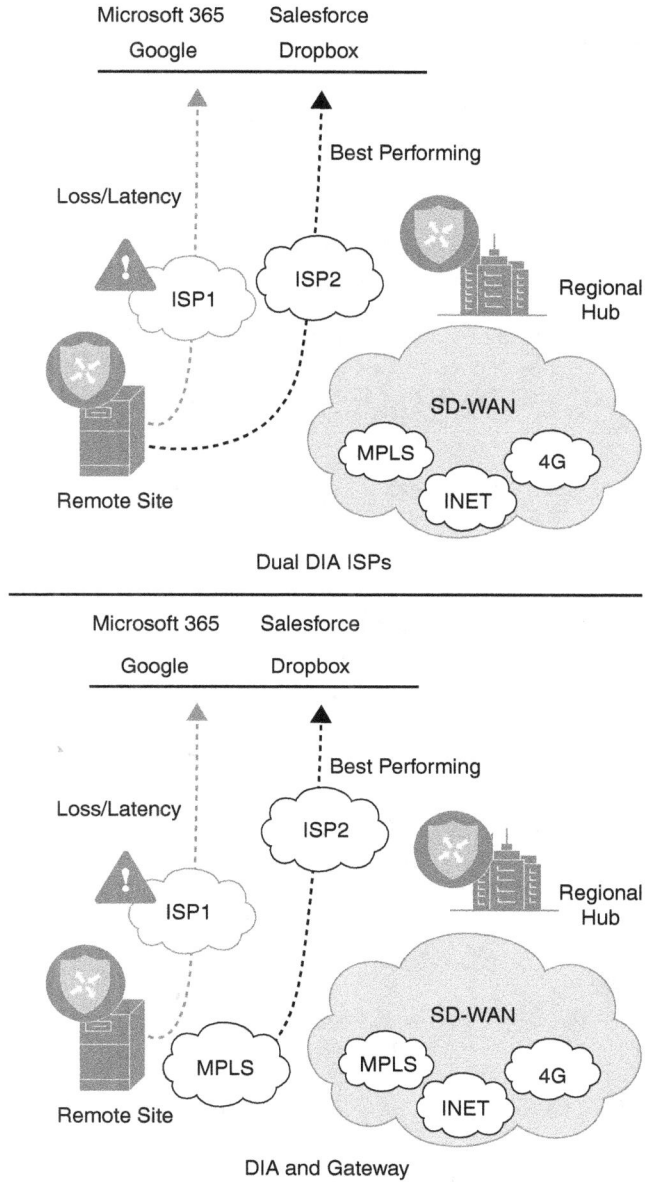

Figure 12-8 *Obtaining Performance Metrics for DIA Sites*

Cisco Catalyst SD-WAN Application Intelligence Engine (SAIE) analyzes data packets beyond the basic header information and identifies the SaaS application based on that analysis.

NOTE   In Catalyst SD-WAN versions 20.7 and earlier, the SAIE flow was called Deep Packet Inspection (DPI).

When a flow starts for the first time, the traffic takes the path indicated by the routing table. After a couple packets, SAIE identifies the application and stores its identity in a cache so that any subsequent flows going to that destination are sent out the optimal exit determined by the vQoE score instead of via the normal routed path. SAIE does not redirect the initial application flow because the redirection would cause Network Address Translation (NAT) changes that would break TCP. Figure 12-9 shows how Cloud OnRamp for SaaS handles the application flow.

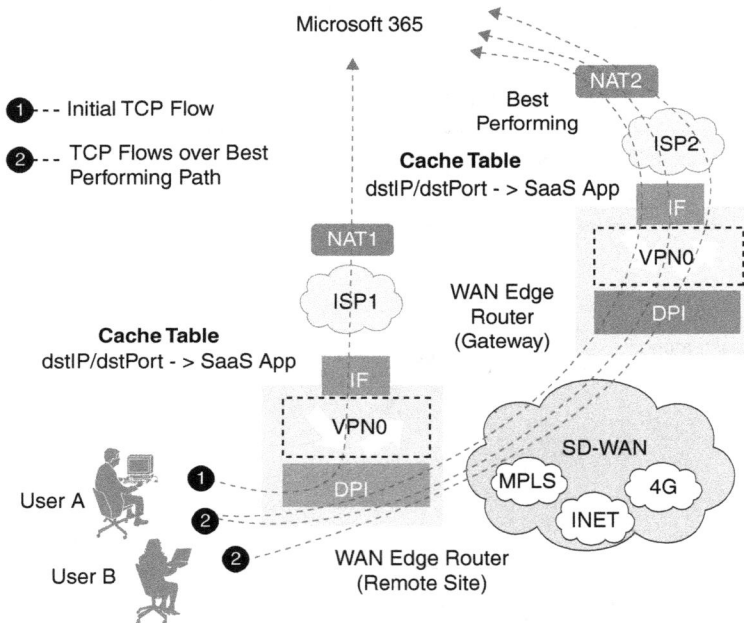

Figure 12-9   *Cloud OnRamp for SaaS and NAT*

NOTE   For dual WAN Edge sites using SAIE, because SAIE is used to classify flows on a WAN Edge device, it is important for traffic to be symmetric; that is, SAIE should be able to see both request and response traffic. If traffic from a branch office takes a routed path to the Internet out one WAN Edge router but the return traffic comes back through a different WAN Edge router, SAIE may not be able to classify the traffic correctly so that a local exit or gateway can be chosen for it. It will continue to be routed normally. Care should be taken with routing metrics to ensure symmetry for normally routed traffic.

All the SAIE considerations just listed are valid for all types of applications. However, starting from software version 20.10, Cisco Catalyst SD-WAN also supports SD-AVC (Software-Defined Application Visibility and Control) for some applications. At this writing, Cloud OnRamp for SaaS can use SD-AVC to identify Cisco Webex traffic and SD-AVC Cloud Connector to collect information about Microsoft 365. To use SD-AVC, you need to enable it by selecting **Administration > Settings** in SD-WAN Manager.

SD-AVC also relies on SAIE, but it can identify Webex traffic from the first packet. This significant improvement allows Webex traffic to avoid taking a suboptimal path to the cloud servers. Also, even though having the symmetric traffic paths is always the recommended design approach, SD-AVC also helps resolve issues with application recognition in deployments with asymmetric traffic routing.

In order to reach the SaaS applications to calculate performance statistics in the case of gateway and DIA sites, the WAN Edge router needs to first resolve the names of the Cloud OnRamp SaaS applications to IP addresses. It performs this task by using the Domain Name System (DNS) server addresses defined in VPN 0. The router initiates a separate DNS query to the same application on each of its local Internet exits. When a host at a site issues a DNS query, the SAIE engine intercepts it. If the local DIA Internet exit is the best path and if the query is for a Cloud OnRamp SaaS application, the WAN Edge router acts as a proxy and overrides the user DNS settings by forwarding the query to the DNS server defined under VPN 0 over the best-performing DIA Internet exit. If the best path is through a gateway WAN Edge router, the DNS query is forwarded to the gateway, which intercepts it and forwards it to the DNS server under VPN 0 over its best-performing Internet exit. The SAIE engine forwards any DNS queries for non-Cloud OnRamp applications normally according to the routing table. Figure 12-10 illustrates this point.

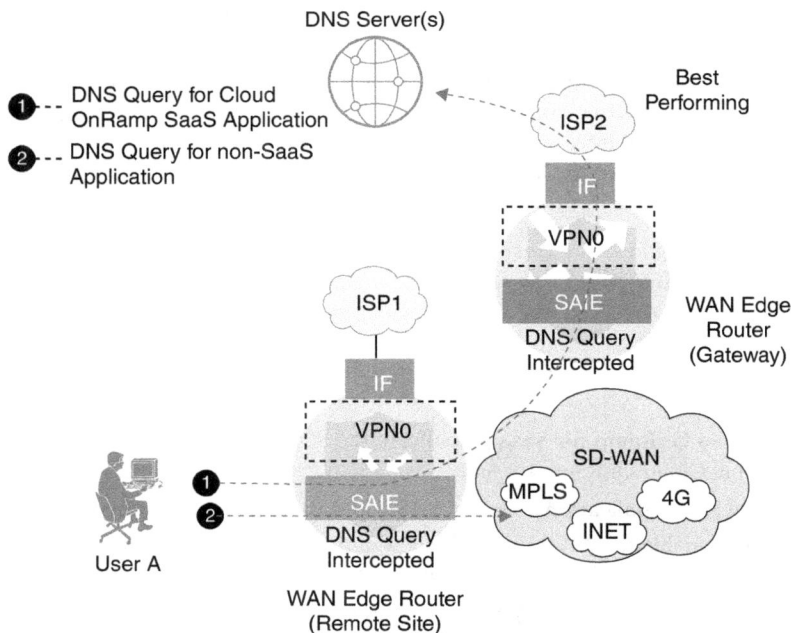

Figure 12-10 *Cloud OnRamp for SaaS DNS Interception*

Because of the built-in workflows integrated into SD-WAN Manager, configuring Cloud OnRamp for SaaS is very simple. However, before configuration can begin, several prerequisites must first be met.

NOTE The information presented in this section contains only general guidelines. For detailed requirements, software compatibility, step-by-step instructions, and more technical tips, refer to the "Cisco Catalyst SD-WAN Cloud OnRamp Configuration Guide" published on Cisco.com.

The prerequisites for SD-WAN Cloud OnRamp for SaaS with SAIE are as follows:

■ WAN Edge routers and SD-WAN Controllers (formerly vSmarts) need to be in SD-WAN Manager mode (also known as vManage mode), as opposed to CLI mode. That means, they need to be managed by SD-WAN Manager and have a device template assigned to them.

■ A centralized policy that includes an Application-Aware Routing (AAR) policy must be activated.

■ A default route that directs traffic out to the Internet (perhaps through a data center, regional hub, carrier-neutral facility, or even locally) and can reach the SaaS applications must be present in the service VPNs before you configure the Cloud OnRamp for SaaS feature. The first couple packets need to take the traditional routing path before the SAIE engine can identify the application and cache it so that subsequent flows can be directed to the Internet by a DIA path or a gateway site path, whichever is more optimal at the time. The initial flow continues to take the routed path until completion.

■ Site-specific routing requirements must be met. Depending on the site type (DIA, client, or gateway) and the Internet connection type, it might be necessary to configure NAT on the VPN 0 physical interface, configure the required IP addresses (static or DHCP), add proper routing for the local exit, enable DIA, define DNS servers, and so on.

■ Application-specific requirements must be met. Some SaaS applications (such as Webex and Microsoft 365) have more specific requirements than others. Refer to the latest "Cisco Catalyst SD-WAN Cloud OnRamp Configuration Guide" for details.

The following steps are required to configure Cloud OnRamp for SaaS in Cisco Catalyst SD-WAN Manager:

Step 1.   **Enable Cloud OnRamp for SaaS globally.** In the SD-WAN Manager Settings page, enable Cloud OnRamp for SaaS.

Step 2.   **Define the SaaS applications.** Enable SaaS applications to be monitored.

Step 3.   **Review and enable the AAR policy.** Review and edit, if necessary, the current active centralized policy that contains an AAR policy.

Step 4.   **Configure DIA sites (optional).** Select the sites that will be configured as DIA sites (that is, sites with transports that allow DIA egress).

Step 5. **Configure gateway sites (optional).** Select the sites that will be configured as gateway sites.

Step 6. **Configure client sites (optional).** Select the sites that will be configured as client sites (that is, sites without DIA egress).

Now let's look more closely at this process. First, start by enabling Cloud OnRamp for SaaS globally by navigating to the **Settings** section of SD-WAN Manager, as shown in Figure 12-11.

NOTE Cloud OnRamp for SaaS is enabled by default starting from the Catalyst SD-WAN version 20.13.

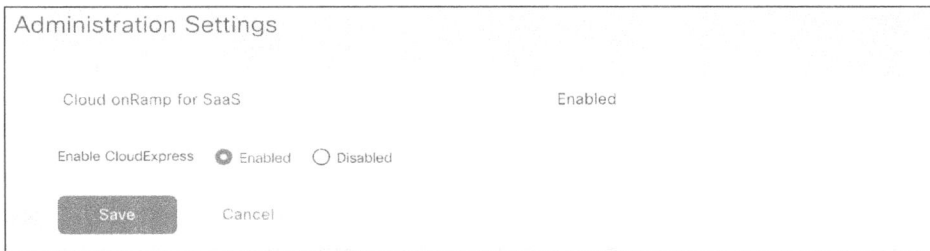

Figure 12-11 *Enabling Cloud OnRamp for SaaS Globally*

To access the Cloud OnRamp for SaaS configuration menu, first select the cloud icon at the top of the SD-WAN Manager GUI window and then select **Cloud OnRamp for SaaS**. Alternatively, you can select **Configuration > Cloud OnRamp for SaaS** from the left side of the GUI. Both options are illustrated in Figure 12-12.

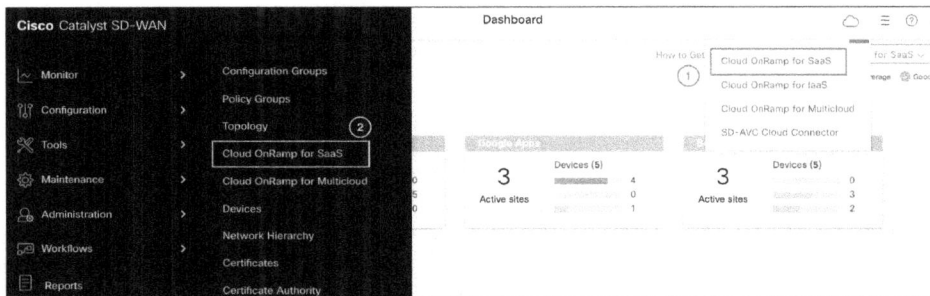

Figure 12-12 *Accessing Cloud OnRamp for SaaS*

When Cloud OnRamp for SaaS is not yet configured, the default screen provides you with the summary steps you need to follow. Select **Applications and Policy** from the **Manage Cloud OnRamp for SaaS** drop-down to enable the SaaS applications that should be monitored by SD-WAN, as shown in Figure 12-13.

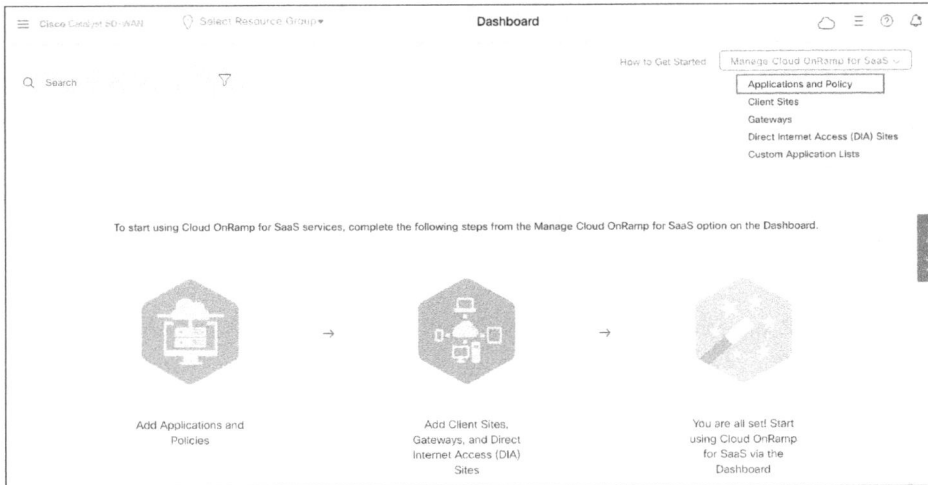

Figure 12-13   *Accessing the Applications and Policy Option*

By default, all SaaS applications are disabled for monitoring, and you must enable the applications that should be monitored, as illustrated in Figure 12-14.

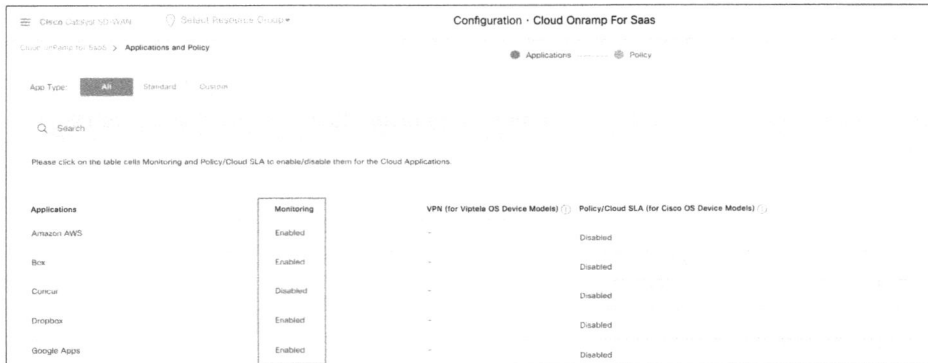

Figure 12-14   *Enabling SaaS Applications for Monitoring*

Next, you need to review and save the Application-Aware Routing policy used in the current active centralized policy, as shown in Figure 12-15. (Remember that having an active AAR policy is a prerequisite.) Once you review and save the policy, SD-WAN Manager enables Cloud OnRamp for SaaS in the selected policy and automatically pushes the updates to SD-WAN Controllers.

NOTE   In this example, we use the topology introduced in Chapter 7, "Centralized Control Policies." Refer to Figure 7-1 to better understand the network diagram and traffic flows between the branches.

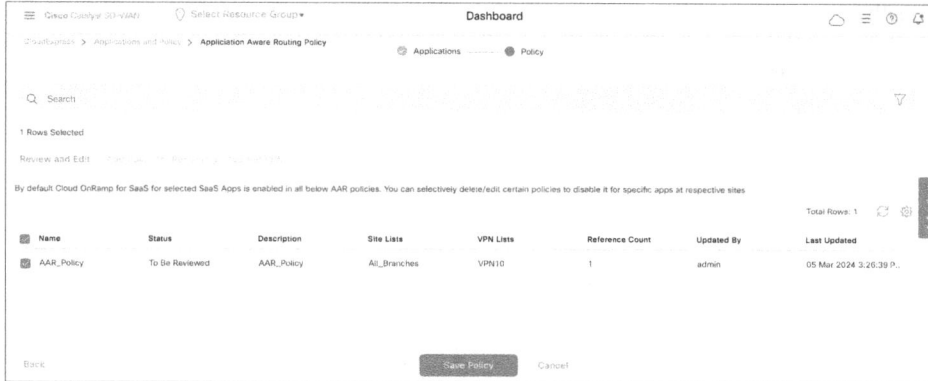

Figure 12-15 *Enabling Cloud OnRamp for SaaS in AAR Policies*

Next, you need to configure and attach the sites based on their type: client site, gateway, or DIA site. Depending on the overlay network topology and the enterprise requirements, you can create all types of sites or only some of them, as needed.

> **NOTE** At this writing, all Catalyst SD-WAN versions (up to 20.14) support Cloud OnRamp for SaaS configuration only for the devices managed by Device Templates, and we focus on this method in this chapter. If you manage your devices with Configuration Groups, you need to use a CLI add-on template to configure Cloud OnRamp for SaaS.

If the goal is to configure DIA sites, navigate to the **Direct Internet Access (DIA) sites** section under the **Manage Cloud OnRamp for SaaS** menu. Attach the sites that are deemed to be DIA sites so that SD-WAN Manager and SD-WAN Controller can push the appropriate configuration and policy to the devices, as shown in Figure 12-16. In this example, only one site will have DIA: Branch 2 (Site-ID 102).

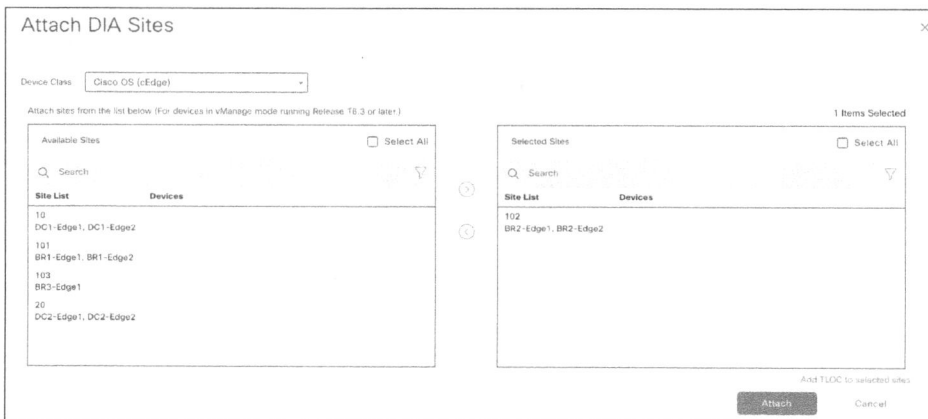

Figure 12-16 *DIA Site Configuration*

Optionally, you can specify the TLOCs that should be used to reach the SaaS applications via DIA. You can do this by clicking the **Add TLOC to Selected Sites** button. Figure 12-17 shows this configuration menu. If you do not specify TLOCs, the **All DIA TLOC** option is used by default.

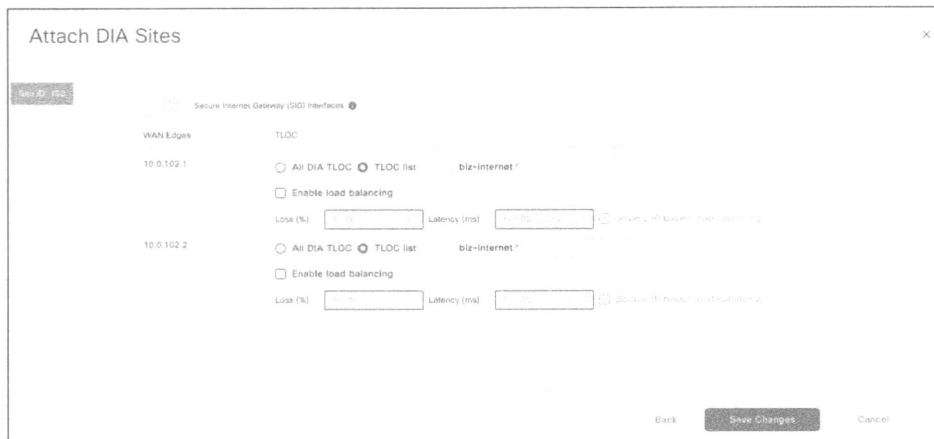

Figure 12-17 *Adding TLOCs to the DIA Sites*

When you finish configuring the DIA sites and click **Save Changes**, SD-WAN Manager automatically pushes the configuration changes to WAN Edge routers. You can monitor and verify this process by using the **Task View** section of SD-WAN Manager.

If you want to configure the gateway sites, navigate to the **Gateways** section under the **Manage Cloud OnRamp for SaaS** menu. Attach the sites that were designed to have the gateway functionality (for example, the data centers or regional hubs). This process is illustrated in Figure 12-18. In this example, DC-1 site will be used as a gateway site (Site-ID 10).

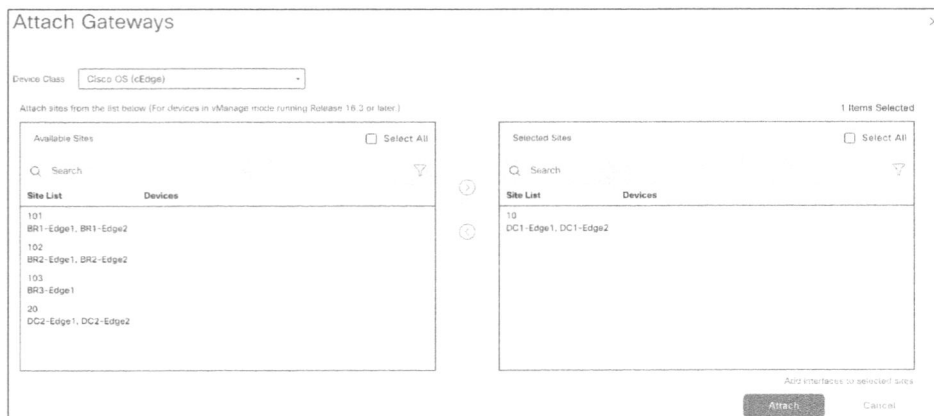

Figure 12-18 *Gateway Site Configuration*

After selecting the sites, you have to configure interfaces (or TLOCs) by clicking the **Add Interfaces to Selected Sites** button. As shown in Figure 12-19, you need to choose the VPN and, optionally, TLOC list that provides Internet connectivity for the chosen gateway site.

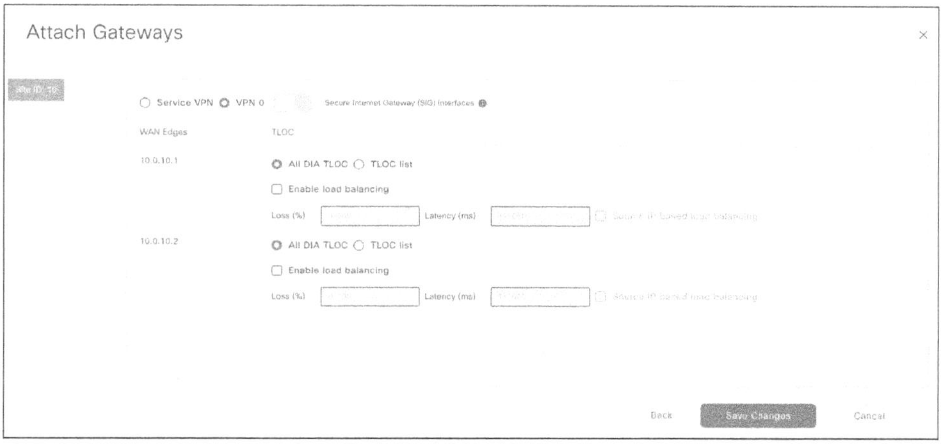

Figure 12-19   *Adding TLOCs to the Gateway Sites*

If you're configuring client sites, navigate to the **Client Sites** section under the **Manage Cloud OnRamp for SaaS** menu and attach the required sites, as shown in Figure 12-20. Keep in mind that you cannot select interfaces when configuring a client site because client sites do not break out locally.

Figure 12-20   *Configuring Client Sites*

SD-WAN Manager provides built-in monitoring for Cloud OnRamp for SaaS. When you monitor Cloud OnRamp for SaaS, you can view vQoE performance scores, view the network path selected for each application and site, and view the detailed loss and latency data for each application and path as well.

The main Cloud OnRamp for SaaS page (accessible via **Configuration > Cloud OnRamp for SaaS** menu) displays each configured SaaS application as a widget. Each widget lists the number of active sites, WAN Edge devices that use that application, and the number of WAN Edge devices that show vQoE scores in the good, average, and bad ranges (see Figure 12-21). Note that these vQoE scores are shown only for the best-performing path according to each WAN Edge device.

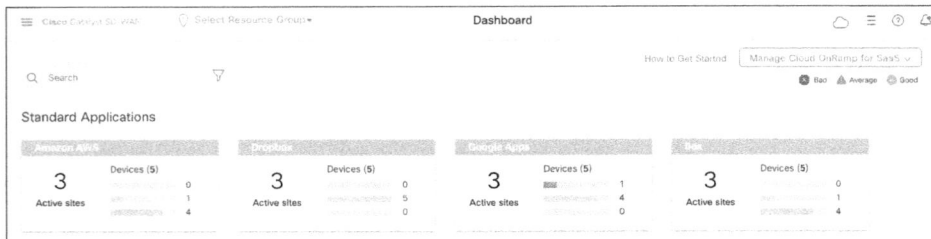

Figure 12-21   *Cloud OnRamp for SaaS Monitoring*

On this page, select an application widget to get additional details about the vQoE scores and optimal paths selected. The resulting page shows the list of sites, the WAN Edge name, the vQoE status (a symbol indicating good, average, or bad), the vQoE number score, and the optimal path in use (local exit or gateway, selected local interface or system IP address of the gateway, and an indication of the IPsec tunnel transports used to reach the remote gateway), as shown in Figure 12-22.

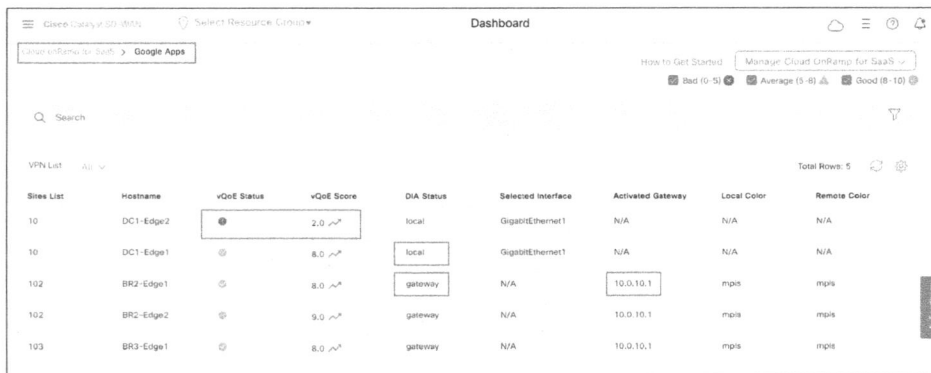

Figure 12-22   *Application-Specific Performance by Site*

In the top-left corner of Figure 12-22, you can see the performance statistics for the Google Apps SaaS application. Remember that different applications can take different paths if their probes show different results. In the DIA Status column, you can see that both WAN Edge routers in DC-1 (Site-ID 10) use the local DIA exit, while remote branches reach Google Apps via the gateway site. Branch 2 (Site-ID 102) was configured as both a client site and a DIA site. Its current status shows that it uses the gateway path; this is because the local DIA path shows worse performance at the moment. If the path characteristics change, the Branch 2 Edge devices can switch to the local DIA exit automatically.

You can also see that all three remote branch routers use the gateway device with system IP address 10.0.10.1 (that is, the DC1-Edge1 router). If you look at the vQoE Status and vQoE Score columns, you can see that DC1-Edge1 has a good score of 8.0, while another gateway device, DC1-Edge2, displays a bad score of 2.0. Because of this, the branch routers do not choose the path via DC1-Edge2.

If you select an arrow under the vQoE score column, a window pops up, showing the vQoE score history on a graph. You can see a 1-, 3-, 6-, 12-, or 24-hour view; a 7-days view; or a custom view of this data. Figure 12-23 demonstrates the vQoE score history for the DC1-Edge2 device that has Internet access only on its GigabitEthernet1 interface. If you hover your mouse over the graph, you can see the detailed statistics of the selected path at a specific point in time.

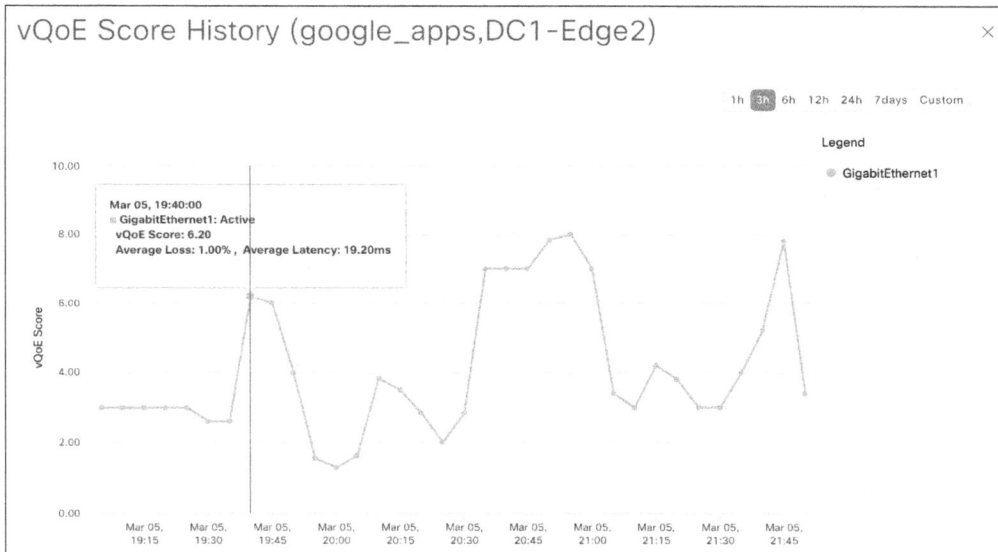

Figure 12-23 *vQoE Score History on the DC1-Edge2 Router (Gateway)*

If you open a similar vQoE score history report for the BR3-Edge1 router, you see a different picture. Branch 3 was configured as the client site for Cloud OnRamp for SaaS. Also, the BR3-Edge1 router has six active data tunnels established with the DC-1 site: one tunnel per color to each DC-1 Edge device (refer to Figure 7-1 for more details). Figure 12-24 shows the vQoE score history for all available paths on BR3-Edge1, as well as the current active path—that is, the path toward the 10.0.10.1 gateway via the MPLS transport.

Branch 2 was configured as both a client site and a DIA site. If you look at the vQoE score graph for the BR2-Edge1 router (see Figure 12-25), you see seven available paths: six tunnels toward the DC-1 site and a local DIA exit on the GigabitEthernet2 interface. At the time this snapshot was taken, the path toward the 10.0.10.1 gateway via the MPLS transport showed the best performance, which is why it is preferred over other paths.

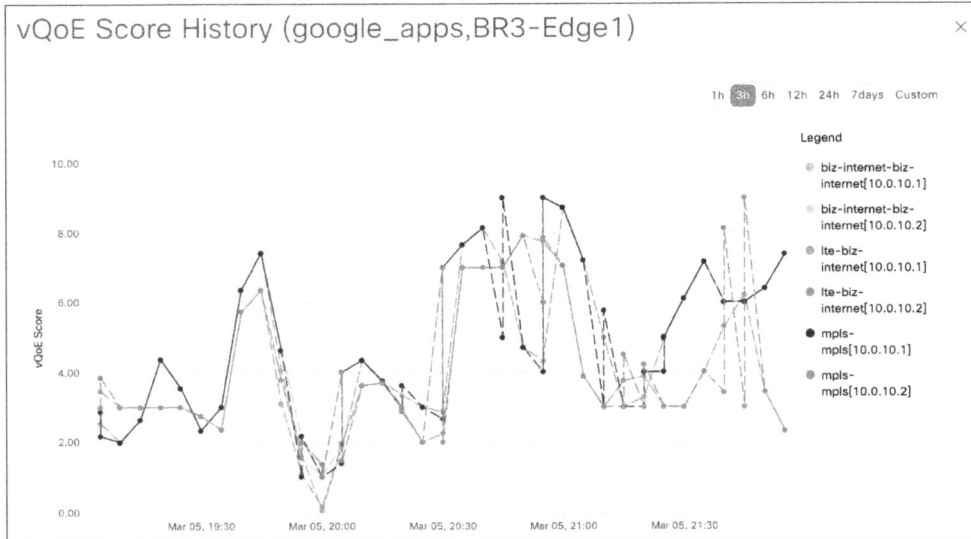

Figure 12-24   *vQoE Score History on the BR3-Edge1 Router (Client Site)*

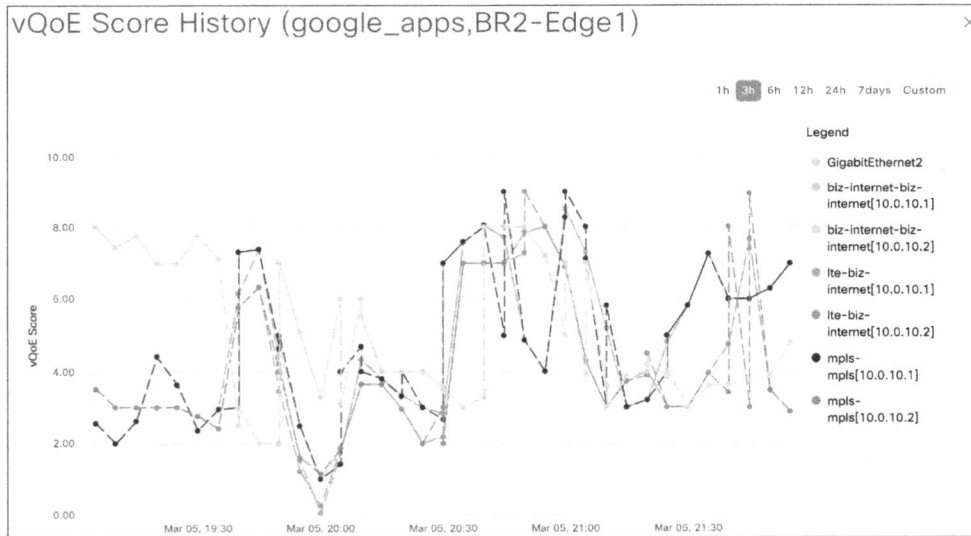

Figure 12-25   *vQoE Score History on the BR2-Edge1 Router (Client and DIA Site)*

You can also have SD-WAN Manager display detailed loss and latency data on a per-SaaS-application basis by navigating to the **Device Dashboard** and selecting the **Real Time** option. The "CloudExpress Applications" output shows each application, the optimal path chosen, and the mean latency and loss associated with the application for each optimal path, as shown in Figure 12-26.

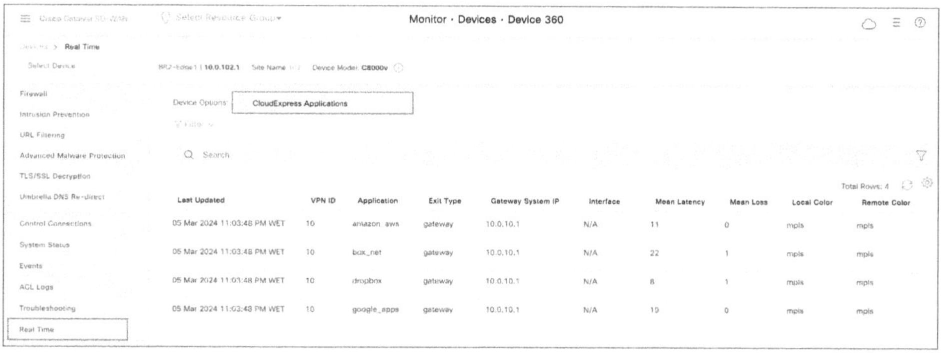

Figure 12-26   *Real-Time CloudExpress Applications*

The "CloudExpress Gateway Exits" output shows each application, what the gateway exits are, and the mean latency and loss associated with the application for each gateway path available, as shown in Figure 12-27. It also indicates the tunnel transport that is taken to reach the gateway site (in the Local Color and Remote Color columns).

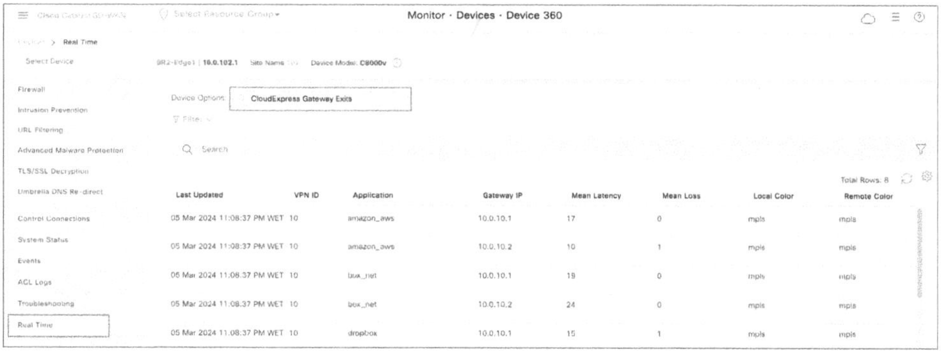

Figure 12-27   *Real-Time CloudExpress Gateway Exits*

The "CloudExpress Local Exits" output shows each application and the mean latency and loss associated with each of its local Internet exits, as shown in Figure 12-28.

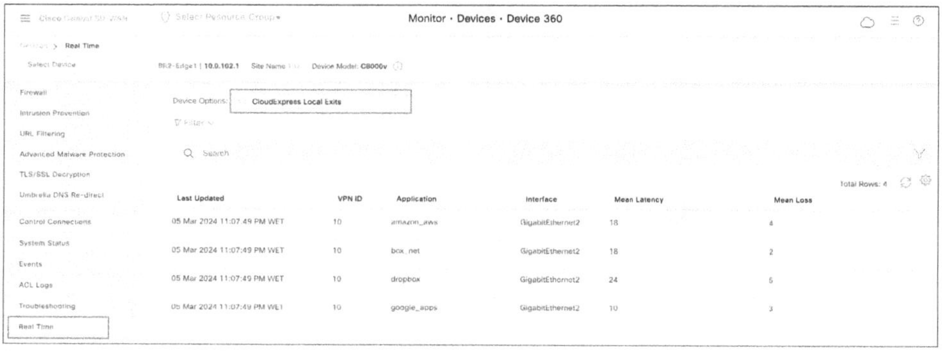

Figure 12-28   *Real-Time CloudExpress Local Exits*

In addition to the general Cloud OnRamp for SaaS features that we discussed previously, Cisco Catalyst SD-WAN offers more granular processing of Microsoft 365 traffic. Depending on the application type and the required user experience, Microsoft 365 divides IP addresses and URLs into three categories: Optimize, Allow, or Default. Cloud OnRamp for SaaS uses those categories to apply individual policies to the applications. If needed, you can create a flexible policy and send different Microsoft 365 applications over different network paths. SD-WAN Cloud OnRamp for SaaS relies on SD-AVC to periodically get the IP and URL categories from Microsoft 365 and to categorize the user traffic in accordance with them.

Also, Cloud OnRamp for SaaS and Microsoft 365 mutually exchange telemetry information for Microsoft Exchange, Teams, and SharePoint applications. Microsoft 365 receives information about the network from SD-WAN Cloud OnRamp and sends back the calculated network paths scores. Based on the Microsoft suggestions, Catalyst SD-WAN can dynamically improve the path selection algorithm for Microsoft 365 traffic.

Figure 12-29 provides a summary of Catalyst SD-WAN and Microsoft 365 cooperation related to the Cloud OnRamp for SaaS use case. Overall, this functionality allows you to improve the end-user experience and provides more visibility into Microsoft 365 traffic for monitoring and troubleshooting purposes.

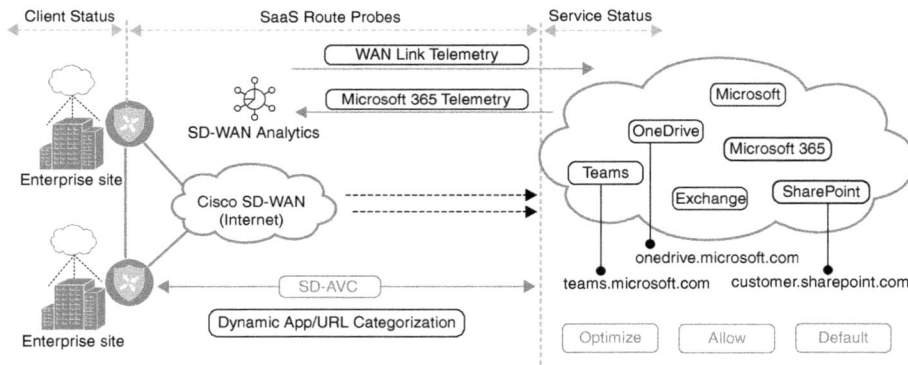

Figure 12-29   *SD-WAN Cloud OnRamp for SaaS with Microsoft 365*

Cloud OnRamp for Multicloud

In today's multicloud landscape, businesses are embracing the versatility and efficiency available by leveraging multiple cloud providers. By distributing workflows across various platforms, organizations gain agility, scalability, and operational efficiencies. This approach facilitates quicker time to market for new services and applications, empowering businesses to adapt swiftly to changing market demands while optimizing resource utilization and minimizing risk. Cloud networking automation stands out as the optimal solution, as it enables customers to seamlessly access workloads and applications across a multicloud environment without the arduous task of manually handling network setup for each cloud provider. By leveraging Cloud OnRamp for Multicloud, businesses can sidestep months of complexity associated with individual cloud networking setups, empowering them to allocate resources toward application innovation rather than navigating networking intricacies across multiple providers.

Keep in mind that digital transformation and cloud migration are not instantaneous processes. Frequently, organizations opt for a hybrid cloud approach, where certain applications or services are migrated to the cloud while others remain on premises. This leads to increased complexity in the network infrastructure needed to ensure seamless and reliable connectivity among users, geographically dispersed applications, on-premises resources, and cloud services. Meeting the demand for a well-balanced combination of connectivity, performance, and security in distributed network architectures necessitates the evolution of WAN infrastructures to support these new multicloud environments.

SD-WAN Cloud OnRamp Overview

Cisco Catalyst SD-WAN provides users with intuitive workflows seamlessly integrated into the system, facilitating rapid connections to multiple public clouds. Presently, Catalyst SD-WAN supports integration with leading cloud providers, such as Amazon Web Services, Microsoft Azure, and Google Cloud, for diverse interconnections. This chapter delves into four specific use cases exemplifying these integrations:

- Enterprise site to cloud

- Region to region

- Enterprise site to enterprise site

- Cloud to cloud

The enterprise site-to-cloud use case facilitates the seamless extension of the on-premises infrastructure to public clouds, ensuring that cloud resources are securely accessible within the SD-WAN overlay network (see Figure 12-30). Cloud branches connect to the SD-WAN fabric via the virtual WAN Edge routers deployed in the public cloud. SD-WAN Manager oversees both the initial deployment and the ongoing management of the Cloud WAN Edge routers, ensuring consistent configuration, security, and policies across all branches, data centers, and clouds.

Figure 12-30 *Enterprise Site-to-Cloud Use Case*

The region-to-region use case is illustrated in Figure 12-31. This deployment model enables the interconnection of a geographically distributed backbone using a public cloud underlay. Depending on the public cloud provider, the solution can have different names, such as AWS Cloud WAN, TGW Peering, Azure Virtual WAN/vHub, or Network Connectivity Center with Google Cloud. All of these solutions aim to deliver secure, flexible, and highly available transit architecture with end-to-end segmentation and optimized performance.

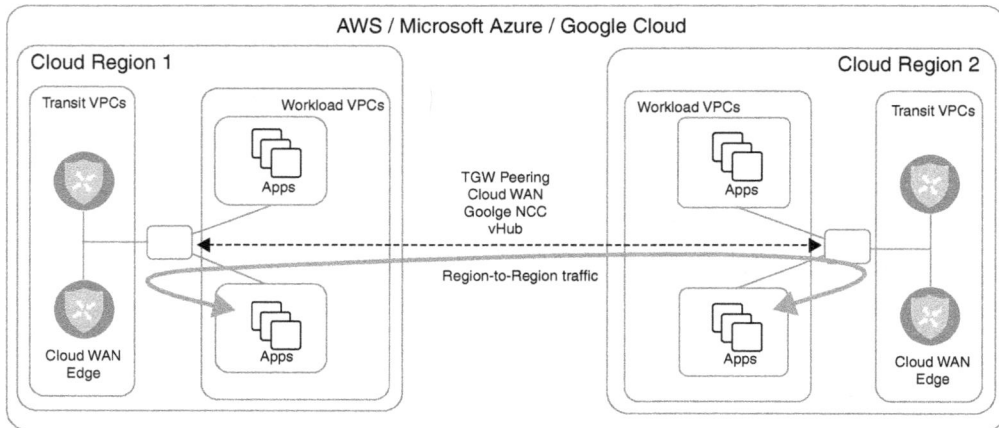

Figure 12-31 *Region-to-Region Use Case*

The enterprise site-to-enterprise site use case is illustrated in Figure 12-32. This type of deployment uses a public cloud backbone as a middle-mile to interconnect geographically distributed sites or even SD-WAN regions. This use case is somewhat similar to the region-to-region use case, but in this scenario, you use the cloud provider's backbone underlays to build the SD-WAN fabric, which enables you to connect sites around the globe. This approach allows you to have one global backbone provider for global connectivity.

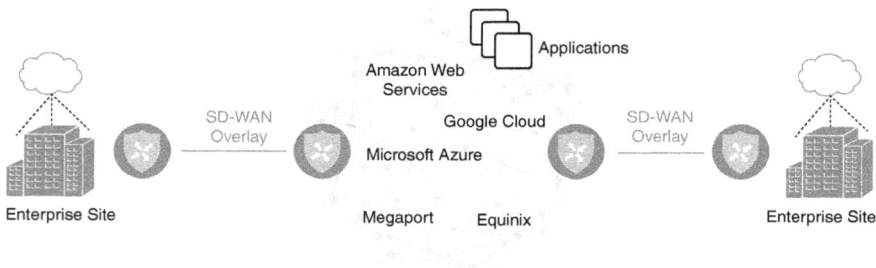

Figure 12-32 *Enterprise Site-to-Enterprise Site Use Case*

The cloud-to-cloud use case, illustrated in Figure 12-33, helps reduce operational complexity, with several public cloud providers or different public cloud regions integrated into the enterprise infrastructure. Traditional networks struggle with today's multicloud world, experiencing performance issues, security concerns, and management headaches. Cloud-to-cloud connectivity solves these problems by providing a dedicated and secure path for data directly between cloud environments, improving performance and security and offering centralized control. Cisco SD-WAN intelligently routes traffic, integrates with cloud providers, offers security features, and enables centralized management of all cloud connections.

Figure 12-33 *Cloud-to-Cloud Use Case*

Enterprise Site-to-Cloud Deep Dive

Different public cloud providers use the same model to build integrations with Cisco Catalyst SD-WAN. When SD-WAN Manager is configured with the appropriate cloud credentials, it fully automates the deployment and configuration by sending REST API calls to AWS/Azure/GCP, and configures the infrastructure required to create a cloud branch. SD-WAN Manager deploys two virtual routers (Catalyst 8000v) that act as virtual gateways and provide connectivity to the cloud from on-premises sites, between VPCs within cloud regions, between the regions, and from cloud to cloud.

Although the general concept is common for all three currently supported cloud providers, the implementation details and the terminology may vary depending on the chosen public cloud. Let us briefly discuss the SD-WAN integration details with all three cloud providers, using the most commonly used scenario—enterprise site-to-cloud connectivity.

Amazon Web Services (AWS) uses the concept of a Virtual Private Cloud (VPC)—a logically isolated instance that can be compared with a traditional network. Customer-managed applications and services reside in one or multiple workload VPCs. Those workload VPCs are created and managed by the company's cloud operations (CloudOps) team. Cisco SD-WAN Manager creates a transit VPC (similar to a transit network) with virtual gateways—Catalyst 8000v routers running in SD-WAN mode. SD-WAN Manager also creates a transit gateway (TGW), which can be treated as an internal AWS router that provides connectivity between transit and workload VPCs, as illustrated in Figure 12-34. TGW and SD-WAN gateways establish an IPsec or GRE tunnel between them and run BGP over it. All workload VPCs use default routes pointing to the TGW. SD-WAN routers learn the application subnets via BGP, redistribute them into OMP, and advertise them to other SD-WAN sites.

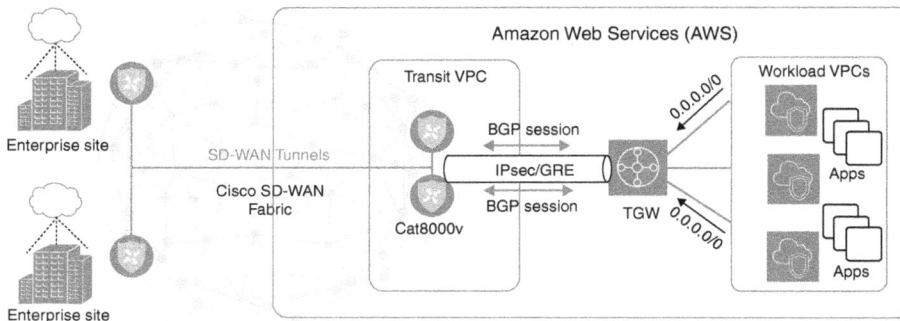

Figure 12-34 *Enterprise Site-to-Cloud Connection with AWS*

In Microsoft Azure cloud, the customer-managed applications are deployed inside Virtual Networks (vNets). SD-WAN Manager deploys Catalyst 8000v routers as Network Virtual Appliances (NVAs) inside a virtual hub. Similarly to AWS, the workload vNet subnets are peered with vHub. SD-WAN Cloud Edge routers learn those routes via BGP, redistribute them into OMP, and advertise into the SD-WAN fabric. Figure 12-35 illustrates SD-WAN Cloud OnRamp integration with Microsoft Azure.

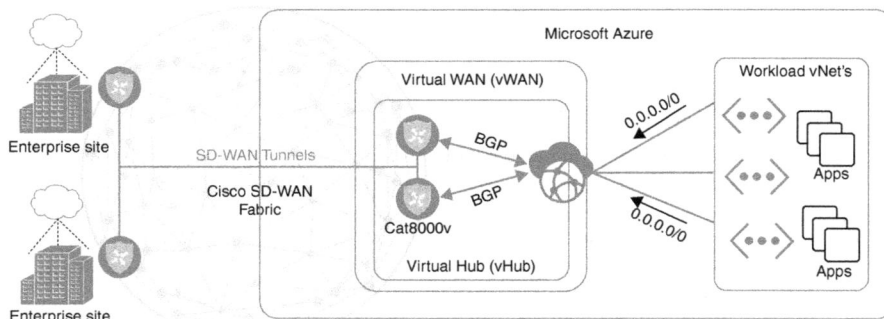

Figure 12-35   *Enterprise Site-to-Cloud Connection with Microsoft Azure*

Google Cloud Platform uses the concept of Compute Engine Instances. An instance is a virtual machine hosted inside the Google infrastructure. When using Google Cloud, an instance with multiple network interfaces requires each interface to be attached to a subnet in a different VPC network. Google Cloud architecture does not allow you to attach multiple network interfaces to the same subnet or to subnets from the same VPC network. For Google Cloud integrations, you therefore need at least three VPCs, as shown in Figure 12-36. The first VPC (called WAN VPC in this example) interconnects the WAN Edge transport interface with the external network (the Internet). It will be used to establish data tunnels with the remote SD-WAN sites. Another VPC, called Site-to-Cloud VPC in Figure 12-36, represents the service side and provides connectivity between the virtual WAN Edge routers and Google Cloud Routers (GCRs). Finally, there are workload VPCs that host custom applications managed by the enterprise CloudOps team. SD-WAN Cloud Edge devices (Catalyst 8000v routers) learn the workload VPC routes from GCR via BGP and advertise them to the remote SD-WAN sites via OMP. SD-WAN Manager also deploys the Network Connectivity Center (NCC) inside the Site-to-Cloud VPC, which is a mandatory underlay requirement to establish BGP connectivity between Google Cloud Routers and third-party routers (Cisco Cloud Edge routers, in this case).

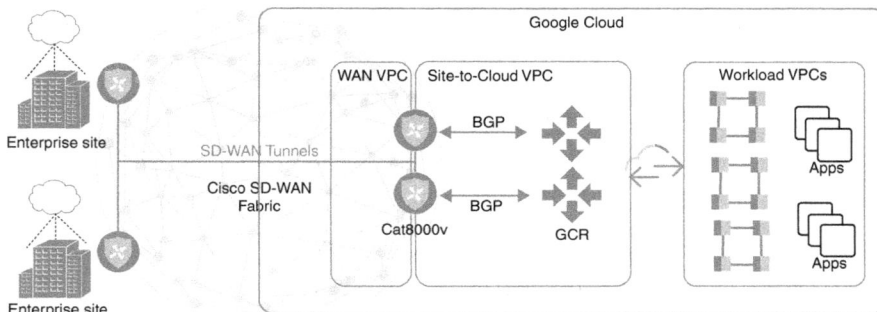

Figure 12-36   *Enterprise Site-to-Cloud Connection with Google Cloud*

Regardless of which public cloud provider you choose, SD-WAN Manager has built-in workflows aimed at automating the provisioning of the required cloud infrastructure. From SD-WAN Manager's perspective, Cloud OnRamp configuration is unified and requires similar steps for all cloud providers.

NOTE Next in this chapter, you will see how to configure SD-WAN Cloud OnRamp for Multicloud using Amazon Web Services. For additional information and other use cases examples, refer to the "Cisco Catalyst SD-WAN Cloud OnRamp Configuration Guide" published on Cisco's website or the corresponding cloud provider's website.

Before you create an integration between AWS and SD-WAN Manager, make sure to complete these preparation tasks:

- Verify that you have your AWS account details and a valid subscription to the Catalyst 8000v from AWS Marketplace.

- Ensure that Cisco SD-WAN Manager has two unused cloud router licenses, which will be used for two WAN Edge routers deployed in the cloud. You can choose between PAYG (Pay-as-you-Go) and BYOL (Bring Your Own License) devices; the device type must match between SD-WAN Manager and your AWS Marketplace subscription. In SD-WAN Manager, you can verify your device type by selecting **Configuration > Devices**. You can add PAYG routers by clicking the **Add PAYD WAN Edges** button. Such devices have a chassis number starting with C8K-PAYG-<..>. BYOL devices are synchronized from Cisco Smart Account.

- Attach the newly created devices to the cloud device templates. This step is required to provide a basic configuration to the virtual WAN Edge routers when they are deployed within the transit VPC. You can use the default prebuilt templates (for example, Default_AWS_TGW_C8000V_Template_V01) or create your own custom device templates, as shown in Figure 12-37.

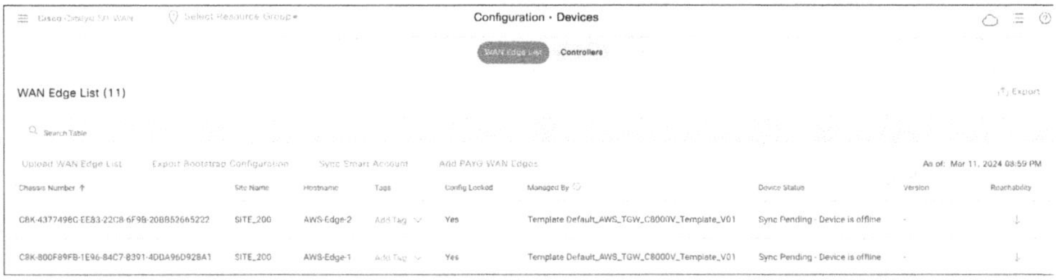

Figure 12-37 *Catalyst 8000v Routers Attached to the Default AWS Template*

The following is a summary of the steps required to configure Cloud OnRamp for Multicloud:

Step 1. **Create an AWS Cloud account.** Create an AWS Cloud account that SD-WAN Manager will use to send REST API calls to AWS.

Step 2. **Configure cloud global settings.** Select the desired use case and the implementation details (transit gateway or cloud WAN, encapsulation protocol, and so on).

Step 3.   **Discover host private networks.** Find the existing workload VPCs.

Step 4.   **Create cloud gateway.** Deploy the transit VPC, two virtual routers, and the Transit Gateway in AWS. In this case, the two virtual WAN Edge routers will act as a cloud gateway, interconnecting the public cloud resources with other SD-WAN sites or the Internet. For this step to be successful, remember to complete the preparation tasks and attach two virtual WAN Edge routers to the Device Templates, as discussed earlier.

Step 5.   **Push the configuration to the cloud gateway.** Attach sites and push the configuration to the cloud gateway.

Step 6.   **Enable cloud connectivity.** Associate VPCs to specific VPNs and configure the required connectivity between them.

Begin by navigating to **Configuration > Cloud OnRamp for Multicloud** in Cisco SD-WAN Manager. Figure 12-38 shows the main configuration menu, which you will use multiple times throughout this chapter, as all Cloud OnRamp workflows start here.

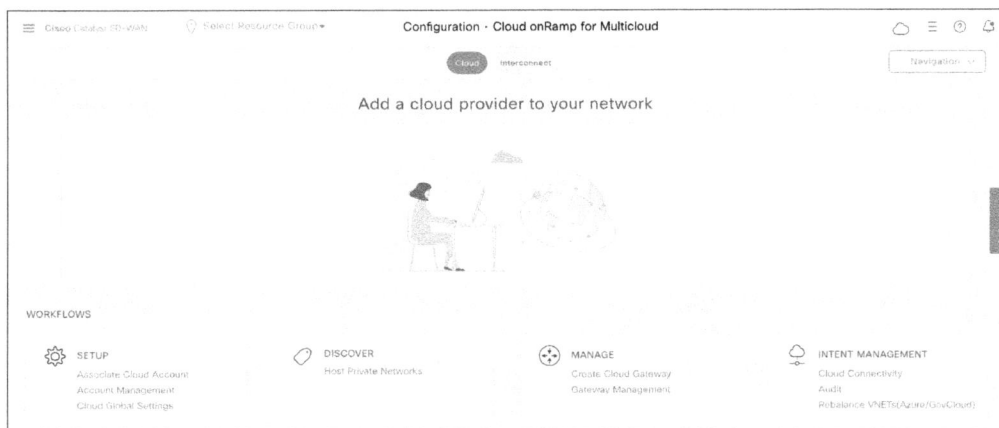

Figure 12-38   *Cloud OnRamp for Multicloud Configuration Menu*

Next, select **Associate Cloud Account** under the **Setup** workflow. As shown in Figure 12-39, you need to select the public cloud provider, enable the **Use for Cloud Gateway** option, and provide login credentials. In the case of AWS, you can either provide API keys or create an IAM role with an external ID provided by SD-WAN Manager, and attach the proper permissions policy. SD-WAN Cloud OnRamp uses API calls to create the AWS transit VPC with two Cisco WAN Edge cloud router instances as well as to map existing AWS workload VPCs to the transit VPC. The account permissions must be sufficient to allow these actions. The "Cisco Catalyst SD-WAN Cloud OnRamp Configuration Guide" covers in detail how to generate the access key and what permissions are required.

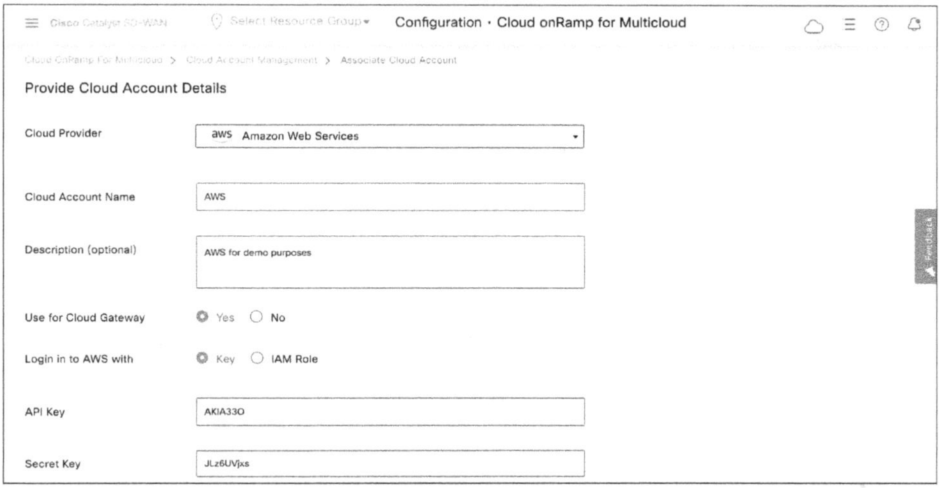

Figure 12-39 *Associating the AWS Cloud Account*

Next, you need to provide the implementation details for the Cloud OnRamp for Multicloud use cases. You can access these details from **Cloud Global Settings** under the same **Setup** workflow shown earlier, in Figure 12-37. Click **Add** in the upper-right corner to create the cloud provider settings. The **Cloud Gateway Solution** drop-down list allows you to choose one of the following options:

- **Transit Gateway—VPN Based (using TVPC):** Allows connectivity of the cloud gateway to the workload VPCs through the transit gateway using an AWS VPN connection (with IPsec tunnels).

- **Transit Gateway—Connect Based (using TVPC):** Allows connectivity of the cloud gateway to the workload VPCs through the transit gateway using an AWS TGW Connect (with GRE tunnels).

- **Transit Gateway—Branch-Connect:** Allows connectivity of different WAN Edge devices to workload VPCs through the transit gateway using an AWS VPN connection (with IPsec tunnels).

- **Cloud WAN—VPN Based (using TVPC):** Allows connectivity of the cloud gateway to the workload VPCs through an AWS Cloud WAN using an AWS VPN connection (with IPsec tunnels).

- **Cloud WAN—Connect based (using TVPC):** Allows connectivity of the cloud gateway to the workload VPCs through an AWS Cloud WAN using AWS Connect attachments (with GRE tunnels).

Later in this chapter, you will see the first option, **Transit Gateway—VPN based (using TVPC)**, used as an example. However, in your deployments, you are free to choose any deployment mode that suits your needs. Refer to the "Cisco Catalyst SD-WAN Cloud OnRamp Configuration Guide" for more detailed descriptions of these options.

The cloud gateway usually consists of a pair of virtual cloud routers that are instantiated within a transit VPC. Keep in mind that these options allow you to choose the protocol (IPsec/GRE) that will be used to establish tunnels between the cloud gateway routers and TGW (refer to Figure 12-34). The tunneling protocol inside AWS can be different from the SD-WAN site-to-site encapsulation, which is configured separately.

The Cloud Global Settings configuration page is shown in Figure 12-40. In addition to the desired use case, you need to provide the deployment details:

- **Reference Account Name:** Specify the name of the account in which SD-WAN Manager should perform the images and instances discovery.

- **Reference Region:** Specify the public cloud region in which SD-WAN Manager should perform the images and instances discovery.

- **Software Image:** Specify the type and version of WAN Edge router that will be deployed in the transit VPC. Only the supported versions are displayed.

- **Instance Size:** Specify the EC2 instance size of the WAN Edge router, based on the capacity needs.

- **IP Subnet Pool:** Specify, in CIDR format, the subnet ranges used to create the transit VPC. You can specify multiple subnets, separated by commas.

- **Cloud Gateway BGP ASN Offset:** Specify the offset for allocation of transit gateway BGP ASNs. The ASN is used to block routes learned by one transit gateway (eBGP) from another.

- **Intra Tag Communication:** Specify whether the communication between host VPCs under the same tag is enabled or disabled. If any tagged VPCs are already present and cloud gateways exist in those regions, then this flag cannot be changed.

- **Program Default Route in VPCs towards TGW:** Specify whether SD-WAN Manager should add the default route to the main routing table of the workload VPCs pointing to the transit gateway.

- **Full Mesh of Transit VPCs:** Specify the full-mesh connectivity between transit VPCs of cloud gateways in different regions to carry site-to-site traffic.

- **Enable Periodic Audit:** Specify whether to run automatic audits, which take place every 2 hours, run in the background, and help identify the gaps or disconnects between SD-WAN Manager configuration and the actual cloud resources state.

- **Enable Auto Correct:** Specify whether periodic audits will automatically try to fix the discovered discrepancies.

Next, you need to discover the host VPCs in the various cloud accounts and regions. To do so, navigate to **Configuration > Cloud OnRamp for Multicloud > Discover**. The configuration screen is shown in Figure 12-41. Usually these VPCs are configured and managed independently from SD-WAN (for example, by the company's CloudOps team), and the custom application resides within those host (workload) VPCs. The intent of the SD-WAN network is to provide connectivity between those resources and the remote branches.

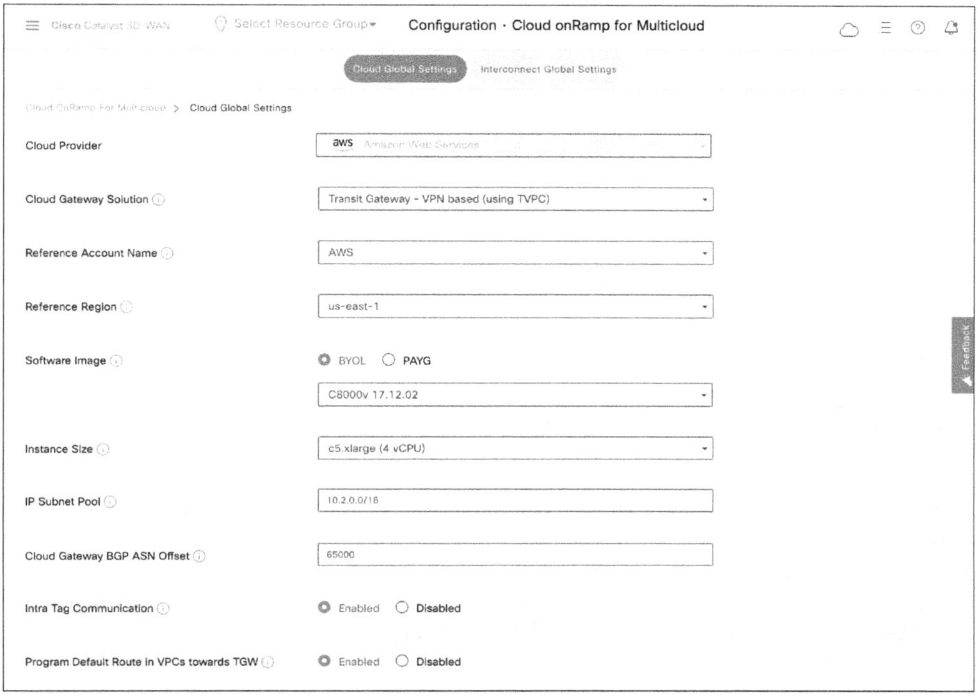

Figure 12-40 *Configuring Cloud Global Settings*

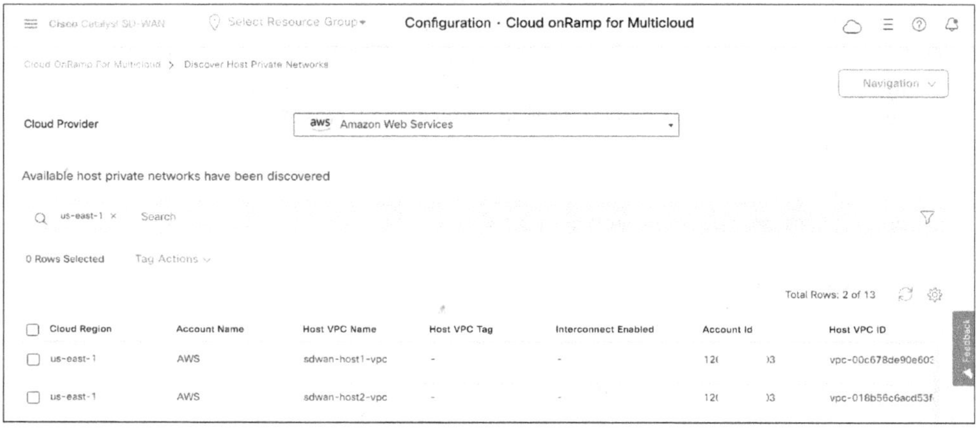

Figure 12-41 *Discovering Host Private Networks*

Once the host private networks (VPCs) are discovered, you need to assign tags to the selected VPC groups, as shown in Figure 12-42. Using an AWS tag is a way to assign the metadata to the cloud resources. SD-WAN Manager assigns VPCs with the user-provided tag value ("Host-VPC" in this example) and the pre-defined "CiscoSdwanV2" tag key.

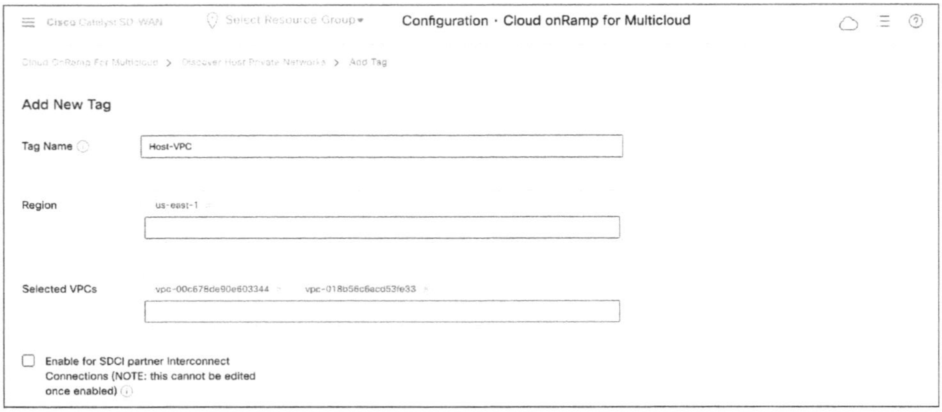

Figure 12-42 *Adding Tags to Discovered VPCs*

NOTE   Only VPCs within the AWS account selected and within the same AWS region as the transit VPC appear in the list of discovered private networks. A VPC must also have a name tag associated with it within AWS in order to appear within SD-WAN Cloud OnRamp. The default VPC automatically created by AWS for each region typically does not have a name tag associated with it. If you want the default VPC for the AWS region to appear within the list of VPCs to map to the transit VPC, you must assign a name tag to it within AWS before it can be discovered.

Next, you need to create the cloud gateway and describe the actual deployment of the cloud gateway in AWS. Before beginning this procedure, ensure that you have completed all prerequisite tasks and have two devices, each with the required type of license (BYOL or PAYG), and with templates attached. Then select **Configuration > Cloud OnRamp for Multicloud > Manage.** This step includes the creation of the transit VPC, two WAN Edge cloud routers, and a transit gateway.

As you can see in Figure 12-43, during the cloud gateway creation process, you need to confirm the EC2 instance details and assign two virtual routers, based on their UUIDs. In Figure 12-37, you can see that these UUIDs belong to the newly created virtual routers that have not been used yet but that already have the AWS device template attached to them. If you don't see the UUIDs here, make sure the devices are associated with the correct device template.

Once the cloud gateway resources are created, the next step is to push the configuration to the cloud gateway. If you don't take this step, the virtual routers in AWS Cloud are not treated as a part of the SD-WAN fabric and do not establish control connections with SD-WAN control components, nor data tunnels with the remote branches. You carry out this step by selecting **Configuration > Cloud OnRamp for Multicloud > Gateway Management**, finding the correct cloud gateway in the list, going to its menu (by clicking the three dots on the right), and clicking **Push Configuration** (see Figure 12-44).

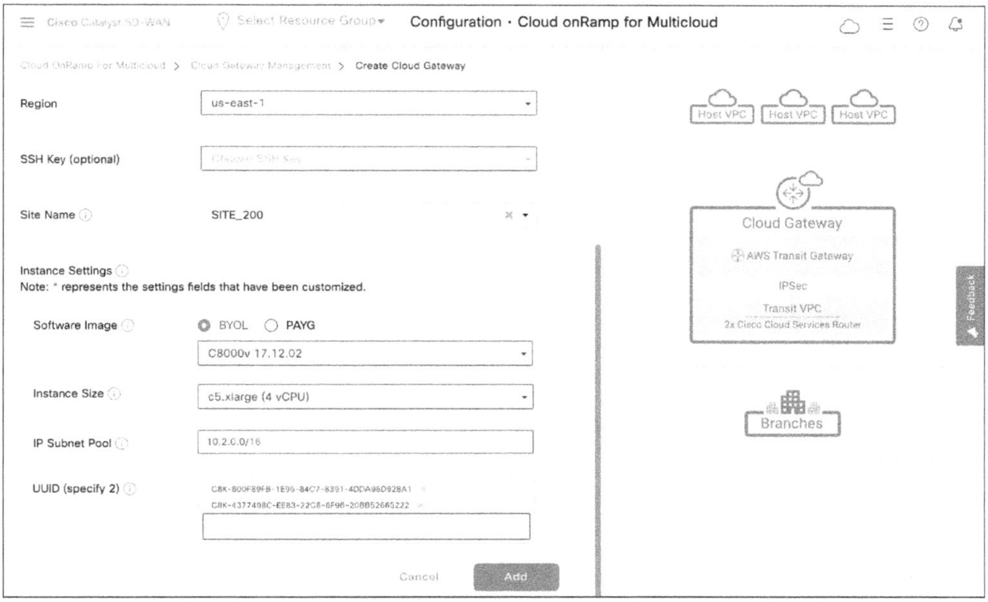

Figure 12-43 *Creating an AWS Cloud Gateway*

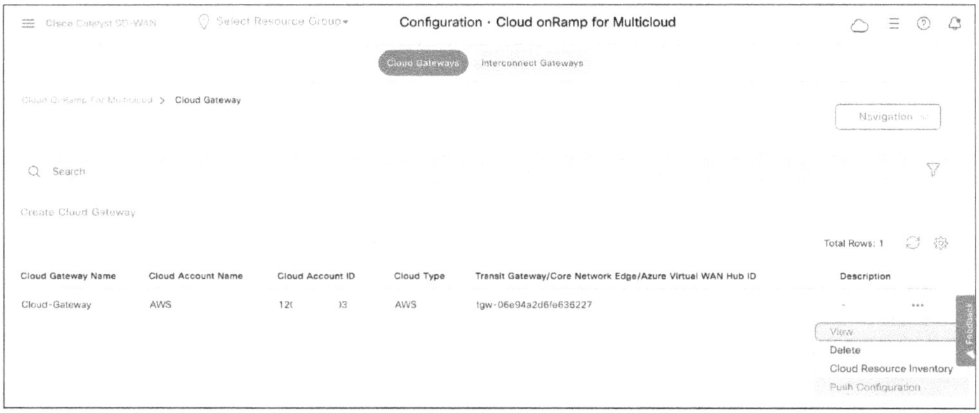

Figure 12-44 *Pushing the Configuration to the Cloud Gateway*

Finally, you need to enable cloud connectivity. To do this, you start by selecting **Configuration > Cloud OnRamp for Multicloud > Intent Management > Cloud Connectivity.** This step is similar to enabling the service-side VPN in the on-premises branches, configuring BGP routing and mutually redistributing routes between BGP and OMP. However, in the case of public cloud branches, you don't need to create these templates manually. SD-WAN Manager has embedded workflows that do it for you. You only need to enable the desired connectivity, as illustrated in Figure 12-45. In this example, you allow communication between SD-WAN VPN10 and Host-VPC in AWS Cloud.

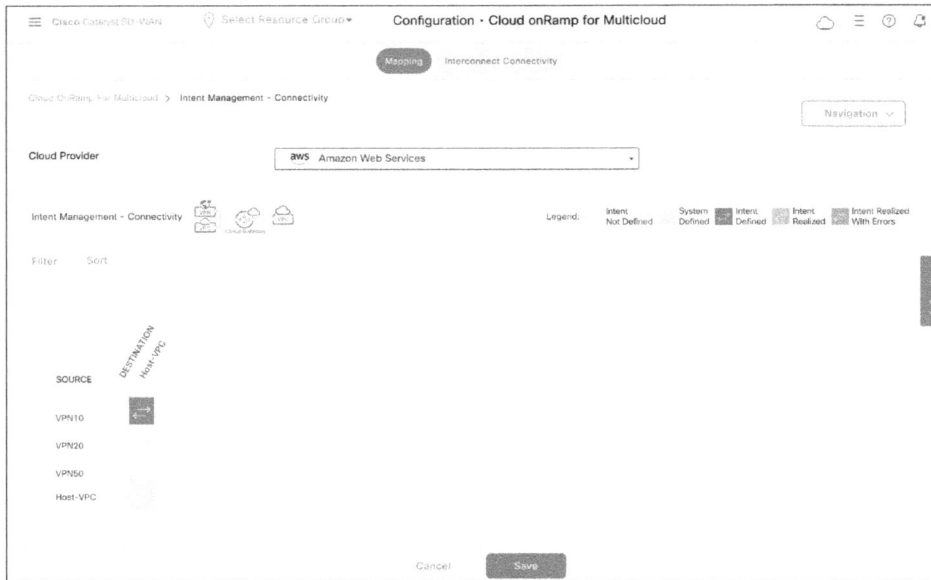

Figure 12-45   *Cloud OnRamp for Multicloud: Intent Management*

You can monitor the status of your Cloud OnRamp integration by selecting **Configuration > Cloud OnRamp for Multicloud.** In a fully operational deployment, you should see all devices and tunnels in the reachable state, as shown in Figure 12-46.

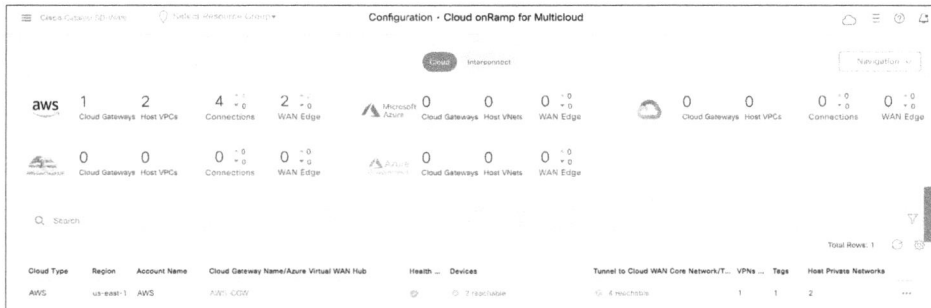

Figure 12-46   *Cloud OnRamp for Multicloud Status*

Once the virtual routers deployed in the cloud have become full members of the SD-WAN fabric, you can customize their configuration, deploy policies, and perform other actions in exactly the same way you do when operating regular on-premises WAN Edge devices. Standard device monitoring options are also available under **Monitoring > Devices.**

SD-WAN Cloud Interconnect

As businesses continue to adopt multicloud and hybrid cloud environments, traditional networks are experiencing significant changes in the requirements to the services they provide. Many cloud-based applications play critical roles in an organization's day-to-day operations, which is why businesses require reliable and secure connections to those applications.

Using traditional Internet links to connect to the cloud services can bring some challenges. For one thing, Internet service provider (ISP) links perform unpredictably. Once traffic goes to the ISP and beyond, an organization lacks visibility into and control over the traffic paths. In addition, the ISP links provide unsecure connectivity by default.

Private connections to cloud providers (such as Direct Connect and ExpressRoute) can be a good solution for a company that requires high-speed and high-quality connections to the public clouds. However, the deployment of such direct interconnections may take some time, and there are additional costs associated with such services. Also, this approach requires customers to plan for capacity and global reach up front, which can lead to underutilization and increased cost.

Cisco Catalyst SD-WAN, together with partners such as Equinix or Megaport, allows you to build a cloud-agnostic backbone using Software-Defined Cloud Interconnects (SDCIs). SDCIs help improve network performance in a cost-effective manner by providing flexible on-demand connectivity between multiple sites and the world's leading cloud provider networks. The goal is to perform middle-mile optimization and provide more visibility into and control over the transport connections between your direct private connection and the remote application you are trying to access.

Figure 12-47 illustrates Cisco Catalyst SD-WAN Cloud Interconnect using SDCI providers. An SDCI provider has a geographically dispersed physical network that serves as a middle mile for the SD-WAN fabric. An organization needs to establish connections to the nearest SDCI point of presence, which can be done via the regular Internet or MPLS links. Then the organization can utilize the dedicated bandwidth provided by the underlay, apply policies, perform traffic optimization, and so on. SD-WAN Cloud Interconnect can be used to establish site-to-site connections between remote branches as well as to provide site-to-multicloud access to public cloud providers, such as AWS, Microsoft Azure, and Google Cloud.

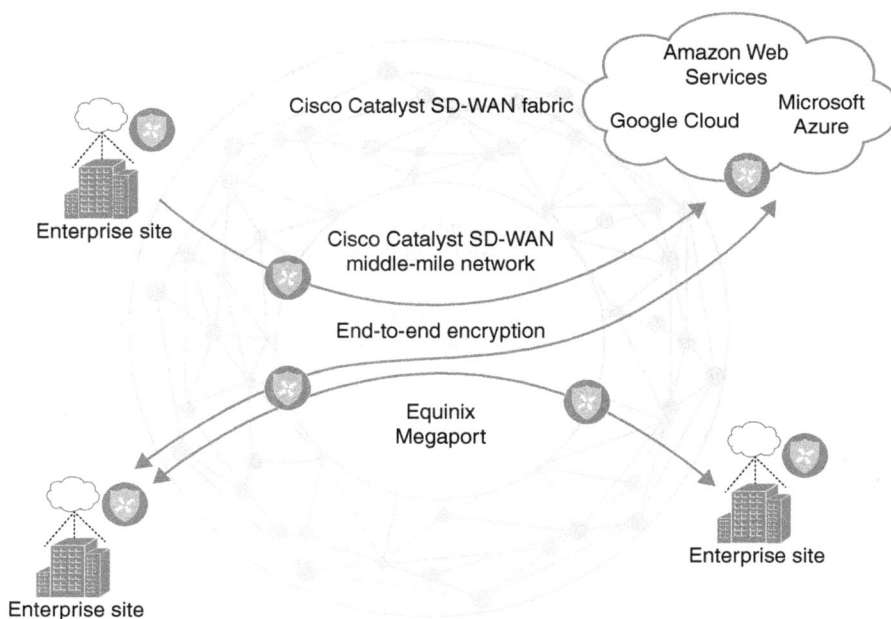

Figure 12-47 *Cisco Catalyst SD-WAN Cloud Interconnect Using Equinix or Megaport*

To use an SD-WAN Cloud Interconnect, you need to deploy a WAN Edge router within the SDCI provider's fabric and establish SD-WAN overlay connectivity between your branches and this Cloud Edge device or from a Cloud Edge device to private or public clouds. The SDCI Cloud Edge devices are virtual routers (typically Catalyst 8000v routers at this time), and their deployment is fully automated by Catalyst SD-WAN Manager. An entire solution can be deployed in the fast and easy manner.

WAN Edge devices in the SDCI provider fabric serve as Interconnect gateways. They provide dedicated private Layer 2 connectivity with SLA-backed assured performance, bandwidth, and 99.999% availability. *Short-haul interconnects* link several branch locations or a branch location and a public cloud in the same region. *Long-haul interconnects* link branch locations in different regions or a branch location in one region and a public cloud site in another region.

When using an SD-WAN Cloud Interconnect, the traffic between remote locations takes the following path:

1. The on-premises WAN Edge router sends the traffic to the closest SDCI provider location where a virtual Cisco WAN Edge router was deployed. This communication is encrypted inside SD-WAN tunnels. The branches can use ISP connection links as a fabric underlay to reach the SDCI data center.

2. The SDCI provider forwards the traffic using SD-WAN tunnels built over its own backbone as an underlay network.

3. The WAN Edge router on the receiving side forwards the packets to the final destination.

SD-WAN Cloud Interconnect allows for end-to-end traffic encryption and also ensures that traffic is automatically steered to alternate paths whenever the primary underlay path is unavailable. All kinds of SD-WAN policies, as discussed in earlier chapters, can be applied to the Cloud Interconnect traffic as well. For example, you can redirect only critical applications over this optimized SDCI path and send noncritical applications to a different region over the public Internet. Or you can set the SLAs, dynamically apply Application-Aware Routing policies, and so on.

Summary

This chapter covers all aspects of Cisco Catalyst SD-WAN Cloud OnRamp, including Cloud OnRamp for SaaS, Cloud OnRamp for Multicloud, and Cloud Interconnect. With Cloud OnRamp for SaaS, Cisco Catalyst SD-WAN fabric improves the branch office user experience by using the best-performing network path to SaaS applications, increasing application resiliency, and providing path and performance visibility. Cloud OnRamp for Multicloud extends the SD-WAN fabric into public cloud instances and provides all the benefits of Cisco Catalyst SD-WAN when accessing cloud workloads. Finally, SD-WAN Cloud Interconnect allows you to gain more control and visibility over the middle mile when accessing remote branches or public cloud resources over the private backbones offered by SDCI providers.

Review All Key Topics

Review the most important topics in the chapter, noted with the Key Topic icon in the outer margin of the page. Table 12-1 lists these key topics and the page number on which each is found.

Table 12-1   Key Topics

Key Topic Element	Description	Page
Section	SD-WAN Cloud OnRamp for SaaS	516
Section	SD-WAN Cloud OnRamp for Multicloud	534
Section	SD-WAN Cloud Interconnect	546

Define Key Terms

Define the following key terms from this chapter and check your answers in the glossary:

client site, cloud gateway, DIA site, gateway site

Chapter Review Questions

1. True or false: Cisco Cloud OnRamp for SaaS requires a Cisco Catalyst WAN Edge router to be placed in the SaaS cloud.

   a. True

   b. False

2. What are the Cloud OnRamp for SaaS site types? (Choose three.)

   a. Gateway site

   b. DIA site

   c. Local site

   d. Client site

   e. Hub site

3. True or false: Cloud OnRamp for SaaS supports dual Internet and MPLS transport sites.

   a. True

   b. False

4. True or false: Cloud OnRamp for SaaS SAIE (formerly DPI) redirects the initial application flow after detection.

   a. True

   b. False

5. How many Cisco Catalyst WAN Edge cloud routers are provisioned in a single transit VPC or vNet with Cloud OnRamp for Multicloud?

   a. It depends on the scale of the network.

   b. Two

   c. Four

   d. Eight

6. True or false: When logging in to an AWS Cloud instance with Cloud OnRamp for Multicloud, both IAM role and API key methods are supported.

    a. True

    b. False

7. What connectivity can Cisco Cloud OnRamp for Multicloud provide? (Select three options.)

    a. Site-to-site

    b. Site-to-SaaS

    c. Site-to-cloud

    d. Cloud-to-cloud

8. Which service do SDCI providers offer?

    a. Hybrid cloud

    b. Software as a service

    c. Cloud-agnostic private backbone

    d. Hosting of SD-WAN control components

References

"Cisco Catalyst SD-WAN Cloud OnRamp Configuration Guide," https://www.cisco.com/c/en/us/td/docs/routers/sdwan/configuration/cloudonramp/ios-xe-17/cloud-onramp-book-xe.html

CHAPTER 13

Cisco Catalyst SD-WAN Programmability

This chapter covers the following topics:

- **Cisco Catalyst SD-WAN API Overview:** This section discusses features and capabilities of Cisco Catalyst SD-WAN APIs.

- **Using the Cisco Catalyst SD-WAN API with Python:** This section provides practical examples of how to interact with Cisco Catalyst SD-WAN using REST APIs.

- **Cisco Catalyst SD-WAN Infrastructure as Code:** This section discusses the infrastructure as code (IaC) approach and its relevance to Cisco SD-WAN deployments.

In the ever-evolving landscape of networking, programmability and automation have emerged as key drivers for agility, efficiency, and innovation, where *network programmability* refers to the ability to control, configure, and automate network devices and infrastructure through software rather than using traditional manual methods. This paradigm shift enables network engineers to dynamically adapt to changing business requirements, deploy new services rapidly, and streamline operations.

Cisco Catalyst SD-WAN is part of this trend. In addition to its foundational capabilities outlined in this book, Cisco Catalyst SD-WAN offers powerful programmability capabilities through its application programming interfaces (APIs). These APIs allow organizations to extend, customize, and automate various aspects of their SD-WAN deployment, unlocking the full potential of their networks for innovation and efficiency.

The adoption of Cisco Catalyst SD-WAN programmability brings several notable benefits:

- **Automation and orchestration:** SD-WAN APIs enable the automation of routine tasks such as provisioning, configuration management, and policy enforcement. By interacting programmatically with the SD-WAN infrastructure, organizations can streamline operations, reduce errors, and speed up service delivery.

- **Customization and extensibility:** SD-WAN APIs provide the flexibility to tailor the network infrastructure to specific business needs. Organizations can develop custom applications, scripts, and integrations that leverage SD-WAN functionality to address unique use cases. This extensibility enables organizations to adapt their network infrastructure to evolving demands and opportunities.

- **Enhanced visibility and control:** SD-WAN APIs offer detailed insights into network performance, traffic patterns, and application behavior. By integrating SD-WAN data with monitoring and analytics platforms, organizations gain actionable insights that enable informed decision making and proactive network management. In addition, APIs allow organizations to dynamically adjust network policies and configurations in response to changing conditions, ensuring optimal performance and user experience.

- **Accelerated innovation:** SD-WAN programmability stimulates innovation by empowering organizations to experiment, iterate, and innovate rapidly. Developers can use SD-WAN APIs to create new applications, services, and solutions that leverage the capabilities of the underlying network infrastructure. This agility allows organizations to stay ahead of the curve and seize emerging opportunities.

> **NOTE** This chapter assumes that you have a basic understanding of programming and APIs, including familiarity with Python programming language, knowledge of JSON data encoding format, and experience with REST APIs. While basic explanations are provided when needed, a comprehensive overview of these topics is beyond the scope of this book. If you are new to network programmability, we recommend checking out the Cisco DevNet program for beginner-friendly resources and guidance.

Cisco Catalyst SD-WAN API Overview

Cisco Catalyst SD-WAN uses APIs as a core component of its architecture. Cisco Catalyst SD-WAN APIs (usually called simply SD-WAN APIs) act as a bridge that allows external systems, applications, and services to interact with SD-WAN Manager (formerly vManage), enabling automation, integration, and customization of network management tasks.

Notably, the SD-WAN Manager GUI is an application that interacts programmatically with the SD-WAN Manager servers, much as other clients do. When a user performs actions in the SD-WAN Manager GUI, such as creating a new device template or updating a policy, the GUI application sends corresponding API requests to the SD-WAN Manager server. The server processes these requests, performs the necessary operations on the underlying resources, and returns appropriate responses.

> **NOTE** The content in this chapter is based on SD-WAN API Release 20.12, unless otherwise noted. For accuracy, please refer to the SD-WAN API documentation corresponding to the release you are using if you are using a different release.

Cisco Catalyst SD-WAN APIs as REST APIs

Key Topic

SD-WAN APIs adhere to REST principles, allowing clients to use HTTP requests and standard HTTP methods (such as GET, POST, PUT, and DELETE) to perform operations on resources, which are represented as URLs.

Here's a brief overview of SD-WAN APIs from the REST perspective:

- **Resources:** Each resource in SD-WAN Manager, such as a device, interface, policy, or template, is represented as an API URL. For example, the URL /dataservice/device represents a collection of network devices managed by SD-WAN Manager.

- **HTTP methods:** SD-WAN APIs support standard HTTP methods to perform actions on resources:

  - **GET:** Retrieves information about resources.

  - **POST:** Creates new resources or initiates actions.

- **PUT:** Updates existing resources.

- **DELETE:** Removes resources.

- **Statelessness:** Each request to SD-WAN APIs is stateless, meaning that the server does not store any client state between requests. Each request contains all the information necessary for the server to fulfill it.

- **Request and response formats:** When requests include the data necessary to perform operations on resources, that data is sent in JSON format in the request body. Responses, also in JSON format, contain data about the operation results.

- **Authentication:** API endpoints are protected by authentication mechanisms to ensure secure access to resources. Clients must authenticate with username and password credentials.

- **Error handling:** SD-WAN APIs provide standard error messages and status codes to indicate the success or failure of requests.

> **NOTE**   Cisco Catalyst SD-WAN uses two distinct types of APIs: northbound and southbound.
>
> Northbound APIs enable external systems to communicate their intentions to SD-WAN Manager. Cisco Catalyst SD-WAN uses REST APIs as northbound APIs because they provide a flexible, lightweight, and easy-to-use interface.
>
> On the other hand, SD-WAN Manager uses southbound APIs to communicate with network devices. Cisco Catalyst SD-WAN uses NETCONF as a southbound protocol, as it offers a standardized programmatic interface for configuring and managing network devices.
>
> This chapter focuses specifically on northbound REST APIs.

Cisco Catalyst SD-WAN API Guidelines

As mentioned earlier, in an SD-WAN API, each resource is represented as a URL. To illustrate this, let's examine a sample resource URL structure for the API endpoint https://manager.ciscopress.com/dataservice/admin/user. It is constructed from several components, as outlined in Table 13-1.

Table 13-1   Cisco Catalyst SD-WAN API URL Structure

Component	Description
Protocol	https:// indicates the protocol over which data is exchanged between client and server.
Host:Port	manager.ciscopress.com is the IP address, or hostname, of SD-WAN Manager. The port number may be omitted if the default port, port 443, is used.
API root	/dataservice is a common URL prefix for most SD-WAN API calls. Exceptions include authentication and logout calls.
Resource	The last part denotes the location of the data or object of interest. For instance, the /users resource holds the list of users in SD-WAN Manager.

Component	Description
Parameters	The URL may include optional additional parameters for scoping, filtering, or clarifying a request. In such cases, the question mark (?) starts a query string, and the ampersand (&) separates multiple parameters within a query string. For example, ?deviceId=10.0.10.1 may be used in some API calls to indicate that only data for the device with the system IP address 10.0.10.1 needs to be returned.

13

NOTE   In this chapter, we refer to a fictitious SD-WAN deployment that operates with SD-WAN Manager at the https:/manager.ciscopress.com URL. When adapting examples from this book to your specific needs, replace this URL with the address of your organization's SD-WAN Manager.

Example 13-1 presents a sample response to the HTTP GET request sent to the https://manager.ciscopress.com/dataservice/admin/user URL, delivering a list of SD-WAN Manager users in JSON format.

Example 13-1   *SD-WAN API Response Example: A List of Users*

```json
{

    "header": {
        "generatedOn": 1710798327336,
        "viewKeys": {
            "uniqueKey": [],
            "preferenceKey": "grid-AdminUser"
        },
        "columns": [
            {
                "title": "Name",
                "property": "description",
                "hideable": false,
                "dataType": "string"
            },
            {
                "title": "Username",
                "property": "userName",
                "dataType": "string"
            },
            {
                "title": "User Groups",
                "property": "group",
                "dataType": "array"
```

```
                },
                {
                    "title": "Resource Group",
                    "property": "resGroupName",
                    "dataType": "string"
                },
                {
                    "title": "Status",
                    "property": "status",
                    "dataType": "string"
                }
            ],
            "fields": [
                {
                    "property": "description",
                    "dataType": "string"
                },
                {
                    "property": "userName",
                    "dataType": "string"
                },
                {
                    "property": "group",
                    "dataType": "array"
                },
                {
                    "property": "resGroupName",
                    "dataType": "string"
                },
                {
                    "property": "status",
                    "dataType": "string"
                }
            ]
        },
        "data": [
            {
                "userName": "admin",
                "locale": "en_US",
                "group": []
            },
            {
                "userName": "constantin",
```

```
            "description": "Backup local admin user",
            "locale": "en_US",
            "resGroupName": "global",
            "status": "active",
            "group": [
                "netadmin"
            ]
        }
    ]
}
```

As shown in this example, the standard SD-WAN API response consists of two primary JSON objects:

- **header:** The header object includes a generation timestamp, a columns section, and a fields section. The columns section defines the display name and attributes for the SD-WAN Manager GUI, and the fields section describes the data type of the response data. This design makes the SD-WAN API self-documenting.

- **data:** The data object contains the actual data retrieved from the SD-WAN system. In Example 13-1, SD-WAN Manager has a default admin user defined along with an additional user name, who also has netadmin privileges.

Certain APIs, such as an API that attaches a template to a WAN Edge device, may require substantial processing time. Rather than blocking the caller application until completion, these APIs execute *asynchronously* and just return the task or process ID. The caller application can use this ID to check the state of the request and retrieve the results upon completion. This approach ensures that the caller application remains responsive and can continue with other tasks while awaiting the long-running operation's completion.

Cisco Catalyst SD-WAN API Error Handling

SD-WAN APIs provide standard HTTP status codes, as shown in Table 13-2, to indicate the success or failure of requests. Most HTTP client libraries provide attributes or methods to access the HTTP status code within the response object returned by the API call. For example, with the name Python library, the status_code attribute of the Response object does this.

Table 13-2   Cisco Catalyst SD-WAN API HTTP Status Codes

Status Code	Status Message	Meaning
200	OK	Success
201	Created	New resource created
302	Found	Redirect to another URL
400	Bad request	Invalid request
401	Unauthorized	Authentication missing or incorrect
403	Forbidden	Request understood but not allowed
404	Not found	Resource not found

Status Code	Status Message	Meaning
429	Too many requests	Requests exceed rate limit
500	Internal server error	Problem with the server
503	Service Unavailable	Server unable to complete request

In addition, the response body may provide extra information about the nature of the error. Example 13-2 shows a sample response for a failed API request for the nonexistent device that is returned along with the HTTP 400 status code.

Example 13-2 *SD-WAN API Error Response Example*

```
{
    "error": {
        "message": "Device data error",
        "code": "DEV0001",
        "details": "No device found for system IP 1.1.11.101"
    }
}
```

When using SD-WAN APIs, be mindful of the following limitations (as of this writing) and make sure your application properly handles rate-limiting and timeout errors:

- There is a limit of 250 concurrent sessions. Because of this limit, it is important to log out at the end of your program.

- Bulk APIs are capped to 48 requests per minute. Bulk APIs allow you to issue a single request to gather information about multiple WAN Edge routers in the overlay network.

- Other APIs are restricted to 100 requests per second.

NOTE   Real-time monitoring APIs are very CPU intensive and should be used only for troubleshooting. They are not suitable for continuous active monitoring of devices.

Cisco Catalyst SD-WAN API Documentation

The official home page for Cisco Catalyst SD-WAN API resources is https://developer.cisco.com/sdwan/. Here, you can find API documentation, "Getting Started" guides, sample code, labs, sandboxes, and more.

Documentation is available at https://developer.cisco.com/docs/sdwan/ (see Figure 13-1). This portal provides API reference and guides for the latest releases of SD-WAN APIs, as well as information for previous releases. (Just click the "Latest" drop-down to see a list of releases.) Pay attention to "Change Logs" for SD-WAN API releases, located under the "API Reference" section, as even well-established APIs may change their behavior between releases.

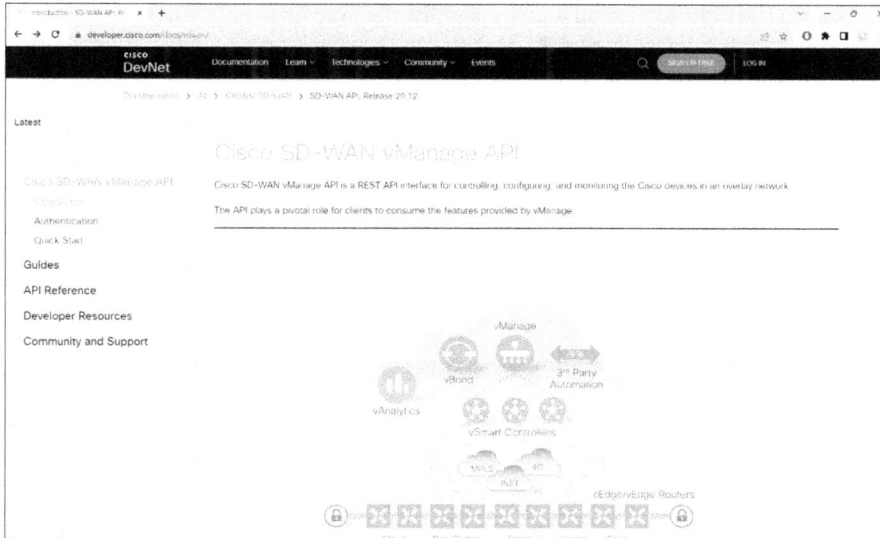

Figure 13-1 *Cisco Catalyst SD-WAN API Documentation Home Page*

Conveniently, SD-WAN API documentation is also included in the SD-WAN Manager software, accessible at the https://*manager-address*/apidocs (where *manager-address* is the hostname/IP address of the SD-WAN Manager server). On this page, as shown in Figure 13-2, API calls are bundled together into groups for ease of navigation.

NOTE As of this writing, there's no link to this URL in the SD-WAN Manager GUI, so you'll have to manually type it into your browser to access the documentation.

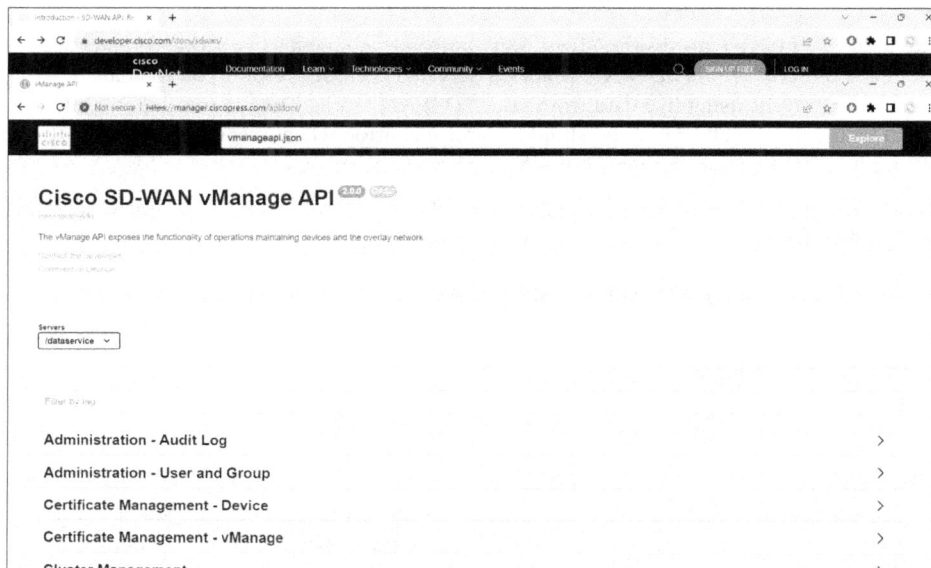

Figure 13-2 *Cisco Catalyst SD-WAN API On-Box Documentation*

Click the arrow on the right to expand a group and list the individual API calls and their respective URL for each call (see Figure 13-3). You can then click on a specific API call title to get detailed information about it, including:

- Description of and notes about the API

- A description of parameters and sample values for them, where applicable

- The request body format and an example (for POST/PUT/DELETE calls)

- Supported response HTTP status codes and examples of responses, where applicable

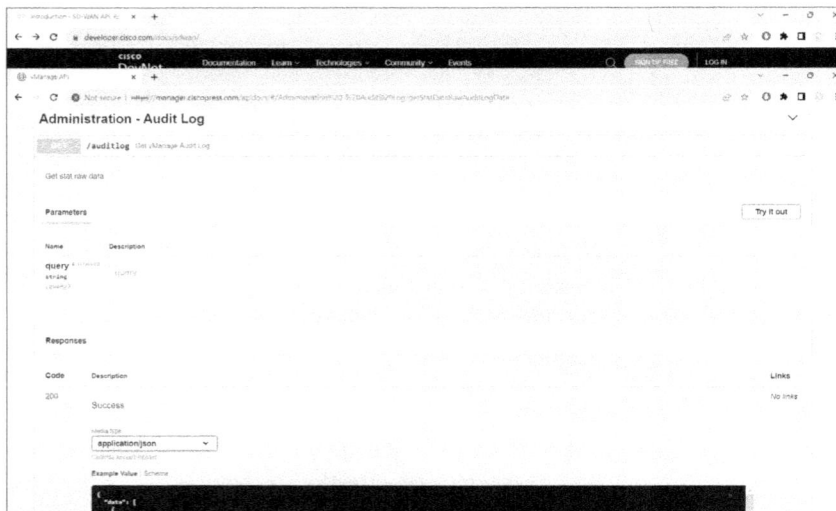

Figure 13-3 *Cisco Catalyst SD-WAN API On-Box Documentation: API Details*

An expanded API page features the "Try it out" button that enables live mode for executing API calls directly on the SD-WAN Manager server. This mode allows you to analyze API behavior interactively, using live data from your SD-WAN fabric. Keep in mind that while GET API calls are generally safe, you should exercise caution when executing PUT, POST, and DELETE API calls due to their potential impact on the system.

Upon providing necessary parameters and clicking the "Execute" button, you are presented with the following information, which is helpful for development efforts:

- The command-line equivalent of making an API call with curl (a Linux command-line browsing utility), including all the parameters

- The complete URL of the request

- The SD-WAN Manager server response code, body, and header

- The request execution time

Figure 13-4 provides an example of obtaining a AAA (authentication, authorization, and accounting) setup by making an interactive **GET /admin/aaa** API call. You can find this API in the Administration–User and Group group.

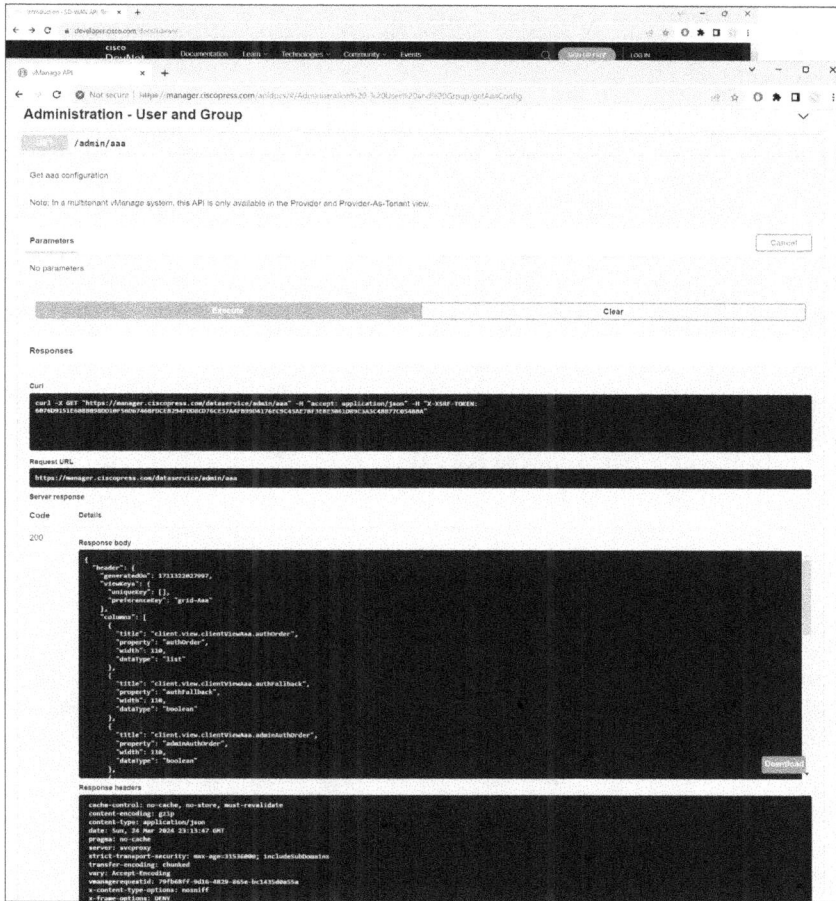

Figure 13-4   *Cisco Catalyst SD-WAN API On-Box Interactive Mode*

Learning from Cisco Catalyst SD-WAN Manager

While the Cisco Catalyst SD-WAN API documentation is comprehensive, navigating through its extensive list of APIs can sometimes be challenging. In addition, the documentation may lack context or overlook certain aspects of API usage. At times, you might want to replicate a specific SD-WAN Manager function programmatically but struggle to find the corresponding API in the documentation. In such situations, observing real-world examples of API usage can be invaluable. And what could be a better source of examples than the Cisco SD-WAN Manager application itself? SD-WAN Manager is just another application that uses an SD-WAN API. What if you could peek into the calls it makes and use them as examples?

Fortunately, modern browsers are equipped with built-in developer tools that allow you to inspect network requests made by web applications. Here's how you can use this feature with the SD-WAN Manager GUI:

Step 1.   Access **SD-WAN Manager.** Log in to the SD-WAN Manager web interface using your credentials.

Step 2.   **Enable developer tools.** Most modern browsers include developer tools that you can access by right-clicking on the web page and selecting Inspect or by pressing F12.

Step 3.   **Monitor network requests.** Within the developer tools, navigate to the Network tab, which shows all network requests made by the web application, including API calls.

Step 4.   **Find SD-WAN API calls.** Look for requests that are made to URLs starting with /dataservice. These are API calls made by SD-WAN Manager.

Step 5.   **Inspect API requests and responses.** Clicking on a specific network request provides detailed information about the request and response. You can inspect the request headers, parameters, and payload to understand how the API call is structured. Similarly, you can examine the response body to see the data returned by the API.

Step 6.   **Reproduce API calls.** Once you have a good understanding of how SD-WAN Manager interacts with the SD-WAN API, you can reproduce these API calls in your own scripts or applications. Use the same or similar HTTP methods, headers, parameters, and payloads to interact with the SD-WAN API programmatically.

Figure 13-5 shows the inspection of the administrative Manage Users page in the Chrome browser. Here you can see that SD-WAN Manager issued an HTTP GET request to https://manager.ciscopress.com/dataservice/admin/user URL to obtain a list of users in the system. The request was executed successfully (according to HTTP code 200 [OK]). You can also see authentication headers, which are explained in the next section.

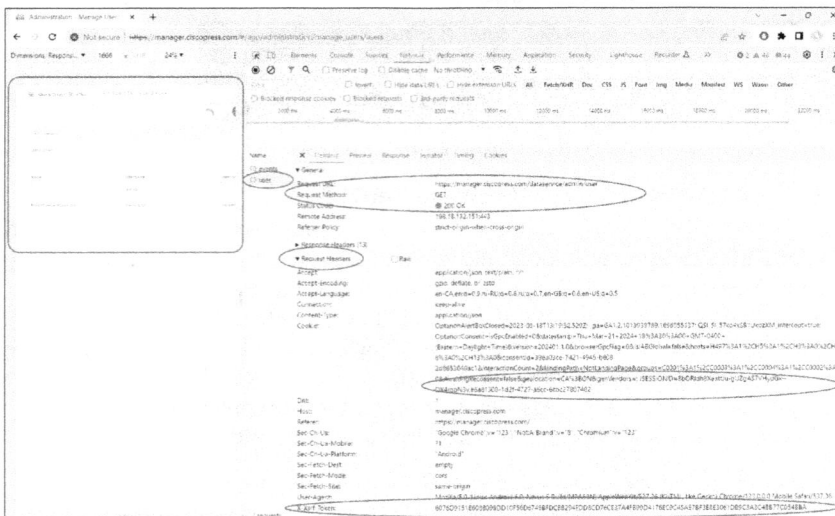

Figure 13-5   *Peeking into SD-WAN Manager's API Use: API Request*

Figure 13-6 shows the response, which is similar to the output provided in Example 13-1 except for the generatedOn timestamp. (Note that the columns and fields sections are collapsed in this figure for brevity.)

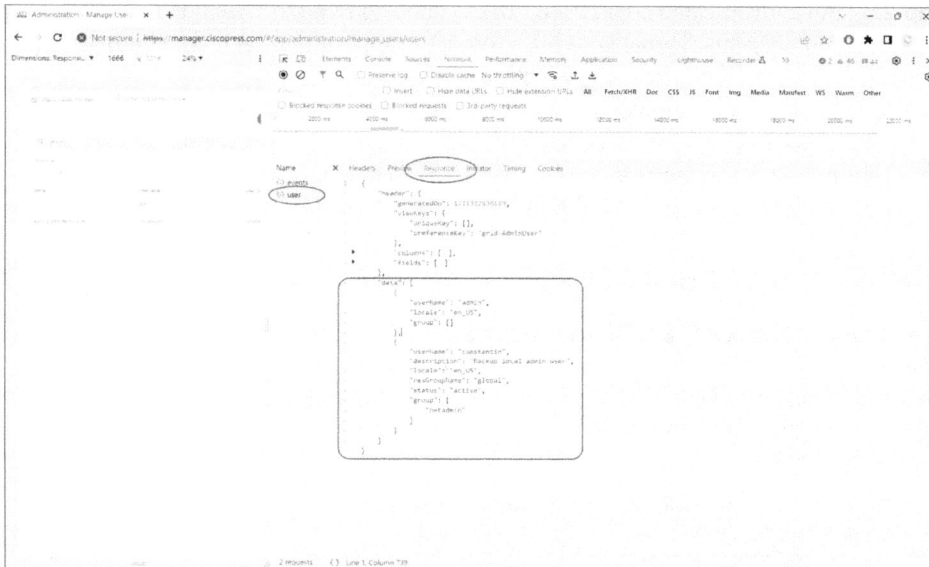

Figure 13-6   *Peeking into SD-WAN Manager's API Use: API Response*

Using the Cisco Catalyst SD-WAN API with Python

This section explores the practical use of SD-WAN APIs, using the Python programming language to illustrate how to interact with different SD-WAN APIs. Python is one of the most popular choices in network programmability due to its simplicity, flexibility, and extensive library ecosystem.

A fundamental aspect of working with SD-WAN APIs is the notion of sessions. Upon successful authentication, applications are granted a session that provides them with the privileges needed to interact with the Cisco Catalyst SD-WAN infrastructure. If multiple API requests are invoked sequentially, they normally share the same session. This session-based approach ensures secure access to APIs, with each application being allocated a unique session upon login.

NOTE   The default lifespan of a session is 24 hours, with an inactivity timeout of 30 minutes. The maximum concurrent session limit is 250. If this limit is reached, the new session will invalidate the least recently used session.

Here's a typical workflow for leveraging an SD-WAN API in a user application:

Step 1.   The user authenticates an application by logging in with their user credentials and establishing a session that grants access to the SD-WAN API endpoints.

Step 2.   An authenticated application can execute API requests based on their logic and requirements. Throughout the session, the application can make multiple API requests, as needed, to accomplish its objectives.

Step 3.   Finally, upon completing its interactions with the SD-WAN API, the application can securely log out and end the session. By terminating the session upon logout, an application revokes access privileges, mitigating the risk of unauthorized access to the SD-WAN infrastructure or other potential security breaches.

Let's review these steps in more detail to gain a better understanding of them.

Cisco Catalyst SD-WAN API Authentication

Before making any SD-WAN API calls, the first step is authentication. The standard method for authenticating with the SD-WAN API is by using username and password credentials with cookie-based authentication. Table 13-3 provides the details of the SD-WAN API authentication call.

Table 13-3   Cisco Catalyst SD-WAN API Authentication

Parameter	Value/Description
API endpoint	/j_security_check
HTTP method	POST
Request payload	Username and password in the JSON format: {"j_*username*": *Username*,"j_*password*": *Password*}
Successful call response	HTTP OK (200) response code, with an empty response body and a JSESSIONID session cookie set in the response headers, indicating the allocated session ID
Unsuccessful call response	The same HTTP OK (200) response code but with a response body that contains an HTML login page with an error message

Example 13-3 presents a Python code snippet that performs an authentication call to the SD-WAN API and reports its status along with the session ID upon successful authentication. Note the handling of login credentials: They are either passed via environment variables or prompted for interactively but are not hard-coded. This approach aligns with best practices for working with APIs, ensuring that sensitive information like credentials is not exposed directly in the code.

This and subsequent examples use the requests Python library and its Session object. Using the Session object streamlines interaction with the SD-WAN API by establishing a persistent TCP connection for API requests and automatically handling cookies, headers, and other parameters across multiple requests.

Example 13-3   *SD-WAN API Sample Authentication Code*

```
import requests, getpass, os

# Check environmental variables for SD-WAN Manager details
# Use defaults if not defined
MANAGER_ADDR=os.environ.get("MANAGER_ADDR", "manager.ciscopress.com")
MANAGER_USER=os.environ.get("MANAGER_USER") or input ("Username: ")
MANAGER_PASS=os.environ.get("MANAGER_PASS") or getpass.getpass('Password: ')

# API URLs and data structures
base_url = f"https://{MANAGER_ADDR}"
base_api_url = base_url + "/dataservice"

login_url = base_url + "/j_security_check"
login_data = {"j_username": MANAGER_USER, "j_password": MANAGER_PASS}

# Helper function, checks and prints status after making API call
def check_API_status (response):
    print ()
    print (f"Request:  HTTP {response.request.method} {response.url}")
    print (f"Response: HTTP code {response.status_code}")

    # Check for critical errors
    response.raise_for_status ()

# Initialize "Session" object from the "requests" library
session = requests.Session ()

# Disable TLS certificate warnings: do it for testing only
requests.packages.urllib3.disable_warnings()
session.verify = False

# Execute SD-WAN API Authentication call
response = session.post (url = login_url, data = login_data)
check_API_status (response)

if response.text == "":
    print ("Authenticated successfully, obtained session ID: ")
    print (f"  {session.cookies['JSESSIONID']}")
else:
    print (f"Authentication failed")
```

Example 13-4 shows the outcome of executing this code. You can see the API call made, the HTTP response code, and the successfully obtained session ID.

Example 13-4 *SD-WAN API Sample Authentication Code Output*

```
Request:  HTTP POST https://manager.ciscopress.com:443/j_security_check
Response: HTTP code 200
Authenticated successfully, obtained session ID:
  pOZHwe2Oe9CwhtNte1voqkJGGUM7ivQqr9dAo7uG.e6a81308-1d2f-4727-a6cc-6cbc27807482
```

With the Session object, the received SD-WAN session ID is automatically stored as a JSES-SIONID cookie and does not require any additional handling.

After successful authentication, the application can make read-only (HTTP GET) SD-WAN API calls. However, for write API calls (HTTP POST/PUT/DELETE), an additional authentication element called a cross-site request forgery prevention token (XSRF token) is required. Without it, those APIs will return an HTTP 403 error code along with a token-related error message in the response body. Table 13-4 provides the details of the SD-WAN API call used to obtain the XSRF token.

Table 13-4 Cisco Catalyst SD-WAN API Authentication Token

Parameter	Value/Description
API endpoint	/dataservice/client/token or /dataservice/client/token?json=true
HTTP method	GET
Request payload	None
Successful call response	Plaintext XSRF token or JSON-formatted token (if called with the json=true option)
Unsuccessful call response	Non-HTTP OK (200) response code

Example 13-5 provides an addition to the sample code from Example 13-3 that obtains the XSRF token. Example 13-6 demonstrates the result of executing this code.

Example 13-5 *SD-WAN API Sample XSRF Token Code*

```
token_url = base_api_url + "/client/token?json=true"

# Obtain authentication token
response = session.get (url = token_url)
check_API_status (response)

if response.status_code == 200:
    print (f"Token: {response.text}")
    session.headers['X-XSRF-TOKEN'] = response.json().get("token")
else:
    print (f"Unable to obtain the authentication token")
```

Example 13-6 *SD-WAN API Sample XSRF Token Code Output*

```
Request:  HTTP POST https://manager.ciscopress.com:443/j_security_check
Response: HTTP code 200
Authenticated successfully, obtained session ID:
  zSX3QB68Pd-1YdQuKFYJfh-zXUVMHbdxhmalMZey.e6a81308-1d2f-4727-a6cc-6cbc27807482

Request:  HTTP GET https://manager.ciscopress.com:443/dataservice/client/
token?json=true
Response: HTTP code 200
Token: {"token":"CCCFB8CEE5D1A7B18A4D388BCF7A63C90BC436662B8CD72548020EBA9DF98E5A38E
6FEE07FD4B35B6135EA61326E2318960A"}
```

Having acquired both the session ID and the XSRF token (which is stored for future use as an X-XSRF-TOKEN header in the Session object), the application is now fully authenticated and ready to execute SD-WAN API calls.

NOTE To see a practical example of how both the JSESSIONID cookie and the X-XSRF-TOKEN header are used in SD-WAN API calls, refer to Figure 13-5.

Ending a Cisco Catalyst SD-WAN API Session

An application should log out and close its SD-WAN API session once all API activities are complete. This ensures the release of allocated session resources and is considered a best practice for security purposes. Table 13-5 outlines the details of the SD-WAN API logout call.

Table 13-5 Cisco Catalyst SD-WAN API Logout

Parameter	Value/Description
API endpoint	/logout?nocache={*random-number*}
HTTP method	POST (for SD-WAN API Version 20.12 and up) or GET (for older SD-WAN API releases)
Successful call response	HTTP redirect (302) code with the location header https://{*manager-address*}/welcome.html?nocache= Note: Your library may handle redirects automatically, as the requests library does by default, so you may see an HTTP OK (200) response code for the redirect target page instead.
Unsuccessful call response	Non-HTTP redirect (302) response code

Example 13-7 extends the sample code from Example 13-5 to include the logout process. Example 13-8 shows the outcome of running this application.

Example 13-7 *SD-WAN API Sample Logout Code*

```
logout_url = base_url + "/logout?nocache="

# Log out
response = session.post (url = logout_url, allow_redirects = False)
check_API_status (response)

if response.status_code == 302:
    print (f"Logged out successfully!")
else:
    print (f"Error logging out")
```

Example 13-8 *SD-WAN API Sample Logout Code Output*

```
Request:  HTTP POST https://manager.ciscopress.com:443/j_security_check
Response: HTTP code 200
Authenticated successfully, session ID:
  SPCFLwp6kNpt_kfdMVI8ceeMdlvc6mVkPU_hQvwB.e6a81308-1d2f-4727-a6cc-6cbc27807482

Request:  HTTP GET https://manager.ciscopress.com:443/dataservice/client/
token?json=true
Response: HTTP code 200
Token: {"token":"C6927A5B9590B57AC826572BE07D94EB8E22D82AB806C2F4EACF9F94A1158DF5D5A
F04DBF293D84808F54EDB4F2727DE6884"}

Request:  HTTP POST https://manager.ciscopress.com:443/logout?nocache=
Response: HTTP code 302
Logged out successfully!
```

This basic application doesn't do much other than login and logout operations. Now let's explore how to use the SD-WAN API to accomplish more practical tasks.

Cisco Catalyst SD-WAN API Categories

Most SD-WAN APIs can be categorized into the following groups:

- **Administration APIs:** These APIs handle tasks related to the management of users, roles, permissions, and systemwide settings in the SD-WAN environment.

- **Certificate management APIs:** These APIs manage digital certificates for authentication and encryption in the SD-WAN fabric, including creation, retrieval, and revocation.

- **Configuration APIs:** These APIs handle various configuration-related tasks in the SD-WAN environment, including manipulation of device settings, inventory, and fabric configuration, as well as handling of templates, configuration groups, and policies.

- **Monitoring APIs:** These APIs provide real-time and historical data on network performance metrics, including traffic statistics, device status, network health, and other metrics for monitoring the SD-WAN environment.

- **Troubleshooting APIs:** These APIs assist in diagnosing and resolving issues in the SD-WAN fabric by providing functionalities such as event log retrieval, path tracing, packet capture, and other diagnostic tools.

The following sections present simple scripts demonstrating practical examples of using these APIs.

Base Python Module for SD-WAN API Interactions

All the basic SD-WAN API interaction tasks will be repeated in each example. To streamline these tasks across all scripts and avoid repetition, let's create a basic Python module that can be reused later. This module uses a Python object to group together data and methods for easier management. This Python object includes authentication and logout functionalities covered in previous sections, along with methods for executing all basic REST calls.

This module, named sdwan_api.py, is presented in Example 13-9. To use it in other scripts, place it in the same directory as a script file and include it with the **import sdwan_api** line in Python.

Example 13-9 *Basic Python Module for SD-WAN API Interactions*

```
import requests, getpass, os, time

class sdwan_api:
  def __init__ (self):

    manager = os.environ.get("MANAGER_ADDR") or "manager.ciscopress.com"
    username = os.environ.get("MANAGER_USER") or input ("Username: ")
    password = os.environ.get("MANAGER_PASS") or getpass.getpass('Password:')

    self.base_url = f"https://{manager}"
    self.base_api_url = self.base_url + "/dataservice"
    self.session = requests.Session ()

    # Disable TLS certificate warnings: do it for testing only
    requests.packages.urllib3.disable_warnings()
    self.session.verify = False

    if not self.login (username, password):
      raise SystemExit (f'Login to {self.base_url} failed, exiting...')

  def login (self, username, password):
    login_url = self.base_url + "/j_security_check"
```

```
      token_url = self.base_api_url + "/client/token?json=true"
      login_data = {"j_username": username, "j_password": password}

      response = self.session.post(url=login_url,
                    data=login_data,
                    verify=False)
      response.raise_for_status ()

      # If authenticated, the response body is empty.
      # If not, the response body contains a html login page
      if response.text:
        print ("Authentication Error")
        return False

      # session object contains the JSESSIONID cookie
      response = self.session.get(url=token_url, verify=False)
      response.raise_for_status ()

      try:
        self.session.headers['X-XSRF-TOKEN'] = response.json()['token']
        return True
      except:
        print ("Error obtaining XSRF Token")
        return False

  def logout (self):
    url = self.base_url + "/logout"

    # use "GET" action in versions <20.12
    response = self.session.post (url, {'nocache': str(time.time_ns())} )
    response.raise_for_status()

  # basic python method for REST interactions, called by other python methods
  # "method" parameter is HTTP method: GET/POST/PUT/DELETE
  # "url" parameter is full API URL
  # "payload" parameter is payload, where needed (POST/PUT methods)
  def api_action (self, method, url, payload = {}):
    try:
      response = self.session.request (method=method, url=url,
                      json=payload)
      response.raise_for_status()
    except:
```

```python
        raise SystemExit (f"{method} request failed: {url},"
                f" code {response.status_code}")

    try:
      data = response.json()
    except:
      data = ""

    # comment to stop debugging:
    print (f"\n>>> HTTP {method} {url}, status: {response.status_code}")
    # uncomment for more debugging:
    # if data:
    #   print (json.dumps(data, indent=4))

    return data

# Python method to execute "GET" REST API call
def api_GET (self, path):
  response = self.api_action ("GET", self.base_api_url + path)
  return response

# Python method to execute "POST" REST API call
def api_POST (self, path, payload):
  response = self.api_action ("POST", self.base_api_url+path, payload)
  return response

# Python method to execute "PUT" REST API call
def api_PUT (self, path, payload):
  response = self.api_action ("PUT", self.base_api_url+path, payload)
  return response

# Python method to execute "DELETE" REST API call
def api_DELETE (self, path):
  response = self.api_action ("DELETE", self.base_api_url + path)
  return response
```

NOTE The Python source code for this module, along with all the examples featured in this chapter, is available in the public repository located at https://github.com/sdwanbook/code.

SD-WAN Administrative API Example

The first script demonstrates how to create, read, update, and delete a local user in an SD-WAN system. It uses the following API endpoints, described in more detail in the "Administration–User and Group" section of the API documentation:

- **GET /admin/user:** Reads all local SD-WAN users.

- **POST /admin/user:** Creates a new user based on the provided payload. If the user already exists, an error is returned.

- **PUT /admin/user:** Updates details of an existing user according to the provided payload. If the user does not exist, an error is returned.

- **DELETE /admin/user:** Deletes an existing user from the system.

To illustrate the effect of each of these calls, the script refreshes and prints the list of users after each step. This script, named demo-app-admin.py, is presented in Example 13-10.

Example 13-10 *SD-WAN Administrative API Python Script*

```
import sdwan_api

sample_user = {
    "userName": "demouser",
    "password": "demopassword",
    "description": "Demo User",
    "locale": "en_US",
    "group": ["netadmin"]
}

# Helper function, prints formatted data
def print_users (users):
    for user in users['data']:
        username = user.get('userName','-')
        description = user.get('description','-')
        group = user.get('group','-')
        print (f"{username:15}{description:25}{group}")

# ----- start of the script -----
# Initialize API object
sdwan = sdwan_api.sdwan_api ()

# Print list of current users in the system
print_users (sdwan.api_GET ("/admin/user"))

# Add one more user and print user list to verify
sdwan.api_POST ("/admin/user", sample_user)
print_users (sdwan.api_GET ("/admin/user"))
```

13

```
# Change user group and print user list to verify
sample_user['group'] = ["operator"]
sdwan.api_PUT ("/admin/user/demouser", sample_user)
print_users (sdwan.api_GET ("/admin/user"))

# Finally, delete user and print user list to verify
sdwan.api_DELETE ("/admin/user/demouser")
print_users (sdwan.api_GET ("/admin/user"))

# Close session and exit
sdwan.logout ()
```

Example 13-11 shows the output of this script.

Example 13-11   *SD-WAN Administrative API Python Script Output*

```
>>> HTTP GET https://manager.ciscopress.com/dataservice/admin/user, status: 200
admin           -                       []

>>> HTTP POST https://manager.ciscopress.com/dataservice/admin/user, status: 200

>>> HTTP GET https://manager.ciscopress.com/dataservice/admin/user, status: 200
admin           -                       []
demouser        Demo User               ['netadmin']

>>> HTTP PUT https://manager.ciscopress.com/dataservice/admin/user/demouser, status:
200

>>> HTTP GET https://manager.ciscopress.com/dataservice/admin/user, status: 200
admin           -                       []
demouser        Demo User               ['operator']

>>> HTTP DELETE https://manager.ciscopress.com/dataservice/admin/user/demouser,
status: 200

>>> HTTP GET https://manager.ciscopress.com/dataservice/admin/user, status: 200
admin           -                       []
```

SD-WAN Device Inventory API Example

The script in this section illustrates how to retrieve inventory information for SD-WAN fabric by using the **GET /system/device/***{deviceCategory}* API endpoint. The *{deviceCategory}* parameter can be either **controllers**, to fetch data about SD-WAN Control Components, or **vedges**, to retrieve data about WAN Edge devices.

By default, this API call returns information about all devices of the specified type. Option-ally, you can specify a single device with the deviceIP option (for example, **GET /system/**

device/vedges?deviceIP=10.0.10.1). Refer to the API documentation (in the "Configuration–Device Inventory" section) for this option and additional options.

Note that there is an alternative API call that may be used to obtain the inventory information: **GET /device** endpoint (described in the "Monitoring–Device Details" section of the API documentation). It provides data about provisioned SD-WAN devices, including both SD-WAN Control Components and WAN Edge routers. However, this call does not include unprovisioned devices in the response and provides more operational details, such as the number of active BFD sessions, at the expense of configuration details such as the associated template. Choose the API call that better suits your needs.

The script, named demo-app-inventory.py, is presented in Example 13-12. It makes two calls to obtain inventory and displays several elements of the inventory.

Example 13-12   *SD-WAN Device Inventory API Python Script*

```python
import sdwan_api

# Helper function, prints formatted data
def print_devices (devices):
    print (f"\n{'Name':12}{'System IP':12}{'Model':10}"
        f"{'Site':5}{'OS Ver':18}{'Template'}")

    for device in devices:
        dev_name = device.get('host-name','-')
        dev_ip = device.get('system-ip','-')
        dev_model = device.get('deviceModel','-').replace('vedge-','')
        dev_site = device.get('site-id','-')
        dev_ver = device.get('version','-')
        dev_tpl = device.get('template','-')

        print (f"{dev_name:12}{dev_ip:12}{dev_model:10}"
            f"{dev_site:5}{dev_ver:18}{dev_tpl}")

# ----- start of the script -----
# Initialize API object
sdwan = sdwan_api.sdwan_api ()

# Obtain data for controllers
controllers = sdwan.api_GET ("/system/device/controllers")['data']
# Obtain data for routers
wan_edges = sdwan.api_GET ("/system/device/vedges")['data']

# print inventory
print_devices (controllers)
print_devices (wan_edges)

# Close session and exit
sdwan.logout ()
```

Example 13-13 presents the output of this script. Here you can observe the API calls made, the HTTP response codes, and inventory information for the SD-WAN fabric. This information includes a list of SD-WAN Control Components and WAN Edge routers, along with the system IP address, device model, site ID, software version, and attached template of each device, where applicable.

Example 13-13 *SD-WAN Device Inventory API Python Script Output*

```
>>> HTTP GET https://manager.ciscopress.com/dataservice/system/device/controllers,
status: 200


>>> HTTP GET https://manager.ciscopress.com/dataservice/system/device/vedges,
status: 200


Name        System IP     Model     Site OS Ver             Template
vBond-1     1.1.1.104     cloud     100  20.12.3            -
vBond-2     1.1.1.105     cloud     100  20.12.3            -
vManage     1.1.1.101     vmanage   100  20.12.3            -
vSmart-2    1.1.1.103     vsmart    100  20.12.3            vSmart_Template
vSmart-1    1.1.1.102     vsmart    100  20.12.3            vSmart_Template


Name        System IP     Model     Site OS Ver             Template
BR3-Edge1   10.0.103.1    C8000V    103  17.12.03.0.3740    Branch3_Edge
BR1-Edge2   10.0.101.2    C8000V    101  17.12.03.0.3740    Branch1_Edge2
BR2-Edge1   10.0.102.1    C8000V    102  17.12.03.0.3740    Branch2_Edge
BR2-Edge2   10.0.102.2    C8000V    102  17.12.03.0.3740    Branch2_Edge
BR1-Edge1   10.0.101.1    C8000V    101  17.12.03.0.3740    Branch1_Edge1
DC2-Edge1   10.0.20.1     C8000V    20   17.12.03.0.3740    DC2_Edge
DC2-Edge2   10.0.20.2     C8000V    20   17.12.03.0.3740    DC2_Edge
DC1-Edge2   10.0.10.2     C8000V    10   17.12.03.0.3740    DC1_Edge
DC1-Edge1   10.0.10.1     C8000V    10   17.12.03.0.3740    DC1_Edge
-           -             C8000V    -    -                  -
-           -             C8000V    -    -                  -
```

SD-WAN Real-Time Monitoring API Example

The script in this section demonstrates how to obtain operational information for WAN Edge devices by using the **GET /device/interface?deviceId={***Device System IP***}** API endpoint (described in more details in the "Real-Time Monitoring–Interface" section of the API documentation). This API call retrieves real-time operational information about interfaces, including state, counters, and other relevant details for a specified device. It provides the same information as if you executed the **show interfaces** command in a router CLI.

While this API call provides a lot of details about the current state of interfaces, the script demo-app-monitoring.py, presented in Example 13-14, displays only a small subset of this information.

Example 13-14 *SD-WAN Real-Time Monitoring API Python Script*

```python
import sdwan_api

device = "10.0.10.1"

# Helper function, prints formatted data
def print_interfaces (intf):
    print (f"Interface statistics for {intf[0].get('vdevice-host-name')} "
            f"({intf[0].get('vdevice-name')})")
    print (f"{'Name':20}{'VPN':6}{'IP Address':15}"
            f"{'Admin':6}{'Oper':6}{'TX octets':>12}{'RX octets':>12}")

    for int in intf:
        if int.get('ip-address') == '0.0.0.0':
            continue
        if_name = int.get('ifname','-')
        if_vpn = int.get('vpn-id','-')
        if_ip = int.get('ip-address','-')
        if_admin = int.get('if-admin-status','-').replace('if-state-','')
        if_oper = int.get('if-oper-status','-').replace('if-oper-state-','')
        if_tx = int.get('tx-octets','-')
        if_rx = int.get('rx-octets','-')

        print (f"{if_name:20}{if_vpn:6}{if_ip:15}"
                f"{if_admin:6}{if_oper:6}{if_tx:12}{if_rx:12}")

# ----- start of the script -----
# Initialize API object
sdwan = sdwan_api.sdwan_api ()

# Obtain real-time interface info
# Real-Time Monitoring - Interface
status = sdwan.api_GET (f"/device/interface?deviceId={device}")['data']

# print interface data
print_interfaces (status)

# Close session and exit
sdwan.logout ()
```

Example 13-15 shows the output of this script.

Example 13-15 *SD-WAN Real-Time Monitoring API Python Script Output*

```
>>> HTTP GET https://manager.ciscopress.com/dataservice/device/
interface?deviceId=10.0.10.1, status: 200
Interface statistics for DC1-Edge1 (10.0.10.1)
Name                VPN    IP Address    Admin Oper    TX octets    RX octets
GigabitEthernet1    0      209.165.201.1 up    ready    151014871    151493284
GigabitEthernet2    0      192.168.20.1  up    ready     67775041     68986431
GigabitEthernet3    10     172.16.10.1   up    ready       403474        85565
GigabitEthernet4    512    192.168.1.10  up    ready       335068      1107855
Loopback65528       65528  192.168.1.1   up    ready            0            0
Loopback65529       65529  11.1.10.1     up    ready            0            0
Sdwan-system-intf   0      10.0.10.1     up    ready            0            0
Tunnel1             0      209.165.201.1 up    ready            0     63959974
Tunnel2             0      192.168.20.1  up    ready            0     28431743
```

SD-WAN Configuration API Example 1

The script in this section can be used for documenting SD-WAN configuration. It lists all the feature templates used by a specified device template. It demonstrates how to retrieve and cross-reference data between multiple API calls, using the following endpoints:

- **GET /template/device:** This API call, described in the "Configuration–Template Master" section of the API documentation, retrieves a list of all configured device templates.

- **GET /template/feature:** This API call, explained in the "Configuration–General Template" section of the API documentation, returns a list of all the configured feature templates.

- **GET /template/device/object/**{*TemplateID*}**:** This API call, described in the "Configuration–Template Master" section of the API documentation, provides the full content of a specified device template. Example 13-16 shows a sample response.

Example 13-16 *Device Template Sample Response*

```
{
  "templateId": "57dfe544-75d8-40ea-942b-09b63ebfc800",
  "templateName": "DC1_Edge",
  "templateDescription": "WAN Edge routers in Primary Data Center",
  "deviceType": "vedge-C8000V",
[... removed for brevity ...]
  "generalTemplates": [
    {
      "templateId": "aa0fa123-394f-4660-8c9a-b6e6d7c81788",
      "templateType": "cedge_aaa"
```

```
      },
      {
        "templateId": "7a368a9c-e29c-4156-96e3-ed8cae8e0ad6",
        "templateType": "cisco_bfd"
      },
[... removed for brevity ...]
```

In the script, the first step is to obtain a list of all the configured device templates and feature templates, enabling the mapping of their IDs to names and vice versa. Next, searching by device template name, the script finds the template ID and uses it in the API call to obtain its full content, which includes IDs of all the feature templates used in it. Finally, by mapping feature templates IDs to their names, the script presents the content of the device template in human-readable format.

This script, named demo-app-template-list.py, is presented in Example 13-17.

Example 13-17 *SD-WAN Configuration API Python Script: Example 1*

```python
import sdwan_api

target_template = "DC1_Edge"

# Helper function, returns template ID for the provided template name
def find_template_id (templates, name):
    for template in templates:
        if template.get('templateName') == name:
            return template.get('templateId')
    return None


# Helper function, returns template name for the provided template ID
def find_template_name (templates, id):
    for template in templates:
        if template.get('templateId') == id:
            return template.get('templateName')
    return None


# Helper function, prints formatted data
def print_device_template (template, feature_templates):
    print (f"\nDevice Template: {template.get('templateName')}")
    print (f"    Device Type: {template.get('deviceType','').replace('vedge-','')}")
    print (f"    Description: {template.get('templateDescription')}")
    print (f"Attached Feature Templates:")
    # Loop through template's feature templates
    for ftpl in template.get('generalTemplates'):
```

```
        ftpl_name = find_template_name (feature_templates, ftpl.get('templateId'))
        print (f"    {ftpl_name} ({ftpl.get('templateType')})")


        # Some templates have sub-templates, need another loop
        sub_ftpls = ftpl.get('subTemplates')
        if sub_ftpls:
            for sub_ftpl in sub_ftpls:
                sub_ftpl_name = find_template_name (feature_templates, sub_ftpl.
get('templateId'))
                print (f"     - {sub_ftpl_name} ({sub_ftpl.get('templateType')})")

# ---------- start of the script ----------
# Initialize API object
sdwan = sdwan_api.sdwan_api ()

# Obtain a list of all device templates
device_templates = sdwan.api_GET ("/template/device")['data']
# Obtain a list of all feature templates
feature_templates = sdwan.api_GET ("/template/feature?summary=true")['data']

# Find ID - needed for the next API call
target_template_id = find_template_id (device_templates, target_template)
# Obtain content of device template
template = sdwan.api_GET (f"/template/device/object/{target_template_id}")

print_device_template (template, feature_templates)

# Close session and exit
sdwan.logout ()
```

Example 13-18 shows the output of this script. Here, you can see details for the DC1_Edge device template, such as device type and description, along with a comprehensive list of the feature templates that are included in it.

Example 13-18 *SD-WAN Configuration API Python Script Output: Example 1*

```
>>> HTTP GET https://manager.ciscopress.com/dataservice/template/device, status: 200

>>> HTTP GET https://manager.ciscopress.com/dataservice/template/
feature?summary=true, status: 200

>>> HTTP GET https://manager.ciscopress.com/dataservice/template/device/
object/57dfe544-75d8-40ea-942b-09b63ebfc800, status: 200

Device Template: DC1_Edge
```

```
     Device Type: C8000V
     Description: WAN Edge routers in Primary Data Center
Attached Feature Templates:
   Global_AAA (cedge_aaa)
   Default_BFD_Cisco_V01 (cisco_bfd)
   Global_OMP (cisco_omp)
   Default_Security_Cisco_V01 (cisco_security)
   Global_System (cisco_system)
    - Default_Logging_Cisco_V01 (cisco_logging)
   DC1_VPN0 (cisco_vpn)
    - DC1_VPN0_Gig1 (cisco_vpn_interface)
    - DC1_VPN0_Gig2 (cisco_vpn_interface)
   Global_VPN512 (cisco_vpn)
    - Global_VPN512_interface (cisco_vpn_interface)
   DC1_VPN10 (cisco_vpn)
    - DC1_BGP (cisco_bgp)
    - DC1_VPN10_Gig3 (cisco_vpn_interface)
   Default_EQUINIX_C8000V_GLOBAL_CISCO_V01 (cedge_global)
   Factory_Default_Retail_Banner (cisco_banner)
```

SD-WAN Configuration API Example 2

The advanced script in this example demonstrates how to programmatically modify SD-WAN configuration by adjusting device template variables and pushing updated configuration to attached devices. It uses the following API endpoints:

- **GET /template/device:** This API call retrieves a list of device templates.

- **GET /template/device/config/attached/{*TemplateId*}:** This API call, described in the "Configuration–Device Template" section of the API documentation, gets a list of devices attached to a specified device template.

- **POST /template/device/config/input:** This API call, explained in the "Configuration–Device Template" section of the API documentation, returns provisioning variables for the template and devices specified in the payload.

- **POST /template/device/config/attachfeature:** This API call, described in the "Configuration–Device Template" section of the API documentation, initiates a task that attaches devices to a template. It does not wait for the task to complete but rather responds with the ID of the created task.

- **GET /device/action/status/{*actionName*}:** This API call, described in the "Configuration–Dashboard Status" section of the API documentation, provides the status of the action, which is the configuration push in this case.

NOTE   When working in the SD-WAN Manager GUI, attaching a device to a device template and changing device values for an attached device are separate workflows that push configuration to SD-WAN devices. However, from the perspective of the SD-WAN API, both processes—attaching a device to a template and updating device variables—are handled by the same device attachment API call. So don't be confused by the fact that we use the device attachment process when updating device configuration.

As in the previous example, the script in this example starts with obtaining the device template ID and identifying devices attached to it. It then retrieves device variables for those devices and updates them as needed. (The interface description is changed to "Configured via API" in this case). Next, the script creates a proper payload and initiates the task to attach devices to a device template, pushing the configuration changes to WAN Edge routers. It will take some time to finish this process, so the script monitors the task's status, checking it every 5 seconds until completion (or timeout). When it is finished, it prints an execution log (returned as a part of the API status call) for every device and the completion status.

This demo-app-template-push.py script is presented in Example 13-19.

Example 13-19   *SD-WAN Configuration API Python Script: Example 2*

```
import sdwan_api, time


target_template = "DC1_Edge"


# Payload structure for the API call that reads current variable values
variables_request = {
    'templateId': '',
    'deviceIds': [],
    'isEdited': False,
    'isMasterEdited': False,
}


# Payload structure for the API call that attaches devices to a template
attach_request = {
  'deviceTemplateList': [
    {
      'templateId': '',
      'device': [],
      'isEdited': False,
      'isMasterEdited': False
    }
  ]
}
```

```python
# Helper function, returns template ID for the provided template name
def find_template_id (templates, name):
    for template in templates:
        if template.get('templateName') == name:
            return template.get('templateId')
    return None


# Helper function, checks the status of the async task
# Waits until task completes, with 1 min timeout
def wait_for_task(sdwan, task_id, interval=5, maxtime=60):

    task_url = "/device/action/status/"+task_id
    time_elapsed = 0
    status = "unknown"


    while True:
        if (time_elapsed < maxtime):
            # read task status from vManage
            status_data = sdwan.api_GET(task_url)

            # current status of operation (in progress/success/fail)
            if len(status_data['data']) == 0:
                status = "Validation " + status_data.get("validation","").
get("status","unknown error")
            else:
                status = status_data['summary']['status']

            # Task is complete when status is "done"
            if status == "done":
                # Task status includes execution log, let's print it
                print ("\nExecution log:")
                for rtr in status_data.get ('data'):
                    print (f"{rtr['host-name']}, status: {rtr['status']}")
                    for line in rtr['activity']:
                        print (line)
                    print ()
                break

            print (f"Operation in progress {time_elapsed}/{maxtime}s, status:
{status}")
            time.sleep (interval)
            time_elapsed += interval
        else:
            status = "Timeout"
            break
```

```
    return status

# ---------- start of the script ----------
# Initialize API object
sdwan = sdwan_api.sdwan_api ()

# Find template ID - needed for the next API call
device_templates = sdwan.api_GET("/template/device")['data']
target_template_id = find_template_id(device_templates, target_template)

# Find all the devices attached to this template
attached_devices = sdwan.api_GET(f"/template/device/config/attached/{target_tem-
plate_id}")['data']

# Prepare "variables_request" data structure to request current variables
print (f"Updating devices attached to the '{target_template}' template:")
variables_request['templateId'] = target_template_id
for rtr in attached_devices:
    variables_request['deviceIds'].append (rtr.get('uuid'))
    print (f" - {rtr.get('host-name')} ({rtr.get('deviceIP')})")

# Request device variables
device_variables = sdwan.api_POST("/template/device/config/input", variables_
request)['data']

# Update values as needed
# In this case, we're updating description of the interface in VPN 512
for var in device_variables:
    var['/512/vpn512_if_name/interface/description'] = "Configured via API"

# Prepare "attach_request" data structure for the template push call
attach_request['deviceTemplateList'][0]['templateId'] = target_template_id
attach_request['deviceTemplateList'][0]['device'] = device_variables

# Template attach - asynchronous call, only returns task ID
task_id = sdwan.api_POST("/template/device/config/attachfeature", attach_request)
['id']

# Patiently wait for the task to complete
status = wait_for_task(sdwan, task_id)

# Report the status
print(f"Task execution status: {status}")

# Close session and exit
sdwan.logout ()
```

Example 13-20 presents the output of this script. As you can see, the configuration change was successfully applied to two WAN Edge routers attached to the DC1_Edge device template. The process took approximately 15 seconds to complete for both devices.

Example 13-20   *SD-WAN Configuration API Python Script Output: Example 2*

```
Updating devices attached to the 'DC1_Edge' template:
 - DC1-Edge2 (10.0.10.2)
 - DC1-Edge1 (10.0.10.1)
Operation in progress 0/60s, status: Validation In progress
Operation in progress 5/60s, status: in_progress
Operation in progress 10/60s, status: in_progress


Execution log:
DC1-Edge2, status: Success
[2-Apr-2024 1:26:50 UTC] Configuring device with feature template: DC1_Edge
[2-Apr-2024 1:26:50 UTC] Checking and creating device in vManage
[2-Apr-2024 1:26:52 UTC] Generating configuration from template
[2-Apr-2024 1:26:55 UTC] Device is online
[2-Apr-2024 1:26:55 UTC] Updating device configuration in vManage
[2-Apr-2024 1:26:55 UTC] Sending configuration to device
[2-Apr-2024 1:27:00 UTC] Successfully notified device to pull configuration
[2-Apr-2024 1:27:02 UTC] Device has pulled the configuration
[2-Apr-2024 1:27:04 UTC] Device: Config applied successfully
[2-Apr-2024 1:27:04 UTC] Template successfully attached to device


DC1-Edge1, status: Success
[2-Apr-2024 1:26:50 UTC] Configuring device with feature template: DC1_Edge
[2-Apr-2024 1:26:50 UTC] Checking and creating device in vManage
[2-Apr-2024 1:26:51 UTC] Generating configuration from template
[2-Apr-2024 1:26:55 UTC] Device is online
[2-Apr-2024 1:26:55 UTC] Updating device configuration in vManage
[2-Apr-2024 1:26:55 UTC] Sending configuration to device
[2-Apr-2024 1:27:00 UTC] Successfully notified device to pull configuration
[2-Apr-2024 1:27:01 UTC] Device has pulled the configuration
[2-Apr-2024 1:27:03 UTC] Device: Config applied successfully
[2-Apr-2024 1:27:03 UTC] Template successfully attached to device
Task execution status: done
```

Sastre Software Development Kit (SDK)

For developers who wish to interact with Cisco SD-WAN without dealing with the low-level details of a REST API and for those who are less familiar with Python, there are other solutions for programmatic interactions—including the Sastre tool.

Sastre is a versatile tool designed to streamline management of configuration elements and visualization of information in Cisco SD-WAN deployments. It can be used as either a self-contained CLI application or as a Python SDK for seamless integration into other applications.

Example 13-21 presents a sample Python application that consumes the Sastre SDK. In this example, the DeviceControlConnections object encapsulates information regarding the state of control connections for the specified device (DC1-Edge1 router). The field_info method provides descriptions of the data fields, and the field_value_iter method facilitates easy iteration over selected data fields.

Example 13-21   *Sastre SDK Python Script*

```
import os, getpass
from cisco_sdwan.base.rest_api import Rest
from cisco_sdwan.base.models_vmanage import DeviceControlConnections


device = "10.0.10.1"

manager = os.environ.get("MANAGER_ADDR") or "manager.ciscopress.com"
username = os.environ.get("MANAGER_USER") or input ("Username: ")
password = os.environ.get("MANAGER_PASS") or getpass.getpass('Password: ')

f0,f1,f2,f3,f4='peer_type','system_ip','local_color','remote_color','state'

with Rest(f"https://{manager}", username, password) as api:
    control_conns = DeviceControlConnections.get(api, deviceId=device)

    # self-documenting API: extract field descriptions from API response
    head=control_conns.field_info(f0, f1, f2, f3, f4)
    print(f"{head[0]:11}{head[1]:15}{head[2]:14}{head[3]:14}{head[4]}")

    # Iterate through control connections
    for row in control_conns.field_value_iter(f0, f1, f2, f3, f4):
        print(f"{row.peer_type:11}{row.system_ip:15}"
                f"{row.local_color:14}{row.remote_color:14}{row.state:5}")
```

Example 13-22 presents the output of this script.

Example 13-22   *Sastre SDK Python Script Output*

```
Peer Type  Peer System IP Local Color   Remote Color  State
vsmart     1.1.1.102      mpls          biz-internet  up
vsmart     1.1.1.103      mpls          biz-internet  up
vsmart     1.1.1.102      biz-internet  biz-internet  up
vsmart     1.1.1.103      biz-internet  biz-internet  up
vmanage    1.1.1.101      biz-internet  default       up
```

When Sastre is used as a standalone CLI application, one of its most beneficial features is configuration backup. Sastre can perform a full SD-WAN backup in the API's JSON format, including all the configuration elements, such as templates, policies, and certificates, and it can also save running configurations of all SD-WAN devices in the fabric. This functionality is invaluable for maintaining configuration snapshots and tracking device configuration changes over time.

For more information about Sastre, you can visit the SD-WAN API documentation site at https://developer.cisco.com/docs/sdwan/overview and the official GitHub repository at https://github.com/CiscoDevNet/sastre.

Key Topic

Cisco Catalyst SD-WAN Infrastructure as Code

Infrastructure as code (IaC) in networking is a practice that transforms the management and provisioning of network infrastructure resources. Instead of relying on manual configurations through traditional CLI or GUI methods, IaC uses machine-readable configuration files to define, deploy, and manage network configurations, devices, and services as programmable resources.

This approach aligns with the broader DevOps philosophy, fostering collaboration, automation, and agility in network operations. By adopting IaC, organizations can apply software development principles such as version control, automated testing, and continuous integration/continuous deployment (CI/CD) to their network management processes. This shift enables faster, more predictable, and more scalable deployments while reducing manual errors and improving overall efficiency.

In the context of Cisco Catalyst SD-WAN, IaC enables organizations to automate the deployment and management of SD-WAN infrastructure components, including WAN Edge routers, SD-WAN Control Components, policies, templates, and configuration groups. Instead of using manual configurations or direct APIs for each operation, organizations can use tools like Terraform or Ansible to define their SD-WAN infrastructure as code and automate provisioning, configuration, and maintenance tasks.

Terraform and Ansible stand out as the two most popular tools for Cisco Catalyst SD-WAN IaC. Each of them serves a slightly different purpose and takes a distinct approach.

Ansible is often used for configuration management tasks, such as pushing configurations to SD-WAN devices or automating repetitive operational tasks. Some key features of Ansible include:

- Emphasis on simplicity and ease of use

- An imperative approach through Ansible playbooks, which describe actions to execute on target devices (for example, creating the user Alyx Vance and then assigning that user to the group netadmin) rather than the final state of the infrastructure

- A procedural approach in which tasks are executed sequentially on target devices

- Suitability for tasks that require intricate configurations or involve complex logic and conditional statements

Terraform, on the other hand, is typically used for infrastructure provisioning tasks, such as deploying new SD-WAN devices, configuring network connectivity, or deploying security policies. Primary features of Terraform include:

- Focus on declarative configuration and state management

- Use of a declarative language to describe the desired infrastructure state (for example, the presence of the Alyx Vance user, a member of the netadmin group), with Terraform managing the provisioning and orchestration of resources to achieve that state

- State management to track the current state of the infrastructure, allowing for easy updates and modifications without disrupting existing resources

- Suitability for provisioning and managing complex infrastructure environments, including multi-cloud setups and hybrid cloud deployments

Table 13-6 highlights the differences between Ansible and Terraform.

Table 13-6   Ansible and Terraform Comparison

Feature	Ansible	Terraform
Configuration	Describes actions to execute on target devices	Describes the desired infrastructure state
Approach	Procedural, imperative	Declarative
Language	YAML-based	HashiCorp Configuration Language (HCL)
State management	Manages infrastructure state during runtime	Manages state persistently
Use cases	Configuration management, automation tasks	Infrastructure provisioning, resource management
Strengths	Simplicity, ease of use, complex logic	Declarative configuration, state management

While both Ansible and Terraform support Cisco Catalyst SD-WAN automation, Terraform is often considered superior for IaC due to its declarative approach, infrastructure state management, and broad support for various infrastructure providers. Its ability to manage complex dependencies and orchestrate changes across multiple resources makes it ideal for automating SD-WAN deployments and ensuring consistency and reliability in network configurations.

Ultimately, the choice between Ansible and Terraform depends on the specific requirements of the SD-WAN deployment and the preferred approach to infrastructure automation and management. Some organizations may choose to leverage both tools in combination to capitalize on their respective strengths for different aspects of the SD-WAN environment.

Using Ansible with Cisco Catalyst SD-WAN

For those comfortable working directly with SD-WAN APIs, the simplest way to interact with them in Ansible is by using the built-in uri module, which implements standard interactions with HTTP/HTTPS web servers, as demonstrated in Example 13-23. The output has the same JSON structure as the output from a direct SD-WAN API call.

Example 13-23   *Using an SD-WAN API with the Ansible uri Module*

```
---
- name: Demo Ansible Playbook for API interactions
  hosts: localhost
  gather_facts: no
  vars:
    manager_address:  "{{ lookup('ansible.builtin.env', 'MANAGER_ADDR') }}"
    manager_username: "{{ lookup('ansible.builtin.env', 'MANAGER_USER') }}"
    manager_password: "{{ lookup('ansible.builtin.env', 'MANAGER_PASS') }}"

  tasks:
  - name: Get Cookie
    uri:
      url: https://{{ manager_address }}/j_security_check
      method: POST
      body:
        j_username: "{{ manager_username }}"
        j_password: "{{ manager_password }}"
      body_format: form-urlencoded
      return_content: yes
      validate_certs: no
      status_code: 200
    register: auth_result

  - name: Obtain List of Devices
    uri:
      url: https://{{ manager_address }}/dataservice/device
      method: GET
      headers:
        Cookie: "{{ auth_result.set_cookie }}"
      status_code: 200
      return_content: yes
      validate_certs: no
    register: output

  - debug:
      var: "{{ output.content }}.data"
```

Many users prefer to avoid the intricacies involved in manually crafting API calls and instead use specialized Ansible modules tailored for SD-WAN tasks. These modules offer simplified syntax, improved error handling, enhanced maintainability, and reduced overall complexity.

Numerous third-party Ansible modules are available. However, Cisco has developed and provides support for several repositories containing specialized modules that enable users to create specific automation workflows for Cisco Catalyst SD-WAN:

- **ansible-collection-sdwan:** This collection leverages the other two repositories to enable users to create custom workflows or use common ones, such as for full deployment of SD-WAN Control Components and software WAN Edge routers, onboarding configuration, and software upgrades on existing SD-WAN networks. See https://github.com/cisco-open/ansible-collection-sdwan.

- **ansible-collection-sdwan-deployment:** This repository provides the underlying modules needed to deploy and tear down Cisco Catalyst SD-WAN infrastructure on AWS Cloud. See https://github.com/cisco-open/ansible-collection-sdwan-deployment.

- **ansible-collection-catalystwan:** This repository contains Ansible modules that help users automate SD-WAN tasks like device onboarding and initial configuration, as well as post-bring-up operations. See https://github.com/cisco-open/ansible-collection-catalystwan.

These collections showcase Ansible's modularity and the benefits of using roles, custom modules, and collections for automating network operations. They are valuable resources for organizations seeking to implement infrastructure as code within their networks and adopt a more agile and DevOps-oriented approach to network management.

Example 13-24 illustrates the use of the ansible-collection-catalystwan collection for executing two tasks: health checks and data collection.

Example 13-24 *Using the ansible-collection-catalystwan Ansible Collection*

```
---
- name: Demo Ansible Playbook for cisco.catalystwan module
  hosts: localhost
  gather_facts: false
  vars:
    manager_address:  "{{ lookup('ansible.builtin.env', 'MANAGER_ADDR') }}"
    manager_username: "{{ lookup('ansible.builtin.env', 'MANAGER_USER') }}"
    manager_password: "{{ lookup('ansible.builtin.env', 'MANAGER_PASS') }}"

  tasks:
    - name: "1: Health check: verify all BFD sessions are up"
      cisco.catalystwan.health_checks:
        check_type: bfd
        filters:
          device_ip: "10.0.10.1"
        manager_authentication:
          url: "{{ manager_address }}"
```

```
          username: "{{ manager_username }}"
          password: "{{ manager_password }}"

    - name: "2: Obtain List of Devices"
      cisco.catalystwan.devices_info:
        device_category: vedges
        manager_authentication:
          url: "{{ manager_address }}"
          username: "{{ manager_username }}"
          password: "{{ manager_password }}"
      register: edge_devices

    - debug:
        var: edge_devices.devices
```

SD-WAN Infrastructure as Code with Terraform

Cisco's Terraform SDWAN provider is specifically designed for automating the deployment, configuration, and management of Cisco Catalyst SD-WAN environments with Terraform. Acting as a connector between Terraform and Cisco SD-WAN, this provider allows network administrators to easily define the desired state of their SD-WAN environment, including devices, templates, policies, and configurations—all through Terraform's declarative configuration language.

The Terraform configuration snippet in Example 13-25 shows the basic setup of an SD-WAN environment. It includes some of the SD-WAN configuration resources, such as the feature template resource, the device template resource, and the sdwan_attach_feature_device_template resource that is responsible for keeping per-device variables values and for attaching templates and pushing configuration to WAN Edge devices.

In this example, you can see how Terraform establishes a relationship between resources and tracks dependencies between resources. For instance, Terraform understands that a device template cannot be created until its referenced feature templates are created. Furthermore, when a change is made to a resource, Terraform examines dependencies, plans, and executes updates accordingly, including pushing the configuration where necessary, to ensure correct propagation of changes throughout the SD-WAN infrastructure. This dependency-tracking mechanism allows Terraform to efficiently manage and reliably update infrastructure resources in a predictable manner.

This example shows only a single feature template for brevity. We've provided the full configuration in the book's public repository, located at https://github.com/sdwanbook/code, to enable you to explore and implement comprehensive SD-WAN setups using Terraform.

Example 13-25 *SD-WAN Configuration with Terraform*

```
resource "sdwan_cisco_system_feature_template" "Global_System" {
  name = "Global_System"
  description = "Global_System"
  device_types = ["vedge-C8000V"]
```

```
  console_baud_rate = "9600"
  hostname_variable = "system_host_name"
  site_id_variable = "system_site_id"
  system_ip_variable = "system_system_IP"
}


resource "sdwan_feature_device_template" "DC1_Edge" {
  name = "DC1_Edge"
  description = "WAN edge routers in Primary Data Center"
  device_role = "sdwan-edge"
  device_type = "vedge-C8000V"
  general_templates =   [
    {
      id: sdwan_cisco_system_feature_template.Global_System.id,
      type: sdwan_cisco_system_feature_template.Global_System.template_type,
      version: sdwan_cisco_system_feature_template.Global_System.version,
    },
.......... Output omitted for brevity ...........
  ]
}


resource "sdwan_attach_feature_device_template" "DC1_Edge" {
  id = sdwan_feature_device_template.DC1_Edge.id
  version = sdwan_feature_device_template.DC1_Edge.version
  devices = [
    {
      id = "C8K-PAYG-928-798b-4276-a4b3-2a649a3d292f"
      variables = {
        system_host_name = "DC1-Edge1"
        system_site_id = "10"
        system_system_IP = "10.0.10.1"
        vpn0_gig1_ipv4_address = "209.165.201.1/27"
        vpn0_gig2_ipv4_address = "192.168.20.1/24"
        bgp_neighbor_address = "172.16.10.2"
        bgp_neighbor_remote_as = "65010"
        bgp_router_id = "10.0.10.1"
        vpn10_gig3_ipv4_address = "172.16.10.1/30"
        vpn512_if_description = "Configured via API"
        vpn512_if_name = "GigabitEthernet4"
        vpn512_if_ipv4_address = "192.168.1.10/24"
      },
    },
  ]
}
```

For further guidance on using the Terraform SDWAN provider, see the comprehensive documentation available at Terraform registry site: https://registry.terraform.io/providers/CiscoDevNet/sdwan/latest/docs.

Summary

This chapter provides a focused overview of network programmability in the context of Cisco Catalyst SD-WAN deployments. It provides an overview of SD-WAN APIs, including guides, error handling, and documentation. The chapter also provides practical API usage scenarios covering authentication, inventory retrieval, monitoring, and configuration management, and provides Python code examples to show practical applications.

This chapter also discusses the infrastructure as code (IaC) approach and its relevance to Cisco SD-WAN deployments. It explores the use of Ansible and Terraform as powerful tools for automating deployment, configuration, and management tasks in SD-WAN environments. By showcasing real-world examples and code snippets, the chapter equips you with the knowledge and skills necessary to leverage programmability effectively in your SD-WAN infrastructure, promoting efficiency, scalability, and agility in network operations.

Review All Key Topics

Review the most important topics in the chapter, noted with the Key Topic icon in the outer margin of the page. Table 13-7 lists these key topics and the page number on which each is found.

Table 13-7   Key Topics

Key Topic Element	Description	Page
Section	Cisco Catalyst SD-WAN APIs as REST APIs	553
Section	Cisco Catalyst SD-WAN API Authentication	564
Section	Cisco Catalyst SD-WAN API Categories	568
Section	Cisco Catalyst SD-WAN Infrastructure as Code	586

Key Terms

Define the following key terms from this chapter and check your answers in the glossary:

Ansible, infrastructure as code (IaC), network programmability, REST API, Terraform

Chapter Review Questions

1. What kind of APIs are Cisco Catalyst SD-WAN APIs?

    a. SOAP

    b. REST

    c. RPC

    d. WORK

2. What communication protocol would you use to interact with Cisco Catalyst SD-WAN APIs?

    a. Telnet

    b. SSH

    c. HTTP

    d. WORK

3. When interacting with SD-WAN APIs, which HTTP methods can be used? (Choose two.)

    a. GET

    b. PULL

    c. PUSH

    d. PUT

4. Which of the following is a valid SD-WAN API URL?

    a. https://manager.ciscopress.com/data/admin/user

    b. http://manager.ciscopress.com/dataservice/admin/user

    c. https://manager.ciscopress.com/dataservice/admin/user

    d. http://manager.ciscopress.com/data/service/admin/user

5. Which HTTP response code indicates a successful SD-WAN API request?

    a. 201

    b. 302

    c. 403

    d. 503

6. True or false: The SD-WAN Manager GUI is a standalone web application that uses SD-WAN APIs to perform its functions.

    a. True

    b. False

7. Which of the following is not a valid SD-WAN API category?

    a. Certificate management

    b. Configuration

    c. Monitoring

    d. Assurance

8. True or false: An SD-WAN API call to attach a template to a WAN Edge device returns the status of the configuration push after its completion.

    a. True

    b. False

9. How is network configuration managed with the infrastructure as code (IaC) approach?

    a. Via the CLI

    b. Via the GUI

    c. Via machine-readable configuration files

    d. Via PowerPoint slides

10. What is true about IaC tools?

  a. Ansible configuration typically defines the final state of the infrastructure.

  b. Ansible uses HCL as the configuration language.

  c. Terraform does not track the state of the infrastructure.

  d. Terraform uses declarative language to describe the desired state.

References

Public repository for the code used in this chapter: https://github.com/sdwanbook/code.

"Cisco Catalyst SD-WAN API," https://developer.cisco.com/sdwan/.

"Cisco Catalyst SD-WAN Manager API," https://developer.cisco.com/docs/sdwan/.

Sastre tool repository: https://github.com/CiscoDevNet/sastre.

"Terraform SDWAN Provider," https://registry.terraform.io/providers/CiscoDevNet/sdwan/latest/docs.

CHAPTER 14

Cisco Catalyst SD-WAN Monitoring and Operations

This chapter covers the following topics:

- **SD-WAN Manager Monitoring Tools:** This section covers built-in SD-WAN Manager tools and mechanisms that allow you to monitor the entire SD-WAN overlay network and its individual components.

- **SD-WAN Manager Troubleshooting Tools:** This section discusses the tools that can be used to verify and troubleshoot the operation of SD-WAN fabric components. It also covers Network Wide Path Insight (NWPI), an analytical instrument inside SD-WAN Manager that offers extensive visibility and insights into the SD-WAN deployment.

- **SD-WAN Monitoring with ThousandEyes:** This section provides an overview of Cisco ThousandEyes and examines how SD-WAN Manager can streamline the deployment and configuration of ThousandEyes Enterprise Agents.

- **SD-WAN Analytics Overview:** This section provides an overview of SD-WAN Analytics (formerly called vAnalytics) and explains how it can be used for SD-WAN monitoring.

Throughout the lifecycle of any IT solution, administrators need to be able to verify the initial deployment of products and their components, perform day-N monitoring, identify opportunities for optimization and improvement, and sometimes even troubleshoot the system because something does not work as expected. With Cisco Catalyst SD-WAN, a variety of both built-in and external tools provide a comprehensive overview of the current deployment status and help to identify potential issues and points of improvement.

This chapter discusses the main tools that are used for monitoring and troubleshooting Catalyst SD-WAN deployments. The goal of this chapter is not to cover specific troubleshooting scenarios but to equip you with the most commonly used tools and solutions that you can use in many different situations. In earlier chapters, you have already learned about specific tips and commands for verifying the deployment of individual SD-WAN features and components. For more detailed guidance, refer to the official Cisco documentation and configuration guides related to the specific features you want to configure or troubleshoot.

SD-WAN Manager Monitoring Tools

Like many other solutions with a centralized management plane, Cisco Catalyst SD-WAN assumes that the vast majority of day-to-day operations will be performed on the management controller and not on every network device individually. As we discussed previously, the Catalyst SD-WAN management plane component is SD-WAN Manager (previously known as vManage). In addition to all the configuration features we have already discussed throughout this book, SD-WAN Manager has multiple embedded tools for monitoring and troubleshooting.

Monitoring Dashboards

The main monitoring dashboard is the default landing page that you see upon logging in to SD-WAN Manager (see Figure 14-1). You can also access it from the **Monitor > Overview**. You can customize the home page appearance by choosing between *Dashboard*, *Table*, *Heatmap*, and *Geomap* views (see callout 1 in Figure 14-1). You can also filter the displayed information based on the resource group, if configured, or based on the specific site (see callout 2 in Figure 14-1).

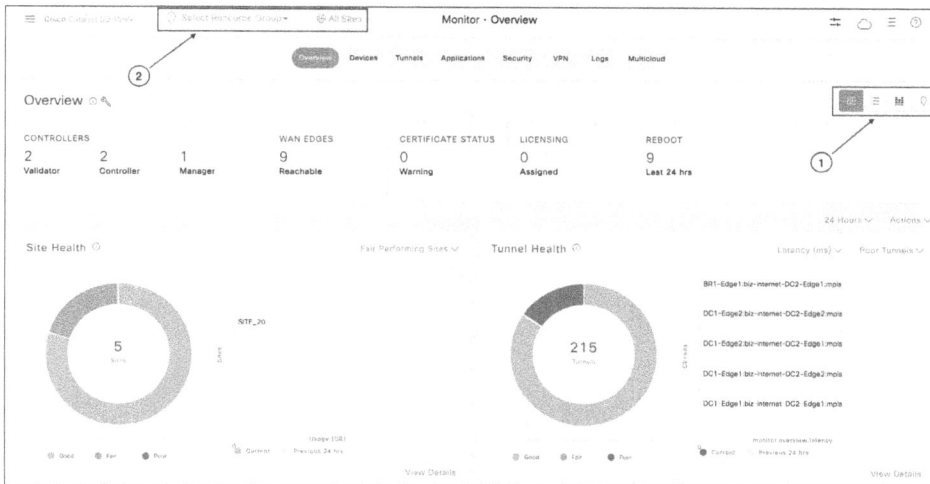

Figure 14-1 *The Monitor Dashboard in SD-WAN Manager*

At the top of the Monitor dashboard shown in Figure 14-1, you can see different tabs: Overview, Devices, Tunnels, Applications, Security, VPN, Logs, and Multicloud. As you'll see in the following sections, each of these tabs provides a different dashboard view.

Overview Dashboard

The Overview dashboard displays the overall health status of the SD-WAN deployment, including SD-WAN Control Components (SD-WAN Managers, Controllers, and Validators) and WAN Edge devices.

You can add, remove, or re-arrange the dashlets on this page. To do so, click **Actions > Edit Dashboard** in the upper-right corner. SD-WAN Manager allows you to add the following dashlets:

- **Site Health:** Displays the overall health status of the site, including the device health, tunnel health, and application health, on a per-site basis.

- **Tunnel Health:** Displays the health of SD-WAN and Secure Internet Gateway (SIG) tunnels, based on the tunnel state and the average latency, loss, and jitter metrics.

- **WAN Edge Health:** Displays the overall health status of the WAN Edge routers based on their CPU and memory load, reachability, per-tunnel Bidirectional Forwarding Detection (BFD) status, and TLOC status.

- **Application Health:** Displays per-site application health metrics and bandwidth usage, as well as application QoE (Quality of Experience) values for each path.

- **Transport Health:** Displays the aggregated average loss, latency, and jitter for all links and all combinations of colors.

- **Site BFD Connectivity:** Displays the state of per-site data connections based on BFD sessions.

- **Transport Interface Distribution:** Displays the interface usage in the past 24 hours for all WAN interfaces in VPN 0.

- **WAN Edge Inventory:** Displays an inventory of all devices in the network, with their states.

- **Top Applications:** Displays SAIE (SD-WAN Application Intelligence Engine) flow information for the traffic transiting WAN Edge routers in the overlay network.

- **Application-Aware Routing:** Displays the worst tunnels based on the specified criteria, such as loss, latency, or jitter.

- **WAN Edge Management:** Displays the WAN Edge router configuration management types, such as Device Templates, Configuration Groups, or unlocked devices, as well as how many devices are managed by each method.

Figure 14-2 shows an example of a customized Overview dashboard appearance. Many dashlets allow you to change the output criteria, such as to show good, fair, and poor devices and sites or display health status based on the loss, latency, or jitter. Also, you can click **View Details** on a particular dashlet to discover more information related to it.

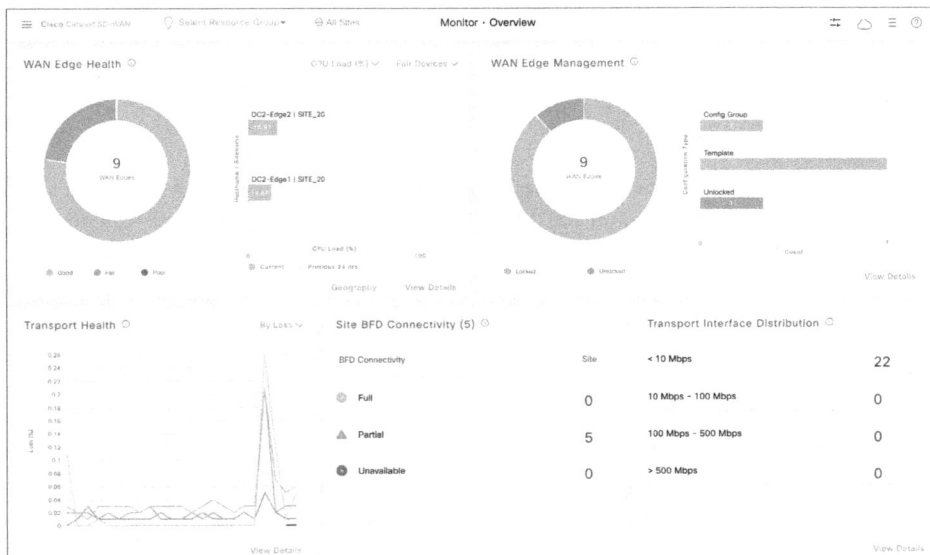

Figure 14-2   *Dashlets on the Monitor Dashboard*

If you configure WAN Edge routers using Configuration Groups, SD-WAN Manager can automatically create and display the site topology, as shown in Figure 14-3. To get this view, open the Overview dashboard, select the specific site—in this example, SITE_102 (see callout 1 in Figure 14-3)—and select the button called out with the number 2 in Figure 14-3. SD-WAN Manager shows the network topology with connection details such as VPNs, interfaces, and colors. If a device has any warnings or health issues, you see notifications here.

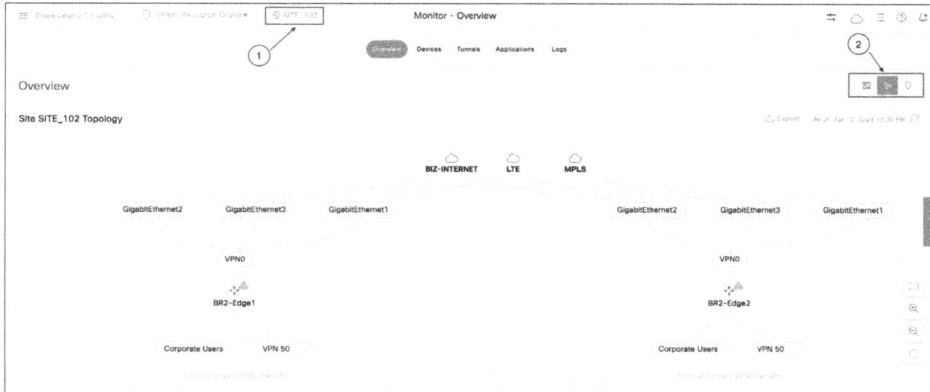

Figure 14-3 *Site Topology on the Monitor Dashboard*

By clicking on a device (BR2-Edge2 in this example), you get immediate access to details about the device and its performance, as shown in Figure 14-4. You can also view the events and alarms associated with this device and open the device troubleshooting tools (which are discussed later in this chapter).

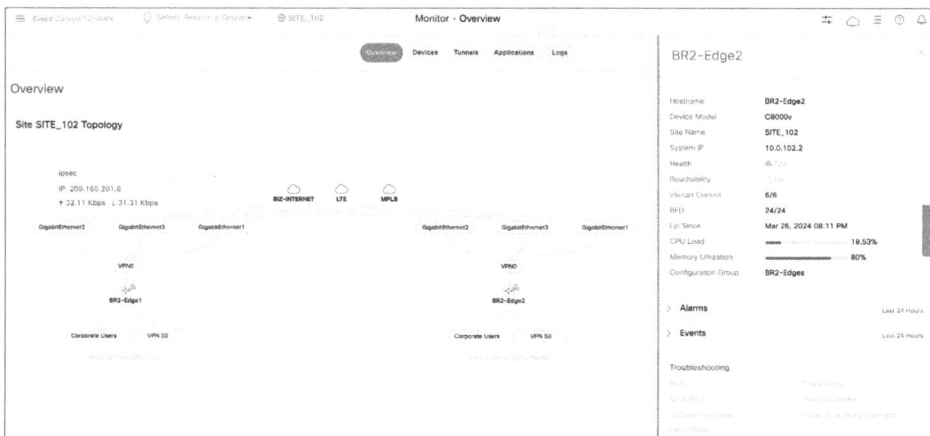

Figure 14-4 *WAN Edge Device Details from the Topology View*

Device Dashboard

The Device dashboard can be found under **Monitor > Devices** in SD-WAN Manager. As shown in Figure 14-5, this dashboard displays the status of all SD-WAN devices (including SD-WAN Control Components and WAN Edge routers), as well the certificates and device licensing status. On this dashboard, you can open the device details, go to the alarms or events associated with particular devices, issue real-time **show** commands on the remote devices, or run troubleshooting tools (which are covered later in this chapter).

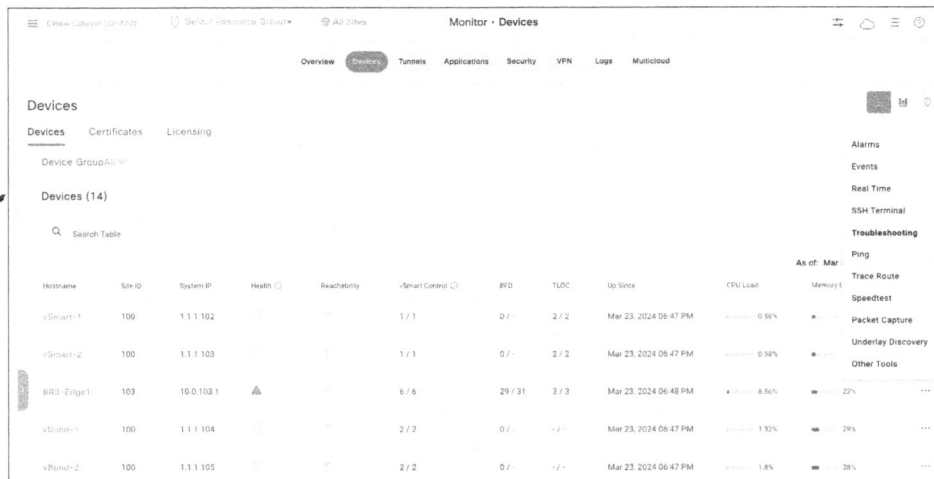

Figure 14-5   *The Device Dashboard in SD-WAN Manager*

Here you can see a column titled Health, which lists the overall device health status as good, fair, or poor, based on device reachability, control plane health, data plane health, and CPU and memory status. Table 14-1 presents the possible device health status values and the metric criteria.

Table 14-1   WAN Edge Health Metrics

State	Reachability	Control Plane	Data Plane	Resources
Good (All conditions are true.)	Device Reachable	All Control Connections Up	All BFD Tunnels Up and All TLOCs Up	CPU Usage < 75% Memory Usage < 75%
Fair (At least one condition is true.)	Device Reachable	>= 1 Control Connection Up	>= 1 BFD Tunnel Up and >= 1 TLOC Up	CPU Usage > 75% Memory Usage > 75%
Poor (At least one condition is true.)	Device Not Reachable	No Control Connections Up	No BFD Tunnels Up or No TLOCs Up	CPU Usage > 90% Memory Usage > 90%

On the global Devices dashboard, you can click on a specific device to open the Device 360 report. Device 360 is a detailed page that provides a comprehensive view of the current device state. As an example, Figure 14-6 shows the current control connections state for one of the WAN Edge routers. In Device 360, you can also issue real-time commands on the remote device or run troubleshooting tools such as **ping** or **traceroute**. (Device 360 is covered in more detail later in this chapter.)

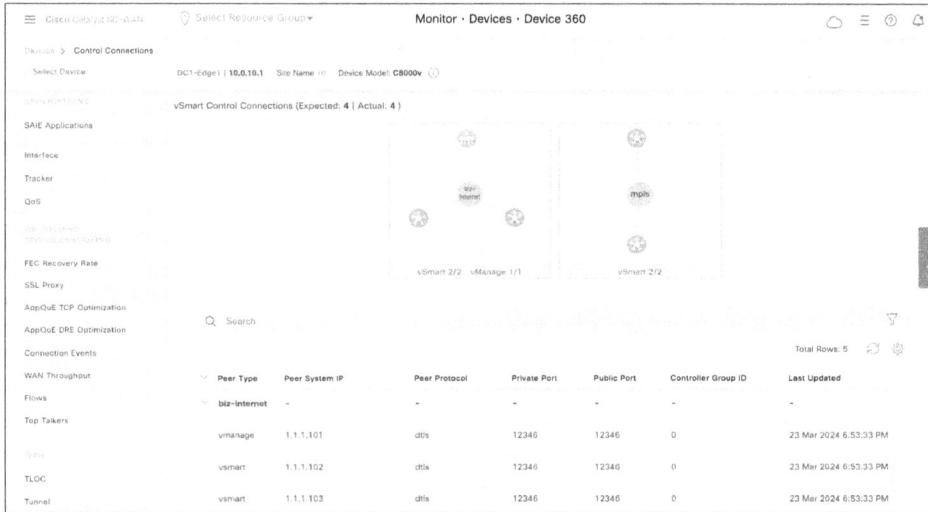

Figure 14-6 *WAN Edge Control Connections in Device 360*

Tunnels Dashboard

The Tunnels dashboard (available under **Monitor > Tunnels** in SD-WAN Manager) shows the state and health status of the SD-WAN tunnels, as well as tunnels to the SIG. Figure 14-7 shows the Tunnels dashboard.

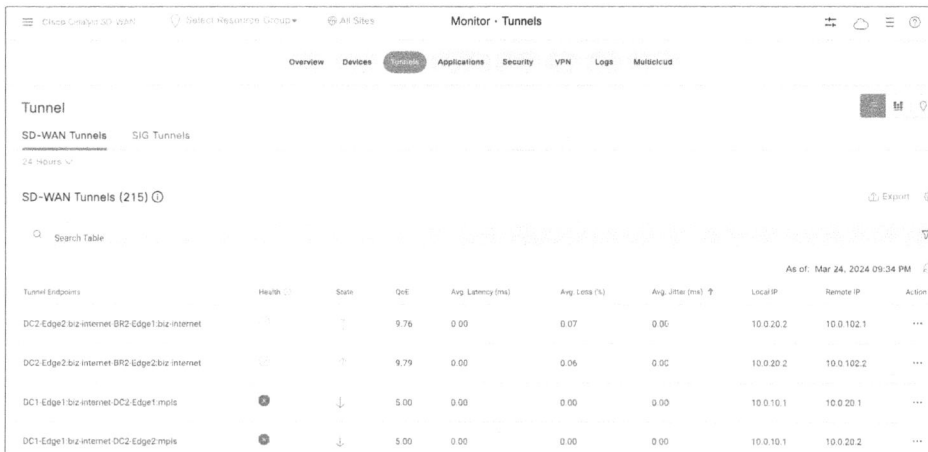

Figure 14-7 *The Tunnels Dashboard in SD-WAN Manager*

SD-WAN tunnel health is calculated based on the tunnel state and QoE. The QoE score is calculated based on the average loss and latency over the specific tunnel. The tunnel health metric values are provided in Table 14-2.

NOTE   The process of measuring and calculating the QoE score, which is the same for all use cases, is explained in Chapter 12, "Cisco Catalyst SD-WAN Cloud OnRamp."

Table 14-2   SD-WAN Tunnel Health Metrics

Health	Quality of Experience Score	State
Good (All conditions are true.)	>= 8.0 QoE	Up
Fair (All conditions are true.)	>= 5.0 QoE	Up
Poor (At least one condition is true.)	< 5 QoE	Down

From the Tunnels dashboard, you can open the *Tunnel Health Troubleshooting* tool under the Action column. As shown in Figure 14-8, this tool provides more details and a historical view of the tunnel health between the selected WAN Edge routers and the local/remote color combination.

Figure 14-8   *Tunnel Health Troubleshooting in SD-WAN Manager*

Applications Dashboard

The Applications dashboard shows the average QoE metrics within the past 30 minutes, collected from all sites and all monitored applications. This dashboard can be found under **Monitor > Applications** in SD-WAN Manager.

Note that the application health data is collected only from the WAN Edge devices configured via the configuration groups with the *application-performance* parcel enabled. To enable this parcel, go to **Configuration > Configuration Groups** and open the specific configuration group. Under **System Profile**, click **Add Feature** and select the feature type **Performance Monitoring**. In the Application Performance Monitoring tab, enable monitoring globally. You can also select the specific applications to be monitored (see Figure 14-9). (Chapter 4, "Onboarding and Provisioning," provides more details on how to configure and deploy configuration groups.)

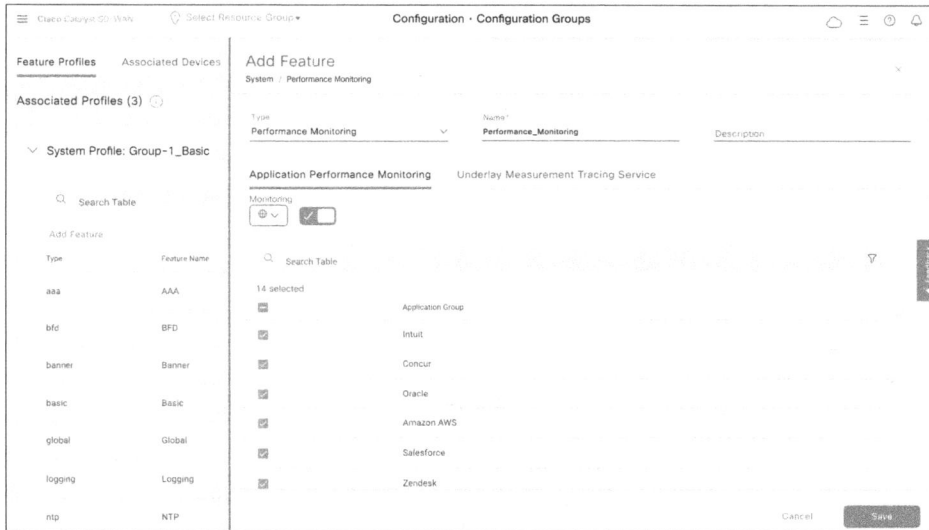

Figure 14-9   *Adding the Application Performance Parcel*

Figure 14-10 shows the Applications dashboard. In this example, you can see three applications: ms-services, ms-update, and google-services.

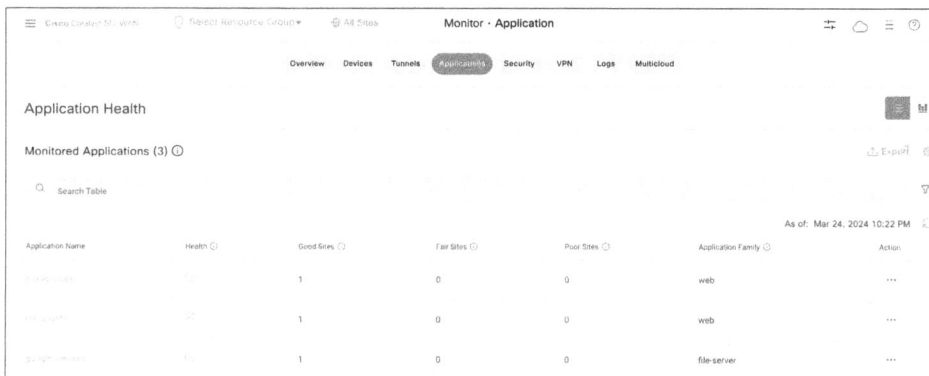

Figure 14-10   *The Applications Dashboard in SD-WAN Manager*

You can view the Application QoE details for a specific site by clicking the application name or by clicking **View Details** in the Action column. Figure 14-11 shows an example of QoE details for the ms-update application accessed from the DC2 site (site ID 20).

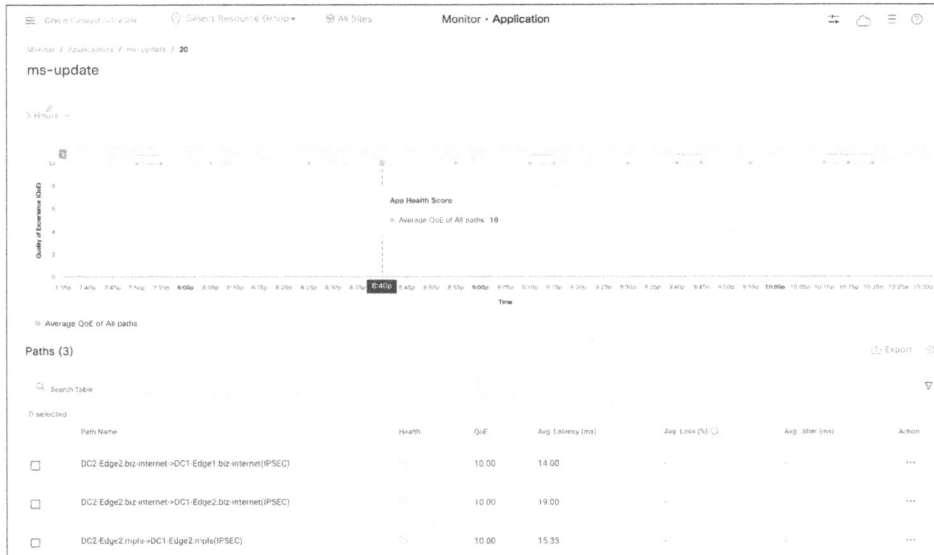

Figure 14-11 *Per-Site Application Health Details in SD-WAN Manager*

Security Dashboard

On the Security dashboard (which you reach by selecting **Monitor > Security** in SD-WAN Manager), you can view the current state of and historical data for all security features, including next-generation firewall, URL filtering, SIG, intrusion prevention, and Advanced Malware Protection. Figure 14-12 shows a snapshot of the Security dashboard. As with many other dashboards in SD-WAN Manager, you can customize the Security dashboard and dynamically add, remove, or reorder the dashlets as needed.

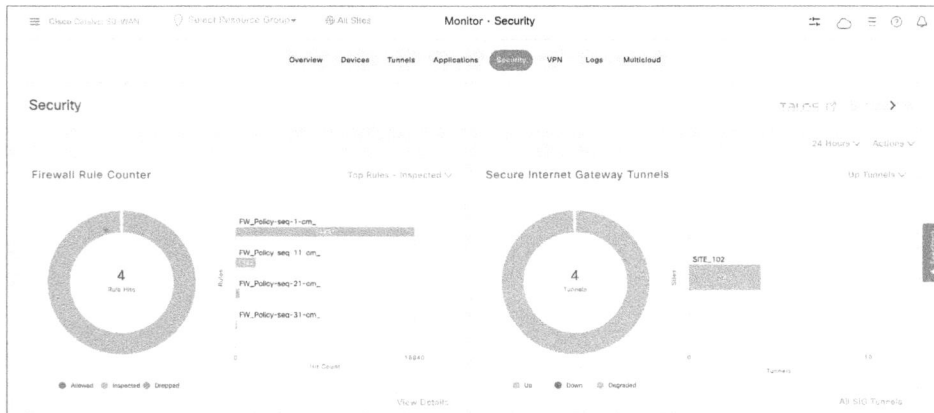

Figure 14-12 *The Security Dashboard in SD-WAN Manager*

VPN Dashboard

The VPN Dashboard (which you open by selecting **Monitor > VPN** in SD-WAN Manager) provides general information about the health of WAN Edge devices, their reachability from SD-WAN Manager, site BFD connectivity, and Top Applications (see Figure 14-13). By default, this information is displayed for all VPNs inside the entire SD-WAN fabric.

If VPN groups are configured, you can filter the output for a specific VPN group or groups. (See Chapter 11, "Cisco Catalyst SD-WAN Security," for details about VPN groups.)

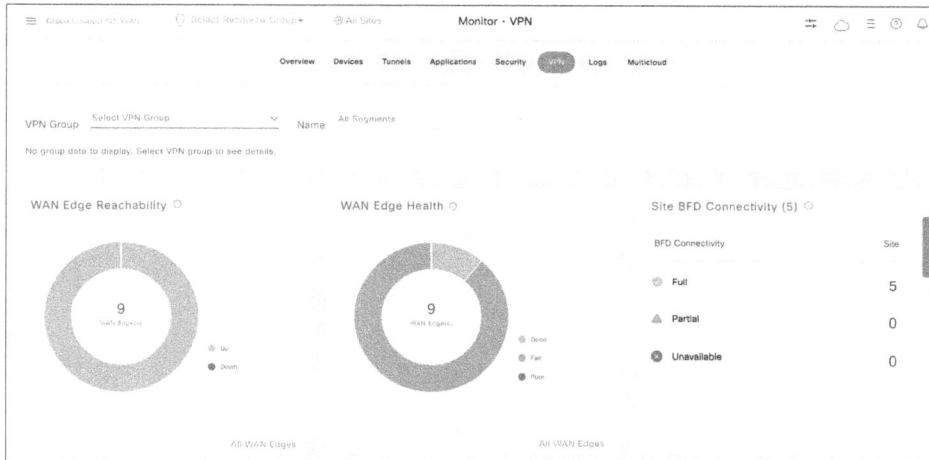

Figure 14-13   *The VPN Dashboard in SD-WAN Manager*

Logs Dashboard

When something happens on an individual WAN Edge device in the overlay network, that device sends a report about the event to SD-WAN Manager. An example of such event might be a change of OMP peer state, BFD state, interface state, BGP peer state, or policy updates.

Based on their severity and their impact on the overlay network, events are classified as follows:

- **Critical:** Indicates that action needs to be taken immediately.

- **Major:** Indicates that the problem needs immediate attention but it is not critical enough to bring down the entire network.

- **Minor:** Is informational only.

Upon receiving event notifications from devices, SD-WAN Manager filters them, correlates the related events, and consolidates major and critical events into alarms. Based on the seriousness of the alarms, they can be classified into the following severities:

- **Critical (red):** Serious events that impair or shut down the overlay network operation

- **Major (yellow):** Serious events that affect but do not shut down the network operation

- **Medium (green):** Events that might impair the performance of a network function

- **Minor (blue):** Events that might diminish the performance of a network function

Both alarms and events can be found in the Logs dashboard (which you reach by selecting **Monitor > Logs** in SD-WAN Manager), as shown in Figure 14-14.

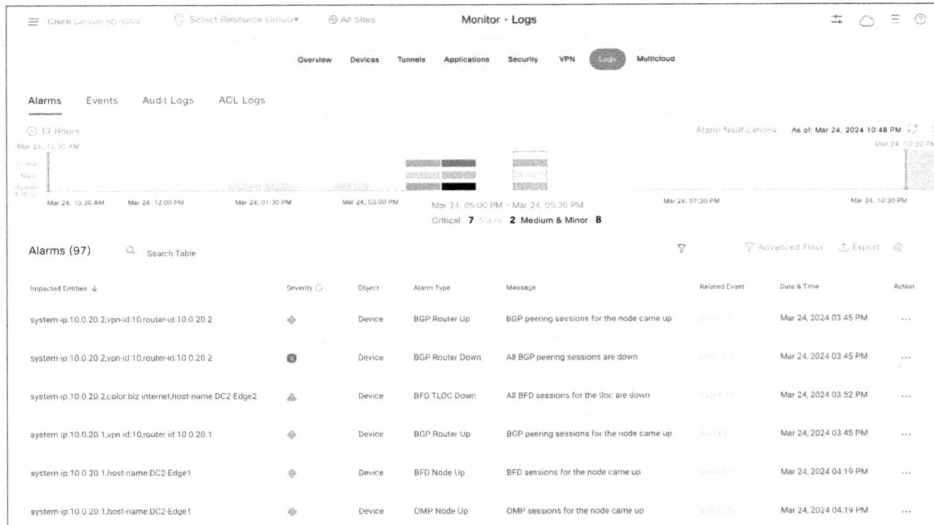

Figure 14-14   *The Alarms Dashboard in SD-WAN Manager*

You can also configure custom notifications about alarms. To enable this feature globally, go to **Administration > Settings > Alarm Notifications.** You can then configure notifications on the Alarms page (which you reach by selecting **Monitor > Logs > Alarms**). To do that, click **Alarm Notifications** in the upper-right corner and then click **Add Alarm Notifications.** In the window that appears, you can select specific Sites or Devices for which you want to enable notifications, select the alarm severity and, optionally, choose the alarm types to receive notification (via email or webhooks) about only specific events (see Figure 14-15).

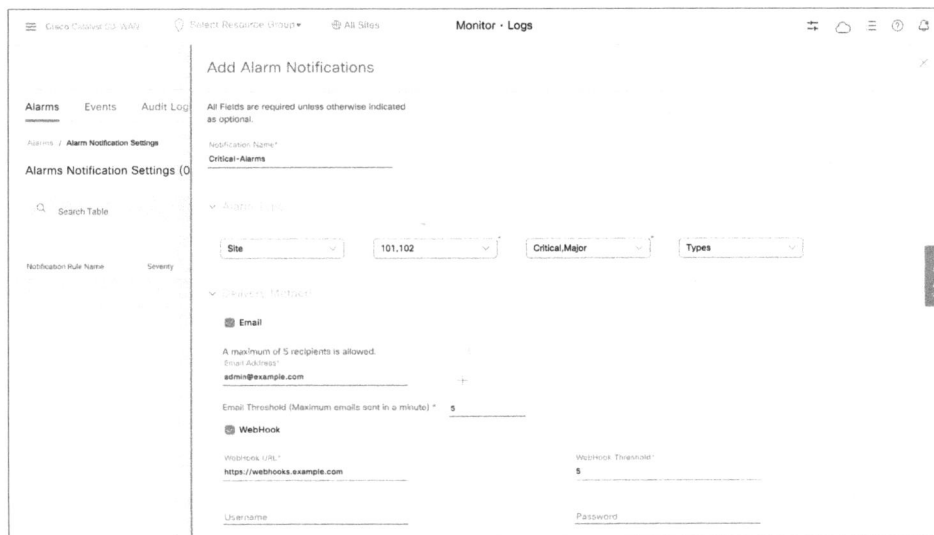

Figure 14-15   *Adding Alarm Notifications*

Many companies, especially those that have strict security requirements, keep historical log records and audit users' activity. Catalyst SD-WAN's detailed logging and audit capabilities allow you to track configuration changes, ensure network compliance with internal corporate standards or external regulations, and provide visibility into who deployed specific changes.

SD-WAN Manager allows a network administrator to audit logs under **Monitor > Logs > Audit Logs**. As shown in Figure 14-16, you can use the Audit Logs dashboard to see all actions performed by all users in SD-WAN Manager. The *Actions* column allows you to open audit log details for every record and examine specific activities in more detail.

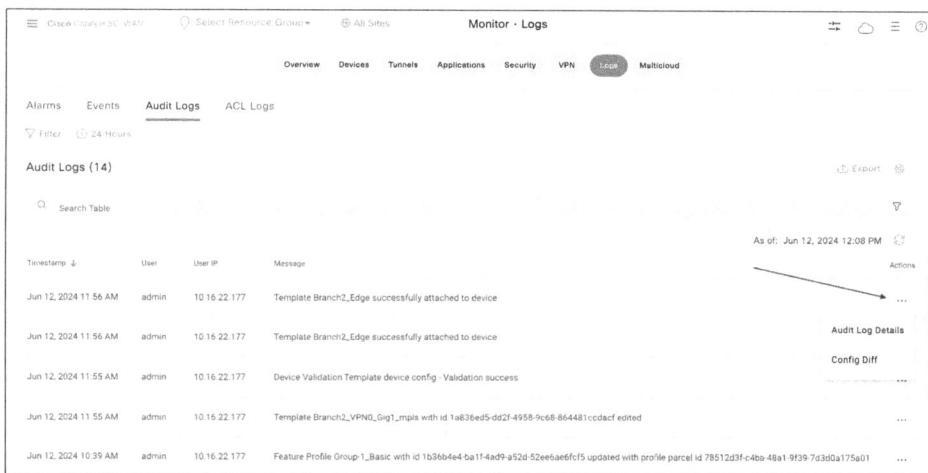

Figure 14-16   *The Audit Logs Dashboard in SD-WAN Manager*

The **Config Difference** option for audit logs shows the configuration changes that have been introduced via new or modified device templates or feature templates. You can review and compare the configuration in one window (using *Inline Diff* view) or in two windows (using *Side by Side* view). Figure 14-17 shows the Side by Side view of Config Difference. In this example, you can see that SD-WAN Manager shows the old and new configurations and highlights a change that was introduced in line 243 of the router configuration, where the state of the GigabitEthernet2 interface changed from **no shutdown** to **shutdown**.

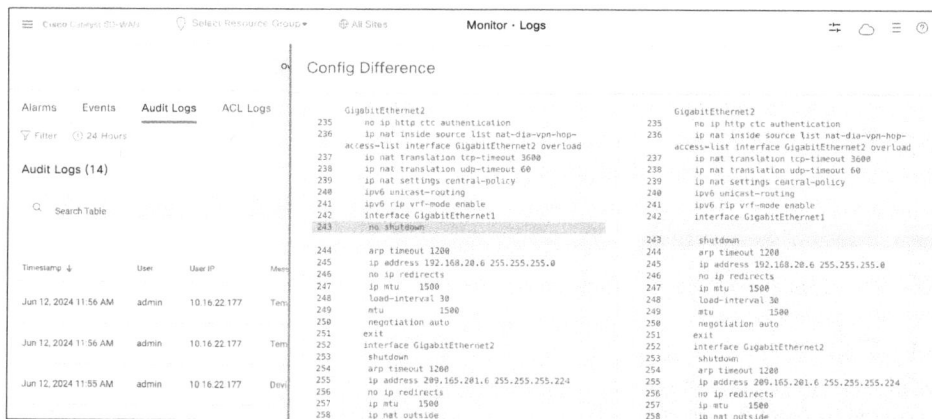

Figure 14-17   *Side-by-Side Config Difference in the Audit Logs Dashboard*

Multicloud Dashboard

The Multicloud dashboard (which you reach by selecting **Monitor > Multicloud** in SD-WAN Manager) shows a summary of the Cloud OnRamp for Multicloud connections (see Figure 14-18). On the main dashboard, you can find information about the Cloud OnRamp setup, such as different branch-to-cloud integrations or branch-to-branch connectivity via the interconnect provider. The dashboard displays information about the current cloud gateway state, connectivity between different SD-WAN sites, the tunnels state, and so on.

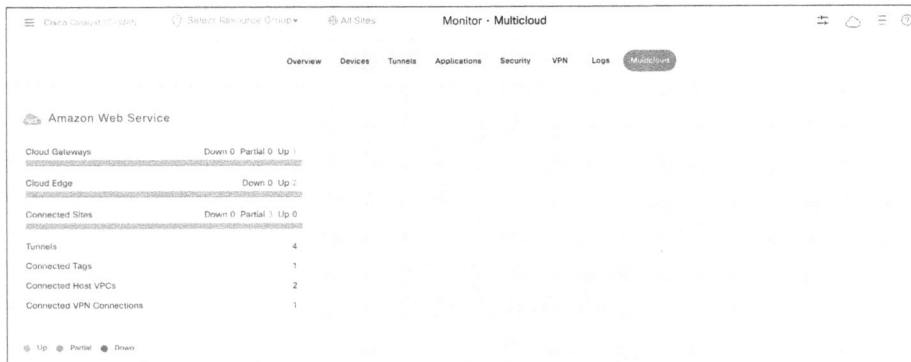

Figure 14-18   *The Multicloud Dashboard in SD-WAN Manager*

From the main Multicloud dashboard, you can open more detailed reports about specific sites, devices, and so on. Figure 14-19 shows an example of such a report. Here you can see the current health status of both cloud and on-premises branch devices, their reachability from SD-WAN Manager, any warnings, if present, and so on.

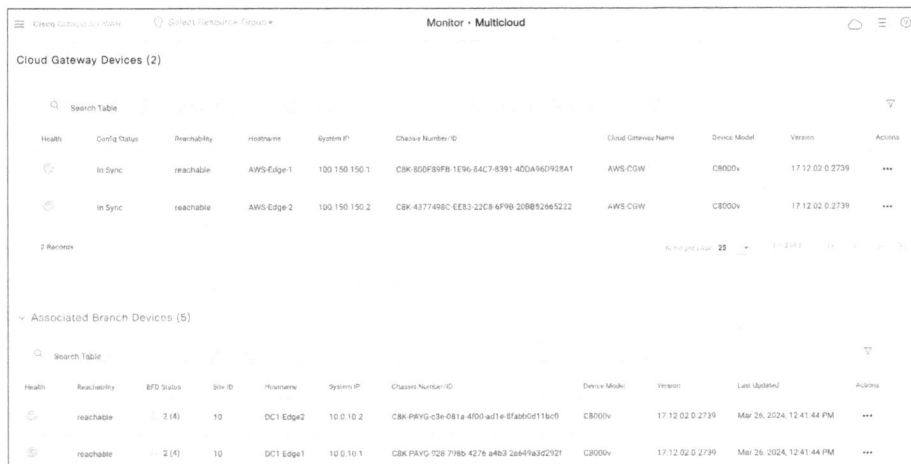

Figure 14-19   *Multicloud Dashboard: Device Details*

Reports

In addition to the live dashboards that are available in the SD-WAN Manager GUI, you can also generate reports for specific periods of time (such as most recent 7 or 30 days) to more easily view information about the status of the SD-WAN fabric or specific sites. In particular,

SD-WAN Manager allows you to generate an executive summary report, which is a multipage file that consolidates information from different dashboards.

You can initiate the report generation process by selecting **Reports > Report Templates** in SD-WAN Manager. During this process, as shown in Figure 14-20, you can define the schedule for this task; for example, you can generate a one-time report immediately or do it later at the specified time, or you can configure a recurring task that will be executed periodically. In addition, you can configure SD-WAN Manager to send the report via email.

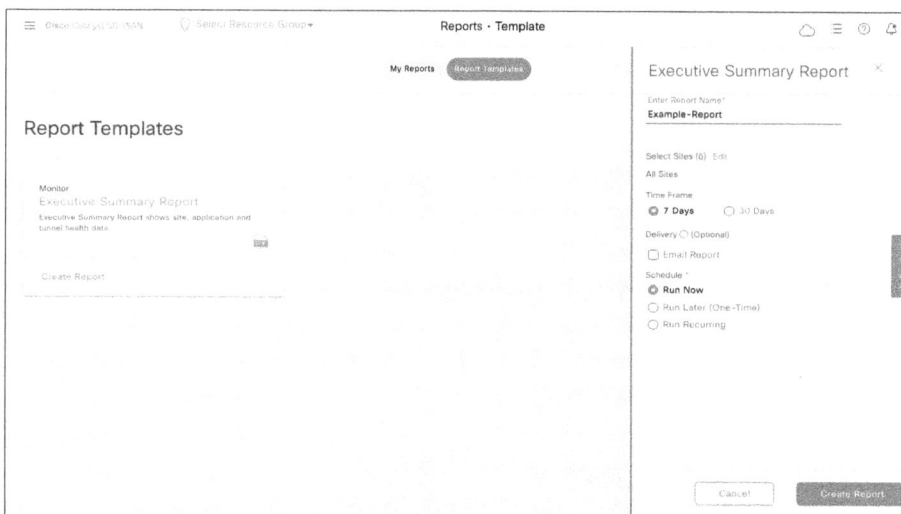

Figure 14-20   *Generating Reports in SD-WAN Manager*

Before generating a report, you can preview the template and get familiar with the information that will be included in the report. For example, Figure 14-21 shows a preview of the site summary from an executive summary report.

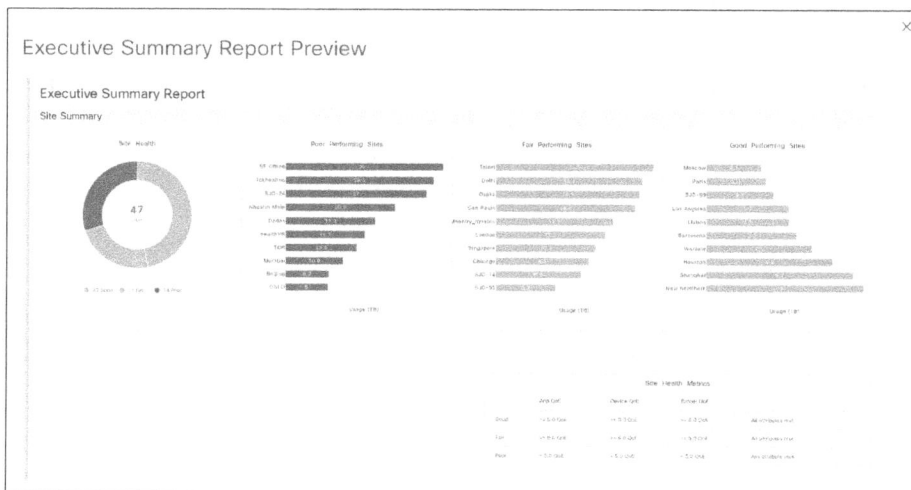

Figure 14-21   *Executive Summary Report Preview: Site Summary*

Once you have generated reports, you can find them under **Reports > My Reports,** as shown in Figure 14-22. On this page, you can verify and customize the existing schedule as well as download reports in PDF format.

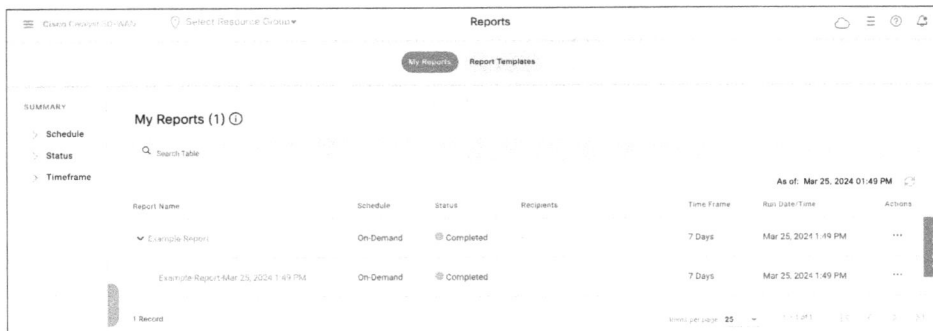

Figure 14-22   *My Reports Page in SD-WAN Manager*

SD-WAN Manager Troubleshooting Tools

As discussed earlier in this chapter, Catalyst SD-WAN enables you to perform monitoring and troubleshooting operations from the SD-WAN Manager GUI, without needing to log in to individual devices and run commands via the command-line interface (CLI). The SD-WAN Manager tools also allow you to execute on-demand checks of the current device state (for example, the state of the control connections or routing protocol neighbors) or connectivity checks using tools like **ping** and **traceroute.**

Device Troubleshooting

As discussed earlier in this chapter, the Device 360 dashboard provides detailed information about the devices that are under the control of SD-WAN Manager. To access this dashboard, navigate to **Monitoring > Devices** and then click on the specific device. In the **Trouble-shooting** section of the Device 360 dashboard, you can access the following types of diagnostic tools (see Figure 14-23):

- **Connectivity:** These tools, which allow you to check network connections and parameters, include **ping**, **traceroute**, Speed Test, Control Connections, and Underlay Discovery.

- **Traffic:** These tools, which provide visibility into data traffic flows, allow you to verify tunnel health, simulate flows, visualize application routes, and perform packet captures.

- **Logs:** You can access live debugging logs for the supported hardware routers.

NOTE   To use troubleshooting tools like Packet Capture, Speed Test, and Debug Logs, you must have the Data Stream feature enabled under **Administration > Settings** in SD-WAN Manager.

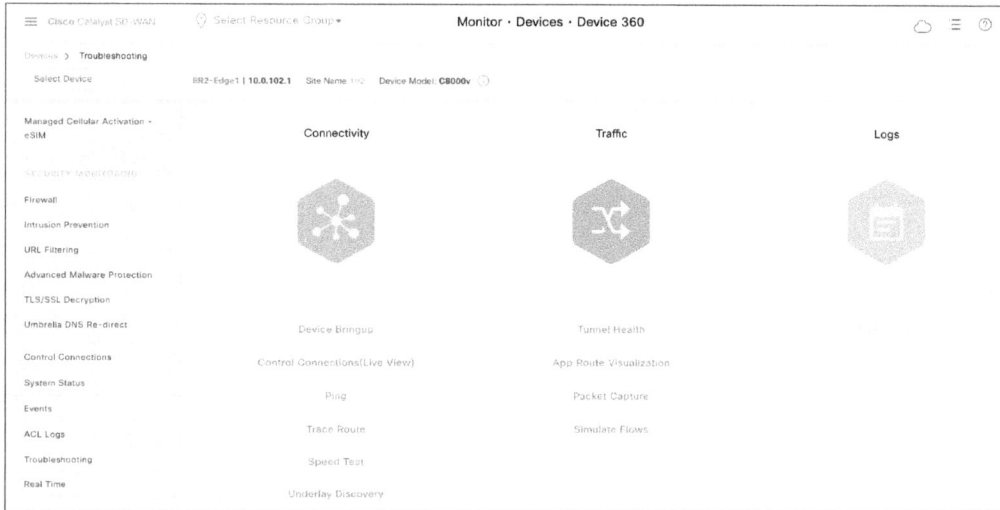

Figure 14-23 *Troubleshooting Tools in Device 360*

To run a connectivity test between devices, you need to provide source and destination details. Figure 14-24 shows results from running the **Underlay Discovery** tool from the source BR2-Edge1 with the local color *biz-internet* toward the destination device BR1-Edge2 and the remote destination color *lte*. As you can see, SD-WAN Manager provides a visualization of the whole underlay path between these WAN Edge routers.

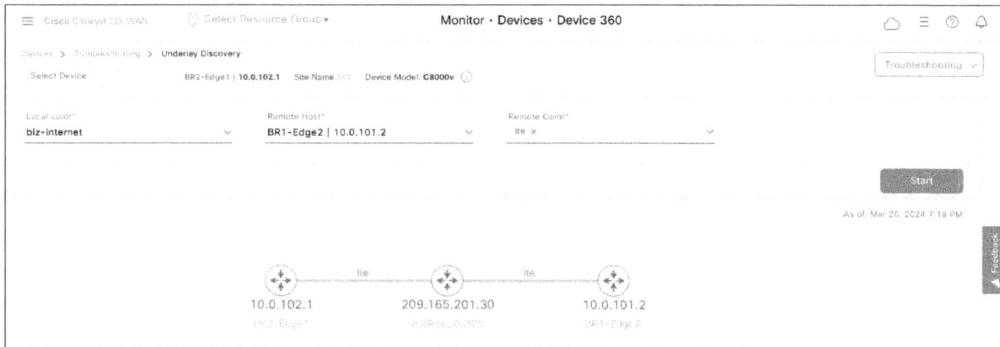

Figure 14-24 *Troubleshooting Tools: Underlay Discovery*

With traditional connectivity tools like **ping** and **traceroute**, you need to select the source VPN and the interface inside the selected VPN, and you need to provide the destination IP address. In addition, you can customize advanced options such as protocol, type of service, fragmentation, and MTU. Figure 14-25 shows an example of the output from **ping**.

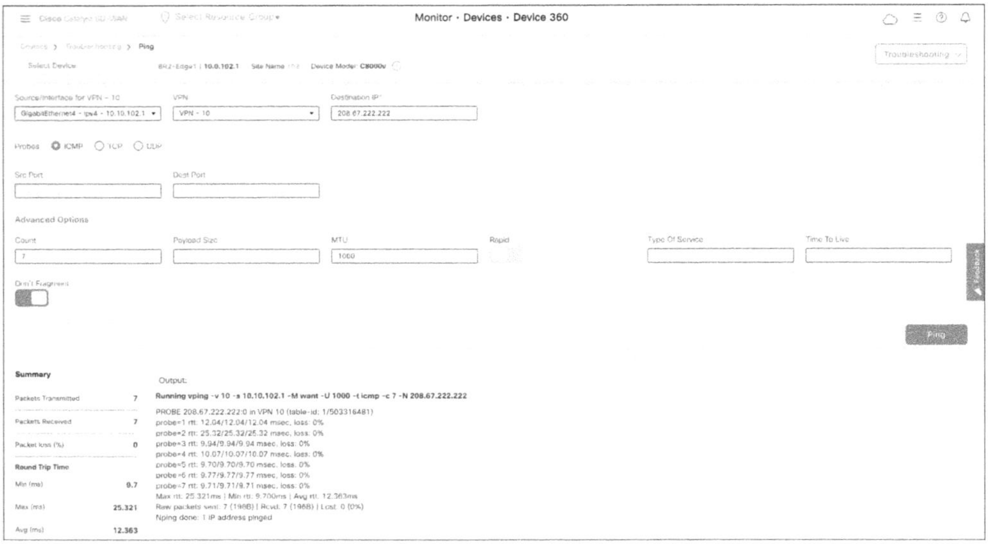

Figure 14-25   *Troubleshooting Tools: ping*

Data plane troubleshooting tools aim to provide better visibility into the traffic flows in the overlay fabric. For example, the **Packet Capture** tool, shown in Figure 14-26, allows you to collect the packets on the specified interface and download the final **.pcap* file directly from the SD-WAN Manager page. You can also apply packet filtering rules in an easy and intuitive way so that only interesting traffic is collected.

Figure 14-26   *Troubleshooting Tools: Packet Capture*

The **Simulate Flows** tool provides an easy way to visualize the data flow path in the overlay network (see Figure 14-27). This tool can be extremely useful for data policy verification because it provides a descriptive graphical representation of the path that real data traffic would take. You can run a simulation for specific applications and make sure that your Data Policy or Application-Aware Routing works as expected.

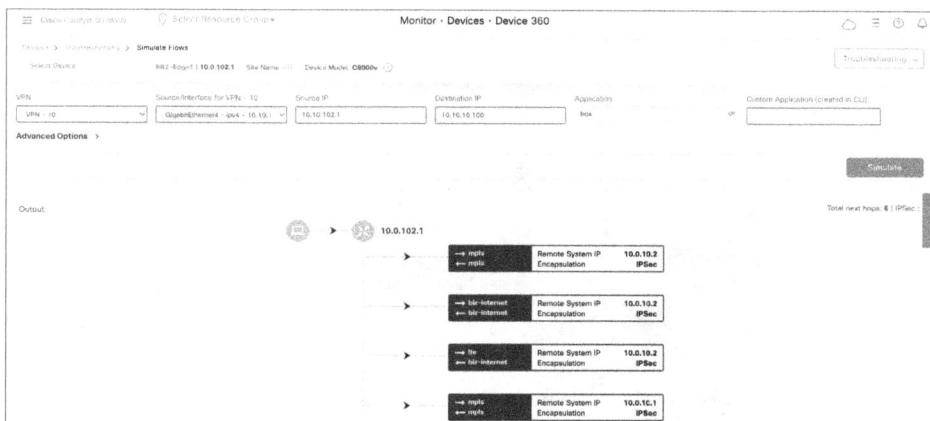

Figure 14-27 *Troubleshooting Tools: Simulate Flows*

Real Time

The Device 360 dashboard also enables you to obtain real-time data from remote devices via the SD-WAN Manager GUI. The **Real Time** tool includes a large number of prebuilt commands you can use to collect information from devices. It gives you information similar to the output you get by executing **show** commands in a remote device's CLI.

The Real Time tool can provide information on hardware inventory and status, interface statistics, routing table entries, routes that were advertised or received via OMP or traditional routing protocols, and Cisco TrustSec data. Figure 14-28, for example, shows the use of the Real Time tool to view IP NAT translations on the DC1-Edge1 router.

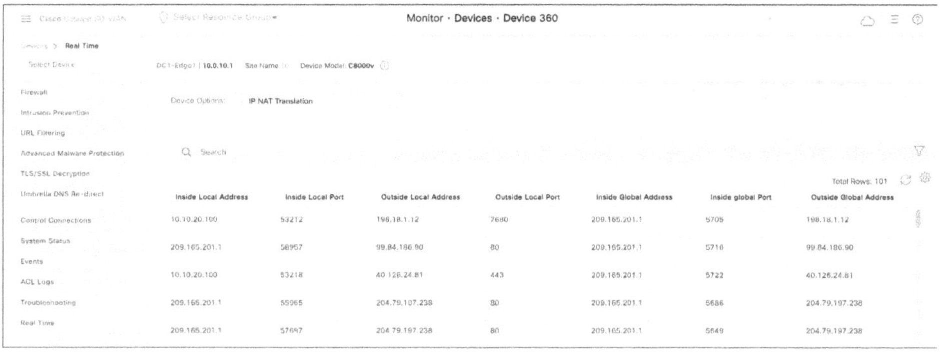

Figure 14-28 *Real Time Output in Device 360*

SSH Terminal

Despite the fact that SD-WAN Manager offers a big variety of configuration, monitoring, and troubleshooting tools by default, in some situations you might need to run custom commands for a particular device. Instead of connecting to the individual devices' CLI, you can run those commands remotely through the SD-WAN Manager GUI by navigating to **Menu > Tools > SSH Terminal** (see Figure 14-29).

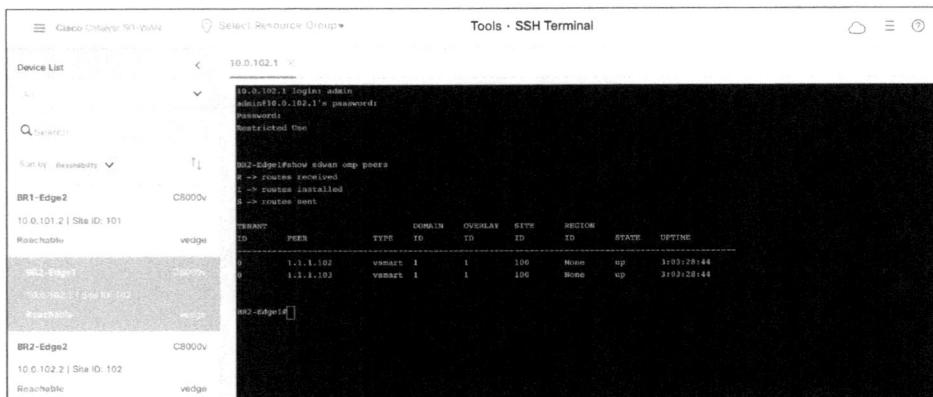

Figure 14-29 *SSH Terminal Tool*

SD-WAN Manager's **SSH Terminal** tool acts as a traditional multi-tab SSH client. It allows you to communicate with the remote device over the SSH protocol, run CLI commands, and get the real-time output directly from the device. However, for this type of communication, SD-WAN Manager uses the underlying NETCONF connections, so it is not necessary to allow SSH (TCP port 22) between SD-WAN Manager and a remote device.

> **NOTE** When running SD-WAN commands in Cisco IOS XE routers, make sure you use the **sdwan** keyword inside the command. For example, **show bfd summary** displays a BFD protocol summary for traditional links, and it can give you empty output if there are no other BFD sessions on the router besides SD-WAN BFD sessions. In contrast, the **show sdwan bfd summary** command shows summary information for the BFD protocol running inside SD-WAN data tunnels.

Network Wide Path Insight

Network Wide Path Insight (NWPI) is a diagnostic tool that provides end-to-end application tracing in the SD-WAN overlay network. You can access it by navigating to **Tools > Network Wide Path Insight** in SD-WAN Manager. NWPI allows you to track down a specific application, discover what network path is used by that application, and measure application performance along the path. SD-WAN Manager collects tracing information from multiple network devices, processes the received data, and displays it in a consolidated view, which allows network administrators to get comprehensive insights into the current network operation that they can use for performance analysis, troubleshooting, new deployment planning, and network optimization.

By default, WAN Edge routers trace the real data flows and send the collected information to SD-WAN Manager. However, it is also possible to generate synthetic traffic in order to measure and analyze application performance without waiting for real user data. Real and synthetic data traffic can be used in the same trace simultaneously.

NWPI involves a number of steps (see Figure 14-30):

Step 1.   **(Prerequisite) Enable Data Stream.** The Data Stream feature must be enabled in the Administration settings of SD-WAN Manager.

Step 2.   **Create a trace.** An administrator creates a trace with the specified parameters and duration. (The allowed trace duration is from 1 minute to 24 hours.)

Step 3.   **Distribute the configuration.** SD-WAN Manager establishes a NETCONF connection to the first WAN Edge router and instructs it to add NWPI metadata to the SD-WAN header of the original data packet.

Step 4.   **Collect the data streaming flow.** Subsequent WAN Edge routers that participate in the data packet forwarding use the NWPI metadata to send the flow information to SD-WAN Manager.

Step 5.   **Correlate and display the data.** SD-WAN Manager correlates the data received from multiple WAN Edge devices and displays it in a single view.

Steps 3 through 5 of this process usually happen without the administrator's intervention. You only interact with SD-WAN Manager to create a trace with the required parameters and view the consolidated insights. SD-WAN Manager does the rest.

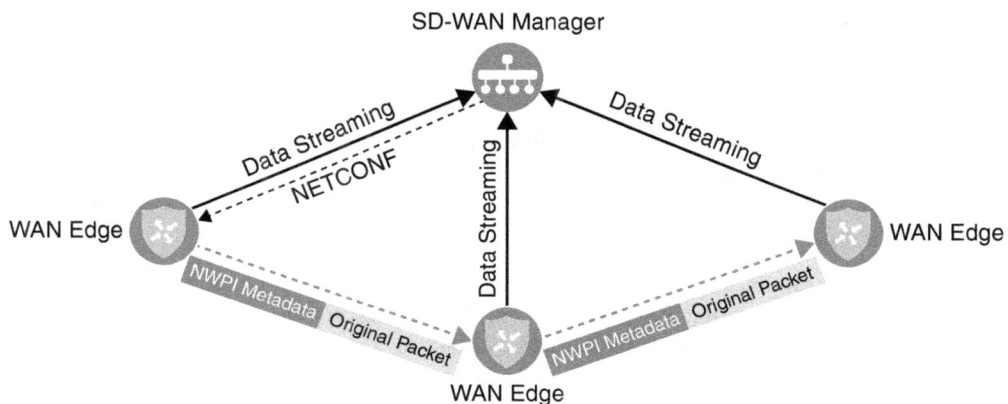

Figure 14-30   *Network Wide Path Insight Operation*

To create a trace in SD-WAN Manager NWPI, click **New Trace** (see Figure 14-31). The mandatory configuration fields are Site ID and VPN; these parameters define the sources from which traffic will be monitored. In addition, you can provide more specific parameters, such as source client address, application type, specific WAN Edge device, interface, protocol, and DSCP value, to trace the data flows based on the provided filters. In addition to configuring real traffic data, you can configure synthetic traffic data (see the bottom portion of Figure 14-31).

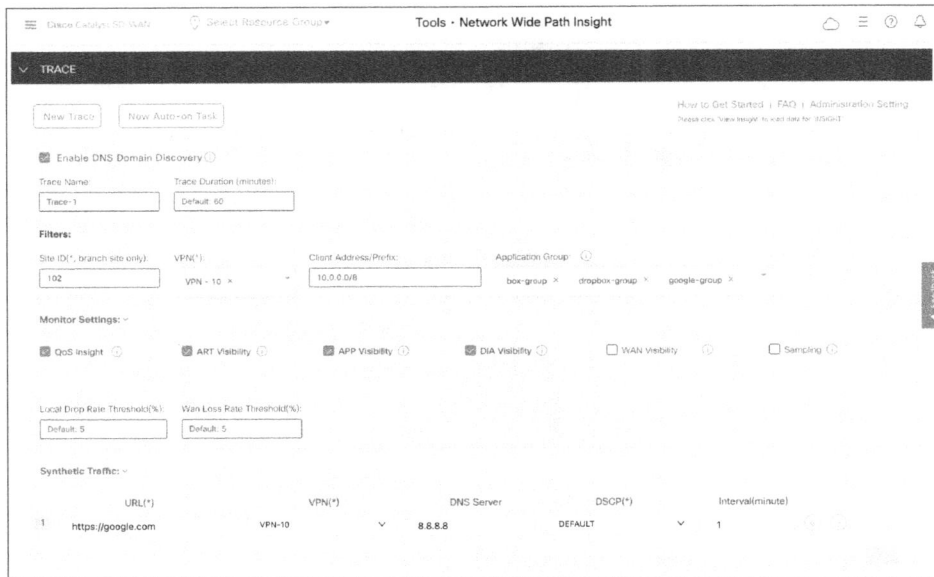

Figure 14-31   *Creating an NWPI Trace*

Figure 14-32 shows an insight summary for a trace. As you can see, an Insights report has the following tabs:

- **Overview:** This tab shows the overall status of the flows that were inspected in this particular trace and the ratio of different application types. The *Events* graph shows the events detected in the monitored traffic and the number of application flows that each event affects.

- **App Performance Insight:** This tab provides detailed metrics about the application, such as an application performance score, hop-by-hop application path, loss/delay/jitter in the traffic flow, and information about the client network delay or server network delay.

- **Event Insight:** This tab shows information about application flows that were affected during each minute of the event. Examples of events include local drop of the packet, SLA violation, QoS congestion, path change, and no response from the server.

- **QoS Insight:** This tab displays networkwide information about which application traffic entered which QoS queues on the devices detected by the trace.

On the main NWPI page, you can see a list of all active and completed flows inside the current trace. Figure 14-33 shows the flow details for the synthetic HTTPS traffic sent to https://google.com/. You can observe the whole traffic path in the overlay SD-WAN network. At the first hop (Hopindex 0), the traffic leaves the local device BR2-Edge2 and moves toward the remote DC1-Edge1, using the data tunnel with MPLS colors on both sides. At the second hop (Hopindex 1), the traffic leaves the DC1-Edge1 router through the Direct Internet Access configured on the interface Gi1. The traffic path beyond that point is not monitored because that is where the traffic leaves the SD-WAN fabric. You can also see the DCSP values for both directions (by default), packet drop, jitter, loss, and other information.

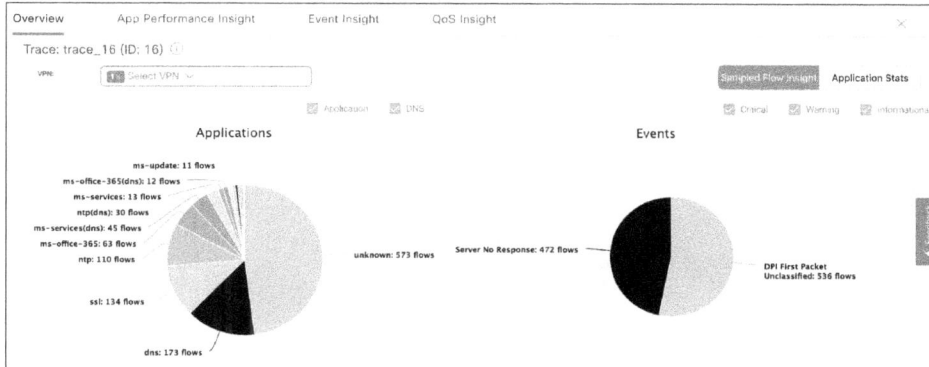

Figure 14-32 *NWPI Trace Overview*

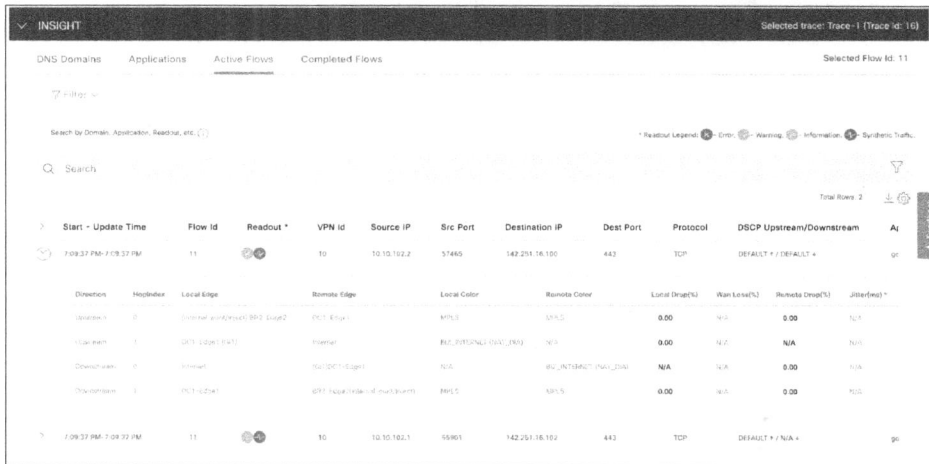

Figure 14-33 *NWPI Active Flow Trace Insights*

The NWPI tool helps you discover problems with traffic flows, such as packet drops, flow asymmetry, and many others. Figure 14-34 shows information on a situation involving no response from the application server. This issue was detected based on the uncompleted TCP handshake.

The Advanced View in NWPI provides deeper information about a selected insight. You can view the global domain and flow trends, and well as geographic distribution of the traffic path. In addition, you can view the details of all features applied to the upstream and downstream flow directions. Figure 14-35 shows an example of this output. As you can see here, you can examine all actions that occurred with the traffic, including tunnel encapsulation, packet forwarding decisions, NAT translation, application of SD-WAN policies, and NBAR classification. The exact output in the Advanced View may be slightly different for your deployment, depending on the application type, underlying protocol, and other factors.

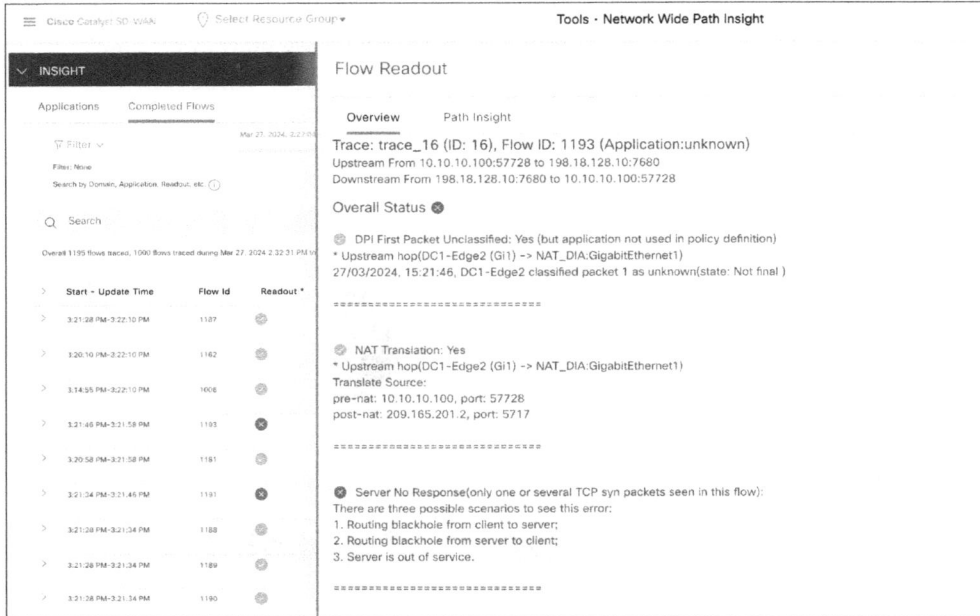

Figure 14-34   *NWPI Flow Readout*

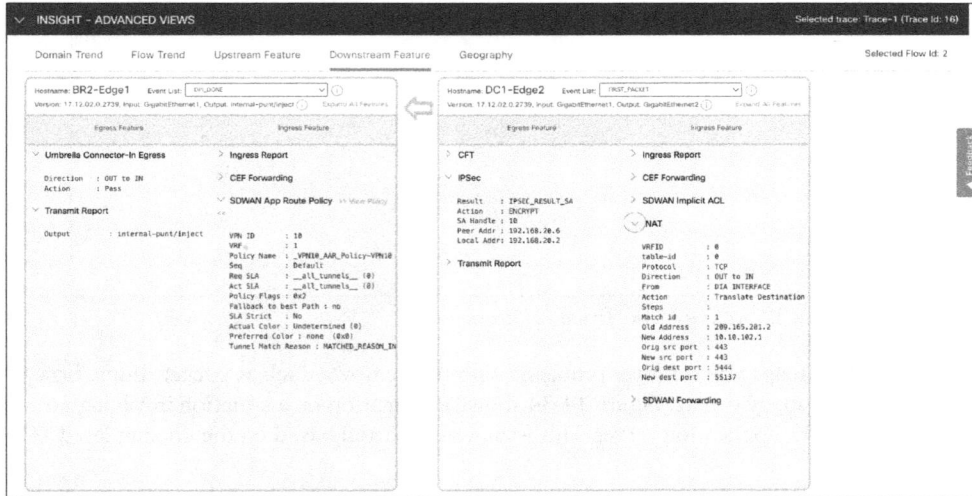

Figure 14-35   *NWPI Flow Advanced View*

NWPI is a powerful analytics tool that gives you comprehensive insights into all aspects of application routing across the entire SD-WAN fabric. It helps you get the insights needed to verify your policy design, monitor application and network performance, and perform optimization efforts.

SD-WAN Monitoring with ThousandEyes

In recent years, increasing the visibility of Internet links has been one of the biggest challenges facing network administrators. While it is relatively easy to manage and monitor network segments that are under enterprise control, it is more challenging to track the traffic when it exits the on-premises infrastructure and moves across Internet connections.

Cisco ThousandEyes is a comprehensive network assurance and monitoring solution that provides Internet-scale visibility and insights into end-to-end WAN connectivity, measures the performance of WAN links, and analyzes the behavior of these links.

Cisco ThousandEyes monitors the availability of resources and services over WAN links, explores traffic paths, analyzes global Internet routing, and measures the performance of specific application types on WAN links.

14

ThousandEyes Overview

Cisco ThousandEyes is a software-as-a-service (SaaS) solution that makes use of synthetic tests. Those tests, which are generated by ThousandEyes agents, represent exactly the same traffic patterns that real users or devices would produce. The main purpose of the agents is to generate the required type of traffic, receive responses, and share the information with the ThousandEyes cloud. Agents do not perform any compute or data analysis operations locally, and they therefore do not require extensive compute resources.

There are three main types of ThousandEyes agents:

- **Cloud Agents:** Cisco ThousandEyes provides and manages these agents. At this writing, there are almost 1000 cloud agents around the world, installed in 66 countries. Customers can use cloud agents to deploy custom tests, verify intra-cloud monitoring (for example, to monitor asset performance or availability within the same region or availability zone), and as sources or destinations for tests aimed at assessing an Internet provider's infrastructure.

- **Enterprise Agents:** Enterprise network administrators deploy and manage these agents. An enterprise agent is a software-based entity that is installed within the enterprise infrastructure (on premises or in the cloud). ThousandEyes supports multiple enterprise agent form factors, including virtual appliances inside VMware, Hyper-V, or Oracle VirtualBox infrastructure; Linux packages; Docker containers; and hardware routers and switches that use Cisco Application Hosting. When deploying tests, you can use any combination of cloud and enterprise agents as sources or destinations for synthetic test traffic.

- **Endpoint Agents:** These software-based agents are installed on end users' computers. They work in conjunction with web browsers and provide better visibility into the performance of specific applications, such as Webex, Microsoft 365, and Google. You can also define a custom list of domains to be monitored by endpoint agents.

Once enterprise agents are installed and configured, they register themselves in the ThousandEyes cloud and appear under your organization account. At that point, you can manage them from the centralized admin web interface, available at https://app.thousandeyes.com/. We will discuss cloud and enterprise agents further later in this chapter.

Another important component of ThousandEyes is tests. Tests define what traffic should be generated by the agents, how often the packets should be sent, custom parameters, and so on.

ThousandEyes ensures that the following test categories can be executed:

- **Routing (BGP) tests:** This type of test tracks reachability and path changes for the relevant prefix. For this type of test, ThousandEyes ingests and analyzes BGP routing data from multiple global BGP collectors.

- **Network (agent-to-agent and agent-to-server) tests:** This type of test measures network performance and the path between any combination of cloud and enterprise agents, as well as between an agent and a target server. For these tests, ThousandEyes agents send TCP or ICMP traffic to measure network parameters such as latency, jitter, and loss.

- **DNS tests:** This type of test is used to perform Domain Name System (DNS) performance measurement. DNS tests provide DNS record validation and service performance metrics for a specific domain, as well as perform DNS traces to verify the delegation of DNS records or observe the DNS hierarchy of a target domain. In addition, you can perform security validation with DNSSEC tests.

- **Web tests:** This category provides a big variety of tests aimed at monitoring web traffic and measuring server response time, network throughput, and other parameters. Web tests include verification of HTTP server availability, web page loading, web transactions, API calls, and FTP server operations.

- **Voice tests:** These tests allow you to evaluate the quality of voice traffic in the network by facilitating measurements against the SIP server, simulating the RTP voice stream, and so on.

Once you create a test, you need to deploy it to the agents. Depending on the test type, you will need to define the source and/or target (destination) agents that will run the tests. The results of the executed tests are summarized and visualized in the **Test Views** and **Dashboards** pages of the ThousandEyes admin portal.

You can also configure individual alert rules for different test types and get notified when the specific conditions are matched (for example, when any errors are present, or when the packet loss exceeds the threshold). The possible notification options are email, webhooks, and built-in or custom integration with a large ecosystem of Cisco and third-party tools (such as ServiceNow, AppDynamics, PagerDuty, and others).

Figure 14-36 provides a high-level architecture diagram of a network with ThousandEyes agents. You can use different combinations of enterprise and cloud agents to run the tests that are critical for your business needs.

NOTE Cisco ThousandEyes is a complex solution. In this chapter, we briefly discuss how it is most commonly used together with Catalyst SD-WAN. For additional use cases and more deployment details, please refer to the official product documentation available at https://docs.thousandeyes.com/.

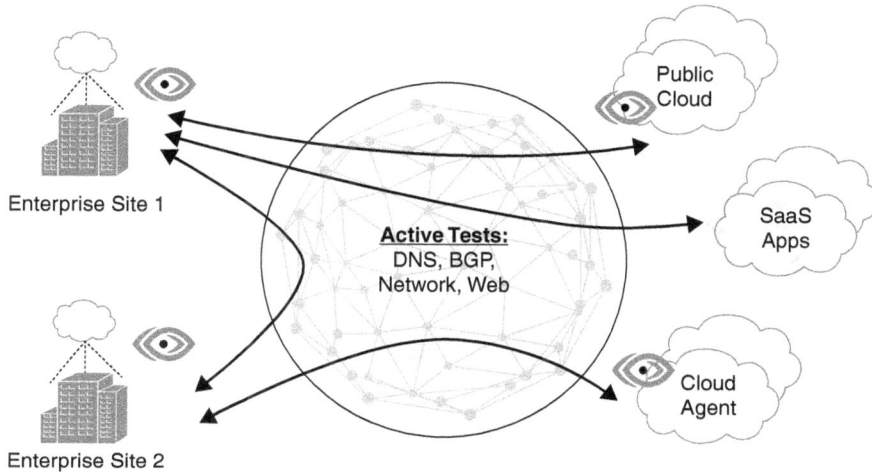

Figure 14-36   *Network Monitoring with ThousandEyes Agents*

Catalyst SD-WAN and ThousandEyes Integration

As we discussed earlier, ThousandEyes enterprise agents can be deployed for application hosting on Cisco hardware devices, such as Catalyst 9000 series and Nexus switches, Catalyst 8000 devices, and ISR or ASR routers. When deployed like this, an enterprise agent runs inside a Docker container on the supported hardware platform.

SD-WAN Manager can streamline ThousandEyes enterprise agent deployment on WAN Edge routers and automate their configuration. These agents are configured as if they were running inside a service-side VPN. Once the agents are deployed on the routers, you can use them to execute tests and monitor network performance from the network users' perspective.

Deployment and configuration of ThousandEyes agents from SD-WAN Manager require the following steps:

Step 1.   **Upload a virtual image to the SD-WAN Manager software repository.** Upload the virtual image for the Docker appliance installation to the SD-WAN Manager software repository. From there, it is distributed to the hardware WAN Edge routers via SD-WAN Manager.

Step 2.   **Create the configuration in SD-WAN Manager.** If you use Device Templates to manage your devices, define a *ThousandEyes Agent* feature template and add it to the device template for the supported router platforms. If you manage your devices with Configuration Groups, add another profile of the type *Thousand-Eyes* under Feature Profiles.

Step 3.   **Deploy the configuration to WAN Edge devices.** If you use device templates, attach the device template that includes the ThousandEyes agent feature template to the WAN Edge routers. If you use configuration groups, associate the configuration with the supported hardware devices and deploy it. You can supply agent-specific parameters, such as IP address and hostname, as variables during the deployment process.

Step 4.   **Create and assign a ThousandEyes test.** Once the enterprise agent is installed and appears in the ThousandEyes admin interface, you can create custom tests and assign them to the agent.

> **NOTE**   Usually ThousandEyes Agents get IP addresses from the service-side VPN range. This way, they can run tests and provide visibility of the network connectivity from a service-side client's point of view. To establish control connections with the ThousandEyes admin interface, the agents need to have access to the Internet and the DNS server(s).

Before you start to deploy ThousandEyes agents, you need to obtain the latest software image and the account group token from the ThousandEyes admin portal. Go to **Cloud & Enterprise Agents > Agent Settings > Add New Enterprise Agent** and select the agent type you want to deploy. You can find the installation details and instructions at the ThousandEyes admin portal, and you can also download the installation files, as shown in Figure 14-37. To deploy an agent on Cisco routers using SD-WAN Manager, you need to download the *.TAR* file from the **Cisco Application Hosting** tab.

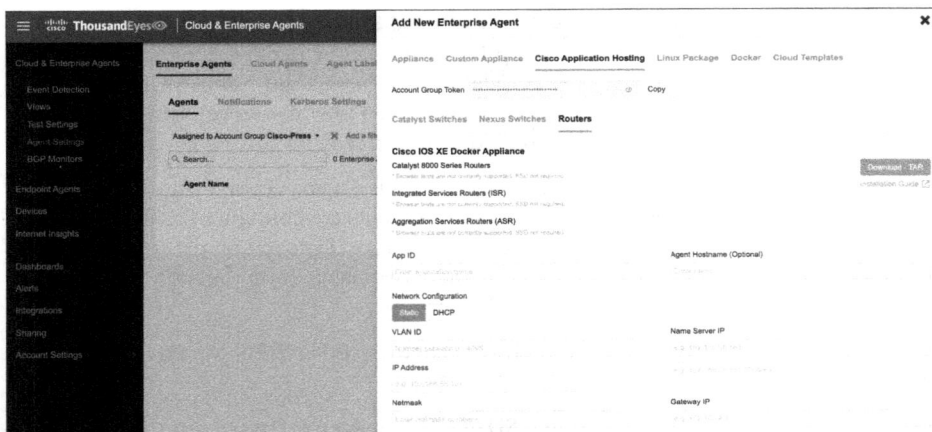

Figure 14-37   *Downloading ThousandEyes Agent Software*

Next, you need to upload the *.TAR* file with Cisco IOS XE Docker Appliance to the SD-WAN Manager software repository. You do this by selecting **Maintenance > Software Repository > Virtual Images** (see Figure 14-38).

Next, you need to create a ThousandEyes Agent configuration in SD-WAN Manager and deploy it on the WAN Edge routers. Depending on the configuration method you use, you can do this via templates or configuration groups.

To configure a ThousandEyes Agent via templates, you need to create a feature template of the type *ThousandEyes* in SD-WAN Manager (see Figure 14-39). (Refer to Chapter 4 for more information about the feature and device templates.) As shown in Figure 14-39, you provide the basic agent configuration information, such as IP addressing, service-side VPN information, and the hostname as it will appear in ThousandEyes UI.

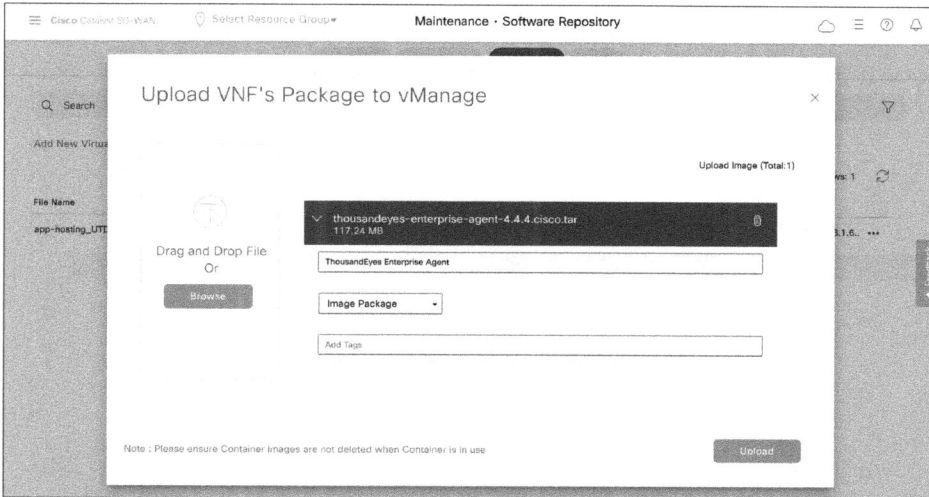

Figure 14-38   *Uploading the ThousandEyes Agent to SD-WAN Manager*

NOTE   This example shows ThousandEyes Agent configuration using global variables with explicit values inside a template. We did this intentionally to reduce the number of screenshots required. However, in a big production deployment, the best practice recommendation is to make the template as generic and reusable as possible.

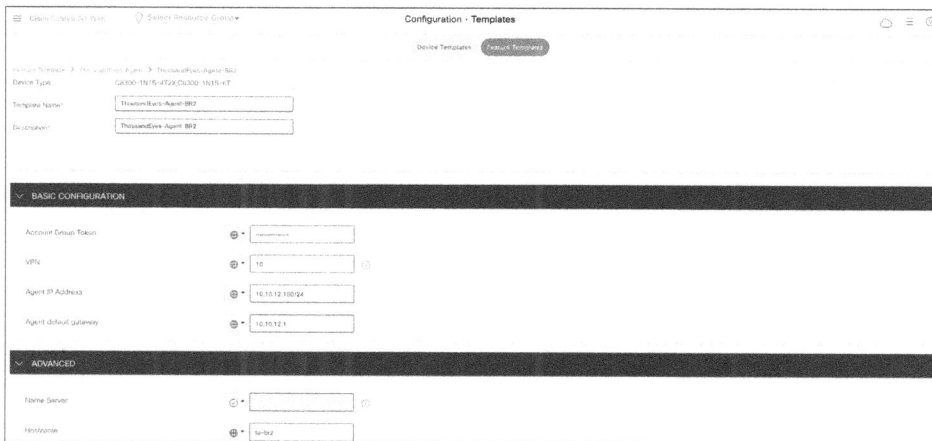

Figure 14-39   *ThousandEyes Agent Feature Template in SD-WAN Manager*

Then you need to add the ThousandEyes agent feature template to the *Additional Templates* section in the device template, as shown in Figure 14-40. When the device template is ready, follow the standard steps to attach WAN Edge routers to this template (refer to Chapter 4).

NOTE   You can create and use ThousandEyes templates only for the supported hardware platforms. If you select an unsupported device type (such as a virtual router), you will not be able to use the ThousandEyes agent template.

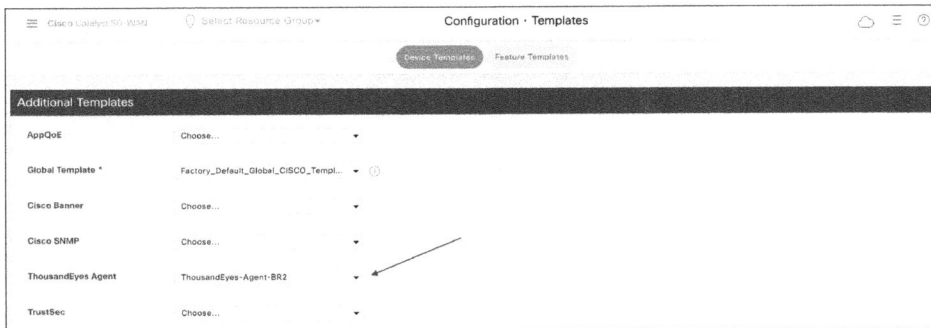

Figure 14-40   *A Device Template in SD-WAN Manager*

Another option is to use configuration groups, as discussed in Chapter 4. To add a new ThousandEyes profile, go to **Configuration > Configuration Groups**, open the configuration group you want to edit, and select **Feature Profiles > Other Profile > ThousandEyes**. Figure 14-41 shows a new feature profile being added.

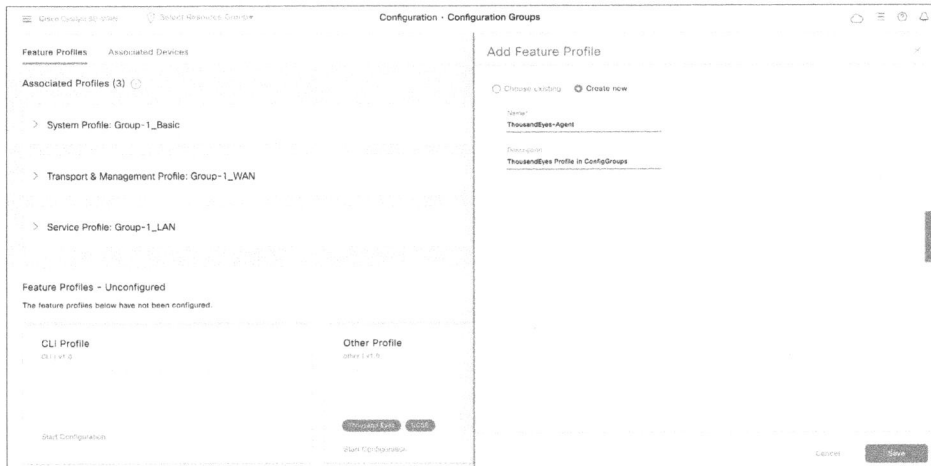

Figure 14-41   *Adding a ThousandEyes Feature Profile*

After you add a new ThousandEyes profile, it appears next to other profiles associated with this configuration group. Click **Add Feature** under the ThousandEyes profile and provide the agent details, such as IP address parameters, agent hostname, and account group token. Much as with feature templates, you can define these parameters as global values or as variables, and you can provide their values during the deployment process. Figure 14-42 shows this configuration step. The next step is to deploy the modified configuration group to the associated devices, as discussed in Chapter 4.

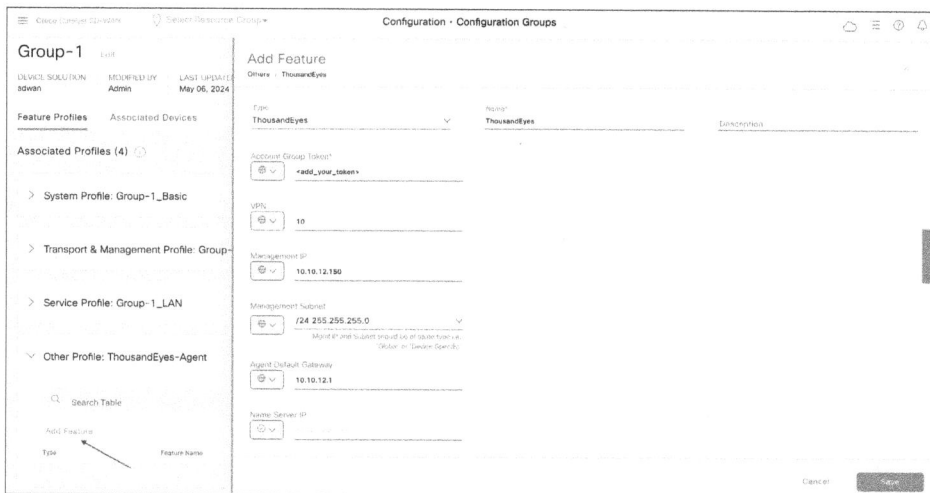

Figure 14-42 *Adding ThousandEyes Feature*

Regardless of the configuration method you use, you can verify the application hosting status and details directly in the WAN Edge CLI by running the commands **show app-hosting list** and **show app-hosting detail**. Example 14-1 shows the command output, which you can use for verification.

Example 14-1 *Application Hosting Details for a ThousandEyes Agent*

```
C8300-Edge#
C8300-Edge#show app-hosting detail
App id                   : te
Owner                    : iox
State                    : RUNNING
Application
  Type                   : docker
  Name                   : ThousandEyes Enterprise Agent
  Version                : 4.4.4
  Description            :
  Author                 : ThousandEyes
  Path                   : bootflash:.TE_IMAGES/te-agent-4.4.4.cisco.tar
  URL Path              :
Activated profile name : custom


<OUTPUT OMITTED>


Network interfaces
    ---------------------------------------
```

```
eth0:
    MAC address        : 52:54:dd:45:8d:c3
    IPv4 address       : 10.10.12.150
    IPv6 address       : ::
    Network name       : VPG4
C8300-Edge#
```

A WAN Edge router gets an additional interface of the type VirtualPortGroup that will serve as a default gateway for the ThousandEyes application running inside a Docker container. Example 14-2 shows the output of the **show ip interface brief** command.

Example 14-2   *WAN Edge Router Interfaces*

```
C8300-Edge#
C8300-Edge#show ip interface brief
Interface              IP-Address       OK? Method Status   Protocol
GigabitEthernet0/0/0   192.168.20.6     YES other  up       up
GigabitEthernet0/0/1   209.165.201.6    YES unset  up       up
GigabitEthernet0/0/2   209.165.202.130  YES unset  up       up
GigabitEthernet0/0/3   10.10.102.1      YES other  up       up
GigabitEthernet0      unassigned       YES other  down     down
Sdwan-system-intf      10.0.102.1       YES unset  up       up
Loopback65528          192.168.1.1      YES other  up       up
NVI0                  unassigned       YES unset  up       up
Tunnel1                192.168.20.6     YES TFTP   up       up
Tunnel2                209.165.201.6    YES TFTP   up       up
Tunnel3                209.165.202.130  YES TFTP   up       up
VirtualPortGroup4      10.10.12.1       YES other  up       up
C8300-Edge#
```

WAN Monitoring with ThousandEyes

When ThousandEyes agents are successfully deployed, they appear in the ThousandEyes admin portal, under **Cloud & Enterprise Agents > Agent Settings > Enterprise Agents**, as shown in Figure 14-43. Here you see all enterprise agents, regardless of the installation method used (for example, Cisco application hosting, virtual machine, Linux application).

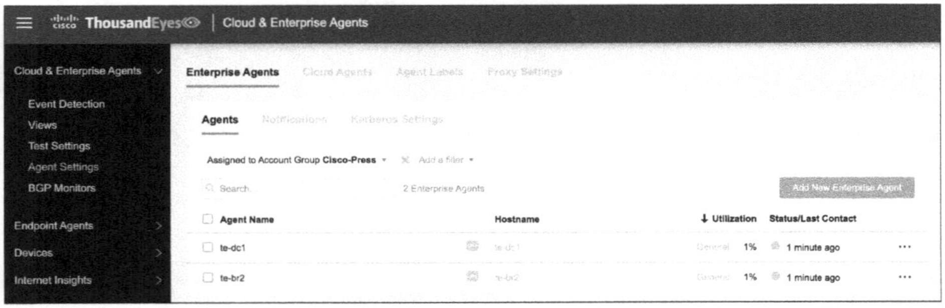

Figure 14-43   *Enterprise Agents in ThousandEyes*

Next, you need to configure the ThousandEyes tests and monitor the test results. Figure 14-44 shows how to add a new network test of type *Agent-to-Agent*. This example shows the creation of a test to check the connectivity between two SD-WAN branches, Branch2 and Datacenter1. On the right side, you can see what views will be available for this test (in this case, network overview details, traffic path visualization, and BGP route visualization).

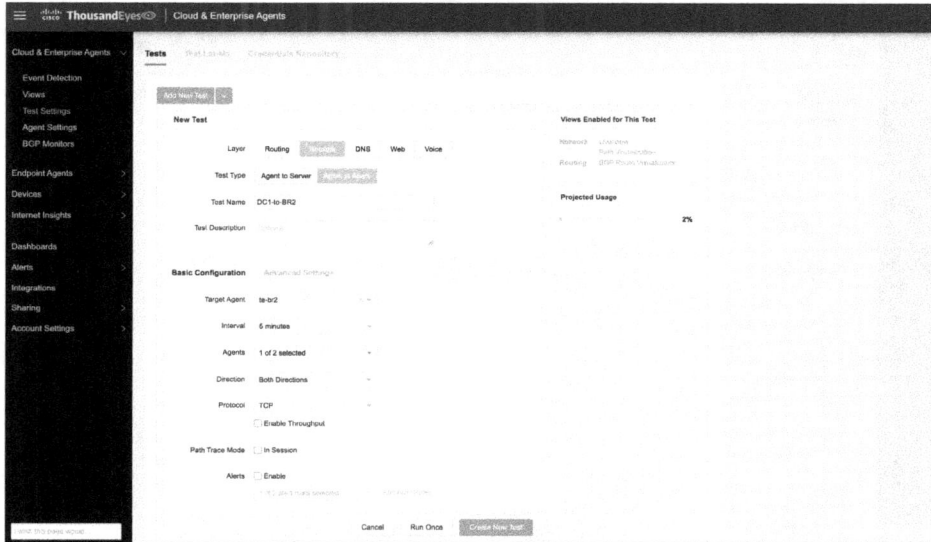

Figure 14-44   *Agent-to-Agent ThousandEyes Test*

Figure 14-45 shows the ThousandEyes view page displaying the results of the test that was just configured. Here you can see the hop-by-hop path visualization between the SD-WAN branches, detailed information about every node in that path, and the path metrics, including latency, jitter, and delay.

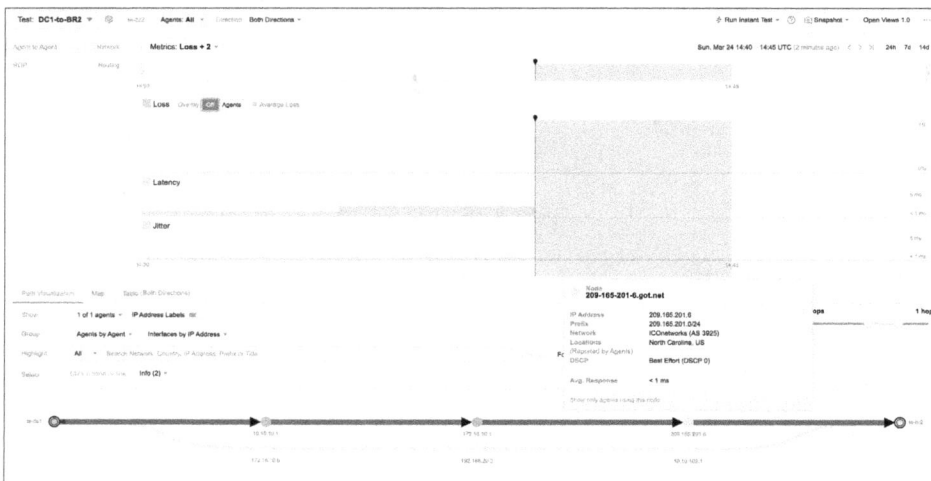

Figure 14-45   *ThousandEyes View: Agent-to-Agent Test Results*

Figure 14-46 shows another commonly used ThousandEyes test: an *Agent-to-Server* test. Here you instruct your agents to send periodic HTTP probes to the Microsoft 365 web page. This type of test can be used independently or together with SD-WAN Application-Aware Routing policies or SD-WAN Cloud OnRamp for SaaS to provide better visibility into data traffic going through Internet links.

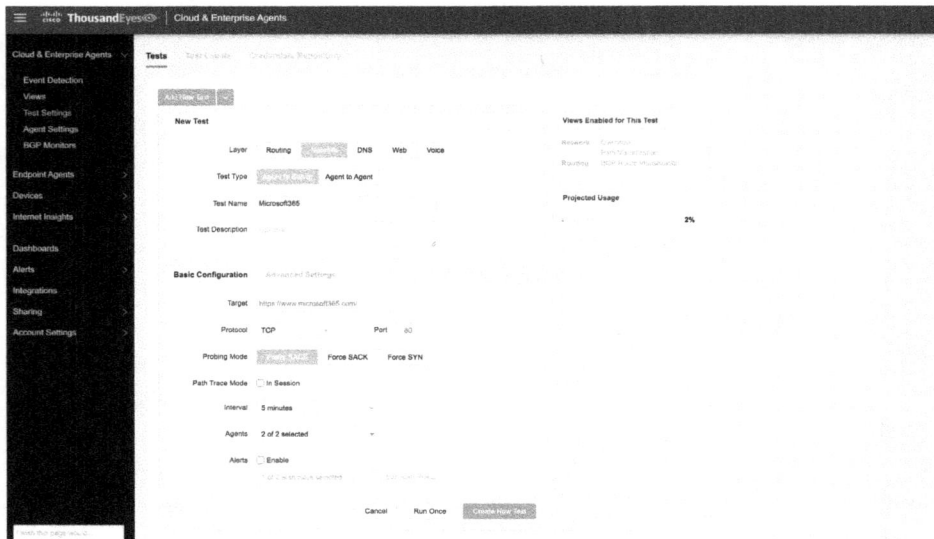

Figure 14-46   *Agent-to-Server ThousandEyes Test*

Figure 14-47 shows the results of this Agent-to-Server test. Much as with the previous output, here you can see a full path visualization between the on-premises WAN Edge router and the remote https://microsoft365.com/ page, as well as the path quality metrics.

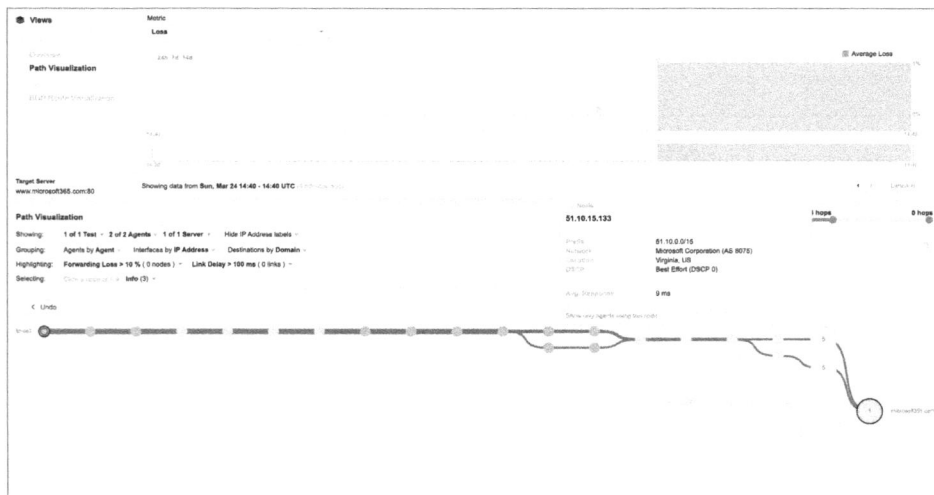

Figure 14-47   *ThousandEyes View: Agent-to-Server Test Results*

As discussed earlier, Cisco ThousandEyes provides a variety of different tools designed to visualize and troubleshoot the traffic flows in a WAN network. You can use the scenarios discussed here in any type of deployments, including with traditional WAN connections and SD-WAN overlay networks.

In addition, the ThousandEyes WAN Insights feature provides predictive path recommendations (PPR) by delivering proactive network analysis and providing recommendations on how the performance of the overlay network can be improved, even before real users are impacted. This feature is covered later in this chapter.

> **NOTE**   You have just gotten a brief introduction to the capabilities of ThousandEyes. Please refer to the official documentation for more information about the solution available at https://docs.thousandeyes.com/.

14

SD-WAN Analytics Overview

Cisco Catalyst SD-WAN Analytics (formerly vAnalytics) is another SaaS solution that provides extensive monitoring and in-depth insights into the operation of an SD-WAN network. It aggregates the telemetry data received from SD-WAN Manager, correlates the application performance with the underlying network behavior, and displays the health status of the entire network in a highly visualized and intuitive manner. In addition to keeping tabs on the actual and historical network state, SD-WAN Analytics also performs root-cause analysis for network issues and suggests corrective actions aimed at improving network performance.

You can access SD-WAN Analytics either via SD-WAN Manager from the **Analytics** menu or by going directly to the SaaS application URL. The URL format is https://<region>.analytics.sdwan. cisco.com/, where the *region* part is us01, us02, eu01, or au01, depending on the location of your SD-WAN Analytics instance. The mandatory prerequisite for using SD-WAN Analytics is to enable Cloud Services in the SD-WAN Manager Administration settings.

SD-WAN Analytics provides access to the following dashboards:

- **Overview:** This dashboard provides a top-level view of the sites, applications, circuits, and performance.

- **Sites:** This dashboard provides an overview of the availability and the usage of sites across the whole network.

- **Applications:** This dashboard provides a view of the specific application performance for a dedicated site or for the entire overlay network.

- **Circuits:** This dashboard provides a summary of and insights into the availability, utilization, and performance of different circuits in the SD-WAN fabric.

- **Predictive Networks:** This dashboard shows a forecast of future network issues and suggests recommended changes to improve the application experience for end users.

Figure 14-48 shows the SD-WAN Analytics *Overview* dashboard, which displays a summary of the network performance at the overlay level. The information is presented in dashlets for specific data types, such as sites, applications, circuits, and clients. Additional information about the various data categories can be found in specialized dashboards, as discussed in the remainder of this section.

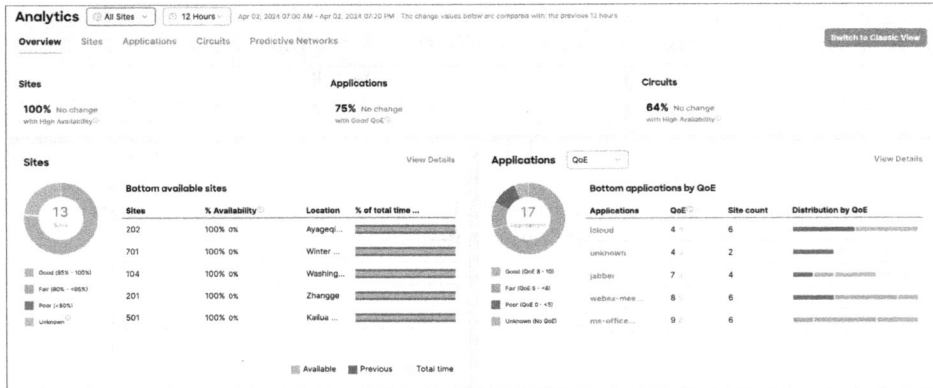

Figure 14-48   *SD-WAN Analytics Overview*

The *Sites* dashboard provides a map view of all sites in the SD-WAN fabric (see Figure 14-49). It allows you to view the availability of the overlay from a single site perspective and displays information about site performance based on utilization, availability, and latency.

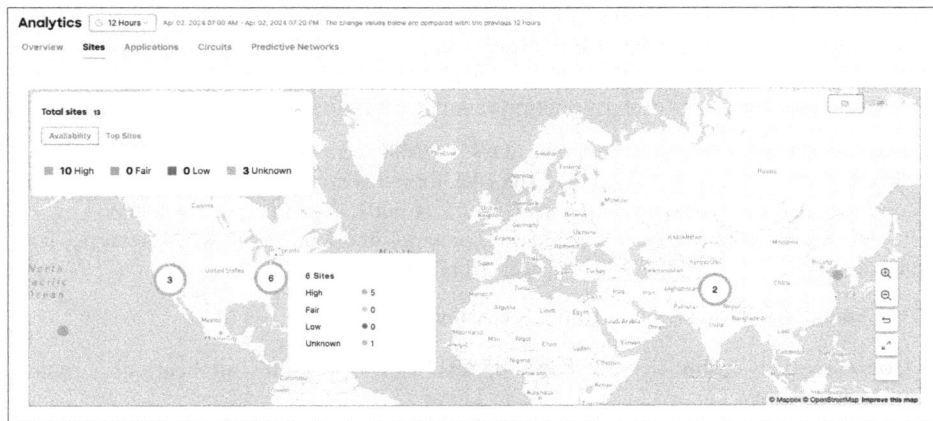

Figure 14-49   *SD-WAN Analytics Sites Dashboard*

The *Applications* dashboard displays information about application performance and QoE (see Figure 14-50). This dashboard uses a number of dashlets to display application data:

■ **Application Experience:** This dashlet displays the application health in terms of QoE score (good, fair, poor), utilization details, and the total volume of the traffic. Colors are used to draw attention to the most critical application performance issues.

■ **Application Trend Analysis:** This dashlet visualizes the changes in application metrics over the specified period of time.

■ **QoE Distribution by Application Classes:** This dashlet displays applications together with their classes. This dashlet helps you understand if an application was classified properly and identify issues that may cause specific classes of applications to perform poorly in the overlay network.

- **Trending Applications:** This dashlet displays the top applications that have had significant rises or drops in their QoE score, usage, latency, or loss.

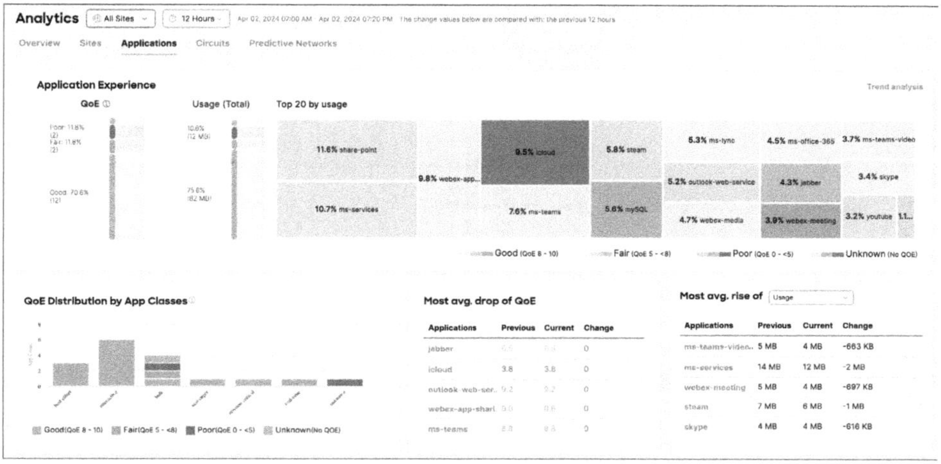

Figure 14-50 *SD-WAN Analytics Applications Dashboard*

The *Circuits* dashboard provides insights into the availability, utilization, and network performance of different circuits across the entire overlay fabric or for individual sites (see Figure 14-51). This dashboard includes the following dashlets:

- **Total Uptime:** This dashlet displays the total time the SD-WAN fabric was active.

- **DIA vs Tunnel Usage:** This dashlet highlights the distribution of traffic routed through Direct Internet Access and traffic routed through SD-WAN tunnels over a specific circuit.

- **Color Usage:** This dashlet provides a breakout of traffic segmentation within the overlay fabric, based on TLOC color.

- **Bandwidth:** This dashlet displays the top five circuits in terms of bandwidth utilization based on the transmitted and received data.

- **Circuits:** This dashlet displays circuits distribution in a Cisco Catalyst SD-WAN fabric. It includes the essential metrics for the circuits, such as service provider information, availability, downtime, bandwidth, and details about packet loss, latency, and jitter.

Finally, the *Predictive Networks* dashboard displays the results of historical data analysis, a forecast of potential network issues, and suggestions for how to avoid those issues in the future (see Figure 14-52). The Predictive Path Recommendations section uses advanced data modeling powered by Cisco ThousandEyes to determine the optimal data path to help improve the performance of a specific application and displays recommendations.

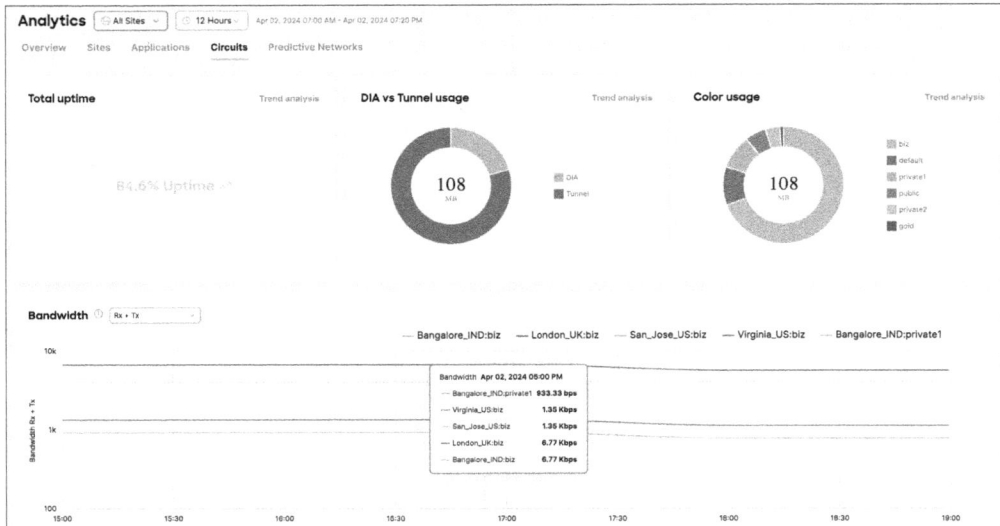

Figure 14-51 *SD-WAN Analytics Circuits Dashboard*

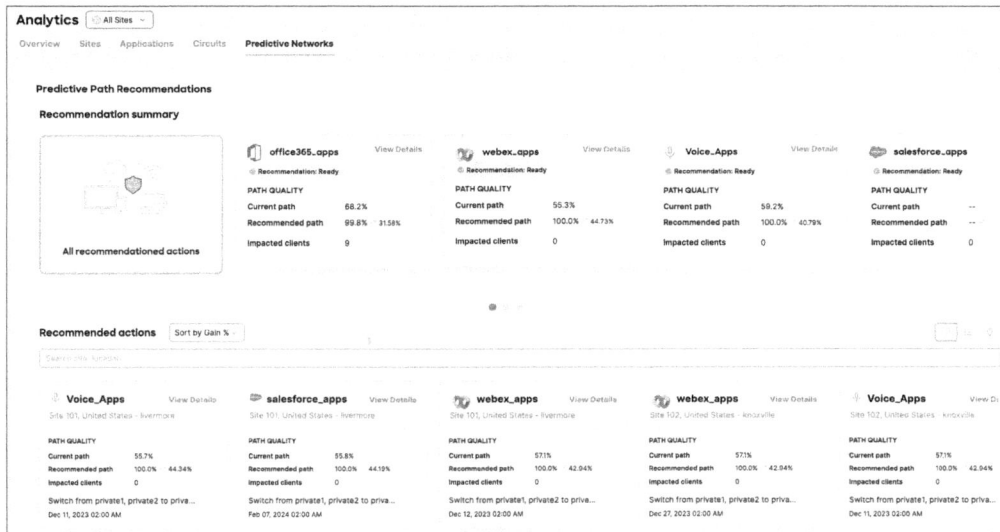

Figure 14-52 *SD-WAN Analytics Predictive Networks Dashboard*

Predictive Path Recommendations analyzes historical data for the past 30 days and evaluates traffic flow patterns over various network paths. Then it compares the quality of the current network path with other available paths and recommends an alternative path that can offer better quality. It also gives recommendations on how to adjust SD-WAN policies to achieve the best performance for a specific application. You can implement these suggestions in the Application-Aware Routing policies in SD-WAN Manager.

Summary

This chapter provides an in-depth look at the tools and methods for monitoring and troubleshooting Cisco Catalyst SD-WAN deployments. Effective monitoring and analytics tools are essential for all network administrators to maintain optimal network performance, quickly resolve issues, and enhance the overall efficiency and reliability of the network infrastructure. This chapter introduces built-in SD-WAN Manager tools for overseeing the entire network and maintaining the SD-WAN fabric components. It also discusses the use of Cisco ThousandEyes for advanced monitoring capabilities and presents an overview of SD-WAN Analytics for ongoing network monitoring.

Review All Key Topics

Review the most important topics in the chapter, noted with the Key Topic icon in the outer margin of the page. Table 14-3 lists these key topics and the page number on which each is found.

Table 14-3   Key Topics

Key Topic Element	Description	Page
Section	Monitoring dashboards	597
Section	Device troubleshooting	610
Section	Real-time troubleshooting tools	613
Section	Catalyst SD-WAN and ThousandEyes Integration	621
Section	SD-WAN Analytics Overview	629

Chapter Review Questions

1. What component(s) of the SD-WAN fabric can be monitored via SD-WAN Manager (formerly vManage)?

   a. SD-WAN Edge devices

   b. SD-WAN Validators (formerly vBond)

   c. SD-WAN Controllers (formerly vSmart)

   d. All of the above

2. Which health statuses can be assigned to resources like devices, tunnels, and applications? (Choose three.)

   a. Excellent

   b. Healthy

   c. Good

   d. Fair

   e. Poor

   f. Down

3. Which SD-WAN Manager (formerly vManage) tool allows you to get live output from WAN Edge devices?

   a. Troubleshoot

   b. Real Time

    c. Live Logs

    d. Device template

    e. TLOC List

    f. Site List

4. True or false: Cisco ThousandEyes agents can be installed on all Catalyst 8000 router platforms.

    a. True

    b. False

5. What external analytics tools can be used to monitor Catalyst SD-WAN deployments? (Choose two.)

    a. Cisco Intersight

    b. Catalyst SD-WAN Analytics

    c. Cisco ThousandEyes

    d. Cisco AppDynamics

6. Which tool provides a graphical representation of the overlay network path that will be chosen for data traffic?

    a. TraceRoute

    b. Flow Simulator

    c. Application Dashboard

    d. Ping

7. True or false: Predictive Path Recommendations requires Cisco ThousandEyes.

    a. True

    b. False

Answers to Chapter Review Questions

Chapter 1

1. **A, B, E.** Businesses are looking to reduce operational complexity, increase usable bandwidth by using dormant backup links or commodity Internet links, and improve the overall user experience, all with a topology-independent environment.

2. **A, B, E.** Administrative distance, traffic engineering, and preferred path selection all come into play when there are multiple links in the branch routers.

3. **A, B.** SD-WAN is designed to give the business control of all routing and service-level agreements (SLAs).

4. **A, B, C, F.** IoT devices and increased cloud consumption are IT trends, not benefits of SD-WAN.

5. **A, B, E.** Cisco SD-WAN can support dual MPLS, hybrid WAN, and dual Internet as options for transport.

6. **B.** DIA is used to offload cloud applications directly to the Internet for more efficient access to cloud providers.

7. **B, D.** Cloud application migration and an increase in network complexity are two of the driving forces behind cloud adoption.

Chapter 2

1. **A, B, D.** The three Cisco Catalyst SD-WAN Control Components are SD-WAN Controller, SD-WAN Validator, and SD-WAN Manager.

2. **A, B, E.** Cisco Catalyst SD-WAN is a distributed architecture. By splitting out the components in the solution, SD-WAN Manager provides a single pane of glass for all management and troubleshooting. By also moving the control plane to a central location, it enables greater scale while reducing complexity.

3. **A, B, E.** SD-WAN Manager provides a single viewpoint for all troubleshooting, configuration, and monitoring functions.

4. **A.** IPsec is used to secure and authenticate data plane connectivity. IPsec tunnels are formed only between WAN Edge routers.

5. **C.** With a route reflector, BGP peers only establish neighbor adjacencies to a route reflector and advertise routes to them. Similarly, with SD-WAN Controller, routing updates are only advertised to and from the SD-WAN Controller. The SD-WAN Controller has the capability to apply policy inbound or outbound to the prefixes it services.

6. **A, B.** SD-WAN Validator provides authentication of all devices in the environment. SD-WAN Validator is the initial point of contact, and it distributes connectivity information for all other controller elements. STUN is also used with SD-WAN Validator to detect when a component is behind NAT.

7. **A.** Cisco Catalyst SD-WAN supports three types of multitenancy: dedicated, VPN, and enterprise.

8. **C and D.** OMP is not supported on the service side of Cisco Catalyst SD-WAN. OMP is run in the transport side; it is used to exchange routing updates with the SD-WAN Controller.

9. **A, B, C.** BFD is used to measure delay, loss, and jitter. With this information, intelligent decisions can be made to switch traffic to different transports that may perform better.

10. **A.** Per RFC 4023, MPLS labels are used to provide different levels of segmentation for various compliance reasons. With segmentation, different types of topologies can be created for each VPN, including hub-and-spoke, full-mesh, and point-to-point VPNs.

11. **D.** Cisco does not provide on-premises hosting in its own data centers.

Chapter 3

1. **A.** The three Cisco SD-WAN Control Components are SD-WAN Controller, SD-WAN Validator, and SD-WAN Manager. These components make up the control, management, and orchestration planes in the environment, respectively. The SD-WAN Controller is the brains behind the control plane and distributes routing information and encryption information.

2. **A, B, E.** OMP has three types of routing advertisements: OMP route, TLOC route, and service route.

3. **B.** When two devices are behind symmetric NAT, the data plane cannot be built. This is due to the fact that symmetric NAT uses ports that change depending on which device the data plane tunnel is being established with.

4. **A.** When using private-to-private colors, it is assumed that there is no NAT between the two colors, so private (pre-NAT) information is used. When communicating with a public color, NAT may be involved, so the public (post-NAT) attributes are used.

5. **A.** Since key exchange is handled via the SD-WAN Controller, there is no need for the IKE session management protocol.

6. **A.** UDP port 12346 is used to communicate with all control elements in the SD-WAN fabric.

Chapter 4

1. **A, B, D.** Device templates can either use feature templates, CLI templates, or APIs. When a CLI template is used, it must be the full configuration of the device.

2. **A, B, E.** Three different types of values that can be set with Feature Templates. When global is used, the value of that field will be the same wherever that template is applied. The default value will use whatever the default value is for the field. Device-specific variables allow a network administrator the flexibility to set a parameter on a per-device basis, without the need for an additional template.

3. **B.** Device templates are specific to certain device types. Separate device templates need to be used for different product versions.

4. **B.** CLI templates do not provide the same flexibility as feature templates. A CLI template must contain the full CLI configuration.

5. **A.** The plug-and-play process uses HTTPS for communication to the PnP server.

6. **A, B, C.** For automatic provisioning to be successful, a device must receive an IP address and DNS server via DHCP. Once the device has this information, it needs to be able to resolve ztp.viptela.com or devicehelper.cisco.com and have connectivity to them.

7. **A.** Configuration groups provide some advantages over Device Templates in that you can target different device types and models with a single configuration group. The system translates the intent and configuration to the desired device type.

8. **B.** A device can only be attached to a configuration group or a device template at one time. You can use configuration groups and device templates at the same time, but they can't both be applied to a device at the same time.

9. **A.** To take advantage of direct Internet access, you need to enable NAT on the WAN interface to translate the internal IP address to the public WAN address.

Chapter 5

1. **A, B, C.** Application performance optimization is the ability to control traffic flows based on WAN performance characteristics. Secure direct Internet access is the capability to securely use local Internet exit points instead of sending all traffic to a central location. Multicloud connectivity is a set of features and functionality that enables you to extend your WAN to cloud workloads in a seamless fashion.

2. **B, D.** Cloud OnRamp for Multicloud Catalyst SD-WAN can simplify and build connectivity to IaaS and SaaS providers.

3. **B.** Catalyst SD-WAN is a solution that focuses on the WAN. It primarily provides operations, troubleshooting, and monitoring for your WAN.

4. **A.** There is no requirement to add a control policy to a region to provide access between regions.

5. **C.** In an on-premises private cloud deployment, the customer is responsible for managing the underlying systems hosting the controllers, which includes security and operations of those systems.

6. **A.** SD-WAN Analytics is a cloud-delivered application, so it doesn't require supporting high availability.

7. **C.** With administrator-triggered failover, a server is in warm standby mode, and the data is replicated automatically to standby mode. When a failover needs to occur, the administrator triggers it manually via the GUI.

8. C. Using two controllers is recommended for redundancy with a large deployment.

9. C. In your configuration, the FQDN or the IP address can be provided for the SD-WAN Validator.

10. B. Most customers have existing WANs, so you need to perform a brownfield migration from that existing WAN to the new SD-WAN solution.

11. B. Most migrations occur in a stepped fashion, where smaller existing sites are migrated first and the data centers are migrated last.

12. C, D. Before performing a migration, you should analyze the existing network, routing design, and traffic flows. Then you can design policy and configuration in SD-WAN.

13. A, B, E. Site IDs should be defined beforehand, with a careful focus on growth and standardization. You should use some kind of strategy when you think about site IDs. It is important to standardize on your VPN IDs so all sites are consistent and follow a specific pattern. TLOC colors or transports should be decided before deployment, specifically focusing on public versus private colors.

14. A. When planning a migration, you should stand up new SD-WAN routers in the data center, and as you migrate sites to SD-WAN, they will connect through the new SD-WAN routers.

15. C. When migrating to SD-WAN, you can deploy multiple localized regional transit hubs to connect through instead of backhauling everything to a centralized hub.

16. B. When deploying WAN Edge devices, you should try to practice having separate physical interfaces in VPN 0, which helps prevent physical interface or physical cabling outages (which can lead to a complete outage). When you split these interfaces, if one interface goes down, you don't completely lose WAN connectivity.

17. D. Bind mode ensures that traffic destined to the loopback will be carried to and from the mapped physical interface. Unbind mode does not have this behavior.

18. A, C, D. Complete WAN Edge replacement, integration with an existing CE router, and complete CE replacement with a dual WAN router are the correct options.

19. B. TLOC extension can use private and public colors.

20. B, D, F. All common routing protocols are supported on the service side, including eBGP, OSPF, and EIGRP.

21. D. You should take special consideration to filter toward the WAN Edge router to prevent routing loops.

Chapter 6

1. B, C, D. URL filtering, application-aware routing, and centralized data policies are all types of Cisco SD-WAN policies. There is no such thing as a traffic engineering policy; traffic engineering can be achieved with a control policy or a centralized data policy.

2. B. Cisco SD-WAN policies, much like traditional Cisco ACLs and route maps, are evaluated ordinally and use first-match logic.

3. **A, B, C, D, E, F.** All of these are different types of lists that are used in Cisco SD-WAN.

4. **B.** Unlike traditional IOS, SD-WAN has explicit list types for matching in the control plane (**prefix-list**) versus the data plane (**data-prefix-list**).

5. **B.** The only way to filter routes from routing neighbors outside the SD-WAN fabric is with a route map in a local policy.

6. **A, B.** VPN membership policies and topology policies are applied to and enforced on the SD-WAN Controllers. Zone-based firewall policies are part of security policies, which are applied directly to the WAN Edge and enforced there. Cflowd policies are part of centralized data policies; they are applied to the SD-WAN Controllers but enforced on the WAN Edge devices.

7. **C, D.** Security policies and localized data policies are applied to and enforced on the WAN Edge routers. Application-aware routing policies are applied to the SD-WAN Controllers and enforced on the WAN Edge routers. VPN membership and topology policies are applied to and enforced on the SD-WAN Controllers.

8. **A.** Application-aware routing policies are applied to the SD-WAN Controllers and enforced on the WAN Edge routers. Security policies and localized data policies are applied to and enforced on the WAN Edge routers. VPN membership and topology policies are applied to and enforced on the SD-WAN Controllers.

9. **D.** All policy configuration is done in SD-WAN Manager. SD-WAN Manager is the single administration point for both the SD-WAN Controller and the WAN Edge routers.

10. **B.** If there is a conflict in the forwarding decisions made by an application-aware routing policy and a centralized data policy, and there are no tunnels or colors that meet the SLA in the Application-Aware Routing policy, the centralized data policy will override the application-aware routing policy.

Chapter 7

1. **C.** The only two answers that apply to centralized control policies are Accept and Reject. Deny is an action in a centralized data policy. The default setting of the default action in a centralized control policy is Reject.

2. **B, C, D, E.** System IP, color, and encapsulation are the three elements that uniquely define a TLOC. In addition, a TLOC list also allows the configuration of Preference. The other attributes cannot be defined as part of a TLOC list.

3. **C.** The TLOC attribute Weight is not part of the OMP best-path selection process. After the winners of the best paths have been determined, the Weight attribute is examined to determine how the flows should be divided proportionally among the best paths.

4. **B.** TLOC Preference values, not OMP Route Preference values, can be configured via feature and device templates.

5. **A.** A route that has a valid TLOC as a next hop will have the status code R for "resolved." If the resolved route is also the winner of the OMP best-path selection process, the route will have status C R, where C means "chosen." If the route is installed in the local routing table, it will have the status of C I R, where I is "installed."

6. C. Both TLOC routes and OMP routes have support for an attribute called Preference.

7. D. A VPN membership policy specifies which VPNs the SD-WAN Controller will accept updates from and forward updates to on a specific WAN Edge device. Unless the VPN is permitted by the VPN policy, the VPN can still be configured on the WAN Edge device, but it will be isolated from the rest of the fabric.

8. B. Control policies that are used to leak routes must always be applied in the inbound direction.

9. B. A centralized control policy can be used to leak routes between different service-side VPNs. A centralized control policy cannot be used to leak into or out of VPN 0 or VPN 512.

10. C. Centralized control policies configured with the **export-to** action are used to leak routes between service-side VPNs.

11. A. Topology groups create a simplified workflow that performs the same behavior as centralized control policies.

Chapter 8

1. B. In a centralized data policy, the easiest way to match all traffic is to not configure any matching criteria. There is no concept of a match-all criteria in SD-WAN, and the default action will only allow certain actions to be undertaken.

2. A. The **nat use-vpn** configuration syntax is always used to apply NAT to send traffic to VPN 0.

3. B. The **nat fallback** configuration provides a backup forwarding path across the fabric in the event that all the local interfaces configured for NAT are down. If all the WAN interfaces go down, **nat fallback** will not work, as there will be no way to backhaul the traffic to a different site.

4. C. In the SD-WAN Controller configuration, there is only a single data policy that is configured per site ID per direction. That single policy includes sub-policies for each VPN, but there are only two policies that are applied per site ID.

5. B. The **local-tloc** command sets the preference for the outbound interface to be used when forwarding traffic. In the event that the TLOC specified in the LOCAL-TLOC policy is unavailable, traffic will fall back to the routing table.

6. D. A single FEC block consists of four data packets and a parity packet that is calculated from those four data packets. In the event that any one of the data packets is lost, the original packet can be reconstructed from the remaining three data packets and the parity packet.

7. C. FEC adaptive begins to operate when the packet losses on a tunnel exceed 2%. Currently, this is not a user-configurable policy.

8. D. When packet duplication is configured, the duplicate packets are automatically sent down the tunnel that is currently experiencing the least amount of packet loss.

9. C. The PKTDUP RX field shows the total number of unique packets that have been received at the WAN Edge device, including the values received over the original path (PKTDUP RX) and the backup path (PKTDUP RX OTHER). The last two values are TX values and have nothing do with the number of packets received.

10. A. To leverage policy groups, you must use configuration groups for device management.

11. C. When selecting Fallback to Routing, you are saying that if the tunnel is down, fall back to what the routing table has indicated is the path.

12. A. To configure AppQoE, TCP optimization, and DRE, you must use data policies. Data policies directly influence the data flow, not the control plane.

Chapter 9

1. D. Application-Aware Routing policies are applied on a per-site, per-VPN basis. Unlike with other data policies, directionality does not play a role with AAR policies. The direction is always from-service.

2. B. An App-route policy is a special type of centralized data policy. An App-route policy is centrally applied on the SD-WAN controllers and enforced on the WAN Edge routers.

3. A, D, G. The BFD hello interval specifies how frequently BFD packets are sent and statistics are gathered. The app-route poll interval defines the period of time to evaluate the BFD statistics and produce an average. This forms a single bucket. The app-route multiplier specifies how many app-route poll intervals to consider (that is, how many buckets to consider) when calculating tunnel performance. The number of tunnels, colors, and SLA classes has no impact on the statistic calculation process. The BFD hello multiplier is used for liveliness detection and is not part of the app-route process.

4. C. The maximum (and default) number of app-route poll intervals that can be used for tunnel performance calculations is six. This value is configured using the app-route poll interval multiplier.

5. D. Tunnels are reevaluated for compliance with SLA classes after each app-route poll interval. The hello interval controls how often BFD packets are transmitted by the router and, thus, how often they are received by the router. The hello multiplier is used for path liveliness detection, not for application-aware routing.

6. A. A single WAN Edge router can have 16 different SLA classes configured.

7. D. A router and, thus, a single WAN Edge router can have 16 different SLA classes configured.

8. C. The Backup SLA Preferred Color option applies when no colors, not just the options configured under Preferred Colors, are able to meet the required SLA.

9. B. When the **strict** option is configured, it drops traffic when *all* available colors fail to meet the requirements of the SLA class, not only the colors specified in the Preferred Colors field.

10. **A.** An AAR policy will only make path selection decisions between multiple equal-cost routes. If one route is more preferred, that route will always be chosen by the forwarding engine, regardless of the AAR policy or the performance of the tunnels.

11. **A.** Policy groups can be used to build a policy that defines and takes into consideration SLA criteria.

12. **B, C, E.** The three modes you can configure when building an EAAR policy are aggressive, conservative, and moderate mode. Each of these has different timer and poll intervals. Select the one that meets your requirements.

13. **A.** SLA dampening ensures that you don't place a transport back into service until you can guarantee that it is no longer experiencing any WAN impairment. As you bring the transport back into service, you slowly reintroduce the transport.

Chapter 10

1. **C.** Localized policies are configured and enforced on the local WAN Edge routers. SD-WAN Validator and SD-WAN Controllers are completely independent of localized policies.

2. **B.** Because centralized policies are applied to the SD-WAN Controller and localized policies are applied to the WAN Edge routers, the configurations are completely independent and use different lists.

3. **A.** A localized policy is scoped to a specific device. While uncommon, it would be possible for every device to have a different localized policy.

4. **A, B.** Localized control policies support the Accept and Reject actions. The Drop action is only available in a localized data policy. The Inspect and Pass actions are specific to zone-based firewalls.

5. **B.** Because all the traffic is traversing tunnels, all the necessary firewall and NAT states have already been established. Ensuring symmetric flows through a single WAN Edge router is important for the fidelity of the deep packet inspection and application recognition data.

6. **A, C.** Localized data policies support the Accept and Drop actions. The Reject action is only available in a localized control policy. The Inspect and Pass actions are specific to zone-based firewalls.

7. **D.** Current code supports eight queues per interface on WAN Edge routers.

8. **A.** LLQ and priority queuing functionalities are only supported in queue 0.

9. **A.** Control plane traffic is automatically mapped to queue 0.

10. **A, B, D.** While shapers are part of QoS, they are configured under the interface configuration and are not part of the localized policy configuration. Class maps are used to map the forwarding classes to hardware queues. QoS schedulers are used to configure the forwarding parameters of each traffic class. QoS maps are used to tie all the schedulers together into a single policy.

11. **B.** ACLs along with centralized data policies and policy groups can be used to select forwarding classes.

12. **A.** Configuration groups greatly simplify the configuration management of an SD-WAN deployment.

Chapter 11

1. **B.** The Cisco Catalyst SD-WAN Enterprise Firewall with Application Awareness is completely VPN aware. Firewall policies are applied on a per-VPN basis.

2. **A, B, E.** Three main actions can be set, per sequence entry, in a firewall policy: Inspect, Drop, and Pass.

3. **B.** High-speed logging is an available logging option for a firewall policy.

4. **B, D, E.** Only three options for signature sets exist today for IDS/IPS: balanced, connectivity, and security.

5. **B, E.** The Fail-close option drops all the IPS/IDS traffic when there is an engine failure. The Fail-open option allows all the IPS/IDS traffic when there is an engine failure. The default option is Fail-open.

6. **A.** An IDS/IPS policy cannot be configured unless a security virtual image is first uploaded to the software repository in SD-WAN Manager.

7. **B.** To support URL filtering functionality, an ISR must be configured with a minimum of 8 GB of DRAM and 8 GB of system flash if doing a cloud lookup and 16 GB of DRAM and 16 GB of system flash if doing an on-box database lookup.

8. **C.** A URL blacklist can be configured to explicitly block certain websites in the URL policy configuration.

9. **B, D.** Between the security dashboard and device dashboard, SD-WAN Manager can provide the blocked and allowed categories by percentage, as well as the URL session count.

10. **B.** As of this writing, the current SD-WAN code supports a maximum exportable file size of 10 MB.

11. **A, B, C.** At a minimum, file analysis must be enabled, a file types list must be specified, and the Threat Grid API key must be configured.

12. **A.** The filename of the malware detected is displayed in the Device Dashboard section of SD-WAN Manager.

13. **D.** To generate the API token, the user must log in to the Cisco Umbrella portal and navigate to the API token generation page.

14. **C.** The WAN Edge router can leverage local domain bypass functionality, where a list of internal domains is defined and referenced during the DNS request interception process. Any domain defined in the list is ignored, and no interception or redirection occurs.

15. **A, E.** When configuring a user group, read and write privileges can be assigned on a per-feature basis.

16. **B.** RBAC by VPN is for visibility only, not for configuration.

17. **A, B, D.** In addition to local database authentication, SD-WAN Manager supports SSO, RADIUS, and TACACS for remote authentication.

Chapter 12

1. **B.** Cloud OnRamp for SaaS is not a book-ended solution. Cloud OnRamp for SaaS uses a unique HTTPS probe to monitor the performance of the path to the SaaS application.

2. **A, B, D.** The three types of Cloud OnRamp for SaaS sites are gateway, direct Internet access, and client sites.

3. **A.** A site configured for Cloud OnRamp for SaaS can have Internet or MPLS transports to reach SaaS applications.

4. **B.** SAIE (Formerly DPI) does not redirect the initial application flow because the redirection would NAT changes that would break the TCP flow.

5. **B.** Only two cloud routers are provisioned per transit VPC.

6. **A.** Cloud OnRamp for IaaS supports both the IAM role and API key login methods for connecting to a cloud instance.

7. **A, C, D.** Cloud OnRamp for Multicloud can facilitate the configuration workflow for site-to-site, site-to-cloud, and cloud-to-cloud solutions.

8. **C.** A cloud-agnostic private backbone enables the enterprise to use a supported provider to build connectivity and use that provider as the transport to the public cloud.

Chapter 13

1. **B.** While SOAP and RPC are also valid API architectures, Cisco Catalyst SD-WAN APIs adhere to REST principles, allowing clients to use HTTP requests and standard HTTP methods (such as GET, POST, PUT, and DELETE) to perform operations on resources, which are represented as URLs.

2. **C.** Because they are REST APIs, Cisco Catalyst SD-WAN APIs support standard HTTP methods to perform actions on resources.

3. **A, D.** GET, POST, PUT, and DELETE are valid HTTP methods that can be used with Cisco Catalyst SD-WAN APIs.

4. **C.** Cisco Catalyst SD-WAN APIs use HTTPS as a secure transport, and /dataservice is a common URL prefix for most SD-WAN API calls.

5. **A.** 201 HTTP indicates the successful creation of a new resource.

6. **A.** Cisco Catalyst SD-WAN uses APIs as a core component of its architecture. The SD-WAN Manager GUI is an external application that interacts programmatically with the SD-WAN Manager API.

7. **D.** An assurance API is a kind of API that you can use with Cisco Catalyst Center, but it does not exist for Cisco Catalyst SD-WAN APIs.

8. **B.** A template attachment API call executes asynchronously and just returns the task ID or process ID. The caller application can use this ID to check the state of the request and retrieve the results upon completion.

9. C. Instead of relying on manual configurations through traditional CLI or GUI methods, IaC uses machine-readable configuration files to define, deploy, and manage network configurations, devices, and services as programmable resources.

10. D. Terraform uses a declarative approach to describe the desired infrastructure state using HashiCorp Configuration Language (HCL).

Chapter 14

1. D. SD-WAN Manager is the central place to monitor all aspects of your SD-WAN fabric.

2. C, D, E. The three valid options are Good, Poor, and Fair. As you are reviewing the monitoring dashboards you will see these three statuses represented by different icons.

3. B. Real-time monitoring in SD-WAN Manager allows you to pull live monitoring data from the WAN Edge device, giving you an indication of what is currently going on with your WAN Edges.

4. B. ThousandEyes is not support on Cisco 8000 virtual platforms such at the Cisco Catalyst 8000v. ThousandEyes is support on the Cisco 8000 physical platforms.

5. B, C. Cisco Thousand Eyes is an external application that monitors certain aspects of your WAN and the Internet, using polling data presented by agents. SD-WAN Analytics is a service that takes data from your SD-WAN deployment and provides you with actionable insights and recommendations based on what is currently happening in your network as well as what has happened in the past.

6. B. Flow Simulator is a tool that allows you to indicate various aspects of a flow, such as source and destination IP addresses, port, and application and tells you what transport the flow will use. It takes into consideration your currently applied policies.

7. A. The Predictive Path Recommendations (PPR) feature uses advanced data modeling powered by Cisco ThousandEyes to determine the optimal data path to improve the specific application performance and display recommendations.

GLOSSARY OF KEY TERMS

A

Ansible   An open-source automation and configuration management tool that uses easily readable playbooks to automate configuration changes while ensuring that the desired state is met.

app-probe-class   A setting that includes forwarding class, color, and DSCP values and that defines the marking, by color, of the applications that are forwarded.

app-route multiplier   A setting that determines how many app-route poll intervals should be considered when making a determination about the SLA compliance of the tunnels. The default value is 6, and the maximum is 6. This value is configured per router.

app-route poll interval   A setting that defines the period of time to collect Bidirectional Forwarding Detection (BFD) probes for analyzing the statistical performance of SD-WAN tunnels and making a determination about SLA compliance. This value is configured per router.

application programming interface (API)   A flexible interface beyond the traditional user interface that can be used programmatically to manage and monitor an application, a device, or an operating system.

artificial intelligence (AI)   The use of compute power to make human-like and informed decisions based on real-time data in the environment.

B

backup-sla-preferred-color   An optional configuration argument that allows for the specification of a selected color or colors to use when forwarding a class of traffic in the event that no tunnels meet the required SLAs.

BFD hello interval   A setting that specifies how often a WAN Edge router should send a BFD probe on a tunnel. This value is configured per router, per color.

BFD multiplier   A setting that specifies how many consecutive BFD probes can be sent without a response before the tunnel is declared to be down. This value is configured per router, per color.

bring your own device (BYOD)   A common enterprise administrative policy that allows for employees to connect to enterprise networks or the Internet with personal devices such as phones and tablets.

C

centralized policy   A policy that can affect the entire Cisco SD-WAN fabric and is activated on SD-WAN Controller.

certificate authority (CA)   An entity that is responsible for signing certificate requests and issuing SSL certificates. Since SD-WAN components are configured to trust an organization's root CA, any certificate generated or signed by the root CA is also trusted. Hence, SD-WAN components inherently trust the identity of one another since they share the same mutual trust of the signing root CA.

Cisco Catalyst Software-Defined WAN (Cisco SD-WAN)   A software controller–based solution from Cisco that uses SDN to deploy, monitor, and manage wide-area networks.

cloud   Shared compute and application resources that exist in a domain away from the physical enterprise network, such as the Internet or a shared data center. Examples include Amazon Web Services (AWS), Google Compute (GCP), and Microsoft Azure.

color   An attribute that allows an SD-WAN solution to identify specific transports and influence how the data plane is built.

command-line interface (CLI)   A tool for configuring network devices individually by inputting configuration commands.

control plane (SD-WAN Controller)   The element of SD-WAN where all control and centralized policy are enforced. Calculation of the routing table and distribution of encryption keys are handled by the SD-WAN Controller in the control plane.

control policy   A policy that manipulates routing information and can be used to affect how traffic is forwarded through a WAN Edge device.

D

data plane (WAN Edge)   The element of SD-WAN where data traffic is terminated and encapsulated across the SD-WAN fabric. The data plane is only built between WAN Edge devices.

data policy   A policy that directly impacts the forwarding of traffic flows through a WAN Edge router.

Direct Cloud Access (DCA)   Cisco technology that forwards SaaS traffic (such as Office 365, Salesforce, Box, and Google traffic) from a branch directly to the Internet or the backhaul path to a data center based on candidate path performance. It ensures the best SaaS application experience and also reduces the IT WAN cost.

Direct Internet Access (DIA)   Technology that makes it possible to access the Internet through local egress at the remote site rather than backhauling through a data center.

E–I

enhanced application-aware routing (EAAR)   A type of routing that has the capability to read into the application data traffic, which allows for more accurate and detailed measurements of these metrics.

extranet   A restricted communications network that is typically used to allow business partners in different organizations to have a private and secure communication channel.

fallback-to-best-path   An option that selects the best path out of all the available colors when an SLA isn't met. When it is selected, you can choose more options that determine the best color.

Forward Error Correction (FEC)   A method of including additional information, called parity, in a message so that if part of the message is lost or corrupted, the whole message can still be recovered.

inbound control policy   A control policy that is applied to OMP updates sent from a WAN Edge device to a SD-WAN Controller and applied before the SD-WAN Controller performs the best-path selection algorithm.

infrastructure as code (IaC)   The ability to define the desired configuration as human-readable code. You can use this code with automated DevOps practices rather than manual operations.

infrastructure as a service (IaaS)   Virtualized hardware that is outsourced to providers and that typically runs in the cloud.

Internet of Things (IoT)   A collection of nontraditional network-connected devices that are typically unstaffed, such as manufacturing equipment, lighting, security cameras, and door locks.

intrusion detection system (IDS)   A system that analyzes network traffic for signatures that match known cyberattacks.

intrusion prevention system (IPS)   A system that analyzes packets and that can also stop the packets from being delivered based on the kind of attack that is detected, thus helping stop the attack.

L–M

localized policy   A policy that affects only a single WAN Edge router and that is configured in the device template.

machine learning   A subset of AI that is used to gather data and information from the network environment to constantly learn, adapt, and improve the accuracy of the AI.

management plane (SD-WAN Manager)   The element of Cisco Catalyst SD-WAN where day-to-day administration of the SD-WAN fabric occurs. SD-WAN Manager is a single pane of glass used for configuration, troubleshooting, software upgrades, and monitoring.

multi-topology   A network design in which different VPN segments have different logical topologies. Some VPNs may be able to establish direct communication with each other, whereas other VPN segments may have to communicate indirectly via a third site, and other VPN segments may not be able to communicate at all.

N–O

NAT fallback   The process of forwarding traffic that would have been subjected to network address translation through a local egress interface across the SD-WAN fabric when no local interfaces are configured for NAT in an operational state.

network programmability   The use of code to write programs or processes that communicate with network infrastructure. Various programming languages support network programmability, and the most common of them are Python and Go.

OMP route   A route that is responsible for carrying information about data prefixes. Such a route is usually a LAN subnet.

orchestration plane (SD-WAN Validator)   The glue that brings together all the other SD-WAN Control Components. The orchestration plane distributes SD-WAN Manager and SD-WAN Controller information to the WAN Edge devices and also authenticates all the Cisco SD-WAN Control Components.

originator   A matching criterion that is used to select the WAN Edge device that did the initial advertisement of a route or TLOC route.

outbound control policy   A control policy that is applied to OMP updates that are sent from a SD-WAN Controller to a WAN Edge device and applied after the SD-WAN Controller uses the best-path selection algorithm.

Overlay Management Protocol (OMP)   The routing protocol of the SD-WAN fabric. OMP is used to distribute all routing information, encryption keys, and other policy information. OMP runs inside a DTLS/TLS tunnel between a SD-WAN Controller and WAN Edge devices.

P–R

packet duplication   The process of forwarding a redundant copy of a traffic flow down a duplicate path in order to protect against packet loss.

preferred color   An optional configuration argument that allows for the specification of a selected color or colors to use when forwarding a class of traffic, as long as those classes are compliant with the SLA class.

preferred color groups   A ranking system for preferred and backup colors in application-aware routing. You can configure up to three levels based on priority or path preference.

quality of service (QoS)   The categorization and prioritization of traffic in a network, typically based on application type and requirements.

REST API   An HTTP-based API that allows you to interact with SD-WAN components via common HTTP commands. Code can be written to interface with this API.

role-based access control (RBAC)   A policy-neutral access control mechanism that is defined around roles and privileges. The components of RBAC, such as role-permissions, user-role, and role-role relationships, make it simple to perform user assignments.

S

SD-WAN Controller   The control plane of the SD-WAN fabric, which acts as a Border Gateway Protocol (BGP) route reflector and is responsible for distributing encryption keys as well.

service insertion   The process of redirecting a network flow to an additional device for the purpose of performing a function on the traffic. Common network services include firewalls, load balancers, and caching engines.

service-level agreement (SLA)   A commitment made by a service or application provider to customers for a minimum level of service or uptime.

service route   A route that advertises a service, such as a firewall or an intrusion prevention system, to the rest of the network. Policy can be deployed to force traffic through these services.

SLA class list   A list that allows an administrator to specify the maximum loss, latency, and/or jitter on an SD-WAN tunnel that a specific class of traffic is forwarded across.

SLA dampening   A mechanism used to slowly reintroduce the transport back into the available paths for forwarding to ensure that you don't reintroduce a transport while it is still having connectivity problems.

software as a service (SaaS)   Software applications that are outsourced to providers and that typically run in the cloud.

software-defined networking (SDN)   A network management approach in which network flows, rules, and operations are defined and deployed from a centralized controller rather than on each individual network device.

strict   An optional configuration argument that specifies that the class of traffic should be dropped rather than forwarded in the event that no classes meet the required SLA.

T

Terraform   An IaaS-based tool developed by Hashi Corp. that can be used to develop plans in a human-readable language called HCL. Terraform can be used to apply this configuration and also track the state of the configuration and alert to any drifts.

TLOC   A Transport Locator route that distributes next-hop information and also connects the fabric to the physical underlay. Data plane deployment can be influenced by manipulating TLOC information.

tloc-list   A list element that can contain references to one or more TLOC routes described by their system IP address, color, and encapsulation. It may also include the optional arguments Weight and Preference.

topology group   A centralized control policy that allows an administrator to configure hub-and-spoke or mesh policies with predefined workflows and fully customized topologies through the manipulation of route and TLOC route information at an SD-WAN Controller.

transit VPC   A virtual private cloud (VPC) that can be used for connecting multiple geographically dispersed VPCs and remote networks in order to create a global network transit center. A transit VPC simplifies network management and minimizes the number of connections required to connect multiple VPCs and remote networks.

V–Z

virtualization   A process in which applications and software are abstracted from the underlying physical hardware resources and run as virtual instances.

zone   A group of one or more VPNs.

Index